The United States

Methuen's Companions to Modern Studies

GERMANY: *A Companion to German Studies*
Edited by Malcolm Pasley

FRANCE: *A Companion to French Studies*
Edited by D. G. Charlton

SPAIN: *A Companion to Spanish Studies*
Edited by P. E. Russell

THE UNITED STATES: *A Companion to American Studies*
Edited by Dennis Welland

The United States

A COMPANION TO AMERICAN STUDIES

edited by Dennis Welland

Professor of American Literature
University of Manchester

METHUEN & CO LTD

I I NEW FETTER LANE · LONDON EC4

First published in 1974
by Methuen & Co Ltd
11 New Fetter Lane, London EC4P 4EE
© 1974 by Methuen & Co Ltd
Printed in Great Britain by
Richard Clay (The Chaucer Press) Ltd
Bungay, Suffolk

SBN 416 28150 8

Harper
Sale

Contents

Maps

Introduction

The best companions are those whose company is most eagerly sought
for the stimulus it affords; this volume has been planned in the hope
that it will become such a companion for the steadily increasing number
of readers interested in the study of the United States. It is not intended
to be descriptive, definitive, or exhaustive, but rather, by the discussion
of selected and seminal ideas, to open up lines of enquiry and point in
the direction of further study. Then, as his knowledge widens, the
reader will, it is hoped, return from time to time to test his developing
impressions afresh against those embodied here.

To speak of these chapters as 'impressions' is not to belittle the scholarship of their authors, all of whom have been actively engaged in the
extension of American studies in British universities for some time,
many of them as pioneers in this field; all of them are already known
for their independent publications. These pieces are impressionistic in
their necessarily compressed and selective treatment of large subjects;
together they constitute a collection of related essays rather than a series
of carefully integrated chapters moving in a specified direction towards
a predetermined end. There is no 'party line', nor, in most cases, have
contributors known in any detail the contents of chapters other than
their own. That there is some overlapping is deliberate: the topics
treated are all parts of a larger theme – what Whitman called 'this
puzzle the New World' – and cannot be artificially isolated. Similarly,
despite present-day emphasis, the Negro is not segregated into a separate chapter, but his omni-presence in American life is reflected in the
different contributors' examinations of his role in their spheres.

That the book does not offer a narrative moving sedately and
sequentially to 1973 from the Jamestown settlement of 1603 is not a
concession to currently fashionable demands for a 'relevance' that is
often myopically conceived. Modern historians, escaping thank-
fully from the dedication to dates, the passion for periods and the

enslavement to chronology that have too often passed for history, tend to think topically in both senses of that word. Thus, the importance of an understanding of the American past to an understanding of the American present is axiomatic in all these essays, but collectively they relate past to present in ways that enlarge the discussion rather than encourage a simplistic *post hoc ergo propter hoc* view or suggest that there is only one possible and received interpretation of history.

When, at the Chicago meeting of the American Historical Association in 1893, Frederick Jackson Turner propounded what has come to be known as the Frontier Thesis of American history, he believed that he was demolishing the so-called 'germ theory' which sought all origins of American history and institutions in the European past. The uniqueness of the American experience Turner found in the geographical fact of virgin land, ready for occupation and ripe for exploitation, lying to the west of the settled area from the earliest days of white colonization until his own time. The existence of this frontier, and the necessity for settlers to adapt to the changing conditions of successive frontiers, far outweighed, in Turner's submission, the significance of European influences in the shaping of the American character. Researches more sophisticated and less emotively partisan have challenged the historical validity of this theory, but for many Americans who have never heard of Turner the land and the idea of America still coalesce unconsciously into an imaginative concept of extraordinary power: in this respect Turner was more of a poet than an historian. The contributors to this volume, seeing America from across the Atlantic, give more emphasis than Turner to its European connections, but they recognize readily what is quintessentially indigenous. In this spirit Wreford Watson's opening geographical commentary explores the ways in which the society's development has been conditioned by its physical setting, and W. R. Brock speculates on the historical factors and attitudes that strengthened, for the inhabitants of that land, the sense of conscious nationalism on which so many visitors remark.

A familiar but valid explanation of the American preoccupation with national identity points to the historically unprecedented ethnic diversity of the American people. To settle and exploit so vast a continent required a population explosion that had to be artificially induced: Charlotte Erickson, in Chapter 3, discusses the 'melting-pot' created by immigration and its implications for the American economy as well as for the development of a national image. In 1784, to encourage immigration, Benjamin Franklin published in London his 'Information to those who would remove to America' and emphasized the predominantly agrarian nature of the new Republic: 'Great establishments of manufacture require great numbers of poor to do the work for small wages; these poor are to be found in Europe, but will not be found in America, till the lands are all taken up and cultivated' (or, in Turner's idiom, until the frontier was closed). On more ideological grounds Thomas Jefferson had also urged agrarianism on America, celebrating the farmers as 'the chosen people of God', but his rival in Washington's first administration, Alexander Hamilton, in his *Report on Manufactures* (1791), argued for an industrial economy, thus beginning a debate the repercussions of which still reverberate. History justified Franklin's prediction; the industrialization of America resulted, by the 1880s, in a combination of progress and poverty that was sharply and even explosively apparent in the cities. In Chapter 4 H. B. Rodgers traces the development of these vast urban complexes and analyses the attendant social problems which (see Chapters 10 and 13) so agonized the conscience of the late nineteenth-century novelists and thinkers.

The agonized conscience, which George Santayana saw as the characteristic of the Puritan, has remained an important part of the American inheritance, manifesting itself especially in connection with the Vietnam War and with race relations. The righteous vigour with which the Puritans (and their successors) waged wars against the Indians contrasts strangely with the ideal of America as the peaceable kingdom which William Penn embodied in Pennsylvania, and which dozens of subsequent experiments in communitarian living also tried to realize. This dichotomy persists in much American thinking. The nation established by a War of Independence has never in its history been conquered by an external enemy, and it is a truism to attribute the uniqueness of the American South, in part at least, to the fact that it is the only region of America to have experienced defeat. How war has historically contributed to the development of modern America is discussed by M. A. Jones in his chapter, and H. C. Allen then looks at the related question of how the United States has come to see her role in world affairs.

What so often agonizes the American conscience is a tragic awareness of the gulf between the possibility and the actuality, the promise and the achievement. Lionel Trilling once remarked, 'Ours is the only nation that prides itself upon a dream, and gives its name to one, "the American Dream" '. He added ruefully, 'To the world it is anomalous in America . . . that so much raw power should be haunted by envisioned romance'; and, in an evocative phrase, he spoke of America as 'divided between power and dream'. The American Dream is sustained by a multiplicity of influences – Franklin's belief in industrious self-help, Jefferson's agrarianism, Emerson's idealism, Whitman's democracy, Turner's faith in the Frontier and countless more – yet the dream always failed to materialize, the promise of the land of opportunity came to seem illusory, the peaceable kingdom was torn by one of the bloodiest civil wars in history. The Puritan, with his belief in Original Sin, would have ascribed this to man's natural depravity and would have stressed the necessity of government to restrain man's baser nature; the Founding Fathers, though proceeding from rather different premises, were equally convinced that life, liberty, and the pursuit of happiness could best be ensured by a constitutionally-ordered society; and Lincoln's rhetoric on the battlefield of Gettysburg also reiterated a dedication to the preservation of government. In two complementary chapters Max Beloff and H. G. Nicholas examine critically the implementation of these ideals of government in the Constitution of the United States, and in the operations of its political machinery.

The subduing of a continent, the achieving of their independence, and the creation of a constitution and political institutions of an unprecedentedly democratic nature, were felt by many Americans to be a lofty enough expression of the national genius and one sufficiently time-consuming to absolve them from the obligation to cultivate the arts for which an effete and undemocratic Old World had the leisure and resources. But predictably there were others who wished to see political independence paralleled by artistic independence and who looked eagerly for what Poe, in 1842, called 'that epoch when our literature may and must stand on its own merits' and challenge comparison with the literature of England. Such motives reinforced the desire for a national identity already mentioned: in Mark Twain's words 'almost the most prodigious asset of a country, and perhaps its most precious possession, is its native literary product'. A great nation deserves a great literature, and a great literature made that nation both greater and more of a nation. How great, and how American, the 'native literary product' has been occupies the critical attention of the authors of Chapters 9–11 inclusive, while Chapter 12 widens the spectrum a little further to include the other arts in a glance not, it is hoped, too cursory.

In the final chapter Marcus Cunliffe, with the eye of the intellectual historian, returns to some of the problems that have occupied other contributors, and in providing a framework for 'the nation's intellectual biography examines those general ideas which were taken seriously by serious men at various epochs'. In so doing he ranges over history, government, literature, religion and philosophy in ways that usefully recapitulate and expand on ideas already introduced.

That the reader should leave this book aware of how many further aspects of America still merit study is one of its primary intentions. Each contributor provides a select bibliography of recommended further reading at the end of his chapter, and at the end of the book there is a short general bibliography drawing attention to standard works and periodicals which, like the map on p. 14, will be found especially useful for reference. 'There is then', said Emerson in 'The American Scholar', 'creative reading as well as creative writing': it is on this belief that this book is based.

University of Manchester   D.W.
March 1973

I Geography and the Development of the U.S.A.

J. WREFORD WATSON

The geography of any country has a great deal to do with its use and development. This is particularly true of the United States which has long regarded geography as one of its main capital assets: from the beginning settlers in America sought out resources that could be turned to good account if not profit. They looked for advantages in sea or land that could help them, and tried to avoid handicaps. Increasingly, they focused activity on areas of comparative favour, and developed the country from its main points of growth. In other words, they had an eye for their geography. Consequently, it played a great part in their history. With an area of just over $3\frac{1}{2}$ million square miles and a population of 220 millions, the United States is now one of the four largest nations in the world. The influence of geography, though real, was by no means uniform, or straightforward, but often diverse and devious. Some areas had a positive effect, in that they drew men to them; others had a negative effect, repelling settlement. Some regions forged ahead at one stage of development, but fell into disuse at another stage. Some parts satisfied one kind of use but were quite hostile to a different type. Again, some parts were thought to be hostile, that in fact were not, or imagined to be of great advantage, only to have events prove them ineffectual.

Geographical influence is, therefore, a very complex thing, affecting different men in different ways, depending on what they can see in geography and also on what they can get out of it. To talk about *the* influence of geography or *the* geography of America is quite misleading. The geography of a region is what any people there can make of it at any time, by selecting from the natural environment what they feel they need for the kind of life they want.

Geography and Culture: Indians and Europeans

This is very apparent if we compare what the Indians made of America with what Europeans did. From the same basic environment they

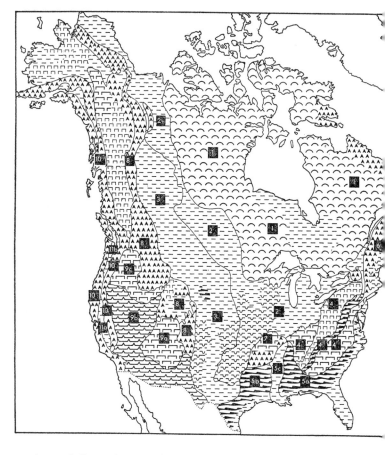

created two different 'geographies'. The geography of Indian America was along north–south rather than east–west lines, it used rivers for travel not for power, it was very dependent on wild life, which the white man destroyed, it virtually ignored fuels and metals, which became the sinews of European success, and it revolved around self-sufficient regions with practically no transcontinental connections such as the Europeans developed, and no contacts outside the continent. The Indian population in what is now the United States at most reached 10 millions and was probably not more than 5 millions, giving a very low density of between 1·4 to 3 people per square mile, compared with the present density of about 63. Thus they did not make much of the environment.

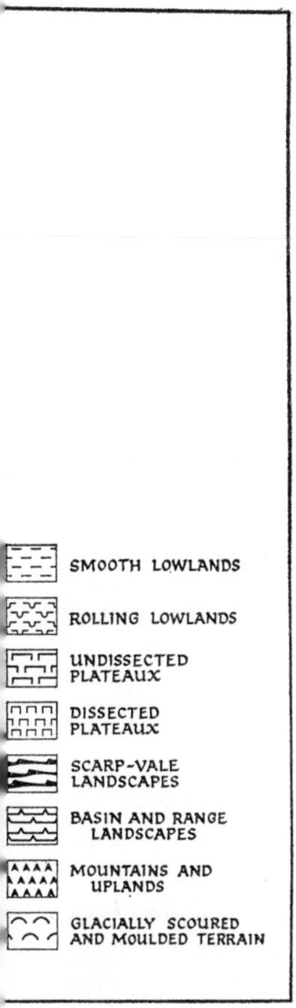

SMOOTH LOWLANDS	
ROLLING LOWLANDS	
UNDISSECTED PLATEAUX	
DISSECTED PLATEAUX	
SCARP-VALE LANDSCAPES	
BASIN AND RANGE LANDSCAPES	
MOUNTAINS AND UPLANDS	
GLACIALLY SCOURED AND MOULDED TERRAIN	

FIGURE I.I. The physiographic regions of North America (after D. K. Adams and H. B. Rodgers, *An Atlas of North American Affairs*, London, Methuen, 1969, p. 3).
I. Laurentian Shield. 2. Central Lowlands. 3. Great Plains. 4. The Piedmont and Appalachians. 5a. Atlantic Coast Plain. 5b. Gulf Coast Plain. 5c. Mississippi Valley. 6. Mountains of New England and Maritime Canada. 7. Ozarks and Ouachita Mountains. 8. The Rockies. 9a. Colorado Plateau. 9b. Basin and Range province. 9c. Columbia Plateau. 10. Coast Range and Sierra Nevada. 11a. Central Valley of the Sacramento and the San Joaquin. 11b. Willamette Valley–Puget Sound.

This was due to the different things they saw in it, or wanted from it. Accept the view that they came into the area from the north and were differently oriented to the whole continent and one is not surprised at the way in which they responded to continental structure. The main grain of America is north–south: the Laurentian Shield, which is exposed in the north, around Lake Superior, plunges beneath the Central Lowlands to the south, forming a huge stable area from the Great Lakes to the Gulf, against which the long wall of the Appalachians was thrown up in the east, and the triple systems of the Western Cordilleras, consisting of Rockies, Cascades, and Coast Range, were pushed up from the west. Coming into this strongly-corrugated structure from Canada, the Indians saw the routes for migration stretching to the south along the Pacific seaboard, along the foothill zone of the Rockies, along the longitudinal sweep of the Great Plains, along the southward-flowing Missouri and Mississippi, and along the plateaux bordering the Appalachians. In relatively few cases did they make much of latitudinal routes: the Great Lakes were one important exception, and the Mohawk Gap, through the Appalachians, another. But by and large it was left to the white man, coming in from the Atlantic bridgeheads, to span the continent in his great drive to the west, and to discover a major use for east–west riverlines, for trans-Appalachian gaps and gaps through the Rockies, Nevadas, and Cascades, and for other routes that came to knit the country together from coast to coast. Indeed, one of the triumphs of the European was that he created a new grain to the country through his roads and railways that largely superseded the natural 'run of the land': coastal terminals and interior junctions of transcontinental railroads and highways became the focal-points for settlement and development, and bridges across the Ohio, Mississippi, and Missouri on the way west, rather than the merging of the waterways on their journey south, dominated the continental heartland.

In their movements the Indians either used the rivers, travelling on them by canoe or raft, or had trails running beside them. They rarely struck out along or across the broad interfluves between. Europeans, by contrast, although using rivers where navigable, frequently preferred the interfluves, especially where the rivers were deeply entrenched and their valleys difficult to use for vehicular traffic.

The rivers of America reflect its structure. In the extreme north they flow away from the United States, in the Red River and the Great Lakes–St Lawrence, around the blunt end of the Laurentian Shield. Then the land becomes tilted southward and inward over the down-faulted and buried portion of the Shield underlying the Central Lowlands. This is the greatest basin in North America – and one of the largest in the world – rimmed by Shield to north, Appalachians to east, and Rockies to west, and sloping down to the Gulf of Mexico, whence the vast Mississippi flows, gathering together the streams whose fertile flood-plains make up the heartland of the continent. In the east their headwaters have eaten back through deep gorges across the Allegheny and Cumberland plateaux to capture the drainage of the central Appalachians. Relatively short, often beheaded, rivers then flow across the outer Appalachians to the Atlantic. In the west, major rivers, starting when the Rockies were elevated, were able to maintain their way to the Pacific across the later fold systems of the Cascades–Nevadas, and the Coast Ranges, reaching the sea, or the Gulf of California, in courses marked by the most profound canyons.

Many of the rivers had falls and rapids. Those falling off the edge of the Laurentian upland, those tumbling down from the Appalachian Piedmont to the Atlantic coastal plain, those plunging from the High Plains to the Central Lowlands in the continental interior, and those breaking through lesser mountain ranges as they flowed westward from the Rocky divide to the Pacific, all had interruptions of one kind or other in their course. Although Indians were in so many ways river-centred, they made no use of the abundance of water power in America. The waterfalls and rapids which have given rise to the 'Fall-Line' cities of the Piedmont, to great interior cities like Cincinnati and Minne-apolis–St Paul, and to western centres like Spokane, were devoid of settlement, or were noted more for the portage villages commanding routes that went *around* the falls than for sites of power attempting to exploit them. Here, then, was a very big difference in the geography of settlement between Indian and European times.

The main interest of most Indians lay in the hunt, and their chief resource was wild life. Consequently, the geography of tribal lands, camps, and trails was very largely that of animals and their migrations. Since big herds of animals need a lot of water, they were found mainly in the humid parts of the country, and a first major distinction within Indian cultures was that between the effective hunting tribes, in the humid forest or subhumid grassland environments, and the simpler gathering-and-collecting communities of the arid mountain basins.

Thus climate, as the ultimate factor behind vegetation and wild life, came to have its say. The climates of the United States are dominated by polar and tropical air-masses. There are two sets of these, divided, although by no means completely, by the western Cordilleras. East of the Cordilleras are the polar continental air-mass, centred over the Laurentian upland, and the tropical maritime air-mass, over the Gulf of Mexico. Their conflicts make up the weather from the Rockies to the Atlantic. The polar continental air advances south in October, reaches the Ozarks in January, and retreats back to Canada in March; tropical gulf air invades the Lower Mississippi in April, spreads to the Great Lakes and the Red River in June, and subsides in September south of the Appalachians. Thus a constant succession of cold waves from the north and warm waves from the south creates cyclonic storms that sweep from west to east, carrying snow and rain. Since they are sparse in

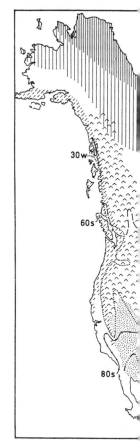

FIGURE I.2. Climatic contrast in North America
(after Adams and Rodgers, op. cit., p. 5).

the west but numerous in the east they produce subhumid grasslands over the Great Plains, and forests in the Central Lowlands and the Appalachians.

West of the Cordilleras are the polar maritime air-mass of the Pacific Northwest, and the tropical high-pressure system of the Southwest. The former produces storms that sweep onshore and thus bring rains from San Francisco to Seattle, clothing the coast ranges with America's tallest and densest forests – the California Redwoods and the Western Cedar, Western Hemlock, and Douglas Fir of the Puget Sound. The Southwest highs draw air *away* from the continent and thus lead to dry offshore winds that aggravate the deserts lying in the rain shadow of the mountains. Fortunately for California, the polar

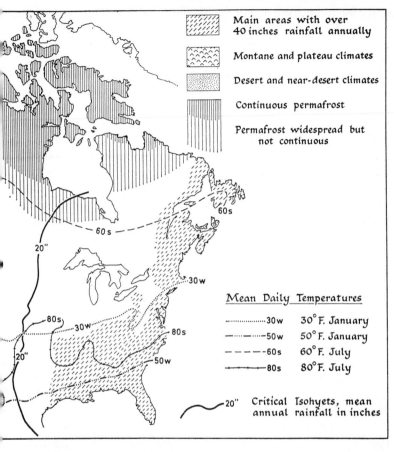

Main areas with over 40 inches rainfall annually

Montane and plateau climates

Desert and near-desert climates

Continuous permafrost

Permafrost widespread but not continuous

Mean Daily Temperatures

30w	30° F. January
50w	50° F. January
60s	60° F. July
80s	80° F. July

20″ Critical Isohyets, mean annual rainfall in inches

airs shift well south in winter, bringing a rainy season even to southern California. But summer sees the return of the tropical highs and of dry weather. A huge wedge of drought divides the humid Northwest from the humid Mid-West and East of America. The intermontane basins between the Nevada–Cascade ranges and the Rockies are cut off from the cyclones blowing in from the Pacific or sweeping across the Missouri–Mississippi plains. On the whole, America is blessed with humid climates and changeful weather, but it does experience the challenge of real drought in the western basins and the arid Southwest.

This division between humid and arid showed up during Indian times in dramatic contrasts between the really quite rich hunters and fishermen of the Pacific Northwest, the comparatively poor collectors of the intermontane basins of the Mountain West, and the reasonably secure and affluent hunters of the Great Plains. The Pacific Northwest lies in the path of the annual salmon swarms; the lower parts of its rivers have been drowned by the sea, making long inlets ideal for the salmon runs; at the same time the dense coniferous forest, nurtured by a mild wet climate, provided the wherewithal for canoes and traps; fishing communities grew up with an abundance of raw materials. Large villages appeared, made of solidly-built wooden houses, roofed with bark, where chiefs displayed their wealth in ceremonies of lavish hospitality. Wood carving and painting flourished and totemic art reached a high stage of development.

The buffalo hunters of the Great Plains did not advance as far in arts and crafts, mainly because they could not adopt a sedentary life but had to migrate from place to place following the annual march of the game across the prairies, but they ate well, and were well clothed. Their camps were large and they became a fairly populous people, noted for their warlike discipline.

In the high plateaux and intermontane basins between the coast and the Great Plains, Indian population was much lower, tribes and camps were smaller, equipment and artifacts simpler and more restricted. Dana, one of the nineteenth-century pioneer geologists, tells us how he was shot at with a stone-tipped arrow by a boy who, with his family, lived in Stone-Age conditions. Their ancestors moved into the refuge of the mountain basins, or fled into the isolation of the deserts, over 8000 years ago, and showed little if any advancement until Spaniard or American eventually caught them up into modern times.

Whether it was the inadequacy of their mind or of the environment that kept them back, compared with other Indians, is a debatable matter: most of the more advanced Indians lived in the more fruitful climates and were given the opportunities of making progress by having a much greater range of products at their command. On the other hand, the so-called Pueblo Indians of the arid Southwest advanced well beyond their Paiute neighbours, in spite of suffering from the same insecurity and paucity of resources. Through their own initiative and inventiveness they became seed-cultivators, instead of seed-gatherers, and, learning the secrets of irrigation, albeit in a primitive way, made use of the climate, with its long growing season and ample sunshine, to develop an agriculture rich enough to support towns, temples, pottery, metal-craft, and jewellery. Thus the deserts which in most of arid America led to the continuation of very primitive ways, also saw the rise of early civilization, producing in the Pueblo culture the hope of finding the fabled 'Seven Cities of Cibola' that drew the first white men into what is today the United States.

If Carl Sauer is correct, the idea of cultivation spread from Mexico and the arid Southwest into the humid Southeast, and certainly agriculture here vied with hunting as the mainstay of people's lives. The constant sweep of cyclonic storms down from Canada or up from the Gulf of Mexico made the lands east of the Mississippi exceptionally well watered. The frequency of warm fronts in these storms broke up the severity of winter and prolonged the summer. The frost-free season south of the Mohawk valley was in excess of 175 days and was practically year-round in Florida. In other words, conditions were certainly favourable for agriculture. Maize, squash, and bean were planted together in clearings in the forest and provided a sufficiently regular supply of food to warrant the setting up of permanent settlements.

Nevertheless, agriculture was never carried to the extent where forests were cut away for, and replaced by, crops. Hunting remained a major occupation, and the men spent more time in the woods than on the fields. Wood buffalo, deer, bear, wild turkey, and pigeon furnished plenty of sport as well as much-needed food. The white pioneer also lived like this for a while, but was soon tempted to replace fur-trapping and deer-hunting by the raising of maize and cattle; forests were cut out in all areas where it was thought crops could offer more profit, and what had been an essentially closed, wooded landscape was turned into an open one of fields of corn and pasture.

The fact is that the 'influence' of the environment in the American East could work in either of these directions. The climate was humid enough, with over 40 inches of rain, and had a long enough growing season, with over 175 frost-free days, to support both a rich broad-leaved hardwood forest of oak and chestnut, cypress and pine, where a full range of herbivorous animals could develop, and also a varied and productive suite of cultivable plants. Hunting (or its replacement by herding), and the gathering of fruits, nuts, and seeds (or its replacement by farming), were alike suitable responses to the situation: the Indians chose a mixed economy of hunting and agriculture, the whites a more sophisticated one including trapping, agriculture, and lumbering.

A major contrast between Indian and European geography lay in the realm of fuels and metals. The Indian never permitted the unique wealth of coal, oil, iron, copper, lead and zinc, bauxite, precious metals, limestone, gypsum, salt and potash which occurs in America to influence the geography of settlement, routes, trade, occupation, or standards of living to any significant extent. He never augmented the barrenness of the Mountain West from the stores of gold, silver, copper, lead, and zinc whose working is now one of the distinguishing features of that region; although he had begun to work the copper of the Great Lakes area, he made comparatively little use of it, particularly in manufacture and trade, and was ignorant of the happy concurrence of coal, iron, and limestone in that region which is now the basis of the world's largest steel and steel-using industry. In ignorance, the hunter wandered over the world's largest coalfield along the western flanks of the Appalachians, or the great anthracite field on their eastern flanks. Similarly, the natural gas that occasionally bubbled up in the southern High Plains, or the stains of oil there or in the lowlands of the Gulf, went quite unnoticed: yet these have been found to be today among the world's largest gas and oil reserves. The geography of mineral wealth in America had virtually no influence until minerally-minded men came on the scene: then steam-power pounced on the coalfields; the internal-combustion engine opened up the oilfields; the ship, the railway, the motor-car and the combine dug deep into reserves of iron; and the aeroplane quickened the attack on copper and bauxite. With these developments, the huge ironfields of the Laurentian upland around Lake Superior, deposits of other metals in the metamorphosed rocks in contact with the crystalline cores of the Western Cordilleras, and the truly vast fuel reserves found along the west flanks of the Appalachians and the east flanks of the Rockies, and in great basins in the Mississippi valley and by the Gulf of Mexico, made themselves effective, and showed America to be the best-endowed continent for modern industry of any in the world.

Since most of the minerals were found at depth, they gave a third dimension to American geography. It became necessary to think of the influence of what lay below the surface, as well as of the surface itself, and of what was on and above the surface: geology, relief, vegetation, and climate all came into play. This was the main result of white occupation, it gave effect to the total environment.

Geography and Psychology: European Concepts

This is not to say, however, that it brought all parts into play with equal effect. European realization of the environment, though much greater than that of the Indian, was itself very uneven, in terms of both concept and organization. With regard to concept, what man does with the environment, and therefore the kind of land he recreates out of that environment, depends on the image of it developed in his mind. It is the mental image of mountains or deserts as barriers that determines to what extent and in what ways they become effective as barriers, and so forth. Yet skills are also important, and one could suggest that the chief barrier presented by mountain or desert is a lack of engineering skills, not relief or climate: given engineering competence both mountains and deserts can be brought under control.

With regard to organization, some areas have been developed almost to an excessive degree, as for example in what Gottman calls the American 'megalopolis', that strip of highly urbanized land running from Boston to Baltimore; other areas, like Appalachia, where resources have been neglected because they have been too difficult to exploit or the people too poor to exploit them, are underdeveloped by comparison. Regions where rich concentrations of resources occur in very accessible situations have shown such a cost advantage that they have been used to a maximum, leading to more and more people crowding into more and more crowded areas, while other parts, costly to develop in terms of men, money, material and time, have been avoided or given up. Thus certain places have had a positive influence, others a negative effect on settlement and development. In most geographical accounts, attention is paid principally to the positive areas. In America, these have been tremendously important: the mid-Atlantic seaboard, the Hudson–Mohawk valley, the Pittsburgh region, the Lower Great Lakes, the Chicago–lower Lake Michigan region, Puget Sound, San Francisco Bay, and Southern California have acted like magnets. However, the great negative areas of America are equally significant: the emptied uplands of New England, the sandhills of the southern Coast Plain, the Cumberland Plateau and the Ozarks, the Staked Plains and the arid basins of the Mountain West, are parts which people have avoided or from which they have drifted away.

The role of ideas and techniques in the geography of America has not been given enough attention. Yet this 'psychological environment', as Professor William Kirk has called it, merits study because it is the measure of the ultimate or natural environment. The America seen with the mind's eye often determined the course of American exploration and development. The early reports of Friar Marcos that there were seven large cities in the country of the Zuni Indians 'with houses of stone and lime, and on the door-sills and lintels of the principal houses many figures of turquoise' sent Coronado after the seven lost cities of Cibola (to which the Christians were said to have fled after their defeat by the Moors in A.D. 734). As Hoffman says, this mythological belief had its part to play in opening up America, for 'with the expansion of Spanish exploration the location of the legendary Seven Cities moved gradually westward'. When Coronado came upon them, the mental geography of the seven legendary cities had to be rudely contracted to the real geography of seven Zuni Pueblos, but at least the vision of the lost cities in the mind's eye had drawn the Spaniards to the edge of the Great Plains, deep in the heart of America. In the same way La Salle, hearing of a warm sea to the south of the St Lawrence, which he took to be the China sea, set out into the West on those trips to discover Cathay which led him through the Great Lakes to the lower Mississippi. Although the mental image of the West which he held was quite erroneous, it spurred him on to make those journeys that took France into the American heartland and, incidentally, provided bases for America's great push to the West in the nineteenth century. In that western drive the Americans in their turn came to have certain mental images that affected their progress. Chief among these were the concept of a 'great American desert' which made the pioneers avoid the Great Plains for the Pacific Northwest. Later, men held the view that 'rain followed the plough' and that by breaking up the prairie sod they would improve the climate and make the West safe.

Pike's expedition of 1806–12 along the Spanish trail to Santa Fe from the Missouri had a profound effect upon the opening of the West in that he described the Great Plains as uninhabitable and fit only for the Indians. They were not a domain for the farmer, who was advised to stay east of the Missouri. The Yellowstone expedition of Stephen H. Long in 1820 reported that 'in regard to the extensive area between the Missouri River and the Rocky Mountains, we do not hesitate in giving the opinion that it is almost wholly unfit for cultivation, and of course uninhabitable by a people depending upon agriculture for their subsistence'. The map of the expedition called the Plains area 'the Great American Desert'. Even as late as 1863 Captain Palliser wrote, 'The fertile savannahs and valuable woodlands of the Atlantic United States are succeeded . . . on the West by a more or less arid desert, occupying a region on both sides of the Rockies, which creates a barrier to the continuous growth of settlements between the Mississippi valley and the States on the Pacific Coast.' About the same time Hind stated, 'It is impossible to examine a map of the North American continent without being impressed with the remarkable influence which the Great American Desert must exercise upon the future of the United States.'

As a result of such reports the Oregon, and later the California, pioneers trekked right across the Great Plains to take up their abode in the humid forests of the Pacific coast, failing to realize the worth of the intervening grasslands. At best they considered them to be the realm of the rancher: *farmers* pushed on to the Willamette valley and Puget Sound. Thus the myth of the 'Great American Desert' more profoundly influenced the use of the Great Plains than the Plains themselves. This is obvious from the fact that after 1870 the real worth of the Plains began to be understood, and the rich black and brown soils were eagerly sought out by the 'sod-busters' in the western rush of the homesteader.

Great improvements in technology helped the farmer. The railroads pushed across the Plains and brought him tools and machines, at the same time taking his produce to eastern and eventually transatlantic markets; barbed-wire fencing kept cattle and sheep out from the crops; the metal windmill brought water into sites independent of river and spring; the disc plough, the seed drill, and the reaper-binder mechanized farming and increased productivity; and finally new skills in farming, and the breeding of frost- and drought-resistant grains, all gave a new command over the land.

New techniques helped to conserve soil moisture. Breaking the sod early so that the soil would catch the spring melt, cultivating ruthlessly to prevent the weeds sucking up moisture, summer 'planking' to stop evaporation, creating a mulch on the soil surface to keep summer rains in, increasing the supply of humus to help soil decomposition, using crops that could be harvested early thus permitting the land to lie fallow and accumulate moisture for a longer time in the autumn, and planting crops that drank as little water as possible, all assisted the advance of farming at the expense of ranching.

Then as Henry Nash Smith shows, the notion grew up that 'Rain follows the plough'. It was imagined that farming would further its success by making the climate more humid, thus chasing away drought. The mental image of the Great Plains as the domain of the wheat farmer drew scores of thousands of cultivators to the region. The result was a completely new geography, with wheat and cotton farms spreading west, virtually to the foothills, pushing the ranches into the bad-lands or the mountains.

That this new geography was ill-founded (being founded on a myth), was proved several times over by disastrous droughts, when it became evident that dust storms could follow the plough as well as rain. The worst of these droughts, lasting from 1930–6, ruined so many farmers that the government had to step in and try to redress the harm done. Millions of acres were taken out of cropland and put back into rangeland and a more rational balance was struck between ranching and farming, based on a scientific appraisal of the real environment.

Even science can, of course, err, making it still more difficult to evaluate the 'influence of geography'. One example of this comes from a reinterpretation of the agricultural regions of the United States. On the not unreasonable assumption that cultivated plants, like all types of vegetation, are conditioned by temperature and humidity, the distribution of crops came to be explained in terms of climate. However, crops are raised by farmers who are conditioned by profit and loss; the distribution of farm activities may thus be explained by the cost of land, labour, and access to market. Some of these costs can undoubtedly be related to climate, and a farmer with an eye to profits will try to make the most of the climate in which he lives. But many costs have nothing to do with climate. They spring from the competition with other users of land and other employers of labour; they result from other calls on capital, and other profits from transport. As a consequence agricultural regions must be thought of in economic terms, in output per man or per acre in comparison with output in other occupations, or land-man returns, or man-hour income.

Geography and Economics: Cost-Distance

If one takes the agricultural zones from Chicago to Nebraska, they consist of the dairy belt, the corn belt, and the wheat belt. This could be taken to reflect a gradation from a cool-temperate humid climate, through a warm-temperate humid one, to a warm-temperate dry regime. Yet it might better be explained in terms of the cost of access to Chicago: dairy farmers are able to pay the high costs of their nearness to Chicago because of the high returns of a local market, but wheat farmers have no chance to compete for local access and are therefore willing to accept the lower returns of being a long distance out.

This is a debatable matter. There is no gainsaying that the three crop belts are closely related to corresponding climatic zones. In the dairy belt, the cows feed mainly on timothy hay, clover, oats, and silage corn. Timothy hay is native to New England and does well in a relatively short growing season with summers averaging between 65 and 70°F. Clover and oats were brought from Britain where they were adapted to even cooler summers of 58 to 65°F. Silage corn, although it usually does better in a warmer summer, can flourish where the July average is about 65 to 68°F. All these crops are humid plants, requiring a rainfall of over 30 inches. Now in New England and the Great Lakes States rainfall is between 35 and 40 inches and July averages are about 68°F. Climate and crops seem to show an obvious correlation, and this whole region has therefore been called America's dairy belt.

Yet up until about 1880 this was the American wheat belt; soft wheat was the major crop in western New York, Ohio, and southern Michigan, and Rochester, N.Y. was the flour-milling capital of America. It did not lose its pre-eminence until the turn of the century when Minneapolis–St Paul finally replaced it. The changeover from wheat farming to dairying was due to two things: the cheapness of Western wheat on newly acquired land secured at a very low cost compared with the East, where land values were rising steeply, and the presence of a rapidly growing market for fresh milk in the industrial cities that were springing up all the way from Boston to Chicago. This market gave farmers the profits from which to pay for the rising cost of land and labour in the East. And this is the main reason for the continuance of dairying in the region: thanks to the enormous demand for milk in New England, New York, and the Great Lakes States there are sufficiently high returns for dairy farmers to compete successfully with other users of land and other employers of labour in the region. It is really the rise of the American manufacturing belt (in an area that happens to be suited to cool temperate humid forage crops and pasture-land) that explains the presence of the dairy belt; that is to say, economics rather than climate.

The existence of the corn belt in the great triangle between the Ohio and the Missouri might with more confidence be attributed to climate. Although corn is widely grown outside this area, from Mexico to Canada, nevertheless it is present here in a much greater concentration than anywhere else. Is it not likely that corn-growing has been concentrated here because here are the ideal conditions? Corn does not mature successfully where the mean July temperature is less than 66°F. On the other hand it suffers from wilting if the average is over 80°F. Corn does best where the mean temperature of the ripening season lies between 70 and 80°F. The mean July isotherm of 77°F runs through southern Iowa and Indiana – about the middle of the 'corn belt'. Corn likes a fairly humid climate with between 25 and 50 inches of rainfall. But it is very particular. It likes rain to fall chiefly at the beginning of the season, from mid-May to mid-July, and then to slacken off to a golden autumn from mid-August to mid-October. Also, it prefers the rain to fall at night. But these are the very conditions in the middle Mississippi basin, where early summer cyclones, mid-summer convection rains occurring mainly in late afternoon or evening, and late-summer anticyclones giving a bright, sunny fall, form the usual weather.

Undoubtedly the American farmer has become increasingly aware of the advantages of growing corn here. Yet he has been exploiting other factors as well, such as the need in the American manufacturing belt for prime-fed pork and beef products, and the nice geographical location, where he is near enough to serve this market, and yet remote enough to avoid competition with dairy farms and market gardens. It is in fact his position on the cost-distance scale that has proved crucial. He is not at the high cost–short distance end of the scale, close to the industrial market, and yet he is away from the low cost–long distance end, far from the market. His product, beef or pork, may not outprice milk, eggs, and vegetables and so he cannot afford being close at hand; yet it fetches a higher price than range-fed beef or wheat, and therefore he does not need to be as far out.

Cost-distance rather than climate may also account for the wheat districts in the Great Plains. Wheat can be grown here not only because short summer rains and a long sunny fall suit the growth and harvesting of wheat, but because successful wheat growing needs a lot of low-cost land, and can afford the cost of a long haul to market. After all, wheat is still grown as a profitable cash crop in the dairy belt, and as a winter crop in the corn belt. It can be raised under climatic conditions distinctly cooler, hotter, and more humid than in the American Great Plains. Yet it is a subsidiary crop in these other locations, tributary to the forage-crop/dairy or the corn/pork–beef economies. The chief reason for its being the main crop in the Great Plains is that it could not afford to be the main crop in any of the other cropping areas. It was not until wheat took up the lower end of the cost-distance scale that it found its chief opportunity, and came to dominate the farmscape. True, this is a region where other crops were not likely to flourish, but wheat could have flourished in other regions. The reason for its concentration in the Great Plains was its economic isolation there; its advantage was that it could make use of an area of little advantage to higher-cost enterprise.

Geography and Society: Social Distance

Cost-distance has not been the only means of dividing and isolating communities. Social distance has grown to almost equal importance, providing a status scale that has separated people from each other in a way that has become characteristically, although by no means uniquely, American. The social distance between white and black, native-born and foreign-born, higher and lower income groups has created a geography of segregation stamped upon every American settlement. Indeed, it can be argued that 'the geography of segregation segregates out the United States in the geography of North America', since in no other part of the continent is the force of social distance, separating group from group, so strong or widespread.

This can hardly be said to be inherent in the basic geography, but once it had created a geography of segregation, then man-made 'social geography' came to condition the further development of settlement and society. In other words man, by separating off black areas from white, foreign-born districts from native, lower-class sites from upper, evolved a geographical pattern that crystallized and hardened the social distances between people in a concrete way, in the very landscape itself, making that landscape a physical environment for continued and further separation. The effect of geographical segregation has thus become part of the 'influence of geography' on society.

Every American city is really a congeries of cities made up of their Harlems, Chinatowns, Ghettoes, Little Sicilies, Germantowns, and so forth. This is, of course, true of other North American and of the larger European cities. But there is a difference: Jim Crow laws in the American South and social covenants in the North have, at least in the near past, made formal what is generally informal elsewhere. Desegregation laws have started to change things and should in the end write a new geography, but social distance between high-status black and low-status black, or high- and low-status white, will doubtless still continue to operate. In a mainly all-white community like 'Yankee City', as L. Warner and P. F. Lunt have shown, differences between wealthy and poor have created different neighbourhoods such as Hill Street (upper town) and Riverbrook (lower town) which, though almost side by side, are worlds apart. In Hill Street, all are native-born, in Riverbrook 37 per cent are foreign-born; in the former, most are of

Anglo-Saxon stock, in the latter 56 per cent are of other ethnic extraction including all the Negroes, 90 per cent of the Poles, 70 per cent of the Ukrainians, and 50 per cent of the French Canadians, Greeks, and Italians. In upper town 83 per cent are in proprietary or professional positions; in lower town 89 per cent are in unskilled or semi-skilled occupations; less than 1 per cent of the houses in Hill Street, but 71 per cent in Riverbrook, are in poor condition; all the Hill Street children finish High School, but 85 per cent do not do so in Riverbrook. Perhaps the most significant difference of all is that, of the arrests made in the city, less than 0·5 per cent are from upper town but 65 per cent are from lower town. None of the Hill Street residents arrested were juveniles, whereas over 30 per cent of the juvenile delinquents lived in Riverbrook. In other words, Hill Street is a wealthy, established, and influential community, able to protect itself and to set a great distance socially between itself and the dwellers of nearby Riverbrook, who are poor, insecure, and with practically no political influence. Such are the status gulfs that yawn between groups in American society. Yet in the struggle for status, Americans can move both up and down. At one time in Yankee City the Catholic Irish were at the foot of the social scale; as they became more established, they could look down on the French-Canadians; these in their turn made a place for themselves, and felt one above the Italian immigrant. No one is tied to his class.

Geography and Time: the Factor of Change

Change is the essence of America. People constantly change status, change occupation, and change residence. And these combinations change from region to region. As a consequence, regions have changed themselves. This is a fascinating aspect of the American scene. Its parts are always combining and recombining with other parts to create different sections of the nation at different times. American geography is thus tremendously dynamic. It is in a state of constant evolution. What is true of it in one generation may not be true of the next. The regions of Indian times were replaced by those of Colonial America. As America discovered its West, regions changed again, reaching from Atlantic hearthlands to trans-Appalachian frontiers. The America of turnpike roads and canals changed again with the railway age, becoming truly transcontinental in its scope and grasp. The agricultural revolution worked out its pattern of dairy, corn, cotton, and wheat belts and cattle and sheep lands. The industrial revolution made the greatest change, creating the American manufacturing belt and reorienting the agricultural belts accordingly. The urban revolution of the present day is focusing activity and control in a few dominating centres whose widening spheres of influence divide up the rest of America. The space revolution which America has done so much to pioneer may create the most sweeping changes of all, making the whole of America but one region in a new vast Western Community including the Americas, Europe, Oceania, Japan, Australia, and New Zealand.

F. Mood and V. Carstensen, in Jensen's *Regionalism in America*, have given an excellent survey of the evolution of regions within the United States. They point out that after the Revolution, the U.S. Government set about administering the country through sectional divisions. Thus there were Eastern (i.e. New England), Middle (Mid-Atlantic Coast), and Southern (South Atlantic Coast) divisions of the Department of Indian Affairs. There were Eastern and Middle divisions under the Navy; and Eastern, Middle, and Southern commands of the Army. Similarly, three judicial circuits were organized, known as the Eastern, Middle, and Southern – although in this case New York was included in the Eastern, and Virginia with the Middle divisions. At the beginning of the nineteenth century, when the West began to be opened up, a Western legal circuit was instituted, consisting of Ohio, Kentucky, and Tennessee. By the mid-nineteenth century, expansion into the West was so great that it was too cumbersome to have a single Western circuit. Three new circuits were created, made up of the Northwest, including Ohio, Michigan, Indiana, and Illinois; a Western–Middle division, of Kentucky, Tennessee, and Missouri; and the Southwest, of Alabama, Mississippi, Louisiana, and Arkansas. Subsequently, a 'Deep South' circuit was organized, extending from Florida to Texas – together with a Mid-West circuit for the lands opening up on the west side of the Mississippi, from Oklahoma to Minnesota; and a Far-West circuit for California, which was extended to Oregon. At the end of the century, the Great Plains and nearer Mountain States came within the Mid-West, while the farther Mountain States were allocated to the Far-West.

These divisions were in the main a reflection of American physiography. The old Eastern, Middle, and Southern districts were the eastern part of the Appalachians, made up of the New England upland, the mid-Atlantic estuaries, and the Southern coast plain and Piedmont plateau. They looked mainly to the sea, traded with each other and with Europe, and offered a wide range of products from Maine pine and potatoes to oak, tobacco, and cotton from Virginia. As the interior developed, the Middle region came to the fore, commanding the Hudson–Mohawk and the Delaware–Susquehanna gaps across the Appalachians. Indeed, for a time, what is now Ohio was included in the Middle district, which was thus the bridge between seaboard and heartland.

Trans-Appalachian America, or the West, changed in character and meaning on being 'unrolled', as F. J. Turner brought out in his *Rise of the New West*. Actually the first West – often referred to as the Old West – does not come into what we now think of as the West at all; it was the western fringe of the Seaboard States, and consisted of back-country New England, upstate New York, and the ridge-and-valley section of the Appalachians beyond the Piedmont plateau. By the early nineteenth century this was integrated with the East through the building of the Genesee Road, the Catskill Turnpike, the National Road and the Wilderness Road from the seaports across the middle Appalachians.

As people streamed over these roads they passed the Allegheny Front and came out on the Allegheny and Cumberland plateaux, and so descended to the Ohio and Great Lakes lowlands. The trans-Allegheny or New West then stretched out right across the continent, first to the Rockies, and subsequently to the Pacific. This vast area came to have different names as different characteristics were recognized. From the Alleghenies the land sloped to the northwest and the southwest. The Old Northwest was that slope going from the Allegheny plateau, over the Pottsville scarp, to the low and fertile plain fronting on to Lake Erie. Here the Erie and Allegheny canal connected the lake with the headwaters of the Ohio. It was paralleled by the Ohio canal, from the Ohio to Cleveland, and the Miami canal from the Ohio to Toledo. The Old Southwest, by contrast, consisted of the slope of land from the Cumberland plateau to the lower Mississippi and the Gulf, and was made up of the states from Kentucky to Louisiana, given unity by the Kentucky, Cumberland, and Tennessee rivers and the Mississippi delta.

The New Northwest comprised the basin of the Upper Mississippi, principally Illinois, Wisconsin, and Minnesota, stretching more or less from Chicago to St Paul: while the New Southwest came into being with the rise of Texas and the other trans-Mississippian territories in the south.

As the pioneers pushed on up the Oregon and California trails to the Pacific, the terms Pacific Northwest and the American Southwest were coined for the Columbia basin, and for California and the southwest

Mountain States. The name Mid-West was often given for all the lands of the Mississippi basin from the Appalachians to the Rockies, while the Far West was used for all that lay beyond the Rockies. In the late nineteenth century the latter was divided into the Mountain West, between the Rockies and the Cascade–Nevada system, and the Pacific West, made up of Puget Sound, the Wilamette valley, the Great Valley of California, southern California, and all the American Pacific coast. In 1875, Swinton proposed that the word 'Western' should be reserved for the Rocky Mountain, Plateau, and Pacific States, and that the designation 'Central' should be applied to the Mississippi basin States. Later, he suggested dividing these states into an Eastern Central and a Western Central, divided by the Mississippi itself.

The Census Bureau of the United States has tried to reflect the importance of American regions by tabulating statistics by groups of states. A widely used system has been that first proposed by the U.S. Census in 1910 which divides the country up into nine major sections, viz.: (i) New England; (ii) the Mid-Atlantic States; (iii) the East North–Central States (the Ohio–Wisconsin–Great Lakes region); (iv) the West North–Central States (the Missouri–Red River region); (v) the South Atlantic Coastal States; (vi) the East South–Central States (Southern Appalachians to the lower Mississippi); (vii) the West South–Central States (lower Mississippi to the Rockies); (viii) the Mountain States (between the Rockies and the Sierra Nevadas); and (ix) the Pacific Coast States (Nevadas to the coast). This system of division, with occasional modification, is still extensively used.

However, it obscures a very important trend in modern geography, and that is the orientation of the land to the city. Urbanization is the most potent force in America today. And with the increasing urbanization of life – and by this is meant something much more than the increasing concentration of population in cities: the commercialization, mechanization, integration, and standardization of life – the rapidly growing power of the city has come to dominate the geography of the country. An especially important aspect of this is its domination of regional geography. 'The city', Lewis Mumford says, 'is the region in human expression'. More and more, the city extends its influence outward and gathers the countryside into its sphere, until it creates its own region, focusing the life and thought and activity of an area recognizably on itself (see map on pp. 120–1).

C. A. Dawson, in his *Essays in Society*, describes this trend in his discussion of North American conditions. 'In each physiographic region', he writes, 'a major city emerges. The expanse of territory tributary to each city depends on transportation advantages, the resources of its hinterland, and the stage reached in its development. Its cycle of development links it increasingly with a widening hinterland. If such a city has distinct advantages it tends to become the centre of a metropolitan region which extends beyond its original physiographic basis. These metropolitan regions in turn compete with each other with regard to position and function. In this fashion the whole of America is in process of being organized into a constellation of metropolitan regions.'

This is becoming daily more true, although not all the country can be conveniently assigned to the sphere-of-influence of one metropolis or another. New York dominates the Atlantic coast and the main breakthrough across the Appalachians. Chicago is the supreme centre of the Mid-West. Seattle commands the Pacific Northwest, and Los Angeles the American Southwest. These are outstanding examples. The South is different: it comes under no one centre. The Gulf South has usually been thought of as tributary to New Orleans, but Houston bids fair to contest this. The Appalachian South is somewhat similarly divided between Atlanta, the commercial and cultural centre, and Birmingham, focus of industry.

Geography and Space: the Regional Factor
(a) the New York Region

The New York region is, in one sense, the entire nation since, as the greatest of all metropolitan centres, it exerts a financial and cultural influence that spreads across America. But at the second level of finance, commerce, mass communication, education, and so forth, its sphere is so strongly contested west of the Appalachians by Chicago in the north, or New Orleans in the south, and further west still by Denver, Seattle, and Los Angeles, that its range of immediate efficacy is limited mainly to the east coast, with a spur extending to Lake Erie.

The New York region is a densely-packed, urbanized strip reaching from Boston to Washington – called by D. J. Bogue the Atlantic Metropolitan Belt – together with a large hinterland. The area is a very diverse one, consisting of coast plain, Appalachian upland, the Adirondack massif, and lakeshore plain. At first sight it might appear to have no unity; but it has been made into a region by man through a chain of cities connected with each other by links along the coast and links across the uplands. Diversity, given unity, has been a source of great strength. The New York region embraces all the major structures, land-forms, types of vegetation, and kinds of weather found in north-eastern North America. Indeed, no other metropolis is the centre of such a variety of conditions. Translated into human terms this has meant a great range of occupations and interests, with resources of iron, coal, and hydro-electric power for industry, with rich timber reserves, a remarkable suite of farm-types, and significant fishing grounds, all brought so close together as to stimulate finance and trade. Such a geography did not of itself 'produce' development, as witness the Manhattan Indians, who, with these very same opportunities at hand, remained quite undistinguished as a simple tribe practising rudimentary gardening, hunting, and fishing. But the geographic opportunities did make it possible for dynamic peoples like the Dutch, British, and Americans to create in and through New York a dynamic economy and society. To this extent the influence of geography has been profound.

New York city itself includes many of the elements of its region. It is centred on Manhattan, a hard rocky island which is part of the Appalachian upland. The city has spread across to the morainic hills and hollows of Long Island, part of the Atlantic coast plain. Through New York run drowned river valleys that are caught up into the estuary of the Hudson, commanding the Hudson–Mohawk Gap to the Great Lakes and the interior lowlands. These natural ties have been most effectively used by the Americans to connect the New England bays and the great estuaries of the Mid-Atlantic States, together with the St Lawrence–Great Lakes basin, with New York, making it an unrivalled transportation and trading centre. Here are both the major ocean terminals from Europe, and rail and road terminals from the interior of the United States. Their exploitation by industry, com-merce, and finance has built up the New York urban area to 16 millions. The advantages used from Boston Bay to the Chesapeake inlet have added another 24 millions, centred in metropolises which, though sub-ordinate to New York, are great in themselves, such as Boston, $3\frac{1}{2}$m., Philadelphia, 5m., Baltimore, 2m., and Washington, 3m. Altogether some 80 million people live in the Atlantic Metropolitan Belt, focused on New York (see map on pp. 122–3).

The coast plain has been the basis of their wealth, even although in the New York region it is so narrow and broken it has been little more than a beach-head for the American attack upon the continent. In fact in New England it is virtually absent, for the New England upland plunges into the sea very abruptly, except for a few areas where glacial deposits built small lowlands, as in Boston Bay. The plain proper begins at Cape Cod, runs through Long Island and New Jersey, and widens out beyond the Chesapeake in Virginia. It is made up of young rocks dipping gently to the Atlantic, often with distinct though low scarps of limestone rising above shallow clay vales. Much of it has been drowned by the sea, and its seaward connections have been as important as its landward ones. From early colonial times agriculture and commerce went hand in hand. The growth of commercial towns excited expansion in village and farm. Ground became used more and more intensively, and, with the onset of the motor age and quick transport to market, developed into America's main truck-farming belt, concentrating on vegetables, fruit, eggs, and dairy produce. Rich agriculture provided capital surplus for investment in industry which in turn offered an expanding market for agriculture. Yet the balance was unequal. The function of the coast plain as port, terminal, emporium, factory, hotel, and office for an America reaching far beyond its confines, both out to sea and into the interior, made this the most highly urbanized and commercialized area in the United States.

Again, this was not true of Indian times. It was the white trader who saw the value of the sea-shot strip of land at the gaps to the interior; it was the white engineer who built the National, Catskill, Mohawk, and Wilderness roads; the white entrepreneur who capitalized the Erie, the Chesapeake and Ohio, the Juniata, and the James and Kanawha canals; and the white financiers who, in fierce competition with each other, constructed the Boston and Albany, the Erie, the New York Central, the Pennsylvania, and the Baltimore and Ohio railroads. As a consequence, the coast plain achieved new value, swarmed with people, and became America's real centre, although far from being geographically central.

It is today America's most highly urban region, with some 86 per cent of the population living in cities and only 2 per cent on the farms. Moreover, 66 per cent live in large cities of over 500,000. Cities tend to merge into each other, producing a belt of citified land from Portland, Maine, to Richmond, Virginia. Here the average density of the population is over 600 per square mile, or about ten times the U.S. average of 63. Town spreads out into country so that there is a wide mingling of urban and rural landscapes. This is increased by the mass movements of commuters into the city to work by morning and out to the country to sleep by night. Nearly two millions move into greater

New York every day. Seasonal movements out into the hills or down to the sea during the holidays mount to scores of millions. Cottage colonies pepper the countryside, joined to sprawling suburbs by super-highways. Summer-used land is full of golf and country clubs, car parks, open-air cinemas, airstrips, motels, hot-dog and cold-custard stands, and a vast city litter.

Special characteristics of the area are the high proportion of business and professional people, a constantly increasing division of labour, a unique concentration of highly-skilled and well-paid personnel, an unparalleled accumulation of capital for investment, very great scientific, technical, and educational aids, the centralization of decision-making functions for the nation, and a creativity that has shaped the culture of the entire country. All this has built up a massive consumer market which has led to tremendous industrial growth.

Industry has pushed inland from the coast plain to link up with the interior plain. It has advanced from Philadelphia up the Schuylkill and Lehigh valleys, forming the Ruhr of America. Road and rail push further inland and across ridge and valley to Pittsburgh, often called the Sheffield of America, with its rich coalfields forming the basis for giant iron and steel mills. Above all, industry has thrust up the Hudson and Mohawk, across the Appalachians, to the Great Lakes. The Mohawk valley is a fantastic array of human power, with the Erie canal, major transcontinental railways, great motorways, enormous coal and oil depots, factories that are never out of sight of each other, and cities that jostle their neighbours the length of the plain. This whole stream of engineering, electrical, textile, and chemical industry pours out between Rochester, Buffalo, and Erie on to the lake-shore lowland where vast milling, iron, and steel works, and electro-chemical interests dominate the scene. Since the Hudson–Mohawk is by far the most important inlet for immigration it is thronged with people, is extremely cosmopolitan, is characterized by maleness, youth, and vigour, offers a wide range of skills, and adds appreciably to the dynamism of the New York region.

Between the interior lowlands (by the Great Lakes) and the Atlantic coast plain lie the Appalachians which, from being an initial handicap for the New York region have been turned to advantage. They consist of an outer, eastern belt made up of old mammalated plateaux, like the New England upland and the Piedmont, together with intensely folded steep-sided mountains, frequently pierced by ancient volcanoes or igneous intrusions, like the New England ranges and the Blue

Ridge; and also an inner, western belt, with a ridge-and-valley section of tightly-packed parallel ridges ending in the Allegheny Mountains, followed towards the interior by slightly undulating plateaux, such as the Allegheny and Cumberland plateaux. The whole structure is divided in two at New York, with the older, more rugged, more massive systems of New England giving way to the younger, more distinctly folded and ridged relief trending off to the south. The split at New York was a structural trough, later scoured and widened by glacial melt-water, and eventually invaded and drowned by the sea as far as Albany. The New York–Albany line is thus the natural hinge of the northern and southern Appalachians, which has always given New York an advantage in both areas. The Housatonic and Connecticut valleys empty into Long Island Sound and thus in many ways fall more into the New York than the Boston sphere: indeed, Boston itself long had to rely on New York for inland connections, since access to the interior was across the whole grain of New England but was part of the natural heritage of New York. Similarly, the Hudson–Mohawk Gap offered itself as a main contact with the West for Philadelphia, Washington, and Richmond, even though the Delaware, Potomac, and James were used to cross the Appalachians. These crossings, even to this day, are slower and more costly than the sea-level route through the Appalachian barrier – and in any case they are almost as accessible to New York (thanks to its place on the coast plain) as to the towns at their opening, as may be seen by the way in which the Pennsylvania, and the Baltimore and Ohio railroads have advanced their terminals to the shores of the Hudson, opposite Manhattan.

Although the Appalachians as a whole have been, and still are, a major barrier to east–west movement, from the Green Mountains of Vermont, through the Taconics and Catskills of New York, to the Blue Ridge of Virginia and the Great Smokies of the Carolinas, they do offer in their middle portion a remarkable series of gaps enabling New York, Philadelphia, Baltimore, Washington, and Richmond to capture the wealth of the interior and link it with that of the coast. Together these cities account for about two-thirds of the overseas-interior trade of the United States, which is an astonishing concentration, considering the length of the American coast. But one must remember that America's main trade contacts have always been with Europe, and her main expansion has been from her eastern ports inland: hence the southern ports like Mobile, New Orleans, and Houston, and the western ports such as Seattle, San Francisco, and Los Angeles, have not had the same opportunity. (In a sense history has robbed them of the full potential of their geography. Had America's main contacts been with South America or with East Asia, the situation might have been very different. The influence of geography is always mediated through history.)

Also of great assistance to the rise of the New York–Baltimore industrial and commercial 'complex' has been the happy concentration of iron and coal within the zone of trans-Appalachian gaps. Geologically this resulted from a change of trend in folding and a lowering of the fold belt as the Appalachians came up against the Adirondacks: in this fractured, depressed zone ancient deltas pushed out into arms of the sea or into old lakes caught between the folds, and buried and compressed the lush lagoon vegetation into beds of high-grade bituminous coal in western Pennsylvania, and hard anthracite coal in eastern Pennsylvania. The Adirondacks themselves, as an outlier of the mineraliferous Laurentian Shield, contained considerable deposits of iron.

Once more, this fortuitous coming together of natural advantages exerted no 'influence' on the Indians, who did not even use the iron, much less the coal, but remained basically Stone-Age men in the area that is today the steel capital of the world. Not even the early Europeans could make use of this wealth, although Washington noted the presence of coal and thought it might be valuable in time. The geography of iron, coal, and connecting routeways remained quite inert and ineffectual until the industrial revolution: it took an Andrew Carnegie to bring it really to life and make it felt in the location of industry, and the rise of cities.

The Appalachians meant hunting to the Indians and lumbering to the early Americans. In New England mixed forests of spruce, birch, maple, and elm; in New York, oak, chestnut; and in Maryland and Virginia, oak, butternut, and pine, provided both hard and soft wood, together with pine tar, turpentine, maple sugar, and nuts. These woods were, and still are, a home for deer, bear, beaver, squirrel, turkey, and goose: they offered good hunting, especially during the long winter when the corn and beans raised in the short summer grew scarce. The woods also gave the Indians timber for their houses, hafts for their hoes and axes, and fuel for their fires. These same products were invaluable for the pioneer, and lumbering early became a major activity. Pioneer culture was wood-based; wood was used for fences, tools, machines, factories, houses, cooking, heating, raising steam, smelting metal – for countless purposes. With Thoreau the woods even entered into the philosophy of the people, calling them back to nature.

This may be said to be one of their main influences today. They are no longer one of the region's major resources; in many parts of the area they have been cut down so badly that second-growth bush or rock barrens have replaced them. But increasingly they are becoming sites for relaxation and recreation. From the nineteenth century when people like John P. Marquand's *The Late George Apley* left the sheer business of Boston for the woods, down to the contemporary scene when Robert Frost wrote *Stopping by woods* (although he knew the world called him to go on), the woods have come to play a larger part in the life of the Northeast. This is chiefly because of the tremendous and unprecedented urbanization of the coast plain and the lake-shore lowland on the flanks of the Appalachians. From these overcrowded areas, where city merges into city, hundreds of thousands pour into the woods and hills every weekend.

As things have developed one is inclined to say it is no wonder that the New York region has forged ahead to take the lead in American affairs. It offers the variety of relief, the stimulation of climate, the wealth of fuel and power, the abundance of wood products, the fertility of lowlands (even if they are restricted) and, above all, the opportunities of ready access both by sea and by land, that have provided its peoples with unrivalled advantages. Once settled by forceful folk such as the early colonists from Britain, Holland, Sweden (and under the Hanoverians, from Germany), these advantages at last became unlocked, and opened the way for unprecedented progress.

The Regional Factor (b) the Chicago Region

This progress has pushed so far west in the Lower Lakes region that it is difficult to say where the New York sphere ends and the Chicago one begins. If Pittsburgh and Buffalo are to be regarded as outliers of the New York metropolitan region, then their spheres have to be taken into account, which would draw the region as a whole as far as Wheeling on the Ohio and Erie on Lake Erie. West of this one is in the Central States of the U.S.A., dominated by Chicago, and made up essentially of the Great Lakes lowland and the vast spread of the Ohio, Mississippi, and Missouri plains. This huge area, between the Laurentian Shield in the north and the confluence of America's main rivers in the south, and between the Allegheny plateau, flanking the Appalachians, in the east, and the foothills of the Rocky Mountains in the west, has probably the greatest natural unity of any region in the United States.

That fact was not recognized in Indian times when tribes with quite different ways of life farmed and hunted in a relatively sedentary economy east of the Mississippi, and hunted in a semi-migratory habit west from the Mississippi. Early colonial rivalries also kept the area divided, with Spanish Louisiana centring on the Missouri, and French Illinois on the land between the Illinois and the Ohio. It was only after the British had taken over from the French, and the Americans, falling heir to this, had also purchased Louisiana, that the natural unity of structure, relief, drainage, and weather had a chance to exert its influence. Then, with the Americans creating a criss-cross of routes by using the east–west lakes and the north–south rivers, and connecting them with the Miami, Wabash, and Illinois–Chicago canals, and subsequently by pushing west the National Road and by extending the New York Central, Erie, Pennsylvania, and Baltimore and Ohio railways into great transcontinental systems, a man-made unity was generated that reinforced the natural unity.

The comparative ease with which the region was tied together by canal, road, and rail was due very largely to the mild relief and the simple structure of the area. The chief structures are the exposed Shield in the extreme north, and the buried Shield underlying the whole of the rest of the region. The exposed Shield is found in the Superior Upland around the western and southern shores of Lake Superior. It forms a rough rocky plateau lined with very ancient ridges full of iron. Here is the largest and richest concentration of iron in the world – a fact that had no influence on the Indians, whose main tools were made of wood, stone, and bone: copper was used for knives and fish hooks, but not iron. Living on an ironfield did not advance them into the Iron Age; this was effected through trade with the whites who brought iron instruments made of French or English ore. The white men who poured into this region after the 1812–14 war with Canada, had begun to mine at Marquette and Gogebic within a generation. The iron was close to the Great Lakes and could be shipped to more populous centres, particularly to Toledo, Cleveland, Erie, and Buffalo which were near to the Pennsylvania coalfield. Subsequently coal was shipped west or came north from the Interior fields, and steel works were set up at Gary, Chicago, Milwaukee, or Duluth-Superior. By the end of the nineteenth century America's primacy in steel-making was assured, especially once the massive Mesabi iron ranges were worked.

The mineral wealth of the Chicago region has proved to be tremendous. In addition to the iron of Minnesota, there is a considerable amount of copper in Michigan, and of lead and zinc in Wisconsin, all associated with the older rocks round the edge of the Shield. Then there are very large coal reserves and a number of pools of oil. Fuel deposits were formed, as deltas pushed into shallow epi-continental seas, burying the Shield which now lies underneath the surface of the Midwestern plains. This buried Shield, though it does not have any influence on the relief of the land above, has a profound effect upon the preservation of coal, oil, natural gas, and salt. For it has been buckled (by pressures from the Appalachians) into 'rises' and basins. The basins have harboured the coal and oil, and the rises have helped to bring these fuels close enough to the surface to be worked. In the east is the Cincinnati rise (so named after Cincinnati, growing up where the Ohio cut down through the upwarp of rock) with the West Pennsylvania–Kentucky coalfield on one flank and the Eastern Interior coalfield on the other. This latter is divided from the Western Interior coalfield by the La Salle anticline, trending southeast from Lake Michigan. Both the large Interior fields are divided from a smaller coal basin, sloping down to Saginaw Bay, by the Kankakee rise, east of southern Lake Michigan. Further west and south, a long upwarp of the buried Shield runs from the Ozarks across Kansas to the Black Hills of Dakota. This Kansan rise marks off the east Kansan coal and oilfield from the great oil basin of Oklahoma and the coalfields of Colorado and Wyoming along the front of the Rockies. Natural gas is found in quantity in the Oklahoma fuel area.

No other region in the world has such a wealth of fuels, and it is surprising that the Indians who lived right on top of it for over 10,000 years were quite unaware of it. Even the early American pioneers ignored it, mainly because they saw no way to exploit it with profit, and in any case their chief goal was land; their profit, cattle and wheat. It was not really till the railway age, when engines required the local coal and could haul it into factories and towns, that Midwestern fuel started to play its part. It was used more and more widely and became the basis for the industry that, in the twentieth century, made this America's second manufacturing region, all but vying with the Buffalo–Pittsburgh–Philadelphia triangle in the East.

The Great Lakes–Mississippi waterways helped to make this possible by providing very cheap transportation. The Great Lakes, which are the largest system of inland lakes in the world, lie in hollows just within or just outside the edge of the Laurentian Shield. Some of them, like Lake Superior and parts of Lake Huron, originated as great fault troughs let down at the rim of the Shield. Others, like Erie and Ontario, developed in soft clay vales separated by sandstone and lime-stone cuestas, of which the most famous is the Niagara Escarpment, the cause of Niagara Falls. Each basin was deeply scoured during the Ice Age by huge tongues of ice that moved slowly south from a vast dome of ice covering central Canada. As the ice gradually melted away, lakes were formed between the Mississippi–Ohio divide and the receding front of the ice occupying the St Lawrence basin. These lakes could not find their outlet in the St Lawrence estuary, as is now the case, and so they spilled over the low divide to the south and poured their waters into the Wisconsin and Illinois, joining the Mississippi; and also the Maumee–Wabash, Miami, and Erie–Allegheny channels, emptying into the Ohio. A whole mesh of meltwater courses thus came to link up the St Lawrence–Great Lakes with the Mississippi–Ohio system, which made for remarkable ease of connection between these two great waterways.

This was one advantage which the Indians *did* use. The rivers were their highways and they explored all the old spillways and used them as low, easy portages between the rivers flowing into the Lakes and those joining the Mississippi. The French were quick to realize the importance of these portages and, by skilful use, were able to move swiftly into the very heart of the continent from their base in the St Lawrence estuary. In the time it took the British (impounded behind the Appalachians) to advance 200 miles up the Mohawk to reach the interior lowlands at Oswego, the French had moved 2000 miles inland from Quebec and were on the banks of the Mississippi. Their skill in using river and portage was extraordinary, and in another context the author has called their North American realm 'the empire of the spillways'. Not unnaturally the British who superseded them, and the Americans coming after, made good use of what had served the French so well. The Americans first exploited the spillways as portage roads, but in the 1840s and 1850s they built canals through them, such as the Miami, the Wabash, and the Chicago canals – the last of which is still in active service.

The railways very largely knocked out the canals, and since they led a rush to the West (that turned aside only in a secondary way to go north to the Lakes or south along the Mississippi), they built up a new east–west pattern of routes. Nevertheless, they often used canal towns to serve as staging points along the way, and some of these became major junctions as, for example, Chicago itself. Built on Lake Michigan, and therefore centrally placed to use the upper and lower Lakes, on an old portage that was canalized to link the Lakes with the Mississippi, Chicago developed superb water connections, made all the more profitable when the small St Lawrence canals were replaced by the Seaway that rendered Chicago a sea port. At the same time, the way in which Lake Michigan forced the railway routes debouching on the Mid-West from the Appalachian gaps to bunch together around its upper end, gave Chicago the chance to become the supreme rail junction of the central lowlands. Altogether twenty-seven major lines converge on the city. No transcontinental line except the Southern Pacific fails to go through or have an immediate link with Chicago. In the same way, the chief trunk highways from Boston (Mass. Tpk.), New York (N.Y. Thruway), Philadelphia (Penn. Tpk.), Baltimore (U.S. 40), Washington (U.S. 50), Atlanta (U.S. 41) and New Orleans (U.S. 61) all meet in Chicago, before fanning out for the passes in the Rockies and their Pacific terminals (see map on p. 131).

Geography has much to do with all this, but it is difficult to explain it all by geography. After all, the principal centre in the early nineteenth century was St Louis, at the western end of the Cumberland Road and the beginning of the Sante Fé, the California, and the Oregon trails. St Louis was also the first western terminal of the Baltimore and Ohio and of the Pennsylvania railroad. Independence, on the Missouri, was another famous road and river junction and a jumping-off place for the further West, as were Kansas City and Omaha, once the frontier of settlement had rolled on across the Plains. Moreover, in the east were notable river and road junctions like Cincinnati and Columbus, while Detroit was well situated to command the trade of the Great Lakes and contact that of east–west land routes.

Perhaps one reason that enabled the developers of Chicago to go beyond their rivals was that the city lay at the centre, whereas all these other places were towards the periphery of the region. It was easier to reach all parts of the Mid-West from Chicago than from any other point. It became the focus of every principal activity in the Mid-West. By the 1880s it was the region's chief agricultural market, with large flour-milling, corn-pressing, and meat-packing plants. Its success as a hog and cattle mart was phenomenal. Although Cincinnati had earlier been the 'hog market of the world', and Omaha 'the cattle capital', Chicago stole their place, chiefly because it could draw in from a wider area, sell to a bigger market, and process the meat in huge curing and canning factories. The Chicago stock yards became the largest in the world, containing over thirty-five miles of cattle alleys and five miles of hog alleys serviced by 150 miles of railway sidings. Although meat packing has now spread to lesser cities, and the Chicago stockyards are gone, the meat industry in its hey-day helped to build up the centrality of Chicago.

Industrially, Chicago is well placed for iron and steel and for steel-using plants, lying as it does almost half-way between the great Interior coalfields and the Lake Superior ironfields. The 'thumb' of Michigan supplies an abundance of limestone suitable for furnace flux. Hence the Chicago district from Milwaukee and Evanston through to Calumet and Gary has a large number of metal-making or metal-using industries. These have helped, in turn, to facilitate the expansion of the food-processing industries. Transportation industries and industries making agricultural machines are also very important, especially in the Detroit area.

Much of this wealth goes back to the natural wealth of the surrounding lowlands. When the Great Lakes finally found their lowest-level outlet in the St Lawrence they shrank in size, leaving rich lake-bottom deposits stranded in long and broad terraces above their present shores. These are among the richest agricultural lands in America. The melt-waters from the Lakes had strewn their spillways with silt and sand, and these, too, became fertile tracts. The greatest river system in the world had, through the Mississippi and its branches, developed flood-plains of highly productive alluvium. The lands in between were covered with glacial till which, though often stony, had weathered to a deep tilth. The soil throughout the eastern parts has come to be a good, workable grey-brown earth, reflecting a temperate humid climate; soils west of the Red River are black to chocolate brown fading in colour to light brown against the Rocky foothills, corresponding to a sub-humid climate.

The weather systems, derived from a vast polar continental mass of cold to cool air in the north, and a very dynamic mass of warm to hot tropical maritime air from the south, provide both challenge and reward. They challenge men with the threat of frost and blizzards from the north, of hail and drought from the west, and of the periodic hurricane from the south, yet they reward, too, with moderate to ample amounts of rain in a five-months growing season and warm burgeoning summers.

For the first time most of the northerners who migrated out of New England, New York, and Pennsylvania, found really productive soil, good ripening weather, and plenty of room, and there was, consequently, an avid desire to take up and develop land. The Mid-West became the nation's breadbasket and meat-larder. Although the Indians had recognized some of this potential in their attempts at farming, they were never aware of the immense agricultural wealth at their disposal. This was the white man's work, particularly in the twentieth century when farming became highly scientific, mechanized, and commercialized. Then distinct agricultural zones began to emerge, consisting of the dairy belt in the north, the corn belt to the south, the wheat belt to the west, and the cattle belt on the mountain margins. As has been indicated, these were partly a result of climatic advantages and partly an outcome of economic opportunities, with the more intensive types of farming, like the fattening of beef, dairy farming, poultry raising, and market gardening, taking up land close to the expanding industrial and urban markets.

The Chicago region, then, has the influence behind it of simplicity of structure, unity of relief and drainage, productivity of climate and soil, an abundance of metals and fuels, a central location within the continent, and plenty of space for growth. These influences came to have more and more meaning and power as they were given effect and value by American farmers, industrialists, and traders. As a result, they helped to build up America's second great metropolitan region, with an urban population between Cleveland and Minneapolis–St Paul of about 30 millions living in cities that are central places for highly-developed hinterlands. An additional 15 millions in lesser towns and the countryside give this region about 20 per cent of America's total population.

The Regional Factor (c) the Los Angeles Region

The third metropolitan region in rank is that of Los Angeles. Indeed Los Angeles itself is now America's second city, with over 8 millions in its built-up area. Supported by San Francisco Bay district with about 4 millions, and San Diego, with nearly 2 millions, and a number of smaller cities, it has a concentration of population whose effect reaches to the Rockies.

Its rise to power is phenomenal and represents one of the great triumphs of man, for most of the region is desert or mountain or both. Here drought, ruggedness, and inaccessibility proved too great a challenge to early man. Although there may have been men here in early Pleistocene times, they amounted to very little in American pre-history and were among the poorest, least well-equipped, least populous and least adaptive Indians the Americans came upon in their drive across the continent. From this point of view one might be disposed to regard the area as having a negative influence. Yet the fact is, both Spaniards and Americans found positive factors in the region, enabling it to come to the fore and to be the most rapidly developing part of the United States today.

In no other region is geography so two-faced, frowning on the backward, but smiling on the forward. The climate which meant sparse vegetation and little wild life, piñon seeds and acorns, wood-grubs, lizards, snakes and the occasional rabbit to the primitive food-gatherer and hunter, meant vineyards and orchards, irrigated pasture, pedigree dairy herds, race courses and golf courses – America's garden and playground – to the modern entrepreneur, backed by science and engineering, economics, and the urge to outdo the Joneses. The climate is under the control of a subtropical high for most of the year, with dry offshore winds, producing long spells of drought, but it is sunny and warm, comfortable, and pleasant. Through irrigation it can be made extraordinarily productive.

The water for irrigation-works comes from the snows of high mountains or from water-bearing strata into which snowmelt and winter rains have soaked. This is the truly mountainous part of America, with the three lofty and massive ranges of the Rockies, the Sierra Nevadas-and-Cascades, and the Pacific Coast Ranges. Between the Rockies and the Sierras are the Colorado Plateau, ringed about by igneous intrusions or fault-faced ridges, and the Great Basin, a low plateau with a great number of short sharp-fronted cuestas overlooking lesser basins. Between the Sierras and the Coast Ranges are the profound depressions of the Gulf of California and the Great Valley of California. Although these deep depressions and the intermontane plateaux and basins are dry, they are the sites of significant snow-fed rivers and are lined by springs. The mountains rise high enough to catch moisture from drifts of humid air moving in at high levels in cyclones from the Pacific or from the Gulf of Mexico. Below their snowy tops, the ranges are clothed with quite thick forests of fir, hemlock, and pine that give way at intermediate levels to poplar, aspen, willow, birch, and oak.

Lower still the vegetation thins out to tall grass prairie. On the slopes about to drop to the valley floors, short-grass prairies occur, and in the bottomlands and basins, bunch grass, sage bush, or cactus desert are found, except by streams whose sides are remarkably green with grass and willow.

An astonishing range of conditions may thus be found within a comparatively short distance. Spaniards first took advantage of this with wheat farms replacing the tall grass, ranching the short grass, and irrigated orchards the bunch grass and desert bush. Americans followed suit but expanded the areas under orchards enormously, and also grew irrigated cotton, and, in more recent years, irrigated hay and alfalfa for an active stall-fed dairy industry. It is this wonderful variety of land use which attracted so many people, and has given such interest and charm to the landscape while making the region so productive.

Mountains and basins have also been shown to have an abundance of metals and fuels. The Western Cordillera are now America's main source of precious and industrial metals, the crystalline cores of the fold belts, and the metamorphosed zones around the big igneous domes being highly mineralized. Gold and silver are still almost as important as when they led the gold rush to California or the silver rush to Nevada. Copper, lead, and zinc are found in big quantities and there are a few significant reserves of iron. Coal occurs in isolated fields in the Great Basin, but the main fuel resources are the still used oilfields in Southern California. Large amounts of cheap hydro-electricity have been developed in association with the irrigation dams on the Colorado and in the Sacramento and San Joaquin valleys.

These many forms of wealth are now becoming the basis for rapidly expanding industries, mainly in the Los Angeles and San Francisco areas. Petro-chemical, agricultural, metal-making and engineering industries have altered what was until fifty years ago essentially a rural landscape into an industrial and urban one. Many Eastern and Northern manufacturing concerns have set up branches in the American South-west rather than transport their goods there. Some of the Southwest industries, especially aircraft and the making of films, have an international importance. Pleasant living conditions and factories designed to provide pleasant working conditions are drawing in so many migrants from other parts of America and from Europe that the Los Angeles region is now the fastest growing one in the United States. Thus an area which, so far as Indian or early American migrations were concerned, was at the end of the road, which was threatened with drought and had a most difficult terrain, became the frontier of amenity in modern America, because it was the great breakthrough to the good life where men could take advantage of, and enjoy, its essential beauty and comfort.

The Regional Factor (d) the Seattle Region

Of the other American regions none has developed a metropolis of similar range and power; Seattle may be thought of as the centre of the Pacific Northwest but it has come nowhere near to Los Angeles in size and influence. The same Cordilleran structures are present, with much mineral though with far less fuel wealth; there is the same variety of vegetation and soil, made use of by a very varied agriculture; the forests are thicker and more profitable, and the fishing far more lucrative; waterpower is more abundant, and there is much more water available for farm, domestic, and industrial use: yet the region has not forged ahead to the same extent. It was settled earlier, during the great Oregon trek, and ought to have developed as far as the Southwest. But perhaps because the climate is cooler, damper and much cloudier, people have not flocked to the region. It is still largely dependent on primary production and trade, and is more likely to become an adjunct of the Los Angeles region than to develop a metropolitan character and sphere of its own.

This is strange since, in Indian times, matters were reversed, and the Indians of Puget Sound lived a good deal better than those in Southern California. But at that stage rain mattered more than the sun, and amenity for the hunter and fisher, the dweller in wood houses and the traveller in wood dugouts, must have been mist-drenched forests and rain-filled rivers where game and fish abounded and there was plenty of local material for tools and houses. Obviously what are 'favourable geographical influences' for one people at one stage of development may not be suitable for others at a different stage. (It must be remembered, however, that in terms of *absolute* development, the present users have made more of the Pacific Northwest than ever before.)

The Regional Factor (e) the South

The American South is the last of the regions to be described. It is a most important one, but that importance is not to be measured in terms of metropolitan growth. No one city dominates the South. Richmond was of course long its main focus, but has really been drawn into Megalopolis and the New York region. Atlanta is its biggest city, and is most influential in the southern Piedmont, but its sphere is challenged by Birmingham, where the Great Valley of the Southern Appalachians passes into the Alabama plain. Neither of these cities would be regarded as their metropolis by Kentucky and Tennessee, far less by Missouri and Arkansas, yet these interior or Mississippian parts of the South are really without large centres: they look outwards to several foci, like Cincinnati, St Louis, or New Orleans, beyond their limits. Even the Gulf, which for so long turned upon New Orleans, now has its divisions. Houston is the new star, in the Gulf Southwest, and Jacksonville pulls the east Gulf right out to the Atlantic.

In spite of having no real centre, the South is a very real region, with structures, climates, soils, agriculture and ways of life that are distinctly its own. Here the Appalachians die out but have a counterpart in the Ozarks and Ouachitas. The way in which the whole fold belt spreads out in Georgia, sags beneath the Mississippi in Louisiana, and then reappears in Arkansas, is found only in the South. The Cumberland and Ozark plateaux are deeply dissected, difficult to traverse, and have long been the refuge of those escaping from the competition so rife in the Great Valley of the Appalachians or in the valley of the Arkansas. The Smokies and the Ouachitas were also relatively negative areas except for the trapper and the lumberman. Together with the plateaux they have tended to keep the cold 'northers', coming down behind the cyclones of the advancing polar air, from invading the southern Atlantic coast and the Gulf shore plain.

One result of this has been the mildness of the Southern climate in winter, where there are from 200 to 350 days free of frost. Summers tend to be hot and humid, and are not as comfortable or pleasant as in California. The tropical Gulf air-mass moves over the coastal plains bringing temperatures of over 80°F in July, and heavy cyclonic and convection rain. But though tending to be 'close' or 'muggy' the summer climate is very productive and gives the South what are probably the best conditions for agriculture in the United States.

The Indians responded to this and developed an agricultural way of life in excess of anything outside of central Mexico. When Monroe endorsed the policy of removing the Indians from eastern U.S.A. west of the Mississippi, the Cherokees objected strongly. They were no nomads of the forest, used to moving around, but a sedentary tribe of 15,000 people who owned 22,000 cattle, 31 grist mills, 10 saw mills, 8 cotton gins, and 2000 spinning wheels. None the less, their agriculture was limited in range. It was the British who widened the whole scope of farming, made tobacco and cotton into commercial crops farmed on a big scale, and introduced rice, sugar, peaches, oranges, pigs, poultry, cattle, and sheep. As for the Americans, they did so well at farming that most of the capital and labour in the South went into the land.

There was, in fact, an overdevelopment of agriculture and other forms of primary production, at the expense of industry. This was partly due to the positive effects of relief, drainage and soil and the negative role of minerals and fuels. The Atlantic coast plain broadens out in the South much more than in the north, and becomes a 'belted lowland' with an all but unique range of local conditions due to belts of sandstone or limestone standing up as low escarpments above belts of shale and clay. Hence the Southern Pineries on the hills and the Black Waxy Prairies in the vales gave the South a main opportunity both in lumbering and in farming. The belted lowland reappeared in Texas, south of the Balcones Escarpment, where cattle ranching, wheat farming, cotton raising, citrus and nut cultivation, and market gardening have all flourished. Between the belted lowlands of southeast and southwest is the extremely fertile alluvial plain of the lower Mississippi and its delta. Well-watered, its soil of the finest silty loam, with a warm, moist climate having a year-round growing season, this is one of the naturally most productive areas in the United States. Actually, its potential has still to be fully realized because too much of it is under cotton, and too much of the cotton is raised by small tenant farmers or share croppers, many of them Negro.

Here is a major problem that the South still has to solve – it has too many small-scale, inefficient enterprises run by poor white and Negro. Social distance has separated these from the wealthier and more successful white owners and operators and has created barriers to improvement reflected in the economy and in society alike. These social barriers have become built in to the landscape itself in separate housing for blacks and whites, separate schools and churches, and separate amenities. Desegregation has begun, and will undoubtedly change the whole geography of the South, but even although segregation by law may go, segregation by social custom may continue for a considerable time. Social 'lag' helps to account for the unfavourable contrast which the American Southeast offers to the Southwest. Although the Southeast has a much more productive climate, and has greater forest and fuel resources, although it has had a much longer history of development and has enjoyed the leadership of some of America's most brilliant minds, it has nevertheless grown more slowly and is generally less affluent than the American Southwest.

One thing that is helping to change the situation is the rise of industry in the South. Heretofore this has been slow to develop, partly because of the wealth to be obtained through agriculture and men's fascination with land, as such, but also in part because of the paucity of coal and iron. As long as the industrial revolution was based on steam and steel, the South only had the Birmingham area, in Alabama, since this alone had large deposits of coal, limestone, and iron near enough to be brought together in the making of steel. But once the second industrial revolution arrived with its emphasis on electricity and oil, on aluminium and plastics, then the South was able to forge ahead because the South was discovered to be rich in power-sites, bauxite, oil, natural gas, potash, salt, and sulphur. The Tennessee Valley Authority developed great quantities of power in the Tennessee basin, and power was also produced at dam sites in the Carolina and Arkansas mountains. Large amounts of power went into the smelting of aluminium, and also into electro-chemical industries. The Gulf oil region of Louisiana and Texas was soon seen to be the richest in America. While much of the oil was taken by tanker or piped to the Northeast and Northern-central states, a considerable amount began to be turned into petro-chemical products in the South, especially in the vicinity of Houston. The zone from Texas to Florida is now often known as the 'rocket belt' and many of America's newest industries, engaged in 'space engineering', are now centred in that area.

It is obvious, then, that the South is a well-endowed region with many opportunities in agriculture, lumbering, mining, and industry. It was held back, compared with the North, mainly for social reasons, such as its symbolization of wealth by land, the rule of a landed aristocracy, and the social gulfs between rich and poor and black and white. These social barriers still affect the way in which 'geographic influence' is being allowed to operate. Nevertheless, the rise of a modern commercial and industrial economy is releasing new forces in the geography of the South which are already creating a new landscape. Whether these forces will be pulled together in, and directed from, one great metropolitan centre or not, remains to be seen. The South has never had the strong city tradition of the North or the West, and it may well remain unique in American geography as the region not dominated by any one metropolis.

Conclusion: major trends

Looking at America as a whole, one sees it as a land of remarkable opportunity and yet of considerable challenge. It is almost continental in size and has plenty of room for settlement and development – yet large tracts are neglected whereas others are overcrowded. The structure of North America is on fairly simple lines with a stable 'Shield' exposed in the north though buried beneath a great lowland in the centre, against which were folded marginal mountains on the east and on the west. A strong north–south lineation resulted, yet the Americans developed their country on essentially east–west axes, often in the face of great difficulties. The exposed Shield and the core areas of the fold mountains are rich in metals, the central lowlands in fuel. Where these are linked together by inland or coastal water routes they have been developed as nowhere else in the world. However, great waste has accompanied exploitation, and America now finds itself a net importer of many of the products on which it is most dependent.

Most of America widens out in the temperate humid belt of climates: few countries have proportionately as much land that is as productive. There is, none the less, threat from frost in the north, and a grave challenge from drought in the southwest. Through central-heating America has virtually made a California of the North, and through irrigation, a new north in California. One of the great tributes to be paid to Americans is that they have made the most drought-stricken part of their country the part that is growing the most. Indeed, they have added a tremendous amount to nature through their enterprise, skill, and organization, and where the Indian saw little in grassland or forest beyond hunting and saw nothing in iron and coalfields, oil and natural gas, the Americans have developed the most productive agriculture and industry in the world. Yet this very expansion is a problem, leading to an unusual centralization of power in a few centres, and also to great gaps between and within communities as social development has lagged behind economic development. America has discovered different uses for its land and has shown different ways of interpreting its geography as its history and culture have changed. This is likely to go on and to result in a different land-scape tomorrow from that which prevails today. Thus, although its geography has undoubtedly gone into the making of America, America is all the time remaking its geography: the two are in-extricably mixed and dependent upon each other. The influence of geography upon America is as varied and variable as the mind of America working upon its geography.

Further Reading

GENERAL WORKS AND AIDS

Geographical Bibliographies

American Geographical Society N.Y. Current Geographical Publications, annual index.

Serials

Association of American Geographers, Annals. Washington, 1911–.
Economic Geography (Clarke University). Worcester, Mass., 1925–.
Geographical Review (Amer. Geog. Soc.). New York, 1852–.
Focus (Amer. Geog. Soc.). New York, 1950–.
Landscape, New Mexico, 1951–.
The Professional Geographer (Assoc. Amer. Geogrs.). Washington, 1949–.
Regional Science, Journal of. Penn., 1958–.

Atlases

Atlas of American Geology, A. K. Lobeck. New York, 1960.
Goode's Atlas, ed. E. B. Espenshade. Chicago, 1964.
Lord, C. L. and E. H., Historical Atlas of the U.S. New York, 1948.
Paullin, C. O., Atlas of the Historical Geography of the United States, ed. J. K. Wright. Washington, 1932.
Urban Atlas: 20 American Cities, ed. J. R. Passoneau and R. S. Wurman. Cambridge, Mass., 1966.
National Atlas of the United States. U.S. Govt., Washington, D.C., 1969–.

Gazeteers

U.S. Board on Geographic Names. Washington, D.C., 1955–.

Miscellaneous Aids

Andriot, J. L., Guide to U.S. Govt. Serials. Washington, D.C., 1964–.
Cox, E. G., Reference Guide to the Literature of Travel, Vol. 2, The New World. Washington, D.C., 1938.
James, P. E. and Jones, C. F., eds., American Geography, Inventory and Prospect. Syracuse, N.Y., 1954.
U.S. Library of Congress, Map Division, List of Geographical Atlases. Washington, D.C., 1958–.

General Works

Estall, R. A., Modern Geography of the United States. Chicago, Ill., 1972.
George, P., Géographie des Etats-Unis. Paris, 1971.
Mead, W. R. and Brown, E. H., The United States and Canada. London, 1962.
Parker, W. H., Anglo-America; Canada and the United States. London, 1962.
Paterson, J. H., North America: A Regional Geography. New York, 1962.
Revelle, R. and Landsberg, H. H., America's Changing Environment. Boston, Mass., 1970.

Shaw, E. B., *Anglo-America: A Regional Geography*. New York, 1959.

Siegfried, A., *America at Mid Century*. New York, 1955.

Smith, J. R. and Phillips, M. O., *North America; its People and the Resources, Development and Prospects of the Continent as the Home of Man*. New York, 1942.

Starkey, O. P. and Robinson, J. L., *The Anglo-American Realm*. New York, 1969.

Watson, J. W., *North America: Its Countries and Regions*. London, 1967.

White, C. L., Foscue, E. J. and McKnight, T. L., *Regional Geography of Anglo-America*. Englewood Cliffs, N.J., 1964.

Wright, A. J., *The United States and Canada: a Regional Geography*. New York, 1956.

WORKS ON SPECIAL TOPICS

Historical Geography

Bartlett, R. A., *Great Surveys of the American West*. Oklahoma, 1962.

Brown, R. H., *Mirror for Americans; Likeness of the Eastern Seaboard 1810*. New York, 1943.

Brown, R. H., *Historical Geography of the United States*. New York, 1948.

Gilbert, E. W., *The Exploration of Western America, 1800–50*. Cambridge, 1933.

Pattison, W. D., *Beginnings of the American Rectangular Land Survey System, 1784–1800*. Chicago, Ill., 1957.

Thwaites, R. G. (ed.), *Early Western Travels, 1748–1846*. Cleveland, Ohio, 1904–7.

Turner, F. J., *The Frontier in American History*. New York, 1949.

U.S. Bureau of the Census, *Historical Statistics of the U.S.* Washington, D.C., 1960. Vol. 1, *Colonial times to 1957*; Vol. 2, *Continuation to 1962 and revisions*.

Physical Geography

Atwood, W. W., *The Physiographic Provinces of North America*. Boston, Mass., 1940.

Braun, E. L., *Deciduous Forests of Eastern North America*. New York, 1950.

Hunt, C. B., *Physiography of the United States*. New York, 1967.

Jaeger, E. C., *North American Deserts*. Stanford, Calif., 1957.

Kimble, G. H. T., *Our American Weather*. New York, 1955.

Miller, D. W., Geraghty, J. J. and Collins, R. S., *Water Atlas of the United States*. Port Washington, N.Y., 1963.

Shelford, V. E., *The Ecology of North America*. Urbana, Ill., 1963.

Shimer, J. A., *This Sculptured Earth – The Landscape of America*. New York, 1959.

Thornbury, W. D., *Regional Geomorphology of the United States*. New York, 1965.

U.S. Department of Agriculture, *Yearbook of Agriculture, 1938*. Washington.

U.S. Department of Agriculture, *Yearbook of Agriculture, 1941*. Washington.

U.S. Department of Agriculture, *Yearbook of Agriculture, 1957*. Washington.

Wright, H. E. and Frey, D. G., *The Quaternary of the United States*. New York, 1965.

Human Geography

Bogue, D. J., *The Population of the United States*. New York, 1960.

Brennan, L. A., *The American Dawn*. New York, 1970.

Driver, H. E., *Indians of North America*. Chicago, Ill., 1969 (2nd edn).

Duncan, O. D. *et al.*, *Metropolis and Region*. Baltimore, Md., 1960.

Fellows, D. K., *A Mosaic of America's Ethnic Minorities*. New York, 1971.

Higbee, E. C., *The Squeeze: Cities without Space*. New York, 1960.

Jensen, M. (ed.), *Regionalism in America*. Madison, Wisc., 1951.

Mohl, R. A., *Urban America in Perspective*. New York, 1970.

Murphy, R. E., *The American City*. New York, 1965.

National Academy of Sciences–National Research Council, Division of Earth Sciences, *Rural Settlement Patterns in the U.S.* Washington, D.C., 1956.

Neils, E. M., *Reservation to City: Indian Migration and Federal Relocation*. Chicago, Ill., 1971.

Ogden, S. R., *America the Vanishing: rural life and the price of progress*. Brattleboro, Vt., 1969.

Oswalt, W. H., *This Land was Theirs*. New York, 1967.

Price, D. O., *Changing Characteristics of the Negro Population*. Washington, D.C., 1969.

Sherman, R. B. (ed.), *The Negro and the City (in U.S.A.)*. Englewood Cliffs, N.J., 1970.

U.S. Govt., *Population Challenge, what it means to America*. Washington, D.C., 1966.

Wakstein, A. M. (ed.), *The Urbanization of America*. New York, 1970.

Economic Geography

Alexandersson, G., *The Industrial Structure of American Cities; a Geographic Study of Urban Economy in the U.S.* Lincoln, Neb., 1956.

Berry, B. J. L. and Hankins, T. D., *A Bibliographic Guide to the Economic Regions of the U.S.* Chicago, Ill., 1963.

Bogue, D. J. and Beale, C. L., *Economic Areas of the U.S.* New York, 1961.

Clawson, M., *Land for Americans: Trends, Prospects and Problems*. Chicago, Ill., 1963.

Cohen, S. B., *Geography and the American Environment*. Washington, D.C., 1968.

Cooley, R. A. and Smith, G. W., *Congress and Environment*. New York, 1970.

Cummins, D. E., *Effect of Urban Expansion on Dairying in the Lake States*. Washington, D.C., 1970.

Fuchs, V. R., *Changes in the Location of Manufacturing in the U.S. since 1929*. New Haven, Conn., 1962.

Gray, L. C., *History of Agriculture in the Southern United States to 1860*. Washington, D.C., 1933.

Haystead, L. and Fite, G. C., *Agricultural Regions of the United States*. Norman, Okla., 1955.

Higbee, E. C., *American Agriculture: Geography, Resources, Conservation*. New York, 1958.

Highsmith, R. M. et al., *Conservation in the U.S.* Chicago, Ill., 1962.

Krause, O. E., *Cropland trends (in U.S.); regional changes*. Washington, D.C., 1970.

McDonald, S. L., *Petroleum Conservation in the United States*. Baltimore, Md., 1971.

Marschner, F. J., *Land Use and Its Patterns in the U.S.* Washington GPO, 1963.

Opie, J. (ed.), *Americans and the Environment*. Lexington, Mass., 1971.

Parson, R. et al., *Conserving American Resources*, 3rd edn. Englewood Cliffs, N.J., 1972.

Perloff, H. S., *Regions, Resources, and Economic Growth.* Baltimore, Md., 1960.
Stover, J. F., *The Life and Decline of the American Railroad.* Chicago, Ill., 1970.
Ullman, E. L. *et al., The Economic Base of American Cities.* Seattle, Washington, 1971.
Wollmann, N. *et al., The Outlook for Water (in the U.S.A.).* Baltimore, Md., 1971.

Northeastern States

Albion, R. G. and Pope, J. B., *The Rise of New York Port (1815–1860).* Hamden, Conn., 1961.
American Geographical Society, *New York City.* New York, 1971.
American Geographical Society, *New England's Prospect: 1933,* ed. J. K. Wright. New York, 1933.
Estall, R. C., *New England: A Study in Industrial Development.* London, 1966.
Evans, E., *Opportunity City, New York.* New York, 1970.
Gottman, J., *Megalopolis: the Urbanized Northeastern Seaboard of the U.S.* New York, 1961.
Hoover, E. M. and Vernon, R., *The Anatomy of a Metropolis: the Changing Distribution of People and Jobs within the New York Metropolitan Region.* Cambridge, Mass., 1959.
Morris, J., *The Great Past: passage through New York.* New York, 1969.
Swatridge, L. A., *The Bosnywash (Boston, N.Y., Washington) megalopolis; a region of great cities.* Toronto, 1971.
Thompson, J. H. (ed.), *Geography of New York State.* New York, 1966.
Truett, R. B., *Washington D.C.* New York, 1968.

The South

Bowman, M. J. and Haynes, W. W., *Resources and People in East Kentucky; Problems and Potentials of a Lagging Economy.* Baltimore, Md., 1963.
Ford, T. R. (ed.), *The Southeastern Appalachian Region: A Survey.* Lexington, Ky., 1962.
Gottman, J., *Virginia at Mid-Century.* New York, 1955.
Hamilton, C. H., *The changing population of the U.S. South.* Chapel Hill, N.C., 1970.
Hart, F., *The Southeastern United States.* New York, 1970.
Merrens, H. R., *Colonial North Carolina in the Eighteenth Century: a Study in Historical Geography.* Chapel Hill, N.C., 1964.
Odum, H. W., *Southern Regions of the U.S.* Chapel Hill, N.C., 1936.
Parkins, A. E., *The South: Its Economic–Geographic Development.* New York, 1938.
Vance, R. B., *Human Geography of the South: A Study in Regional Resources and Human Adequacy.* Chapel Hill, N.C., 1935.
Vandiver, F. E., *The Ideas of the South.* Chicago, Ill., 1964.

North Central States and Great Plains

Elazar, D. J., *Cities of the Prairies.* New York, 1970.
Garland, J. H. (ed.), *The North American Midwest: A Regional Geography.* New York, 1955.
Langman, R. C., *The Great Plains; the anatomy of a region.* Toronto, 1971.

Malin, J. C., *The Grassland of North America: Prolegomena to its History*, with addenda, rev. ed. Lawrence, Kan., 1956.

Maver, H. M., *The Port of Chicago and the St. Lawrence Seaway*. Chicago, Ill., 1957.

Mayer, H. M. and Wade, R. C., *Chicago, growth of a metropolis*. Chicago, Ill., 1969.

Weaver, J. E. and Albertson, F. W., *Grasslands of the Great Plains; their Nature and Use*. Lincoln, Neb., 1956.

Webb, W. P., *The Great Plains*. New York, 1959.

The West

American Geographical Society, *Los Angeles*. New York, 1969.

Atwood, W. W., *The Rocky Mountains*. New York, 1945.

Bartz, F., *Alaska*. Stuttgart, 1950.

Booth, C. W., *The Northwestern United States*. New York, 1971.

Carter, G. F., *Plant Geography and Culture History in the American South-west*. New York, 1945.

Durrenberger, R. W. (ed.), *California, its people, its problems, its prospects*. Palo Alto, Calif., 1971.

Freeman, O. W. and Martin, H. H. (eds.), *The Pacific Northwest, an Overall Appreciation*, 2nd edn. New York, 1954.

Lantis, D. W., Steiner, R. and Karinen, J., *California: Land of Contrast*. Belmont, Calif., 1963.

Morris, J. W., *The Southwestern United States*. New York, 1970.

Parkman, F., *The Oregon Trail*. Edited by E. N. Feltskog. Madison, Wisc., 1969.

Powell, J. W., *Report on the Lands of the Arid Region of the U.S.* Cambridge, Mass., 1962.

Stegner, W. E., *Beyond the Hundredth Meridian; John Wesley Powell and the Second Opening of the West*. Boston, Mass., 1954.

Zierer, C. M. (ed.), *California and the Southwest*. New York, 1956.

2 Americanism

WILLIAM R. BROCK

Visitors to the United States are frequently impressed by the outward show and symbols of conscious nationalism. Children are taught to salute the flag, and it is flown by private individuals to demonstrate their patriotism. The word 'American' is used with a wealth of overtones, so that to describe oneself or a custom or an institution as 'American' is to claim a whole set of positive values. The 'all American boy' has become something of a joke, but it is a character which most American parents covet for their sons. Conversely, to be 'un-American' is not to be merely foreign or unfamiliar but dangerous, immoral, subversive, and deluded. Fourth of July orations are the classic expressions of American patriotism, but hyperbole is not confined to these rhetorical exercises and to foreign ears the discourse of public men seems to be marked to an extraordinary degree by appeals to the special character and destiny of the American people.

Close acquaintance with the American people will reveal that the cult of Americanism can divide and dismay as much as it unites and inspires. It is likely to embarrass intellectuals, is anathema for most radicals, and strikes a sour note to many racial minorities. There is a tradition going back to the Revolution which prefers to describe the national identity as allegiance to political principles; to equality, freedom, inalienable rights, and authority derived from the consent of the governed. This belief that the essence of American nationality lies in dedication to universal principles is constantly at war with the idea that Americanism belongs exclusively to the American people and must be defended against alien influences rather than shared with mankind. In this controversy the aggressive nationalists have normally had the advantage of superior organization and generous funds; but in the long war of ideological attrition they have failed to win the final battle. When all has been said, 'Americanism', as expounded by its most vigorous exponents, has too little to offer too few Americans. One has the paradox of a nation united while the very foundations of national existence are in constant debate.

The Protestant Tradition and Jeffersonian Democracy

In recent years it has been fashionable among intellectuals to denigrate those Americans who are white, Anglo-Saxon, and Protestant (colloquially abbreviated to WASP). Yet, for better or worse, the central tradition in America is white, Anglo-Saxon, and Protestant, and no purpose is served by concealing the fact; indeed, without this heritage it is difficult to imagine how the idea of American nationality could have been generated. If it is sometimes necessary to emphasize the lack of unity and common purpose among the American colonies before the Revolution, it is also true that they shared the same language, law, political institutions, and social traditions. Religion appeared diverse, but everywhere Protestantism, and those forms of Protestantism which stressed the role of congregations in the Godly society, were supreme. Even the episcopal church was distinguished by a form of worship rather than by devotion to hierarchical organization.

Protestantism still provides the substratum of American culture; its influence has been pervasive and moulded attitudes which have little direct connection with religion. The Old Testament told of a people chosen by God and living under His Providence. It told of exodus, wandering, and life in a new land. It preached the need for order, yet was severe in its judgment upon the rulers of men. To this the New Testament added the personal responsibility of man to God, and the social responsibility of man to man. Though ardent dedication has waned, evangelicalism can still rouse enthusiasm, charitable causes fail without support from the churches, and a surprising number of colleges and universities retain denominational affiliations. More significant for the theme of this chapter is the extent to which biblical religion still provides the imagery and argument for so many attempts to explain American nationality. There have been Roman Catholics in America since the seventeenth century, the majority of nineteenth-century migrants were of that faith, and the Eastern Orthodox Church has a substantial number of congregations; yet neither Roman nor Greek Christianity can approach Protestantism as a formative influence upon American culture. It may be that the time of the other faiths has yet to come, but until the election of John F. Kennedy many competent observers believed that no Roman Catholic could become President.

The Protestant congregation existed in a small community planted in the wilderness. The driving spirit behind Puritan settlement was the desire to create communities which rejected the corruptions of the old world and subdued the barbarism of the new, civilized men but preserved their purity, and defied authority but established a Godly discipline. The extension of American civilization across the continent provided constant opportunity for the renewal of this experience. The historians of the American frontier have stressed lawlessness, individualism, and the renewal of primitive impulses through contact with the wilderness. From this experience were deduced such American characteristics as individualism, self-reliance, equalitarian ideas, and resistance to the extending grasp of organized capitalism; but this was mythology as much understanding, and the truth lay rather in the constant efforts of countless Americans to extend and preserve the vitality of community life. To attain this objective material success was of the first importance: a settlement which failed, died; the community which established profitable economic associations with the rest of the world made the good life possible.

It was therefore no accident that the small town became the most typical product of American civilization. It was here that the constructive labour of the great westward migration was most prominently displayed, and it was here that businessmen won a prestige unparalleled elsewhere in the world. The colourful story of the westward movement seized upon lawless individuals as elemental characters in an epic; the real heroes of the struggle were the small farmers, merchants, ministers, lawyers, and politicians who created communities where none had existed before.

Communities could not remain isolated; their survival depended not only upon internal effort but also upon the development of the whole region in which they were situated. Competition, regarded by later theorists as the driving spirit in American life, was always modified by the need for co-operation first within communities and then in larger regions. Individualism, subsequently prized as the key to American success, was a convenient fiction for businessmen who fought against acceptance of public responsibility; reality was found in the needs of communities to harness individual effort and direct energies into co-operative channels. The reality of this situation was obscured by later obsession with the conflict between individuals and government, for in practice the discipline of American community was often achieved by social pressure rather than by governmental regulation. Alexis de

Tocqueville saw the greatest danger of American society in the 'tyranny of the majority', exercised not through the agencies of government but through the relentless pressure of public opinion in small face-to-face societies where politics, law, and religion were all controlled by popular consensus. Beyond this there could be no appeal because there were no superior institutions but similar communities demanding and enforcing similar codes of behaviour. Individualism for Tocqueville was not a dynamic principle but exposure without the protection of established institutions.

Throughout history the Protestant, small town, and individualistic tradition has been challenged by the plantation culture of the South, the influx of immigrants, the rise of cities, intellectuals, and most recently by the black revolution. Thomas Jefferson, the greatest theorist of Southern society, endorsed some ideas of the close-knit communities of the Protestant congregational tradition. He believed in the autonomy of local societies, and defended the right of men to regulate their own lives; but his ideas were formulated in a rural and hierarchical society, in which the focus was not the small town but the plantation, and where a scattered rural population contained a minority of large landowners and a large number of small but independent freeholders. The upper class controlled politics, local administration, and economic life, while enjoying education and leisure in a society where the majority were ignorant and bound to a life of toil. Jefferson could see only too clearly the danger in abuse of power by this upper class, yet believed that the remedy must not be found in external control but in the balance of forces within society itself. Independent free-holders might have little education or knowledge of the wider world, but they could feel the burden of taxation and see where or when their freedom was restricted; representative government enabled them to use the vote to prevent the exploitation of the weak. Did local auton-omy mean the right of the gentry to rule? In a sense, yes; but it would be government by the consent of individual freeholders whom no man could control. Were the rights of states no more than the rationalization of the rights of a patrician class? Yes; but of a class which could not govern solely in its own interest. Protestant congregationalism had subordinated the individual to the moral purpose of a community; Jefferson strove to keep the individual as the free judge of what had been and should be done.

Jefferson's political philosophy made no attempt to embrace large cities and manufacturing establishments. Towards cities he could adopt only a fatalistic premonition of corruption to come; industry he hoped to keep in Europe so long as it was possible to do so. The abundant land of America might prevent the concentration of men in dependent masses for a period, and the charter of American freedom lay in the promise of the West. If the powers of government were allowed to grow, freedom would inevitably be diminished, and if the ordinary voter could not control a government so close to him as that of the state, he could not hope to influence the remote government of the Union. Thus Jefferson planted in the American mind the conviction that enlarged government would inevitably mean domination by ambitious men pursuing selfish interests.

It is a grand paradox of American history that the Jeffersonian slogans of equality and freedom (formulated for a rural society with strictly limited government) came, in the long run, to inspire city dwellers, industrial masses, intellectuals, and federal administrators. The irony is symbolized by the lonely splendour of Jefferson's national monument within walking distance of the world's largest complex of bureaucratic administration. A more revealing memorial is his hilltop mansion at Monticello where, whilst looking across some miles of fertile wooded country to the portico of the University of Virginia which he designed, the philosopher statesman could meditate upon the forces of democracy and education which limited the power of his own patrician class. Illustration of the Jeffersonian paradox helps, however, to explain his commanding influence over the American mind. If Jefferson was an upper-class slave-owner with philosophic interests and a humane temperament, he seemed also to epitomize the aspiration of humble men to escape from the constraints and oppressions of the Old World. If his Virginia was, in some respects, like the rural society of Europe, it was also a society in which men could own land and go about their affairs without asking permission from the squire or the parson. It was a society which discontented or ambitious men could leave if they wished, where class lines could be crossed, and no hereditary barriers obstructed vigorous men of humble birth.

To many conservative Americans Jefferson seemed a dangerous radical. In practice his radicalism was in speech and mind rather than in action, but the suspicion of his enemies was not entirely unjustified. Jefferson made clear the Revolutionary threat to traditional social barriers, and the implications of a system in which the mass of the people could overthrow the fabric of social order if they wished to do so. This has been a persistent tension in American life, for, if Americans hanker after stability, their society has been, for two centuries, in a state of constant movement. Economic opportunity and education, rather than political action, have been the forces of change. The declining fortunes of some groups and the rise of others have explained many of the tensions, anxieties, and conflicts of American life; but if political action has been the servant rather than the master of social change, its democratic character has always been significant. It is not so much that equalitarianism has been manifest in the electoral process, but that democratic principles have deprived the established interests of the political power to defend themselves. Popular politics have constantly turned against élites and prevented the accumulation of power in their hands, but a major anxiety of the present day is that this process may be ceasing to operate. The élite of the twentieth century, with its control of economic life, mass media, and party machinery is certainly far stronger than the old Federalists, the 'slave power' or the predatory capitalists of the late nineteenth century.

Protestant congregationalism assumed the existence of a moral code, known to man through revelation and sustained by conscious direction from a spiritual élite; Jefferson took human personality as the only social reality one could know. His ruling class was there because someone had to accept responsibility, and it was convenient to combine public responsibility with private interest; but the members of this class were not better or wiser than other men. No one could claim authority to decide what was best for others. Even the rights of majorities rested only upon the empirical observation that humble men could best judge when they had been wronged. Yet modern technology and the tasks of modern government tend constantly to concentrate the power with fewer and fewer men.

Romanticism and Nationalism

During the first half of the nineteenth century American life felt the influence of romanticism. Considered purely as a literary influence romanticism was limited in its effect, though much popular literature imitated the sentimental aspects of inferior English novels; but as a mode of thought it was far more pervasive. Romanticism seized intuitively upon great entities, endowed them with attributes, and gave them the power to act. American nationalism flourished on romantic concepts of this kind: 'the Union' became something greater and more potent than individuals or states; it commanded loyalty and would eventually demand a tremendous sacrifice of lives. 'The Constitution' became something more than political mechanism, and was regarded as an oracle to answer the vexed questions of a growing society. Men argued about 'the Union' and 'the Constitution' as they argued about religion, to provide the convinced with reasons for action rather than to convert heretics. So, too, 'the South', 'the West', became romantic concepts long before they had any reality as political entities, and Southerners talked about 'the North' as a malignant and purposeful personality though Northerners were divided by political, economic, social, and regional conflicts. The use of these romantic concepts in political discourse was akin to the way in which the poets used 'Nature'; a force that could be felt rather than defined, acted even when it appeared inert, and stood above individuals while controlling their destinies. Much evidence of this romantic mode will be found in present-day political discourse; indeed it became and has remained the essential core of public rhetoric.

Romantic imagination has illuminated other aspects of American experience. Virtue struggled with vice, outlaws were transformed into folk heroes, and the good survived when tested and proved. The West became a land of legend, the battlefields of the Civil War were cultivated with loving care, cowboys fought their unending battle with rustlers, the U.S. cavalry arrived in the nick of time to save the emigrant train from savage massacre, and railway locomotives (vintage 1880) moved across the landscape as witness to the triumph of man over nature. In this romanticized past dirt, disease, ignorance, and the agony of death were sublimated into a golden vision of the American triumph. Parallel with this was another epic – owing much to Jefferson – of innocence under constant threat from the unattractive forces of commerce, class, and capitalism. The vision was equally romantic in its personification of the forces at work in society, though not a story which ended with the best of all possible worlds but with the betrayal of the last and best hope of mankind. Harold Laski, in *The American Democracy* (1949), described the way in which the latter mood had come to dominate historiography:

> No one, I think, can seriously measure the character of the work done in the last seventy years, and particularly since the end of nineteenth-century peace in 1914, without seeing that it has been the half-conscious preoccupation of the historian, above all of those who have sought to explain and not merely to narrate, to discover what went wrong in the development of the American promise.

Laski went on to say 'No one now takes seriously the legend of a special American destiny.' To say that 'no one' believed this was to claim too much; indeed a good deal of recent history can be understood only if one remembers that a great many, perhaps a majority, continued to believe that there was 'a special American destiny'. In the present context it is, however, enough to say that 'the promise' and 'the special destiny' were equally products of the romantic vision of the past.

The American past was imagined in isolation, and Europe was considered only to present a contrast or to draw a moral. Yet the development of the United States was a part of the great explosion of intellectual and physical energy which transformed civilization. Whether one thinks of scientific revolution, economic innovation, population growth and movement, humanitarianism, democracy or the rise of the administrative state, one can see that America was the child of universal change; but too often the American past has been viewed as a spontaneous growth in which external influences existed only to be selected or rejected. In particular belief in the exclusiveness of the American past has minimized the effect of European rationalism. In one way or another most of the great changes which have occurred since 1700 are the product of the rationalist faith that man is master of his world, and that once he had understood its principles he could make it as he wished. The American, with nature on the one hand and the corruptions of the Old World on the other, had the power to make a new society as it ought to be.

There were precedents in American history for the deliberate construction of institutions. The Puritans had made their communities and imposed a religious and social order upon them. The foundation of each new colony had required a charter to define the form of government. The Revolution created a new necessity for political engineering at a time when men were prepared to break with tradition and think out political institutions from fundamental principles. From 1765 to 1788 the Americans went through an intensive period of political thinking, and the result was an unprecedented experiment in constitution making. For the first time since ancient Greece men sat down to decide what kind of government they would have, and the federal Constitution of 1787 was a supreme example of the rational spirit applied to politics. Unlike the tentative experiments on these lines during the Commonwealth and Cromwellian period in England, the American Constitution endured and this monument to eighteenth-century rationalism survives as the oldest written plan of government in the world.

Implicit in the conviction that political systems could be made to serve the needs of men was the assumption that they could be changed whenever the occasion arose, but it was equally desirable to set constitutions above the normal process of legislation. The federal Constitution included a provision for amendment but the process – the consent of two-thirds of both houses of Congress and ratification by three-fourths of the states – has proved so cumbersome that amendments have been comparatively few. In the smaller societies of the states they have been more frequent, and all states have held constitutional conventions from time to time when the whole framework of government has been reviewed and reformed. The federal Constitution has, however, been constantly the subject of judicial review and legislative interpretation so that it has proved to be far more elastic than one might assume from its existence as a formal document. The idea of a written constitution as fundamental law has not meant a static and rigid form of government.

Nevertheless the existence of written constitutions, and especially of the federal Constitution, has given a characteristic flavour to American political discourse. Even though constitutions can be changed, most controversies begin with the assumption that difficulties must be resolved without doing so. For a nation which has been constantly growing since its foundation, American politics often have a curiously backward-looking character. This was, perhaps, more marked in earlier days than in the late twentieth century; but it is still the first step in any political argument to appeal to precedent and written law rather than look forward to new principles. At no stage in American history has any major party advocated changes in the political institutions of the nation, and in most political controversies both contestants have sought to present credentials for their adherence to the letter and spirit of the existing system. To some extent, therefore, modern Americans have abdicated the right to indulge in radical reform out of respect for the rational wisdom of the past. The implication of this fundamental conservatism is far-reaching.

The rejection of the radical approach to politics was demonstrated at an early stage when early nineteenth-century Americans ignored the rise and impact of British philosophic radicalism. While British reformers, inspired either by Jeremy Bentham or by humanitarian concern, were busy laying the foundations for what is now recognized as the 'welfare state', Americans emphasized demands that economic activity should be free from governmental intervention. *Laissez-faire* seemed to its proponents to embody scientific rationalism, but was in fact based on faith rather than reason. Europeans moved quickly to the conclusion that governments must exercise social and economic responsibilities, but many Americans became convinced that principles operating automatically in competitive societies would produce greater benefits for all than any attempt at rational administration. It took long to shake this assumption, and even today many Americans believe that it is preferable to accept suffering (in others) than to restrain free enterprise.

The Americans are a political people. The Revolution, the Declaration of Independence, the constitutions of the states, and the Constitution of 1787 explain their national existence. They have more opportunities for engaging in political activities than any other people in the world: there are Congressional elections every two years, Presidential elections every four years, state elections at equal or greater frequency, elections for city governments, and primary elections to choose the party nominees for most of these contests. In many states the people may also be required to vote on constitutional amendments, on certain legislative proposals, and proposals initiated by private citizens. In several states it is also possible for voters, if they obtain sufficient support, to demand that measures are considered by the legislature or that proposals for the recall (that is, the dismissal) of elected officials should be put to popular vote. There are thus few occasions when politically active persons can be at rest, and it requires constant vigilance to keep in touch with all the possible developments.

Unfortunately, this profusion of democratic activity has not always had the desired result. In every country the hard work of politics has to be done by men who are prepared to devote all their time to the task, but in most democratic countries a substantial amount of political work is done by men for whom it is a part-time and intermittent activity; in America frequent elections have meant that the sheer burden of political work, even in the lower echelons, has demanded the services of a very large army of professionals, while the opportunities for amateurs are proportionately reduced. This sets up a chain reaction, for the more professional politicians dominate political activity, the less attractive it becomes to amateurs. In theory, of course, the professional politicians depend, like every other politician, upon winning the consent of the governed; but professionals find many ways of gathering support while the issues remain obscure.

In a rural society and in small towns the gap between social leadership and political leadership did not appear to be great; but in cities it was difficult to bridge. By the later nineteenth century most of the cities were ruled by professional politicians, while the educated élite of merchants and bankers withdrew from public life. There was always one major exception to this rule; whether in rural or in urban communities lawyers moved naturally into politics and the great majority of public men belonged to this profession. In the Congress of the United States it was an exception to find a member who was not also a practising lawyer or had embarked upon a legal career before turning to politics. These phenomena have had a marked effect upon the political character of the American people. Politics become professional; lawyers make the most adept professional leaders; and other interests exert pressure from the outside rather than operate through official channels. Legislators tend to act as though holding a brief for clients, who may be either their constituents in the broadest sense or special interests. It has often been difficult to focus on national issues, because so many lawyer politicians give first priority to the satisfaction of favoured supporters. At the same time business, organized labour, and private associations are forced to lobby and to use pressure-group tactics in order to get favourable attention from legislators. The system works better than might be imagined, but is obviously open to abuse.

In many countries intellectuals have a close interest in politics but find it difficult to bring their influence to bear upon political decisions. This is particularly marked in the United States where intellectuals have often been acutely sensitive to their exclusion from the centres of power, while practical politicians are frequently contemptuous of idealists and exploit the popular distrust of men who claim superior knowledge. Indeed 'alienated intellectuals' and 'anti-intellectual' public men have become familiar stereotypes. Sometimes, however, one wonders whether the picture has not been overdrawn; intellectuals seem to have as much share in opinion-making as anywhere, and if they are disappointed they can take their revenge by writing the books which determine 'the verdict of history'. Despite this doubt it is important to know that American intellectuals have often felt alienated from the political establishment, frustrated when obscurantism seems to defeat reason, and shocked by the unsavoury way in which public life is conducted. There is therefore a continuing paradox in American life. Nearly everyone expresses profound attachment to the political principles of the nation, but many of the most intelligent and articulate people believe that the principles are constantly betrayed by the politician.

If intellectuals may think that they are excluded from the world of politics, they are certainly alienated from the world of business. Again, this is not unique to American civilization, but it is particularly noticeable because businessmen enjoy so much prestige and social priority. In the older élite society, of Europe and eighteenth-century America, men of books could often find acceptance (and patronage) in upper-class society; in modern America they are unlikely to be found in exclusive country clubs. This is not merely a matter of place and fashion; the American intellectual lives in a different environment from the businessman – his work is different, his pleasures are different, and he has wholly different attitudes of mind.

The position of intellectuals in modern American life is surprising in view of the central position they occupied in early America. Several of the 'founding fathers' would count as intellectuals by any reckoning, and most of them had a respect for intelligence. Even Washington, a supreme embodiment of practical wisdom, could tackle an abstract idea when he chose to do so, and express himself in clear, well-ordered prose. One can, however, remember that other revolutions have gone through the stage at which they were controlled by men of ideas and passed at last into the hands of bureaucrats and pragmatic opportunists. Once ideas have become institutionalized, the powers that be have little use for abrasive criticism.

There is a more favourable way in which one can diagnose this situation. America, with her existing institutions and capacity for economic growth, has been a success. From the first uncertain gestures towards economic growth to the achievements of twentieth-century science and technology there has been an upward trend in comfort, material rewards, and standards of life. It is true that there have been periods of depression, but recovery has been followed by more striking advances. It is true that at every stage some Americans have been left behind in poverty while others seem to have won an unfair share of prosperity; but looking at the whole span of American history one can safely say that no nation has ever diffused increasing wealth more evenly among its people. The economic success of American civilization has prevented the operation of many factors which might apply in a less expansive and less dynamic society. There has usually been opportunity in excess of available talent, and this has softened social conflicts. The restless and ambitious middle class of modern civilization has found an outlet in entrepreneurial activity; organized labour, as a general rule, has preferred to fight for a share in increasing wealth rather than for control over the means of production; dissatisfied farmers and agricultural labour have been able to seek opportunity in the cities and in industry.

It would be wrong to attribute this success purely to the good fortune of abundant land and natural resources, for other large nations, with comparable advantages, have made much slower progress towards the heights. Some credit is due to educational achievement. From early days, in the Northern and Western states, public policy aimed to produce an educated people. In these states the large majority of adults were literate at a time when the majority of Europeans were denied all education; the remarkable early progress in elementary education laid the foundations for spectacular developments in high school education and, in the twentieth century, for mass higher education. There can be little doubt that this educational progress has provided a key to economic advance. Unfortunately the states of the South made much slower progress in this direction. In the nineteenth century the sons (but not always the daughters) of the upper class were well educated but for the majority schooling was rudimentary, and only the shock of Civil War defeat and Reconstruction produced a public school system in most of the states; even then, in many areas only a minority took advantage of educational opportunities.

All educational systems experience difficulty in serving the dual purpose of training an élite and providing a general education for citizenship. The emphasis over the greater part of American educational history has been upon the more general objective, and has been criticized for sacrificing quality to quantity. Today the leading positions of Americans, in so many fields of high intellectual endeavour, refutes the criticism, but there are substantial differences between the American and the British approach. The success of American graduate schools is evident, but the contrast between the general character of education in earlier stages and intense specialization for the minority who go on to graduate work tends to widen the gap between the intellectuals and the rest of society.

Racial Minorities

The tensions of American society which have been so far considered exist within the white, Anglo-Saxon, Protestant culture; but the pressures upon this culture have been a major theme of American history. The oldest Americans – the Indians – offered a physical threat in early days, but they have provided few internal problems for the dominant culture. Partly through accidental circumstances, partly through their reaction to white settlement, and partly through deliberate design, the Indians have been placed outside American civilization; few attempts have been made to assimilate them, and removal rather than integration has always been the guiding principle of white policy. Only in recent years has the small Indian minority been able to organize protest against this treatment.

It was otherwise with Negroes. They had been brought to America to labour in the fields and in the household, and all the resources of law and social discipline were employed to keep them in these occupations. Africans were uprooted, tribally mixed, sold indiscriminately, and condemned to life-long toil. Historians differ about the legal origins of the slave code – slavery having vanished from seventeenth-century English law there were no precedents to build upon – but there seems little doubt that from their earliest contacts white men regarded black men as naturally inferior and destined by God to become a subject race. Slavery imposed some obligations upon masters; they had to clothe and feed their slaves, to provide for the infants and the aged, and in their own interest to see that the workers were healthy and as cheerful as their servile status would permit. But slaves could do nothing without the permission of their owner who laid down the conditions of work and leisure, administered all punishment short of death, and had absolute control over the slave's domestic life. Slaves could not legally marry or own property, and could be sold at will.

This is not the place to examine all the consequences of slavery, but the institution has left an agonizing legacy. Indeed it is difficult to imagine a worse initiation into the problems of a bi-racial society. Nearly two hundred years ago Jefferson commented upon a Virginian proposal for the gradual emancipation of slaves and for their removal to other parts of the world:

> It will probably be asked, Why not retain and incorporate the blacks into the State, and thus save the expense of supplying by the importation of white settlers, the vacancies they will leave? Deep-

rooted prejudices entertained by the whites; ten thousand recollections, by the blacks, of the injuries they have sustained; new provo-
cations; the real distinctions which nature has made; and many
other circumstances, will divide us into parties, and produce con-
vulsions, which will probably never end but in the extermination of
the one or the other race.

The words strike a prophetic note in the light of twentieth-century
race riots, black militancy, and white 'backlash'.

Slavery was extinguished in the Northern states when revolutionary
and humanitarian ideas assaulted the bastions of eighteenth-century
society. Here the slave-owners were few while the majority of blacks
had been employed in skilled or semi-skilled trades and were thus more
easily accepted in a predominantly white society. Even so the Northern
Negroes continued to suffer social and legal discrimination which
branded them as an inferior race. In the South the slave-owners were
more numerous, the majority of the slaves unskilled labourers, and a
wide range of interests were intimately affected by the slave economy.
Even so it is probable that slavery would have ended in the South if
practicable plans had been proposed for separating the races geographically after freedom.

Abraham Lincoln, who emancipated the slaves, continued to hope
for some scheme of colonization which would have taken the Negroes
to a country of their own; and the technical problems of transportation
(in an age which saw the transatlantic migration of millions of Europeans) were not insuperable. But there were other difficulties. Negroes
had lived on American soil almost as long as the whites, the majority of
them had no wish to leave provided that they could be free, and the
racial mixture which had occurred made it difficult to define 'Negro'.
Frederick Douglass, the most eloquent and eminent Negro of the
period, came out emphatically for integration rather than separation,
and this ideal inspired the Fourteenth Amendment (guaranteeing equal
citizenship and equal protection of the laws) and the Fifteenth Amendment (making it illegal to deprive men of the vote on grounds of race).

The twentieth century has seen some dramatic changes in the racial
situation. A great northward migration brought thousands of Negroes
into the cities of the North and West, and today half the Negro
population of the United States is concentrated in a dozen large cities.
With increasing numbers of whites moving out to suburban areas it
seems certain that many of these cities will be under black political

control in the near future. By the middle of the next century predominantly black cities may be confronting predominantly white rural and suburban areas. It is an intriguing thought that the city most likely to come under black control is the federal capital, Washington, D.C.

Both in the North and in the South strenuous efforts have been made to integrate education, employment, and social life, but success has been limited. There has been a marked improvement in the status of Negroes, and in the opportunities open to them, but self-conscious black leadership is increasingly unwilling to accept integration into a predominantly white society (which, in their analysis, can end only in subordination not equality). Increasingly Negroes wish to stress the achievements and potentiality of the black race, and to abandon the integrationist ideal of becoming white men with black skins. Present anxieties may, however, blind one to some possibilities within the system. The law of the United States is emphatically committed to racial equality. Negroes have reached high posts in the government service, in the professions, in universities, and to an increasing extent in business. As consumers Negroes may have less average purchasing power than whites, but it is increasing and is already higher than that of the poor in many other countries. The black magazine *Ebony* can now claim to be the best medium for advertisers who wish to sell in this growing market. These are straws in the wind which hold some hope that education and economic power will, in the long run, accomplish more than conscious policy. It is certain that the pattern of race relations will evolve in ways which have not been wholly anticipated and that, in the meantime, the problems of a bi-racial society will remain as the severest challenge to Americanism.

The failure of the 'melting pot' to melt away the differences between white and black causes one to look more closely at this much-valued concept in American tradition. Though the Irish remain fully conscious of their racial traditions, they have risen to power and influence in American life, largely through municipal politics and the national Democratic party. Germans and Scandinavians have experienced few difficulties in assimilation; but can the same be said of Italians, Poles, and other Mediterranean and Slav peoples? Few from these ethnic minorities have entered the citadels of political and economic power. Some Jews have become prominent in business, education, politics, professions, and organized labour; but there remains a good deal of latent anti-Semitism and a sharp social distinction between Jews whose families settled before 1850 and the more recent immigrants from eastern Europe. Further out still are the Chinese and Japanese minorities. For many Americans of old stock the norms of American civilization are still set by the Anglo-Saxon Protestant tradition; yet the original justification for independent nationhood was based upon universal propositions about human rights in society. Thus the ethnic problems of the American nation not only give rise to irritation and frustration, but also to fundamental questions about the nature and purpose of Americanism.

Equality and Rights

Racial problems have strained the principle of equality which has always been the most difficult of the Revolutionary concepts to interpret. The authors of the Declaration of Independence said that all men were created equal, but their primary intention was to claim that as colonists they had been treated inequitably by the British government, and that the political status of a community should have no effect upon the rights of individuals. At the same time colonial laws linked the right to vote with the possession of property, and there was thus an early distinction between natural rights (of which a man could not be deprived) and political rights, which were at the discretion of the governing authority. Further, when the Declaration said that governments derived their just powers from the consent of the governed, 'consent' meant 'acceptance', not a positive act of will.

This distinction between natural and political rights was maintained in later westward settlement. Expediency required that the political organization of a Territory should be subordinate to the government of the United States, so that the *political* rights of the inhabitants were inferior; but they were also guaranteed equal *legal* rights with all American citizens. The distinction was blurred when adult male suffrage became normal but maintained in the Fourteenth and Fifteenth Amendments after the Civil War. The Fourteenth Amendment gives an absolute and unqualified guarantee of equality in the courts and prohibits legislation discriminating between different kinds of citizens; the Fifteenth makes it unconstitutional to deprive men of the right to vote on grounds of race, creed, or colour, but leaves the states free to fix other conditions for suffrage. However, today the term 'civil rights' is usually taken to include the right to vote and to participate in politics. The Supreme Court has accepted this wide interpretation in recent years and has ruled that if the apportionment of seats in a state legislature overweights some areas, the people in under-represented areas have been denied 'equal protection of the laws'. In an earlier age the unfair representation of districts or communities was often a grievance, but it was not then suggested that it abridged the rights of individuals. Today it is accepted that 'one man, one vote' and an equal weight for every vote are principles which override the argument that certain areas or interests deserve special recognition in the electoral system. Yet there remains an obvious exception to this rule: in the Senate huge states – greater in population than a majority of the world's independent nations – have exactly the same representation as Rhode Island, Delaware, or Nevada.

A further difficulty in the interpretation of 'equality' arises when discriminatory behaviour arises from the convention and customs of society. It would be thought improper to deny to members of a private club the right to lay down their own rules for membership; but exclusive clubs can be powerful instruments for social discrimination or even the means by which the political domination of an élite can be informally but effectively organized. Equally difficult problems have arisen when residents in a community voluntarily accept conditions which prevent them from selling or renting their houses to Negroes or to other persons not acceptable to existing residents. In these and other instances government has been faced with an uncomfortable choice between freedom and equality, and too often the eventual compromise has permitted the evasion of equalitarian laws by private agreement. Racial discrimination which exists by private agreement and social custom has been more effective and more pervasive than discrimination by law. In many Northern and Western areas there has been no legal discrimination against Negroes for over a century, but segregation by residence and employment has become very clear and has been a major agency in producing the concentration of blacks in certain well-defined city areas. Discrimination exists against lower-class whites as well as against blacks, but whereas for a white the acquisition of wealth is a passport into most exclusive circles, the educated and well-to-do black may still be denied admission.

It is not the purpose of this chapter to investigate further the sociological problems of race, but merely to indicate the way in which the existence of racial differences has complicated the interpretation of 'equality'. The original commitment to equality has come to mean that so far as possible, and as far as the law can reach without abridging individual rights, men should be treated as though they were equal. Many Americans would maintain that the attempt to treat men as equal has already resulted in the unwarranted abridgment of individual rights, especially in the field of education. Special criticism has been focused on attempts to mitigate the effects of residential segregation upon education by moving children by bus to school districts other than their own. Others would, however, maintain that a still more determined assault must be made on social custom in the interests of equality.

The conflict between equality and freedom is implicit in all democratic societies. It is acute in America because of the emphasis upon economic freedom. Equality of opportunity, accompanied by unfettered freedom to acquire and use wealth, necessarily produces unequal achievement. Moreover, once wealth has been acquired it can buy privilege (including educational and social privilege) for sons and daughters. Sociological studies have demonstrated a strong and increasing hereditary element in the upper ranges of business, professions, and the armed services. It is, of course, possible to find some men of humble origin in the highest positions, but the United States can no longer claim any special distinction for a social characteristic which is shared by every other advanced society.

The tendency towards social stratification in all modern societies has worked to crystallize and perpetuate the leadership of an 'establishment', and in America this means continued influence for the older white American stocks. English, Scottish, Northern Irish, and German names are still those most commonly found in the upper ranks of the professions, business and (in some regions) politics. In a few areas in the West the dominant strain is Scandinavian. The Southern Irish have firmly established themselves as leaders in the Catholic Church and in city politics. In most Northern and Mid-western communities the business and professional élite includes some Jews, and less frequently Italians and Slavs, but they are seldom in the inner circles which contain the social leaders of a community. In addition to upper-class prestige, imponderable influence still attaches to the heirs of the British culture from which American civilization derived, and despite all the changes and tensions they remain the custodians of 'Americanism' in both its conservative or liberal manifestations.

Anglo-Saxon Americanism is, however, split by a deep rift. The Civil War was fought between two rival traditions, derived from a common source but no longer compatible with each other. It was a war about the character of the nation which had evolved since the Revolution. The war left these differences unresolved, and they persist to this day. It is easier to state that the differences exist than to define them. At one time it was fashionable to describe Southern civilization as 'agrarian' and the Northern as 'capitalist'. In the mid-nineteenth century 'agrarian', so far from describing a structured society dominated by large landowners, was used of land reformers who advocated the confiscation and redistribution of land on equalitarian principles. The North, still an overwhelmingly rural society with a far more equitable distribution of land than the South, was thus closer to the 'agrarian' ideal. The Homestead Law of 1862, which Southern politicians had successfully resisted before the outbreak of war, was the most 'agrarian' measure ever passed by a United States Congress. The word 'capitalist' can be equally confusing; for while Marxists agree with apologists of the Old South in describing that society as 'pre-capitalist', others may see little practical difference between commercial agriculture and other forms of business enterprise. Examination of the decision-making process in the two societies will, however, demonstrate the existence of important differences which need not be obscured by quarrels over the use of terms. In the South all major decisions – whether in economics, politics, social conventions, or cultural activities – were made by the upper class of planters. In the North economic decisions were made by bankers, merchants, and entrepreneurs of various types; political decisions were made by majorities drawn from rural areas and small towns; cultural leadership rested mainly with the heirs of the old élite in the Eastern states; and no one was an effective arbiter of social manners. Thus decision-making in the South was concentrated; in the North it was diffused. The South could appear to speak with one voice, while the North was distracted by conflicting councils; but this also meant that the forces of change flowed much more easily in Northern than in Southern society. Religion, reform, science, and economic innovation had been transforming Northern and Western society in a hectic and often confusing way, but the Southerners were selective in what they accepted and conservative in adaptation. Many of the differences can, of course, be traced to the bi-racial character of the South and the enslavement of the black race.

Southerners would maintain that the crude analysis of their nine-teenth-century society in terms of class and race misses the essential flavour of their culture. Their own descriptions normally occupy two stages: certain characteristics are attributed to the North, and their absence in the South is then used as positive evidence for Southern 'values'. In this sequence of argument the North is dominated by the search for wealth, is ruthlessly competitive, abandons courtesy and devalues aspects of behaviour to which no cash reckoning can be attached. If slavery was a social evil (as many pre-war Southerners secretly believed), in practice it might have redeeming features when compared with Northern employers who acknowledged no public or social responsibility for their 'wage slaves'. Northerners were given credit for ingenuity and enterprise, but not for reflection or wisdom. Northerners got quick results at the expense of the standards which should sustain the quality of civilized life. Having thus defined the unattractiveness of Northern life, it was not difficult to demonstrate the immunity of the South from these unwholesome influences.

There were many aspects of the Southern image of the North which could be denied or qualified, but they were undoubtedly real to Southerners and played a decisive part in moulding the Southern character. At least it gave the opportunity to emphasize some social values which were in danger of being swamped by nineteenth-century progress, and this has given the Old South an abiding attraction for many Americans. Modern dissatisfaction with a society dominated by big government and corporate capitalism may well lead to renewed sympathy for local autonomy and non-commercial values; but this sympathy is unlikely to extend to the use of these principles to justify the bitter politics of white supremacy.

Radicalism and the Establishment

A European coming to the study of American history is often surprised by the weakness of radical tradition. In British and French history it has been assumed that the existence of opposition is normal and healthy, and that a portion of this opposition will aim at radical alterations in the structure of society. It is also assumed that over a long period some of the radical objectives will be achieved and that history will vindicate the men who advocated them. Few of these assumptions can be transferred to American history. It is true that party battles have usually been vigorous, but they have been fought on a very narrow front. Elections may settle particular issues and decide which set of men will hold political power; but most of the time Americans are asked to choose between different kinds of men who are likely to administer very similar policies. There have been exceptions such as 1832, 1860, 1896, and 1936; but the first and the last of these were decisive confirmations of what had been done rather than new departures. Other examples, such as 1828, 1912, and 1932, inaugurated new political eras, but for the voters these elections repudiated incumbent Presidents in favour of men whose future policies had not been revealed. The change of direction came when the new administration had assumed office. Major parties do not campaign on promises of basic change, and parties that do so normally receive very small votes. In 1972 George McGovern's mild dalliance with radicalism was severely punished by the voters (including many in his own Democratic party). Radical criticism of the political and social structure is normally resented by the majority of the people, and it is expected to fail in achieving its objectives.

The history of abolitionism provides an interesting exception. The abolitionists were not revolutionaries but they did use agitation as a political weapon and attacked the existing power-structure. In the interests of a major reform some abolitionists did not hesitate to attack the Constitution and the Union itself. In their early days they were also closely associated with England, a foreign power regarded by many Americans as the inveterate enemy of their country. It is therefore possible to draw some close parallels between abolitionism and some of the twentieth-century radical movements. For conservatives this comparison is inconvenient because the abolitionists witnessed the triumph of their great cause even if their part in this achievement was obscure; but the exception proves the rule, for radical anti-slavery succeeded under circumstances which no one wishes to repeat.

One is forced to ask whether this traditional attitude to radicalism will be altered by late twentieth-century events. It is not only that contemporary radicalism is more vigorous, more articulate, and more violent than earlier radical movements, but also that it is strong among the young, intelligent, and middle class. In Europe this combination has provided leadership for most radical and revolutionary movements. Another factor is that, if the radical philosophy is not understood (or, indeed, not explained in comprehensible terms), many of the causes advocated by contemporary radicals command a great deal of sympathy. If a majority of Americans supported the Vietnam war, many did so with a great deal of doubt, and certainly with reservations about the way in which the United States became involved, while for an articulate minority it became the most immoral betrayal in history. A very large number of Americans feel guilty and anxious about the racial question. The great corporations, which are targets of radical propaganda, are by no means popular. Many Americans feel resentful at the constant pressure of advertising upon their lives, and are intensely suspicious of the whole paraphernalia of public relations. Pollution of the environment and neglect of safety is attributed to callous indifference on the part of those who control the economy. For many young people drugs become morally justified simply because they are condemned by the establishment.

There are still deeper reasons why modern radicalism may come to have a different place in history than earlier minority movements. The vastness of the modern administrative organization, the remoteness of government, the evidence that vital decisions can be taken without the knowledge of Congress or opportunity for public debate, all create feelings of frustration. In the country with so many opportunities for political participation, the chances of *effective* participation seem to be diminishing. Political discussions on the television are usually unimpressive and seem to be declining in frequency. It does not seem likely that future presidential candidates will agree to face-to-face televised debates as Kennedy and Nixon did in 1960. At a lower level public men are more likely to cultivate evasion than communicate with the public, and press conferences have evolved a sophisticated technique of concealment. The news provided by many newspapers is often poor in quality and so highly selective that it is frequently impossible to follow important questions through from day to day. In addition to all this, a great many Americans suspect that the real decisions are not made by the politicians at all but by the generals and the industrialists; this is a misconception, but the idea is prevalent and disturbing.

Business has shown an increasing tendency both to concentrate and to diffuse decision. The single masterful entrepreneur has been replaced by the managerial team, and decisions are not made by single men on specific occasions but by committees operating over a period of time and responsible for various aspects of the industrial process. At the same time the magnitude of decisions and their consequences are greater than ever before. Indeed, the complexity of modern business has helped to fragment responsibility; and though business leadership remains essential it comes to lie in the ability to devise the strategy within which multiple decisions on detail are made. The individual leader probably lacks the knowledge to criticize the findings of a technical committee under his nominal control, but he can impress upon its members the need for urgency, the character of the general questions which must be answered and the implications of their decisions for other sectors of the industrial process. This kind of leadership fosters harmony and speed in internal affairs, but has no impact upon the external picture of the corporation. In the early twentieth century Rockefeller, Carnegie, J. P. Morgan, and Henry Ford were household names, but how many people could name the present general managers of the firms founded by them? The corporations have become impersonal, and ordinary citizens – whether as consumers or as men interested in public affairs – find their lives moulded by great bureaucratic concerns which they cannot understand and can hardly identify.

Another factor is the long period of preparation required for modern innovation. An individual – or even a powerful organized group – has no chance of influencing the design of next year's car, because the plans have been approved years before, the necessary modifications in expensive machinery have already been made, and the strategy of sales promotion has already been fixed by numerous contracts and commitments. The same difficulty in identifying responsibility and influencing long-term events extends to politics, and too many people feel that the will to act is lost in a maze of intrigue and bureaucracy. Never before have decisions involved such momentous consequences, nor has the process by which decisions are made apparently been so uncontrollable.

Under these circumstances it is no surprise that violent protest supersedes peaceful petitioning. The one way in which indignant individuals can use the mass media is to produce an event which makes the headlines and the peak-hour newscasts. Violence may generate reaction, but the goal of protestors is not popularity but influence. It could once be assumed that democracy was working so long as no minority preferred resistance to the acceptance of majority decisions; but this is no longer valid. Violence has become not the last but the first step in the political process, the demand that talks must begin, not the ultimate sanction against their outcome; too often the price of peace must be concessions made without public discussion. This attitude is justified in radical thought by the theory that any state, even the most democratic, is organized force; and that the only argument recognized by force is counterforce. The liberal plea for rational discussion is seen as evasion, because 'the establishment' long ago discovered ways in which discussion could be limited and rendered harmless. The greater the show of open impartiality, the greater the danger of secret pressure, and the greater the need for violence that no one can ignore.

It can be argued that contemporary Americans are paying the price for a traditional tolerance of violence. It is frequently said that the Americans are a violent people, and this is stated as though it explains much. There has been a kind of perverse pride in the violence of the frontier. Violence in relations between capital and labour has not left so favourable a record but few Americans doubt its existence. A candid examination may throw doubt upon these beliefs and it is doubtful whether the American character is especially prone to violence; indeed the long record of peaceful settlement and growth, together with an almost superstitious reverence for law and constitutions, might suggest the opposite. It is true that Americans have often been singularly negligent in their provision for law enforcement; but this is to say that governments failed, not that people were abnormally addicted to violence. Labour violence certainly existed, but it is not certain that it was more frequent than in many other industrial societies; it was magnified in America largely because both employers and wage-earners had an interest in emphasizing it – the former to buttress their appeals for protection, the latter because it was an effective threat.

The American tradition of violence is thus a convention rather than a historical truth, and the occasions on which it has become real arose because people demanded too much and then refused to pay the price. Prohibition was a classic example: millions were asked suddenly to abandon a habit which they regarded as harmless and convivial, while a tiny handful of federal officers were employed at low salaries to enforce the law. Equally conducive to violence was the reluctance to meet nationwide crime with national police; criminal jurisdiction still remains in the hands of weak state governments and not until the reorganization of the Federal Bureau of Investigation in 1933 was there an effective national enforcement agency.

In one respect, however, Americans have shown a stronger propensity to violence than other advanced countries. This has been the readiness of men who regard themselves as custodians of the American tradition to use violence against their enemies; the vigilante tradition – in which 'law-abiding' citizens take the law into their own hands – goes far back in American history. This could bring about the summary execution of known criminals, but it could also lead to the barbarous punishment of men who were no more than suspects or whose crimes against social convention would not have been punishable in the courts. Lynch law dates from the period of the Revolution, and was originally no more than organization of a community to ostracize suspected

Tories; later it became a method of bypassing the law or imposing conformity. In the North it was well known, before the Civil War, that mob action against abolitionists was often inspired and led by the 'best citizens'. In the South, in the later nineteenth century, terrorism (often with the connivance of leading citizens) became an accepted method of evading the Fourteenth and Fifteenth Amendments. Late nineteenth-century employers used violence against labour organizers, and in later years suspected 'reds' have suffered more from private persecution than from the operation of the law (however severe that may have been). Thus lawlessness in defence of 'law and order' or of social conventions is an interesting and disturbing aspect of American history, but is clearly divorced from any tradition of radical protest. The earlier examples of endemic violence therefore prove nothing about the radical violence of the twentieth century. There may, it is true, be a remote link through the place of violence in the literary tradition, but it cannot be strong. The older examples of violence flowed from situations in which the law was weak; modern radical violence stems from a situation in which the establishment is so strong that only the smell of burning property can penetrate its defences.

Modern radicalism, even when not manifested in violent action, is a new phenomenon in American history. The majority of the radicals are educated and come from middle class families. They are seldom drawn from the lower social strata, and this is true even of the black radicals. They come from the class which has been (in traditional historiography) the greatest beneficiary of American development, and however indignantly they repudiate their social origins they belong to the bourgeoisie for whom a capitalist society was created. It has been rare enough in the past to find any American challenging the fundamentals of American society; now significant numbers of the 'chosen people' are prepared to break loose and some are determined to destroy.

This is not a conflict over means but over ends, and raises profound questions of purpose and belief. It cannot be answered by the kind of rhetoric that has so often been used to persuade the critics that their interests are identical with those of the criticized. It is true that radical ideas are ill-assorted and inconsistent: Mao Tse-tung jostles with echoes of Thomas Jefferson, Lenin becomes merged with Herbert Marcuse, philosophic anarchism is quickly transformed into denials of free speech. This incoherence is, perhaps, the most American charac-teristic of the new Left which manages to combine as many contradictions as the Democratic party. American, too, is the belief that the best plan is to have no plan, that every problem has an empirical solution, that every individual has a contribution to make if left free to make it, and that every prior commitment is an impediment to action. There are, however, guiding principles which rule in chaos. No concession must be made to authority, capitalism is the enemy of mankind, the establishment is immoral, men have been bribed by comfort and corrupted by sales technique; if this is reminiscent of Thomas Jefferson, it is ominous in a society which, since Jefferson's time, has pinned so much faith upon the triumphs of enterprise and the justice of democratic society. It is not a phase or a party which is under attack, but national faith and tradition. The American elements in contemporary radicalism offer some hope that bridges can be built between them and the mainstream of American civilization; but they will not be built without effort and time is running short. No society can preserve for long either its efficiency or its self-respect when an articulate intelligentsia is determined to reject both.

Cohesive Forces

The preceding pages have stressed the divisive elements in American society, and have interpreted them mainly as challenges to the original White Anglo-Saxon and Protestant culture. The unsolved enigma of American nationalism is whether old and new elements are fusing together to create a new and stronger alloy. If the rewards of American civilization were purely material there would be little ground for optimism, for there is little evidence from history that either the enjoyment or the prospects of economic growth will long prevent men from rushing into emotional conflict. It is, however, worth enumerating some successes which should not be overlooked. The educational system of the United States is often criticized in detail, but it was the first to aim at creating a literate people, the first to contemplate universal secondary education, and to pioneer in opening wide the gates of higher education. Today flourishing graduate schools demonstrate that quality is not sacrificed to quantity. American small towns are proverbially cultural deserts, but most large cities can display a cultural achievement which should be the envy of many European provincial towns. American culture has been enormously enriched by wealthy men whose private collections now fill the public galleries and whose benefactions have provided museums, concert halls, and public parks. American science has been profusely endowed, and in every branch of science and medicine some Americans are numbered among the world leaders. In this age it is demonstrably untrue to say that America is the land of opportunity for businessmen alone, for in few countries are there greater opportunities in intellectual, cultural, and scientific activity. Nor is it true to say that status and prestige goes to business success alone, for the arts and the professions can lead to fame and fortune. If the radicals represent the alienation of the intelligentsia from the establishment, many intellectuals have acquired a vested interest in American society; if American society sometimes looks as though it is falling apart, the opportunities offered to so wide a range of talents provide a cohesive force. Mesmerised by the less attractive features of American society, commentators have often failed to observe that America is still the land of innovation, though today the pioneer is as likely to be a scientist, scholar, writer, musician, or artist as an entrepreneur.

The sophisticated idea of America as a land of intellectual opportunity may be difficult to reconcile with popular patriotism. The normal invocation of Americans takes pride in its simplicity; to be an American is to have rejected the subtleties of worn-out cultures, to be decent and straightforward, kindly but not soft, and able to discern the essentials with the eye of common sense. The one hundred per cent American is individualistic, but also a good neighbour and an excellent family man; he drinks beer or whisky and despises wine; he has no taste for foreign cookery and prefers a plain (but expensive) broiled steak. But this kind of archetypal American is rapidly becoming a minority within a minority, though no more modern stereotype has taken his place. Indeed, complex modern societies are less and less able to see themselves as caricaturists see them. National character can no longer be expressed in simple terms, and a new vocabulary is required to describe society as it is. America is not alone in experiencing a conflict between earlier images and modern reality, but the clash is more obvious and more important because the older concepts have played so important a part in American history and are still treasured by many Americans.

It is a curiosity of contemporary America that so many political and cultural successes have been victories over 'Americanism'. The men who claim the purest patriotism are a minority among Americans, and have fought to prevent every development which the majority would regard as progress. Sooner or later the majority, with the intellectuals as their spokesmen, must take over the field and give popular expression to the positive values of American society as they understand them. When this is done it is certain that a part of the restatement will draw heavily upon the principles of the past and that the most sophisticated of modern societies will continue to use language framed in the rural communities of the eighteenth century; but it is equally certain that somehow the ideas of modern philosophers and social scientists must be distilled into a form which is readily understood and relevant to modern conditions. There is much discredited lumber on the stage – together with a few valuable period pieces – but somewhere in the wings waits the prophet of a new society.

Further Reading

The books suggested are divided into two sections: books by Americans and books about America by foreigners. In the first section, preference has been given to books which not only seek to explain aspects of American civilization but have in turn influenced the Americans' ideas about themselves. Within each section books which attempt overall interpretations or assessments of American history and civilization are placed first, followed by books which consider special problems and themes.

BOOKS BY AMERICANS

Max Lerner, *America as a Civilization: Life and Thought in the United States Today.* New York and London, 1958.

Daniel J. Boorstin, *The Americans.* Vol. I: *The Colonial Experience* (New York, 1958); Vol. II: *The National Experience* (New York, 1965); Vol. III in preparation.

Oscar Handlin, *The American People: The History of a Society.* New York and London, 1963; Pelican Book, 1966.

Reinhold Niebuhr and Alan Heimert, *A Nation so Conceived.* New York, 1963; English ed. with preface by Marcus Cunliffe, London, 1964.

David M. Potter, *People of Plenty: Economic Abundance and the American Character.* New York, 1954.

Frederick W. Merk, *Manifest Destiny and Mission in American History.* New York, 1963.

John Hope Franklin, *From Slavery to Freedom: a history of Negro Americans,* 3rd edn. New York, 1966.

Gunnar Myrdal, *An American Dilemma: the Negro Problem and Modern Democracy.* New York, 1944. There is a condensed version of this book by Arnold Rose called *The Negro in America,* New York, 1964.

Melvin Drimmer (ed.), *Black History: a Reappraisal.* New York, 1969.

Oscar Handlin, *Race, Nationality and American Life.* Boston, Mass., 1957.

C. Wright Mills, *The Power Elite.* New York, 1956.

William H. Whyte, Jr., *The Organization Man.* New York, 1956.

Hugh D. Graham and Ted R. Gurr (eds.), *The History of Violence in America.* A report to the National Commission on the causes and prevention of violence. New York, 1969.

Richard Hofstadter, *Anti-Intellectualism in American Life*. New York, 1962; London, 1964.

Willard L. Sperry, *Religion in American Life*. Cambridge, 1946; Boston, Mass., 1963.

Sydney E. Ahlstrom, *A Religious History of the American People*. New Haven, Conn., and London, 1972.

Merrill D. Peterson, *The Jefferson Image in the American Mind*. New York, 1960.

Henry Steele Commager, *The American Mind*. Newhaven, Conn., and London, 1950.

C. Vann Woodward (ed.), *The Comparative Approach to American History*. New York, 1968.

Henry Nash Smith, *Virgin Land: The American West as Symbol and Myth*. Boston, Mass., 1950.

Ronald Berman, *America in the Sixties: an intellectual history*. New York and London, 1968.

BOOKS ON AMERICAN CIVILIZATION BY FOREIGNERS

Alexis de Tocqueville, *Democracy in America*, 2 vols. 1835 and 1840; many later editions; the latest paperback edition (Fontana Library) ed. J. P. Mayer and Max Lerner, 1966, has a good introduction.

Harriet Martineau, *Society in America*. London, 1837; new edn., with introduction by Seymour Lipset, New York, 1962.

Lord Bryce, *The American Commonwealth*. First edn., 1889; 2nd edn., much revised, 1893–5; the last edition to be revised by the author was published in 1914.

Harold J. Laski, *The American Democracy*. London, 1949.

William R. Brock, *The Evolution of American Democracy*. New York, 1970.

Frank Thistlethwaite, *The Great Experiment*. Cambridge, 1954.

Hans Kohn, *American Nationalism: an interpretative essay*. New York, 1957.

Denis W. Brogan, *Introduction to American Politics*. London, 1949.

——, *American Aspects*. London, 1964.

Marcus Cunliffe, *American Presidents and the Presidency*. New York, 1968; London, 1969.

M. J. C. Vile, *Politics in the U.S.A.* London, 1970.

3 Immigration and the American Economy: An Historical View

CHARLOTTE ERICKSON

From the time of the settlement of the colony of Virginia on the mainland of North America in 1607 until the first Quota Act was passed in 1921, migrants from overseas helped to populate the region which became the United States of America. For three centuries America was a frontier of Europe to which malcontents and adventure-seekers, people without opportunities or those with ambitions beyond their opportunities could repair, if they could find the means and brave the journey and the transplantation. This was a highly productive safety-valve. The rich resources of North America had been but lightly exploited by the Indian tribes of Stone Age cultures whom the first European settlers found. The Europeans had the skills and were acquiring the technology with which to make this continent support millions of human beings. Unlike the Spaniards in South and Central America, the English did not succeed in enslaving the Indians of North America. While they were not wholly exterminated, they were nevertheless, decade after decade, relentlessly driven from the richer parts of the continent. Today some 200,000 descendants of these first immigrants to North America live segregated from the mainstream of American life on reservations, among the very poorest of her inhabitants.

Other parts of the world were also to be colonized by Europeans by the end of the nineteenth century, but no region received such a heterogeneous mixture of peoples. They came not only from many different parts of Europe but from Africa and Asia as well. Within the United States of America there emerged an extraordinary mixture of races, nationalities, cultures, and religions. The largest and most varied immigration took place during the last half of the nineteenth century.

The rapid industrialization which then attracted so many immigrants added its own problems associated with rapid economic change to those of adapting so many strangers to each other and to the society. The varied immigration and rapid industrialization of those years offered what was perhaps an unprecedented challenge to man's ability to adapt to a changing physical and social environment. Even today, a half-century after the mass immigration was halted, one cannot understand American society without recognizing that it is still an ethnic society, in which most people are conscious of their ethnic origins. Ethnic appeals are still significant in politics, and ethnic organizations are by no means moribund.

Thus the history of immigration spans nearly the whole of American development. The fact that the American colonies and afterwards parts of the United States persistently received immigrants for many generations explains much about the way of life and the traditions of the American people. This immigration was also at some points in her history essential to her economic development, and, at most times, helpful to it. The immigration which posed so many problems of social adaptation was almost invariably an economic boon. This essay focuses upon that economic contribution.

The Colonial Period

The population of the English colonies in North America had reached only about 200,000 souls at the time of the Glorious Revolution of 1688. Scattered along more than a thousand miles of coastline from the Carolinas to Maine, penetrating the interior for a few miles only where rivers permitted, these colonies had depended, from the time of their plantation, upon immigrants to quicken their growth. During the colonial period the incoming people were not called immigrants. Depending upon the time of plantation of a particular colony they were called colonists or settlers, and only later, immigrants. Since by the eighteenth century England no longer supplied most of the new settlers, we may describe the inflow as immigration.

The so-called Great Migration of perhaps 20,000 persons to Massachusetts and 10,000 to Virginia in the ten years after the founding of the Bay Colony in 1630 came to a halt with the outbreak of the English Civil War. After the Restoration emigration came to be regarded as harmful to the state, and the Act of Toleration of 1689 weakened religious motives for emigration from England, motives which since 1607 had been intertwined with material motives in the peopling of the various colonies. The poor outlook for future colonizing from England towards the end of the seventeenth century was illustrated in the founding of the Carolinas. When the proprietors began to try to settle their lands in 1670 they found it virtually impossible to attract white immigrants except from the islands of the West Indies or from other mainland colonies. By the last part of the seventeenth century convicts, paupers and debtors were being sent to the colonies by the judges and magistrates of the mother country. Statutes of 1662 and 1717 specifically authorized judges to ship convicts to America. Perhaps 30,000–50,000 convicts were transported to America from England during the first three-quarters of the eighteenth century. On the other hand, Parliament went so far as to prohibit the emigration of skilled artisans in 1719, though this legislation was difficult to enforce.

The population of the colonies was not exclusively English even in the last part of the seventeenth century. The few hundred inhabitants of the Swedish colonies on the Delaware (founded in 1632) and the larger Dutch settlements in New Netherlands (founded in 1609) had been taken over as colonies of the English Crown in 1664 and the settlers allowed to remain. By 1700 Sephardic Jews had begun to settle in New England towns, a few Scots–Irish had arrived from Ulster, and some of the Huguenot refugees had brought their savings to American seaport towns. William Penn advertised for immigrants from the Rhineland and the Low Countries for his colony in Pennsylvania, founded in 1681. Furthermore, African Negroes were among the earliest people to land from overseas on the North American mainland. The first shipment of Negroes to Virginia arrived in 1619. Thus while most of the free population of the colonies was still English by birth or descent at the end of the seventeenth century, the need for labour to develop the vast land resources, combined with discontent elsewhere in the British Isles and on the continent of Europe, was already beginning to produce a cultural mixture in the population.

In the eighteenth century, therefore, the American colonies found that they had to attract non-English immigrants if population growth was to be supplemented by immigration, which was so very important to the growth of the labour force. The institutions of indentured servitude and slavery, on which much of the immigration of the eighteenth century was to be based, had by this time become distinctly recognized in law. The development of various forms of unfree labour during the seventeenth century reflected the shortage of labour in the colonies, especially where a crop marketable in Europe, such as tobacco, could be grown. With a persistent adverse balance of payments drawing their cash to England and without a banking system, planters could not think in terms of paying high wages in cash to new settlers. Their difficulties were met in part through the importation of indentured servants who had agreed before they emigrated to work for no wages at all (merely board and lodging) for a number of years, usually from four to seven, in return for the passage and provisioning. Thus the possibility of becoming an indentured servant opened the way to emigration to servants, artisans, and labourers who could not save the money needed for ocean fare and provisions.

Indentured service was thus well-established during the seventeenth century as a means of populating the colonies. Not all servants entered their indentures voluntarily. This was true not only of convicts, but also of persons who were kidnapped as servants in England and Scotland. Nevertheless, if they survived, white indentured servants could look forward to winning their freedom eventually. The origins of slavery in the mainland colonies are not yet very clear. As late as 1660, forty years after the first importation of Africans, when there were still only about three hundred of them in Virginia, a clear status of lifelong inheritable condition of slavery was not legally recognized as the fate of all Negro servants. The decline of indentured servitude and the rise of slavery in the tobacco colonies is still not fully understood. At any rate, forms of unfree labour were established before 1700 and recognized in all the colonies, which already contained a mixture of races and nationalities. The immigration of the eighteenth century was to increase both of these tendencies.

Apart from the growing importation of Negroes as slaves, the three most significant streams of immigration in the eighteenth century were the German, the Scots–Irish and the Scottish. None of these was primarily a movement of well-off bourgeoisie, such as the Huguenot and Jewish immigrations. The emigration from the Palatine could be counted in thousands, though how many we do not know. It was a sporadic movement from the 1680s until the wars of Louis XIV. Emigration increased when Louis sent an army to the Palatine in 1707 to destroy the food crops. As with most migration of the seventeenth and eighteenth centuries, religious and material motives mingled when some pietists joined the exodus to escape from Catholic princes. After these German refugees arrived in England, the government arranged for some of them to go to the Hudson Valley in New York in 1710, to begin the production of naval stores. Although this project proved unsuccessful, some Germans did settle in the Hudson and Mohawk valleys. Pennsylvania, however, became their chief destination as they continued to arrive in the wake of this first upsurge of migrants in the second decade of the century.

The most recent historian of the Scots–Irish emigration from Ulster, R. W. Dickson, traces the origins of a substantial emigration to the years 1718–20 when a series of bad harvests coincided with the raising of rents for many farmers as their long leases expired. Natural calamities and food shortages kept the emigration going in the twenties. The religious dimension was also present, since most Ulster emigrants appear to have been Presbyterians who were legally tolerated but still debarred from public posts, and whose schools and marriages were not recognized. At the outset this movement seems to have been directed towards Boston in Massachusetts, but before long Pennsylvania and the back country of Southern colonies claimed far more of the Ulstermen. The Scots–Irish emigration reached a peak in the years just before the outbreak of the Revolution. During the five years from 1770–4, an estimated 40,000 Ulstermen went to America. This emigration revived again as soon as the War of Independence ended.

The Scots–Irish emigration from Ulster should not be confused with the departure of Scots from Scotland. The latter was smaller numerically, began somewhat later, but also reached its peak during the twelve years before the outbreak of the Revolution. Careful estimates by the historian, Ian Graham, suggest that about 20,000 Scotsmen, from both the Highlands and the Lowlands, went to America between 1768 and 1775. Among the Highland emigrants were tacksmen, the tenants of Scottish lords, who, after the defeat of the Rebellion of 1745, found that higher cash rents were being substituted for their old military services. Rather than accept these changes some tacksmen took as many of their own sub-tenants as they could persuade to join them and tried to restore feudal relationships on estates in the Mohawk Valley of New York and elsewhere. Perhaps because their emigration had not been so long sustained as the Irish and the German, the Scots tended to remain loyal to Britain in the Revolution and not to split over the issue of independence, as did other immigrant groups.

All three of these migrant streams included many immigrants who were unable to raise the money to pay for their passages and provisions. Having shown a tendency to fall when trade developed between two ports, fares were probably not much higher in the late eighteenth century than they were to be in the nineteenth. But the three or four pounds needed was a lot of cash in eighteenth-century terms. Besides, even to take up an offer of free land an emigrant needed some minimal capital equipment, provisions, and seed. Thus thousands of Scots–Irish and Scottish emigrants went out as indentured servants. Although the recruitment of indentured servants was prohibited in Britain in 1785, it continued in Protestant Ireland until the Passenger Act of 1803 raised fares so much on regulated ships as to take the profit out of transporting indentured servants. Other poor migrants, particularly Germans, went out as redemptioners. They received passages to America on the understanding that friends and relatives would 'redeem' them on arrival. Failing that, the ship's captain could sell them into servitude.

That colonies differed in their ability to attract the immigrant stream may be inferred from estimates of the population of the several colonies. Between 1700 and 1790 the population of the thirteen colonies is thought to have increased from a quarter of a million people to 3·9 millions. The population of those colonies first to be settled grew more slowly than that of the newer colonies. Thus the share of New England's population in the total for the colonies fell in the three-quarters of a century before the Revolution, as did that of the tobacco colonies, Virginia and Maryland. The more rapid population growth of the newer colonies to the south, that is, the Carolinas and Georgia, as well as of that of the middle colonies, Pennsylvania, New York, and New Jersey, was probably largely the effect of immigration from overseas and from other colonies. The two regions most attractive to both overseas and internal migrants would seem to have been Pennsylvania, whose population rose 12·3 times between 1700 and 1770, and North Carolina, whose population increased by an estimated 17·4 times.

This selective distribution of immigrants who came during the eighteenth century can be explained in a number of ways. New England, which at first had attracted the Scots–Irish, had less good land than colonies to the south. Her farmers and tradesmen could less frequently afford to buy slaves or employ indentured servants. Nor did she have a good reputation for welcoming strangers or for religious toleration. At the time of the Revolutionary War, Massachusetts, Connecticut, and Rhode Island probably had the highest proportion of native-born inhabitants. The relative attractiveness of Pennsylvania and North Carolina may be attributed to three factors: the better opportunities to get land in younger colonies; the direction and volume of trade of the colony's chief port; and a lower incidence of slavery as compared with other near-by colonies.

A few observations will suffice to illustrate the importance of land systems. In the seventeenth century planters could get land in Virginia and Maryland for each settler or servant they brought to America. Furthermore, indentured servants were often granted freedom dues of 50 acres on completing service. There is evidence that headrights were not so automatic in the old tobacco colonies in the eighteenth century. Eager for white population, colonies to the south offered land more generously to Europeans, partly as a defence against Spaniards and Indians, partly as insurance against internal slave revolts. The proprietors of both Carolina and Georgia at first pursued too illiberal policies of land disposal. The overthrow of the proprietors in South Carolina in 1719 grew out of a conflict between the proprietors, who wanted to keep feudal dues, and the governor and council, who favoured a more liberal policy of land grants to encourage settlement. Georgia's original land policy also discouraged both large and small speculators to the detriment of settlement. Small farmers were displeased with grants of only 50 acres, and men with larger means were not attracted by having to lay out £200 for the importation of servants in order to receive 500 acres of land. After seventeen years, when the proprietors yielded control to the crown, Georgia had only 5000 inhabitants.

In contrast, North Carolina adopted a successful, liberal land policy once she became a royal colony in 1728. The legislature made grants of 200 acres at a penny an acre for each settler established by a promoter, and also made small land grants to bona-fide settlers. Squatters' claims (that is, claims to lands which had been settled without securing title to the land) were confirmed. This was to become the pre-emption system in the nineteenth century, equally a means of encouraging the development of new lands by settlers. Pennsylvania also had complex land provisions, the very variety of which attracted settlers. Not only did headrights persist in the eighteenth century, but a former indentured servant could get 50 acres on completing his service; and squatters' rights were also being recognized by the land office in the mid-eighteenth century.

Close links between trade and immigration also had something to do with the distribution of population. Philadelphia's share of imports from England rose from 14 per cent in 1701–5 to 34 per cent in 1771–5. Pennsylvania's trade was growing more rapidly than that of colonies to the north and south of her. This brought in vessels which were not highly specialized in the carrying of either freight or passengers. Trade links grew between Northern Ireland and Philadelphia. Early in the century flax seed burdened ships going west, but as the bulky seed was displaced by linen manufactures, more room became available for emigrants. Scottish emigration was influenced by Glasgow's stunning rise in the tobacco trade after the unification with England in 1707. As Glasgow began to dominate the tobacco trade of Virginia and Maryland, Scottish merchants, factors, and storekeepers became immigrants in those colonies.

Partly because of her thriving trade, Philadelphia came to be the best place to land indentured servants and redemptioners. In any case, white indentured servants hesitated to be landed farther south where Negro slaves were being imported in increasing numbers. The slave trade, largely controlled by English, Portuguese, and Dutch traders, expanded after 1697 when the Royal African Company lost its monopoly. Perhaps 250,000 slaves were imported to the mainland during the eighteenth century. The Negro population grew from an estimated 28,000 in 1700 to nearly half a million by 1780. With the growth of the slave trade, Negro slavery displaced indentured servants almost completely on the tobacco plantations. While Negroes were to be found in all the colonies, seven out of nine of them were in the South in 1700 and nine out of ten in 1780. Thus, the extension of slavery in the South diverted the poorer white immigrants, especially the German and Scots–Irish, to Pennsylvania. From there many of them filtered southwards down the Piedmont to take up land in the hinterland of the plantation areas in the Carolinas and Georgia. Because such immigrants were able to become self-sufficient farmers on fertile but isolated lands in the back country, slavery as a labour system fastened ever more firmly on the commercial sectors of Southern agriculture, the cultivation of tobacco, rice, and indigo. No technological breakthrough was visible to increase output of these products for European consumers. Since abundance of land lured European immigrants westward, slavery became increasingly essential to the cultivation of these export crops.

No firm estimate of the overall volume of immigration during the eighteenth century is possible. It seems almost certain that some of the historians who rediscovered St John Crèvecoeur's description of an American on the eve of the Revolution, a description which dramatized the melting-pot idea, exaggerated the size of the foreign-born element in the population at that time. One clear error which, as Jim Potter has pointed out, historians have repeated from each other is the statement that one-third of the population of the thirteen colonies was foreign-born in 1760. This would imply an immigration of 10,000 a year for the previous fifty years, or 20,000 a year for twenty-five years, without even allowing for deaths among immigrants. Even in the peak immigration years, just before the battles of Lexington and Concord, this sort of annual rate was probably not reached. Pennsylvania's population may have been a third foreign-born at that time, but this was not an average for the colonies as a whole.

When historians discovered this diversity of colonial immigration, they also began to recognize that immigrant problems did not begin with the new immigration from southern and eastern Europe in the early twentieth century. To American liberals in the 1930s this was an important aspect of the discovery of their past – to find that the human situations which sometimes produced prejudice and conflict had been a part even of colonial history. Clannishness was to be found among the Scots immigrants from the Highlands, who in colonial agriculture were as resistant to assimilation as any later immigrant group in the cities. The German language persisted in use in immigrant churches and in the press throughout the eighteenth century. The Scots–Irish and the Germans lived in different bands of settlement and in considerable mutual hostility. Colonial towns began early in the eighteenth century to require strangers to post bonds to guarantee that they would not become charges on public funds. By the 1770s artisans were openly showing resentment towards newly arrived immigrants. Here in America, where land was abundant and there was plenty of work for all, frictions arose out of cultural differences and mutual suspicions. The position in colonial America would seem to offer abundant evidence that economic circumstances were not the source of all such conflicts between groups of different cultural or racial origins. These problems of social adaptation were to increase as migration increased and became more diverse, as cities grew and the economy became more complex during the course of the nineteenth century. Sometimes they gave rise to conflict; sometimes and in some places remarkable examples of co-operation and the resolution of conflicts could be found.

Immigration and Industrialization

The British government halted emigration altogether in 1775, but it revived, especially from Ireland, at the end of hostilities. In the

1790s French and English political exiles lent colour and heat to the urban scene in the new country. The real lull in immigration came during the Napoleonic Wars – a lull fostered by the restrictive Passenger Act of 1803, impressment on the high seas and finally the War of 1812 itself. When emigration resumed after 1815 the opportunities for the poor to get to America may, for the moment, have been more limited. At least if we hazard a guess that the peak emigration of the eighteenth century, that of the early seventies, reached a rate of 10,000 per year, the recorded immigration to the U.S.A., begun in 1820, did not exceed that level until the decade of the 1830s.

In the meantime, the United States experienced a generation in which the foreign-born may not even have been replacing themselves and the share of immigrants in the population was falling. Although the census of 1830 did not record the foreign-born, that year may have marked a low point for a hundred years on either side. Even during this period the fear of immigrants was not altogether absent, however. The Alien and Sedition Acts of 1798 reflected a fear of immigrant radicalism, a theme which was to recur for more than a century with varying degrees of emphasis. The hysteria subsided as immigration declined in the early years of the nineteenth century. The next wave of genuine public hostility towards immigrants began with the anti-Catholic crusade in the 1830s as immigration revived, an immigration in which southern Irish Catholics were significant for the first time. This wave of popular abuse of immigrants was not to die out until the Civil War. It is an over-simplification to regard these tensions and divisions simply as native versus foreign-born. Some foreign-born people were themselves very outspoken against other immigrants. Swiss emigrants, who arrived in Pennsylvania in 1817, found the colonial German population in the hinterland of Philadelphia distinctly unfriendly. By the end of the forties a Kentish-born carpenter who had arrived in Rochester, New York, in 1839, was deploring the arrival of poor English people, unfit, in his view, to succeed as immigrants. German Catholics objected to the minority of radicals who came to the United States after the failure of the revolutions of 1848. The draft riots of 1863 arose out of conflict between Irish immigrants and native-born Negroes. Maldwyn Jones and others have noted a distinction between suspicious unfriendliness to strangers on the one hand and outright hostility and hatred of them on the other. The former may be based upon some real situation, such as an increase of immigrants; but to produce irrational hostility which can lead to conflict, immigrant groups must appear to threaten fundamental values. In the forties and fifties, for a number of reasons, the American people were seriously divided. One way of coping with these unsettling divisions was to express a heightened nationalism. The migrant became a scapegoat for problems associated with westward expansion and slavery in the mid-century, as he was to become the scapegoat for problems associated with rapid urban growth a half-century later.

As immigration revived after the Napoleonic Wars some contrasts with the earlier movement were evident. For one thing, unfree labour was much less conspicuous. The slave trade had been prohibited in 1807; where Negro population was increased other than by natural increase, this was now an illegal trade. British law also now forbade the indenturing of migrants before departure. Emigration of skilled workers was forbidden altogether until 1825, though clearly this law too was evaded in practice. Efforts were made during the American Civil War to reintroduce indentured servitude, but the system was then demonstrated to be unworkable and unsuitable to industrializing America long before it was declared illegal by the Federal Congress in 1885. The main function of what was now called contract labour – that is, of prepaying passage in return for a labour contract – in the nineteenth century was to secure certain scarce industrial skills. Most employers found this a prohibitively expensive way of securing skilled workers. While unskilled workers may have come out on indentures in the eighteenth century, the system did not prove adaptable for non-agricultural employment. As wage-paying employment increased in towns, in lumbering regions, on canal and railway projects, unskilled workers were unlikely to remain with an employer to complete the term of their contracts. As settlement moved west and transport improved, it became simply too difficult to retain contract labour. The risk was not worth it. One thing about Negro slavery in a white society was that the fugitive could easily be identified. The danger in this case was to the free Negro who might be returned to slavery. Nevertheless, the decline of systems of unfree labour for European immigrants cut off one route to the U.S.A. for poor rural workers who could not hope to save the passage money. Guardians of the Poor in England continued to send out paupers until the Poor Law Amendment Act of 1834 stipulated that such emigrants could be assisted to go only to British colonies. So also some local authorities in German states forwarded their poor across the Atlantic. But this means of emigrating was not available to those who had not come to rely on public funds for support.

Partially offsetting these barriers to emigration in the second, third, and fourth decades of the nineteenth century was a new form of transport, perhaps the cheapest yet available. It was similar to the eighteenth-century transporting of migrants in that it was a byproduct of trade. But for emigrants, ships would have gone west nearly empty. The system of protection, of which the Corn Laws were a part, continued to discriminate in favour of empire timber after the Napoleonic Wars. The fleets which went out each spring to Canada, to be there as the ice broke up on the rivers, carried emigrants at about £3 a head. It was a long, dangerous journey, and we do not know how many migrants travelled that way, later to cross the border into the U.S.A. No records of this movement survive. Timber ships left from many small ports in Ireland as well as Britain. This mode of travelling obviated the necessity of going up to a major port and possibly dribbling away savings in cheap boarding-houses waiting for tides and sufficient cargo to permit a ship to sail. Without indentures even timber ships did not make emigration easy for the very poor, since one had to plan on purchasing provisions for one to three months in advance and foregoing employment for that length of time. This required savings.

Between the Napoleonic Wars and the 1840s voluntary immigration was gradually increasing from most parts of the British Isles, including Ireland, from the Rhineland, and the first parties had arrived from Scandinavia. The volume of assisted emigration of paupers and criminals was probably reduced as was that of indentured servants. In time, as more and more jobs paying cash wages came to be provided by the American economy, passages prepaid by relatives already in America became the means by which people without savings could emigrate. The voluntary migrants who could finance their own journey probably came from much the same social classes in the early nineteenth century as they had in an earlier period, from among farmers who felt the pinch of increased rents, from village craftsmen, but probably not very often from agricultural labourers. It also seems doubtful that the early beneficiaries of the Industrial Revolution in Great Britain, cotton spinners, railway workers, engineers and ironworkers, emigrated to the United States in large numbers, though some clearly did make specific contributions to the introduction or adaptation of new techniques in the United States. Whether the technologically unemployed (such as handloom weavers of Lancashire in the twenties and thirties, or, as it is so often said, the German craftsmen who suffered from the import of British factory-made goods) emigrated in large numbers at this time is still an open question. It is perhaps a comment on the improved wages possible with the higher productivity of new methods that in the great industrial recession of 1839–42, the hungriest years of the nineteenth century, skilled industrial workers of Lancashire and Yorkshire seem to have been able to find the means to emigrate in larger numbers.

The characteristic nineteenth-century emigration did not begin until the late forties, however. From that time the movement of people across the Atlantic took on more the character of a mass movement. Migration still provided a safety-valve for discontented people from the middle ranges of European society; but in certain regions it now reached deep into the social structure engulfing people with no capital, no industrial skills, and little education. The early years of emigration from most regions saw a movement out of agriculture which formed part of a great redistribution of people from less productive agricultural occupations to more productive urban and industrial ones in the New World.

Why did this mass movement begin when it did? For decades a slow building up of a dangerous famine-prone situation had been going on in Ireland where a population explosion was being fed by an expansion of potato cultivation and subdividing holdings. The same rate of population increase was maintained less dangerously in England by diversifying the economy. The Irish famine finally brought Peel to push through the repeal of the Corn Laws, thus diminishing the role of domestic harvest in business fluctuations in Britain. Neither the free traders in the Board of Trade, nor the anti-Corn Law agitators were so effective in bringing this piece of legislation as was famine in Ireland. But the results of repeal were far-reaching. It made the American wheatlands and potential wheatlands worth cultivating. While areas already settled responded first to the increased demand from England for corn in the 1840s, the repeal of the Corn Laws made it profitable to extend the railway network into the prairies of the Middle West which were not served by natural waterways. Symbolic of the connections between the repeal of the Corn Laws and the economic development in the U.S.A., which relied on mass immigration, was the fact that Richard Cobden, the high priest of free trade, was a large shareholder in the Illinois Central Railway which was constructed through the

Illinois prairies during the fifties with the help of Irish and German immigrant construction workers. Twenty-one thousand miles of railway were laid in the United States during the fifties, mostly in agricultural regions. Their construction made the United States better able to employ needy immigrants directly upon arrival. Professor Habakkuk has argued that the differential between the wages of un-skilled and skilled workers was smaller in the U.S.A. than in Britain in the first half of the nineteenth century. The beginnings of the great migration from Ireland, Germany, and England in the forties and fifties eased that situation and made it possible to contemplate building those railways to which the repeal of the Corn Laws promised traffic. A remarkable conjunction of circumstances explains the beginnings of the great nineteenth-century migration, the greatest the world has ever known.

The proportion of the American population which had been born outside the country rose from 9 per cent in 1850 to 13 per cent in 1860 and did not then vary much from that figure until 1920. Throughout this period the foreign-born element made up about 14 per cent of the population, 23-4 per cent of the labour force, and approximately a third of the labour force in mining and manufacturing. At the end of this period the United States was far more industrial and urban than she had been at the beginning; but from whatever country they came, European immigrants were persistently more industrial in their choice of jobs and urban in their pattern of settlement than was the native-born population. Though many immigrants continued to go into agri-culture, where the expansion of output, acreage, and labour force continued until the early twentieth century, the most significant feature of the great migration of this seventy-year period was the transfer of labour from agriculture to transport, industry and mining. It was American industrialization which gave the opportunity for improved living standards to larger numbers of marginal farmers and labourers from Europe. They in turn provided the labour force, the brawn needed to make that industrialization feasible at a time when capital was not all that abundant. The railways, the houses, the fac-tories, the mines for industrial America were not constructed with labour-saving techniques, but very largely by the unskilled workers who arrived from Europe, decade after decade. By building this super-structure for an industrial state the immigrants helped improve the productivity of the whole economy.

Immigration and Employment

Between 1776 and 1840 about a million passengers arrived in the U.S.A. Estimates from port records suggest that from 1840 to 1920 more than thirty million people came to the U.S.A. The immigration proceeded in a series of great waves, each of which brought a larger total than the preceding one. The peak years of immigration were 1846–54, 1868–73, 1879–88, and 1899–1907. In 1854, 420,000 passengers were reported as arriving in United States ports; in 1873, nearly 460,000 passengers declared themselves to be intending immigrants; in 1882, the number reached nearly 800,000, and in 1907, 1,285,000. Net immigration figures, calculated from the additions of foreign-born inhabitants recorded in decennial censuses, give much smaller numbers. According to them the United States added just over a million foreign-born persons to her population in the seventies; 2·5 millions in the eighties; 1·1 million in the nineties; and a peak of 3·1 millions during the decade after 1900. The difference between the huge gross figures of immigration and the much smaller net figures are accounted for in part by the deaths of foreign-born people in the United States, the return to Europe of some immigrants and travellers, and repeated entry by others.

This rise of free migration to epic proportions coincided in time with the beginnings of the world trade network. Intercontinental migration grew alongside the expansion of trade. Individual traders, migrants, and investors were all responding impersonally to the same underlying stimulus: the development of under-populated areas overseas, as a result of trade, promised high interest rates to capital and high returns to labour. That these connections between trade, investment, and migration were significant is demonstrated most clearly by the timing of overseas migration. The migration of this period seems to have come to be ever more sensitively timed to indicators of employment opportunities in the United States.

Immigration to the United States showed marked seasonal fluctuations. Immigrants arrived in large numbers during the months of May, June, and July; by December there was often a net emigration. Furthermore, migrants seem increasingly to have timed their arrival in the United States by the American business cycle, rather than according to short-term conditions in the countries from which they emigrated. This was the conclusion of Harry Jerome's important study, *Migration and the Business Cycle*, as long ago as 1926. More recently other writers, including Brinley Thomas, have been noting longer swings in migration which fluctuated with the level of railway and building construction, foreign capital investment, and commodity imports in the United States. The data on which these studies of the timing of emigration are based are fuller for the period after the Civil War than before it. At least for the period from 1870 to 1914 the studies of these indicators of economic activity suggest that the prospect of improvement in the U.S.A. was a stronger force in the migration of this period than were changes in the year-to-year economic condition in countries of emigration; in other words, the pull was greater than the push. Of course, all that such correlations tell us is that for some reason most emigrants timed their departures overseas in a highly rational way. Underlying causes of emigration may have been long, medium, or short-term, while the decision to depart in the month of April in a particular year may have been made in keeping with information available on the prospects of finding a job at a good wage in the area to which one was going – or the arrival of a steamship ticket.

If American conditions really dominated the causes of emigration, one would expect to find a rather neutral distribution of immigrants by regions and countries of origin. The distribution was, in fact, very uneven. Each emigration peak contained a different mix of nationalities. During the forties and fifties Ireland and Germany were in first and second place respectively; during the sixties, German emigration exceeded the Irish; in the seventies, England climbed to second place with Germany still first. During the eighties, Germany and Ireland again contributed the greatest numbers. Italy led in the nineties, while Germany remained in second place. After 1900, Austria-Hungary became the most important country in numbers, while Italy took second place. Such a survey fails to mention smaller, less populous countries, like Sweden, Norway, and Greece, which were among the leading countries of emigration when looked at from the standpoint of the ratio of emigrants to the population of the nation losing them.

Rather than adhere to the outdated distinction between an old emigration from northern and western Europe and a new emigration from southern and eastern Europe, it is more accurate to see this great movement of people from Europe as itself a frontier moving southward and eastward as new areas were touched by the growing international economy. The emigration frontier struck parish after parish and county after county within major countries of emigration. In Ireland, for example, Ulster was still very important in the emigration of the fifties; during the sixties Leinster took the lead; in the eighties Connaught and Munster began to contribute large numbers of emigrants. The German emigrants of the 1840s came chiefly from the lower Rhine Valley; in the fifties, the central provinces of Mecklenberg, Hanover, and Schleswig-Holstein began to join the stream; during the sixties, emigration from east Germany, from Prussia, Pomerania, and Posen climbed, to reach its climax in the eighties. The fact that this frontier of emigration kept shifting suggests the importance of changes in the European economy as fundamental causes of emigration. But for changes in the European economy, overseas areas could not have exerted a pull on the populations of certain regions. Each region is a study in itself of changes in land tenure, methods of agriculture, agricultural markets and alternative employment opportunities. It has often been noted that mass emigration frequently reached major proportions as a result of a local crisis in agriculture which produced a kind of Malthusian situation. The flight in the wake of the Irish famine is the best-known instance. But there were also near famine conditions in the Rhineland in the late forties, and in parts of Sweden in 1866 and 1867 when the exodus from that country first became very great. Similarly, a failure of the currant crop in Greece in the early nineties seems to have been a specific crisis which initiated a large emigration.

Mass emigration did not always begin with such a period of severe hardship. In fact, these crises in agriculture merely revealed a population pressure which in other regions led to emigration without famine. In many parts of Europe populations were increasing rapidly, and opportunities in either agriculture or industry were not keeping pace. When domestic industrial growth began to provide new jobs fast enough, the emigrant stream was usually diverted to places nearer home. Emigration from Germany and from Sweden tended to decline after the 1880s as industrial growth at home strengthened.

Although regions of emigration were regions of confined opportunity, they were at the same time regions in which growth had probably started. They were not stagnant agricultural economies. The most isolated and backward corners of Europe had not begun to contribute overseas migrants before the First World War. Emigration began in those regions 'first in contact with urban and commercial influences' and spread to new regions as they experienced the same disturbing impact. Such contacts often provided the information basic to emigration. They also brought the necessary transport. Even more, perhaps, they introduced the ideas of economic advance among people who for the first time began to think in terms of improved standards of life and to be dissatisfied with the status quo. Other people, it is quite clear, emigrated because they feared the consequences of economic change. Even people who left agriculture to take jobs in American industry sometimes intended initially to save in order to buy land at home or in the United States. Those who went overseas may not always have been the most flexible, intelligent, and imaginative of people, though they probably were very materialistic. All of our present knowledge points to the importance of economic motivation in this great migration. The experience of emigration itself probably sharpened the energies and ambitions of some who had been trying to escape from stresses of change.

Innovations in transport also help explain both the timing and the volume of this emigration. During the 1840s, a new development in passenger transport on the Atlantic lowered the overall cost of emigration and also shortened the time spent in crossing the ocean. From 1838 onwards steamships were gradually taking over the most lucrative traffic on the Atlantic – cabin passengers, the mails, and fine freight – which since 1817 had been carried by the Liverpool–New York fast sailing packets with their reliable times of departure and arrival. When the competition of the steamer in the forties and fifties induced them to undertake the carrying of steerage passengers, the packets, the famous clipper ships, became the major carriers of immigrants to North America for a while. The packets attracted immigrants, even at a slightly higher fare, because they adhered to a schedule. The emigrant was not likely to have to use up his savings in the port city in waiting for the departure of his vessel. The packets made it possible for Liverpool to attract immigrant traffic from Scandinavia and Germany as well as from Ireland. By 1865, steamships had superseded sailing packets in carrying steerage passengers on the Atlantic runs. Steamers had the same advantage of stated time of departure, but also further shortened the time at sea. While no doubt still attended by discomforts at steerage rates of fare, the Atlantic voyage became more reliable, more comfortable, and less hazardous; and this too made Europeans more responsive to changes in the American labour market.

When this great migration began in the middle of the nineteenth century the U.S.A. was still very largely a rural, agricultural nation. In 1850 only about 18 per cent of her population lived in towns of 2500 or more people and three-fifths of the non-slave labour force was engaged in farm work. By the First World War the U.S.A. had become, by a number of criteria, the greatest industrial nation on earth. She still had millions of people living in the countryside, but since the mid-century she had acquired a heavy iron and steel industry, a quarter of a million miles of railway track, some very large cities and giant corporations. When agitation against immigration revived in the last decade of the nineteenth and first decade of the twentieth centuries, it became common to speak of an immigrant problem related to new 'races' of immigrants from southern and eastern Europe who had begun to appear in the coalmines and in the cities during the eighties and nineties. The Dillingham Commission, appointed by Congress in 1907 to investigate the impact of immigration, persistently made this distinction between new and old immigrants. In a number of respects, particularly in its economic aspects, such a distinction had little meaning or bearing upon the question. It was the American economy which had changed since the great immigration began, not so much the characteristics of immigrants. From the beginning of mass migration in the late forties, most emigrants came from villages and countryside, whatever their country of birth. In most migrant streams men tended to be in a considerable majority. Only Irish and Jewish immigrants, the one old and the other new, were exceptions, for special reasons, to this marked preponderance of men in the early stages of emigration from a particular area. Young people between the ages of fifteen and thirty-five were most numerous among the emigrants from every region. Population growth which comes by way of an immigration from outside a country of young adults during their peak working years is likely to be more stimulating to an economy, certainly a net economic gain, exceeding growth from natural increase of population. America received young people, and especially men, who had been clothed, fed, housed, and educated elsewhere until the time when they could make their maximum contribution to production. The effect of immigration was to increase the ratio of economically active persons in the population and to reduce the ratio of dependants.

Throughout the second half of the nineteenth century, in spite of growing industrialization, the agricultural population continued to expand in America. The only possible reservoirs among the rural population of workers who might have shifted on a large scale to railway, coalmining, and industrial jobs were the sharecroppers and labourers, white and black, of commercial agriculture in the South and the small farmers in arrested frontiers of primitive subsistence farming in the southern Appalachians and the Ozarks. The European immigrant was more available, both for historic and economic reasons. The South used her rural proletariat to a limited extent in her relatively weak industrialization. Most of the European immigrants bypassed the South and came to the cities and regions where industrialization was proceeding rapidly. Yet the people locked up in Southern agriculture were the only important potential competitors with the immigrants from European agriculture in American industry and transport. While many native-born Americans were chasing the setting sun in opening up marginal lands for agriculture, the European immigrants tended to be where they were needed for industrial expansion. In 1890, before the so-called new immigration had become significant, three-fifths of the foreign-born inhabitants of the States were to be found in urban areas; only a quarter of the native-born white population lived in towns and cities.

The Dillingham Commission regarded the older immigrants as largely skilled workmen and the new immigrants as unskilled rural workers. Certainly if one compared the British immigrants arriving in America after 1900 with those arriving from Italy or the Austro-Hungarian Empire at that time, the latter contained a smaller share of skilled workmen. But the contrast was not so great if one compared emigrant groups at the time they were at high tide. Another suggestion was that immigration in the late nineteenth century hastened the mechanization of industry in America as entrepreneurs simplified tasks to accommodate an unskilled labour force. This is an over-simplification. American industry had shown a tendency towards mechanization of tasks performed by craftsmen or their helpers in Europe before the great migration began. Such mechanization, in any case, increased the overall demand for skilled labour to make the machinery. Furthermore, many important changes in industrial technology, such as the introduction of steel or electricity, had little to do with the character of the labour force. If one examines industrial jobs to find the proportion of the labour force who were foreign-born, it was not the more mechanized occupations and industries, where labour productivity was high, which stood out as the biggest employers of immigrant labour. Rather it was occupations in which little assistance was given to human muscle by machines – the building of houses, city streets and railways, coalmining and meat packing. The clothing trades were immigrant industries from the beginnings of the mass migration in the fifties, the sewing-machine being the only machine in a highly competitive industry in which individual productivity was relatively low. In factories immigrants usually had the job of firing furnaces or fetching and carrying.

If one sees that immigrants filled mainly these less productive jobs (less productive because they were unaided by much capital equipment), one can understand why it is said that immigrants and native-born workers were largely non-competing groups. Far from reducing the wages and living standards of most native-born workers, immigrants, by contributing to investment booms, helped indirectly to create more jobs for skilled and semi-skilled grades and more supervisory positions.

The American economy showed a remarkable capacity for absorbing new labour during this period. The greatest challenge to its ability to find jobs for immigrants had come at the very beginning of the great migration. For example, the commercial seaport of Boston was not prepared to employ all the Irish who descended upon it in the late forties. Their arrival in time encouraged the expansion of industrial investment in the city. By the time the immigrants from southern Europe began to flow in, the distribution of immigrants to areas offering jobs, both through the informal immigrant networks and through steamship companies and labour bureaus, was working much more efficiently. Few of the arguments which the Dillingham Commission accepted as proof of the economic disadvantages of immigration have stood the test of modern scholarship. The economic effects of immigration in this period were probably in the main salutary both for immigrants and for Americans. Not only were millions of Europeans enabled to raise their material standard of living by taking their labour where it would be more fully employed, even if without much mechanical assistance, but the immigrants also helped create their own jobs by providing the labour force to encourage and lengthen upswings in investment.

The argument for restriction of immigration which rested upon the cultural and social effects of immigration had more substance. In these respects the fact that the origins of immigrants were changing with time was important. Throughout this period American entrepreneurs had continuously to adapt rural peoples from varied cultures to an industrial and urban way of life. The conflicts which could arise from the clash between rural and urban values were persistently in the background wherever industry was growing. But conflict was by no means everywhere present. Americans permitted each immigrant group to develop freely its own institutions: churches, benefit societies, social organizations, schools, and newspapers, for example. For the first-generation immigrant these organizations helped to provide a defence against the strangeness of his situation, to keep his world intact. Often, through the attitudes of their leaders, these ethnic organizations became the link with the host society. Leaders of ethnic organizations were almost as prone to talk about Americanization as were the opponents of immigration in the days before the First World War. The most telling arguments against continued unrestricted immigration were the social ones: that the immigrants lived in poor housing conditions, that they were a burden upon the social services, that they continued to use their own languages and resisted Americanization, that there were radicals among them. All of these arguments might have been applied to the old immigration, say in the 1850s, as well, had these characteristics seemed so relevant in an agricultural and commercial economy. In the period immediately after the First World War, this part of Progressivism, the restriction of immigration, was approved by Congress as even businessmen ceased to rally on behalf of keeping the doors open, and the first Quota Act became law in 1921.

Until that time, few restrictions were placed upon immigrants. In 1882, when the new immigration from southern Europe was still insignificant, certain classes of people were excluded – convicts, lunatics, and persons likely to become public charges. Three years later immigrants who came as contract labourers also became subject to deportation. These laws did not openly discriminate between immigrants by nationality. This policy introduced in the Quota Acts was foreshadowed in the Act of 1882 which prohibited Chinese immigration altogether for a period of ten years in the first instance. The Chinese had been immigrating in increasing numbers since the 1850s. They had been essential to the building of the Central Pacific portion of the first transcontinental railway where they worked on a system akin to indentured servitude. When it was completed Chinese immigrants continued to arrive, 123,000 of them during the seventies, and settled mainly on the West Coast. The Chinese probably kept their native social and economic organization and ties intact more successfully than any other immigrants to America. Californian workers complained of their economic competition; but social fears and racial prejudice may have been more important in the exclusion of Chinese immigrants.

Restrictions on Immigration

The Quota Act of 1921 restricted immigration to 3 per cent of the numbers of each nationality recorded in the Census of 1910. In 1924 the act was revised to reduce the numbers further and discriminate more severely against recently arriving groups; immigration was restricted to 2 per cent of each foreign group as recorded in the 1890 Census. A more elaborate and slightly subtler means of attaining the same ends, by fixing quotas according to the national origins of the American population in 1920, took several years to prepare and went into effect in 1929, just as the Great Depression finally brought this great migration to an end. After 1924 Italy, Greece, the newly-created Poland, Czechoslovakia, and Hungary had infinitesimal quotas. Four-fifths of the quota immigrants permitted to enter the country were assigned to Great Britain and Ireland, Germany, the Netherlands, Switzerland, and Scandinavia. In the 1920s, Great Britain again led the world in numbers of emigrants, as she had in the 1850s.

The character of immigration was transformed by this legislative interference with the free movement of people. For example, skilled workers rose sharply as a percentage of the smaller number of immigrants. Fifty per cent of the immigrants entering in 1925–6 were returned as skilled workers as compared with 27 per cent of those arriving between 1911 and 1913. Dependants became a much larger group among the few immigrants permitted to enter. Just before the First World War, women, children, and old people accounted for 21 per cent of immigrants; in 1925–6 they accounted for 45 per cent. Since the only occupational clause in the Quota Acts gave preference to skilled agriculturists and their families, the number of farmers among immigrants was swollen temporarily from 1925 to 1930. The flow of immigrants has shown much less sensitivity to the business cycle since the Quota Acts were enacted. During the thirties, with the spread of totalitarian governments, more people wanted to emigrate to the U.S.A. for political reasons. Again this increased the skilled and professional element among immigrants. Above all, the numbers have been small: quotas were not increased during the thirties and early forties to aid political refugees. When a limited number of displaced persons was admitted after the Second World War, they were mortgaged against future quotas from their countries. Not until 1965 was the nationality quota, as the means of selecting immigrants to the United States, rescinded by Congress. After reaching 650,000 in 1921, immigration from European countries was cut to about 150,000 a year from 1925 through 1929. Nor did the compensating movement of people into the United States from other parts of the Americas, from Canada, Mexico, and Puerto Rico, succeed in raising the level of foreign immigration to anything like the pre-war figures. Total immigration hovered around 300,000 persons a year until the Great Depression cut it more, as compared with pre-war figures which topped a million people in six years.

The drastic reduction of foreign immigration was accompanied by a greatly increased internal mobility and a considerable redistribution of people within the United States from the poorer to the richer regions. Restricted immigration stimulated emigration from the Southern states, where birth rates among both the white and black populations had remained higher than in the rest of the country. Encouraged by recruitment and advertising for labour, as well as by the advanced guard of Southern Negroes who had gone north to work before the war, Southerners began to supply increasing numbers of workers for Northern industry during the First World War when immigration was stopped becauses of hostilities. This exodus continued until about 1926. The Southern states lost half a million Negro inhabitants during the war decade and 649,000 during the twenties. The wartime interruption of European immigration did improve temporarily the chances of the poorest people in American agriculture of raising their standards of life through obtaining more productive industrial employment. Continued improvement during the boom of the twenties was not so evident, in spite of the Quota Acts.

Quite apart from discrimination because of colour, their situation was tragic. When these unskilled rural workers, who certainly had no better a preparation for urban industrial life than had the millions of Europeans who came before the war, began pouring into the cities of the North, American manufacturing industry and mining began to lose that remarkable capacity they had previously shown to absorb such labour into employment. The number of jobs in manufacturing industry did not rise at all during the decade of the twenties, and those in coalmining and on the railways actually fell. Of the old typical immigrant industries which eased the untrained man's economic adaptation, only building and road construction continued as rising employers. With the greatly reduced supply of unskilled labour being offered during the twenties, labour became relatively more expensive than machinery. The 1920s became a decade of outstanding increases in productivity both in expanding industries such as automobiles and electricity, and in declining ones such as railways and coalmining. Much of the emphasis in mechanization was placed on doing away with precisely those labouring jobs which had once afforded work for the unskilled countryman. Mechanical loading and transport in the mines advanced rapidly; in the steel works cheap electricity helped in the replacement of men by machinery in the most degrading, heaviest jobs. The American economy made great strides towards modernity in that decade, towards eliminating some of the worst kinds of industrial occupations. Yet in so doing, it removed some of the kinds of jobs which had helped the semi-literate European agricultural worker in his economic adaptation to industrial life. Not so many of these jobs were there for the Southern workers as they moved north after the war, and the process was irreversible. The absence of this link increased the Negro's problems as he continued to move north in even greater numbers from the beginning of the Second World War. The ending of mass immigration of European unskilled workers probably speeded mechanization.

The weakness of trade unions in the twenties may also have assisted mechanization. Some of the pre-war progressives had maintained that immigration weakened trade unions; yet in certain industries the Slavic and Italian immigrants showed themselves amazingly loyal union people. On the whole, the unions were no better off in the twenties after mass immigration stopped. The industries where they had been strong – clothing and mining – were stagnant or declining industries, and unions made no advances in the great mass-production industries. The ending of immigration did not immediately strengthen trade unions, though some writers think it helped to make possible the great upsurge in trade-union membership in the late thirties.

Although the real wages and leisure of most industrial workers rose during the twenties, these benefits cannot be traced directly to the effects of the Quota Acts. Immigrant restriction probably introduced harmful distortions to the economies of both sending and receiving nations. The disruptions to the international economy, which resulted at least in part from this placing of artificial barriers to the international mobility of labour, almost certainly worked against the long-run welfare both of people living in the United States and those in the rest of the world. The Quota Acts encouraged the trend towards agricultural protection in Europe because people who might otherwise have emigrated now had to stay at home. Migrants from southern and eastern Europe moved into France and emigrated to Brazil; the Japanese, excluded from the United States since 1907, also emigrated to South America. The numbers involved in these movements were much smaller than the massive movement into the U.S.A. had been. The Anglo-Saxon nations, Canada and Australia as well as the U.S.A., closed their doors just when people from the poorest and most over-crowded countries were beginning to take full advantage of the inter-national mobility of labour. Instead tariffs raised the price, and so the supply, of farm products produced in Europe; some emigrants were also deflected to other primary producing regions in South America, which also increased the supply of primary products. In both ways competition to American agricultural exports was being increased. At the same time the ban on cheap labour from Europe and the exodus from American farms to cities raised the price of labour in American agriculture and put a premium on economies of manpower, raising agricultural productivity. Thus the restriction of immigration fostered the problem of agricultural surpluses. Immigration of Europeans to American cities had eased the farm problem in the first decade in the century; now those people who might have augmented the domestic market for American farm produce remained in Europe.

Though some individuals have made great contributions in many fields of American life, immigration to the United States since the Second World War has not had the same kind of economic significance as it had in the past. Yet the social aspects of an ethnic society persist, and ethnic organizations and consciousness have by no means dis-appeared. The cessation of mass immigration and the great increase in the rate of naturalization which took place during the Second World War have not obliterated these evidences of disparate national and cultural origins. Today some of the children of the new immigrants of the early twentieth century seem to see the black man as a threat and to be resentful of the special efforts which are being made to incorporate him belatedly as a full citizen. In the harsh period of industrialization, each new immigrant group helped to increase the number of jobs and was in part responsible for the occupational upward mobility available to able members of the last immigrant group but one. Now this immigrant social ladder no longer operates. As Milton Gordon has suggested, neither the melting-pot nor a culture enriched by its pluralism seems to have been the outcome of the meeting of so many people within the borders of the United States. The descendants of the immigrants who contributed so much to America's economic greatness through their unique contribution to the size of the economically active population and their ability and willingness to do hard labour during the period of the great drive to industrialization, have not merged without a trace in a single national culture. America is still an ethnic society.

Further Reading

Barth, Gunter, *Bitter Strength: a History of the Chinese in the United States, 1850–70.* Cambridge, Mass., 1964.

Berthoff, Roland T., *British Immigrants in Industrial America.* Cambridge, Mass., 1953.

Dickson, R. W., *Ulster Emigration to Colonial America.* London, 1966.

Erickson, Charlotte, *American Industry and the European Immigrant.* Cambridge, Mass., 1957.

——, *Invisible Immigrants: the Adaptation of English and Scottish Immigrants in 19th Century America.* London, 1972.

Gordon, Milton M., *Assimilation in American Life.* London, 1964.

Graham, Ian C. C., *Colonists from Scotland.* Ithaca, N.Y., 1956.

Handlin, Oscar, *Boston's Immigrants.* Cambridge, Mass., 1941.

——, *The Newcomers. Negroes and Puerto Ricans in a Changing Metropolis.* Cambridge, Mass., 1959.

Hansen, Marcus, *The Immigrant in American History.* Cambridge, Mass., 1939.

——, *The Atlantic Migration.* Cambridge, Mass., 1940.

Higham, John, *Strangers in the Land: Patterns of American Nationalism, 1860–1925.* New Brunswick, N.J., 1955.

Jones, Maldwyn A., *American Immigration.* Chicago, Ill., 1960.

Potter, Jim, 'The Growth of Population in America, 1700–1860', in D. V. Glass and D. E. C. Eversley (eds.), *Population in History.* London, 1965.

Taylor, Philip, *The Distant Magnet: European Emigration to the United States.* London, 1971.

Thistlethwaite, Frank, 'Migration from Europe Overseas in the Nineteenth and Twentieth Centuries', *Rapports du XIme Congrès Internationale des Sciences Historiques.* Stockholm, 1960.

Thomas, Brinley, *Migration and Economic Growth.* Cambridge, 1954.

——, *Migration and Urban Development,* London, 1972.

4 A Profile of the American City

H. B. RODGERS

The Urbanization of the American Nation

Within the span of a single lifetime American society has been transformed from a rural to an urban base. Until the early decades of the
present century the setting for the life of the typical American family
was the countryside: the farmer, the hired hand, the shopkeepers and
service workers of the small country town formed the mass of the
population, particularly away from the urban clusters of the industrial
Northeast. When the first census was taken in 1790 only 5 per cent of
the population was classified as urban; and as late as 1840 only one
American in ten was a townsman, while in contemporary Britain the
urban and rural elements in population had almost reached parity. In
the later nineteenth century the urbanization of the U.S.A. went
forward more vigorously under the influence of a belated industrial
revolution. By 1890 40 per cent of Americans were town-dwellers,
but only as late as 1920 did the census for the first time report a
small majority of the total population (51 per cent) to be urban.
Today rather more than 73 per cent of the population is classed as
urban, though Europeans may question the Bureau of the Census
definition of a town, in essence any place with more than 2500
inhabitants.

Clearly the urbanization of American society has come late, but at
a quickening pace. The middle-aged townsman of today is likely
himself to be a migrant from the countryside, or at least to have rural
roots a single generation back. A number of consequences stem from so
massive and so recent a transplantation of population from the environment of the country to that of the town. The rural–urban drift has
replaced the westward movement as the dominant American folk-
migration of the recent past. In this sense the city has replaced the
wilderness as a frontier. Here, as at the fringe of settlement, man has
had to face the challenges of an unfamiliar environment: though it is

a man-made environment it is one that he has had at least as much difficulty in controlling and shaping to his needs and aspirations as his ancestors faced in mastering the frontier of forest, prairie, and mountain valley. Indeed in some senses the American nation has failed to adapt to the urban environment and has rejected the city in favour of the quasi-rural setting of the suburb; escape from the former to the latter is the chief reward of career success, and so the inner city becomes the home of the under-privileged by a process of population replacement, and its problems of environmental decay multiply. It is a matter of significant coincidence that the decade in which the American nation became more than half urbanized was also that in which the cheap car began to roll in its millions from the assembly lines of mass production, making it easy for the fairly prosperous to turn their backs on the city that generates their wealth but to which they have never become completely reconciled.

The transformation of a population from a rural to an urban mode of living has immense implications, social, political, and economic. The old rural communities were stable and close-knit: kinship linkages provided a social framework and specific institutions – the church, the cross-roads store – were the pivots about which life centred. There were no strangers in the countryside; in the city there are none but strangers. In a single year, 1969–70, 18 per cent of all American families moved from one home to another and the great majority of these moves were from city to city, from farm to city or within the city. It is not wholly unfair to describe the American nation as a shifting population, and clearly it develops social forms very different from those of the old and stable rural communities. The economic relations of town and country, too, have changed radically. Urban America of a century ago was dominated by the small country town and regional centre – as late as 1860 only nine cities had populations greater than 100,000 – and these were the creation of, and so subservient to, the rural populations that had called them into being as service centres to meet the needs of the farming communities. Today's great cities – the tenth largest now has a population of more than two millions – utterly dominate their rural hinterlands. Agriculture is enslaved to the demand of the urban market for perishables, non-farm land is dominated by the recreational needs of the city and by its ever-rising demand for water supply; while the rural community itself is penetrated and diluted by a commuting or retired population of urban origin. The political balance of city versus country, too, has been transformed. Less than half a century ago the farm vote was crucial, and rural questions like price support and farm assistance programmes were vital election issues. Today elections are won and lost on the problems of the city: law and order, renewal and the housing question, community relations and the like.

There are few states today in which rural voters outnumber urban: West Virginia is almost the most rural of the states, with only 39 per cent of its population urban, and it also has the distinction of having the most unfavourable population trend of all the states, a loss of 6 per cent from 1960–70. A few other states have an urban proportion less than 50 per cent – Vermont, the Carolinas, the Dakotas, Mississippi, Arkansas for example – and all are among the states of feeblest population increase or actual decline. Conversely the most urban states are among those of fastest growth: California has 91 per cent of its population urban, Texas 80 per cent, and Connecticut 78 per cent, and their 1960 to 1970 growth rates were 27 per cent, 17 per cent, and 20 per cent respectively. But even in many states in which a high proportion of population is classed as rural by residence, the data are misleading and undervalue the degree of urbanization. In 1960 only 26 per cent of the rural population, nationally, was classified as a farm population. Much of the remainder consisted of an essentially urban population, deeply dispersed into the countryside, occupying converted farmsteads and scattered fragments of suburban development. There is an urban penumbra beyond the suburban fringe to which the title 'exurban' has been given. Here the countryside has been preserved physically but transformed socially: it has been invisibly urbanized. Over much of the urban Northeast rural communities have become vestigial; for example only 25,000 of Connecticut's 525,000 rural population consists of farming families. In brief, the old distinction between town and country has become indistinct and irrelevant.

That the American nation is now city-dominated is plain enough, but by what sort of city? There is a radical difference between the town of 50,000 and the city of 500,000 in the quality of life and the problems it produces. Is the nation town-dwelling or city-dwelling? Taken at face value the figures would suggest the former: of the total population in 1970, 10 per cent lived in cities of over 1,000,000, compared with 30 per cent in small towns of less than 50,000, 15 per cent in larger towns in the 50,000 to 250,000 size range and 12 per cent in the smaller cities of between 250,000 and one million. From this one might conclude that the typical American is a small-town dweller, troubled

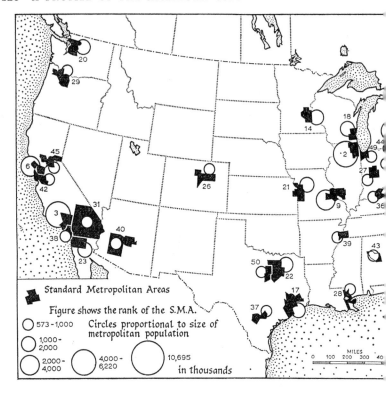

Standard Metropolitan Areas

Figure shows the rank of the S.M.A.

○ 573 - 1,000   Circles proportional to size of metropolitan population
○ 1,000 - 2,000
○ 2,000 - 4,000   ○ 4,000 - 6,220   ○ 10,695
in thousands

MILES
0   100   200   300   40

only by the parochial problems of such a community. This is entirely misleading. The cities of the U.S.A., like those of Britain, have fused and coalesced with smaller towns in their outward growth, to become major urban complexes. The smaller towns caught up in the expanding city – or created *ab initio* by its suburban overspill – preserve their separate legal identities but in every other sense become part of the greater urban mass and cannot escape its collective problems. The term used in Great Britain to describe these urban complexes – the conurbations – has no currency in the U.S.A. The Bureau of the Census, however, recognizes what are cumbersomely described as the Standard Metropolitan Statistical Areas: these are the metropolitan cities of America – major industrial and regional centres from which growth has spilled out beyond their legal boundaries so that the central city is surrounded by a patchwork of suburban and satellite munici- palities. Taking these 'real' cities as our measure of the scale of urban-

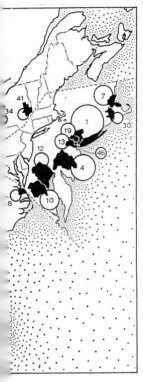

FIGURE 4.1. Major Standard Metropolitan Statistical areas (SMSAs) of the U.S.A. (after D. K. Adams and H. B. Rodgers, *An Atlas of North American Affairs*, London, Methuen, 1969, p. 93).
1. New York. 2. Chicago. 3. Los Angeles.
4. Philadelphia. 5. Detroit. 6. San Francisco. 7. Boston.
8. Pittsburgh. 9. St Louis. 10. Washington, D.C.
11. Cleveland. 12. Baltimore. 13. Newark.
14. Minneapolis-St Paul. 15. Buffalo. 16. Cincinnati.
17. Houston. 18. Milwaukee. 19. Paterson.
20. Seattle. 21. Kansas City. 22. Dallas. 23. San Diego.
24. Atlanta. 25. Miami. 26. Denver. 27. Indianapolis.
28. New Orleans. 29. Portland. 30. Providence.
31. San Bernardino. 32. Tampa-St Petersburg.
33. Columbus. 34. Rochester. 35. Dayton.
36. Louisville. 37. San Antonio. 38. Anaheim.
39. Memphis. 40. Phoenix. 41. Albany. 42. San Jose.
43. Birmingham. 44. Toledo. 45. Sacramento.
46. Jersey City. 47. Akron. 48. Norfolk. 49. Gary.
50. Fort Worth.

ization, different conclusions emerge. Over a quarter of all Americans live in the great cities of a million or more people, another quarter in lesser cities of from 100,000 to 1,000,000, and only a fifth in towns of less than 100,000. Most Americans, therefore, face the problems of the big city as their own; traffic congestion and urban blight, substandard housing and racial tension, crime and vice are part of the background to their lives.

The Metropolitan City and Megalopolis

Metropolitan cities (the SMSAs) are recognized much more liberally by the American census than the conurbations are by the British. Each SMSA contains a core city of at least 50,000 (or twin cities of the same total) together with all adjacent counties provided that at least half their populations live at urban densities in areas contiguous with the main urban mass, and given also that there is a journey-to-work relationship

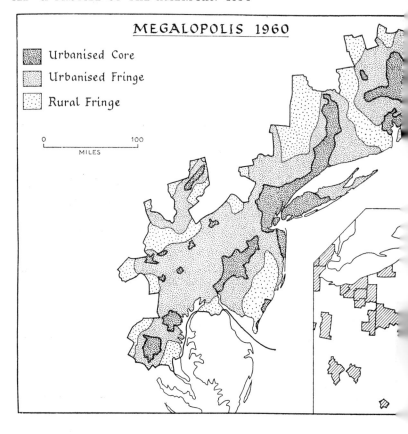

MEGALOPOLIS 1960

- Urbanised Core
- Urbanised Fringe
- Rural Fringe

0 —————— 100
MILES

with the central city. The county basis of delimitation means that many metropolitan cities are grossly over-defined spatially. San Bernadino – itself almost a suburb of Los Angeles – is 200 miles from east to west and 180 from north to south as defined by its constituent counties, but most of its area is semi-desert. To avoid this exaggeration of the physical extent of urbanization the concept of the 'urbanized area' has been adopted: this is in essence the continuously urbanized core of the SMSA – the core-city together with its physically contiguous extensions – but since it is not defined in terms of municipal boundaries it has a limited value in population analysis. No fewer than 222 metropolitan areas were identified in the 1960 census, and these had grown to 247 by 1971. Many of these are cities of very modest size, with populations not much exceeding 100,000 in their extended form.

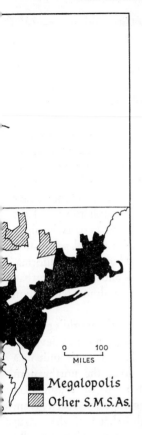

Megalopolis
Other S.M.S.As.

FIGURE 4.2. Megalopolis: the urbanization of the north-eastern seaboard (after Adams and Rodgers, op. cit., p. 115).

But the five leading cities (New York, Chicago, Los Angeles, Philadelphia, and Detroit) all now have more than 4 million people each; the ten leading cities have populations exceeding 2 millions while there were 33 'millionaire' cities in 1970 and over 60 with more than half a million each.

In the cases of the largest urban agglomerations even the concept of the metropolitan area is inadequate to define their true extent and size. Greater New York, for example, consists of a complex of linked and contiguous metropolitan cities, each with its ring of suburban and dispersed industrial development. There are four separate metropolitan areas (and two extra-metropolitan counties) in the New York 'standard consolidated area': these are centred on New York itself, with ten million people, and on the cities on the New Jersey shore of the

Hudson river – Newark, Paterson, and Jersey City. This super-city of some 15 million inhabitants functions in many respects as a single urban unit: its separate urban and industrial foci are linked by a complex commuting pattern so that the city complex as a whole serves, to some degree, as a single labour market area; its communications system is Manhattan-centred and so cohesive in relation to the city system as a unit; and its manufacturing complexes are closely integrated by inter-firm and inter-industry linkages. But it is divided between over 1400 separate city, municipal, and local administrations with varying degrees of autonomy: there is no agency with executive power to plan for its future development and renewal, though the Metropolitan Plan Association has done useful research and missionary work. Similar but smaller city clusters exist at the southern tip of Lake Michigan, where Chicago is the dominant centre in a coastwise chain of cities stretching from Gary to Milwaukee with a total population approaching 9 millions. The greater part of coastal southern California, too, is quickly becoming a single discontinuous but integrated urban system, dominated by Los Angeles and containing almost ten million people.

With its 15 millions, New York rivals Tokyo as the world's greatest city, yet there is an even larger dimension in American urban development, for the New York cluster is only the largest single unit in a semi-continuous urban region that extends along the northeastern shorelands from north of Boston to the extensions of Washington beyond the Potomac, and to which the title Megalopolis has been given. Megalopolis almost certainly foreshadows the shape of the urban future not only in the United States but also in Europe, where broadly similar urban regions are evolving across the England lowlands from London to Lancashire and in the lower Rhineland. Megalopolis, U.S.A., is therefore an urban prototype. It is no simple, single linear city: it contains five discrete urban clusters. Each consists of a nuclear metropolitan city (Boston, New York, Philadelphia, Baltimore, Washington) together with its suburbs and smaller, satellite metropolitan areas with their suburbs, each major unit cohering not only physically in terms of the continuous extent of bricks and mortar but also functionally in terms of inter-urban linkages. These are, then, five distinct city regions of giant size. Between them are 'freestanding' towns and cities of smaller but substantial size (for example Hartford, Providence, Trenton) all increasingly bound to the major nuclei by industrial and commercial linkages and in some cases by commuter flows. Inevitably the Boston–Washington axis is a corridor of inter-city movement on an immense scale: parallel systems of inter-urban motorways, high-frequency air services – for example the Boston to New York 'commuter' route – and even, most unusually for the United States, high-density improved rail services almost able to compete for speed with the airlines.

The countryside that still dominates the land-use pattern in the interstices between the city clusters is dominated by urban needs. Intensive dairying and market gardening, state parks and other recreational areas, watershed protection zones to conserve water supplies to the cities, are the chief uses of rural land; while the rural society is permeated by an intrusive element of 'exurban' type. In short, the shadow of the city lies across the rural landscape, and each year new farms fall to the suburban developer on a scale that is beginning to create a land shortage in the regions of most intense pressures in urban growth. Megalopolis is so far unique, at least in North America, but it may not long remain so. City systems of a similar character are growing in southern California, along the southern shoreland of Lake Michigan and in the strongly industrialized region between Lake Erie and the Ohio river. Already more than 35 million Americans live in the environment of Megalopolis, and the total may quickly rise as the other incipient urban regions take firmer shape. Clearly this is the dominant urban form of the future. But America is wholly unprepared, politically and administratively, to face and solve the problems presented by urban growth on so huge a scale: even the lesser problems of the city region defeat the fragmented system of city government, and the entire philosophy of the American political system, with its emphasis on states' rights and local autonomy, might have been tailor-made to frustrate any attempt to grapple with problems of city and regional planning.

The Advance of the Urban Frontier

Urbanization is today most intense along the northeastern shore, partly because it had its earliest origins here in these tidewater lands of primary settlement. By 1800 the great trading cities of the northeastern estuaries were already engaged in vigorous commercial rivalry for the developing trade of the interior, and they were soon jockeying for advantage in their promotion of improved communications with the contemporary West, like the Erie Canal from the upper Hudson to Buffalo of 1825 and the Baltimore and Ohio railroad on which traffic began in 1830. From this earliest eastern base of city growth an urban frontier advanced westwards, a wave of town development closely following the progress of the frontier of settlement. At its simplest this was a process of two stages: an early development of commercial cities as regional, sub-regional and local service centres, and a much later, more slowly spreading stage of industrial growth.

The trading towns of the Mid-West were quick to grow; and in the sense that many originated as French or British forts (Pittsburgh is the modern derivative of the French Fort Duquesne built in 1754) they preceded the frontier. Pittsburgh had become a maturely developed trading town and fitting-out centre by 1800, the first regional centre to evolve beyond the Appalachians and already with a certain post-frontier sophistication in its life, work, and urban form. By 1830 a strong rival had developed lower down the Ohio, where Cincinnati had been founded as a speculation in 1789 and had grown by 1830 into a flourishing commercial and manufacturing town of 25,000. For a time this new city replaced Pittsburgh as the chief regional focus for the quickly developing and superbly productive farmlands of the Ohio valley, but it was soon to lose its dominant regional role to cities yet to rise further westwards. St Louis has earlier origins than Cincinnati as a French river-town and trading-post, but it rose from relative obscurity to the status of regional metropolis of the Mid-West in a period of explosive growth during the forties when its population grew from 17,000 to 77,000. So long as rivers were the chief carriers of the commerce of the region St Louis remained its dominant city, standing close to the focus of the Mississippi, Missouri, and Ohio system: when railways became the chief city-forming force after 1850, St Louis lost its peculiar advantage. An obscure fort at the southern tip of Lake Michigan, Fort Dearborn, became the infant city of Chicago in 1833; the long barrier of Lake Michigan channelled railway development through Chicago, which quickly became, after 1852, the node of the developing system and the chief point of rail-to-lake trans-shipment. From a small town of 30,000 in 1830 Chicago had become a great city of 300,000 twenty years later, soon to outpace all its rivals in its growth to the status of the second city of the nation, a position it is about to lose to Los Angeles.

This wave-like westwards progress of an urban revolution was repeated everywhere as the colonization of the West advanced, though much more slowly and more feebly in the South, creating a first urban framework of trading cities which have remained to this day, west of the Mississippi, dominantly commercial in function. But as early as the first quarter of the nineteenth century a second stage in urbanization had begun in parts of the East. In the anthracite valleys of east Pennsylvania, and a little later in the forested valleys of the bituminous coalfield centred on Pittsburgh, those industrial communities that Lewis Mumford describes as 'Coketown, U.S.A.' were growing, an American equivalent of the English Black Country. In New England textile towns were developing, closely similar both socially and architecturally to their prototypes, the mill-towns of Lancashire. By the closing decades of the nineteenth century the industrial city was spreading westwards as a second phase in urban growth: the steel towns and ports of the Erie coastlands, the engineering cities of the Hudson–Mohawk valley, the automobile centres of Michigan were among its products. Few industrial cities were created *ab initio*: they evolved through a new stage of rapid growth in old commercial towns. This involved a change in the urban economic base, a transformation in the structure of urban society and a reshaping, often for the worse, of the urban environment and the city structure.

The industrialization of the commercial city is still regionally incomplete, and its varying progress helps to explain present contrasts in the pace of city growth. Few Northeastern cities are still increasing quickly in population: New York and Boston grew (on the SMSA basis) only by 12 and 8 per cent respectively during the decade 1950–60, far below the national mean of 23 per cent for the metropolitan cities. Most Pennsylvanian towns and cities based on mining and heavy metallurgy are stagnant or actually declining in population, as are many New England towns that have not managed to shed their obsolete textile-based economies. Indeed, throughout the Northeast there is scarcely a single major city, east of Buffalo and north of Washington, that is still growing at the national average rate. The city clusters of the industrial Mid-West in Ohio, Indiana, and Illinois are growing at about the national average rate and so the region as a whole is roughly maintaining its share of the nation's urban population. Beyond the Mississippi, in a region at a much earlier stage in the urbanization process, city growth is faster: Denver and Wichita grew by half in the single decade 1950–60, Kansas City and Oklahoma City by almost a third. But it is in the West and parts of the South that town growth has reached its most feverish pace. Taken collectively the major cities of Texas are growing twice as fast as the average for the nation, while the resort and retirement towns of Florida – which have

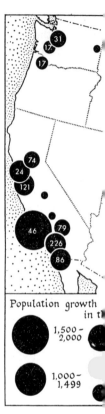

FIGURE 4.3. City growth in the U.S.A., 1950–60
(after Adams and Rodgers, op. cit., p. 97).

acquired a new significance in the space age – increased at rates ranging
from 90 per cent to almost 300 per cent; but in the heart of the Old
South most cities have grown much more sluggishly, and the urban
revolution in the Cotton Belt is by no means as dynamic as some
popular reports would suggest. Beyond the western mountains
modern rates of city growth are almost reminiscent of the nineteenth-
century Mid-West: Tucson and Phoenix both doubled – or almost
doubled – their populations during the fifties, but even they are totally
overshadowed by the performance of the urban cluster in South
California. This semi-desert, to which almost every urban-industrial
need including water must be imported, accommodated almost one-
sixth of the total national growth of urban population during the
period 1950–60, but the impetus has slackened since. Growth weakens

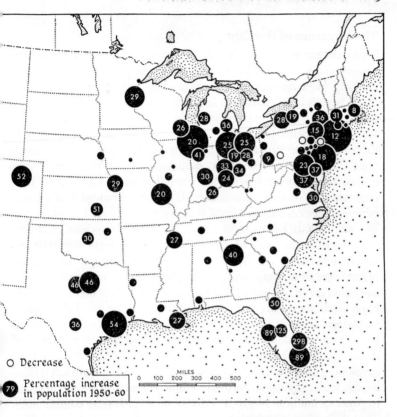

O Decrease

79 Percentage increase
in population 1950-60

MILES
0   100   200   300   400   500

quickly northwards, for the cities of the Golden Gate grew at much below the rate for the Los Angeles cluster, while those of the Northwest (except Seattle) could not match the national mean.

These trends, very briefly summarized here, reflect complex economic factors: the decline and locational shift of old Eastern industries like textiles and heavy metallurgy only partly replaced by research-based industries that are giving many Eastern cities a much more sophisticated economic base; the strongly localized industrial revolution that is reshaping favoured areas of the South; the addition of new manufactures, especially in the electronic and aero-space groups, to the commercial economies of Prairie and Mountain cities and – last but most important – the almost inexplicable urban momentum of southern California.

The Structure of the City

That cities are not merely shapeless aggregates of houses, factories, and commercial streets, but have a coherent form and a rational structure, has long been recognized. Urban 'models' have been developed by many writers in an attempt to find structural patterns that fit the form of the American city in the abstract, in a sense a search for a structural archetype. Sociologists were among the first to develop general theories of urban structure. E. W. Burgess (*The City*, 1925), working with Chicago as his laboratory, postulated a fivefold system of concentric zones. At the heart is the Central Business District, the chief concentration of retail, distributive, financial, commercial, and entertainment services and so a great focus of non-industrial employment. Beyond the 'CBD' lies a second zone, the 'zone in transition', called by other workers the 'zone of decay'. 'Transition' is both economic and social: wholesaling, light manufacturing, workshops, and service industry are forced outwards by rising land values from the city centre and convert old housing in this second zone for their needs, spreading blight and environmental deterioration as they do so. This 'sequent occupance' leads to a fragmented land-use pattern, a mosaic of commercial, industrial, and decayed residential land uses. But 'transition' is also social and ethnic. The more prosperous families flee from the enveloping blight to the outer zones and the social vacuum left is filled by the underprivileged, formerly ethnic colonies of recent migrants to America but now Negro, Puerto Rican, and Mexican communities. Thus the zone in transition is also the setting for community conflict, which has not been solved – and in some cases has in fact been worsened – by the massive projects of clearance and renewal that are beginning to transform it.

Beyond the zone in transition lies what Burgess called 'the zone of workingmen's houses': here low-income – but not desperately poor or distressed – artisan families are dominant, and from it they graduate to better housing on the suburban fringes as they acquire the means to do so. But the inner edge of this third zone feels the pressures generated within the zone in transition. Well-established, relatively prosperous Negro families attempt to escape from the worst conditions of the multiracial slum to the better but dreary environment of the third zone. Thus many Negro ghettoes have an advancing front, socially distinct within the Negro community, which penetrates the artisan zone, itself a source of racial tension. Zone four is one of better housing – most of

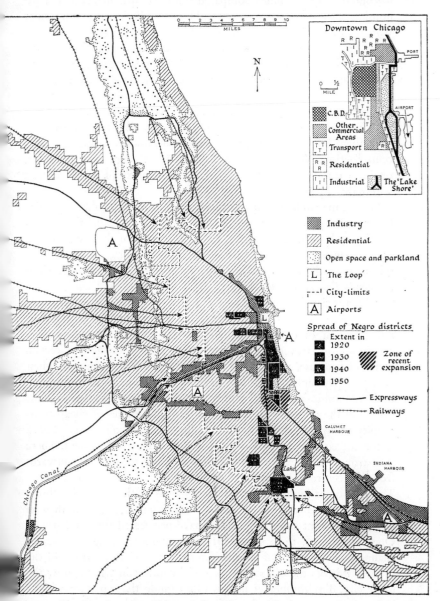

FIGURE 4.4. The American city: Chicago (after Adams and Rodgers, op. cit., p. 111).

it single-family dwellings compared with the apartments and 'row' housing of the other zones – occupied by a middle-income community which is drawn from the white-collar occupations. Beyond lies zone five – the fulfilment of the American dream in the urban context – the distant and dispersed high-income suburbs, clustered about small-town centres or lost in the woodlands. Here is the quasi-rural environment that offers the illusion of a return to the countryside, but at urban standards of living and income. Burgess wrote in the twenties: not only have our concepts of the nature of the city advanced enormously since then, but the city itself has also been radically changed by de-centralization. Yet the zonal concept, naïve though it may appear, retains a certain relevance, at least in the context of social contrast within the city.

No one in search of a causal explanation, however, could now main-tain that Burgess's views provide an adequate conceptual framework for the analysis of the complex land-use pattern of the modern city. Hoyt, a land economist, developed his 'sector theory' of urban struc-ture to meet the inadequacies of the zonal concept. To Homer Hoyt (*Dynamic Factors in Land Values*, 1960) land value and land use are closely associated: land value (expressed as rent) varies not only radially across the concentric zones but also circumferentially. The radial system of communications centred on the inner city gives certain sectors, traversing the 'zones', specific advantages for certain forms of land use, which tend to become dominant because of their ability to pay higher rents than possible rivals. The sector theory has both economic and social dimensions. Certainly industrial sectors evolve in the outward growth of the city along lines of cheap com-modity transport, navigable rivers, railroads, and expressways. Social sectors are equally strongly developed, though less self-evident. There is a strong tendency for high-income housing to advance outwards from the centre in a consistent direction generation after generation. Thus the older high-income residential areas of the inner city threw out their interwar suburbs of similar social character, and from these in turn more recent suburban salients have penetrated the rural fringe. Once established, these sectors of high-income housing very rarely change their direction of advance, so that the social patterning of the suburbs mirrors the old system of social contrast in what is now the inner city. Environmental factors often guide these patterns: high-income sectors advance along fast and efficient lines of commuter movement towards high ground and other sites of high amenity.

The lakeshore spread of expensive housing north from central Chicago – the 'gold coast' – is an example. Middle-income sectors tend to cling to the margins of the high-income salients, while low-income housing advances into or alongside the industrial sectors. There is even an ethnic dimension to these contrasts: suburbs with a slight but distinct ethnic 'flavour' – Italian, German, Polish, Scandinavian – evolve as suburban shadows of those districts of the inner city that were dominated by the group concerned, and as a spatial extension of the old ethnic quarter. New York's Norwegians once lived in lower Manhattan beside the East River: advancing in a consistent direction they spread first to western Brooklyn and then along the shore to modern suburbs with a slight and now residual Norwegian cultural character overlooking the narrows of the harbour.

Hoyt's sectors, a key to land use as guided by land value superimposed on the social model developed by Burgess in his zonal theory, provide the basis for an acceptable resolution of the city structure, at least where the city has evolved from a single nucleus. But the modern metropolitan city has caught up lesser towns in its growth and each of these has its own semi-independent structure, keyed to its own nucleus. A 'polynuclear' model of urban growth has been developed by C. D. Harris and E. L. Ullman (*The Nature of Cities*, American Academy of Political Science, 1945) to explain the nature of the pattern that evolves as the great city swallows small towns in its expansion. The greatest cities – New York, Chicago, Boston and others of similar stature – show the influence of site factors so idiosyncratic that each has grown as a unique case. But certainly the rise of the youngest of the great American cities, Los Angeles, can only be understood in polynuclear terms. Here is a city without a centre, for 'downtown' Los Angeles is a run-down business area of little better than small-town stature, ravaged by freeway development and largely irrelevant to the shaping of the structure of the urban mass as a whole. In such a city without a focus there can be neither zones nor sectors, for both assume centrality as a dominant influence. Instead there has developed a relatively loose-linked aggregate of semi-independent cities, specialized by function so that some are dominantly industrial, others ports, yet others residential suburbs. The 'central' retailing and commercial facilities are in fact dispersed between rival nuclei, but the life of the city is given coherence by the most intricate system of urban motorways yet developed, and still unfinished. This is often taken as the inevitable model towards which the city of the motor-age must trend.

The City Centre: Concentration and Decentralization

At the heart of the city lies the Central Business District, a compact area even in the greatest cities, in which land values, the intensity and selectivity of land use, the density of employment on each acre of land, the volumes of traffic flow and pedestrian movement all rise to their highest levels and in which, conversely, the density of population falls to a minimum. Land-value gradients are fundamental to an understanding of the nature of the CBD. Within this zone of high overall values there is a most marked rise in values from its margins to its core. Though the detail of individual cases clearly varies, the typical city has a node of highest land value at the intersection of its two chief shopping streets, and from this a spine of almost equally high values extends along the principal shopping and commercial artery: Broad Street, Philadelphia, and Main Street, Salt Lake City are particularly clear examples. From this node and chief commercial axis values decrease outwards, and it has been suggested that the 'contour' of value at which the cost (or rent) of land falls to 5 per cent of the peak levels at the core broadly delimits the CBD. This value curve explains both the physical form and the land-use 'mix' of the city centre. The skyscraper is the most obvious response to it: this is merely a building of very high plot-ratio (the ratio between site area and the total of floor space provided) forced to rise to the greatest height technically feasible in order that the huge cost of expensive land may be offset by the largest possible revenue from rents. In the tall building, too, the largest possible number of occupiers may be accommodated in those 'prestige' addresses by which American business sets such great store. A skyscraper is less the product of architectural virtuosity than of economic necessity.

Such high plot-ratios – producing perhaps twenty to thirty times as much office floorspace as there is site area – create almost unbelievable concentrations of employment in the most crowded city blocks. The Wall Street area contains about 400,000 jobs on three-fifths of a square mile: the scene at 5 p.m. as a human torrent washes out of the buildings and down the subway entrances, or along to the Staten Island ferry terminal, is one of the most striking indictments of the unplanned city. There is a clear answer to such extreme congestion: to control and lower plot-ratios. In the British city – even, though weakly, in London – this is done through planning powers. In the U.S.A. any intervention is plainly impossible within the lifetime of the present buildings; but in any case few city administrations have strong enough planning powers, backed by sufficient political authority, to impose real restraints on developers. To control plot-ratios would be to 'manage' the price of land: it would infringe perhaps the most jealously guarded of all the rights of the American citizen, the right to speculate. But control of the height of development is vital to rational planning; without it there can be little effective restraint on traffic flows, the demand for car parking and the pressure on public transport. In a real sense it is plot-ratio, not the car, that is helping to destroy the American city centre through the creation of an intolerable environment. But this is essentially a problem of the great city: smaller cities, especially those away from the industrial East, have little tendency towards the vertical development of their centres.

Within the CBD there exists a coherent structure, a rational pattern of land uses, selectively grouped by competition for the most favoured sites and so adjusted to the value pattern. At the very heart, on the dearest land, are the department and 'variety' stores, the chain businesses and the most specialized shops, with an admixture of the central banks, entertainment, and restaurants. Only here does retailing spread to the upper floors. Moving away from the nucleus, values decline and office uses replace retail above street level so that the maximum concentration of white-collar employment occurs here. Towards the margins of the zone large space-users with a low ratio of sales turnover to floorspace enter the retail 'mix' – furniture shops and car showrooms for example – while the boundary of the CBD is often outlined by a zone of marginal uses, wholesaling, the used-car lots of 'automobile row' and a variety of small-scale industries of service type – for example printing - that need a near-central site. A public park (for instance Boston Common), a group of civic buildings or a line of railroad tracks all set limits to the spread of the CBD, for selective 'central' users will not locate beyond any physical break in the office-retail cluster. But the margins of the CBD are not stable. There are zones of 'retreat' or 'discard', run-down areas lapsing from central to 'zone of decay' status, for example along the waterfronts of riverside cities; but there are also zones of advance towards newly favoured locations, for example new concentrations of car parking.

Perhaps the most radical change in the structure of the American city during the post-war period has been the relative weakening of the CBD. The city centre of 1945 was essentially the product of the strong centripetal forces working within the nineteenth-century city: the city, then, was compact, for 43 per cent of Chicago's population lived within four miles of the centre in 1900, and the higher-income groups had not abandoned the inner residential areas. There was little personal mobility: people travelled by a public transport system that necessarily focused on the centre. Radial accessibility was high, peripheral accessibility low; and in this situation the only rational location for mass retailing and general commerce was the city core. But today the city is not compact but diffuse: only 25 per cent of Chicago's population now lives within four miles of the centre and this is in general the poorest quarter, largely a Negro community of low purchasing power. Not only are the suburbs areas of much higher income level but they are also growing quickly in total population, while the inner city is stagnant or declining. Moreover, personal mobility is now universal and movement is no longer guided by the inflexible, city-centred net of public transport services. Congestion and high parking costs render the CBD inaccessible to the average shopper, but movement within the suburbs is easy and quick.

From these changes the 'regional' suburban shopping centre has risen as a rival to the CBD. These began modestly in the thirties, when Sears Roebuck began to establish small department stores in suburban locations. Since the fifties almost all the major department stores that were for so long the very symbol of the CBD have set up their suburban branches, and some have abandoned their central operations. From this a general decentralization of many sectors of CBD retailing has developed. The major 'out-of-town' centres thus created are very large, covering at least 50 acres of space: they have a nucleus of department-store branches, variety stores, large drug-stores and chain businesses, with a range of more specialized shops. Banks, entertainment facilities and restaurants are all present and office development is also beginning to move to them from the CBD, so that they are substantial foci of employment. These are the new nodes in the suburban way of life: increasingly the average man and his family need never travel to the city centre to be reminded of the city's problems of decay and renewal, racial tension and housing needs as they travel through the 'twilight zone'. The rise of the suburban centre has almost made it possible for the suburban family to turn its back, once and for all, on the city and its problems.

Community Problems and the Zone of Transition
One of the characteristic features of the belt of deterioration that surrounds the glitter – a little dulled though it may now be – of the

central business area is that it has for long been a zone of ethnic mixture and has become the setting for racial conflict. Ever since American cities first grew to the size at which they began to exhibit a distinct pattern of functional 'zoning' their older residential areas have attracted underprivileged minority communities of recent immigrant origin. The slums of late nineteenth-century Chicago, of the lower East River frontage of New York, of the decayed waterfront zones of Pittsburgh became an ethnic mosaic of communities that had nothing, scarcely even a language, in common, except their immigrant origin. Chicago had its Polish neighbourhood, its Italian and German quarters, its clusters of streets dominated by Russian and Ukrainian families; and each ethnic boundary was a line of social friction. To these new and unassimilated minorities the ethnic ghetto was both a refuge and a prison. It was a refuge in the sense that they chose to live in it, among a close-knit community of their own speech and culture: indeed here they were for a time insulated against the full shock of adaptation to a strange environment and a frighteningly different society. Segregation had its historic social role. But the ethnic quarter was also – and increasingly became – a prison, in the sense that for a generation or longer few immigrant families possessed the means to escape from the ghetto and the slum housing of the greybelt to the pleasanter environment of the outer city. During this century, and especially since the thirties, the ethnic segregation of European minority groups in the American city has weakened to the point that now only a relic pattern may be perceived. Second and third generation immigrants have lost all sense of national and cultural identity with the old ghetto community: they are no longer at a disadvantage in terms of language or experience, or in educational standard and occupational status. They have thus escaped from the slum to the suburb, and indeed the process of suburbanization is a symbol of the deeper changes of the process of assimilation into the main mass of the American people.

Once dominated by minority communities of eastern and southern Europeans, the greybelt of the great city still serves its traditional function in that it now houses a new complex of minorities, not only Negroes from the farmlands of the cotton states but also Puerto Ricans, Mexicans in the cities of Texas and California, and rural French Canadians in the New England towns. All these have replaced the migrant from Europe as a source of cheap labour, both in the manufacturing and service industries; and so the slum fulfils its traditional role as a reservoir of unskilled but un-unionized labour, willing to do menial work at low wages. This is a semi-transitory labour force, often taking more or less casual jobs, so that unemployment and under-employment rise to levels that would be regarded as entirely un-acceptable to the American nation as a whole. Unemployment among Detroit Negro workers was as high as 20 per cent in the early 1960s, an obvious cause of the high crime rate in the racial minority quarter and its troubled recent history.

Today the Negro, not the European migrant, dominates the social geography of the belt of decay in the great industrial city of the North-east and Mid-West. The processes by which the Negro communities of the Northern city have evolved are best illustrated by a case-study of Chicago, where over a million black people live in a city-within-a-city stretching almost ten miles southwards from the central commercial nucleus. The Negro is no stranger to Chicago but he remained a trivial element in the city's population until the present century, a mere 2 per cent even in 1910. As in the Northern industrial cities generally, the first great wave of Negro migration into Chicago came during the First World War which interrupted the migrant stream on which the urban economy relied for cheap labour. By 1920 the Negro proportion of the city's population had doubled to 4 per cent and it was to double again by 1940, for the economic stimulus to northward migration of 'prosperity decade', the twenties, was replaced by such rural misery during the depression of the thirties in the cotton-growing areas that migration continued unabated whatever the state of the Northern labour market. The enormous increase in the demand for industrial labour during the Second World War brought the Southern rural migrant to the city in his tens of thousands, and by 1950 the Negro population was close on half a million. Since the great Negro influx of the war of 1941–5 there has been a radical change in the significance of the growth of a black population: before then, Negro growth was merely an increment in total growth in population, but since then it has represented a progressive replacement of white by black. There was no overall population growth in the City of Chicago between 1950 and 1960 (indeed there was a slight decline) but the Negro proportion grew to virtually one-quarter. Since then the Negro population has passed the million mark so that the great black city of south Chicago constitutes about a third of the total population of the City in the legal sense, but not of course of the metropolitan area. At the present rate of replacement Chicago must become a predominantly Negro city within the next decade or two, as Washington is already.

A second great change can be discerned in the nature of recent population growth in Negro Chicago. Until about the time of the Second World War black population increase was chiefly by migration and the natural increase of the Negro community was quite slight, for there were low marriage and birth rates and a certain loss by migration elsewhere. Under these circumstances Negro population growth could be expected to adjust itself, to some degree, to the state of the market for unskilled manual labour, and there were indeed fluctuations in the growth of the black community geared to the general state of prosperity in the city. But today the nature of Negro population growth is quite different. This is no longer a male-dominated community, the marriage and birth rates are much higher, and so the chief factor in growth is now no longer fresh in-migration but a high net reproduction rate. In short the city is now committed to a high and accelerating rate of increase of its Negro community whatever the state of the employment market for Negro labour. In fact the Negro job supply must grow faster than Negro population, for this is a relatively young community generating large increments to the labour force as children leave school. But the supply of unskilled and labouring work that was for so long the mainstay of Negro employment is diminishing as industry becomes ever more automated. High and persistent unemployment is the obvious consequence of this situation, and crime, vice, violence, and riot are its inevitable expression.

As the Negro community has multiplied, so it has become ever more tightly segregated within a single dominant and sharply defined area of the city. It is not commonly realized that the segregation of the coloured community is a relatively new thing. In 1910, while the Negro was a tiny minority, he was widely dispersed throughout the slums on the border of central Chicago, which he shared in competition with other minority groups: even in the core of the most Negro area he constituted only 30 per cent of the total population. A state of *de facto* integration prevailed, though it was soon to weaken. By the twenties the core of the quickly expanding Negro zone was 75 per cent black and the ghetto had begun to evolve. During the thirties the geographical spread of the coloured population southwards from the city centre sketched out what are still, broadly, the limits of the Negro city. A long, narrow sector of the city became Negro-dominated, following the blighted axis of an elevated railroad southwards some 7 miles from the 'Loop', the Chicago CBD, almost reaching the Lakeshore on the east and in the shadow of the infamous and evil-smelling stockyards 'upwind' and to the west. There has been some marginal enlargement of the belt since the thirties, and further substantial southwards advance in the post-war period, but the boundaries of 1960 were remarkably similar to those of 1930 despite the huge increase in coloured population in the intervening decades. The great change of this period was not expansion but consolidation and progressive segregation, so that large parts of the core of the belt became virtually 100 per cent Negro. By 1950 about half the Negro population was living in conditions of total segregation (compared with 20 per cent in 1930) and the proportion has probably risen since despite legislation for integration.

In the shaping of the Negro city a distinct cycle of social and racial change may be identified: each white district in the path of Negro advance will pass, ideally, through five phases. The first of these is the phase of 'penetration'. It involves a very few Negro families, generally middle-class and with an income level and educational standard not inferior to those of their white neighbours. These are, in essence, successful Negroes attempting to escape from the ghetto and the slum to what is, for them, the equivalent of the white suburb. There is, alas, often no escape, for they are the pioneers of a much greater in-movement of Negro families. The 'penetration' stage often leads quickly to the 'invasion' stage; and this is especially the case when 'penetration' is induced by the 'blockbusting' process, the speculative buying of property by landlords (white or black) who install Negro families, wait for property values to fall as the white community leaves because of the threat of Negro advance, buy more houses for tenement use on the falling market, and finally resell at a large profit since the rent-roll of a tenement house gives it a considerable capital value.

However 'penetration' begins, naturally or in its speculative form, it is usually a transitory stage: 'invasion' follows and the Negro proportion quickly rises to about 10 per cent of the total. This is still very largely a 'middle-class' community: except where 'blockbusting' has hastened the racial change, most Negro families own their property (though only 7 per cent of Chicago's Negroes are owner-occupiers) and subdivision of houses to create tenements is rare. Perhaps the greatest hope for white–Negro integration in the city is the fact that the 'invasion-stage' community can prove at least semi-permanent. There are districts around the fringe of the Negro city that have been stable in this stage for many years. Given that the Negro element is 'white-collar', it is accepted by its white neighbours in a stable and integrated community. Unhappily this is the exception rather than the norm, for 'invasion' is often followed by 'consolidation': this is in essence the advance of the black frontier to swallow and digest a neighbourhood of racial mixture. Quickly the Negro proportion rises to 100 per cent as whites flee, values fall and a process of community replacement takes place. Not only do white families go, but so, too, do the middle-income Negroes, to begin the 'penetration' process elsewhere. This is the dynamic of the black city. Thus there is a clear social contrast, within the black society, between the 'invasion' and 'consolidation' stages. At the latter stage the low-income, artisan Negro family has become dominant, of markedly inferior income, occupational and educational standard to the coloured people of the earlier phases in the replacement process. But there is little subdivision of housing and not much increase in population density at 'stage three'. These follow in a last stage that produces the black slum in its worst form.

Stage four is inevitable once stage three has developed. In this 'build-up' of Negro population property is subdivided to the tenement level, overcrowding quickly worsens and population densities soon rise to phenomenal levels. This is the Negro slum at its worst, both in physical and social terms. The middle-class pioneers of the Negro advance have long abandoned these areas, to begin yet another stage of colonization in the white or mixed neighbourhoods of the fringe; and many of the 'established' working-class Negro families, too, have sought a less blighted environment elsewhere. A socially abnormal community replaces them with a high proportion both of young and single people and a male dominance. This is a 'rooming-house' community of recent migrant origin; its income level, educational attainment and occupational status are all low, but its unemployment rate is persistently high. It is in the 'stage four' areas that crime, vice, and violence reach their peak; and so do many other symptoms of social stress and break-down – illegitimacy, family disruption, the drug problem, and mental disorder. The core of the Negro slum thus becomes a focus of human misery and degradation of a depth almost unknown elsewhere in 'advanced' industrial societies. When a black slum on the north side of central Chicago was cleared for redevelopment a decade ago, a social survey showed that one-third of the adult male population was un-employed and the average income level was only half the mean for the city, itself a low-income area through the migration of the prosperous to the suburbs. Almost half the population in the tract lived wholly or partly on 'relief' and charitable payments of one sort or another.

Only half the families interviewed were 'normal': the rest consisted of temporary and informal unions (and their numerous progeny) or the relics of broken homes. The problem of the Negro slum is at least as much one of social reconstruction as of physical redevelopment.

There is a fifth stage in the life-cycle of the Negro slum: its clearance and renewal when its condition has become so grossly deteriorated that the city authorities move against it. The consequent problems are discussed below in the section on urban renewal in general. All that need be recorded here is the oft-repeated complaint that the clearance of the black slum creates two new ones at the margin of the Negro city. Any reduction of such grossly congested housing stock at the centre enormously adds to housing pressures within the slum: the cycle of change described above accelerates and the border of the black belt advances to relieve the pressures created. Only a very great increase in the construction of cheap and subsidized housing for the displaced Negro community can solve this cyclical problem. It is not, of course, a problem peculiar to Chicago: this has been used as a case-example since the growth of the black metropolis in the south of the city is so well documented. Virtually every major industrial city of the Northeast and Mid-West, and increasingly those of California too, have very similar problems to face. New York's black population is much greater in total than Chicago's, over one and one-half millions, though it is divided between two major concentrations, Harlem and the decayed areas of inner Brooklyn. Philadelphia has 34 per cent of Negroes in its total population, Detroit 44 per cent, and Los Angeles 18 per cent; and of the greatest cities only Boston and Pittsburgh are without large black minorities: these are the two slowest growing of the major cities and their industrial weakness has to some degree protected them from the Negro invasion of the North. Since the mass of the American population is becoming ever more concentrated upon the great metropolitan cities, this is a complex of problems that a high proportion of American families has to learn to live with and to find solutions for.

Urban Renewal: the Federal Bulldozer

One of the most powerful of the first impressions of the visitor to the United States is the energy and vitality with which the American city continually renews itself, so that little of the urban fabric is allowed to age to the condition of the historic. Urban redevelopment has been given an immense new impetus by the federal policies of the post-war years. The high costs of renewal may now be made to fall largely on the federal taxpayer and many cities have been quick to claim their share of the funds available. For a modest outlay on their own part, backed by massive federal contribution, they can attack the problem of decay in the twilight zone that surrounds the CBD. City planning in the general sense has always been, and remains, more than a little suspect in the U.S.A., for it imposes a total control on land use and overall restraints on development. In all but a few cities planning agencies of greater or lesser power exist, but many have weak political support and so lack teeth. But urban renewal is much more palatable than town planning in the total sense. The latter is as important for what it prevents as for what it achieves and many of its successes are negative. But the results of renewal are tangible and self-evident: it operates in the zone of decay and few citizens would question the need to clear 'skid-row', though many would contest the planners' right to guide the process of suburban growth. For all these reasons urban renewal is a much bigger part of planning in the American than in the British city.

The machinery of renewal derives essentially from the Federal Housing Act of 1949, amended by later legislation but not changed in principle. In brief, the Federal Housing Administration makes grants to cover the greater part of the capital loss to be expected in the total redevelopment of an urban area. The award of a grant is hedged about by restrictions and requirements: the city must survey its blighted tracts and produce a programme for their treatment; it must enact housing byelaws and at least pretend to enforce them. These pre-liminaries complete, it can propose specific areas for clearance and renewal, but these must consist of predominantly residential districts before clearance, even if the intention is to redevelop them for some other urban purpose. If decayed industrial or commercial zones are to be cleared these must be intended for residential re-use. Compulsory purchase may be used for the assembly of the site in city ownership, and this complex operation complete, the bulldozers may be brought in to level the tract. Once cleared the land is most commonly put on the market; only quite rarely does the city retain ownership for purposes of building municipal housing. Usually a private developer, often an insurance company or property corporation, buys the site to build office accommodation, middle-income apartment housing or some other development that will maximize his revenue from rents. The price paid is often far below the costs of acquisition and clearance, and this is the capital loss that will be borne (to the extent of at least two-thirds) by the Treasury. Thus the whole operation has a speculative quality: much depends on whether the site proves attractive to a developer, and if not it may lie idle and weed-covered for many years. Many cities are scarred by unsuccessful renewal projects, a constant source of criticism. But perhaps the overriding failure of the renewal process is that it so rarely provides good housing at low rent for the thousands of low-income families it displaces; indeed by clearing the most congested slum it seriously diminishes housing stock and so creates new slums by the housing pressures it generates. A recent book on the subject began with the charge that 'at a cost of more than three billion dollars the Urban Renewal Agency (of F.H.A.) has succeeded in materially reducing the supply of low-cost housing in American cities', and this is fair comment (Scott Greer, *Urban Renewal in American Cities*, 1965).

What has gone wrong with a programme that now clearly has a crucial role in easing the tensions within the American city? Whatever the shortcomings of the British slum-clearance programme, its failures have not brought bloodshed and arson to the city in the form of race riots that spring in part from bad housing. The crux of the problem is the relocation of the population displaced from the clearance tracts. In British cities the housing authority has a direct responsibility to provide alternative housing (usually municipal) to families moved from a clearance tract, but in an American renewal area the city need only pay a small 'disturbance allowance' (often not collected by Negro families who have little knowledge of their rights), and in any case the stock of subsidized 'public' housing in all American cities is still far too small and too slowly growing to absorb more than a small proportion of the displaced community.

Chicago's experience of the problem of rehousing clearance populations is typical. About 700 acres of slum had been leveled between 1945 and the early sixties, most of it Negro. A single large scheme, the Lake Meadows project, displaced 4600 black families, only 25 per cent of whom were able to get into subsidized public housing. The rest melted away into the encircling slums, contributing to their enlargement and deterioration. Among these families the mean rent, after their displacement, had risen from 37 to 67 dollars, but half of the housing that they went to was substandard and itself awaiting ultimate clearance. Thus the 'relocation' problem is self-renewing. Its role in enlarging the black ghetto was made very clear by the survey by the Chicago planning authority of the Cabrini area. Two-thirds of the displaced families were traced to new addresses in districts that were dominantly white in 1950. Indeed as clearance has progressed at the heart of the Negro zone so its borders have advanced in sympathy, and the two processes are very clearly associated. Elsewhere the same general principle holds true. Up to 1960 only 12 per cent of the families displaced by New York's clearance projects had gone into public housing and the spatial spread of the Negro in Brooklyn and part of the Bronx quickened with the development of the renewal programme on Manhattan. However, the growth of the new Harlem of huge public housing blocks during the sixties is at least a development in the right direction, whatever their aesthetic deficiencies and social problems.

To the British planner the solution of the relocation problem, which makes the slum self-propagating, is simple: it is to build subsidized civic housing on a much more massive scale. It has been demonstrated in the United States, as was shown in Victorian Britain, that private capital cannot provide decent housing for the low-income groups as an ordinary investment, and so this sector of the housing market must become a public responsibility. But there is a real social stigma attached to public housing in the American city: it is seen by many as little better than a barracks for the social derelicts, and to go into it is thought to involve the acceptance of charity. Yet almost every handsome block of middle-income apartments built under federal renewal powers is very heavily subsidized through the payment of grants to cover the capital loss in the write-down of site value. The splendid apartment blocks that replaced rotting Negro slums on the site of the Lake Meadows project are subsidized in this way: since they have become prestige housing for Negro business and professional families there is here the paradox that the well-to-do Negro has been provided with excellent housing at a very fair rent while the low-income family has had to accept an increase in rent for miserably poor housing to make the scheme possible. Renewal in the American city is full of such oddities.

Despite the recent acceleration in the programme under the impact of racial disorder, American public housing is pitifully inadequate in scale and it fulfils quite the wrong function. Even in Chicago, a progressive city, only about 3 per cent of the total housing stock has been publicly provided. The function of civic housing in the past has been almost institutional – to shelter the unfortunates and misfits until they can get on to their feet again. A means test is rigorously applied, so that as soon as a family recovers from misfortune it must leave and take its chance in the tenements of the slum. Thus the families who could do so much to set a standard have to go and other derelicts replace them. Inevitably the incidence of social stress and family breakdown is as high in public housing projects as in the worst of the socially deteriorated slum: unemployment is common – even normal – and petty crime endemic. There is ample evidence for the common complaint that public housing is built, and subsidized by the community at large, only to become a nest of crime and vice: why then build more? Fortunately the image is improving as the total public housing stock grows and a larger and more 'normal' cross-section of the low-income community, white or black, moves into it. But as the scale of the programme grows another problem becomes more critical. Should public housing be segregated or integrated racially? Segregation is illegal, but racial tension is at its worst at the interface between the lowest-income sectors of both communities. Moreover, the Negro need is greatest, and most renewal projects clear black rather than white populations. But if the Negro is favoured and entire schemes allocated to him, this is not only racially divisive but also likely further to inflame the prejudice of the poor white community. A common device is for cities to allocate public housing tenancies in ratio to the racial balance in the pre-clearance community.

Urban renewal is socially disruptive, racially divisive, legally complex and politically corrupting (for it is open to easy abuse), and its chief effect has been to reduce low-cost housing supply. Is it an abject failure? In fact it has its great successes, which are perhaps most obvious outside the field of housing. Motorway access to the city centre would have been even more expensive to provide in the absence of the financial mechanism of the renewal process, and where it is associated with new shopping and commercial development built to accommodate the car (for example at Hartford, Conn.) it has done much to revitalize the CBD. The great Pittsburgh auditorium, with its opening steel dome, the Lincoln Center complex of entertainment facilities in New York, conference halls, city campuses of universities and new airway terminals are among the real achievements of urban redevelopment, though not all projects of this type have access to federal funds. But there is powerful opposition to the basic principle of renewal, that it is better to clear and build afresh. The renewal process disrupts existing communities and impoverishes social life: why not improve, adapt, correct the more obvious outbreaks of blight but within the existing urban and community structure? This approach has its eloquent advocates, especially among sociologists, and it has an institutional expression through the Community Conservation movement. This attempts to enlist public support and participation for spot-clearance and general environmental improvement in areas where blight is still patchy and incipient, and so controllable. It is, in a sense, grass-roots democracy: people and the planner collaborate within a scheduled Community Conservation area. It has had some success but it can easily become the instrument of forces it was never intended to support. The spot-clearance of incipient slums can all too often be, in fact, the early eradication of a pocket of Negro colonization. It is significant that in Chicago the scheduled Community Conservation districts envelop the Negro city. Yet it is inevitable, geographically, that they should do so, and this is not necessarily evidence that the movement is directed towards racially divisive ends.

The Flight to the Suburbs

It is appropriate to conclude this sketch of the nature of the American city with a brief account of the process of suburban growth, for the typical metropolitan area has been emptying itself into its rural border-lands at a rate that makes even the vigorous spatial expansion of the British city seem laggardly in comparison. Virtually all American urban growth of population is suburban: the 'central cities' have reached stability or actual decline over much of Northeastern and Midwestern America and everywhere suburban growth has far out-paced city growth. Taking the metropolitan cities identified at the time of the 1960 census, the average growth rate of the core cities, between 1950 and 1960, was only 11 per cent, but of their suburban margins 47 per cent. Thus the great city has become the exploding metropolis, with a decaying core surrounded by an expanding periphery, in which the outward movement of population is balanced by the racial change in the composition of the community of the central city.

But not only are people leaving the city for the suburbs: employment, too, is on the move. American industry has long been de-centralizing from the cramped, expensive sites of the inner city, where firms must face a high level of local taxation and all the excess costs of congestion, to large, open, 'greenfield' sites on the urban margin where both site-costs and tax rates are likely to be very much lower. This flight of manufacturing from the city has been intensively studied in Detroit, a city that lost almost a quarter of a million jobs during the fifties, partly through decentralization. Of the 4000 firms that had remained in Detroit about 40 per cent were discovered to be dissatisfied with their present site and almost half of these were considering a move from the city. The costs of congestion were the chief complaint: few firms thought they could afford to assemble a large enough site on expensive land in the city to rebuild and expand and many were prevented from operating at peak efficiency by the cramped nature of their sites and buildings. Only wholesale renewal of the older factory zones and the total replacement of old multi-storey factories by modern single-storey space on much larger sites seemed likely to prevent a mass migration of industry from the city. Even office employment is now joining the exodus from city to suburb: several firms in the insurance industry, that is the chief basis of the prosperity of Hartford, have left the inner city for peripheral sites, and the growth of office clusters in the suburbs is now a familiar feature of most big American cities.

Thus the suburb is no mere dormitory – a bedroom and weekend resort from which the mass of the employed population migrates daily to the city. Indeed suburbs may be classified on the basis of the level of employment they provide. Some are primarily residential in function with a job-ratio (the ratio between employed population and work available) of about 80 or less. Among these are the high-income suburbs of low-density housing where zoning ordinances have kept not only industry but also a lower-income population at a distance; 'acre-lot zoning' – a housing density of one dwelling per acre – is a device often employed to preserve social homogeneity. But other suburbs have very high job-ratios and 'import' labour each day just as the central city does. The city of Vernon, part of the Los Angeles complex, has a resident population of 229 but offers some 60,000 jobs in manufacturing industry. This is in effect an industrial satellite developed as a factory zone around a complex of railroad yards, but it is an independent suburban municipality nevertheless. Other suburbs are 'balanced', with job-ratios of from about 80 to 120. Given the rapid decentralization of employment from the centre this is becoming the most common type, for even where industry is absent dispersed retailing and commercial employment provide a considerable volume of work. Few suburbs are truly self-contained in terms of job supply – labour is mobile and moves freely between them – but increasingly the suburban population lives to a pattern of life in which the central city, with its frightening problems, has a diminishing place.

Thus the American city is developing to a new spatial and structural model in which emphasis is shifting from the city to the suburban periphery, and in which the old commercial nucleus and the inner industrial zones of the central city have a weakening influence. A new social framework is evolving in sympathy with these physical changes. A study by H. J. Gans of the evolution of community consciousness in Levittown, New Jersey, describes the rise of a social framework in an archetypal fragment of American suburbia. This is virtually a new town of 12,000 homes built by the firm of Levitt and Sons, mass producers of suburban housing. It is, of course, a commercial development: in a sense it is 'planned', in that the firm collaborated with the little township in which the new town was to be sited. But the relationship of company to township was one of strength with weakness. The builder is rich, technically powerful and politically agile; the township poor, divided against itself on the issue of development and eminently persuasible. Planning became, therefore, a little rudimentary, certainly in the provision of community facilities. But the firm was prepared to temper its desire to please its accountants with a certain social idealism, for some of its earlier developments had suffered severe criticism by the professional planners. However, there was little in the way of general social facilities to guide the evolution of a community life, which therefore developed largely spontaneously without the physical foci of neighbourhood centres and the like.

The process is fascinating. It depended not on the provision or neglect by the planner of specific pieces of community equipment but on the sheer social vitality of the American suburban population. The analogy with the simple social values of the old frontier community is irresistible. Within weeks of the first few families of pioneers arriving the compulsive social activity of suburban America had begun, at first through the chance media of 'drinks parties' and coffee gatherings. Soon semi-formal subsectional groups began to emerge as a first institutional framework. The immense social diversity of the American suburb clearly helps to explain its tremendous capacity for group formation. In a sense there is no 'majority', only a complex, multi-dimensional system of 'minorities' distinguished by income, education, ethnic origin, religion, cultural, and sporting interest – or merely by being overweight, for a 'Buxom Belles' group was one of the first to emerge. Within this framework social contact flourishes and multiplies through interlocking memberships. In total, seventy-seven organizations of this kind were formed, and over two-thirds of Levittowners belong to at least one. Religious diversity, too, helps the social process. All the many major churches were soon represented and most sent active 'starter' ministers to build and organize. But often the stimulus came not from outside but from within: even the Catholic diocese was obliged to begin work here earlier than intended because of the strength of organized demand. Even religious schism has its place, as it had in colonial New England: the Jews soon divided between conservative and reform groups and doubtless many friendships were cemented in the struggle. Whatever Levittown may or may not be, whether the planners sneer at it or not, it is certainly not the social desert that so many of its British equivalents remain for so long. Just as the American city is pioneering new structural forms by decentralizing, so perhaps it is evolving a new social model in which the focus (the village, the neighbourhood centre, the small town) has no real place, for the community contacts described above are those of a mobile society with little consciousness of 'place' and perhaps only a year or two of attachment to it.

One of the most obvious and most serious consequences of the explosive decentralization of the American city is the administrative anarchy that it produces. Few central cities in metropolitan areas have been able to extend their boundaries to annex territory as their suburban growth has proceeded. Only the newer cities of the West and parts of the South have been able thus to incorporate their own outgrowth. More commonly suburban growth takes place beyond the city limits, within the many suburban municipalities – mostly of recent creation – enveloping the city. The fragmentation of the political structure of the metropolitan area thus created reaches almost unbelievable levels. The 'real' Chicago spreads over 2 states, 6 counties, 10 towns, 30 cities, 49 townships, and 110 villages. Overlaid upon this complex pattern are 235 tax districts and more than 400 school districts. Boston consists of about 80 separate authorities of greater or less autonomy, Los Angeles almost 90, Pittsburgh about 160; while the title of a book on the pattern of local administration in the New York city cluster is '1400 Governments'.

That this parochial division of responsibility defeats any attempt at rational planning for the city and its region is obvious. Devices have been used to bring some order to the system for specific purposes: the Massachusetts Bay Transit Authority provides public transport for the whole of Greater Boston and the Southern California Metropolitan Water District serves the whole of the Los Angeles system of cities.

But there is nothing to compare with the regional authority set up in 1953 to administer Metropolitan Toronto, nor any equivalent of the British Maud Commission to suggest reform of the entire system of local government: indeed such a body would be wildly unconstitutional in the United States. But it is here, at the level of administrative infrastructure, that the search for solutions to the many problems of the American city must begin if it is to be wholly effective. The *laissez-faire* process will not work: public direction and community investment on a massive scale are in the long term inevitable. The alternative is alarming: the vision of a poor, debt-ridden, highly taxed central city at the core of every major urban mass, Negro dominated and of low average income, surrounded by the brave new suburbs in which a white population lives in great affluence, enjoys low local taxes, forms its complex social patterns and lives the American dream with its back to the city that it has rejected.

Further Reading

ON THE GROWTH OF AMERICAN CITIES

Glaab, C. N. and Brown, A. T., *A History of Urban America*. New York, 1967.
Green, C. McL., *American Cities in the Growth of the Nation*. New York, 1957.

ON THE STRUCTURE OF THE CITY AND THE NATIONAL PATTERN OF URBANIZATION

Murphy, R. E., *The American City: an Urban Geography*. New York, 1966.
Duncan, O. D. *et al.*, *Metropolis and Region*. Baltimore, Md., 1960.
Gottmann, J., *Megalopolis: the Urbanised Northeastern Seaboard of the United States*. New York, 1961.
Yeates, M. H. and Garner, B. J., *The North American City*. New York, 1971.

ON SOCIAL PATTERNS AND RACIAL PROBLEMS

Duncan, O. D. and Duncan, B., *The Negro Population of Chicago*. Chicago, Ill., 1957.
Handlin, O., *The Newcomers* (New York Metropolitan Region Study). Cambridge, Mass., 1959.
Gans, H. J., *The Levittowners*. London, 1967.

ON PROBLEMS OF URBAN RENEWAL AND CONSERVATION

Anderson, M., *The Federal Bulldozer*. Cambridge, Mass., 1964.
Jacobs, J., *The Death and Life of Great American Cities*. New York, 1961.
Vernon, R., *Metropolis 1985* (New York Metropolitan Region Study). Cambridge, Mass., 1960.

5 American Wars

MALDWYN A. JONES

Historians have surely been right to devote a major part of their energies to the recording of war. Warfare can admittedly be an arid and unrewarding subject; battles and campaigns studied for their own sake can hardly avoid being so. Yet war has been not only one of the favourite collective occupations of the human race but also one of the most revealing. It has been a formative influence in the development of every society of which we have record. It has at the same time faithfully reflected the characteristics of the peoples engaged in it; nations have been distinguished from one another by nothing so much as by the way they have fought and by their reasons for doing so. Thus to examine a nation's experience of war and its response to it is to learn something about its values, its social order and the way in which it has developed.

It is of course one of the ironies of history that these generalizations about war's illuminant properties should have come to apply at least as fully to the United States as to other countries. Americans have always prided themselves upon being an unwarlike people. Benjamin Franklin's comment in 1783 that 'there never was a good war or a bad peace' came oddly from the representative of a new nation which had just made good by force of arms its claim of independence, but it represented accurately enough the distaste of most of his countrymen for the belligerency to which Europe had been prone. Americans of the Revolutionary generation, indeed, assumed that one of the distinguishing characteristics of their *novus ordo saeculorum* would be freedom from the warfare endemic in Europe. Jefferson's isolationism was predicated, for example, upon a distinction between the bellicosity of the Old World and the more pacific, more rational and more natural order he believed was being ushered in in the New. The nations of Europe, he wrote, 'are nations of eternal war. . . . On our part, never had a people so favorable a chance of trying the opposite system, of peace and fraternity with mankind and the direction of all our means and faculties to the purpose of improvement instead of destruction.'

For all these brave prognostications the United States has found that, as Henry Adams once remarked, she has had to 'bear the common burdens of humanity'. Far from being a purely Old World scourge war has proved a persistent, almost a continuous, theme in American history. It had indeed already become so by the time of Franklin and Jefferson. Not only had the Americans had the experience of several generations of Indian warfare; they had also been embroiled, between 1689 and 1763, in the contest for empire that went on intermittently between England, France, and Spain.

The pattern thus established in the colonial period was to be repeated after the Revolutionary War of 1775–83 had brought the United States into being. The shameful succession of Indian wars continued for more than a century after Independence; until in fact the tribesmen had been dispossessed and almost exterminated. The United States went to war with Britain a second time in 1812–14, with Mexico in 1846–8, with itself in 1861–5, and with Spain in 1898; then in the twentieth century it has been at war with the Central Powers in 1917–18, with the Axis in 1941–5, and in Korea in 1950–3. In addition it has become involved in a number of undeclared wars, ranging from small-scale affairs like the naval war with France of 1798–1800 and the border campaign of 1916–17 against the Mexican bandit Pancho Villa, to what had escalated by the end of the 1960s into a major conflict in Vietnam.

This bloody catalogue, extending over the whole span of American history, demonstrates that the American claim to uniqueness is subject to at least one major qualification. Yet if the United States has resembled other countries in its inability to avoid war a closer look at her military involvements nevertheless suggests a distinctively American way in war, a set of attitudes and practices which, not least in their ambivalence and contradictions, mirror the society from which they have sprung.

The Colonial Period

The empty continent to which the first Europeans supposedly came at the beginning of the seventeenth century was in fact inhabited by over 600,000 Indians, and it was with them that the earliest American wars were fought. Relations between Indians and whites were at first friendly but as the white man cleared the land and encroached more and more upon traditional hunting grounds the Indians attempted to stem the advancing tide of settlement. In colony after colony the early phase of co-existence gave way to friction, skirmishing and, finally, open warfare. In New England the clash of two antagonistic economic systems led early on to the Pequot War of 1637 whereby the destruction of the Pequot nation opened the Connecticut Valley to white settlement. In an even bloodier outbreak a generation later a score of New England frontier settlements was wiped out; but King Philip's War ended, as all Indian–white wars would ultimately end, in the decimation of the tribesmen. On the Virginia frontier conflict persisted longer; first heard during Opechancanough's assault of 1622 the war whoop finally died away only after the Shawnees had been crushed in Lord Dunmore's War of 1774. Similar scenes, in which the whites vied with the Indians in ferocity, were enacted in the Carolinas during the Tuscarora War of 1711–12 and the Yamassee War of 1715. These local conflicts were, however, overshadowed by Pontiac's Rebellion of 1763, in which an Ottawa chieftain led a powerful confederacy of Western tribes in the most formidable Indian uprising of the century. Before they were subdued by British regulars Pontiac's braves had overrun every western fort except Detroit and Fort Pitt, killed or captured 2000 troops and settlers and ravaged a thousand miles of frontier from Niagara to Virginia.

But the Indians were not the only adversaries the colonials were called upon to fight. Five times in three-quarters of a century they became involved in war, for the most part sporadic in nature, with either the French or the Spanish: King William's War (1689–97), Queen Anne's War (1702–13), the War of Jenkins' Ear (1739–43), King George's War (1744–8), and the French and Indian War (1754–63). Though each of these conflicts originated in the rivalries of the European Powers there were also local frictions, arising out of the intercolonial situation, to add a further American dimension. There was intense rivalry both between English and French fur traders and between New Englanders and French Canadians over the Newfoundland fisheries. There was a good deal of antipathy between English Protestants and French and Spanish Catholics. Above all, the English colonists, whether on the northern frontier or in the South, felt insecure so long as their Indian neighbours were encouraged in their hostility toward them by French or Spanish allies.

It was the outlying settlements which bore the main burden of these conflicts. During the first two intercolonial wars the French and their Indian allies carried out savage attacks on the frontiers of New York and New England; settlements like Schenectady, New York, and

Haverhill, Massachusetts, were looted and burned, their inhabitants killed, scalped, tortured or carried off into captivity. Later on it was the turn of Virginia, Maryland, and Pennsylvania to be terrorized; Braddock's defeat in 1755 exposed four hundred miles of frontier to French and Indian attack, and the small defence force under the command of Colonel George Washington was inadequate to prevent a series of appalling massacres.

In an effort to put a stop to this ruthless form of warfare the colonials carried out retaliatory attacks on the Indians and made several attempts to cripple the enemy by striking at French strongholds in the St Lawrence. But for much of the period Britain was too absorbed in her European wars and apparently too indifferent to the fate of her American colonists to send them much help. Not until 1758, when Pitt came to the conclusion that the best way to defeat the French would be to strip her of her colonies, was a sizeable British army sent to America. Until then the colonists had to depend largely on their own efforts. Even so they won some notable victories, such as the capture of Port Royal in 1710 and, more especially, the storming of Louisbourg in 1745. The Louisbourg expedition – a joint effort by Connecticut, New Hampshire, Massachusetts, Maine, Rhode Island, New York, New Jersey, and Pennsylvania – was the foremost American military achievement before the Revolution. It was also the most characteristically American. Planned and executed by amateurs the enterprise, according to one contemporary, 'had a lawyer for contriver, a merchant for general, and farmers, fishermen and mechanics for soldiers'.

The wars in which the several colonies were engaged were not without some effect upon their attitude both to one another and to the mother country. Admittedly more than one effort at intercolonial military cooperation, such as the abortive attack on Montreal in 1690, ended in failure and mutual recrimination. Local particularism, moreover, wrecked firstly the attempts of the Albany Congress of 1754 to produce some arrangement for joint defence and then the efforts of Lord Loudoun to induce the colonies to combine during the French and Indian War. In that conflict, indeed, most colonies remained reluctant to send their militia to join in the defence of their neighbours. Nevertheless the colonists had been made aware long before the Revolution that their defence problems were common to each of them and that some form of joint action might be necessary for their solution. Moreover, Louisbourg showed what could be done.

While a common experience of war was thus pointing the need for unity it was also helping to weaken colonial ties with Britain. The British tendency to allow the colonists to fight their own battles was hardly calculated to strengthen the imperial connection. This was particularly the case when the British proceeded to throw away the fruits of colonial victory; the return of Louisbourg to the French in 1748 by the Treaty of Aix-la-Chapelle could only rankle with those whose blood had been spilt in capturing the great fortress. And even when the British undertook joint military action with provincial forces the experience was not always a happy one for the colonials; thus the heavy loss of life during Admiral Vernon's unsuccessful attack on Cartagena in 1740 led to bitter colonial complaints about British bungling.

The colonial wars had a further effect. They transformed the colonists into what Daniel J. Boorstin has aptly called 'a nation of minute-men'. In Europe – at least after the end of the Thirty Years' War – the waging of war had been a specialized occupation, a matter for professional soldiers alone and one which avowedly exempted the civilian population; wars had been fought for limited objectives and were regulated by an elaborate code – the so-called 'civilized rules of warfare'. But the kind of warfare waged by the Indians did not fit into this pattern. The Indian was an ever-present and merciless foe; no home was safe from his torch and no one – not even women and children – could expect to escape his tomahawk and scalping knife. These circumstances presented the colonists with a horrifyingly novel definition of war and compelled them to devise new ways of waging it. War was no longer a formalized set of manoeuvres carried out on a distant battlefield but a desperate defence of hearth and home. And when every corner of the land might at any moment become a battle-field every able-bodied citizen had perforce to equip himself to become a soldier.

The militia system, based upon the concept of a self-armed citizenry, thus became the customary pattern of colonial defence. It was to have a seminal influence upon American military attitudes and hence upon American military policy. The colonists as transplanted Englishmen had traditionally looked upon standing armies with aversion and distrust. Their experience as minute-men suggested that a standing army was ineffectual and unnecessary. Their ideas on the subject were to be reinforced and further developed by the passage of the Mutiny Act of 1765, which required the New York Assembly to provide quarters for British troops, and by the alleged responsibility of the redcoats for the Boston 'massacre'. It was in consequence of these events, indeed, that the colonial preference for the militia was to become enshrined as part of the American credo.

The War of Independence

The Revolutionary War was several wars in one. It was among other things a war for national independence, a civil war and in the end a world war. It was not only the first war of modern times to result in the rupture of an imperial connection and, as such, was to become an inspiration to other colonial peoples; it was also a war of ideas, a truly revolutionary war. It was not that the war accomplished a social revolution – the structure of American society was basically unaltered – but that the new nation which proclaimed itself in 1776 was founded upon a set of political principles which were at the same time a statement of its own aspirations and a challenge to the existing European order. The successful assertion of those principles in war was thus an event of world-wide significance. At the same time it was a war fought on the American side – and on the British too for that matter – by a disunited people. The divisions within the United States did not correspond to geographical areas; even more divisive was the fact that both Whigs and Tories, Patriots and Loyalists were to be found in every part of the country, and sometimes within the same family. It was this circumstance which was to lend an added tinge of bitterness to the struggle. Not that it was in any sense a parochial affair. Even before France and Spain took a hand officially the American cause had attracted the support of a motley band of European sympathisers, some of them idealists, some soldiers of fortune, and among them such figures as Lafayette, Steuben, De Kalb, Pulaski, and Kosciuszko. And before the fighting was brought to an end it had spread to the West Indies, Gibraltar, the North Sea, and the Indian Ocean.

Even within its American context it was a war fought over an immense battlefield; from Quebec to Savannah and from Boston to Vincennes. It was to be, moreover, the longest war, at least until Vietnam, in which the United States was to engage, extending over eight and a half years from the firing at Lexington to the signing of the treaty of peace. Yet the number of troops involved was relatively small. No large armies were ever engaged. The largest force deployed by the British consisted of the 34,000 men with which the Howe brothers attacked New York in 1776. On the American side Washington's army never exceeded 20,000 men; for most of the time he commanded between 5000 and 9000; and at one given moment he led a dwindling band of only 2000.

It was in some ways an odd war, especially by the standards of the eighteenth century. Instead of being fought in the accepted manner by professionals it resolved itself into a series of clashes between one army made up largely of militia and another composed of regulars, mercenaries, Loyalist volunteers, and Indian auxiliaries. Much of the fighting, especially in the South, took the form of guerilla warfare. There were comparatively few pitched battles and battle casualties were relatively few. In no battle were as many as 500 Americans killed and even at Bunker Hill, the bloodiest engagement of the entire war, the British, who suffered the heavier losses – amounting to two-fifths of their entire force – counted only 1150 dead and wounded. But at its two most decisive moments the war exhibited its essentially eighteenth-century character. Both at Saratoga and at Yorktown a trapped British army chose to surrender rather than risk a pitched battle and, on the latter occasion, which brought the war effectively to an end, 7000 British troops stacked their arms to the accompaniment of an American band which played a march called 'The World Turned Upside Down'.

At the outset of the struggle, however, such a *dénouement* would have been almost unthinkable. The colonists had challenged one of the strongest powers in the world. Great Britain enjoyed an advantage in population of the order of three to one, and it possessed overwhelmingly superior military and naval power and an infinitely greater war-making potential. The colonists, on the other hand, lacked not only an army and navy but even an effective government. The Articles of Confederation, adopted by the Continental Congress in 1777, conferred only limited powers upon the proposed central government. It had the power to declare war but not the means to carry it out; for troops and taxes it could only make requisitions on the states. In any case the states could not be persuaded to ratify the Articles until 1781, so that they did not go into effect until the fighting was almost over. Meantime the Continental Congress remained the *de facto* government, giving to the American war effort such direction and coordination as it was to possess. Given its lack of authority Congress may be pardoned its many shortcomings; its administrative failures, its excessive reliance on paper money, its neglect of the army and its general indecision and timidity. The real fault lay not with the men who were entrusted with the conduct of the new nation's affairs but in the preference of the states for a weak central government even when the continued existence of the United States seemed manifestly to demand firm central direction.

This ingrained localism was in other ways a serious handicap to the American cause. It manifested itself not only in the tardiness with which the states responded to calls for men and money but also in the dissension that broke out in the ranks of the Continental Army. Throughout the conflict Washington was plagued by the same kind of particularism that had hamstrung colonial efforts in earlier wars. 'I have labored, ever since I have been in the service,' wrote an exasperated Washington at the end of 1776, 'to discourage all kinds of local attachments and distinctions of country, denominating the whole by the greater name of *American*, but I have found it impossible to overcome prejudices.' Adding further to the commander-in-chief's problems were the levelling tendencies of Americans. Discipline proved hard to maintain in the face of endless disputes between soldiers over rank and precedence, the refusal of the states to establish a sufficiently high pay scale for officers and the persistence of an unmilitary familiarity between officers and men.

An even more serious difficulty was the instability which resulted from civilian suspicions of a standing army and fear of a military dictatorship. These attitudes dictated the form and character of the armed forces raised by Congress and the states. Though Washington's Continental Army possessed a sound nucleus of long-service veterans and was reinforced from time to time by other volunteers, it consisted mainly of state militia enlisted for short periods, sometimes for as little as three months. This method of raising an army proved to be highly ineffective and unreliable, and a source of perpetual worry to Washington. 'I am religiously persuaded', he wrote in 1780, 'that the duration of the war, and the greatest part of the misfortunes and perplexities we have hitherto experienced, are chiefly to be attributed to temporary inlistments.' The history of the war strongly confirmed this opinion. Several times the transient character of the army had forced commanders into decisions that could hardly be justified on purely military grounds and these had on occasion contributed to American reverses. The timing of Montgomery's disastrous assault on Quebec, made in a snowstorm on 30 December 1775, was determined by the fact that the enlistments of his New England troops would expire the next day and experience had shown that they could not be relied on to remain a moment longer. But bad though it was when men enlisted for only three months, it became much worse when they deserted after two. It was quite common for militiamen to go home before their terms expired so that even in the face of the enemy Washington always faced the possibility that his army would melt away.

As though this was not sufficient handicap the American cause had also to contend with treason, mutiny and the activities of what would now be called a fifth column. Washington probably exaggerated when he asserted that, if Benedict Arnold's offer to hand over the fortress of West Point to the British had not miscarried, it 'must have given the American cause a deadly wound if not a fatal stab'. But it would nevertheless have been a great calamity for it would have given Clinton command of the Hudson. Hardly less menacing were the mutinies of the Pennsylvania and New Jersey Lines in 1781 – the consequence, however, not of disloyalty but of long-smouldering resentment with conditions of service in the Continental Army. Throughout the war, moreover, the Loyalists proved a grave threat to the patriot cause. Their number has sometimes been exaggerated but their services to the British have not. They were to be found in every state and all classes of society; they were an important source of supplies and intelligence to the British army; and perhaps 30,000 of them took up arms for George III at some time or other during the conflict.

That the Americans, with their ill-disciplined and transient army and their ineffectual government, should have managed nevertheless to emerge victorious from the war seems at first glance inexplicable. But the British suffered from a number of offsetting disadvantages and the odds in their favour were not as great as they seemed. Formidable problems of supply and communication were involved in waging war in unfriendly territory three thousand miles from home, and the American terrain was unsuited to the kind of warfare to which the British were accustomed. The Royal Navy had been allowed to decay and the army was so far below strength that 30,000 Hessians had to be recruited. The absurdity often charged against Lord George Germain of trying to run the war from London has no basis in fact; rather was it the case that the British effort was seriously impaired by the lack of a unified command and overall strategic direction. The British generals were an unimposing lot; Howe was overcautious, Burgoyne blundering, Clinton dilatory and Cornwallis reckless. But their operations were handicapped by the confusion of purpose that characterized the instructions emanating from London; until late in the war the British government was unable to make up its mind whether its object in America was to conciliate or to coerce. Yet the greatest difficulty confronting the British was that, in a war to restore the Americans to their former allegiance, the occupation of territory brought no lasting advantage. Though every important town fell successively into British hands in the course of the war, the British lacked the resources to garrison so vast an area and the moment they evacuated a region they believed to have been pacified, rebellion flared up again in their rear.

Thus if the Americans could but retain the will to fight and some capacity to do so, their ultimate triumph was inevitable. They owed much to the assistance they received from France. Even before France entered the war in 1778, Louis XVI authorized the despatch of large quantities of arms and supplies. It was a vital contribution. Ninety per cent of the powder used by the Americans in the early years of the war came from France, and the guns and ammunition which brought about the surrender at Saratoga came from French arsenals. In addition the facilities granted to the Americans in the ports of France and the French West Indies were largely responsible for the successes achieved by American privateers against British shipping. To be sure, the French motive in granting such aid was not so much to achieve American independence as to weaken Great Britain, and this was equally the French purpose in eventually joining in the war. Yet though she remained indifferent to American interests and did not exert herself unduly to concert operations with the Americans, France's only serious military intervention was decisive; the expedition sent under De Grasse and Rochambeau to Virginia in 1781 to reinforce Washington sealed Cornwallis' fate at Yorktown.

Even so the greatest contribution to the American cause was made neither by the French nor by the American terrain, but by Washington. He was not a military genius; in fact he lost most of the battles he fought. But he was a great war leader. Out of unpromising material and in the face of great odds he brought an army into being. By keeping it in being through a long succession of dark days, of which the darkest were those at Valley Forge, he sustained American morale and kept the patriot cause alive. His courage, steadfastness and resource were not, however, the only qualities Washington possessed for which the young nation had cause to be thankful. Though frequently driven to protest at Congressional neglect of the army, he was never less than deferential to the civil authorities. Moreover the promptness with which he quitted the army in 1783 in order to return to private life showed that he had no desire to make political capital out of his war service. In so doing he not only assuaged the fears of most of those who had feared the emergence of 'a man on horseback'; he had helped set the tone of American civil–military relations for generations to come.

The War of 1812

The War of 1812 is full of paradox. It began only after the main cause of friction between the belligerents – the British Orders in Council – had been removed; it was vehemently opposed by those economic groups in whose interests it was ostensibly being fought; and its most decisive battle did not take place until after the conclusion of peace. Not surprisingly historians have found it a somewhat baffling affair and have disagreed about every aspect of it – why it was fought, by whom it was won, and whether or not it had any important consequences.

Until about a generation ago it was taken for granted that, on the American side, the war was fought primarily, if not exclusively, for the protection of the maritime rights of neutrals. Historians took at face value Madison's war message of June 1812 which laid the main emphasis upon imprisonment, illegal blockades, and the stopping and searching of American vessels for contraband on the high seas. But it was difficult to understand why a war for maritime rights should be opposed by the merchants and shipowners of the Northeast, whose rights were allegedly being violated, and supported by the South and West which had no direct interest in maritime affairs. The motives of the War Hawks, the group of young ultranationalists from the West and Lower South and led by such figures as Henry Clay, John C. Calhoun, and Felix Grundy, were thus subjected to fresh scrutiny. Hence it came to be argued that the real roots of the war were to be found, not in maritime rights, but in such factors as an alleged sectional bargain between West and South which wanted respectively to annex Canada and Florida, both of which served as bases for Indian attacks on the frontier, and an agricultural depression in the agrarian states which was widely blamed on British restrictions on neutral commerce. But in recent years the pendulum has swung strongly back to maritime rights. No evidence has been found to support the theory of a sectional bargain on expansion, and although the Indian menace and the fall in agricultural prices are acknowledged to have been contributing factors, there is now a broad consensus that British interference with American shipping was the main cause of the conflict. What angered the War Hawks most about British maritime policy was not, however, the damage done to American commerce and agriculture; rather was it the hurt inflicted upon American national pride.

Although the conquest of Canada was not, therefore, the object for which the Americans had declared war, it nevertheless became for them the means – indeed the only means – of bringing it to a successful conclusion. Canada was so obviously vulnerable that Jefferson only expressed a common opinion when he predicted that its conquest would be 'a mere matter of marching'. Canada's long land frontier was defended by only 4500 troops and reinforcements could not easily be spared so long as Britain's hands were tied by the struggle with Napoleon. Compared with the United States Canada had fewer resources of manpower on which to draw; her population totalled only half a million as against seven and a half millions in the United States. Moreover the loyalty of the Canadian population was in doubt; in Lower Canada two-thirds of the population was of French descent and in Upper Canada there was a substantial minority which was American by birth and sympathy.

Nevertheless two successive American invasions of Canada ended in failure. The first, in 1812, was a complete fiasco; the Americans were not only expelled from Canada but were forced to surrender Detroit and other frontier posts to their pursuers. A second attempt in 1813 achieved nothing tangible; after capturing York (Toronto), the then capital of Canada, the invaders set fire to Parliament and a number of other public buildings before withdrawing across Lake Ontario.

These failures, though unexpected, are not really difficult to explain. The United States was totally unprepared for war and Madison's administration proved incapable of conducting it efficiently, at least until the President rid himself of his incompetent Secretary of War, William Eustis. American ability to wage war was further limited by the hostility of the wealthiest and most strategically located section of the country. What New England thought of 'Mr Madison's War' could be seen in its refusal to contribute troops or subscribe to federal loans and in its persistence in trading with the enemy. Partly for financial reasons, and partly because of the traditional American antipathy to standing armies, the decision was taken to rely mainly on the state militia. But the militia were ill-trained and ill-disciplined and many of them had no stomach for an invasion of Canada. They were, moreover, badly led. The generals who commanded on the Canadian front during the first two years of the war – Dearborn, Pinckney, Hull, and Wilkinson – were uniformly incompetent. Elderly regulars who had never commanded – indeed had never seen – large bodies of troops, they were mainly responsible, along with the vigour of the Canadian defence, for the defeats and *débâcles* that befell American arms in 1812 and 1813. By the end of 1813 they had been replaced by younger and more capable men. By that time also Commodore Perry's victory at the Battle of Lake Erie had given the Americans command of the Great Lakes. But these developments came too late to affect American prospects. With the end of the war against Napoleon in 1814 the British were able to send out 20,000 reinforcements and all hope of conquering Canada had gone.

Only at sea could the Americans regard the first two years of the war with any satisfaction. The United States was not of course in a position to challenge the British for command of the sea; it had no ships-of-the-line and only a dozen frigates against the Royal Navy's 120 ships-of-the-line and 116 frigates. With fleet actions thus ruled out the Americans struck at British trade and shipping by using privateers which captured in all some 1300 British vessels. But what is best remembered about the war at sea is the succession of single ship actions between American and British warships. The American frigates were more manoeuvrable and more heavily armed than their British opponents, and their gunnery proved superior. Accordingly they won nearly all of these engagements, either sinking the British warships or forcing them to surrender. But although these victories were a source of justifiable pride to the Americans and of discomfiture to the British, they could not alter the fact that the British enjoyed naval superiority around the American coast.

So complete had this superiority become by the last year of the war that the earlier roles of the belligerents were reversed. The Royal Navy blockaded the entire American coast, British forces controlled much of the coast of Maine, and in October 1814 a large British raiding force sailed into Chesapeake Bay and, in retaliation for the earlier American attack on York, set fire to the public buildings of Washington, including the Capitol and the White House. But British plans for a major thrust into the United States by way of Lake Champlain received a fatal check when Commodore McDonough destroyed the British flotilla at the Battle of Plattsburg (11 September 1814). And in the extreme South hostilities came to an end with a crushing American victory. In the Battle of New Orleans (8 January 1815) a British army of 10,000 men, most of them veterans of the Peninsular Wars, was routed by General Andrew Jackson and was driven back to its ships with heavy losses.

The battle had no effect on the outcome of the war. In fact a treaty of peace had already been signed at Ghent two weeks earlier but the news had not yet reached the United States. Weary of an inconclusive war both sides were ready to end it on the basis of the *status quo ante bellum*. Since the war in Europe was over, the maritime rights of neutrals were no longer a live issue. The Treaty of Ghent ignored the issue and in fact did little more than declare that hostilities should end.

Since most Americans learned of Jackson's victory at New Orleans before news arrived of the Treaty of Ghent it was possible to conclude that the United States had won the war. Moreover the sequence of events tended to obliterate from American minds any recollection of the dire extremity in which the federal government had so recently found itself. Yet only a few weeks earlier the country had stood on the verge of bankruptcy, efforts to raise an effective army were meeting with little success and the Hartford Convention, called by New England opponents of the war, had seemed to threaten the Union with dissolution. In the event the Convention did no more than hint at secession but proposed a number of amendments to the Constitution, all of them designed to protect New England from the growing influence of the agrarian states. But in the wave of patriotism that followed the Battle of New Orleans the New England Federalists were discredited as traitors.

Besides dealing the final blow to the declining Federalist party the War of 1812 had other important consequences. It stimulated the growth of manufactures and it broke the Indian barrier that had stemmed the westward movement some distance east of the Mississippi. More important still, the war brought about a great outburst of national feeling. During the war itself a prominent Washington lawyer, Francis Scott Key, had been inspired while observing the British bombardment of Baltimore to compose some verses entitled 'The Star Spangled Banner', which later became the American national anthem. More generally the American naval victories and the defeat of Britain's Peninsular veterans at New Orleans were a tremendous source of national pride and self-confidence.

The War of 1812 is sometimes referred to as 'the second war for independence' and on the whole it merits the title. It was not of course a struggle for national survival in the sense that Britain was seeking to reimpose her rule over her former colonies. But this was the first time that the young republic demonstrated that it had the will and the capacity to defend what it deemed to be its national interests, even against the strongest military and naval power in the world. At the same time the war marked the end of American dependence upon the European state system. Up to this time the United States had been embroiled again and again in the wars of Europe, and her primary concerns had thus been foreign affairs and defence. After 1815 she could afford for almost a century to turn her back on Europe and give priority to her own domestic affairs.

The Mexican War

There are sound reasons why the Mexican War has remained hidden in relative obscurity. There is first of all the simple fact that, historically speaking, it has always been overshadowed by the greater conflict that broke out only a dozen or so years later. Historians have tended, indeed, to dismiss the war with Mexico as a mere prologue to the Civil War, important only to the extent that it focused attention for the first time upon a group of young men – Grant and Lee, Lincoln and Davis, Jackson and McClellan – who were destined later to be pitted against one another. There is also the circumstance that Americans have developed an uneasy conscience about the Mexican War. It has come to be regarded as a shameful episode, a piece of calculated aggression whereby a weak neighbour was plundered of half her territory. Such a blot on the national record, it has been felt, is best forgotten.

Yet the Mexican War does not merit this neglect. It was a truly significant event, worthy of being studied in its own right. It exemplified the expansionist spirit of Manifest Destiny and it shed some revealing light upon the character of civil–military relations in the American democracy. It brought the young republic immense gains and equally great problems. Though it rounded out the continental boundaries of the United States it at the same time rekindled the sectional controversy over slavery.

The immediate cause of hostilities was the Texan boundary dispute. Yet this was but the culmination of a process which had long poisoned relations between the United States and Mexico. The Mexicans resented the acquisitive ambitions of their northern neighbour while the Americans, for their part, were intensely hostile to everything Mexican because of the cruelties perpetrated by Mexican soldiers during and after the Texan Revolution. Mexico's failure to pay her debts had increased friction still farther and her chronic political instability complicated diplomatic relations and lessened the chances of a peaceful solution. But it was the Texan question that engendered most bitterness. Mexico was far from being reconciled to the loss of Texas, which had declared itself independent in 1836 and was annexed by the United States nine years later. Nor was she disposed to concede the Texan claim that the Rio Grande constituted the Texas southern and western boundary. President Polk, however, supported the Texan claim and in 1845 sent a detachment of soldiers under General Zachary Taylor to the disputed territory.

Polk was a convinced exponent of the expansionist credo summed up in the phrase 'manifest destiny'; that is, he believed that the United States was preordained to control the whole of the North American continent and had the right and even the obligation to extend its institutions and ideals to peoples in adjacent countries. He entered office in 1845 determined to acquire New Mexico and California and possibly other provinces of northern Mexico. He hoped to persuade the Mexicans to sell these huge areas but if he could not acquire them peaceably he was prepared to resort to war. The Mexicans for their part were in an uncompromising, even belligerent, frame of mind and when Polk sent an envoy to Mexico City in a last attempt to secure his objectives by diplomacy he was rebuffed. Polk thereupon decided on war and in May 1846 found a fresh pretext for it in the news that the Mexicans had crossed the Rio Grande and attacked Taylor's troops. Bending the facts to suit his purpose Polk stampeded Congress into declaring war with the claim that Mexico had 'shed American blood upon American soil' and that 'war exists by act of Mexico itself'.

The Mexicans entered the war confident of victory. They possessed much larger regular forces and doubted the American will to fight. But Mexican strength was not as great as it appeared; the army was badly organized and its war material was antiquated. The Americans, with a population more than twice that of Mexico, proved capable of putting superior forces in the field. Moreover they had more competent generals, better guns and equipment and an infinitely greater capacity to finance the war and supply their armed forces.

For the United States the war was a succession of triumphs. It began with the occupation of the two provinces for which it had gone to war. In May 1846 Colonel Stephen W. Kearny led an expedition to Santa

Fe and met little opposition in reducing New Mexico. He then set off
for Los Angeles and, with the aid both of the American settlers there
who had staged the Bear Flag revolt and of other American military
and naval forces, he completed the conquest of California by the
autumn of 1846. Meanwhile Taylor was heavily engaged in northern
Mexico and in February 1847 crowned a successful campaign with a
crushing victory at Buena Vista, when he overwhelmed a Mexican
army three times the size of his own. A still greater feat of arms was
General Winfield Scott's advance into the heart of Mexico. Landing
his army at Vera Cruz, Scott marched 260 miles over difficult mountain country, defeated the Mexicans at Cerro Gordo, fought half a
dozen other pitched battles against superior forces and finally, on
14 September 1847, having previously stormed the great fortress of
Chapultepec, took possession of Mexico City. This forced the Mexicans
to make peace and by the Treaty of Guadalupe Hidalgo (2 February
1848) they agreed to cede California and New Mexico and to acknowledge the Rio Grande boundary of Texas.

Yet against a stronger adversary victory might not have been so
easily won. As it was, American military effectiveness was hampered
by the want of harmony that developed between the civil and military
leaders. Politics and soldiering had never been completely divorced in
the United States and the Mexican War afforded a classic example of
their interaction. Both the direction of the war from Washington and
the conduct of generals on the battlefield were affected by political
considerations. As a Democratic politician Polk could scarcely be
oblivious to the fact that both his leading generals were known
Whigs – Scott had been a leading contender for the Whig presidential
nomination in 1844 – and that the only time the Whigs had won the
presidency had been in 1840, when they nominated a military hero in
General William Henry Harrison. That pattern could well be repeated
– as in the event it was – if the war led to the aggrandizement of either
Taylor or Scott. Polk's aim therefore was to win the war without in
the process allowing a Whig general to acquire sufficient lustre to
defeat the Democrats in the next presidential election. He sought to
deny Taylor the credit for his victories and attempted, though in
vain, to persuade Congress to give a Democratic politician the highest
command in the army. Later, when Scott court-martialled two
Democratic generals who had been intriguing against him, Polk
intervened to dismiss the charges against them and instead ordered a
court of inquiry to investigate charges against Scott. Not that either

Taylor or Scott was prepared to remain passive under this treatment. Neither made any secret of his lack of confidence in Polk's administration or of his conviction that strategic decisions taken in Washington were influenced primarily by the desire to discredit them politically. Indeed Taylor's success in the presidential election of 1848 was due largely to the impression he and his friends created of a gallant soldier, victorious in spite of being stripped of his troops by a partisan president.

It was thus one of the ironies of the Mexican War that, despite its roll of triumphs, it resulted in the repudiation at the polls of the Democratic party that had made it. Nor did it unite the American people. The war was bitterly unpopular in large parts of the Union, especially in New England. It was widely believed that the war was nothing more than a Southern plot to acquire more slave territory. In fact many Southern leaders, recognizing that areas like New Mexico and California were unsuited to slavery, were lukewarm about further acquisitions. The main support for the war came from the West, from the people of the Mississippi Valley who were enthusiastic about expansion and supplied most of the volunteers for the war. Nevertheless opposition to 'Mr Polk's War' intensified the longer it went on and intellectuals like Emerson, Thoreau, and Lowell denounced its aggressive origins and objectives. In Congress too opposition increased, with opponents of slavery attempting by means of the Wilmot Proviso to exclude slavery from any territory to be acquired from Mexico. The Wilmot Proviso tended to cut across party lines and to divide opinion instead in sectional blocs. Northerners supported it and Southerners firmly condemned it. In such fashion was the dangerous issue revived of whether slavery should be permitted to expand into new territories.

The Mexican War was thus a mixed blessing for the United States. It brought her immense advantages – over half a million square miles of additional territory, the splendid harbour of San Francisco and an outlet to the trade of the Orient, and the mineral wealth of California where gold was discovered in January 1848, just before the peace treaty was signed. But the price was high, and not only in blood and treasure, though it did in fact cost the United States 13,000 dead and nearly $100 million. More damaging ultimately would be the renewal of sectional strife over an issue that had divided the country before and would now do so again. The Mexican War, Emerson predicted, would act as a poison on the United States. That he was a true prophet was proved thirteen years later by the firing at Fort Sumter.

The Civil War

The Civil War has etched itself more deeply upon the American mind than any of the other conflicts in which the United States has been engaged. It contributed to the American Valhalla some of its best-remembered heroes; it produced in the Gettysburg Address and Lincoln's Second Inaugural some of the most quoted and the most sublime sentiments ever uttered by an American. It inspired Walt Whitman's *Drum Taps*, perhaps the best war poetry ever written in America, and Stephen Crane's *The Red Badge of Courage*, the prototype of the realistic war novel. It supplied the theme for Margaret Mitchell's *Gone With The Wind*, a book which sold one million copies within six months of publication and which became the basis of a film seen by more than twenty-five million people. Endlessly analyzed, debated, reinterpreted, and refought, it has been more studied than any other episode in history, save possibly the life of Christ. The number of books and articles written about it is said to have exceeded 36,000 – more, that is, than the number of days which have elapsed since Appomattox. And today, more than a century after its close, the Civil War shows no signs of losing its fascination either for the scholar or for the thousands of Civil War buffs for whom it is an all-absorbing hobby.

This inordinate interest in the Civil War has not, however, been matched by a comparable effort to comprehend its significance. All too often it is looked upon merely as an historical pageant, picturesque, dramatic, and romantic, but without any particular point except that it testified to the valour of the opposing armies. Historians, no less than laymen, have tended to concern themselves with the purely military aspects of the struggle, with the details of what happened on each of its many battlefields. But the Civil War was not exclusively a military concern. Though less of a watershed, perhaps, than has sometimes been claimed, it was nevertheless an event of the most profound significance for the whole future of the United States and, indeed, for the world. It settled much that had previously been in doubt and determined in so many areas of national life the lines along which the country would develop.

The Civil War settled firstly that the United States would remain one nation. The ultimate disruption of the Union had been long predicted. Tocqueville, for example, concluded in 1835 that the character of the Union had changed so fundamentally and so rapidly since 1787 that it could not possibly endure. On numerous occasions between

1787 and 1861 the Union had seemed in imminent danger of a break-up. Indeed there was never a time before the Civil War when it was free from the threat that one discontented section or another – the West, New England or the South – would attempt to secede. Finally in 1860–1 eleven states out of a total of thirty-three actually did so and many Europeans took it for granted that unity could never be restored. The secession of the South threw the entire political future of North America into the melting-pot for, had the Southern Confederacy been able to maintain its independence, the remaining states might well have split up into separate groups. But the Civil War ruled out finally the possibility of fragmentation. Sectionalism would remain a vigorous force, to be sure, but never again after 1865 would it endanger the existence of the Union.

The Civil War also wrote finis to the long constitutional debate about the nature of the Union. The Constitution of 1787 had divided sovereignty between the state and federal governments and had thus created two spheres of political authority each acting directly on the individual citizen. But the Founding Fathers had chosen – because they would not have agreed on the answer – to ignore the question of where ultimate sovereignty lay in the event of a clash between the federal government and the states. Their successors – Jefferson and Hamilton, Webster and Calhoun, Lincoln and Jefferson Davis – were forced by events to tackle the question directly and by 1861 Americans had rejected the concept of divided sovereignty and were agreed instead that ultimate power must lie either with the nation collectively or with the states individually. But North and South disagreed in their choice of alternatives and it was this disagreement which was the explicit if not the basic cause of the Civil War. Once the war began, of course, the fine points of constitutional exegesis which had for so long absorbed the political leaders became mere abstractions. It was force of arms rather than force of argument that now counted and when the Union armies re-established the national authority throughout the land they made it clear that sovereignty rested not in the states but in the federal government. In so doing they wrought a constitutional revolution, for the Union that was restored in 1865 was one in which, compared with the Union of 1861, the power of the federal government had been greatly and, as it proved, permanently increased.

The North took up arms in 1861 in order to save the Union and throughout the conflict this remained its principal war aim. The Union symbolized for Northerners the distinctive political philosophy and form of government to which their ancestors had dedicated the United States at the moment of its birth; they felt with Lincoln that on the maintenance of its territorial integrity depended not only the success of the American experiment but the fate of popular government throughout the world. About slavery they felt much less strongly. Yet as time went on the conviction grew that slavery had been the fundamental cause of the war and ought not to survive it. Lincoln hesitated about slavery for eighteen months, chiefly because he could not afford to alienate the border slave states which had remained with the Union, but he finally realized that the war could not be won if he left the South's 'peculiar institution' untouched. The Emancipation Proclamation was a partial and indeed a conditional measure, and did not in practice have much effect in striking the shackles from the slave. But from the moment it was issued slavery could not hope to survive a Northern victory, and although the war was to end with slavery still not completely eradicated, the Thirteenth Amendment was well in train and when ratified a few months later could sweep away the last vestiges of the institution. To be sure, the change was more in the Negro's legal status than in his actual condition for most Americans, even in the North, were not yet prepared to grant him social and political equality. But the war had at least abolished an institution whose existence had been a standing reproach to the United States and which might otherwise have survived for several decades. Moreover the passage of the Fourteenth and Fifteenth Amendments, growing directly out of the post-war situation, meant that the United States had, perhaps uncomprehendingly, entered into a commitment to the concept of racial equality, a concept which it would be the task of a later generation to try to honour. The Civil War thus added a new dimension to the national purpose.

To draw attention to the non-military aspects of the struggle is not of course to deny that the Civil War was a great landmark in the history of warfare. It was one of the most terrible wars of history, an intense, protracted and bloody struggle that cost 1,000,000 casualties, of whom 635,000 were dead. It has moreover the distinction – if such it be – of qualifying as the first truly modern war. It differed from previous conflicts in two ways: in the techniques and weapons used and in being a war of unlimited objectives. It was the first in which the railroad and the telegraph were regularly used in the deployment of troops; it was the first to witness trench warfare on a large scale; it saw the first appearance of breech-loading and repeating rifles, various precursors of the machine-gun, the ironclad warship, and a primitive kind of submarine. But much more important than these purely technical innovations was the fact that the Civil War came to have the unlimited character that marks modern war. Unlike the formalized wars of the eighteenth century, fought with limited means for limited objectives and ending in some kind of accommodation, this was an all-out struggle in the sense that both sides ruled out the possibility of compromise and were unprepared to stop anywhere short of complete victory. This attitude was bound to affect the way the war was fought. Admittedly the contestants continued to observe most of the accepted rules of civilized warfare, particularly as they affected sieges, capitulations, and the treatment of prisoners. But the clear distinction which had hitherto existed between the armed forces and the civilian population tended to become blurred. Union generals did not confine their attentions to the Confederate armed forces; they struck at anything which might contribute to the enemy's ability to wage war. Hence Sherman's march through Georgia, undertaken avowedly with the intention of crippling the state's productive capacity; in burning crops, killing off farm animals, tearing up railway lines and destroying iron foundries and textile mills, Sherman was introducing a new concept of a military objective. So was Sheridan when he raided the Shenandoah Valley with the object of reducing 'the granary of the Confederacy' to such a state that, as Sheridan himself put it, 'a crow flying across it would have to carry his own rations'. In such ruthless acts as these the horrifying shape of modern war can be clearly discerned.

The contestants in the Civil War were by no means equally matched. The North had a great preponderance of potential strength. Its reservoir of manpower was three times greater than that of the South, its transportation system was superior in every respect, and it had overwhelming financial and industrial advantages. But the odds against the Confederacy were not as great as they appeared. Its people were more united than those of the Union and it had the advantage of fighting on the defensive in familiar territory as well as on interior lines. At first, moreover, the South possessed more than its share of the nation's military talent; there was no one on the Union side in 1861 who could compare with Lee and Jackson.

During the first two years of the war, indeed, when the Union was still in process of mobilizing its resources and when Lincoln had yet to find a competent general, the South might well have won its independence by an outright military victory. Even as it was the Confederates won most of the laurels during the first half of the struggle. They repulsed every attempt by Union forces to approach Richmond, the Confederate capital, and in the process inflicted a series of bloody reverses on the attackers, notably at Second Bull Run, Fredericksburg, and Chancellorsville. On two occasions Lee led his troops into the Northern states though both times he was checked, first at Antietam in September 1862 and, more decisively, at Gettysburg in July 1863. Only in the West did the Union armies make much progress. An amphibious Federal force seized New Orleans early in 1862 and when Grant took Vicksburg in July 1863 it gave him control of the Mississippi along its entire length and cut the Confederacy in two. Gettysburg – 'the high tide of the Confederacy' – and Vicksburg were to prove the turning points of the war. But the Confederacy was a long way from defeat and nearly two more years of bitter fighting would be needed to bring her to her knees.

Not that the issue would necessarily be decided upon the battlefields of Virginia and in the swamps of the Mississippi. If Europe decided to take a hand in the struggle the independence of the Confederacy would be assured. At the outset the South had confidently expected that Britain would be forced by her dependence on Southern cotton to intervene to break the Federal blockade. But British manufacturers held large stocks of cotton when the war broke out and King Cotton thus proved less influential than Southerners had hoped. The most that Palmerston and Russell were prepared to contemplate was an offer of mediation if Lee's invasion of Maryland in 1862 resulted in yet another Northern defeat. Since it did not the idea of intervention even in this form was rejected. There were nevertheless two occasions when Britain might have been drawn into the conflict. The first was in November 1861 when a Union warship contravened neutral rights by removing two Confederate diplomats from the British mail steamer *Trent*; the second came in the summer of 1863 when it became increasingly evident that two powerful warships under construction in British yards were intended for the Confederacy. But an American climb-down ended the first crisis and similar action by Britain the second, so that in the event the Confederacy had to depend exclusively upon its own exertions.

To Lincoln a problem no less pressing than the threat of foreign intervention was that of dealing with domestic disaffection. Though the North responded with virtual unanimity to his call to arms in 1861, Lincoln had before long to contend with some of the most virulent criticism ever made of an American president. Criticism was not, however, synonymous with disloyalty and one must distinguish, as contemporaries often did not, between opposition to the war and opposition to particular administration policies. Politics were not suspended in wartime and even when Democrats supported the war effort, as they generally did, they felt free to express their disapproval of certain wartime trends and policies. Many loyal Democrats, especially in the Middle West, were disquieted at the way in which the war was fostering the philosophy of industrialism and increasing the power of the federal government at the expense of that of the states. Even more were outraged by the Emancipation Proclamation; enthusiastic supporters though they might be of the war for the Union, they were less keen – as the draft riots of July 1863 in New York City showed – on a war for Negro freedom.

But even when legitimate political opposition is discounted there remained in the North sizeable numbers of Southern sympathizers, some of whom were engaged in treasonable or subversive activities. Lincoln believed that the civil courts were inadequate to deal with the problem of what would now be called fifth columnists. He therefore repeatedly suspended the privilege of the writ of habeas corpus – at first only in specified areas, later throughout the Union – in the case of persons who discouraged enlistments or engaged in disloyal practices. In all more than 13,000 persons were arrested under martial law and imprisoned for varying periods. These arbitrary acts were denounced by political opponents as tending toward dictatorship and were later held by the Supreme Court to have been unconstitutional. But Lincoln took a broad view of the powers of the president. He believed that in wartime the executive authority can legitimately be extended – this was his justification for the Emancipation Proclamation – and in any case he felt that strict adherence to the Constitution mattered less than the preservation of the Union.

Besides highlighting the difficulty of maintaining civil liberties when their exercise might jeopardize the safety of the state, the Civil War threw further light on another continuing theme in American history, that of the relationship between the civil and the military authorities. In particular it raised such crucial questions as whether there can be any clear dividing line between civil and military affairs, to what extent the civil authorities are justified in intervening in military operations and, conversely, whether there are any circumstances in which soldiers might properly intervene in politics.

In discussing these matters most historians of the Civil War have concluded that political interference in military affairs seriously handicapped the Union war effort. They have cited the appointment of 'political generals' like Butler, Banks, and Sigel, Lincoln's interventions in strategy and tactics and, above all, the malevolent meddling of the Joint Congressional Committee on the Conduct of the War. There was, indeed, much for soldiers to complain about. Few of the 'political generals' possessed military talent or experience, some of Lincoln's military decisions were open to criticism and there is no question but that the Committee on the Conduct of the War often acted unfairly and irresponsibly, besides exceeding its proper authority. Set up ostensibly to investigate an early Union fiasco the Committee spent most of its energies promoting the fortunes of generals with Radical political leanings and, still more, in hounding commanders – especially those with a West Point background and Democratic connections – who were deemed to be prosecuting the war with insufficient vigour.

Yet the politicians too had a case. After all, few 'political generals' could hope for more than a subordinate role; the important commands tended to go to the professionals. In any event there were good reasons for making generals of politicians. There were not enough West Pointers to go round and, in order to secure popular support for the war, it was vital that recognition should not be withheld from political leaders in whom the people had confidence. It was, moreover, unrealistic to complain about political interference in military matters when every military problem – the use of Negro troops, the disposition of escaped slaves who came into Union lines, the treatment of the Border states – had political overtones. As for the Committee on the Conduct of the War, it was not altogether absurd for it to refer to a 'West Point mentality' or to suspect that some at least of the professionals were out of sympathy with the purposes for which the war was coming eventually to be fought. This was particularly true of McClellan, commander of the Army of the Potomac in 1861-2, in whose Civil War career may be found an answer to the claim that professional soldiers were apolitical. McClellan seemed to think that the war could be conducted as a purely military exercise without regard to political realities. He did not conceal the contempt he felt for politicians, especially Republican politicians – not excluding Abraham Lincoln, who happened to be his commander-in-chief. McClellan had moreover very definite views about the political purpose of the war. Like many members of the Democratic party, whose presidential party candidate he was to become in 1864, he wanted the Union restored but slavery left intact. These convictions contributed to his belief that the war could be won without excessive bloodshed and were reflected in his lack of drive which to the Radicals stemmed from sinister motives.

Lincoln did not share the Radicals' suspicions of McClellan's loyalty but he was exasperated by his ponderousness and grew increasingly doubtful of his fitness to lead the Union armies in a war which was assuming the character of a democratic crusade. Hence in the spring of 1862 Lincoln dismissed him from the post of general-in-chief. It was two years before the President found a capable successor in Grant, who had by then emerged as the North's greatest general. Grant was not unaware of his political potential – he was to become the Republican presidential candidate in 1868 – but he was not given to political intrigue and unlike McClellan was prepared to acknowledge that ultimate responsibility for the conduct of the war lay with the President. Lincoln, for his part, was content to allow Grant a free hand.

Under this arrangement the war was slowly brought to a successful end. The Union victory at Chattanooga in November 1863, worthy to be ranked with Gettysburg and Vicksburg, gave the Federal forces control of the Tennessee River line and provided a base from which to split the Confederacy a second time. It opened the way the following year to Sherman's Atlanta campaign and the march to the sea and in the spring of 1865 to his northward advance into the Carolinas. Lee could do nothing about this threat to his rear for he was pinned down in Virginia for nine months by Grant's persistent attacks. The grim Virginia fighting of 1864-5 inflicted terrible losses upon both armies but it was the North, with its superior resources of manpower, which was better able to withstand the pressure. Lee was finally outflanked and on 9 April 1865 the famous surrender scene was enacted at Appomattox Court House.

The Indian Wars

As would be the case after both the World Wars of the twentieth century, the American response to the cessation of hostilities in 1865 was a hasty demobilization. Within a few months of Appomattox four-fifths of the Union army, which had numbered more than a million, had returned to civilian life. And with Congress reverting to traditional fears of a military establishment the regular army was drastically reduced in size until by 1876 it amounted to only 25,000 men. It was this kind of precipitate disbandment of a formidable military force that Sir Denis Brogan had in mind when he remarked that the lesson of American history was that no nation more cheerfully beats swords into ploughshares – though he was careful to add the corollary that no nation beats ploughshares into swords with such speed.

In the absence of danger from without the main task of the United States army after the Civil War – apart from garrisoning the South – was to subdue the Indians whose presence on the Great Plains constituted an obstacle to white settlement. This task, which was to require a quarter of a century of almost continuous warfare, was but a prolongation of the kind of operations on which American soldiers had been almost continuously engaged since the Revolution. As in the colonial period the story of Indian–white relations in the century after 1776 is a shameful one – a dreary record of dishonoured treaties, successive white encroachments upon Indian hunting grounds and the crushing of those tribes which could not be cajoled, bribed or intimidated into relinquishing their ancestral lands.

The process began immediately after the Revolutionary War with the despatch of a number of military expeditions to the Ohio Valley. One of these, led by General Anthony Wayne, brought about the defeat of the Indians at the Battle of Fallen Timbers (1794), a victory which led to the Indian cession of most of the present state of Ohio. A further Indian defeat at Tippecanoe (1811) at the hands of General William Henry Harrison touched off a frontier war which merged with the War of 1812. In that conflict Indian auxiliaries fought on the side of the British – the last occasion, incidentally, on which the red men would be able to ally themselves with a foreign power against the United States. The War of 1812 in fact proved disastrous to the Indians. In the Old Northwest their power was finally destroyed at the Battle of the Thames (5 October 1813) in which the British were badly defeated and Tecumseh, the Shawnee chief and leader of the Indian confederacy, was killed. In the South General Andrew Jackson's victory at the Battle of Horseshoe Bend (27 March 1814) broke the resistance of the Creeks, the only Southern tribe still possessing serious military potential.

By breaking the Indian barrier the War of 1812 gave fresh impetus to the movement of white settlers beyond the Alleghenies. In the next three decades scores of treaties were negotiated, generally with nominal Indian leaders and rump groups, whereby the tribes relinquished the bulk of their holdings east of the Mississippi and consented to their removal westward. Most tribes were too feeble to resist but in the 1830s the removal policy was nevertheless to involve the United States in two minor Indian wars. One was the Black Hawk War of 1832–5, a series of frontier skirmishes precipitated by the return to their traditional lands in Illinois of a group of Sacs and Foxes who had been experiencing famine in Missouri. This was the war in which Abraham Lincoln served briefly in the Illinois militia and in which, as he liked to recall, he made some ferocious charges on the wild onions and engaged in bloody struggles with the mosquitoes. But although the Black Hawk War had its farcical side, it was nevertheless waged as a war of extermination by the whites and ended with the massacre of a group of Indians, including women and children, who were attempting to escape across the Mississippi. Hardly less brutal was the American record in the Seminole War. For seven years United States forces struggled among the Florida swamps and everglades to round up a few hundred refractory Seminoles. The Seminole chieftain, Osceola, was finally captured when American troops violated a flag of truce, but his warriors kept up the fight until they were almost annihilated. By the time military operations were suspended in 1842 and the remaining Seminoles were removed to what was later to become Oklahoma, the United States had suffered hundreds of casualties and had incurred an expenditure of millions of dollars.

This pattern of barbarous and costly warfare was to be repeated on an infinitely larger scale when the frontier crossed the Mississippi and white miners and settlers began to invade the Great Plains. The Plains Indians – nomadic and warlike tribes such as the Sioux, Cheyenne, Arapahoe, Pawnees, Apaches, and Comanches – were perhaps the most formidable foes the white man had encountered in the course of his advance across the continent. Armed with short powerful bows which were admirably adapted to shooting from horseback, these superb horsemen were more than a match for trained cavalrymen equipped with carbines. In the end the superior technology of the whites – the railroad, the telegraph and the Colt revolver – was bound to count for more than the skill, daring and relentlessness of the tribesmen. Yet the conquest of the Plains Indians was brought about just as much by the mass slaughter in the 1870s of the buffalo upon which they had depended for food, shelter, clothing, and fuel. Their way of life destroyed, the Indians had neither the means nor the will to go on resisting the white advance.

In the Indian Wars that raged on the Plains from the 1860s to the 1880s the contestants vied with each other in ruthlessness and savagery. The earliest of these conflicts broke out in 1862 when the eastern Sioux, led by Little Crow, went on the warpath in Minnesota and massacred over 500 settlers before being hunted down by the militia. Retribution was swift, harsh, and indiscriminate. Over 300 Indians were publicly hanged, thirty-eight from a single scaffold. In 1864 there occurred an even greater horror, the Sand Creek Massacre, when a party of Colorado militia under Colonel John M. Chivington butchered several hundred unsuspecting Indians at a Cheyenne encampment. Observers described how the militiamen beat out the brains of children and disembowelled pregnant women. Colonel Chivington, a minister in private life, became a local hero in Denver where he exhibited a collection of scalps between acts at a local theatre. Such savagery was self-perpetuating and in Montana two years later a party of 82 soldiers under Captain W. J. Fetterman was completely wiped out by the Oglala Sioux, led by Red Cloud.

The expulsion of the Indians from their hunting grounds entered its final phase in 1867 when Congress passed a law providing for the removal of all the Plains Indians to two small reservations, one in the Black Hills of South Dakota, the other in Oklahoma. This was the signal for nine years of warfare during which the army, given the task of herding the tribesmen on to the lands assigned to them, had to fight over 200 pitched battles. But if it was difficult to keep the Indians on the reservations, it proved no less of a problem to keep white intruders out of them. Indeed it was an influx of gold-hungry miners into the Black Hills reservation that led to the last serious Indian conflict, the Sioux War of 1876. This was the war which was to become celebrated for 'Custer's Last Stand'. Sent to round up the Sioux who had concentrated in Montana, Colonel George A. Custer, with a scouting party of 264 men, found himself facing a Sioux army ten times as large. Led by Crazy Horse and Sitting Bull this was the largest Indian army ever assembled in the United States. After rashly attacking the Indians Custer's entire command was annihilated at the Battle of the Little Big Horn (25 June 1876). But the Sioux gained little by their victory. Short of food and ammunition they were forced by the end of the year to submit.

West of the Rockies the Nez Percé tribe took to the warpath against invading miners in 1877 and, under their remarkable leader, Chief Joseph, conducted a thousand mile retreat through Oregon, Montana, and Idaho before starvation and disease compelled their surrender. But the last Indians to carry on the fight were the Apaches of the Southwest, whose subjugation required 5000 troops and occupied fifteen years. With the capture in 1886 of the Apache chief, Geronimo, and his handful of followers, organized Indian resistance may be said to have come to an end.

For both white man and red the conclusion of the Indian wars marked the end of a long chapter in American history. For almost three centuries white settlers on the frontier had lived in dread of Indian attack. Wars and rumours of wars had been a constant in their lives and could not but help shape social and political institutions of the frontier. The universality of the Indian menace had, moreover, discouraged frontier particularism and had contributed to a readier acceptance of federal authority. Indian warfare also furthered the political careers of those Westerners – Andrew Jackson and William Henry Harrison were the outstanding examples – who had made reputations as Indian fighters. Finally the frontier personality, with its individualism, its resourcefulness and its streak of brutality, had been the product of a situation in which warfare was endemic.

For the Indians warfare had always been an integral part of their culture. Whether waged against hostile tribes or encroaching whites, and whether or not it was embarked upon for a specific economic objective, war always possessed for the Indian a special intrinsic value. In the primitive warrior society of the Plains Indian, war was at the same time a career, a test of manhood, the source of glory and 'the touchstone of honour and prestige'. Thus when the scalping knife and the tomahawk were finally sheathed a whole system of values and an entire status structure were swept away.

The Spanish–American War

The Spanish–American War of 1898 was the first occasion for more than half a century that the United States had gone to war with a foreign country. She did so in spite of the fact that her vital interests were not at stake and in spite also of Spain's having virtually accepted every American demand before hostilities began. The war was partly the result of the expansionism of the 1890s, of the spirit that made many Americans eager to see their country behave like a great power. But it was equally the product of American crusading idealism. Americans had a natural sympathy with colonial peoples striving to throw off a foreign yoke and from the moment the Cubans revolted against

Spain in 1895 public sentiment in the United States was whole-heartedly on the side of the rebels. American sensibilities were, more-over, outraged by reports of the atrocities committed by the Spaniards in their efforts to suppress the rebellion. These reports, one-sided as they were and grossly exaggerated by the popular press, stimulated a demand for intervention. But McKinley was reluctant to become involved; like his predecessor, Cleveland, he preferred to exert diplo-matic pressure on Spain to make concessions to the rebels. In this pacific attitude he was strongly supported by business interests, con-cerned lest war should imperil the prosperity to which the country was just returning after the depression of 1893. That the war nevertheless came was due to the insistence of a jingoistic public.

McKinley might have been able to resist the popular clamour but for two dramatic incidents, both occurring in February 1898, which whipped up sentiment against Spain to fever pitch. The less important of these was the publication by the Hearst press of an indiscreet letter written by the Spanish Ambassador to Washington, Dupuy De Lôme, in which he made some disparaging remarks about McKinley. More profound was the effect produced by the destruction of the American battleship *Maine*, mysteriously blown up in Havana harbour with the loss of 260 of her crew. Americans universally assumed – though there was no evidence for it – that the Spaniards were to blame and gave themselves over to an emotional outburst typified by the popular slogan: Remember the Maine! To Hell with Spain! McKinley refused to be panicked and for a while longer persisted in his efforts to find a peaceful solution. But he could not withstand the public demand for intervention and, under tremendous pressure from members of his own party, he finally gave way. On 20 April 1898 Congress adopted by huge majorities a joint resolution recognizing the independence of Cuba, and authorizing the President to employ the armed forces to expel the Spaniards from the island. Added to this resolution, and passed unanimously, was the Teller Amendment disclaiming any intention on the part of the United States of annexing Cuba.

The United States was almost wholly unprepared for war – or at least for land operations. The American navy was the sixth-largest in the world and was superior to the Spanish in ships, gunnery, and personnel. But the regular army consisted of only 28,000 men, scat-tered around the country in various military posts and lacking any fighting experience save that of quelling Indian outbreaks. This tiny force was augmented by 200,000 volunteers but the War Department, staffed by elderly bureaucrats, proved itself incapable of mobilizing, training, and equipping them. Bungling and inefficiency were especially marked in the expeditionary force which was assembled at Tampa, Florida for the purpose of liberating Cuba. Staff work was so deficient and transport and supply services so chaotic that it is astonishing that the expedition was able to sail at all. The troops, embarking for a summer campaign in the subtropics, were clad in heavy woollen uniforms; most of them were equipped with obsolete, single-shot Springfield rifles; and all were fed upon atrocious food, the worst of which was the canned meat nicknamed 'embalmed beef'.

Against a more formidable enemy the United States could hardly have avoided military disaster. But in Spain she faced an adversary even more ill-prepared and inefficient than she was herself. The Spaniards, despite having a Cuban garrison of 200,000 and a large navy, proved incapable of offering effective resistance either on land or at sea and after a brief struggle were forced to capitulate.

The first fighting took place in the Far East, when Commodore George Dewey, sailing into Manila Bay on 1 May, destroyed an antiquated Spanish fleet. An American expeditionary force was promptly despatched to the Philippines and, assisted by Filipino insurrectionists, captured Manila on 13 August. Meanwhile in Cuba the fighting had lasted only a month. An American expeditionary force of 17,000 was finally put ashore toward the end of June and, moving toward Santiago, defeated the Spaniards first at El Caney and then at San Juan Hill. In the thick of the fighting was a volunteer cavalry regiment, the Rough Riders, commanded by Colonel Theodore Roosevelt, whom the newspapers made into a war hero. But it was at sea that the decisive blow was struck. Admiral Cervera's fleet, which had been blockaded in Santiago, put to sea to avoid capture on 3 July and within a few hours every vessel had been either sunk or incapacitated by a superior American squadron. The Spanish forces in Cuba surrendered on 16 July, by which time Puerto Rico had also been occupied. On 12 August an armistice was signed.

For the United States the conflict had been, in the words of John Hay, 'a splendid little war'. Lasting only ten weeks it had been an unbroken succession of American victories. These had been won, moreover, at remarkably little cost. Fewer than 400 Americans had been killed in battle or had died of wounds, though over 5000 others had fallen victim to disease, especially yellow fever and typhoid. Hence not only for Hay but for Americans generally the war had been an exhilarating experience. Military victory had also whetted the public appetite for empire. The result was that, between April and August, the war had subtly changed its character. What had begun as a war to free Cuba had become a war to acquire colonies.

Admittedly the United States was precluded by the Teller Amendment from annexing Cuba as it might otherwise have done. But it was not disposed to restore its other conquests to Spain or, indeed, to abandon them to anyone else. Particularly was this so of the Philippine Islands, of which most Americans had hitherto been only dimly aware, but which many were now anxious to keep for strategic or commercial reasons. McKinley, after much hesitation, accepted this point of view and the peace treaty, signed at Paris on 10 December 1898, besides recognizing Cuban independence provided for the cession to the United States of the Philippines, Puerto Rico and the Pacific island of Guam. These acquisitions were, however, strongly opposed by a variety of influential groups. Some did so from selfish or unworthy motives: political partisanship, the fear of commercial competition and racial prejudice against colonial peoples. But most anti-imperialists appealed to idealism and to tradition. They feared that a colonial empire would necessitate large armaments and the abandonment of the traditional American policy of avoiding foreign entanglements. They also claimed that it was both unconstitutional and contrary to the spirit of the Declaration of Independence to govern a foreign territory without the consent of its inhabitants. But after a protracted wrangle in the Senate, the peace treaty was finally ratified.

The predictions of the anti-imperialists were not in fact borne out. Having become a colonial power the United States found herself obliged neither to enter into foreign alliances nor to join in the arms race. Though in the eyes of the world she had become a great power she remained reluctant after the Spanish–American war to play the part to the full. But the hopes of the imperialists turned out to be just as ill-founded. Possession of the Philippines did not give the United States its expected advantage in the competition for Oriental trade. From being a prize the islands came eventually to be regarded – and with good reason as the Second World War showed – simply as a military liability. More immediately the acquisition of dependencies brought the United States a host of constitutional, legal and administrative problems for which her previous territorial experience offered no solution. To these was added a serious military problem when in 1899 the Filipino nationalists under Emilio Aguinaldo rose in rebellion against their erstwhile deliverers. The revolt was to last three years and its suppression would require the efforts of 70,000 American soldiers and the expenditure of $170 million. It was a savage guerilla war and to win it the United States resorted to some of the harsh methods which, when practised earlier in Cuba by Spain, had so shocked American opinion.

Thus in its results the Spanish–American War was not, perhaps, quite as splendid as John Hay had asserted. Having gone blithely to war as a disinterested crusader the United States found herself enmeshed eventually in the very imperialism she had begun by fighting. Even Cuba gained only a nominal independence. Placed under the beneficent and efficient rule of American officials she remained for several years a mere appendage of the United States.

First World War

The wars the United States had waged before 1898 had all been genuine American wars in the sense that they had arisen out of local American issues and had been fought, at least in part, on American soil. The Spanish–American War, in which these conditions did not obtain, was thus clearly a different type of conflict. It was a war which came about basically because the United States began to recognize the need to play a role more commensurate with her position as a great power. Still more was this to be the case in the twentieth century when the increasing assumption of global responsibilities was to lead to American involvement successively in two world wars and in two other major conflicts on the Asiatic mainland.

Yet it was a testimony to the reluctance with which the United States took on these responsibilities that she intervened in the Great War of 1914–18 only after three years of tenacious neutrality. It is true that even at the outset the American people were not neutral 'in thought as well as in action', as President Wilson had somewhat unrealistically asked them to be. The vast majority – even Wilson himself – were sympathetic to Britain and France and wanted to see German militarism defeated. But almost no Americans wanted the United States to intervene and despite friction with Germany that at times brought belligerency very near Wilson could still be re-elected in November 1916 as the man 'who kept us out of war'.

Why the United States nevertheless declared war on Germany only four months later is something that has been variously explained. In the 1930s, when disillusionment with the First World War was at its height and isolationism was rampant, it became fashionable to argue that America had been deluded into entering the war by the distortions of British propaganda and the machinations of American bankers and munitions makers who had a financial stake in an Allied victory. But neither British propaganda nor business pressure (if there was any) played a decisive part. American intervention was rather the result of German U-boat warfare and of Wilson's reaction to it.

From the moment it was adopted in February 1915 the German submarine campaign was condemned by Americans as a barbarous method of warfare. The issue was dramatized the following May by the sinking of the British liner *Lusitania*, with the loss of 128 American lives. Despite the indignation this aroused in the United States Wilson had no thought of going to war. 'There is such a thing', he declared, 'as a man being too proud to fight.' But in the ensuing controversy with Germany he took a stand which deprived the United States of full freedom of action and made war more likely in future. Wilson held that an American citizen who travelled into a war zone on a belligerent ship, even an armed ship carrying munitions, was simply exercising a traditional right; he remained, moreover, under the protection of the United States government. This interpretation of international law has struck some historians as highly questionable but Wilson insisted upon it and, by threatening to break off diplomatic relations after the French steamer *Sussex* was torpedoed in March 1916, he compelled the Germans to modify their submarine methods.

Wilson then made strenuous efforts to mediate but by the beginning of 1917 his hopes for a 'peace without victory' had foundered upon the intransigence of the belligerents. In any case the German military and naval leaders now decided upon a desperate throw. Fully realizing that the step would inevitably bring America into the war, but believing that Britain could be starved into submission before America could make her weight felt, they decided as from 1 February to institute unconditional submarine warfare against all vessels, neutral as well as belligerent. Wilson, though reluctant to lead the American people into war, was bound by his previous policy to defend what he believed to be American rights on the high seas. Thus on 2 April, after several American ships had been torpedoed, he felt obliged to go before Congress to ask for a declaration of war. Four days later both Houses had passed the war resolution by overwhelming majorities.

Wilson's war message attempted to place the conflict upon a loftier plane than that of mere self-interest. It was to be a war for righteousness, a moral crusade. Its aim would be not merely to defeat Germany but to create a new world order. The United States would fight for 'freedom and justice and self-government amongst all the nations of the world' and for 'a universal dominion of right by such a concert of free peoples as shall bring peace and safety to all nations'. The expression of these idealistic war aims, reflecting as they did the American sense of mission, helped give unity and a sense of purpose to a nation which was still hazy as to objects of American entry. But there was danger in Wilson's rhetoric. By raising impossible hopes of what the war could achieve he sowed the seeds of that disillusionment that was swiftly to follow victory.

The United States entered the war at a critical time for the Allies. The German submarine campaign looked like achieving its object; Allied shipping losses in April 1917 amounted to 881,000 tons and Britain had only six weeks' supply of food. On land, too, things were going badly. The French army, exhausted by its heroic defence of Verdun, was incapable of offensive action; defeatism was rife and ten divisions had mutinied. In Russia revolution had broken out and the Russian armies were disintegrating. The Bolsheviks who came to power in November 1917 at once made a separate peace that enabled the Germans to transfer huge masses of men and equipment to the Western Front. A little earlier Italy had nearly been knocked out of the war when her armies were over-run at Caporetto.

The United States Navy at once made a contribution to the Allied cause by sending a number of destroyers to Ireland to aid in anti-submarine patrols. It was the assistance he received from Admiral Sims of the United States Navy that enabled Lloyd George in the summer of 1917 finally to overcome Admiralty resistance to the adoption of a convoy system which dramatically reduced the number of sinkings. The Americans also took the initiative in laying a huge mine barrage that eventually closed the North Sea to German submarines.

But the Americans were in no position to offer immediate help in the land fighting. Despite the 'preparedness' campaign of 1916 few steps had been taken, by the time the United States became a belligerent, towards raising an army capable of influencing the European war. The first units of the American Expeditionary Force landed in France in June 1917 but almost another year was to elapse before there were enough doughboys on the Western Front to have any military significance, except in so far as their presence boosted Allied morale. By March 1918 there were 300,000 American soldiers in France and by

Armistice Day more than two million. It was a great achievement to have raised and equipped an army of this size and to have transported it across the Atlantic almost without loss. Nevertheless the American military contribution was a relatively limited one. In June 1918, American troops assigned to repulse a menacing German thrust at Paris hurled the enemy back across the Marne at Château-Thierry and Belleau Wood. But these were comparatively small engagements and it was not until September 1918 that Pershing was strong enough to launch a major offensive. The Meuse-Argonne battle, which engaged 1,200,000 American troops for 47 days, was one of the most bitterly fought in American military history. Producing some notable American successes it was nevertheless only part of the general Allied offensive that brought the war to an end.

In the course of the conflict the United States lost 112,000 men to enemy action and disease. These were considerable losses but they were smaller in number than the British had lost in a single battle. In all, the French lost 1,385,000 dead and the British over 900,000. Small wonder, then, that in later years the Allies would find it difficult to accept the American claim to have 'won the war'. Yet it is hardly possible to deny that American intervention had been the decisive factor in the Allied victory. However limited their military role, American troops afforded the Allies the margin of victory. In April 1918 the Germans enjoyed a superiority on the Western Front of over 300,000. But by November American troops had given the Allies a preponderance of 600,000. Added to this was the immense psychological effect of American entry; the arrival of seemingly endless numbers of fresh American troops heartened the Allies and convinced the Germans that they could not win.

The First World War required an unprecedented national effort from the United States; the entire economy had to be mobilized to back up the armies in the field. At first, however, the conversion of American industry to war production was characterized by waste and confusion and there were some spectacular failures. Ambitious programmes for the manufacture of war material developed so slowly as to have no effect on the war. American artillery units on the Western Front had to rely largely on French 75 mm field guns and most of the planes flown by American aviators were British Sopwiths and De Havillands or French Spads, Bréguets, and Nieuports. A huge ship-building programme was a costly fiasco; the largest government shipyard at Hog Island, near Philadelphia, completed its first vessel only after the armistice. But a new era opened in March 1918 when Wilson reorganized the War Industries Board, established earlier to coordinate industrial production. The WIB was now given sweeping powers over the allocation of raw materials and under its new chairman, Bernard Baruch, production expanded and industrial mobilization was brought to a high pitch of efficiency.

Federal agencies came, indeed, to regulate every section of the economy. The Food Administration, headed by Herbert Hoover, achieved great success in increasing food production, cutting out waste and pegging prices. The Fuel Administration, under Harry A. Garfield, rationed coal and oil supplies and introduced daylight saving time on a national basis. The National War Labor Board averted strikes and guaranteed collective bargaining and the closed shop. The Railroad Administration, brought into being early in 1918 when the American railway system was about to collapse under the strain of increased traffic, ran the railroads as a single system.

The war saw, in short, the first large-scale government control of the economy. Yet the introduction of a form of war socialism did not mean the eclipse of big business. On the contrary, since the expansion of war production was now the overriding aim, the Administration encouraged the growth of those large-scale, amalgamated industries which alone could supply the needs of modern war. This was a striking reversal of peace-time policies, which had aimed at breaking up the trusts and encouraging the small entrepreneur. And besides accelerating the trend towards mergers and oligopoly the wartime experience of government business cooperation had one further consequence. By adding something new to the American political tradition it provided a model for New Dealers to follow when another major crisis made it necessary to mobilize the economy in the national interest.

Wilson's administration attempted also to mobilize public opinion. It set up a Committee on Public Information under George Creel to stimulate patriotism and unite the nation behind the war effort. In pursuing these ends, however, Creel's committee and other propaganda agencies were guilty of excess. By appealing to fear and hatred they whipped up an unreasoning hostility to Germany and to any at home who might be thought to be sympathetic with her. The result was the growth of an intolerant nationalism, later to be known as 100 per cent Americanism. Popular hatred of the Germans took a variety of forms, some of them absurd: school boards banned the teaching of the

German language, Beethoven's music could not be played in Boston and sauerkraut was re-named 'liberty cabbage'. More serious was popular insistence upon the suppression of any form of dissent. Pacifists, radicals, and anyone else whose enthusiasm for the war seemed in doubt were subjected to ridicule, abuse and in many cases physical attack.

It was because he had feared the growth of such a coercive spirit that Wilson had been reluctant to lead the American people into war. But he did little to keep the superpatriots in check. Indeed he gave official sanction to their conduct by approving not only the Espionage Act of June 1917, which imposed heavy penalties for treason and sedition, but also the Sedition Act of May 1918, which went so far as to set similar penalties for anyone who attempted to discourage the sale of war bonds or who uttered or published 'any disloyal, profane, scurrilous language' about the government, the Constitution or the uniform of the army and navy. Under laws which made the mere expression of opinion a crime a number of newspapers were suppressed and more than 1500 persons imprisoned, among them Eugene V. Debs, the socialist leader, who got ten years for making an anti-war speech. Unity on the home front was thus purchased at a heavy cost to civil liberties. Yet such was the prevailing atmosphere that few Americans seemed disposed to question the way an idealistic president was conducting a war for freedom and democracy.

Second World War

The American role in the Second World War was very different from what it had been in the First. The United States had intervened in the earlier conflict only when it was more than half over and her military contribution was concentrated into its last few months. Her involvement in the Second World War came at a much earlier stage; she was fully engaged from the moment she entered it and she was a major belligerent for four of the war's six years. The Second World War was in fact the greatest war Americans have ever fought. It was not the longest American war: the Revolutionary War, the Civil War, and Vietnam were all longer. Nor, in terms of human life, was it the costliest: the number of American dead and missing, 319,000, fell short of the total killed in the Civil War. But the Second World War was unprecedented in its geographical extent and required an unparalleled national effort. In a truly global struggle the United States had simultaneously to conduct large-scale military and naval operations in two widely separated theatres, each of them thousands of miles from home. It was a tremendous task and it necessitated the mobilization of over 15 million men, four times as many as in the First World War, and the spending of a sum roughly twice as large as all previous federal expenditures from 1789 to 1941.

The military outlook when the United States was pitchforked into war on 7 December 1941 was gloomier even than that of 1917. Disaster threatened on every front. In Russia German armies were close to Moscow and were menacing the Caucasian oilfields. In North Africa the Suez Canal seemed about to fall into Rommel's hands. On the Atlantic U-boats were taking a heavy toll of Allied shipping. And in the Far East the Japanese, having crippled American naval power by the attack on Pearl Harbor, were poised to overrun the Philippines, Malaya, and the Dutch East Indies.

The first necessity was to stem the tide of Japanese conquest and restore the balance of power in the Pacific. These objects having been achieved by June 1942, through the naval victories at the battles of the Coral Sea and of Midway, Roosevelt and his advisers were free to develop the grand strategy jointly agreed upon with Britain. This involved giving precedence, at least on the military side, to the war against Germany. The decision was criticized in the United States by those who wanted prompt and stern retribution against Japan, but the assumption that Germany was the more dangerous enemy was borne out by events. Had the Germans been given longer to perfect their secret weapons they might have won the war.

During the First World War the United States had remained somewhat aloof from the Allies even after becoming a belligerent; she fought as an 'Associated Power' and in the end concluded a separate peace with Germany. In the Second World War, however, she took the lead in forging the Grand Alliance. On New Year's Day 1942, representatives of the twenty-six nations at war with the Axis met in the White House to sign the Declaration of the United Nations. The signatory powers reaffirmed the principles of the Atlantic Charter, pledged their full resources to the prosecution of the war and promised one another not to make a separate peace.

In practice the Grand Alliance consisted of an intimate collaboration between the United States and Britain, and more particularly between Roosevelt and Churchill. For the most part the two countries worked together in remarkable harmony but there were fundamental disagreements over strategic planning for the war in Europe. From the outset the Americans favoured an attack across the English Channel, the most direct and, as they believed, the most speedy method of ending the war. But Churchill, remembering the dreadful losses incurred in frontal attacks during the First World War, preferred a flanking approach. The Americans at first deferred to him with the result that the first American land operations in the war against Hitler were those undertaken jointly with the British in North Africa, Sicily, and the Italian mainland. But as the United States grew in military strength hers became the dominant voice in determining strategy. After the Italian surrender in 1943 Churchill wanted to concentrate on the Italian front and on the Balkans, but the Americans were able to insist upon transferring the main weight of the Allied efforts to a cross-Channel invasion of France, duly undertaken in June 1944.

Churchill's Mediterranean and Balkan schemes are open to serious criticism: the 'soft underbelly of the Axis', about which he frequently spoke, had no real existence. But at least they had the virtue of taking into account the political implications of strategy, one of their aims being to check Soviet expansion by beating the Russians to Vienna. Similar considerations led Churchill, in the last weeks of the war, to urge Eisenhower to make every effort to seize Berlin and Prague. But neither Roosevelt nor his generals was disposed to listen. It was not merely that they did not share Churchill's deep suspicion of the Russians. It was that they had neither sympathy with nor understanding of the elder Moltke's definition of war as 'the continuation of policy by other means'. Thus in their anxiety to bring hostilities to an end as quickly as possible they remained relatively indifferent to postwar political considerations. Military victory, apparently, would be sufficient to solve all problems.

By contrast with the war in Europe, that in the Pacific was from the start preponderantly an American affair. Though the policy of defeating Germany first had limited the resources available for the Pacific war, the Americans were nevertheless strong enough by the autumn of 1942 to take the initiative. Their first step was to remove the threat to Australia posed by the Japanese presence in the Solomons. Once Guadalcanal was captured in February 1943, the way was open for two separate offensives into the heart of the Japanese empire. One, under General Douglas MacArthur, aimed first at clearing New Guinea and then the Philippines. The other, under Admiral Chester W. Nimitz, took the form of an island-hopping campaign designed to drive a path through the Central Pacific to the Japanese home islands.

By the time the European war ended these objectives had been substantially accomplished and the Japanese navy and air force all but destroyed. But the Japanese had conducted a fanatical defence and each American success, from Tarawa and Kwajalein to Iwo Jima and Okinawa, had been won at immense cost. Such was the scale of the slaughter on these tiny islands and atolls that military experts anticipated in the summer of 1945 that the invasion of Japan, then about to be attempted, would entail another year of fighting and a million additional American casualties. It was in these circumstances that Truman, who had succeeded to the presidency on Roosevelt's death, took the decision to employ the atomic bomb against Japan. The terrible display of force which brought the war to an end announced the opening of a new era in which the very existence of the human race would be in question. Yet, mixed blessing though it was, the perfection of the atomic bomb was nevertheless a great triumph for American science and technology. Once the first controlled chain reaction had been produced – at the University of Chicago on 2 December 1942 – the project was pushed forward with incredible speed until, on 12 July 1945, a test bomb was successfully detonated in the New Mexico desert.

Hardly less impressive were the achievements of American industry. The expansion of industrial production amounted to nothing less than an economic miracle. Between 1939 and 1945 manufacturing output almost doubled. While maintaining a flow of goods that sustained a high standard of living at home, American factories produced prodigious quantities of war materials: 100,000 tanks, 274,000 military aircraft, 41 million rounds of ammunition, and 55 million tons of merchant shipping – a tonnage equal to two-thirds of the entire Allied merchant marine. Hence the United States was able not only to supply its own armed forces with all that was needed for victory but also to send huge quantities of war material to the British and the Russians.

These superb results were not achieved without difficulty. The Administration's earliest attempts at economic mobilization were ill-conceived and the result was confusion and chaos. The succession of overlapping agencies set up by Roosevelt before Pearl Harbor lacked the power to plan effectively. Nor was the problem solved by the establishment of the War Production Board in January 1942. Only after the creation of the Office of War Mobilization in May 1943 did machinery exist capable of exercising centralized and comprehensive control and coordinating the entire war effort. By the end of the war, indeed, government control over the economy had been carried to unprecedented lengths. Materials and manpower were alike subject to priorities and were allocated among the different sections of the economy in accordance with the needs of war. A War Labor Board regulated labour relations and prescribed wage levels. Rents and food prices were controlled and in addition such commodities as meat, fats, petrol, fuel oil, shoes, and sugar were rationed.

Not the least important consequence of wartime economic expansion was that the unemployment problem, which had defeated the best efforts of the New Deal, was at last solved. Unemployment, which as late as 1940 had stood at 8 million, virtually disappeared after Pearl Harbor and a labour shortage developed which greatly increased the bargaining power of the workers. With the increase in the workforce trade unions increased their membership from 8·9 million in 1940 to 14·8 million in 1945. Partly through strikes and partly because the government, anxious to avoid work stoppages, encouraged acceptance of their demands the unions gained in strength as well as in size. Though they had to be content with a compromise on the thorny question of the closed shop the unions were able to secure considerable wage increases; by the end of the war real wages had risen 50 per cent.

Never were Americans more determined or more united in taking up arms than in the Second World War. Pearl Harbor brought to an immediate end the bitter debates over foreign policy that had so long divided internationalists from isolationists: all were now resolved to win the war the Japanese had begun. Also, in 1941 Americans went to war in a less emotional frame of mind than they had done in 1917. They saw it not as a crusade for righteousness but as a struggle for survival. This soberer, more realistic attitude ensured that there was little of the intolerance, the hate-filled vigilantism of the First World War. There was little overt hostility toward the 100,000 conscientious objectors or the far more numerous enemy aliens from Germany and Italy. But there was one shocking exception to the general moderation, namely, the treatment of the West Coast Japanese. Early in 1942, because of a widespread but unjustified fear that they might be disloyal, Roosevelt ordered the army to remove 112,000 persons of Japanese ancestry, 71,000 of them American citizens, from the Pacific coast to internment camps in the interior. By upholding this action in 1944 the Supreme Court dealt a further blow to civil liberties.

Another melancholy consequence of the war was a worsening of race relations. During the First World War there had been clashes in the South between Negro soldiers and white civilians and a number of race riots in Northern cities, the worst being that at East St Louis, Illinois in July 1917. During the Second World War the increase in racial tension followed a similar pattern. The presence in the South of nearly 1,000,000 Negroes in uniform led to an intensification of prejudice. In the North the sudden arrival of 1,000,000 job-seeking Southern Negroes aroused the animosity of white workers, leading to minor clashes in a number of cities and large-scale rioting in Detroit in June 1943, which cost the lives of 25 Negroes and 9 whites. Nevertheless the war brought considerable economic gains for Negroes. Employers were at first reluctant to give them jobs but a turning point came on 25 June 1941 when, to avert a threatened march of 50,000 Negroes on Washington, Roosevelt issued his celebrated Executive Order No. 8802 forbidding racial discrimination on all defence projects and creating a Fair Employment Practices Committee to enforce the ruling. The Fair Employment Practices Committee lacked real enforcement powers but it nevertheless performed a great service in widening employment opportunities for Negroes.

The Second World War altered American social patterns in a variety of other ways. It made an already mobile population more mobile still; the lure of war work uprooted millions of people, transferring them alike to Northern cities and to the Pacific coast. It produced a trend towards earlier marriages and, perhaps in consequence, a great acceleration of the divorce rate. It led to larger families and thus to a population increase in the 1940s more than twice that of the previous decade. The war gave a stimulus to education and a boost to cinema attendance; it led also to a revival of interest in religion.

Yet these results, important as they were, were less momentous perhaps than the change brought about in the attitude of the American people to the outside world. The Second World War precipitated the United States into a position of world leadership and destroyed the illusion that she could live in isolation from the rest of the world. After the First World War she had refused to join the League of Nations and had turned her back on Europe. But in 1945, when she signed the new United Nations Charter, she demonstrated that she no longer sought to avoid the role of an active world power.

The Korean War

The Korean War marked the point at which the cold war turned hot. In Europe American economic and military assistance had sufficed to hold back Communism. But in order to check Communist aggression in Asia the United States found it necessary to lead what was known as the free world into war. Technically it was a United Nations war. On 27 June 1950, three days after North Korean armoured divisions had attacked across the 38th parallel, the Security Council passed an American resolution calling upon members of the United Nations to furnish such assistance to the Republic of Korea as was necessary to repel the invaders. Sixteen nations responded and their troops fought alongside those of South Korea under the blue United Nations flag.

Yet it was essentially an American war. American generals held all the chief commands. The United States supplied 48 per cent of the United Nations ground forces – 43 per cent were South Korean – and virtually all the air and sea power. Moreover, the Korean War had greater consequences for the United States than for any other belligerent, save only South Korea itself. It turned out to be much more than the brief 'police action' that most Americans had at first contemplated. It was a bitter, long-drawn-out conflict which at one point threatened to develop into the Third World War. By the time it was over the United States had lost 54,000 dead and more than 100,000 wounded. In addition, the Korean War placed great psychological strains upon the American people. Brought face to face with the realities of world leadership they became divided, confused, and frustrated.

The North Koreans seemed likely at first to overrun the entire peninsula before American power could be deployed. But by September 1950 the front had been stabilized and MacArthur had opened a brilliant counter-offensive which in a few weeks cleared South Korea of the invaders. Although this meant that the purpose of the original 'police action' had been achieved MacArthur, with the approval of the Truman Administration and the United Nations General Assembly, advanced north beyond the 38th parallel with a new objective in mind, the unification of Korea. But at the end of November, as MacArthur's troops drove towards the Yalu River separating Korea and Manchuria, the Chinese Communists intervened on a large scale and the triumphant advance became a headlong retreat. Only narrowly did the United Nations force escape complete disaster. But by January 1951, having fallen back into South Korea, they had reformed their lines and the war changed into an apparently endless process of attrition.

At this point the behaviour of General MacArthur provoked a major crisis in American civil–military relations. MacArthur was an imperious and flamboyant personality who, during the years in which he had run the military occupation of Japan, had learned to act independently of Washington. From the start of the Korean War his relations with Truman had been strained because of the General's habit of issuing public statements which were at variance with official policy. By the beginning of 1951 it had become clear that the two men were in fundamental disagreement about the conduct and purpose of the war. Truman was determined to wage a limited war for limited objectives. He was not prepared to embark upon a general conflict in the Far East. He believed that in the struggle with Communism Europe was more important than Asia. An all-out war with China, besides being enormously costly, would require the transfer of all available American forces to the Far East and would thus invite a Russian attack on western Europe. The Joint Chiefs of Staff agreed with him. A showdown with the Chinese, said General Omar N. Bradley later, would involve the United States in 'the wrong war, at the wrong place, at the wrong time, and with the wrong enemy'.

But MacArthur had never been very interested in Europe, nor for that matter in limited wars. He tended to ignore the larger political implications of the war and declared: 'There is no substitute for victory.' To achieve victory he was prepared to blockade China, bomb the Manchurian bases, and unleash Chiang Kai-shek from Formosa against the Chinese mainland. On learning that the President was about to try for a negotiated peace MacArthur did his best to wreck it, and, not content with that, attempted to arouse Congress and the public against Truman by writing a letter to a Republican congressman arguing the case for an all-out war on Communism in the Far East. This was an open challenge to the President's foreign policy, as well as to the cherished constitutional principle that the military power is subordinate to the civil. For this he was abruptly relieved of his command by Truman on 11 April 1951.

MacArthur's dismissal brought down a storm of protest around the President's head. Public opinion had at first supported Truman's decision to intervene in Korea but, as the war wore on and became an inconclusive, seemingly endless struggle, the mood changed. Americans were unaccustomed to the experience of fighting a war in which complete victory was unattainable. The national experience and the national character alike ran counter to the concept of a limited war. There was thus a growing sense of frustration and a readiness to believe that there was a quick and easy way of ending the conflict. MacArthur's strategy had, therefore, a tremendous popular appeal; instead of the long, costly, and apparently futile war the President was waging the General seemed to offer victory. Hence MacArthur returned home to a tumultuous reception which reached its climax when he was invited to address a joint session of Congress. He made a melodramatic and emotional speech vindicating his conduct, harshly indicting the Administration and calling for stern action against China.

Despite his Roman triumph MacArthur soon faded away. In the debate on foreign policy that followed his dismissal Republican leaders remained critical of the Administration's Far Eastern policies and Truman's handling of the war. But they soon withdrew their support for MacArthur's strategy, thus tacitly accepting the fundamental soundness of Truman's position. The American people also, having apparently lost their heads for a while, came eventually to accept that a limited war was the only kind possible in a situation in which the United States had lost the atomic monopoly she had enjoyed until 1949. But the intensity of feeling engendered by the MacArthur affair showed how deeply their morale and self-confidence had been shaken by the Korean War. A further result of the war was to add to the effectiveness of the campaign being waged by Senator Joseph R. McCarthy against subversion at home. McCarthy's wild allegations about the extent of Communist infiltration into the State Department were more readily believed when the Administration insisted upon fighting a limited war against Communist aggression.

The Korean War was an important issue in the 1952 presidential campaign. With the inconclusive war still in progress and the truce talks begun in June 1951 having been suspended, war-weariness had become widespread. Thus when General Eisenhower promised during the campaign to go to Korea in an attempt to bring the war to an early and honourable end he added to his already great appeal. But his Korean visit produced no immediate results and it was not until July 1953 that the Communists finally agreed to an armistice. It was not a peace settlement but an uneasy truce. Korea had not been unified but the original aim of the war, to repulse aggression, had been achieved. The policy of containment had proved far more expensive than anyone had anticipated, but its authors could at least claim that it had worked.

Vietnam

The war in Vietnam is at first glance a replica of that in Korea. Once again the United States came to the aid of a free – or at all events non-Communist – republic menaced by the spread of Communism; once again American forces became involved in a costly and seemingly endless war on the Asian mainland. Yet there were significant differences between Vietnam and Korea. There was no overt act of aggression against South Vietnam such as had led the United States into the Korean War. To be sure the North Vietnamese gave substantial aid to the Vietcong rebels; but they did so more or less surreptitiously and the most palpable threat to the South Vietnamese government was an indigenous one, arising from Vietcong guerrilla activity. In these circumstances American military power was blunted. It would prove infinitely more difficult to suppress guerrilla activity than to wage a conventional war. Because of the confused character of the struggle, moreover, neither the United Nations nor most of America's allies could be persuaded that this was another case for collective action. Unlike Korea, this was not a United Nations war; except for Australia, South Korea, and Thailand, which sent token contingents, no other country but the United States sent troops to help the South Vietnamese.

American intervention in Vietnam developed only slowly. A basis for intervention was laid in 1954 when the United States took the lead in establishing the South East Asia Treaty Organization (SEATO), which guaranteed the security not only of member nations, but also of Laos, Cambodia, and South Vietnam. In consequence of this commitment, and in an effort to prop up a series of pro-Western governments in Saigon, the United States sent large-scale military and economic aid to South Vietnam. But the successive Saigon regimes were unable either to win popular support or to prevent the Vietcong from seizing control of large parts of the country. American leaders had misgivings about direct military involvement but, as the Vietnam situation deteriorated, they were unable to avoid being drawn in. The 'domino theory', which held that the fall of South Vietnam would bring down other Southeast Asian countries, so impressed President Kennedy that he increased the number of American military 'advisers' in South Vietnam from a few hundred to over 15,000. But it was during the administration of his successor, Lyndon B. Johnson, that there occurred the episode which was to lead to the large-scale escalation of the war.

An alleged attack on American warships in August 1964 by North Vietnamese torpedo-boats in the Gulf of Tonkin led to the passage of a resolution by Congress authorizing the President to 'take all necessary measures' to protect American forces and 'prevent further aggression in Southeast Asia'.

This was not a declaration of war but it gave President Johnson virtually unlimited power to wage one. American military 'advisers' had already become combatants and had suffered serious casualties. Now came a massive build-up of troops and an intensification of the air war. By the end of 1965 there were 180,000 American troops in Vietnam, a year later 350,000, and by the end of 1967 nearly half a million – a larger number, that is, than had been engaged at the peak of the Korean War. At the same time bombing attacks on North Vietnam were stepped up to the point at which the tonnage of bombs dropped by American planes exceeded that in Europe during the Second World War.

Yet this tremendous military effort did not bring the war to an end. Although by the end of 1968 the United States had lost over 30,000 dead and had sustained 200,000 other casualties, it had failed to crush Vietcong resistance. Indeed, during the Tet offensive earlier in that year the Vietcong had been able to menace every major city in South Vietnam and were dislodged only after bitter fighting.

The Tet offensive of 1968 had important domestic repercussions. It invalidated the Johnson Administration's claim that the Americans were gaining the upper hand and it brought to a head the long-developing criticism of the war. Feeling against the war owed a great deal to the way in which the news media brought its horrors home to the public. Television in particular showed Americans what was being done in Vietnam in their name – the bombing attacks, the napalm raids, the destruction of villages, the killing of civilians. This daily catalogue of destruction and cruelty produced a chorus of condemnation from liberal opinion generally and from the universities in particular. By the spring of 1968 the war had become so unpopular as to persuade Johnson to change course. On 31 March he announced both the first steps in the de-escalation of the war and his own decision not to accept renomination for another term.

The Vietnam War not only brought Johnson's political career to a premature and sorry end: it became the dominant issue in the presidential election campaign of 1968 and created such divisions in the Democratic party as to bring about its defeat. Yet though the war was unpopular most Americans were not in favour of the unconditional withdrawal from Vietnam demanded by the anti-war protestors at home and by the Vietcong and the North Vietnamese. A growing majority wanted an end to American involvement in the war but were not prepared to accept a humiliating defeat. They therefore supported President Nixon's policy of 'Vietnamization' – that is, the assumption by the South Vietnamese of an increasing share of responsibility for their own defence – and his attempts to obtain a negotiated peace. But over four years elapsed before the peace talks begun in Paris in May 1968 produced an outcome which was satisfactory to the United States. While negotiations dragged on Nixon went steadily ahead with the programme of troop withdrawals, and in that way ultimately sapped the strength of the anti-war movement at home. But protests continued to be heard at the intensification of the air war that accompanied the withdrawal of American ground forces, and still more at the successive acts of selective escalation with which Nixon punctuated the policy of disengagement – the attack on Communist sanctuaries in Cambodia in the spring of 1970, the mining of North Vietnamese harbours in May 1972 and the massive bombing attacks on Hanoi and Haiphong the following December.

Whether these actions influenced the peace negotiations is disputed, but at all events a cease-fire was agreed to in January 1973. The cease-fire agreement could hardly be portrayed as an American victory. It provided for the withdrawal of all remaining American forces and for the exchange of prisoners of war, but it did not insist upon a corresponding withdrawal of North Vietnamese forces from the areas under Communist control south of the 17th parallel. Nor did the agreement settle the political future of South Vietnam; indeed, it surrounded the question with ambiguity and did not even try to define the cease-fire line in the South. It was in fact a fragile settlement which held out little promise of a lasting peace in Indo-China. But if the United States did not win the war, it could reasonably claim not to have lost it. American intervention had thwarted the Communist attempt to achieve the reunification of Vietnam by force and, at least at the moment of American withdrawal, a reasonably stable non-Communist regime existed in Saigon. This limited and possibly short-lived success may not have amounted to 'peace with honour', as President Nixon claimed it did, but it was the most that Americans could hope for from a war they had proved unable to win and which had taught them a bitter lesson about the limits of power. After thirteen years of overt American intervention, involving 46,000 American deaths and the expenditure of $130,000,000, the greatest military power in the world conceded its inability to defeat an army of Asian peasants.

The Significance of American Wars

In any comprehensive assessment of the significance of American wars it is important to bear certain limits in mind. Firstly, though the United States has gone to war many times she has become a battlefield much less frequently. The only wars fought on her soil, apart from Indian wars, have been the Revolutionary War, the War of 1812, and the Civil War. With these exceptions war has tended for Americans to be a more or less remote affair, conducted hundreds or even thousands of miles away. Since the War of 1812 the United States has not had to repel a foreign invasion or withstand a foreign blockade. Moreover she is almost unique among twentieth-century belligerents in never having been bombed from the air. What this extraordinary immunity implies is that for Americans war has not been the scourge and the horror it has been for other peoples – the Russians, the French, the Japanese, or even the British. Indeed, apart from the tiny bands of frontiersmen who were the object of several generations of Indian attack, and the Southerners of the Civil War period who saw their land fought over for four bloody years, the American civilian population has never had much direct contact with war.

Secondly, even the armed forces of the United States have been relatively fortunate in their experience of war. The Civil War was the only one in American history to exact a really heavy price in lives. Even in the two world wars American losses were relatively low. In the First World War the number of American deaths from battle and disease was only 112,000 – a mere fraction of the losses of the other belligerents and a figure greatly exceeded by the civilian deaths in the United States during the great influenza epidemic of 1918–19. Then again, in the course of the greatest war in history, the Second World War, in which there was a total of 14 million battle deaths, American losses amounted to only 319,000 – about the same number as were killed on America's roads during the 1940s. From a demographic point of view, therefore, America's wars have not had a substantial impact. Their chief effect on population has been to check the flow of immigration.

The much-debated question of whether wars stimulate or retard economic progress is not easily answered by reference to the American experience. The effects of particular wars upon the American economy are not entirely clear and in some cases are still in dispute. Thus though the War of 1812 is commonly said to have encouraged the growth of American manufacturing, that growth might more accurately be attributed to the embargo which preceded the conflict and the tariff duties imposed soon after it. Then again controversy surrounds the question of whether or not the Civil War accelerated industrialization. The accepted view until recently was that it did, but statistical evidence has been adduced to suggest a lower rate of industrial growth during the Civil War decade than in the decades before and after. Those industries producing goods needed by the war effort were certainly stimulated by the Civil War but the war production boom was largely offset by the decline in the production of civilian goods and overall manufacturing development may even have been held back. But whatever the short-term effects may have been it is still probably true that in the long run the war speeded American industrial development, especially by extending the factory system and mass production techniques.

The economic effects of American participation in the First World War were comparatively slight. Certainly the outbreak of war in Europe gave a great stimulus to American industrial activity. In 1914 the United States was on the verge of a business depression, but Allied orders for armaments and other war materials brought a return to prosperity. The European war revived established industries, notably coal and petroleum, and created new ones such as chemicals. Yet the great increase in production that marked the war years had already been accomplished by the time the United States became a belligerent; there was no appreciable expansion thereafter.

During the Second World War on the other hand the American economy made great strides. Enormous quantities of war materials were produced but, even at their peak, war needs took only about a third of American production. Though the manufacture of automobiles and electrical appliances was halved, the production of most other civilian goods continued or even increased and the gross national product rose by 70 per cent between 1939 and 1944. Moreover, the Second World War was the first to contribute to American technological progress; it saw the appearance of radar, the development of antibiotics, and, most significantly of all, the harnessing of atomic energy.

Each of America's major wars has been greater in scope than the previous one, and in addition has involved more people, required a greater share of the national resources and cost more money. Hence wars have created the conditions for successive extensions of governmental power, especially the power of the federal government. The Civil War, requiring as it did a major national effort, was the first to bring about this kind of shift. The Union government did not resort to direct economic controls; the task of providing the essentials of war was left to private enterprise. Nevertheless Union leaders saw – as the Confederate devotees of state rights did not – that central direction was essential to the successful prosecution of the war. The task of raising troops could perhaps be left mainly to the states, but once mobilized the armies had to be placed under a unified command. In order to finance the struggle it became necessary to devise what had formerly been lacking – namely, a federal internal revenue system. For these and other reasons the power of the federal government, as distinct from that of the states, was greater in 1865 than it had been in 1861 and tended to remain greater thereafter. Then in the twentieth century the demands of modern warfare became such as to necessitate much wider extensions of government activity. In both world wars it became necessary in the interests of defence and survival to suspend for the time being the free operation of market forces. In order to raise men and materials in sufficient numbers and in order to check the inflationary tendencies of war finance, the federal government resorted to conscription and imposed direct controls over prices, wages, and production. Admittedly these controls were abandoned with the end of the wartime emergency, but they served to accustom Americans to the concept of government intervention in the economy and acted as models for such attempts at peacetime planning as the New Deal.

Just as wars have tended to strengthen the power of the central government so in most cases have they contributed to the growth of national feeling. Thus the Revolutionary War transformed provincial self-consciousness into a nascent American nationalism. It is true that the loyalties of the Revolutionary generation remained confused; the impulse toward national unity did not imply the eclipse of local attachments – as the dissension within the Continental Army testified. Yet the mere existence of the Continental Army was proof of a certain solidarity of feeling. That army had been called into existence because the colonists were agreed upon the necessity of common action. Moreover the actual waging of war had welded the states into a kind of fighting unity even before the ratification of the Articles of Confederation brought the Union formally into being.

While it was in progress the War of 1812 seemed more likely to weaken American nationalism than to strengthen it. Though the Hartford Convention did not, as it turned out, represent a serious threat to the existence of the Union, it was nevertheless proof of the extent to which the war had intensified New England sectionalism. Yet the war also brought forth notable expressions of patriotism, especially in the West and the South, and it provided a concrete focus for national pride in the shape of American victories at sea and at New Orleans. The great outburst of national feeling that characterized the immediate post-war years suggested that the war had on balance made a sizeable contribution to national unity.

If wars in general have been significant tests of national loyalty the Civil War constituted an especially sensitive touchstone of nationalism in that secession challenged both the concept and the fact of American nationality. Nationalism was, indeed, the main issue for both sides. So far as Southerners were concerned the loyalty they had hitherto given to the Union was transferred to the Confederacy, though a residual Unionism led them to identify such old national symbols as the Fourth of July and Washington's Birthday with the Confederate cause. Southern independence ultimately turned out to be an unattainable ideal but successive generations of Southerners have nevertheless continued to look back nostalgically to the Lost Cause. In the North on the other hand the Civil War inspired new and deeper feelings of loyalty to the Union. Admittedly Northerners were not touched equally with patriotic fervour; the federal government had to contend with widespread defeatism and war-weariness and at times found it difficult to keep alive the flagging spirit of nationalism. But the firing on Fort Sumter brought forth what E. L. Godkin called a 'fanatical veneration' for the Union cause. Moreover, the immense sacrifices which the Civil War demanded enhanced the value of the Union to those Northerners who had hitherto tended to take it for granted. As Emerson wrote in 1864: 'Before the War our patriotism was a firework, a salute, a serenade for holidays and summer evenings. . . . Now the deaths of thousands and the determination of millions of men and women show that it is real.' Loyalty and patriotism thus took on a new meaning and victory, when finally achieved, was seen in the North as the final triumph of the nationalistic impulse.

It took a foreign war, however, to rekindle in the South a sense of

American nationality. The Spanish–American War was 'a milestone on the road to reunion'. Veterans of the Union and Confederate armies shed their blood in common. Two of the four major-generals called into the United States Army from civilian life – Fitzhugh Lee and 'Fighting Joe' Wheeler – had worn Confederate grey. The whole country experienced a resurgence of national feeling, based upon a consciousness of national unity and strength. And in December 1898, at the Atlanta Peace Jubilee, President McKinley set the seal upon the process of reconciliation by standing while the band played 'Dixie' and by affirming the care of Confederate graves to be a national duty.

If war could contribute to the ideal of a homogeneous nation by softening sectional antagonisms it could do so also by integrating the diverse elements in the American population. Most American wars have in fact accelerated the transfer of immigrant loyalties. The many immigrants who along with native-born Americans participated in the national effort against a common foe were helped thereby to slough off their Old World attachments and to identify themselves more thoroughly with America.

Yet war could have a divisive as well as a unifying effect. The systematic attempt made during the First World War to arouse patriotism by whipping up hatred of a foreign enemy did not promote unity but simply drove a wedge between 'hyphenated Americans', especially those of German origin, and the rest of the population. Moreover, the coercive character of the First World War nationalism, its emotional insistence on conformity as well as on unity, was directed not only against groups of foreign origin but against all who opposed the war, and in the long run weakened national morale. Not that the First World War was unusual in having been fought by a disunited nation. On the contrary there has been a good deal of dissension over every major American conflict from the Revolution to Vietnam. Opposition to war has on occasion been due to sympathy with the enemy. That was the case, for instance, with the Loyalists during the Revolution, with Southern sympathisers in the North during the Civil War and with New England Federalists during the War of 1812 – though in the last of these examples sectional self-interest counted for at least as much as sympathy with Britain. More frequently, however, dissent has stemmed from idealistic motives, either from outright pacifism or from a conviction that particular wars were immoral or unjust. The Mexican War, the Spanish–American War, the war in Vietnam – all were opposed by Americans who believed that their country was acting unrighteously and hence contrary to its traditions. Yet one must guard against attributing too much to idealism. The unpopularity of the Vietnam War, and still more of the Korean War, was due partly to America's inability to win an outright victory. Having triumphed in almost every major collective effort which they have undertaken, Americans have come to expect solutions which, if not necessarily quick, are at least clear-cut. And when such solutions are seen to be unattainable the national psyche has not found it easy to overcome feelings of frustration and impatience.

The strain of pacifism in the national character, the consequent insistence that wars in order to be justifiable have first to be just – these are among the reasons for asserting that Americans, though possessed of many military qualities, are not a military people, still less a militaristic one. The same conclusion is suggested by the unprepared state in which the United States has generally gone to war, as well as by her haste in disarming the moment the fighting has stopped. Her fondness for military presidents might seem to conflict with this conclusion but it is significant that the generals who reached the White House tended, even when they were professional soldiers – which not all of them were – to be those with an acceptable civilian persona; the presidential ambitions of 'men on horseback' like McClellan and MacArthur were never to be fulfilled. Their election would have been too open a contradiction of the constitutional principle, insisted upon in every American war, of civilian control of the military.

It has never been feasible, then, to say of America what Mirabeau alleged of Frederick the Great's Prussia, namely, that war was the national industry. Rather have Americans regarded war as an aberration, as an interruption – welcome or otherwise – of the nation's normal routine; as a task which the national interest or the interest of mankind generally made it necessary to undertake but which in any case ought to be discharged as promptly and efficiently as possible. Hence, for all the crusading idealism that Americans have commonly brought to the waging of war, they have gone about it in the same methodical, businesslike way in which they have approached all their great national problems, from the taming of a wilderness to the conquest of space. War for Americans has not been so much a matter of heroics – though there have been plenty of them – as of logistics; of amassing overwhelming material resources, of accumulating sufficient quantities of the latest military 'hardware', of applying technological 'know-how'. In a word it was a matter of acting on the famous aphorism of the Confederate general, Nathan Bedford Forrest, that the problem of war was that of 'getting there fustest with the mostest'.

Such an attitude was entirely compatible with, and was indeed not unrelated to, another distinguishing feature of the American way in war, namely, the conviction that war-making was a self-contained activity, having no particular connection with politics or diplomacy. For this reason Americans have until recently made little effort to relate their foreign policy to their military capability. Time and again the United States has gone to war without having considered in advance whether it had the immediate capacity to wage one. And its aim once war was embarked on has tended simply to be the military defeat of the enemy, with sometimes only a glance at the political and diplomatic implications of military operations. Such attitudes have come naturally to a people essentially pacifistic by nature and confident, moreover, that ploughshares could quickly be beaten into swords and back again. That notion has been rendered untenable by the threat of nuclear warfare but for most of their history Americans seem to have had considerable justification for holding to it. Only in the nuclear age, when the responsibilities of world power were at last accepted, did the United States renounce the prophet Isaiah and begin to act instead upon the advice of a fourth-century Roman writer on military science: *Qui desiderat pacem, praeparet bellum.*

Further Reading

Robert Leckie, *The Wars of America*. New York and London, 1968.

T. Harry Williams, *Americans at War: The Development of the American Military System*. Baton Rouge, Louisiana, 1960.

Marcus Cunliffe, *Soldiers and Civilians: The Martial Spirit in America, 1775–1865*. London, 1968.

Walter Millis (ed.), *American Military Thought*. New York, 1966.

Russell Weigley, *History of the United States Army*. New York, 1967.

Walter Millis, *Arms and Men*. New York, 1956.

Howard H. Peckham, *The Colonial Wars, 1689–1762*. Chicago, Ill., 1964.

Christopher Ward, *The War of the Revolution*, 2 vols. New York, 1952.

Willard M. Wallace, *Appeal to Arms: A Military History of the Revolution*. Chicago, Ill., 1964.

Harry L. Coles, *The War of 1812*. Chicago, Ill., 1965.

Justin H. Smith, *The War Against Mexico*, 2 vols. New York, 1919.

Bruce Catton, *This Hallowed Ground: The Story of the Union Side of the Civil War*. New York, 1956.

Clifford Dowdey, *The Land They Fought For: The Story of the South as the Confederacy, 1832–1865*. New York, 1955.

Henry Steele Commager, *The Blue and the Gray*. Indianapolis, Ind., 1950.

Fairfax Downey, *Indian Wars of the U.S. Army, 1776–1865*. New York, 1963.

T. Harry Williams, *Lincoln and His Generals*. New York, 1952.

Edmund Wilson, *Patriotic Gore*. New York, 1962.

Walter Millis, *The Martial Spirit*. Boston, Mass., 1931.

Edward M. Coffman, *The War to End All Wars: The American Military Experience in World War I*. New York, 1968.

A. Russell Buchanan, *The United States and World War II*, 2 vols. New York and London, 1964.

Robert Leckie, *Conflict: The History of the Korean War*. New York, 1962.

Samuel P. Huntington, *The Soldier and the State: The Theory and Politics of Civil–Military Relations*. Cambridge, Mass., 1957.

6 America in World Affairs

H. C. ALLEN

A companion to American Studies should, if it is to perform its proper function, number among its readers not only students of the geography, history, and literature of the United States, but also of its contemporary government and society – as well as those interested, as we all must be, in current American foreign policy. For these last this chapter may be a worthwhile starting point, albeit one of necessity rapidly left behind by the serious student, since within its inevitably short and narrow compass it obviously cannot attempt an adequate history of United States foreign policy. For this the reader must refer to the many other works on the subject, a number of which are included in the reading list which is appended. My object here is to try and suggest, in an historical perspective, some of the ways in which Americans have come to look at, and hence to deal with, the outside world.

Two things may be noted at the outset. First, the people of the United States, like human beings and human groups everywhere, can only act in foreign (or any other kind of) policy as a result of their individual or collective apprehension of what is going on around them. We are all, every one of us, dependent upon our senses and upon our minds, which alone can interpret the data which our senses provide, for our understanding of events in the world, and hence for any action we may take in response to those events. We are accustomed to talk, and consciously to think, of the 'facts' of a situation, but in reality those 'facts' appear remarkably different according to the point of view from which they are observed by the individual or the group concerned. Of many of these differences of viewpoint we are well aware, but the importance of others, arising directly from our mere place in time and space, we seldom fully appreciate.

Second, this confusion is almost always worse confounded by the fact, which is a fact, that our mind is very far from being a purely rational instrument for the interpretation of phenomena. Each individual mind is an animate filter, not only shaped by its experiences during childhood and later growth, but constantly subject to the emotions and desires which arise from our sentient nature. Through this distorting filter of our fears and desires and hopes, all the facts, on the basis of which we take even deliberate action, must pass, and in politics as elsewhere many of our actions are not deliberate, but passionate, if not instinctive. In statesmanship, and especially international statesmanship, we take great pains (at least in some countries), by the use of staid machinery, by maintaining deliberate brakes on precipitate action, and by frequently reminding ourselves of the risks of rashness, to get as close to objectivity as we can. This is only sensible, for caution is peculiarly necessary in foreign affairs, where the barriers of language and geography, of national pride and aspiration, and of deep-seated group fears and anxieties about the 'outside world' are at their most formidable. In international society, too, the universal human propensity to preserve public face, which can aid us in producing consistency of conduct but which also carries grave risks of compounding patriotic arrogance, is at its most intense.

The national psyche which controls national policy is thus, as is that of the individual, built up over the years of its history like a palimpsest, experience on top of experience, and the folk-memory serves much the same purpose as the individual memory in creating and preserving the national identity and personality. But fact *is* prior to thought, and the mind must inhabit a body and that body move in a real world. So – and it is fundamental in the case of nations – geography dictates certain lines of historical development. Geography and history have together produced the America with whose role in world affairs we are here concerned.

Nineteenth-Century Attitudes

The metropolitan United States today occupies the great central tract of territory which, stretching from the Atlantic to the Pacific shore, in effect completely controls the North American continent; these two great oceans, combined with the Caribbean sea and the Arctic ice cap, have given America many of the advantages of an insular position, relatively isolated within the Western Hemisphere from the rest of the world and increasingly dominant within that hemisphere. Yet, isolated as the United States was until the accelerating technical revolution which began somewhat over a century ago with the invention of the steamship, she was always an integral part of Western civilization. Settled initially in the sixteenth and seventeenth centuries by the European powers, especially Spain, France, Holland, and Britain, the colonial foundations of what is now the United States remained for many years heavily dependent on their mother countries, politically, economically, and socially, as well as militarily. By 1763, however, Great Britain had in effect established the pre-eminence of her particular colonial empire among the others in North America.

Partly as a result of this weakening of Britain's rivals in the Western Hemisphere and partly as a result of their new-found strength, as well as of their distance from Europe, the thirteen British colonies before long established their political independence by military revolution against the first British Empire, and in 1783 the United States came into existence as an international power. This violent rupture left a long-enduring mark on the American national character. First, it left Americans with a strong instinctive hatred of tyranny or arbitrary rule, which they tended to associate particularly with 'imperialism', or what came in mid-twentieth century to be called 'colonialism'. There was an almost indelible association in the American mind after the Declaration of Independence between national independence on the one hand and individual freedom, self-government and (ultimately) democracy on the other. Thus the Americans in their attitude to the outside world have always been inclined to sympathize with 'demo-cratic' movements and to mistrust imperialist policies. Second, the American Revolution naturally resulted in Great Britain being much hated in the United States, and Anglophobia was for many years a very important factor in America's foreign relations. Even today, after three-quarters of a century of more or less close association between the two English-speaking peoples, it can occasionally show itself in American attitudes. Between the Treaty of Paris of 1783 and the Treaty of Ghent of 1814, which ended (with a stalemate) the Anglo-American War of 1812, the Anglo-American relationship was the dominant and primary concern of the foreign policy of the United States; and for a further thirty years, until the Webster–Ashburton Treaty of 1842 and the Oregon Treaty of 1846 (which ended the main disputes, over boundaries and other matters, between the two coun-tries), it remained in many ways that policy's major theme. In all probability Anglophobia was kept intensely active much longer than might have been the case by the fact that young America, for all its political sovereignty, remained during these early years a neo-colonial country heavily reliant, economically, socially, and culturally, on Britain. Few things produce more tension and frustration than enforced dependence, especially upon a parent whose control has, with a great deal of acrimony, been ostensibly thrown off. Thus the persistent embroilment of the United States in the affairs of Europe – much against her will and despite her early assertion, in Washington's proclamation of 1793, of her neutrality in the French Revolutionary and Napoleonic wars – kept hatred of Britain and suspicion of Europe very much alive in America during the first quarter of the nineteenth century.

After this period these feelings abated slowly, partly because memories of the Revolutionary era faded and partly because Britain and Europe became in reality steadily less important to America. After 1814 the American people – it is a cliché of their historians – turned their backs politically on Europe and faced decisively westward, to acquire and develop their continental domain. As their fortunes, population and territories in America waxed, their hostility to things European, and especially British, tended to wane. In any case their feelings towards their homelands had always been complex, indeed ambiguous. Britain might be the repudiated father-figure, but it was also the source, not only of economic strength (a good 40 per cent of all America's foreign trade was with Britain between 1820 and 1850), but also, as we have seen, of political, social, and cultural inspiration. Similarly, Europe, and at first Britain (including Ireland, if in decreasing degree England, Wales, and Scotland), remained throughout the whole nineteenth century the almost exclusive source of America's massive immigration, and by no means all the sentiments of emigrants towards the land of their birth are hostile. The underlying tension in American foreign policy was between suspicion of a Europe whose dust its citizens had shaken from their feet and inevitable participation in (and indeed identification with) the affairs of the Western world; that this did not have more serious consequences than it did was largely because of American self-absorption in westward expansion, as well as the very real remoteness of the United States from Europe.

This fundamental American concern for the growth of the United States had already shown itself in President Jefferson's prompt purchase of the vast territory of Louisiana from France in 1803. This had the effect of virtually doubling at one stroke the size of his country, which had already stretched in 1783 from the eastern seaboard about 1000 miles to the line of the Mississippi in the west. In the second decade of the nineteenth century Florida was added, in three separate bites, to the territory of the United States, bringing American domination of the Caribbean closer, and foreshadowing the special, unique role which she was later to play in the Western Hemisphere as a whole.

At this juncture, in 1823, the foreign policy of the United States was the subject of the most important American pronouncement since President Washington's solemn and long-heeded warning to his countrymen in his Farewell Address of 1797. In this Washington had declared: 'The great rule for us in regard to foreign nations is, in extending our commercial relations to have with them as little *political* connection as possible. . . . Europe has a set of primary interests which to us have none or a very remote relation. . . . Why forego the advantages of so peculiar a situation? . . . It is our true policy to steer clear of permanent alliances with any portion of the foreign world. . . .' The new pronouncement, which was to become known as the Monroe Doctrine, was enunciated by President James Monroe in his Seventh Annual Message to Congress, in December 1823; it was fundamentally a result of the successful revolutions which had established the Latin-American states' independence of Spain.

This famous declaration in one sense reinforced the principle of isolation which had by now entered so deeply into American policy and inclination; it not merely reasserted that 'In the wars of the European powers in matters relating to themselves we have never taken any part, nor does it comport with our policy so to do', but also warned these powers of continental Europe that 'we should consider any attempt on their part to extend their system to any portion of this hemisphere as dangerous to our peace and safety'. This time the American President not only advised his own countrymen to steer clear of what Jefferson too had proclaimed to be undesirable entanglements with other nations, but warned those nations, except for their existing colonies, to keep their hands off both North and South America. The United States was henceforth to consider it her function to enforce, as well as she could, the isolation of the whole Western Hemisphere.

In another sense, however, the Monroe Doctrine illustrated the extent to which in fact the United States, even in the forthcoming years of her maximum isolation, was inextricably involved in what Jefferson had called the 'broils of Europe', for American concern for political liberty everywhere in the world is openly expressed: 'The citizens of the United States', Monroe declared, 'cherish sentiments the most friendly in favour of the liberty and happiness of their fellow-men on that side of the Atlantic.' Even though the practical emphasis was on the Western Hemisphere – 'The political system of the allied powers is essentially different in this respect from that of America. This difference proceeds from that which exists in their respective Governments' – the ultimately universal implication was clearly there. More important at this point of time, the Administration, as Secretary of State John Quincy Adams well knew, could only launch such a warning to the European continental powers because Britain, who then indisputably controlled even the American seas, was in agreement with the substance of it. American isolation depended, as it was to do for the remainder of the century, on the acquiescence of the Royal Navy. The nature of this dependence was generally little understood in America, but it was in fact to continue to exist until the United States herself became a first-class naval power in the twentieth century.

This dependence was also little noticed by Americans (happily perhaps in view of the past history of Anglo-American relations), in part because it was in Britain's interest as well as power to prevent the serious interference of other nations in the Western Hemisphere and hence any threat to America, and in part because the United States was fully absorbed at first in her own territorial expansion on the North American continent, and later in her internal dissensions, which led ultimately to civil war. Her expansion, after the Adams-Onis settlement with Spain in 1819, was accomplished in two main phases. In the first, by the energy of American settlement in the huge Mexican province of Texas and the resulting establishment, by this very effective American 'fifth column', of Texan independence from Mexico, the way was opened for the annexation of Texas by the United States in 1845. The consequent deterioration of American relations with Mexico played its part, in the second phase, in leading to the outbreak of open hostilities between the two powers in 1846, but the root reason for the war was the violence of expansionist sentiment in the United States, particularly among Democrats; those who cherished these sentiments believed – and did not hesitate to shout from the roof tops – that it was the 'Manifest Destiny' of the American people to occupy the whole tract of territory to their west as far as the Pacific Ocean. Some Americans set few limits to the desirability of American expansion anywhere in the Western Hemisphere, and President Polk fought the successful election campaign of 1844 on a platform demanding not merely a vigorous policy against Mexico but also against Britain over the territory of Oregon, to a large section of which both London and Washington laid claim.

Because it was not practical to tackle Britain and Mexico at the same time, but also because British policy was moderate and also probably because there was notable opposition, within the United States itself, to American expansion even against Mexico, the final and vital Anglo-American compromise over their joint boundary in North America was effected in the Oregon Treaty of 1846. America's weak neighbour to the south received much shorter shrift, and after a brief but triumphant invasion, the Treaty of Guadalupe Hidalgo in 1848 added well over half a million square miles to the territory of the United States. Five years later, with the Gadsden Purchase of a further small tract of land from Mexico, the final limits of the contiguous continental United States were reached. That these were the final limits was in part due to the increasingly bitter opposition in North and South respectively to any expansion of the United States which would strengthen the other section, but also to the subsequent reassertion of anti-expansionist sentiment among the American people. From 1848 onwards, in foreign relations American isolation and American awareness of that isolation intensified as the Civil War approached. It was to dominate the foreign policy of the United States for almost half a century to come.

The period of expansion had strengthened the tendency of the American people to think in terms of the Western Hemisphere, although in reality their interests were in very many respects much more closely tied to those of Europe: this period of insularity, in its turn, greatly strengthened the American habit of thinking in isolationist terms, and in fact her economic dependence on Europe and especially Britain lessened swiftly in the post-Civil War years, which saw the rapid rise of the United States as a great industrial power. But though her specific economic and political ties to the outside world lessened in the middle years of the nineteenth century, the inevitable broad and general effect of the ever-accelerating technological revolution upon which mankind was entering at this time was a sharp and continuing contraction of the whole globe, and this was before long to make isolation impossible for America or any other power. The steam engine, the internal combustion engine, and ultimately the rocket were, in little more than a hundred years, to bring the United States within immediate range of bombardment from Europe and Asia by weapons of unprecedented and terrifying destructiveness.

American Imperialism

The end, albeit a lingering one, of the possibility of actual American isolation was not, however, only a result of the fact – often very alarming to Americans accustomed and addicted to the remoteness of what Jefferson called their 'distant and peaceful shore' – that the 'outside world' seemed to be closing in with disturbing speed upon the United States. It was also a result of the astonishingly rapid growth in the power of the United States herself, which was accompanied by a rebirth of the American expansionist spirit. This outburst of American imperialism in the last decade of the nineteenth century was not as widespread or as strongly held in the United States as its forerunner had been in the era of Manifest Destiny, and there was more sustained and more rapidly effective opposition to American overseas expansion than there had been to American continental expansion. Nevertheless imperialism found its outlet in the Spanish–American War of 1898, as a result of which Cuba was liberated from Spanish rule, though becoming subject to powerful American influence, and the United States acquired a modest but undoubted colonial empire, including Puerto Rico in the Caribbean and the Philippines in the western Pacific.

More enduring legacies of the period than this American Asiatic colony, which was to be granted its independence within less than half a century, were first, the creation of a great United States Navy, which was by 1906 second only to that of Britain, and second, President Theodore Roosevelt's ruthlessly rapid acquisition of the territory for the construction of the American-owned Panama Canal, which was opened to traffic in 1914 and enormously enhanced the power of America's fleets. The United States after this date was still to remain for many years, in peace-time, what she had always been, a nation with a minute standing army and a very weak militia, but she was never again to be other than a first-class naval power; American sea, and later air, strength was to be the main symbol, as well as instrument, of America's status as a great power. But the rapidity and completeness of her victory in the Spanish–American (as in the Mexican) War and her immediate disbandment of her armies when it was over (as had also been pretty much the case after the Civil War) left intact, indeed in many respects strengthened, the isolationist instincts of the American people. Even when the United States had become involved in war (and it happened in all these cases initially as a result of events within the Western Hemisphere), she had beaten her foreign enemies with astonishing speed and completeness, had solved her external problems to her own satisfaction, and had then turned back immediately to her own scarcely interrupted and paramount domestic concerns. This habit of thought and action was to persist for many years to come.

Yet in retrospect we can see that the fact of American imperialism itself illustrated the extent to which the United States was actually involved inextricably in the affairs of the world, and especially the Western world, for her imperialist ideas were very far from being an isolated phenomenon but were shared in greater or less degree at this period by most of the European powers, and especially Britain where a new imperialist phase had been in process of development ever since Disraeli's later years. One particular idea which they shared was that of the unique duty and destiny of what they often regarded as the superior white, and especially 'Anglo-Saxon', races to dictate the future of 'lesser breeds without the law'; this philosophy suited very well not merely Britain's 'raj' in places like India but also the then current state of America's domestic race relations, with its rapprochement between the North and the white South. But one beneficial outcome of this in some ways distasteful imperialist trend was the rise in these years of a close, and internationally crucial, Anglo-American friendship.

This close relationship, which so percipient an observer as Bismarck saw as of supreme significance for the world, was, however, much more broadly and beneficially based than on this narrow racialist doctrine, for it depended on many strong, if sometimes subtle, social, and political bonds, such as the common language, kindred ideas, and similar institutions. Likewise, the rapprochement was not merely supported by the more imperialist parties in the two countries, the Republicans and the Tories, but also by the Democrats of the Wilsonian era and the Asquithian Liberals, for with the growing democratization of Britain these more radical parties also came to see, in a general way, increasingly eye to eye. The Republican Administration in the Boer War reciprocated the Conservative support given to the United States during the Spanish–American War, but there were pro-Boers in Britain, just as there were in the United States elements hostile to American as well as to British imperialism. There was also in effect general agreement between the British (as between the American) political parties over the so-called Roosevelt Corollary to the Monroe Doctrine; by this pronouncement in 1904 the United

States publicly assumed a sort of 'international police power' in Latin America. It was a restrained and, as it turned out, ultimate manifestation of what one American historian has called the 'great aberration' of American imperialism. Thus, happily for mankind, by the beginning of the First World War not only were Anglo-American relations better than they had ever been since Independence, but both their governments were overtly dedicated to the advancement of democracy.

Wilson, the War and the League

To the fearful, spreading, and unexpectedly protracted war which broke out in Europe in 1914 the United States at first and for many months steadfastly maintained her traditional attitude of isolation, her President calling at once for neutrality 'in thought as well as in action'. But in fact many Americans (including even President Wilson) early sympathized with and, as time went on, more and more favoured the Allied cause, while the ruthless German submarine campaign against neutral shipping inevitably and increasingly brought her into direct conflict with the greatest maritime neutral, the United States. This demonstrated forcibly how impossible it was for even a great isolationist power to remain aloof from a widespread war in the technological circumstances of the twentieth century; for all her newly developed strength, she was drawn as remorselessly into the whirlpool of world war as she had been in the days of her weakness a century before. This time, however, she fought with, not against, Britain.

To the surprise of some Europeans, she fought the war after she entered it in April 1917 with all her accustomed force and even ferocity; as soon as it became clear that the Allies could hold out, at sea and then on land, until her full power was developed on the Western front, her participation resulted in a relatively rapid breakdown in the German will, as well as capacity, for victory. The President himself, once the United States had become a belligerent, had swung full-circle from his deep apprehensions about the effect of America's involvement in the war on the morale of the American people (so divided in their national origins as well as their sympathies) and his consequent reluctance to abandon America's isolated neutrality, and had pledged 'her blood and her might for the principles that gave her birth . . .'. He promised that the American people would fight with all their strength 'for the things which we have always carried nearest our hearts – for democracy, for the right of those who submit to authority to have a voice in their own Governments, for the rights and liberties of small nations, for a universal dominion of right by such a concert of free peoples as shall bring peace and safety to all nations and make the world itself at last free'.

President Wilson, in other words, made, with characteristic fervour and oratorical skill, a passionate appeal to the American democracy to reverse its whole history and habit of isolationism. If, he seemed to say, with what appeared to many compelling logic, the United States cannot avoid being drawn inexorably into Europe's wars once they have started, America must ensure that they do not break out at all. This he proposed to do by espousing strongly an idea which had been current in America and Britain for some time, the creation of an institutionalized form of that 'concert of free peoples', which would preserve international peace. This was the League of Nations, which he made his primary objective in the arduous negotiations which led in the end to the Treaty of Versailles. The terms of the Treaty were agreed upon between the Allies by early May 1919 and, under Allied compulsion, it was formally signed by the German representatives on 28 June of the same year. It incorporated the full blue-print of the President's League of Nations, despite considerable opposition from France, for the United States, which was not weakened by the war in the way that both the Allies and the Central Powers had been, was incomparably the strongest nation at the conference table and able to wield supreme influence. President Wilson, in order to get his way, had had to make certain concessions to those who wanted a punitive peace imposed on Germany but he felt that the establishment of the League, with all that he hoped from it for the peace of the world, was well worth the price. 'I think', he said, shortly before leaving Paris for the United States early in July, 'that we have made a better peace than I should have expected when I came here to Paris.' It remained to be seen whether the Senate, a two-thirds vote of which was necessary under the Constitution to ratify the Treaty, would agree with him.

There had already been ominous premonitory rumblings of opposition to the League back in America, centring among the President's Republican opponents, especially Senator William E. Borah of Idaho, who was irreconcilably opposed to the League in any form, and Senator Henry Cabot Lodge of Massachusetts, Chairman of the Senate Foreign Relations Committee, who was not prepared to accept the Treaty without important reservations or amendments. The

President's past record of partisanship in domestic politics made it more difficult for him to obtain the cooperation which he needed from his antagonists in order to get the Treaty ratified; always more effective (as he was) in appeals from the public platform than in the intimacy of politicians' give-and-take in 'smoke-filled rooms', he resolved to 'take the issue to the people' and, by arousing popular pressure, to force the Senate to accept the League. This line of action he based on an underlying, fundamental belief that, if offered only the alternatives of the League, the whole League, and nothing but the League on the one hand, and no treaty of peace at all on the other, the Senate could not possibly do other than ratify the Treaty.

In this he proved wrong. Whether or not he would have modified his opinion in the light of different circumstances, had he not been suddenly stricken and seriously incapacitated by a severe stroke in the middle of a nation-wide speaking tour to rally support for the League, it is impossible to say. What is certain is that, physically handicapped though he remained for the rest of his term of office, he obstinately refused (whether hardened in his resolution by his illness or cut off from sources of information by the physical isolation imposed on him in the name of his health by his wife) to accept any substantial changes in the Treaty. As a result the opposition was able to get its way. After a national debate that lasted eight months and after protracted consideration in the Senate, the Treaty of Versailles finally failed to receive the two-thirds vote necessary for its ratification on 20 March 1920; 49 Senators voted in favour of the Treaty with amendments and 35 against (many of them at the behest of the President), but this was still seven short of the votes required for ratification. This was a tragedy not only for President Wilson personally but, in the view of many able observers, for mankind also, since it in effect postponed for more than twenty years the full and uninhibited participation of the United States in world affairs, except for such limited but decisive initiatives as that which she took to bring about the Washington Treaties in limitation of international naval armaments in 1921. Her mood of withdrawal made it much less likely that the Allied powers, Britain and France, would stand up early enough after 1933 to the ambitious and revengeful designs of Adolf Hitler's resurgent Germany, and thus prevent the outbreak of the Second World War.

This thesis can never be proved, but it is unquestionably true that the return of the Republicans in the presidential election of 1920 showed clearly the desire of most Americans for a return to what their new

President, Warren G. Harding, called – unambiguously if inelegantly – a state of 'normalcy'. 'America's present need', he said, in a speech-making style startlingly different from that of his predecessor, 'is not heroics, but healing; not nostrums, but normalcy; not revolution, but restoration; not agitation, but adjustment; not surgery, but serenity; not the dramatic, but the dispassionate; not experiment, but equipoise; not submergence in internationality, but sustainment in triumphant nationality.' One of his opponents called Harding's speeches 'an army of pompous phrases moving across the landscape in search of an idea', and they certainly had none of the intellectual content of Wilson's some-times academic addresses, but into this intellectual vacuum rushed all the deep desires and old instincts of the American people.

Ideas of Neutrality

After a great war there is a yearning for calm and contentment on the part of any nation, and these words of Harding plainly show this (although it should be remembered that the war-sufferings of America had been less than those of the other great participants). Harding's speech shows also, in the case of the United States, a harking-back to the national idyll of an isolated America. With these feelings went a powerful reaction against the moral idealism of Wilson's 'great crusade' to make the world 'safe for democracy'; to many, indeed most, Americans, in an understandable mood of post-war hedonism, it seemed quite enough to return in foreign affairs to a pre-1914 world now seen through somewhat rosy spectacles. There could not have been a clearer example of national wishful-thinking than Harding's speech. The outside world could no longer, in the twentieth century, be excluded, shut out, from the life of America, any more than the deeply restless fears and turbulent instincts of men everywhere, including the United States, could (or can) be easily controlled and sublimated in the interests either of domestic tranquillity or inter-national peace.

For a period in the booming economic prosperity of the 1920s the American people were able largely to ignore, if not to forget about, the troubles of Europe and, after a brief post-bellum phase of activity in the settlement of Oriental affairs by the Washington Treaties, virtually to opt out of participation in the shaping of things to come even in the Western Pacific. But with the advent of the Great Depression and the rise of aggressive forces in Japan, Germany, and Italy in the 1930s, it became increasingly difficult for a nation as powerful, and as intelligent

and relatively well-informed, as the American to maintain this rever-
sion to the traditional aloofness of the United States, though Secretary
of State Stimson's personal efforts to check the aggression of Japan in
Manchuria in 1931 conspicuously failed to gain the support of his
countrymen. It is, however, a measure of the intensity with which
fantasies, to which we cling in defiance of reason and reality, can grip
not only individuals but massive groups of people, that most Americans
continued to hope against hope, and even to believe, that they could
continue to insulate their country against the currents created by
international events and against the subsequent shocks of war.

Mere isolation had failed to keep America out of war in 1917 and the
American people had accepted the rejection by the Senate of Wilson's
alternative policy of total involvement: now isolationism – a mood
desirous of isolation when isolation is no longer possible – prevailed (it
seemed all-pervasively), and it found expression in positive measures
to attempt to prevent a repetition of the course of events between 1914
and 1917. If America's neutral rights and her maritime interests had
dragged her into the First World War, the argument ran, in any
subsequent war she would not assert, indeed she would voluntarily
renounce, if not deny, them. Thus in successive pieces of legislation,
especially the Neutrality Acts of 1935, 1936, and 1937, the United
States reacted to the crises in Abyssinia, the Rhineland, and China by
providing for such things as the prohibition of loans, and of the sale of
arms and munitions, to belligerents; the prohibition of the sale to
them even of certain raw materials, except for cash paid before they
left America; and the prohibition against the arming of American
merchant ships for self-defence as well as against the travel of American
citizens in belligerent vessels. Thus the American people tried to ensure
that the United States would never become embroiled with any nation
at war, and even that she would never have a special financial interest
in the victory of any particular belligerent.

When war came to Europe with Germany's invasion of Poland on
1 September 1939 the United States was soon to find out (among other
things) that, as Wilson had warned his countrymen on a very different
issue a quarter of a century before, 'It is a very perilous thing to determine the foreign policy of a nation in terms of material interests.' And
even on this score, those who framed the neutrality legislation had been
mistaken in believing that America's economic, let alone political,
interest in the victory of any particular power could be ignored.
President Franklin D. Roosevelt (after his complete early absorption

in America's desperate economic crisis) had, once he realized the full gravity of the international situation, endeavoured for several years to break the grip of the delusion of isolationism on the American mind. At the outbreak of war he issued, as Wilson had done in 1914, a Proclamation of Neutrality, but, in contrast to Wilson, added, 'I cannot ask that every American will remain neutral in thought' as well as action; the anti-Semitic tyranny of Nazism in Germany was already too repugnant to American opinion. Furthermore, he called Congress into special session to amend the neutrality legislation by 'a return to international law'. In other words, no sooner did war actually come than it began to exert its powerful actual pressures upon American opinions and interests.

After a bitter struggle in Congress the neutrality legislation was, mercifully for the United Kingdom, amended to allow the sale of war materials to belligerents, but only for cash and for carriage in non-American ships – the so-called 'Cash and Carry' provisions. Because of British sea power, this in fact helped only the democratic Allies, but its importance to them, and of course to the economic prosperity of a United States still in the throes of depression, is shown by the fact that in the first year of the war 44 per cent of all America's now rapidly expanding exports went to the British Empire. The United States swiftly became what President Roosevelt was later to call her, the 'great arsenal of democracy', and an arsenal with a deep economic interest in the Allied cause.

Very soon, however, it was to become clear that America had much more vital interests at stake than even her own economic prosperity. In the summer of 1940 Hitler's armies overran Western Europe and left Britain standing virtually alone against Germany, which was now joined by Italy. Just as the months after the German invasion of Czechoslovakia in March 1939 had brought painfully home to Britons the realities which their delusory faith in appeasement had long concealed, so now realization of the stark threat which a Europe entirely controlled by the Axis powers would pose to the free institutions and even existence of a still weakly armed United States broke abruptly in upon the American dream of security through renewed isolation. The threat was not rendered any less ominous by the seemingly successful onslaught of the *Wehrmacht* on Soviet Russia in June 1941.

But despite the persistent efforts of the President, step by step, to protect American interests (by imposing, for example, what amounted to economic sanctions on Japan) and to awaken American opinion to the real dangers which faced the United States in Europe, it was not until the final deterioration of the Far Eastern situation and the treacherous and sudden attack by Japan upon America's great Hawaiian naval base of Pearl Harbor, on 7 December 1941, that the American people took the decisive step and entered the war – or rather had it taken for them by the Japanese. As the President ended his message to Congress next day, 'I ask that the Congress declare that since the unprovoked and dastardly attack by Japan on Sunday, December seventh, a state of war has existed between the United States and the Japanese Empire.'

Such was the traumatic effect of Pearl Harbor on the American psyche that from this time forward for three decades the United States has not seriously shirked what she regarded as her international responsibilities. After the unconditional surrender of her enemies in the Second World War, she took full responsibility for the rehabilitation, and political reorganization and re-education, of Japan; she participated in the occupation and democratization of Germany; and she threw her great weight behind the successor of the League of Nations, the United Nations, which was actually situated in New York City. All this was perhaps, after the lessons of the thirties, not so very surprising. What was truly remarkable was the swiftness and flexibility with which, in the years from 1947 onwards, the American Administration, and indeed the American people, recognized and reacted strongly and effectively against what they considered as the new (or at least renewed and vastly more powerful) threat to the 'free world' – of which America was now both heart and leader – constituted by a world Communist movement led by Stalinist Russia, and joined apparently after 1950 by Mao Tse-tung's China. This change was indeed a volte-face from Roosevelt's determination, displayed at the Yalta Conference of 1945, to try to 'play-along' with Stalin. His successor took a different view.

The Containment of Communism

In 1947, under the Truman Doctrine, the United States stepped in to fill the power gap which was to be left by the first serious contraction of British military strength and political influence in the eastern Mediterranean, and gave aid to Greece and Turkey against the threat of a Communist movement inspired from neighbouring Russia. In the next year she set a pattern for the defence of free Berlin by bearing the main brunt of the astonishing Anglo-American airlift which kept the beleaguered city alive and independent. In 1949 she institutionalized the resistance of Western Europe and North America to the activities of the Soviet Union and international Communism, exemplified in the Czechoslovak coup of 1948, by the creation of the North Atlantic Treaty Organization.

During these years, when the other powers (including Russia) had been so exhausted by the war, America's monopoly of atomic weapons and her enormous economic strength gave her a position of dominance in the affairs of the world unprecedented in modern history. As Barbara Ward remarked with truth, America's foreign policy had become everybody's destiny. Had the United States again thrust the cup of international leadership from her, the outlook for free societies and democratic institutions and indeed for the independence of some nations would, in the view of many, have been bleak indeed. Nor did she confine her activities to military and politico-strategic leadership: through the Marshall Plan of massive economic aid for the reconstruction and rehabilitation of ailing Europe in 1948, made possible by her unique generosity as well as far-sighted self-interest, she effected a vastly more rapid and complete European recovery from the war than would otherwise have been conceivable.

Her ascendancy continued into the early 1950s (when, with one-sixteenth of the world's population, America still produced perhaps half of all the world's manufactured goods) but was already by that time being seriously challenged. In 1949 the Soviet Union exploded her first atomic bomb and by 1957 she had advanced so rapidly in modern technological skills that she was able to put the first man-made satellite into space – to the great consternation of American public, as well as official, opinion, which now for the first time gave credence to Russian claims to possess intercontinental ballistic missiles with nuclear-fusion warheads. The homelands of the United States seemed now under the possible threat of virtually immediate and unpreventable annihilation. This, together with the collapse of the Nationalist regime in China, the flight of Chiang Kai-shek to Formosa in 1949, and the signature of the treaty of 15 February 1950 between the Soviet Union and the Communist People's Republic of China, left no doubt that there had been a drastic alteration in the international balance of power. Now, about a quarter of the world's territory and industrial production and about a third of its population was Communist-controlled. The fears, justified and unjustified, which this situation aroused in American minds were exacerbated by the Communist

North Korean invasion of America-orientated South Korea in June 1950.

President Harry S. Truman courageously decided to support South Korean resistance with American troops, in the name of the United Nations. An ultimately stalemated war, in which 'Red' China intervened directly before the end of 1950, continued until 1953, when it was ended approximately on the line where it had begun, probably as a result principally of President Eisenhower's threat, secretly communicated to the North Koreans, to employ tactical atomic weapons if they did not negotiate peace. American leadership in this – for recent times – unusually clear-cut struggle against external aggression by one state on another was, on the whole, welcomed by the nations of the world, and particularly of Western Europe.

But there were also distinct signs of nervousness on the part of these other nations when there seemed any likelihood of the spreading of the war and especially of the use of atomic weapons. Had they known of President Eisenhower's threat, their reaction would no doubt have been very sharp. The initial fear of most of the non-Communist countries after 1945 had been that the United States would revert to isolationism and leave them to their fate, but now they tended to swing to the opposite extreme and to fear that the firm determination of American policy, which (with little consistency and perhaps less truth) they sometimes criticized as totally rigid and inflexible, would precipitate a third and nuclear war. Elements of obstinacy and stiffness did influence the foreign policy of the United States, especially in her refusal (still technically maintained even today) to recognize Communist China or to support her admission to the United Nations, which was the counterpart of her deep-rooted loyalty to Chiang Kai-shek. There was no hint of a weakening of this attitude until 1972. However, it will be surprising if, in the long perspective of history, it does not appear to be principally the result of the almost total intransigence of the Mao Tse-tung regime, which has maintained until very recently all the violent fervour of a revolution.

Nothing has better illustrated this than the self-destructive and, it seems, final split in the Communist camp itself; Peking's denunciations of Moscow were for some years scarcely less ferocious than its curses against Washington, which are now somewhat more muted. The United States has, it is true, been less willing than some other governments wished swiftly and unreservedly to reciprocate the slow and halting but undoubted change for the better which has taken place in

Russian policy since the death of Stalin in 1953, and which resulted in the 'thaw' in the Cold War. But, though her anxieties may have been excessive, her fears were far from unfounded. There certainly had been, ever since 1917 (albeit in changing guises), a Communist 'world-conspiracy', and the doctrine of peaceful co-existence, of which Nikita Kruschev was Russia's principal spokesman, did not end the struggle but merely proclaimed that henceforth Communist aims would not be sought by open war.

And the perceptible softening in the American attitude towards Russia, which became apparent during the three years following Premier Krushchev's visit to the United States in 1959, was sharply – and very understandably – checked by the covert and extremely hazardous attempt of the Soviet Union to install nuclear missiles in the Cuba of the anti-American Fidel Castro in the autumn of 1962. (It can be considered a setback similar to, but vastly more perilous than, the reconnaissance flights of American planes over Soviet territory which had ended in the shooting down of one of their U2s in 1960.) It was perhaps prompted by the disastrous failure of the American-sponsored invasion of Cuba by Cuban refugees in 1961 at the Bay of Pigs. Whatever the Russian reasons, for six days in late October 1962 mankind stood breathless on the brink of a nuclear holocaust, but the very skilful control exercised by the rapidly matured young President Kennedy made it possible for common sense to prevail in Moscow, and in due course the missiles were withdrawn in return for an American guarantee not to invade Cuba. For the first time a full-scale nuclear confrontation between the two super-powers had taken place and it did seem as if both had realized not only the absolute 'impossibility' of using the ultimate weapons but also perhaps the risks of wantonly, or even cautiously, threatening their use. Nuclear rivalry, and indeed technical development, did not cease but America, Russia, and Britain (but not France) did make it possible for the peoples of the world to breathe more easily by the signature, in 1963 in Moscow, of a treaty banning all nuclear tests except those conducted underground. The effect of this, however, was gravely marred by the accession of a still frenetic China to the ranks of the nuclear powers shortly after.

American–Russian relations in the succeeding three years seemed once again slowly to improve, though the wariness never gave way to anything approaching cordiality. The relationship of Washington with Peking, however, deteriorated to its worst state since the Korean War, especially over the intervention of the United States in support of

South Vietnam, the first steps in which had been very cautiously taken by President Kennedy not long before his assassination in 1963. The Kremlin, locked in a struggle with the Chinese government for the leadership of the Communist world, could not but denounce the increasingly determined and extensive military support given by President Johnson to the South Vietnamese government in 1965-7, but Moscow was, compared with Mao Tse-tung's Peking, undoubtedly a moderating influence on North Vietnam's Ho Chi Min. Once again the United States, in circumstances of peculiar difficulty and in some respects exceptional ambiguity, had shouldered a burden of what she then regarded as responsibility in foreign affairs which was to turn out to be much more heavy as well as more painful than that in Korea fifteen years before.

This pattern of determined American behaviour was not confined to the Orient. In Europe the United States in the 1960s stood firm over West Berlin and did not again threaten, as she had done in the 1950s, an 'agonizing reappraisal' of her commitments in the face of possible French defection from the West even when President de Gaulle began to withdraw from NATO in 1965. After the Suez débâcle of Britain and France in 1956, brought about by American opposition to their use of armed force to prevent Egyptian seizure of the internationally-controlled Suez Canal (the worst Anglo-American dispute since the Venezuela crisis sixty years earlier), the United States re-established cordial relations with Britain with what seemed miraculous rapidity. In the Middle East in the succeeding months, she played, under the Eisenhower Doctrine, a much clearer and more forceful role, difficult and confusing as the situation in the region remained. She remained in subsequent years a strong supporter of Israel despite her deep interests in Arabian oil. United States support of India against China, beginning in 1962, went far to complete a sort of global *cordon sanitaire* around the Communist countries. History may well judge this to have been necessary if Communist influence was to be contained, but it did tend to confirm the worst fears which fervent Marxists must, in the logic of their faith, display of 'American capitalist imperialism'.

Even in Latin America, a vast area always regarded by the United States as being of peculiar importance to her, American policy had once again become more forceful in the years since the Second World War. President Franklin D. Roosevelt had, with very beneficial results (especially in the war), repudiated the interventionist policy of his predecessors in Central and South America (first enunciated in his namesake's Corollary) in favour of a policy of cooperation with the countries of Latin America. However, the political instability, social inequality, anti-American sentiments, and desperate poverty of much of Latin America made it a most fertile soil for the spreading of Communism. Cooperation remained the official policy of the United States, but successive Administrations intervened more freely again in the affairs of Central and South America. This began under John Foster Dulles in Guatemala, in 1954, and, as a result of the Castro revolution in Cuba in 1959, culminated in President Johnson's despatch of Marines to the Dominican Republic in 1965. It is perhaps here, in the very backyard (so to speak) of the United States, that we can see most clearly the motives which have recently propelled, and determined the direction of, American foreign policy.

World Leadership

For though the rational and realistic elements in the international policies of the United States since the Second World War have been not merely more powerful than in the pre-war years but also perhaps more influential than those which went to the making of the foreign policies of any great power in modern times, there have been other elements of considerable consequence in America's attitude to the outside world. No people (as we said at the beginning of this essay) and no individual is immune from the effects of their irrational (if understandable) anxieties, as opposed to their justifiable fears. The Americans' belief in, and passionate devotion to, freedom has given them an apparently ineradicable mistrust, even hatred, of doctrinaire atheistic Marxist Communism, which stands in so many respects as the extreme opposite end of the economic, social, and political spectrum from the traditional American system of economic free enterprise and political and religious liberty. The realistic American fear of Soviet Communist expansion in the late 1940s spilled over in the early 1950s into an excessive, in many cases obsessive, panic-state of anxiety about the 'menace of Communism', even at home in the United States; and it was this which was fundamentally responsible for the distasteful and hysterical dominance in those years of the 'red-baiting' demagogue, Senator Joseph R. McCarthy of Wisconsin.

This undue alarm is, however, quite comprehensible to the historian when seen against the long background of American isolation and, in some degree, of American mass immigration, for even in this post-war period (after thirty years of immigration restriction) more

than 5 per cent of the American population was foreign-born. Since
the beginning of the nineteenth century an insular America had grown
and prospered astonishingly, and in all this time no really serious threat
to her homeland and institutions had existed, even in the Second
World War. Suddenly, in the space of a mere decade after that war,
a great and growing bloc of nations, deeply and bitterly hostile
ideologically to the United States, had brought the North American
continent within range of swift and near-total destruction. By the end
of the decade they were seriously attempting to make inroads into
Latin America itself: in a further five years they were to have a military
base in Cuba, only ninety miles from the shores of a United States
accustomed to the security provided in an earlier age by ocean barriers
thousands of miles in extent. Small wonder that for a period the
tendency that had always existed in America for a patriotic popular
majority to ride rough-shod over the rights of dissenting minorities in
times of crisis showed itself once again, and that United States foreign
policy, especially towards China, was rendered much more stiffly rigid
by the emotional pressures from a population frustrated by the unaccustomed, protracted, and painful (if relatively not very severe)
sacrifices demanded of it first in Korea, and later and more painfully in
Vietnam, the most complex and difficult of all America's embroilments
in the outside world.

The United States now discovered that the world leadership she
had reluctantly but resolutely assumed was a thankless task which
often entailed great suffering. To man the walls of what she liked to
call the free world (of what was once aptly dubbed America's Second
Roman Empire) against the threat of what many people (and not only
in the United States) considered the barbarities of Communism, had
necessitated the continual and painful intervention of the legions of the
United States herself, as in the agonizing case of Vietnam.

It is still a deeply-debated matter of opinion in America itself
whether in this case the actions of the United States were prompted by
justified fears or by unjustified anxieties, hatreds, or ambitions, though
after the signing of a cease-fire agreement in January 1973 the authenticity of the local causes of the war has seemed much greater once
more. And let it be remembered, to America's credit, that the great
issue of peace or war in Vietnam was longer, more deeply and more
publicly debated in the United States than anywhere in the outside
world.

Seen, however, in the long perspective of history, peace in Vietnam, if peace there be, may well seem much less important than the astonishing diplomatic revolution brought about by President Nixon's rapprochement with Peking and Moscow during 1972. It was a development fraught with mankind's hopes. It seems to bear the promise that the decisions which have to be taken in American foreign policy will be taken, as they have on the whole conspicuously been in the recent past, on a predominantly rational and a very real basis.

All in all, the objects and ideals of America's foreign policy since the origin of the republic have been in general both remarkably consistent and also beneficent – even benign. The road of many nations to perdition, however, has been paved with intentions which were far from wholly bad, but these have been frustrated and brought to naught by rash and often violent actions, precipitated by their deep, sometimes irrational, and often unconscious, anxieties, desires and ambitions. There is, in this era of President Nixon's thaw, good ground for hope, derived from America's history, that the United States, in the formation and execution of its foreign policy, will continue to be able to keep its less rational motives under control and to pursue successfully the usually wise and moderate aims to which it has dedicated itself in the past.

Further Reading

GENERAL

Allen, H. C., *The United States of America*. London, 1964.
——, *Great Britain and the United States: A History of Anglo-American Relations (1783–1952)*. London, 1954.
Bailey, T. A., *A Diplomatic History of the American People*. New York, 1940.
Bemis, S. F. (ed.), *The American Secretaries of State and Their Diplomacy*, 10 vols. New York, 1927–9.
——, *A Diplomatic History of the United States*. New York, 1936.
Brebner, J. B., *North Atlantic Triangle: The Interplay of Canada, the United States and Great Britain*. New Haven, Conn., 1945.
De Conde, Alexander, *A History of American Foreign Policy*. New York, 1963.
Graebner, Norman A. (ed.), *An Uncertain Tradition: American Secretaries of State in the Twentieth Century*. New York, 1961.
Jones, M. A., *American Immigration*. Chicago, 1960.
Pratt, J. W., *A History of United States Foreign Policy*. New York, 1955.
Van Alstyne, R. W., *American Diplomacy in Action*. Stanford, Calif., 1944.

EARLY NATIONAL PERIOD

Bemis, S. F., *The Diplomacy of the American Revolution*. New York, 1935.
——, *John Quincy Adams and the Foundations of American Foreign Policy*. New York, 1949.

Burt, A. L., *The United States, Great Britain and British North America from the Revolution to the Establishment of Peace after the War of 1812*. Oxford, 1940.

Perkins, Bradford, *The First Rapprochement: England and the United States, 1795–1805*. Philadelphia, Pa., 1955.

——, *Prologue to War*. Berkeley and Los Angeles, Calif., 1961.

Pratt, J. W., *Expansionists of 1812*. New York, 1925.

NINETEENTH CENTURY

Adams, E. D., *Great Britain and the American Civil War*, 2 vols. London, 1925.

Dangerfield, George, *The Era of Good Feelings*. New York, 1952.

Graebner, Norman A., *Empire on the Pacific: A Study of American Continental Expansion*. New York, 1955.

Perkins, Dexter, *Hands Off: A History of the Monroe Doctrine*. Boston, Mass., 1941.

Weinberg, Albert K., *Manifest Destiny: A Study of Nationalist Expansionism in American History*. Baltimore, Md., 1935.

Whitaker, Arthur P., *The United States and the Independence of Latin America, 1800–1830*. Baltimore, Md., 1941.

EARLY TWENTIETH CENTURY

Bailey, T. A., *The Policy of the United States towards the Neutrals, 1917–1918*. Baltimore, Md., 1942.

——, *Woodrow Wilson and the Peacemakers*. New York, 1947.

Beale, Howard K., *Theodore Roosevelt and the Rise of America to World Power*, Baltimore, Md., 1956.

Bemis, S. F., *The Latin American Policy of the United States*. New York, 1943.

Birdsall, Paul, *Versailles Twenty Years After*. New York, 1941.

Campbell, Charles S., Jr., *Anglo-American Understanding, 1898–1903*. Baltimore, Md., 1957.

Ferrell, Robert H., *American Diplomacy in the Great Depression: Hoover–Stimson Foreign Policy, 1929–1933*. New Haven, Conn., 1957.

Kennan, George F., *American Diplomacy, 1900–1950*. Chicago, Ill., 1951.

——, *Russia and the West under Lenin and Stalin*. Boston, Mass., 1961.

Link, Arthur S., *Wilson the Diplomatist*. Baltimore, Md., 1957.

May, Ernest R., *The World War and American Isolationism, 1914–1917*. Cambridge, Mass., 1958.

——, *Imperial Democracy: The Emergence of America as a Great Power*. New York, 1961.

Nevins, Allan, *The United States in a Chaotic World, 1918–1933*. New Haven, Conn., 1950.

Perkins, Dexter, *Charles Evans Hughes and American Democratic Statesmanship*. Boston, Mass., 1956.

Pratt, J. W., *Expansionists of 1898*. Baltimore, Md., 1936.

Seymour, Charles, *Woodrow Wilson and the World War*. New York, 1921.

Sprout, Harold and Margaret, *The Rise of American Naval Power, 1776–1918*. Princeton, N.J., 1939.

Whitaker, Arthur P., *The Western Hemisphere Idea: Its Rise and Decline*. Ithaca, N.Y., 1954.

MID-TWENTIETH CENTURY

Adler, Selig, *The Isolationist Impulse*. New York, 1957.

Buchanan, A. R., *The United States and World War II*, 2 vols. New York, 1964.

Fairbank, John K., *The United States and China*. Cambridge, Mass., 1958 (revised edition).

Feis, Herbert, *The Road to Pearl Harbor: The Coming of War between the United States and Japan*. Princeton, N.J., 1950.

Langer, William L. and Gleason, S. Everett, *The Challenge to Isolation, 1937–1940*. New York, 1952.

——, *The Undeclared War, 1940–1941*. New York, 1953.

McNeil, William H., *America, Britain and Russia: Their Cooperation and Conflict, 1941–1946*. London, 1953.

Rostow, Walt W., *The United States in the World Arena: An Essay in Recent History*. New York, 1960.

Sherwood, Robert E., *Roosevelt and Hopkins: An Intimate History*. New York, 1948.

Spanier, John W., *American Foreign Policy since World War II*. New York, 1962.

7 The United States: Constitution and Government

MAX BELOFF

The political institutions of a country can be studied in two different ways, both equally legitimate. It is possible to look at them as it were from the centre outward, and to concentrate upon the basic legal structure and the formal organs through which policies are made and carried into effect, thus treating the people themselves as a relatively passive element in the process; it is equally possible to start with the sovereign people – particularly in a democracy – and to regard the machinery of government mainly as the instrument through which the electorate or sections of it register their desires and achieve their objectives. In this chapter we shall be concerned mainly with the former of these two approaches, since we shall be looking at the constitutional structure of the United States, and at constitutional development largely in abstraction from the issues that have had to be resolved, the political parties and pressure groups through which they have been voiced, and the general political culture that has given them individuality and meaning. We shall then consider the executive branch of the federal government and particularly at its apex in the Presidency in order to see how, in modern times at least, the responsibilities for the vast areas of national life that it regulates are distributed and handled.

The next chapter in this volume will deal with the history of American political parties and of the causes they have espoused, together with the other extra-constitutional groupings into which American society has organized itself; and in the light of these considerations it will go on to treat of the representative elements in the system, the electoral process, and the Congress, the institution which best mirrors the diversity of the nation, as the Presidency normally best mirrors its fundamental unity. It is hoped that this rather unusual but not, we believe, illogical handling of the general theme will best bring out some of the unique elements in the American system.

238 CONSTITUTION AND GOVERNMENT

The Uniqueness of American Politics

It is indeed part of the uniqueness of American politics that it lends itself to this kind of treatment with so little violence to reality. For this there are a number of reasons about which it is well to be clear at the outset. In the first place, the American system is essentially one of constitutional government; we would look in vain for an equivalent of the notion of the sovereignty of the King in Parliament which is the very heart of the British form of government. The United States is still ruled according to the modes laid down in, and within the limitations imposed by, the Constitution that was drafted at Philadelphia at the Constitutional Convention of 1787 and that came into operation in 1789. Formal amendment of this document has been rare not so much because of the complicated requirements in the document as to its own amendment, but rather because of an instinctive sense that the existence of this time-honoured Constitution is an essential part of the nation's own self-image, fulfilling alongside the flag (itself ten years older than the Constitution) the symbolic significance that Britain assigns to the Crown. Too frequent changes would, it is felt, weaken one of the main links that bind together this huge and disparate country.

Since on the other hand the country itself has grown and changed beyond recognition – it is now a Union of fifty states and not as originally of thirteen – there has had to be some way of reconciling fidelity to the Constitution with the needs of government. In other words, a central problem in American history has been that of the extent to which the Constitution could or could not be interpreted to permit actions or practices that it did not clearly provide for; much has been done as elsewhere through the informal development of conventions, of accepted ways of doing things, and these have been particularly important when it has been a question of deciding about the relations of the different parts of the government to each other. But when the citizen has been more directly concerned, where the limits of legislative or governmental authority have been in question, then the Constitution has had to be interpreted by the courts of law, and in particular by the most original and notable of American institutions, the Supreme Court of the United States. Constitutional history – which in America is largely the history of what has happened to the Constitution at the hands of the courts – is thus more central to the development of the United States than to that of most other countries.

In the second place, the United States is by virtue of its constitution a federation, that is to say, it is a country where the powers of government are distributed between two independent forms of authority – federal and state. And this is not simply a matter of convenience, as when the powers of government in most other large countries are to some extent devolved upon local authorities. In Britain, for instance, the local authorities are the creations of Parliament, and could be swept away by Parliament if it was so minded. The states that form the American Union are in a different position; they derive their authority from the Constitution itself and are no more subject to the federal government than it is to them. It is indeed well to remember that the states in the shape of the original British colonies existed before the federal government itself, that common central institutions were only created in order to prosecute the revolutionary war against Britain and to consolidate its fruits. In the earliest period of American history some men found it convenient to argue that this priority of the states was not temporal merely, but that the states were the true sovereigns, and the federal government only their agent. And although the Civil War of 1861–5 put an end to the practical assertion of this theory in the temporary secession from the Union of the Confederate States, echoes of it have survived to our own day.

Limitations of space will prevent us giving to the institutions of the states the place that is their due; even less can we go into the problems of local and particularly municipal government within the states. But it must not be forgotten that just as the federal Constitution leaves much domestic activity to be regulated by the states, so state constitutions in their turn reserve to local communities further important areas of action – for instance the whole field of primary and secondary education.[1] It is the rigidity of a many-tiered system of government, which does not easily lend itself to reshaping in the light of the transformation of so much of the country into a series of massive conurbations with problems that cannot be solved by the constituted authorities acting singly, that is today one of America's most important domestic problems. Much can be and is done through the many devices that go by the name of cooperative federalism, by which the federal taxing and grant-giving powers can be used to impose federal standards of governmental services, and to make up for the wide disparities that exist between different regions and states; but one cannot ignore the difference that is made to the lives of the citizens by the adequacy or

[1] The state constitutions can of course be amended by state action alone: the states are not themselves federations.

lack of it that characterizes their state and local institutions. Even in respect of the contemporary reliance upon fiscal and monetary policy for the regulation of the economy, it is worth remembering that much public expenditure is not subject to direct federal control.

The balance between the units of which the governmental structure is composed is matched by the further element of diffused authority that results from observing the principle of the 'separation of powers', that is to be found not merely at the federal level but also in state and municipal government. The election of the President by machinery different from that which elects the Congress, the co-ordinate authority of the two chambers, the possibility of the President's party not commanding a congressional majority, and the absence of constitutional provisions for the resolution of deadlocks are features of the American federal system whose consequences have often been manifest to the world. At the state level where the principal executive officers are elected independently of the governor and not like the members of the President's Cabinet selected by him, a diffusion of executive and policy-forming responsibilities further enhances the difficulty created by the separation between executive and legislature; and in a country where so much of political consequence falls to be decided by the courts – labour relations provide a good instance – the independence of the judiciary may not be a wholly unmixed blessing. At the municipal level, too, it is possible for an incoming mayor – as the new Republican incumbent of the New York mayoralty discovered in 1966 – to be largely dependent upon officers and councillors of the opposing party. It is not surprising that at this level at least, efforts have been made to get round some of the problems by the institution of municipal government of the 'city manager' type.

But by and large it remains true that the American system of government is one in which power is uniquely diffused, and in which therefore the creation of a consensus before action can be taken is more necessary than in systems that lend themselves more easily to infusion with the purposes of a majority. The United States, the home of rationalization in the economic field and of managerial theory, does not normally apply these conceptions to the management of its public affairs. Nor can it be said, despite generations of academic pundits advocating constitutional reform, that this basic preference for balance as against concentration where public power is concerned is likely to disappear. Whether under modern conditions a system of this kind and the instinctive philosophy that goes with it give more protection to particular and selfish interests than to the individual citizen or naturally weak minority groups is a question that could be argued. But there seems little doubt but that most Americans are convinced that the merits of their institutions far outweigh any possible weaknesses. And when as in post-1945 Germany they have had the opportunity to help remodel another country's political future they have followed the pattern of their own Constitution without much hesitation.

The Constitution and Congress

The Constitution of the United States is often referred to as though it were the product of a single sustained intellectual effort at a particular point in time. But this exaggerates the degree of freedom available to the members of the Convention. The limits within which they could act had been prescribed by history. The state constitutions were the result of rewriting the existing colonial constitutions to allow for the colonists' repudiation of imperial authority. With some variations all the colonies which took part in the Revolution, despite their differences of origin, had much in common; their institutions bore the mark of British experience in central and local government, and in the organization of private collectivities such as chartered companies. The state governor succeeded the colonial governor; the state legislature, the colonial assemblies. The governor was always now an elected officer rather than a royal nominee as had normally been the case; but like his predecessors, his authority was not dependent upon that of the legislature. The separation of powers was a direct inheritance from the earlier period, not the result of a sudden addiction to political theory. The forms of local government – township in New England, county elsewhere – continued in being. The franchise (as in contemporary Britain) was based upon property, and two generations were to pass before adult male suffrage (for white citizens at any rate) became general. In some of the states an ecclesiastical establishment – episcopalian or other – survived the Revolution and again was not eliminated everywhere until the 1830s.

In most respects the makers of the new federal Constitution had little choice but to take for granted the basic institutions of the states. But even in respect of a national framework there was no clean slate for them to write upon. Most of the functions of any common government would, it was believed, relate to external affairs; once independent the former colonies had to do for themselves in such fields as defence and foreign and commercial policy what had previously been done for them by the imperial government. The original constitution, the Articles of Confederation of 1781, formalized a system by which the common concerns of the states were delegated to an assembly of their representatives – the Continental Congress – with certain minimal executive organs of its own, acting more in the fashion of a modern international organization than like a fully-fledged government, in that its authority was over the states considered as separate units of government and not over the individual citizen.

It is true that the new Constitution departed from this principle. In the light of the weaknesses of the Confederation in its international dealings, arising from its failure either to mobilize for common purposes a sufficient proportion of the national resources, or to make good internally the consequences of its international engagements, and in the light of certain anxieties as to the actions of some of the states in their effect upon the economy, and the interests of the propertied classes, the authors of the new document departed from some of the principles of its predecessor. It undoubtedly provided for something much closer to a real national government than to a mere alliance. The governing principle in the allocation of powers was that the United States should act as one in her dealings with other countries, but preserve her internal diversity of structure and policy. Thus a monopoly of foreign contacts, and of the power to levy armed forces for the support of the country's external policies, was conferred upon the federal government, together with powers of indirect taxation and also of direct taxation – the latter being, however, limited in such a way that full fiscal autonomy was not finally available to the federal government until the passing of the 'income tax amendment' (16th amendment, 1913).

But in some important respects the Constitution went beyond what was strictly necessary to meet the country's international position. In the first place, the Constitution outlawed impediments such as tariffs to trade between the different states. It thus created that 'common market' to which later generations of Americans were to ascribe so much of their country's economic dynamism. And it did it in language – the 'inter-state commerce clause' – so broadly framed as to make it possible, when the problems of controlling a national economy were raised, for the courts ultimately to interpret this power as one within the scope of the federal government, and of it alone. In the second place, the Constitution assigned priority to federal treaties and legislation over state law, so that in fields where the federal government exercised or acquired competence the states would have to give way. And this became even more important when, after the Civil War, some of the guarantees of individual liberties asserted as against the federal government in the Bill of Rights – the first ten amendments of 1791 – were extended to the actions of state governments by the 14th amendment (1868). Thirdly, the wording of the taxation article with its reference to providing for 'the general welfare' as well as the 'common defence' of the United States was to give yet another and even more powerful engine of centralization when the time came. Finally, and for the moment more importantly, the Constitution generalized the provisions of the Northwest Ordinance of 1787, by which although the direct government of territories belonging to the United States as a whole was duly provided for, it was envisaged that such government would be temporary in nature and that the ultimate destiny of such territories would be individual statehood as members of the Federal Union enjoying equal rights with its original constituents. The admission of Alaska and Hawaii in 1959 showed that this principle did not end at the water's edge.

The Bill of Rights, although added to the Constitution as part of the bargain over ratification with those who believed that the degree of centralization was greater than necessary, must be regarded as an integral part of the Constitution, particularly in three of its aspects. The guarantee of the freedoms of speech and of the press, and of the rights of petition and assembly, although envisaging solely the legislative powers of Congress and therefore capable of being infringed by state action as it has been under political stress, has provided an important criterion of all governmental policy, state as well as federal. The declaration that 'residual powers' lie with the states or the 'people' has provided a basis for subsequent arguments in favour of states' rights. It has meant the presumption that any new function of government should be exercised by the states rather than by the federal government. The prohibition of any national religious establishment has made the United States a secular state in its collective capacity despite the powerful social influence of organized religion in later times. While this provision was for a long period of little practical significance, the beginnings of federal subsidies for educational purposes has more recently raised the problem of the degree of prohibition envisaged.[1]

[1] It should perhaps not be necessary to say – though experience convinces me of the contrary – that the Constitution does not proclaim the right to 'life, liberty and the pursuit of happiness'. This famous phrase comes from a more radical

The institutions set up to handle the responsibilities conferred upon the federal government were inspired by the same principles as those of the states, and in particular by a suspicion of executive government characteristic of the period. The principle of equal representation in the old Continental Congress was retained in the Senate, where the two senators from each state were in fact for some time, and in theory until the 17th amendment (1913), elected by the state legislatures, and not by the people at large. Even after direct election had become the reality, the position of senator retained, as it still does, something of an ambassadorial character. In the House, the principle of representation in proportion to population was introduced with an increment of three-fifths in respect of the slaves of those states in which slavery was legal. Until the abolition of slavery by the 13th amendment (1865) the slave-holding states were thus over-represented in terms of their free population. After the 15th amendment (1870) the right to vote could not legally be denied on grounds of race but this provision was evaded because (with this exception) the right to vote in each state was a matter for the state itself; and the federal franchise was simply a concomitant of the state franchise. Female suffrage, which had been introduced into a number of states beginning in 1910, became mandatory through the 19th amendment (1920).

The legislative powers of the two Houses were made identical except for the provision that bills for raising revenue must be introduced first into the House of Representatives. But if it was thought that (on the British model) this would lead to the predominance of the lower House, the expectation was falsified in the event. The specific powers of the Senate, in the shape of its association with the President in making important appointments and in international treaties – which came to mean the right of ratification – and its role (more potential than frequently invoked) as the court for trying impeachments, gave the Senate from about the 1820s a priority from which it has not receded – a priority which the individual senator's six-year term (as compared with the congressman's two) has helped to fortify.

The Executive

The nature of the future executive – single or plural – much exercised the makers of the Constitution. But the familiar triumphed again. The

---

document, the 'Declaration of Independence' of 1776; and its principal author, Thomas Jefferson, was neither a member of the Constitutional Convention nor originally an enthusiast for its results.

executive power was vested in a single elected President in whose person were concentrated both the formal authority of the British monarch and the reality of power in the hands of the British Prime Minister – each fortifying the other. In contrast to the legislative authority of Congress spelled out in the Constitution, and further defined and redefined by the Supreme Court, the powers of the President were in some respects left vague. While he was granted a partial veto over legislation and the right to make appointments to administrative, judicial, and diplomatic office and to require the heads of the executive departments to report to him, while he was bound to report to Congress from time to time on the state of the Union and empowered to make recommendations to it for legislative and other action, there remained a great deal of scope for successive Presidents to make their office what their talents suggested and what their circumstances permitted.

In times of war or of civil or external crisis, the President's powers as commander-in-chief provided a separate source of authority in respect of which much could be claimed. Some Presidents have believed that their oath of office to 'preserve, protect and defend the Constitution' also gives authority to take action not otherwise provided for. Changing circumstances internal and external have on the whole tended to enhance the position of the office if not of the man. Few Presidents could nowadays hope to play as unobtrusive a role as did most of those who held office between Andrew Jackson and Abraham Lincoln or between Lincoln and Theodore Roosevelt. As the need for consistent national policies has made itself felt, the President's right to recommend legislation has come to mean that most important legislation (as in other countries) is in fact sponsored by the departments and not by individual senators or congressmen. Even more serious consequences may result from the fact that the wide scope given to the President under his powers as commander-in-chief to move troops and take other action for the nation's defence has rendered somewhat illusory the constitutional reservation to Congress of the power of declaring war. The advent of nuclear warfare has only accelerated a process already visible in the prelude to America's entry into the Second World War, if not the First.

The mode of election of the President was soon modified in a manner that enhanced his authority. The original provision was for indirect election through an electoral college with a provision for decision by House (with each state casting one vote) in the event of the original election not giving one candidate a clear majority over all his rivals combined. It was a system designed for a country in which reputations would tend to be local and intersectional bargaining between notables the rule. The rise of national parties rapidly defeated the intentions of the system and incidentally made it necessary in order to avoid deadlock that the President and Vice-President should be elected separately, and not as originally laid down. The residual importance of the electoral college (which never meets collectively) is to give to each state a number of presidential votes equal to its total representation in Congress, thus approximately proportionate to population. Since each state's electoral votes go to one candidate irrespective of the actual division of the popular vote, the nature of the electoral contest is not the same as it would be under a direct system of voting such as has been introduced into the Fifth French Republic. The political consequences of this situation will be further discussed in the next chapter. Meanwhile one must simply note that the fact that the President is popularly elected (in fact if not in law) does help to confer upon him the aura of democratic authority in the event of a conflict with other public or private powers. He is at once king and tribune.

Fears that an officer with such constitutional powers – even without the later unforeseen accretions of authority – might endanger the balance of the Constitution and lead to a form of personal rule were familiar to the Constitution-makers; but it was decided that to try to meet the problem by limiting the President's period of office was to incur other dangers. It was therefore decided to make the President's term one of four years but to make him re-eligible. The precedent set by George Washington – the first President and the first figure in the American pantheon – of two terms only was regarded as binding by his predecessors until the Presidency of Franklin Roosevelt, who at the time of his death had just entered upon his fourth term. By subsequent action – the 22nd amendment (1951) – the limitation to two terms was written into the Constitution.

The only other elected member of the executive branch is the Vice-President, and his allotment to this side of government is perhaps questionable since his duties under the Constitution were limited to presiding over the Senate. His real importance lay in the provision that in case of the removal or death of the President or his inability to discharge the duties of his office, they should 'devolve' upon the Vice-President. The first President to die in office was W. H. Harrison (in

1841); his Vice-President John Tyler acted on the assumption that he now became President in the full sense for the remainder of Harrison's term, and this interpretation has been accepted ever since. With the limitation of the number of terms to two, the question of the position of a Vice-President succeeding in this fashion required resolution. Under the 22nd amendment, if a Vice-President succeeds less than halfway through a term, he must count the remainder as one of his terms and can only be re-elected for one more.

A more difficult question raised by the incapacitating illnesses of Presidents Wilson and Eisenhower has been the question of establishing a President's disability and the role under such circumstances that devolves on the Vice-President. An amendment (the 24th) to provide for such eventualities became effective in 1967. The succession to the Presidency in the event of the demise or removal for other reasons of the President and Vice-President is not laid down in the Constitution but is subject to legislative regulation, and has more than once been altered. By the present law enacted in 1947 the first two in the list are the Speaker of the House of Representatives and the President *pro tempore* of the Senate (the senator elected to preside over the Senate's deliberations in the Vice-President's absence). They are followed by the members of the Cabinet in order of precedence.

Apart from the anomalous position of the Vice-President the principle of the separation of powers effectively excludes from Congress all persons holding administrative positions. The heads of the principal departments and other office-holders cannot be members of either House nor appear before it in plenary session. Only the President himself can address Congress in person – though this power was left unexercised in the more than a century that elapsed between the Presidencies of Thomas Jefferson and Woodrow Wilson. On the other hand, the heads of departments, like other government officials, can and do frequently appear before congressional committees as part of both the legislative and the investigatory process. In this sense the roles of the two sides of government are nowadays closely interwoven.

Of the Cabinet as such the Constitution makes no specific mention. It was clear from the Constitution as well as from the nature of the powers of the federal government that the President would have to nominate heads of departments more or less corresponding to the agencies that had grown up during the period of the Articles of Confederation; and it was natural that the President should from time to time consult these men collectively. As the scope of government grew, officials enjoying cabinet rank slowly multiplied, although even today the number is only twelve. But although office-holders of cabinet rank are always in the Cabinet, the President retains the right to invite any other advisers he chooses either to regular membership of it or to occasional participation in its meetings. But this flexibility only illustrates the more important fact that the Cabinet has remained an extra-constitutional body with no collective authority, consulted or not by the President as he chooses, and ultimately subject to his will. It is one among the many instruments through which the President exercises his constitutional powers; it has no independent existence, and since its members have no political constituency they ordinarily have no base from which to resist the presidential will. Normally, it may be added, the Senate will accept the President's nominees for cabinet office with little question; and although it was challenged during the vexed and unhappy Presidency of Andrew Johnson, the President has also preserved intact his right to dismiss them at will.

On the other hand, the President has in important respects a less free hand in relation to the administration of federal policies than concentration on the Cabinet alone would lead one to believe. Precisely because departments headed by cabinet officers are to this extent amenable to the President's will, Congress has shown a decided preference for entrusting specific functions of government, particularly in the economic field, to boards or commissions whose composition as well as competence is prescribed in the acts establishing them. The 'independent regulatory' commissions may have to be 'bi-partisan' in composition, with their members holding office for overlapping fixed terms.[1] It has also been strongly held that the kind of decisions they take – in such fields as tariff regulations and the control of communications where private interests are ordinarily involved – are of a quasi-judicial character. For this reason the Supreme Court has held (in the *Humphrey Case*, 1935) that the President cannot dismiss the members of such bodies before their term expires; and he cannot therefore ensure that their policies will follow the lines he thinks appropriate since they are also not subject to his direction. Finally, the fact that the independence of Congress extends to appropriations as well as to legislation means that some elements in a President's policy can be frustrated by a failure to provide the salaries for the staff that the relevant agency would require for their enforcement.

[1] The legal recognition of political parties in the United States in contrast with the British situation will be further examined in the next chapter.

The Supreme Court

The actual position of the Supreme Court was the most controversial issue bequeathed by the Constitution-makers; and it was later suggested more than once that the important role it assumed was to some extent usurped. Such a contention is difficult to sustain since there is evidence that the makers of the Constitution were aware of both the theory and the practice of what came to be called 'judicial review'. In the first place the constitutional provision that the federal Constitution and federal laws and treaties together constituted the 'supreme law' could have been carried out by conferring upon some political organ at the centre a power of veto over state legislation. Instead, it was consciously decided that it would be sufficient to leave the matter to the courts; in the event of a conflict the courts would be bound to rule in favour of the federal instrument in question. The power to annul state laws was claimed by the Court in its judgement in the case of *McCulloch v. Maryland* in 1819, and has since been maintained despite intermittent political attack. The practice of judicial review in this context was thus a product of federalism; and it had precedents in the jurisprudence of the British Privy Council in relation to colonial appeals. In relation to laws passed by Congress the juridical review was a consequence not of federation but of the existence of a written constitution as such. In his classic judgement in *Marbury v. Madison* (1803), Chief Justice Marshall argued that under constitutional government, only a law made in pursuance of the Constitution and in consonance with its provisions and limitations was law indeed; anything else that purported to be legislation was null and void from the outset, and had no claim to be enforced by the courts. In spite of objections that this argument meant that the Supreme Court regarded its own view of the Constitution as having greater validity than that of Congress or the President, this position has also been maintained intact.

It is of course essential for understanding the actual course of constitutional development to appreciate the fact that the Court's power of disallowance is a power of only a negative kind; it depends, as has been shown in more than one context, upon the executive's willingness and power to make its judgements effective, and the generality of its decisions may mean that legislation is subsequently required in order to give them concrete meaning. This has been the case particularly where the disallowance of state laws is concerned, as can easily be illustrated from the history of civil rights issues in parts of the South since the

Court ruled unconstitutional, first, the 'white primary' in 1944,[1] second, racially restrictive covenants in 1948, and finally, educational segregation in the case of *Brown v. Board of Education* (1954). For, although the Supreme Court stands at the apex of a federal judicial system which ensures that federal legal remedies are widely accessible, federal law-enforcement agencies are generally weak. The practice of cooperative federalism has rested upon the general assumption that the actual administration of the country can largely be left to the states and localities; when these are recalcitrant to federal wishes, difficulties at once arise.

The 1954 decision reversed the 1896 decision in *Plessy v. Ferguson* in which the Court had held that the constitutional requirements of non-discrimination were met by the provision of 'separate but equal' facilities in education and other public services. Such a reversal (which had been foreshadowed by a series of decisions beginning in 1937) is within the power of the Court. Indeed if the Court were bound by the principal of *stare decisis* as rigidly as British courts it is probable that other methods of bringing constitutional doctrine into line with changing social sentiment would have had to be discovered. Nor of course are race relations the only example of such a reversal. For instance, when in 1938 in *Erie Railroad Company v. Tompkins* the Court over-ruled its decision in *Swift v. Tyson* (1842), it abandoned the doctrine that there was a federal common law that could be used in preference to the different interpretations placed upon common law principles by the courts of the states. In the many spheres of private law still primarily a matter for the states, the Supreme Court cannot thus itself exercise a unifying influence, and the search for uniformity has to be carried on through attempts to secure the adoption of uniform codes. In this respect, as in others, it must not be forgotten that the states are capable of making agreements with each other and of devising machinery for cooperation between themselves. Perhaps less strikingly than in Australia or Canada, some of the contradictions inherent in the existence of a federal system of government responsible for an essentially unitary economy are being tackled in the United States, not through the exercise of federal powers, but by negotiation at different levels between the states themselves.

---

[1] Primary elections will be dealt with in the next chapter; in virtually one-party states in the South, the democratic 'primary' was the real election and access to it the only meaningful franchise.

The Constitutional Debate

Indeed the difficulty of trying to summarize the development of the Constitution between 1789 and our own time lies in the fact that the drama of conflict, which is never for long absent from this story, may conceal the equally important and uninterrupted adaptation of this highly complex system to its new tasks. The existence of a constitutional structure giving so important a role to the judiciary has tended to cast many arguments that were essentially arguments of substance into a legal form; but the pedantry of statement should not obscure the very real issues at stake.

The early period of constitutional development was partly, as has been seen, taken up with the extension of democratic principles, notably as regards the franchise, and also in respect of access to administrative responsibilities, state and federal, and to the state judiciaries. But at the same time the federal government was establishing its own authority both by enforcing the supremacy of federal law and by the actual interpretation placed upon some provisions of the Constitution, notably in the important scope given to the federal responsibility for inter-state commerce in the case of *Gibbons v. Ogden* in 1824.

The period that began with the Presidency of Andrew Jackson saw some recovery of initiative by the states in spite of the defeat of South Carolina's attempt to 'nullify' a new protective tariff. The veto in 1832 by Jackson of the renewal of the charter of the Second Bank of the United States put an end to the central control of credit, which was not restored until the beginnings of the Federal Reserve system in the act of 1913; and this important aspect of an expanding economy and society became for more than a century very largely a state matter. In this period also the states began to try their hands at some of the regulatory activities and at the sponsorship of communications and other public works that the growth of industry and commerce now demanded. The jurisprudence of Marshall's successor as Chief Justice, Roger B. Taney (who held the office from 1836 to 1864), carved out in the name of the 'police power' an area of state action sheltered from invasion on the part of the federal government through the 'inter-state commerce clause'.

But the achievements of this period were overshadowed by the increasing importance of the question of slavery. In the original slave states there were growing fears that propaganda from the North would undermine the status of slavery upon which they believed both their economy and their society to be based; and measures were taken to insulate the South from the circulation of ideas hostile to its professed ideology. At the same time it was argued that the Constitution itself must be looked upon as an implicit bargain between the sections and that no constitutional changes would be in order unless both North and South agreed to them. In this way it was hoped to forestall the day when the free states might come to outnumber the slave states to an extent sufficient to enable them to use the amending process to the South's disadvantage. An intersectional bargain – the compromise of 1850 – appeared to have averted the storm; but the underlying issues remained unresolved. By its decision in the *Dred Scott* case in 1857, the Supreme Court seemed to have strengthened the South's position both by declaring that Negroes were not citizens of the Union and so not entitled to the constitutional remedies that would otherwise be available, and by asserting that the 'Missouri compromise' legislation of 1820 (by which slavery was permanently excluded from the vast northwest territories owned by the Union) was unconstitutional, as involving a discrimination against potential settlers whose property was in the form of slaves. But the widespread repudiation of the moral validity of the judgement signalized to many Southern leaders the continued precariousness of their minority position. They therefore seized the occasion of the election of Abraham Lincoln on a platform advocating the territorial limitation of slavery to bring about the secession of the principal slave states, and to form out of them a new confederacy.

Secession itself was justified on the basis of the inherent and inalienable sovereignty of the states, and a concept of the Constitution that emphasized implicit sectional compromises that it was held had been violated by Northern action. The new Confederacy, though making no provision for its own dissolution, was hampered very considerably during the ensuing war by its own dedication to the maximum degree of state autonomy. On their side Northern apologists generally adhered to the view that the Union was prior to the states and that it was intended to be perpetual. The conflict was on the face of it a forcible attempt by a majority to prevent the disruption of the country. The North was thus obliged in theory to treat the war as merely the suppression of an internal rebellion although in practice the ordinary conventions of international conflict were applied.

The Northern victory both re-established the original Union and appeared. as has been said, to give final sanction to the Northern view of the nature of the federal bond. But it was impossible simply to return to the status quo. Lincoln's emancipation proclamation of 1863 was a largely propagandist use of the war power since the slaves it professed to emancipate were not within reach of the federal authority. But the post-Civil War exclusion of the rebellious states from full political participation and the imposition upon them of regimes of occupation in the name of 'reconstruction', enabled a series of constitutional amendments to be pushed through which formally ended both slavery and all forms of legal and political discrimination based upon colour.

This phase in the emancipation of the Southern Negro proved to be of only temporary significance except in respect of the institution of slavery itself. The enforcement of legislation based upon the new constitutional amendments depended upon the presence of federal troops. With the final withdrawal of these forces twelve years later, the stage was set for the return to power of the former slave-holders. Between 1877 and the end of the century Southern society became increasingly based upon the practice of segregation in almost all its aspects, and upon the economic and social subordination of the once more disenfranchised Negro. In the North, however, the Negro could enjoy, if not economic or social equality, at least legal equality and, still more important, the leverage of the franchise. The northward movement of Negroes beginning on a large scale during the First World War helped to pave the way for the second phase in their emancipation to which reference has already been made.

But with the last quarter of the nineteenth century the centre of the constitutional debate shifted from the complex of questions revolving round the status of the Negro to those involved in the need to devise laws and to adapt or create institutions that would enable the United States to face the economic and social consequences of its rapid transformation into a predominantly urban and industrial society. The most obvious evidence of this shift is to be found in the fact that the 14th amendment, guaranteeing to all citizens as against the states the right not to be deprived of life, liberty, or property without 'due process of law', and which had been intended for the protection of the enfranchised Negro, was held by the Court, beginning with the case of *Allgeyer v. Louisiana* in 1897, to involve serious limitations upon the right of the states to regulate economic life and industrial conditions.

For this to be the case it was necessary for the Court to accept the view that 'persons' included 'corporations' – that is to say the new large-scale organizations of private business against which the ordinary citizen might well actually require protection – and also that 'due process' had a substantive as well as a procedural content. In other words, it now meant that complete freedom of contract, the economic and social theory of *laissez-faire*, had been written into the Constitution, and that the states could not enter into those fields of regulation in ways that the governments of all other industrializing countries had found necessary in order to avoid undue hardship for workers, farmers, and consumers. In striking down, in the case of *Lochner v. New York* (1905), a state minimum-wage law, the Court rendered itself open to the charge that it was acting upon philosophical assumptions that much of the nation disputed.

But if the power of the states was limited by 'due process' in addition to 'inter-state commerce', under which it had been held that the states could not interfere with the production of goods for possible sale beyond their borders, the federal government was also limited by constitutional inhibitions from stepping into the breach. The limitations upon the federal government's financial powers produced by the *Income-Tax Case* were, as we have seen, removed by the 16th amendment in 1913. In the same year in which the *Income-Tax Case* was decided (1895), the *Sugar Trust Case* provided an occasion for the Court to limit the powers of the Congress to use the federal powers over 'inter-state' commerce for regulatory purposes. In the case of *Hammer v. Dagenhart* in 1918 a federal child-labour law was invalidated. It thus appeared that a combination of constitutional clauses and amendments could be utilized in order to create a twilight zone in which neither tier of government could act effectively, and that this included matters which in all other civilized countries were clearly seen to be appropriate for legislation.

The issue was brought to a head in the 1930s, when in a series of decisions the Supreme Court declared invalid much of the legislation of the 'New Deal' through which President Franklin Roosevelt had sought to meet the problems of the Great Depression. After his electoral victory in 1936, Roosevelt met the challenge head-on by producing a scheme that, although constitutionally within Congress's powers in respect of organizing the judiciary, would have had the immediate effect of enabling him to nominate new justices and so reverse the existing majority on the Court. The Court in fact removed the immediate need for action by recanting its previous attitudes. Since 1937 the taxing power and the commerce power between them have provided sufficient grounds for the Court to accept all New Deal type legislation; the largely unified economy of the United States is now as subject to unified regulation as that of most other advanced countries. By the Court's decision in *National Labour Relations Board v. Jones and Laughlin Steel Corporation*, the rights of labour to organize were fully accepted for the first time; the difference is that in respect of social legislation and labour questions there is a close interaction between state and federal legislation and their enforcement. The Roosevelt plan for the Court – easily discredited as a device for 'packing' – failed to gain acceptance by Congress. But the main battle had been won.

Since 1937, the importance of the Constitution and hence of the Court has not lain in the economic and social field, although labour relations have remained an important field for the intervention of the law, but in their relations to three other issues of national concern, and sometimes of acute political controversy. One of these, the changed position with respect to racial segregation, has already been mentioned (p. 249), and it is the one in which federal enforcement has come up against deliberate obstruction by some state governments. The second field is that of civil liberties. Although civil liberties have replaced economic and social regulation as a principal field of jurisdiction, it cannot be said that the Court has gone as far in protecting the rights of dissident minorities and individuals as some people would have thought it entitled to under the provisions of the Bill of Rights. The very severe legislation against political subversion, beginning with the Smith Act of 1940 (under which the leaders of the American Communist party were prosecuted in 1948), has largely been allowed to stand. The judicial scepticism, which in a previous generation made the great Justice Oliver Wendell Holmes unwilling to follow his brethren in preferring their own views of the Constitution to those of the legislatures, resulted in the Court (affected like all Americans by the impact of the 'Cold War') allowing governments, and in particular the federal government, much latitude in choosing methods for combating the alleged menace of Communism. The efforts of the judiciary have largely concentrated on procedural questions, so as to see that the ordinary guarantees of legality were not set aside; but the fundamental position of Congress has not been seriously challenged. Despite the Bill of Rights and judicial review, the path of the political dissident in the United States is much harder than for his counterpart in Britain.

In the last of these issues the Court has substantially changed its historic position. The Court has always tried in the past to avoid getting entangled in what have been called 'political' questions, that is to say questions involving the legitimacy or internal constitution of the other branches of government. But it has long been plain that the electoral provisions of many state constitutions, by giving a large measure of extra strength to rural areas in defiance of the principle of equal representation, have been an important bulwark of extreme conservative positions, for instance on race relations. On one important point the Court has reversed itself with important consequences. In 1946 in *Colegrove v. Green*, the Court had ruled that apportionment – that is to say, the demarcation of districts (constituencies) for the House of Representatives or state legislatures – was a political matter and that the gross over-representation of rural areas was not something which could be corrected through legal action. In *Baker v. Carr*, in 1962, the Court ruled the contrary in respect of state legislatures, and in *Wesberry v. Sanders*, in 1964, it applied the principle of equal representation to congressional districts as well. In *Reynolds v. Sims* in the same year the upper Houses of state legislatures were brought within the ruling. Further litigation followed and as a result the political map of the United States has been very considerably altered, probably to the benefit of suburbia.

These examples are only some of those which could be brought forward in order to demonstrate that the Constitution, despite its written form and rigidity, is by no means a static one, that the separation of powers and federalism are not simply formulae to be applied irrespective of circumstances, but ever-changing concepts in keeping with the ever-changing structure of American society.

The Modern Presidency and the Executive Office

The office of President of the United States, the most important elective office in the world, owes much of its present status to the exploitation by successive Presidents of the opportunities presented to them in the Constitution. In more recent times the nature of the electoral contest and the development of the media of mass communication have (as shown in the next chapter) forged further links between the President and the people at large, and these have undoubtedly assisted in the transformation of the office from the fairly lowly esteem in which it has been held at certain times in the past. But while it is tempting to seek, in the accidents of personality, for the reasons why some Presidents have clearly exercised greater authority than others, it is possible to overestimate the importance of this aspect of the office by comparison with the demands made upon it by the changing American and world scene. It is legitimate to wonder how a system that could produce an Abraham Lincoln, a Woodrow Wilson, or a Franklin Roosevelt could also throw up a Ulysses S. Grant, a Warren Harding, or a Dwight Eisenhower. But the men who figure in the lists of the so-called 'great Presidents' are also those who were faced with great problems. No doubt one can hold that men rise to their opportunities but it is also true that institutions can respond to new needs. The President is a man; but the Presidency, particularly the modern Presidency, is an institution. The fact that the President occupies so unusual an eminence is reflected in the public's insatiable appetite for intimate details about him; the literature of the subject is highly personal. But this does not mean that the executive branch of government in the United States is or could be in the hands of a single individual, whatever the Constitution may appear to suggest.

When one says the 'modern Presidency' one has in mind the Presidency since the time of Franklin Roosevelt; for it is in the past forty years only that the assumption by the federal government of new powers in the economic and social field, followed by the involvement of the United States in the affairs of nearly all the rest of the world with an enormous consequent accretion of the government's original external responsibilities, have altered, and for good, the whole balance of the system. Indeed in retrospect the introduction by Franklin Roosevelt of 'big government' as a permanent feature of the American scene even in peacetime looks to have been more important than the actual content of the 'New Deal' policies themselves. And this growth in the size of the machinery of government, although much of it went on in the classic departments or involved the creation of new agencies over which presidential control was limited, also meant equipping the President for the first time with a permanent set of executive instruments of his own.

It is always dangerous of course to underestimate the element of continuity in the history of institutions; and one must not overlook the fact that some of the President's role as the coordinator and energizer of the whole governmental system had earlier roots. The President's annual message on the State of the Union which could serve to direct the attention of Congress and the people to those questions thought most important by the President goes back to the earliest period; but its modern companion, the budget message, has more recent origins. Until as late as 1921 each department prepared its own request for funds which was then presented to Congress by the Treasury; the Bureau of the Budget was set up in 1921 to coordinate expenditure but was thought of primarily as a method of ensuring economy. In 1939 the Bureau was transferred to the newly created Executive Office of the President and has since then performed a more positive role as the organ through which priorities in legislation as well as in financial matters are settled. In 1970 it was reorganized as the Office of Management and Budget. Since the President's budget is subject like other legislation to amendment by Congress, the budget is a less powerful device in the United States than in the United Kingdom, but with the emergence of a positive fiscal policy since the Employment Act of 1946 and with the new direct importance of federal spending for the health of the economy as a whole, it is today central to the governmental process.

The simplest way of looking at the executive branch today is to take the official 'manual' of 'United States Government Organization'. The first part is devoted to Congress and the judiciary, and we then come to the executive branch.

The first institution dealt with is the Cabinet. First come the heads of the twelve cabinet-rank departments: the Secretary of the Treasury, the Secretary of State, the Secretary of Defence (who was placed over the former Service Secretaries in 1947), the Attorney General (who has since 1870 been head of a Department of Justice), the Postmaster General (the Post Office itself has become a public corporation), the Secretary of the Interior (not to be confused with the Minister of the Interior of European countries, since the 'Interior' in this case refers to the geographical section still in process of settlement when the department was created in 1849, so that the department itself is primarily concerned with natural resources), the Secretaries of Agriculture, Commerce, and Labor (representative within the Cabinet of the nation's three most powerful pressure groups), and the three most recent additions, the Secretaries of Health, Education, and Welfare (which replaced in 1953 the Federal Security Agency set up in 1939), Housing and Urban Development (1965), and Transportation (1966). Others may be added and the Vice-President participates in all its meetings. President Eisenhower's attempt to give the Cabinet a more important role in the country's affairs and to endow it with a secretariat on the British model proved unacceptable to his successors. The Cabinet remains rather marginal as a body to the main concerns of American government, and the following up of such decisions as it makes is a matter for the President working through a special assistant for this purpose.

We then come to the Executive Office of the President. So important is this organ today that it is difficult to remember that its creation dates only to 1939. As we have seen, a central role within the Executive Office is taken by the Bureau of the Budget. It also includes a number of different institutions linked only by their common relationship to the President. The three-member Council of Economic Advisers, set up under the Employment Act of 1946, enables the President to secure advice on the economic situation and on economic policy, independent of that of the Treasury, the Commerce and Agriculture Departments, and the Federal Reserve Board. The National Security Council has general responsibilities in the field of defence but its role has been a variable one since its creation in 1947; it is indeed only since 1949 as a part of the general centralization of the machinery of government in this field that it has been part of the Executive Office, and it was only in 1953 that it took on something like its present form. President Eisenhower showed the same preference for orderly patterns of organization in this sphere of his responsibilities as in home affairs, and the NSC in his time was endowed with a powerful underpinning of boards, committees, and with a secretariat for seeing that the proper matters were presented to it for decision and that decisions once taken were duly followed up.

President Kennedy had a different and more personal conception of administration and the NSC, like the Cabinet, was to some extent demoted in favour of the President's own office on the one hand, and of the departments on the other. By 1965-6, the Council itself had only five permanent members, the President, Vice-President, Secretary of State, Secretary of Defence, and the Director of the Office of Emergency Planning (the former Office of Civilian Defence Mobilization); though others can be called to its meetings.

It has certainly been thought proper that decisions in the security field should appear to emanate from the NSC. Thus, while the decisions over the Cuban missile crisis in 1962 were made in an *ad hoc* committee consisting of cabinet members, White House and other officials, and a couple of eminent but by then private citizens, once a programme of action had been laid down it was submitted to the NSC, and the *ad hoc* committee was retrospectively designated as a sub-committee of the NSC. The Office of Emergency Planning itself is another branch of the Executive Office.

The Central Intelligence Agency established under the act of 1947 is perhaps the most widely-known part of the Executive Office although it has physically long outgrown its parent body. Despite the set-back to its prestige as a result of the 'Bay of Pigs' fiasco in 1961, and despite the fact that other agencies of the government are also involved in intelligence activities, the relative independence that the CIA enjoys in operational as well as intelligence-gathering activities, and its virtual freedom from congressional control, makes it a rather equivocal feature of the structure of a democratic state.

The President today is thought to require advice on science and technology as well as on economics. The President acquired a Special Assistant for Science and Technology in 1957; and an Office of Science and Technology under a director was set up within the Executive Office by statute in 1962. The Executive Office has also served since 1958 as the headquarters of the National Aeronautics and Space Council presided over by the Vice-President.

The Executive Office has the merits of extreme flexibility; thus if the President wishes to give an impetus to some new or newly important area of governmental activity he can do so by putting responsibility into a new section of the office. For instance, in 1963 the Office of the Special Representative for Trade Negotiations was set up by Executive Order under the Trade Expansion Act of 1962 to deal with multilateral efforts to reduce trade barriers, notably through the GATT. In 1964 the passage of the Economic Opportunity Act – the first instalment of President Johnson's war 'against poverty' – produced the Office of Economic Opportunity. Both these would of course be dependent upon other branches of the government for much of their work, but their location in the Executive Office makes clear the direct concern of the President with the success of their efforts.

Finally, the White House Office itself is regarded as part of the Executive Office, although its personnel is wholly a matter for each successive President. Here the distribution of assignments is also a matter of the President's personal choice. In 1964–5, the office included ten special assistants and two administrative assistants as well as the Special Counsel and the Legislative Counsel. All these except the last might be given a variety of jobs to perform. But the staff can also include individuals with specific responsibilities: at that time, a Special Assistant on the Arts, and more surprisingly a Special Assistant to the President, additionally styled Director of the Food for Peace Programme. But even more significant is the fact that the special assistants, the press secretary and so on, must be capable of working within the framework and along the lines laid down by the President himself. And this is more important than in the case of cabinet members. Thus, while President Johnson after succeeding President Kennedy was content to keep much of his Cabinet unchanged, the Harvard intellectuals and personal political agents of his predecessor – the so-called 'Irish mafia' – were increasingly replaced by Texans and others more congenial to the new incumbent. Within little more than two years after Kennedy's death, the White House staff had lost the last of his appointees.

During his first term as President, Mr Nixon's arrangements were different again. White House appointments were made in terms which gave the individuals selected very precise terms of reference and which meant a strict control of access to the President. Like President Eisenhower, President Nixon likes orderly processes of delegation. In the course of time it became clear that one special assistant, Dr Henry Kissinger, was a more important figure in the making and execution of foreign policy than the Secretary of State himself. Particular attention has also been given to the public relations aspect of staff-work with men brought in from the world of commercial advertising.

The Departments

The Manual next deals with the organization of the departments proper. The most significant difference in these as compared with their British counterparts is the absence of a unified hierarchy leading up to a permanent secretary. They are instead divided into separate bureaus, administrations or other subdivisions, and continuity is preserved within these rather than in respect of departmental policy as a whole. It is true that since 1949 a number of powers formerly vested by law in the heads of bureaus have been transferred to the heads of the respective departments; nevertheless the lack of unity within departments, as well as between them, is striking for someone familiar with the powers of permanent secretaries in Whitehall. To some extent this difference relates to the method by which the civil service is organized and recruited; but it is also closely connected with the preference in Congress for dealing with bureau chiefs directly. Each separate bureau will tend to have its related pressure group in the country, and its patrons in Congress; and under a system in which congressional control of expenditure is real and effective, this is of considerable importance. Indeed the shape taken by the American departments is as good an example as any of the reality as compared with the theory of the separation of powers. As will be seen in the next chapter, Congress (the legislature) is much more consistently concerned with the affairs of the executive than under a Parliamentary system such as the British, where the theory of the separation of powers is rejected in principle but exists in fact to the advantage, almost exclusively, of the executive.

After the departments come the independent agencies, listed alphabetically from the American Battle Monuments Commission to the Virgin Islands Corporation, including such giants as the Atomic Energy Commission, the Interstate Commerce Commission, the Federal Communications, Federal Trade, and Federal Maritime Commissions as well as lesser organs of federal power: forty-one in all – all owing their being to congressional action, and most of them capable within various limits of both assisting and frustrating the intentions of the President and his administration. Another eighty or so lesser bodies are also listed under the heading 'Guide to selected boards, committees and commissions'; and these also cannot be neglected by someone seeking to evaluate the activities of the federal government, seeing that they include such bodies as the Commission on Civil Rights, and the President's Committee on Equal Employment Opportunity, as well as a number of important advisory bodies in the economic, scientific, and cultural fields.

If one recollects that this brief survey includes only those aspects of the executive branch of government that are federal, and that each state has its own array of departments and agencies, often closely interlocking with the work of the federal government, one can see how far one is today from the frontier myth of the United States as a country where all depends on the private initiative of the individual, and in which government is reduced to its simplest aspects. The absence of certain elements of what would in Western Europe be regarded as the normal components of a welfare state – the most obvious being the lack of provision for general medical care, 'socialized medicine' as it is opprobriously named – should not prevent one from realizing to what an extent the United States is a fully administered society. Even those elements in the population that most clearly symbolize the traditional virtues – the farmers for instance – depend for their livelihood upon a vast apparatus of assistance and controls. Both business – for instance in respect of trusts and other forms of combination – and labour are subjected to more legislative controls and to a bigger administrative apparatus than is true of Britain.

Changes in the Administrative Machine

The growth of administration can of course be seen in crude statistical terms: of an employed population of 46·7 million in 1929, 3·1 million were in government employment (and 0·3 in the armed forces). In 1965, of an employed population of 69·5 million, government accounted for 9·8 million (with about two and a half millions in the federal service alone) and the armed forces for 2·7 million. In the period 1929–64, the expenditure of the federal government alone rose from 3·299 million dollars to 97·684 million dollars. Thanks to the Vietnam War the hundred billion dollar budget arrived in 1966; in 1971 it stood at 225 billion dollars. To put the matter in further perspective, it might be added that the federal expenditure for 1929 was itself over four times the average for the period 1906–10.

But the success of a country's administration does not depend upon the numbers of its servants or its total cost as much as upon quality and upon its underlying philosophy of government. American experience in this respect has been very different to that of most European countries, where modern civil services were based upon the previous and largely aristocratic patterns of administration that had served the *anciens régimes*. Nor does it rest upon the Benthamite foundations of the British system. Although the public service of the early Republic bore some resemblance to that of the colonial period out of which it sprang, the Jacksonian Revolution of the 1830s and 1840s saw the triumph of a different view of administrative office. The then dominant philosophy held first, that no special skills were needed to perform public duties and that any man might thus serve the state at some point in his career; secondly, that public service was a proper source of profit, and consequently a suitable field for party patronage. The effect of this outlook upon the development of American political parties will concern us in a later chapter; here we must note its lasting effects upon the machinery of government itself. It was to colour the attitude towards municipal and state employment even more than towards the federal service, although in more recent times, the importance of state–federal cooperation has tended to imbue state officials with something of the common professional outlook of the federal officials with whom their work is so closely connected.

If we limit ourselves to the federal civil service, we can see that there are two aspects of the reforms that have within the last hundred years produced the modern American administrative system, which make it very different from the parallel development in Britain. In the first place, the changes in Britain have been largely the work of the executive; the civil service is still mainly governed under the royal prerogative. In the United States, Congress has had a more independent role; and this has been even truer in recent decades than formerly. The first civil service legislation took the form of a rider to an Appropriation Act of 1871 enabling the President to lay down rules for admission to the civil service. The Civil Service Act of 1883 (the Pendleton Act) created the Civil Service Commission and gave it the power to frame a system of admission to the service by 'merit', i.e. by examination. From that date until 1930, there was little fresh legislation and the Civil Service Commission was regarded basically as an agency of the President. Since that date, however, a large amount of detailed legislation has been passed – some 1500 acts by 1963 – and the Civil Service Commission has been encouraged to take a more independent position. On the other hand, Congress has been mainly concerned to keep down the growth of the service, and to control its recruitment and management in detail; it has not been much concerned with reform.

In the second place, the British conception of a unified service recruited at different levels but serving government as a whole (with the exception of the foreign service) and not individual departments has not found favour in the United States. In particular the elitist aspect of the British administrative class has always been suspect. What American reformers accepted was that government might need specialized skills or knowledge, not that administration was itself a skill in its more rarified aspects. For this reason, recruitment under the merit system was to departments, and to specific kinds of openings within them. This meant that the system was applied mainly to medium range appointments; the lowest offices (e.g. postmasterships) and the highest – roughly corresponding to the British administrative class – were largely left open to political patronage.

The periods of expansion in the administrative machine have witnessed lapses from what are called 'civil service' principles but these have subsequently been made up. Thus by 1924, about 80 per cent of all federal posts were subject to civil service rules; the enormous expansion of governmental activity in the New Deal period brought the figure down to just over 60 per cent, but this rose again to almost 80 per cent when the war brought about a new period of massive direct recruitment. By the beginning of the Eisenhower Presidency in 1953, the proportion was up to about 90 per cent if one includes the separate merit systems operated by some of the independent agencies.

A change in party control under this system is regarded as creating a problem, since at the higher levels it is thought proper that the departmental heads as well as the President should have a reasonable number of posts to offer, lest they be surrounded by nominees of their predecessors, the other party. Since those appointees who have come in under the merit system cannot be dismissed, recourse may be had to increasing the total number of posts. The incoming Republicans in 1953, for instance, created a new category of policy-making positions to be held at the President's pleasure.

President Eisenhower was himself concerned to bring about a less political system and to improve the quality of the higher appointments. Since Franklin Roosevelt's Presidency, the President has had a 'Special Assistant on Personnel Administration' or someone with similar responsibilities on the White House staff; and between 1953 and 1957 this post was held by the president of the Civil Service Commission himself. President Eisenhower's views were also affected by the report of the Second Hoover Commission in 1955, which worked out that there were some thousand individuals in the federal government occupying positions concerned with policy-making, who were outside the merit system and could be called political executives. Between four and five hundred career civil servants occupied positions of equivalent status.

The commission recommended the creation of a Senior Civil Service and estimated that there were in all some three thousand positions of a senior kind that could usefully be filled by persons promoted from within the career service, and specifically trained for the purpose. The substance of this report was accepted by President Eisenhower in 1957, but his proposal for a 'career-executive service' was blocked in the House of Representatives where strong opposition was expressed to the notion of an elite corps whose members could be moved from one department to another. In 1961, the Civil Service Commission itself established a 'Career Executive Roster'. But the standard American approach to the problem remains largely unchanged.

The changeover from Republican back to Democrat in 1960–1 again involved a large-scale search for persons capable of filling the higher posts in the administration from the Cabinet down. For one must not forget that in the absence of a well-defined class of *ministrables* brought forward through parliamentary activity, an incoming President may have some difficulty in filling even the top positions. President Kennedy had never met his Secretary of State, Mr Dean Rusk, before he summoned him to discuss the offer of the post. What was different in 1961–2 was not the magnitude of the changeover – there were 1200 posts to fill apart from the Cabinet and agency heads – but the amount of previous preparation for it and especially the close contact between the outgoing and incoming administrations in striking contrast to the precedents of 1932–3 and 1952–3. The process of transition in 1968–9 was once again an orderly one though it was reported that President Nixon ran into some difficulties in finding among Republicans all the men he needed to fill the policy-making posts available to him.

Such an injection of new talent drawn from business, the professions, and the universities as well as from politics does of course enable an incoming administration to make its mark in a way which might otherwise be impossible, given the enormous and unwieldy mass that the federal government presents. A good example from the Kennedy Presidency would be the Department of Defense. The creation of a single department out of the empires previously controlled by the service chiefs and their separate political heads was a long-drawn-out process beginning with the National Security Act of 1947. As in other countries, rivalries between the different services were stimulated by the economic interests affected by the choice of weapons to develop; there were tensions between the civilian and the service sides of the department, and above all there was the unwillingness of Congress to accept its exclusion from the settlement of such issues. The political weight of President Kennedy's nominee for Secretary, Mr Robert McNamara, rested upon his prestige as a successful businessman and upon the President's confidence in him, and was indeed considerable. But the new directions which he gave to the work of the department would not have been possible had he not been able to make use of his own team of academic economists and of other individuals with reputations external to the department itself.

On the other hand, there still remain uncured the two principal weaknesses of the system. In the first place, though it may be relatively easy to persuade people for a time to accept the burdens of governmental service – and the American career pattern is more flexible than the European one – it is not easy to persuade such people to remain in Washington long enough for the government to get full value from their services, seeing that in most cases an initial period of apprenticeship will be required. Between 1933 and 1952, the average tenure of the head of a department was three and a half years; but under-secretaries served for just under two years on the average, and assistant secretaries for about two years and eight months. During the Eisen-hower and Truman Presidencies the average tenure further declined to just over two years for assistant secretaries. As far as Cabinet secre-taries, agency heads, and General Counsel are concerned, the average tenure was only just over a year and a half under Truman and only just over two years under Eisenhower. During the whole period 1933 to 1961, over one in three individuals appointed at this level left before two years were up; although some Roosevelt cabinet members had unusually long terms. It might be argued that in Britain there is a very high turn-over at Cabinet level, but here one must again remember the absence of any equivalent in the United States of high permanent officials on the policy-making side.

The other major disadvantage of the system is the fact that the way to the top in government service is so unlikely to be through entry into it on a career basis, as to make the notion of a civil service career much less attractive to the best young graduates than in Britain or France.

The course of events in respect of the foreign service has marked a rather more definable shift towards professionalism. Congress's sus-picion of elitist career services was fortified in this case by a fairly widespread conviction during the nineteenth century that the United States, not being involved in the international power struggle, hardly required a diplomatic service at all. Appointments abroad could thus be used as a reward for political services, whether combined with intellectual distinction, as in the cases of Nathaniel Hawthorne and John Lothrop Motley, or not so combined, as on occasions when it was difficult or inadvisable to provide or maintain a home billet for some-one. The twentieth-century expansion of United States interest in world affairs involved the creation of a full career service, and its modern form took shape as a result of the Rogers Act of 1924 which (twenty years before the 'Eden' reforms in Britain) amalgamated the diplomatic and consular services. In 1954, after a period of even more rapid growth, it was recommended that there should be a further amalgamation, this time with the staff of the State Department itself. The implementation of this recommendation has meant that the United States now has a single unified service of people available to serve either at home or overseas. On the other hand, major embassies are still often filled by political appointees, partly because in some cases the expenses of the post are too great for someone without private means, partly as a way of paying political debts, but partly because, as at home, Presidents may wish to nominate individuals often with considerable experience of the world of affairs, or with other expert qualifications, who can be relied upon to give an impetus to a particular line of policy.

Indeed, in some cases this may be essential if policy is not to be frustrated or gravely weakened. For if the development of the White House staff and the Executive Office has to some extent made possible a degree of coordination in Washington which has not always existed, there remains a rather considerable problem of coordinating America's foreign relations in the field. The spectrum of American activity abroad now ranges far outside the normal field of diplomacy to embrace foreign aid both economic and military, and in some areas the wide-ranging activities of the Central Intelligence Agency as well. If any kind of uniformity of approach is to be maintained, it is essential that the ambassador control his team, and to do this effectively he needs the support and confidence of the President himself. But of course with more than a hundred ambassadors it is unlikely that the President will be on close terms with any but a small minority of them; the choice of ambassador may thus provide a direct indication of countries to which the President thinks it is likely that special importance will attach during his term of office.

It will be seen that this intermingling at home and abroad, in the domestic departments of government as well as in external relations of 'outside' appointees – whether from the business world or the groves of academe – with career men, and the fact that most of the more sensitive posts fall to the latter, gives to the style of American administration at the higher levels a very different feeling from what one is used to in Great Britain or other Western European countries. There is none of the steady insistence on political neutrality of the British civil servant, none of the traditional view that one can serve a master of one party just as well as his lately defeated rival. But party is perhaps the least of it. We have seen, both at cabinet level and at important posts just below it, individuals in recent years who have served Presidents of both parties, or have come to serve a President of one party after being identified with the other. What is more significant is that government servants are expected to, and do in fact, take sides on issues and express themselves upon them much more freely than would be considered tolerable in some other systems. And this is not true only of the political appointees; the same phenomenon is also to be found among career men, where genuine passion about issues is both more common and more overt than in Whitehall. There is in American administration an element of ideology, at least at some periods, and on some subjects – whether it be civil rights, economic relations within the western world, or the containment of Communism – that is quite different from what one finds elsewhere, and which is perhaps easier to parallel within the Communist bloc than in the West.

When one turns from considering the composition of the executive branch and the characteristics of its servants to the place of executive government in the general structure of American society, one is struck by a number of features that are, if not peculiar to the United States, at least present there to an unusual degree. In the first place, there is of course the fact of federalism; much of government is state, almost as much is local. In both there is a wide range of different types of organization and competence in operation to account for. At both levels, power tends to be diffused rather than concentrated; federal-state cooperation becomes more and more essential. What is also clear is that the existing system is very rigid in that it has so far proved impossible to reshape state and local government to meet the needs of the great metropolitan areas where most of the major problems of today arise, and where the fragmentation of authority is a major handicap in dealing with them. In the second place, there is something which can only be fully appreciated in historical terms, namely the irregular growth of governmental powers – particularly federal powers – and the consequently very irregular pattern of the administrative machine.

As has been seen, the element of 'prerogative' in American government is relatively small. Presidents have increased their power by assuming authority not strictly granted to them by the Constitution, but except in dealing with external relations this increase has not normally outlived the emergencies that have called it forth. And even if intervention in domestic affairs – labour relations, for instance – has been justified by the President's responsibility for avoiding civil strife, or the need to keep the economy at full stretch because of defence requirements, the Court and Congress can usually find means of halting the process.

The result is that most of the expansion of executive authority that has taken place owes its origin to congressional action in some new field. Americans are more willing both to seek to legislate in order to reshape the economy or social relations than most other western countries, and to create new machinery to give effectiveness to the new legislation. Both the departments proper, except for the original ones, and the independent agencies, reflect the new preoccupations of Congress at different times. One can trace in the laws themselves, and in the institutions to which they gave rise, the whole transformation of the nation from a pioneering society, largely devoted to mining and agriculture under a great variety of conditions, to its modern overwhelmingly industrial incarnation, with all the familiarity and uniformity of the problems to which industrialism everywhere gives rise.

In the third place, there is a contrast between the trust that is shown in the powers of action through the laws – whether to limit the powers of big business or trade unions, or to provide for a proper pattern of race relations – and the rather general mistrust of administrators. The overmanning of so much of the administrative structure – a fact which strikes anyone who has to do with American government at any level – and the extraordinary burden of paper-work, spring from the same fundamental attempt to make the operations of government as closely regulated and as impersonal as possible. In small matters this leads to extravagance; in the larger ones, it imposes upon the President the need to spend much of his energy in trying to get behind the routine channels and to make certain that his own policies are in fact being implemented. There is thus within the executive branch of the federal government itself as well as within the federal system a degree of friction that is perhaps tolerable only because it would be inadvisable that so large a country as the United States should respond too easily to a touch of the wheel.

For the student of government the most impressive and important thing about American government is its size.

Further Reading

BOOKS

Anderson, W., *Intergovernmental Relations in Review*. Minneapolis, Minn., 1960.

Beloff, M., *The American Federal Government*. London, 2nd edn. 1969.

—— (ed.), *The Federalist*. Oxford, 1948 (several other editions available).

Bernstein, M. H., *Regulating Business by Independent Commissions*. Princeton, N.J., 1955.

——, *The Job of the Federal Executive*. Washington, D.C., 1958.

Corwin, E. S., *The Constitution and What it Means Today*. Princeton, N.J., 12th edn. 1958.

Fenno, R. F., *The President's Cabinet*. Cambridge, Mass., 1959.

Freund, P., *The Supreme Court of the United States*. New York, 1961.

Kelly, A. H. and Harbison, W. A., *The American Constitution. Its Origin and Development*. New York, 3rd edn. 1963.

Heren, L., *The New American Commonwealth*. London, 1968.

Konvitz, M. R., *Fundamental Liberties of a Free People*. Ithaca, N.Y., 1957.

Lees, J. D., *The Political System of the United States*. London, 1969.

McCloskey, R. G., *The American Supreme Court*. Chicago, Ill., 1960.

Neustadt, R. E., *Presidential Power*. New York, 1960.

Pear, R. H., *American Government*. London, 2nd edn. 1963.

Peltason, J. W. and Burns, J. M., *Functions and Policies of American Government*. New York, 1962.

Schwartz, B., *American Constitutional Law*. Cambridge, 1955.

——, *The Reins of Power. A Constitutional History of the United States*. London, 1964.

Van Doren, C., *The Great Rehearsal: The Story of the Making and Ratifying of the Constitution of the United States*. London, 1958.

Vile, M. J. C., *The Structure of American Federalism*. London, 1961.

OTHER

United States Government Organization Manual. Washington, D.C., annual.

8　American Politics, Past and Present

H. G. NICHOLAS

It is not too much to say that the culture of the United States is a political culture. It was through a political act that the country, as an independent power, came into existence. It was through political documents, the Declaration of Independence and the Constitution, that the people affirmed their new nationhood. It has been through the political processes of self-government, by election and representation, that the nation has consolidated itself and assimilated its continuous influx of diverse races, cultures, and faiths. Unlike the typical European state whose unity derives from language, religion or geographical compactness, and whose government is an expression of that unity, the United States, for all its Anglo-Saxon heritage, is a composite creation, established at a fixed point in time, engaged for most of its life in a process of simultaneous absorption and expansion, where government has had to create unity out of diversity and has done so by appeal to a political faith, whose dogmas are to be found in the historic documents of the infant nation. Thus to be an American is not so much, even now, to inherit a tradition; it is initially and recurrently to affirm a set of political beliefs. Similarly politics is valued, not merely as a necessary adjunct to government, but for its own sake, as an activity as self-justifying as worship (and, incidentally, just as socially useful). Thus the complexity, diversity, and continuity of American political activity, so puzzling to the foreigner, require no qualification to the native. As well complain of the exercises of a religion that

> The voice of prayer is never silent
> Nor dies the strain of praise away.

The universal, inclusive character of the political process similarly makes it a principal reservoir of material for folk (and not-so-folk) culture, for the humour and pathos of legend, of the popular press and broadcasting, of stage and screen and, to a considerable extent, of literature. It is, like baseball, a universal solvent, but with a twelve months season. It is associated with the highest moments of the national experience and with the lowest common denominators of human nature. It interpenetrates the profession of law, it touches at repeated points the avocations of the clergy, the inculcation of its principles is a major concern of all levels of education while, in the federal and in many of the state capitals, it constitutes the major, sometimes the exclusive, form of employment.

The Emergence of a Party System

It can be safely affirmed that this development formed no part of the intentions of the Founding Fathers of the Republic. That there were self-evident political truths, that their affirmation should constitute the credentials for membership in the American polity – this was certainly accepted. But that the upholding of such a faith would require this degree of mass participation by its believers, that it would loom so large in the preoccupations of the nation – this they neither desired nor intended. There is dispute about the degree of democracy which the framers of the Constitution regarded as necessary or suitable for the underpinning of that instrument, but we know that for the most part they regarded politics, in the form of party politics, with distaste and disapproval. In the celebrated 10th paper of *The Federalist*, Madison advanced as one of the strongest arguments for the new Constitution the contention that it would reduce and contain the baneful effects of party spirit by creating a set of water-tight compartments in government which would prevent the flood of faction from ever being able to rise above a certain point. Thus the federal system would insulate the governments of the states from each other and from the centre, while within each government the principle of the separation of powers would prevent the capture of one segment automatically leading to the loss of all. Furthermore, the systems of election were designed to prevent any precipitate translation of the popular will into government action. Not only was the choice of the President and Vice-President to be filtered through the electoral colleges (as described on pp. 245–6) but the tenure of office in the House of Representatives, Senate, and Presidency was diversified to guarantee that even if the elections for each were held simultaneously (and originally they were not) the successful candidates would serve for different terms – the President for four years, the congressmen for two, and the senators for six (but not the same six, since only one-third of the Senate would come up for election at any one time). Thus no tidal wave of popular feeling could possibly carry all elective offices at one sweep.

If Madison worried about the menace of parties as such, Washington, after experience of two terms as President, a father-figure above and beyond party, drew attention to the particular menace which he thought parties would assume in the circumstances of the young republic. In his 'Farewell Address' he remarked

> In contemplating the causes which may disturb our Union, it occurs as a matter of serious concern that any ground should have been furnished for characterizing parties by geographical discriminations, Northern and Southern, Atlantic and Western. You cannot shield yourselves too much against the jealousies and heart-burnings which spring from these misrepresentations.

In general the course of American history has falsified Madison's hopes and Washington's fears. Parties developed early and became a permanent, central feature of the American political scene, but sectional parties, save at the breakdown of the Union which resulted in civil war, have not been an American characteristic. Despite the federal system parties have combined across state boundaries and despite the separation of powers all elective offices have been fought for on party lines. So far has this gone that for all practical purposes in normal times 90 per cent of the contenders for political office at every level, local, state, and federal, compete under one of two labels, Democratic or Republican.

Despite Madison, constitutional obstacles and certain historic factors worked from the beginning towards a two-party system. It was the norm inherited from the homeland of Whig and Tory. It corresponded to two successive national lines of fissure, first for and against Independence, and second for and against the Constitution – or, in a modified form, in favour of emphasizing its centralizing features (the Federalists) as against emphasizing states' rights and a weak executive (the Jeffersonian Republicans). The collapse of Federalism in the War of 1812 was followed by a welter of factionalism until lines were again drawn with some semblance of clarity in the contest between Whigs and Jacksonian Democrats. In the struggle which ensued upon the end of Washington's reign the Presidency emerged as a polarizing institution. While House and Senate could have accommodated themselves to a multiplicity of parties, the method (early adopted) of direct election to the Presidency created a permanent bias in favour of a national two-party system. The rise of the convention, as a device for nominating presidential candidates, intensified this, and thus the contest for the supreme elective office set the pattern for the rest.

It soon became apparent that a two-party system could only survive in so large and diverse a country if each rival was able to accommodate within its ranks a considerable range of different opinions and interests. Thus the American party early acquired its most tenacious characteristic, a generous indifference to doctrinal consistency and a willingness to be as many things to as many men as possible. In essence the national party has always been a combination between geographical or racial or economic or ideological interests constructed with a view to creating a nation-wide majority.

What happens when an issue emerges which does not lend itself to compromise? This was the problem that faced Whigs and Democrats in the 1850s. Slavery, to most of the South and to much of the North and West, emerged, despite all party attempts to blur it, as just such an issue. Eventually it broke the Democratic Party into Northern and Southern wings, while out of this and the ruins of the Whig Party emerged the Republican Party, exclusively Northern and committed to resisting the extension of slavery. Fortunately for American democracy no issue of comparable intractability has since presented itself. Religion and race, the historic absolutes, have not (save in this instance over Negro slavery) provided the lines of contention in American politics, while on other issues the instinct of survival has dictated an avoidance of rigid postures and a willingness to bend the party line in whichever direction the pursuit of a majority has dictated. This has enabled Republicans and Democrats ever since the Civil War effectively to divide the national scene between them. Though other groupings – e.g. the Populists in the nineties and the Progressives in the twenties and forties – have challenged their duopoly it has been to little purpose save at the state level, and then only in a few areas.

This pressure to be all things to all men robs much American party debate of consistency and even, upon occasion, of content. To the European observer in particular the identity of the parties presents an elusive problem. Their very labels evade distinction in a country where all are republican and everyone must appear democratic. The attempt to raise temporary differences into permanent differentiae is seldom profitable. At various times the Republicans have been the tariff, the Democrats the free trade party, but more often each has been trying to get the best of both worlds. Historically the Democrats favoured state rights, the Republicans strong federal government, but save in the South the Democrats are now the party of big government while the Republicans emphasize the perils of centralization. Under the New Deal the Democrats in effect established America as a welfare state and the Republicans, whatever their private feelings, have now little option but to tread the welfare road. Again, first with Wilson and then with Franklin Roosevelt and Truman, the Democrats emerged as the party supporting American involvement in world affairs, but the Republicans, for all their affinity with isolationism in the twenties and thirties, have also an 'interventionist' tradition of their own at least as old as Theodore Roosevelt. Even certain territorial adherences, once indisputable, are now impaired. The Republican ascendancy in New England has been only intermittently maintained since Franklin Roosevelt's New Deal and Lyndon Johnson's appeal for consensus. The 'solid South' of the Democratic Party cracked under the impact of Al Smith's Roman Catholicism in 1928 and with increasing assimilation to the economic and social patterns of the rest of the Union it developed a steadily increasing Republican vote from the 1950s onwards.

Thus it comes about that there are few components of America's vast diversity which are not represented in both parties; in the conventional language of European politics, each party can be found to range from right to left. But if regard is had to the centre of gravity of each party a clear enough difference emerges. The Democrats contain substantially more of the poor, the uneducated, the lower classes, the Roman Catholics, and the recently immigrant groups. The Republicans contain substantially more of the well-to-do, those with university degrees, the middle and upper-middle classes, and what popular parlance conveniently dubs the 'WASPS' – White Anglo-Saxon Protestants. The greater part of organized labour is Democratic, the greater part of business and the professions is Republican. Certain racial attachments are fairly clear and consistent. An Irish–American will rarely be other than Democratic. The Negroes, Republican while memories of the Civil War and Emancipation were dominant, have now increasingly moved into the party that accords with their social and economic position. The net result is to create a demographic bias in the country as a whole towards the Democrats, as reflected in their relative dominance of Congress and the Presidency since 1932.

The organization of American parties reflects a curious conservatism, a kind of cultural time-lag. In a country where the economy and organized economic groups have become accustomed to a nation-wide scale of operation, where even big government has been accepted, however reluctantly, the parties still maintain a federal, even local, structure reminiscent of an earlier age. In one sense there are no national parties. The units are the state parties, and in many states even these are only loose amalgamations of city and county organizations. This reflects the fact that it is at this level that the parties have most to do. The American party, rarely being a policy-making instrument, for the reasons described above, finds its main *raison d'être* in the activities of nomination and election. There are only two nation-wide offices to be filled, those of the Presidency and the Vice-Presidency, and these come up for election only every leap year. The other elections, to Senate or House or state or local office, are all at the state level or lower, and all recur with greater frequency. Moreover almost all the law and machinery of elections, even to federal offices, are state con-trolled and administered. Finally, with the growth of a federal 'merit system', the principal remaining source of patronage is at the state or local level. True, the heyday of the 'machine', the party organization entirely staffed and run by officials who drew their salaries from the public purse while they gave their labour to the party, is now past. But as long as a largely apathetic public has to be activated, as long as a remarkable multiplicity of offices has to be filled by election, there is an obvious advantage in having an organization of professionals in constant readiness, and both tradition and convenience place a premium on this being in local hands.

The local party derives both its strength and its weakness from the fact that it is very rarely an association of dues-paying members, as in Britain. Membership rather comes from voting in the party primary, the nominating election held in most states to select the party's standard bearers in the election itself. The primary is supervised by the state itself – a recognition that unless provision is made for the public to participate in the nominating process the actual election could become a Tweedledum and Tweedledee contest between the hack nominees of the rival machines. (Furthermore, the primary may extend even to the choice of the party's own officials.) In one-party areas, particularly in the South, the primary may be the decisive election, what follows being a mere shadow contest. Primaries may be 'open' or 'closed'; if 'closed', only those who have previously put themselves on the elec-toral roll under that party label can vote in them; if 'open', any registered voter can participate whether it is a primary of his party or not.

The primary did a good deal to break the stranglehold of the machines, and indeed to break continuity and responsibility (however defined) in party organizations. Other factors have worked in the same way. Members of an affluent society are no longer very interested in the modestly paid patronage jobs with which the machine was wont to reward its workers; now that the state provides 'social security' benefits the welfare crumbs from the political boss's table are no longer of much esteem as 'favours' with which to win votes. So the classic type of party organization is in decline. Sometimes the trade union has provided a cadre of workers to take its place. More often the proportion of professionals to volunteers has been inverted. Increasingly candidates build entirely personal organizations alongside or against the 'regular' organization. Increasingly the services of professional public relations men or of specialists in the new media of radio and television are employed on a commercial basis. Such new techniques are often more costly than the old and one of the mounting problems of American politics is to maintain access within the system for candidates who lack wealth of their own or the sponsorship of powerful interest groups.

The Choosing of a President

An aspirant for the Presidency has to construct out of this diversity of state and local parties an organization which will enable him to campaign across the continent. Each party has indeed its 'National Committee' on which all state committees are represented, but this is a formal, largely powerless, structure. Its main job is, every four years, to arrange the holding of the party's presidential nominating convention. At this distinctively American conclave, delegates from each state party will assemble for the relatively formal ritual of agreeing on the party's programme and the crucial operation of selecting the party's candidate. All serious contestants for the honour will have put in months of campaigning before the convention, trying to win delegates who will vote for them and trying to impress all the king-makers with their capacity to lead the party to victory. The cost and intensity of these pre-convention contests have grown to a point where only abnormal wealth and superhuman stamina will enable a candidate to survive until the final round. In the convention itself he must be able to marshal his forces and maximize their impact, so that beneath the surface carnival and rhetoric there is a constant and intricate struggle for the delegates' favours. Only an incumbent President is spared this ordeal; custom decrees that he is entitled to the one and only re-nomination which (since 1951) is practicable under the Constitution and with this capacity to succeed himself goes, in effect, the right to dictate the convention's choice of his vice-presidential running mate.

The party's presidential nominee becomes *eo ipso* the party's leader. He selects the chairman of the party's National Committee, generally entrusting to him the management of his own campaign. In choosing a candidate the party will generally have an eye exclusively to his ability to win in the ensuing campaign. This, at a historic low point in the Presidency in the 1880s, led James Bryce to conclude that great men were not chosen Presidents, because electoral appeal counted more than the ability to govern, and the essence of campaign success lay in a facility for offending as few and pleasing as many as possible. Thus amiable nonentities of the Rutherford B. Hayes or Warren G. Harding type who met these criteria of 'availability' were likely to be preferred. But for some time this has ceased to be true. The challenges of econo-mic depression and war, hot or cold, have left the public with a preference for men of proven executive ability and positive purpose, and 'greatness', however defined, has certainly not been lacking in the modern Presidency. Sometimes the demand for executive ability has given the governors of great states, like Franklin Roosevelt in New York, or Stevenson in Illinois, an obvious advantage. Successful war leaders, like Grant or Eisenhower, enjoy a powerful appeal, often irrespective of party. Senators who have made a mark, like Kennedy and Johnson, command a clear lead over congressmen, however distinguished. In general it is well to come from a big state – i.e. one which is both large and electorally ambivalent – since a 'favourite son' is judged likely to bring his state's vote in the electoral college with him. Until 1960 the candidate, it was thought, needed to be a Protes-tant. He will still do well not to be too obviously linked with any recent immigrant group. He need not, like a British party leader, have held cabinet office – indeed no successful candidate since Hoover has. But he must cut a figure which convinces the electorate that he would be a match, man for man, for his opposite numbers in Western democracies and Eastern dictatorships.

It is at the quadrennial national conventions that the parties make final choice of their standard-bearers. The original method of selection was by a caucus of the party's representatives in Congress, but with the rising tide of democracy this was felt to be too restrictive and in the 1830s the convention system established itself. Originally this was a two-tier structure, party conventions in each state nominating delegates to the national conclave. But with the development, before and after the Civil War, of the more disreputable type of machine politics, the conviction grew that such a system played into the hands of the bosses who, packing the state conventions with their henchmen, were thus able, in effect, to dictate their choice to the nation. Hence the demand, beginning in Wisconsin in 1905, for applying the primary election system to the presidential nominating process. Sometimes this means allowing the voter to select the delegates (with more, or less, explicit commitments on the delegates' part about whom they will vote for); sometimes it provides merely a way of registering popular preference for or against likely candidates. In neither case is it binding on the delegates who must, if the national convention is to serve any purpose, be left an ultimate freedom of choice. So the main value of the presidential primaries in those states which have them (now fewer than half) is as local forecasts of national opinion.

The convention delegates, however chosen, are, collectively, plenipotentiaries. Meeting in mid-summer in one of the few cities which can satisfy their exacting requirements of a huge hall and ample hotel accommodation, they engage for almost a week in what is outwardly a species of political carnival. However, behind the bands, the parading, the oratory and the applause, there will be intensive political activity. The candidates will be trying to woo delegates, the delegates to assess the potential of the candidates. Eventually comes the ballot, taken in alphabetical order of states and repeated as often as necessary until an absolute majority is obtained. It is a crude instrument for achieving party unity and providing leadership in a highly fragmented structure, and the admission of television cameras into the proceedings has made it look cruder still. Yet, with all its faults, the convention remains an indispensable tool of the American democratic process. Nor, in the light of its results, can it be said, overall, to fail in its job.

However, securing his party's nomination, strenuous though that usually is, is only the beginning of a presidential candidate's labours. As soon as the worst of the summer's heat is over the campaign proper begins. For the first century or so of the young republic a beneficent tradition decreed that the candidate himself should not canvass on his own behalf; his friends in the party might 'go on the stump' for him but he should stay at home and fight only a 'front porch campaign' – i.e. confine himself to a few dignified responses to visits from delegations of well-wishers. The exceptions to this rule were nearly all unsuccessful candidates – such as Stephen A. Douglas in 1860 and Horace Greeley in 1872. But the spread of the transcontinental railroads, coinciding with the developments of mass democracy, made a 'swing around the country' possible and, by degrees, obligatory. Begun by William Jennings Bryan in 1896, the practice spread, and since 1928 no candidate has been able to resist it. (Though President Nixon in 1972 kept his travelling to a minimum.) First it was the campaign train, stopping at insignificant 'whistle stops' as well as the great regional centres, then this was supplemented by the 'motorcade', as the American railway network declined, then came the chartered aeroplane, making possible a criss-crossing of the continent which simplified the planning of meetings at the price of exhausting the candidate.

It is not only the public meeting that taxes the candidate's strength. Originally, the supporting publicity, confined to newspaper handouts, pamphlet literature, or poster campaigns, made little demand on the candidate himself. But broadcasting, which first made serious impact in 1928, created new opportunities – and consequently obligations – for the candidates, and television, beginning in 1952, developed quickly into an even more exacting taskmaster. Instead of providing substitutes for the candidates' personal appearances, these media piled additional burdens on their shoulders. Moreover, in a country where radio and television are high-cost commercial enterprises, they added formidable items to the campaign bill.

In planning the strategy of his campaign a candidate will have particular regard to the need for carrying the key states. Thus although it will not do to give the impression that any part of the country is being slighted, effort must necessarily centre on such states as New York, New Jersey, Pennsylvania, Massachusetts, California, Michigan, Illinois, Ohio, and Texas, since these between them provide nearly half the electoral votes needed for victory. This also means a concentration on the urban electorate and a proportionate accenting of campaign issues to meet urban expectations. But of course a presidential candidate does not campaign for himself alone. He is the head of his party and in that capacity (quite apart from obligations arising out of his nomination) he has a general duty to assist congressional and senatorial, even state, candidates who are seeking election at the same time. No more complex or burdensome task attends a presidential candidate than that of weaving together the claims and aspirations of the diverse factions and local leaders whose only point of unity may be their common assumption of the Democratic or Republican label. The unity which party doctrine fails to provide the candidate is called upon to supply; hence the extraordinary amount of effort that goes into the merely (but how misleading is that 'merely'!) social operation of cultivating the members of the local party organizations, of composing their feuds, of harmonizing their campaign efforts and of granting them the appropriate degree of endorsement. Much of the 'hoopla' about an American campaign which fascinates and baffles a foreign observer is, in fact, an instrument for eliciting the maximum response, for attracting to the candidate's and the party's support that voluntary participation in the indispensable chores of campaigning which cannot be taken for granted in a heterogeneous and loosely cemented society. The necessity for this is regularly demonstrated in the voting figures in American elections which, with the occasional exception of individual states or cities, run at a consistently lower level of turnout than in British or West European elections.

It is now the universal practice to hold presidential and congressional elections on the same date, the Tuesday after the first Monday in November. (Elections for state and local offices are also almost invariably held on this day, though they do not necessarily poll on the even-numbered years of congressional or the leap years of presidential and congressional contests.) But though thus synchronized, elections are not uniformly regulated. Since each state determines the manner and qualifications for voting, considerable diversity exists. Until the federal Voting Rights Act of 1970 lowered the voting age to 18 there were different age limits in different localities, as there are still differences in the residence qualifications, in the primary regulations (where they exist), in the type of ballot (generally 'long', comprising every office from President to dog-catcher, with party allegiance made explicit), in the use (or non-use) of voting machines, in the provisions for the count etc. In the past these differences have often had considerable political significance, e.g. the use of the poll tax requirement or literacy tests to prevent poor whites or, more generally, Negroes from voting. Gradually, however, in matters of substance uniform procedures (though not uniform reliability) have come to prevail.

Despite the synchronization of elections and the prevalence of the long ballot, 'split ticket' voting is a common phenomenon, by which the voter endorses the candidate of one party for one post and of the opposite for another. Most frequently this discrimination is exercised as between the candidates for the Presidency and Congress. Nor is this surprising, since the President normally represents the national (and, as we have seen, often the urban) point of view, while the congressman or senator serves primarily as the spokesman for local or state interests. It is thus in Congress that the adaptation of the two-party system to the flux and diversity of American society and of the American economy can best be observed.

The Workings of Congress

Although Congress consists of two chambers, the House of Representatives and the Senate, general usage has conferred the label 'congressmen' exclusively on the members of the former. The Constitution specifies, by way of qualification, merely that a congressman shall be an inhabitant 'of the State in which he is chosen' but a convention no less binding has narrowed this to mean 'of the district which he represents'. This rivets localism on the 435 members of the House, obliging them to put loyalty to their constituents above claims of party or nation, when these conflict. The fact that, if defeated, the congressman cannot move and try his luck elsewhere, ties him to his home base; the brevity of his two-year term reinforces this – 'a congressman is the shortest distance between two years'. This inevitably obliges most congressmen to act on the sagacious advice of Speaker Rayburn: 'Vote your district first'.

The typical congressman will be a lawyer by training, thus embodying that intimate relationship between law and politics which is a characteristic of the American federal system. He will enjoy a substantial salary and what, by House of Commons standards, would be regarded as palatial office accommodation, with pay for a staff of up to nine assistants. But it is a rare congressman who, in relation to the cost of Washington living and the demands of his constituents on him, does not complain of both as inadequate. The disposition to use one's congressman as an all-purpose ombudsman and solicitor of governmental favours is one deep-rooted in American history and is itself stimulated by members seeking to establish a record as 'watchdogs' for their constituents' interests. This direct relationship between congressman and constituent, largely unaffected by consideration of party, is an expression of two distinctively American phenomena – the size of the country, which creates the felt need for a representative who can overcome the remoteness of government, and the indistinctiveness of party, which makes it easy for the representative to meet most constituents' wishes without unduly straining his party loyalties.

But though, by British standards, party discipline is light not only in the House but also in the Senate, both chambers use party as an indispensable instrument for organizing themselves. Independents, though not unknown, are very rare, and membership of a third party is hardly more common. There were only six congressmen and senators between 1935 and 1970 who were neither Republicans nor Democrats. The Senate's presiding officer comes to it from outside; he is the Vice-President of the United States and, perhaps for this reason, his senatorial functions are largely formal and his powers slight. The Speaker of the House, however, is elected by the chamber and will be the real and effective leader of the majority party. In its dealings with the President the House will readily envisage him in the role in which the Roundhead parliaments cast their Speakers vis-à-vis the King, as the custodian of their privileges and the spearhead of their complaints. In his internal relations the Speaker will embody in addition many of the characteristics of the British Leader of the House of Commons and even of the Chief Whip. There are, in Congress, majority and minority whips, but it is generally the Speaker who will play the biggest part in directing business and in organizing support for a measure. The power of the Speakership reached its climax with the election of Speaker Reed in 1889 when a vacuum of leadership in the White House virtually necessitated an assumption of power by the leader of Congress. Reed appointed committee members and chairmen, and controlled the business of the House with an iron hand. But his successor, 'Czar' Cannon, provoked a revolt of the Progressives and in 1910 a radical revision of the rules scaled the Speaker's powers down to their more modest present level.

Both House and Senate rely overwhelmingly on standing committees for the conduct of their business. The system evolved piecemeal; *ad hoc* committees were established to deal with particular bills, then it seemed natural to send similar bills to the same committee. So specialization developed. By the mid-nineteenth century the House had 34 standing committees and by 1900 it had 58. Committee-creation became habit forming, since a committee carried privileges and power, especially for the chairman. Hence standing committees emerged on such limited topics as 'Levees and Improvements of the Mississippi River' or 'Industrial Arts and Expositions'. In 1946 Congress pruned the lush growth and reduced the standing committees to 19 (15 for the Senate, where a comparable flowering had occurred). Roughly speaking the committee structure is designed to parallel that of the executive departments, so that there is a committee in each house for each principal area of government.

The congressional standing committee is not, as in the House of Commons, merely a possible instrument for refining legislation. It is, in effect, Congress's dominant legislative tool in respect of each area of public affairs, and it is also the weapon by which Congress exercises its right to oversee the work of the executive. The parent House (and to a lesser degree the parent Senate) is simply unable to handle its vast volume of business itself. It has to delegate to its committees. And although it is not as true now as it was in 1885, when the young Woodrow Wilson wrote his book on Congress, to say that 'ours is a government of the Standing Committees of Congress', it is true that Congress distributes its power among these component committees and has no efficient means either of overseeing the use they make of it or of calling it back if it is abused.

In the House and Senate, in addition to those committees which deal with obvious legislative topics, like Agriculture or the Judiciary, there are others, like Foreign Affairs or Armed Services or Government Operations, whose principal function is obviously supervisory or investigative. But often for such a role the most potent congressional agency is the Appropriations Committee (or one of its sub-committees), since this can add the pressures of the purse to the power of exposure and publicity.

It is as a committee member that a congressman properly realizes himself. Parties are represented on the committees in roughly their ratio in the parent chamber, but individuals seek places on those committees which their own (or their constituents') interests suggest and where the greatest power is to be wielded. Each party has its own 'Committee on Committees' which allocates committee memberships at the opening of each session. Normally once on a committee a congressman continues there. His goal will be the coveted committee chairmanship which accrues to the member of the majority party with the longest continuous service on the committee. This seniority system has the merit – perhaps its only merit – of simplicity, but it reflects the willingness of Congress to diffuse power at random, for the committee chairman is a powerful man. He is more than a presiding officer, just as the committee is more than a debating forum. He is the man responsible for seeing that the committee gets through its work and to this end his colleagues will accord him surprising latitude. He arranges the agenda, appoints the often crucial sub-committees, determines the choice of witnesses to be heard, often conducts the hearings and then, when the bill is reported out of committee, will probably be in charge of it on the floor. Thus the leaders of the House are, in large measure, and in conjunction with the Speaker and the whips, the chairmen of the principal standing committees.

A partial explanation of the committee's power is to be found in Congress's heavy legislative burden. The principle of the separation of powers means that no members of the administration have seats in Congress; consequently, just as there are no government members so there are no government bills. All congressmen and senators have an equal right to introduce legislation on any topic at any time and legislation submitted by the White House has no automatic priority over any other. Two consequences follow: a vast array of legislative proposals and the necessity of some means for winnowing the wheat from the chaff. In a typical session almost 10,000 bills and resolutions are introduced into the House or Senate. The parent chambers cannot possibly consider even the merest outlines of these measures, so they refer them immediately to the relevant committee. This can pigeon-hole a bill – one of its most important functions – or it can report it out unfavourably – a rare event – or it can recommend its passage. In the last event the committee will almost certainly have worked on the bill, amended it and made it, in large measure, its own.

Committee law-making is a two-tier operation. In the first stage the committee conducts hearings on the proposed legislation, at which interested parties from Congress, the departments or the public may testify. (Analogous hearings are also, of course, a feature of committee operations when non-legislative issues, e.g. the conduct of foreign policy, are under consideration.) Committees have power to compel the attendance of witnesses and the production of documents, though the executive branch has never conceded this power to Congress where it involves a witness or a document which the President rules inadmissible. Committee hearings are among the show pieces of a congressional year, often more revealing and dramatic than a congressional debate. The theory behind the hearings procedure is that Congress is gathering the information necessary for the shaping of legislation but of course the opportunities thus afforded for lobbyists and interested parties of all kinds are what give the public hearing its persistent popularity.

After the hearings, the committee will go into what is called 'executive session' where, meeting behind closed doors, it will decide whether it wishes to proceed with the bill and if so in what form. What is said in executive session is not officially reported, nor are votes made public. This does not mean that executive sessions remain secret, but it leaves to the Washington press corps the job of compiling a committee Hansard. Many bills will be smothered in committee. Indeed committees on average report out less than 20 per cent of the bills they receive.

Once reported out of a committee a bill will be placed on a 'calendar' from which it will be called up for consideration on a predetermined day of the legislative month. This is too slow a process for important legislation, so that in most cases a special provision is invoked – a special 'rule' is sought from the Rules Committee, which enables a bill to jump the legislative queue. The rule will probably also specify how long the bill may be debated on the floor, how far amendments are permitted etc. This control over the important legislative traffic of the House gives the Rules Committee a strategic importance, yet it is characteristic of Congress's preference for diffusing power that the Rules Committee is not under the control of the majority leaders and may indeed pursue policies at odds with theirs. When it does so, it cannot easily be brought to heel. The debate on the floor which occurs at this stage is the only consideration by the full House which a bill receives. Even so it is rare for sustained and newsworthy debate to occur. Congress is not very debate-minded.

In general, legislative procedure in the Senate follows the same lines as those set out for the House, save that, as befits a chamber of only 100 members, more is done by informal arrangement and greater latitude is allowed to individual members – cf. the senatorial 'filibuster'. The Senate has no Rules Committee; it determines its legislative priorities by unanimous consent or majority vote. In general, the floor debate in the Senate will give an opportunity for a more serious and sustained consideration of a measure than the floor stage in the House.

When, as generally happens, the House and Senate versions of a measure differ, the bill goes to a special 'conference' committee on which both are represented. To this a surprising amount of power is often delegated by each chamber; its recommendations cannot be amended by the parent chambers and must be accepted or rejected *in toto* – a necessary and potent method of extorting agreement. Moreover it meets in private and often hurriedly, as when, at the end of a congressional session, a flood of bills has to be cleared at short notice.

When all these hurdles have been cleared the measure is ready for the President's signature. This, however, is no mere formality, like the consent of a British sovereign to the proposals of her Parliament. The presidential veto is a reality; originally, it is true, conceived of as a kind of emergency safeguard invoked only against legislation which might invade the President's prerogative or be otherwise unconstitutional, but now employed on openly political grounds as a device which gives the President a voice, albeit a late one, in the law-making process. Nor is the veto as merely negative as it might appear. At an early stage in a bill's passage the President can let it be known that he finds some feature so obnoxious that if it is not amended he will have no choice but to veto the whole bill. But, of course, the President may not have the last word; if the bill is re-passed over his veto by a two-thirds majority in each chamber, it becomes law. This, for example, was the way in which Congress retorted to Franklin Roosevelt's vetoing – for the first time in American history – of a revenue bill. (However, subsequent Presidents have made their vetoes stick even in this sensitive area.) If, however, a bill reaches the President, as many do, in the last ten days of a congressional session he may dispose of it by a 'pocket veto' – i.e. by not returning it until Congress has adjourned – and in that case the last word remains with him.

There is, however, one important field of legislation to which this device is seldom applicable – appropriations. Here the executive's need for funds gives Congress an irresistible weapon if it chooses to use it. Recognizing this, Congress has often tacked on to an appropriation bill a legislative rider which is inappropriate and irrelevant, as a way of slipping through a measure which could never stand on its own feet. In its extreme form, this kind of behaviour reflects a deep-seated indiscipline or irresponsibility characteristic of Congress's handling of financial legislation.

Neither in the Constitution nor in the working rules of Congress is there any provision for ensuring that the raising and spending of federal funds shall be conducted as a coordinated operation. Just as in each chamber separate committees handle the imposition of taxes and the voting of expenditure, so the looseness of party discipline prevents any effective oversight by the majority leadership over the diverse pieces of financial legislation. The President, it is true, presents his budget as a unified whole, but this is really no more than a compilation of the sums he would like Congress to vote, accompanied by proposals as to how they might raise the money. Congress's first act is to take the budget to pieces and to set its committees and sub-committees to work separately upon its constituent parts. Nor is this mere perversity. It is the power of the purse which more than anything else gives Congress its say in the conduct of the executive departments; it is by obliging each department to come forward year by year and justify its requests for appropriations that Congress gives reality to its claim to oversee the administration. In so doing it need not confine itself, like the Opposition in Parliament, to proposing cuts in the departmental estimates; it can increase them. Thus there comes into being that distinctive variety of congressional activity which has enriched the world of politics with its peculiar terminology – the 'pork barrel', 'log-rolling' and the rest. This is the point at which the individual congressman's power to do special favours is maximized. The classic manifestation of this was the annual passage of the 'Rivers and Harbors' bill, the measure which appropriated funds for public works in congressmen's home districts, and for which Congress brought into being and cultivated as its special preserve the Army Corps of Engineers, a kind of congressional public works department. The bill and the Corps still continue, but the expanded range of acceptable government expenditures now, of course, extends far beyond rivers and harbours; it includes defence, public health, even space research, and involves public money on an unprecedented scale. In all these areas, of course, the President and his department heads continue to plan and propose, but it is Congress which disposes and before whom bureau-heads, generals, admirals, and technocrats must parade and testify, not infrequently along the lines which Congress likes to hear rather than those laid down by their executive superiors.

Where the ordinary operations of the committee system fail, for any reason, to provide Congress with the oversight of an executive agency which it deems desirable, resort may be had to the investigating power. The twentieth century has seen a progressively expanding use of investigations by Congress, as the area of government activity has extended and the exploitation of the instruments of publicity has developed. The congressional investigation is, in most cases, essentially an exercise in publicity; it consists of isolating an issue, focusing public attention on it by the skilful marshalling of witnesses and evidence, and maximizing public interest by enlisting the cooperation of the press, the radio and, increasingly, television. The temptations, in such circumstances, to abuse the powers of subpoena and to convert the investigating process into a trial by publicity of persons or institutions who may lack any adequate redress has by no means been resisted. The particular excesses associated with the name of Senator McCarthy are only the most extreme examples of congressional reluctance to protect the citizen against abuse of power by his own elected representatives. In general the courts have provided the only bulwark worth the name against the excesses of congressional investigators. In *Watkins v. U.S.* (1957) and *Yellin v. U.S.* (1963) the Supreme Court upheld the rights of witnesses who refused to testify. Even so, the protection so afforded is minimal and the power of congressional inquiry has not been sensibly affected.

The root source of the generous latitude extended to Congress in its investigating role lies partly in the need to bridge the gulf created by the separation of powers, but also in the conviction that extraordinary diseases may require desperate remedies. The congressional investigation has served reformers of the left as readily as crusaders of the right, and some of the most notable developments in American public policy have had their origins in a congressional investigation. The Stock Exchange investigation begun by the Senate in 1931 led to the Securities Exchange Act of 1934 and related legislation. The Nye Committee investigation of the munitions industry in the mid-thirties largely created the intellectual climate out of which came the Neutrality Acts and much of the pre-war isolationism. No less newsworthy was the investigation into inter-state crime conducted by Senator Kefauver in the 1950s, while the House Un-American Activities Committee won repeated publicity for itself by its continuously sensational exposure of Communist conspiracies, real and alleged. That limelight is not necessary for an investigation's effectiveness was demonstrated by the Senate's Special Committee to investigate the National Defense Programme in the Second World War, which under the chairmanship of Senator Harry S. Truman was unobtrusively effective in enforcing efficiency in the production of war materials. Its example, however, has not been infectious.

The powers so far outlined, of investigation, of executive oversight, of taxing and spending,[1] of legislation – these are all shared by House and Senate. One power only is reserved by the Constitution to the lower chamber – the power to impeach. In the context of eighteenth-century political behaviour this no doubt seemed to the Founding

[1] The constitutional provision that money bills must *originate* in the House is a merely formal limitation on the Senate's powers, since the Senate can amend or reject them at will.

Fathers a matter of consequence, but in fact in the whole history of the United States only twelve civil officials have been impeached and of these the Senate, which is the adjudicating body, has only convicted four. The two most famous cases of impeachment were those of Supreme Court Justice Samuel Chase (1802) and of President Andrew Johnson (1868), both of which failed. The crudely partisan motivation of the impeachment of President Johnson, which failed by only one vote, did much to bring the impeachment process into contempt and it has since been invoked only against judges of inferior federal courts.

The Power of the Senate

The Constitution designed the Senate as a truly 'upper' House. Not only was it conceived as the custodian of the states' interests and its members, as such, invested with a quasi-ambassadorial character, but also, by its compact size, its peculiar powers and its distinctive conditions of membership and tenure it was designed to achieve some of the dignity and *gravitas* implicit in its Roman appellation. Whereas a mere stripling of 25, 7 years a citizen of the United States, may become a representative, no one may become a senator before the age of 30 and after 9 years U.S. citizenship. More important, beside the two-year tenure of a representative, the six-year term of a senator (the longest elective term of any U.S. official) gives security and detachment, while the holdover of two-thirds of the membership from one Congress to the next makes the Senate a continuous body, immune to sudden swings of popular feeling. Although the establishment of direct election by the 17th amendment of 1912 has made the Senate, in one sense, as 'democratic' a body as the lower House, the foregoing factors, coupled with the huge disparities in constituency size – from empty Alaska to burgeoning California – guarantee that the Senate will always wear its democracy with a difference. The failure of the original Senate of 26 members to function, with George Washington, as a kind of Privy Council to the elected monarch has not prevented even the present three-figure membership from regarding themselves as more than a legislature, as, in some sense, a combination of a council of state and an exclusive club.

This reflects, in large degree, the peculiar powers with which the Constitution has invested the Senate vis-à-vis the President. Of these, the first and deservedly the most notable is the proviso inserted into the article which outlines the President's powers (Art. II, 2, § 2) that it is 'by and with the advice and consent of the Senate' that the President has power to make treaties, and that the concurrence of 'two-thirds of the senators present' is needed for this purpose. The reality of this senatorial veto is written across the face of United States and indeed of world history; conceived as an instrument for defending states' rights in a federal system to which they were surrendering their power to conduct their own foreign relations, it has persisted in effect as a popular check, however erratic, upon executive autonomy in this crucial field.

Its present status is rather curious. The whole trend of contemporary international relations has been towards writing down the treaty as a major instrument of diplomacy and indeed it is arguable that American foreign policy has not been dependent, for any major development, upon treaty-making since NATO was established in 1949. Much of the present structure of American diplomacy rests upon the provision of aid, military or civilian, to client countries – a practice going back to the Lend-Lease Acts of the Second World War – and for this what is needed is the passage of financial legislation which does not require a two-thirds majority in the Senate but does require ordinary majorities in Senate and House as well. Thus, to a degree not previously experienced, the House has been given a voice in the legislative oversight of foreign policy. The power to declare war rests, like legislation, with both Houses of Congress. But increasingly the declaration of war, though not the waging of it, has gone out of fashion, and with it has come a reduction in the congressional role in foreign policy, cf. the example of Vietnam.

Moreover the President, by virtue of his diplomatic powers or as commander-in-chief, is perfectly entitled to make executive agreements with foreign powers on a range of topics hardly less extensive than those covered by a treaty. And these agreements he is in no wise obliged to submit to the Senate. Such were the historic 'destroyers-bases' deal with the United Kingdom in 1940 or the Yalta and Potsdam agreements. Nor have these agreements, although personal in character, any less force in law than treaties. To the extent that more than half the international agreements made by the United States in this century have been of this character it must be recognized that the oversight of the Senate has been proportionately reduced. Nor is it much restored if allowance is made for that important category of executive agreements which is made under the authority of an enabling act of Congress. Such, for example, were the important tariff reductions arranged by the President under the Reciprocal Trade Agreements Act of 1934 and its numerous successors, giving him power to negotiate tariff cuts up to a certain level. This was a device explicitly designed to emancipate tariff negotiations from the crippling readiness of the Senate to wield its veto at the instigation of some interest group, often minute as well as irresponsible.

In these ways the Senate has seen its powers curtailed. If, despite this, it remains a formidable force in foreign affairs, it is due partly to the tenacity of a notable tradition, partly to a popular reluctance to give any irremovable executive untrammelled power in this crucial field, partly to the ability with which the Senate has played its hand. It has entrusted most of its responsibilities here to its Committee on Foreign Relations. Since its establishment in 1816 this committee has attracted to its service the ablest talents in the Senate, men who have often acquired by long membership an experience surpassing that of the Presidents or Secretaries of State themselves. The committee has not always been wise but it has seldom been out of step with public opinion and it has often given it its lead. Increasingly, with acceptance of American participation in world affairs, the practice has developed of associating prominent members, of both parties, of the committee with major foreign policy negotiations and it is a rash executive who exposes himself to the charge of presenting them with a *fait accompli*.

There is another area in which the President has to obtain the Senate's 'advice and consent' – though only by a bare majority; that is in the making of the principal executive and judicial appointments. Historically this constitutional provision was the base on which was reared the formidable edifice of senatorial patronage. Senators refused to accept the President's nominee for a post in their own state unless their consent had previously been obtained, and stood shoulder to shoulder to uphold each other's claims under a procedure curiously described as 'senatorial courtesy'. But with the spread of 'merit' rules in appointments, few posts are now left to which such patronage can apply, though where it does senatorial courtesy is still invoked. In general also the Senate abstains from rejecting the President's choices for his 'official family', even when they are of opposite parties. Only one cabinet appointee has been rejected since 1925 – Lewis L. Strauss, whom President Eisenhower unsuccessfully proposed for Secretary of Commerce to a Senate which had already found him intractable as Chairman of the Atomic Energy Commission. But though rejection is rare, full advantage is often taken of the opportunity to haul a candidate through the briars by questioning him about himself or the administration's record, and foreknowledge of senatorial intentions has kept many a name from being sent forward. The Senate has even claimed a right to be consulted about presidential dismissals, but this claim the courts, in the silence of the Constitution, have decisively disallowed.

These powers, coupled to the ordinary legislative authority which it shares with the House, have made the Senate an unusually potent chamber. This potency, surprisingly, is enhanced by its collective indiscipline; the Senate is a chamber of individuals, in which the lines of influence are a complex weave of politics and personality. It reacts violently to pressure, either from party or from President; a senator's first loyalty is to his state and it is still true, as Woodrow Wilson remarked in 1908, that any senator of long standing 'feels that he is the professional, the President the amateur'. His constituency may well represent an area richer and more populous than many a European country and he will regard himself – and be accepted by Washington protocol – as at least the equal of a cabinet member. When therefore he turns, with his colleagues, to arrange the business of the Senate, his first requirement is that he shall have unlimited freedom of speech. The Senate abhors mere majority rule and allows its members a degree of license, not merely in speech but also in action (cf. Senator Joseph McCarthy), which no other assembly of a civilized nation would tolerate. Yet in a country where the 'tyranny of the majority', in Tocqueville's phrase, can be an oppressive reality the Senate, despite the absurdities of the filibuster, can and does serve a valuable role as a forum for minority opinion.

Pressure Groups

An individualistic Senate and a diffuse, loosely organized Congress constitute natural targets for that most American of institutions, the lobby. The United States is not, of course, peculiar in having group interests or in giving them access to government, but in the power, diversity and tenacity of its interests and in the ease of the access it affords them it is exceptional. The interests seeking to influence government are as diverse as America itself. They may be economic, ideological, religious, racial, or merely geographical. If they are of any consequence at all they will, in this age of big government, have come to realize that, whether or not they operate at local and state levels, they must also seek access to the government at Washington. Here the constitutional guarantees of freedom of petition and freedom of assembly combine with the diffusion of power among many government agencies and within the two legislatures to afford generous opportunities to the determined pressure group. In Congress in particular the term 'lobbyist' is no mere metaphor; the Capitol and its adjacent House and Senate office buildings are literally open to those who peddle influence or seek favours, and the congressman is largely denied the protection from their importunities which in Britain his party label may win him. The lobbies know that the legislator's battle for re-election, to House or Senate, is a relatively lonely one, and they will seek to influence him through his constituents. They also know that it is costly and they may be able to help his campaign with contributions or skilled support. Even between elections the constituent can be mobilized. The organized grass-roots campaign – 'write to your congressman' – is one of the oldest tactics in American politics. Applied with skill and irrespective of party, as in the great campaigns of the Anti-Saloon League, it can, upon occasion, be very potent, though the coming of the scientific public opinion poll, with no axe to grind, has limited its power to terrorize by hyperbole.

In general the lobby is not, however, coercive nor does it buy its votes. In Washington the crude bribe is as rare as it is unnecessary. The lobby will seek cooperation rather than corruption and will assist by offering briefs, contacts, and expertise rather than dollar bills. Every congressman wants to become an expert but few have the time or the talent; the lobby can often make good the deficiency. True, every committee now has its specialist staff and behind both House and Senate there is now the Legislative Reference Service, a professional research and legislative drafting organization designed to help Congress to keep up its end against the ever-advancing specialisms of the executive branch. Even so, the lobby can draw on skills of public relations which no congressional civil servant can supply. And in any case much modern legislation can only function if the groups most affected by it have been fully consulted in its preparation.

When, however, it is a matter of 'penetrating' the legislature, the compartmentalism of Congress often means that a lobbyist has only to capture the key figures on a key committee to secure his bill or his appropriation, while the lateral links between congressional committee and executive agency carry a successful lobbyist into the executive portals as well. Indeed certain committees, like certain departments, are recognized spokesmen for relevant interests – agriculture, labour etc. – and here it is not so much a matter of siege and capture as of continuous renegotiation of the terms of occupancy. Thus against a great deal of group pressure Congress neither has nor seeks to have any defences; what, if not for lobbyists, are lobbies for? However, of recent years, the disposition has grown to use publicity as a kind of moral policing device against the excesses of the lobbyists. Investigations have exposed practices which, even if not actionable, were clearly improper and the federal Regulation of Lobbying Act of 1946 now requires everybody seeking to influence legislation in Congress to register and file quarterly reports; these include details of published propaganda, of contributions received and expenditures made. The result has been to put most major pressure groups 'on the record'. Even so a twilight zone of evasion remains. The effectiveness of publicity in curbing malpractices is valid only up to a certain point.

There is one interest group in the United States which, by European standards, has been oddly reluctant to take the further steps that would have led to its emergence as a political party. That is organized labour. This is not because industrial conflicts have not been a central concern of American politics. It is not because the ideas of socialism, in both its democratic and its revolutionary varieties, have not been given a generous airing in the United States. Historically it may have been partly attributable to the fact that the industrial worker was a smaller part of the total labouring force than in European industrialized countries; the farmer, until the 1920s, was also a major component and any true worker's party would until then have had to be a Farmer-Labour Party. (Indeed at the state level, e.g. in Minnesota, such parties briefly emerged.) But although industrial workers developed certain common interests, they did not, as in the Old World, develop a comparable degree of class consciousness. No doubt racial and religious divergencies intensified this, but basically it was due to their acceptance of the individualistic, competitive values of American society. Thus though unionization began early and at once sought benefits from government it was in terms not essentially different from those of other interest groups. In the American Federation of Labour (AFL) Samuel Gompers early established the principle of indifference to party attachment, of 'rewarding the friends and punishing the enemies of labour' whatever their party. Even when, under the encouragement of the New Deal, the more militant Congress of Industrial Organizations (CIO) emerged, to take a very active part in many of the politico-economic disputes of the thirties and forties, the basic elements of the

Gompers doctrine were adhered to. Though organized labour recognized the Democrats as in general the party of its friends it did not identify itself, especially at the federal level, with either party. Both AFL and CIO established 'political education' organizations in the forties as legal channels through which money and propaganda could be directed in support of approved candidates. In certain states, e.g. Michigan, where the Democratic Party has largely been taken over by the trade unions, this has been politically crucial, and it is not difficult to establish instances in which individual candidates have owed their election to the organized labour vote (as well as some in which this same support has constituted a millstone of liability). Similarly, in New York City the Ladies' Garment Workers Union has long sustained the local Liberal Party which, however, is peculiar in that it does not ordinarily nominate its own candidates but endorses those of another, generally but not invariably the Democrats.

In presidential elections the first open endorsement by the CIO came in 1948 when they backed President Truman; the AFL made their first in 1952, endorsing Adlai Stevenson. Even so, and despite the AFL–CIO merger of 1955, the union vote is not committed in all circumstances to Democratic candidates. Moreover, although the union's help with funds may be material,[1] its political organization lacks roots and it cannot 'deliver' the labour vote with assurance even when – as by no means always happens – the labour leadership speaks with one voice. Again, in striking contrast to the TUC's relationship with the British Labour Party, few trade unionists – and no union leaders – sit in Congress. On the other hand, and in keeping with their status as an interest group, the unions will demand of a Democratic administration (and pretend to demand of a Republican administration) that its Secretary of Labour will be acceptable to, if not intimately connected with, the union leadership.

The Ultimate Responsibility

From the foregoing it will be apparent that American interest groups are well equipped to proffer and promote in Congress legislation which has a sectional concern. But what of legislation with a wider application? Or, to put what is much the same question in another form, where does responsibility lie for devising, not merely separate bills, but

---

[1] Since the passage of the Taft-Hartley Act in 1947 it has to be indirect; the AFL–CIO channels funds to approved candidates (of either party) through a so-called Committee of Public Education (COPE).

an overall legislative programme? In an earlier America and on one view of the Constitution a simple answer would be returned to this question – that this was the responsibility of the whole of the Congress, meeting and deliberating together, throwing up their own leaders and hammering out their programme as they went along without too much regard for party lines. Now a Clay, now a Douglas, now a Thaddeus Stevens would arise and by the patent acceptability of his proposals and the power of his personality would lead the legislators along his view of the common weal and Congress would commemorate him, as is its pleasing wont, by attaching his name to the legislation which he had fathered. Such a view reflected a Jacksonian view of the omnicompetence of the average man and of the simplicity of the tasks of government. But it still had validity down to the days when Bryce could say that 'the larger part of law and administration belongs to the State governments' and that 'four-fifths of the President's work is the same in kind as that which devolves on the chairman of a commercial company or the manager of a railway'. However, with the arrival of the twentieth century, of expanded federal power, of big government, of vast international responsibilities, it ceased to make any sense at all.

Yet Congress has been slow to recognize that there was any problem here. In one sense, admittedly, the attempts by the turn of the century Speakers, Reed and Cannon, to grasp power and centralize leadership were a dim recognition of a felt need, but their efforts were not only confined to the House of Representatives, they were also in the service of a narrow, almost tribal view of party government, related to no large principles of general application but simply to preventing the 'Ins' becoming the 'Outs'. It was left to Woodrow Wilson to recognize that, given the American system, leadership could not come from Congress but must be given to Congress from outside and could only be given by the one official who could claim an even wider electoral mandate, the President. Using the limited instruments that the Constitution provided, the President's right and duty to inform Congress and recommend measures to it, Wilson put a new drive and authority behind his communications, making them not mere expressions of opinion but transmitted pressures of the general will. He revived, for the first time since Jefferson, the practice of addressing Congress in person and he concerned himself actively and directly with the legislative fortunes of measures he thought important.

In the crisis of the Depression another presidential leader, Franklin

Roosevelt, had a fresh opportunity to bring home to Congress, not only the need for external direction, but also the inescapable interlocking in modern government of legislation and administration and the impossibility of formulating the one without experience in handling the other. The imperative and personal messages were reinforced by those direct, 'fireside' evocations of popular support which the invention of radio (and *a fortiori* soon of television) made uniquely available to the man in the White House, compared with the chaos of conflicting voices in House and Senate. Moreover the presidential messages were often actual legislative drafts, representing a degree of explicit executive authorship which, in the eyes of an earlier age, would have been virtually unconstitutional. On the whole programme Roosevelt maintained the closest liaison with Congress, evolving what, at its peak, was described as ' "a master ministry" of congressional leaders, cabinet officers and executive officials working through the White House'. Furthermore, much of the legislation which Congress voted was in general terms – in effect enabling acts, delegating extensive powers of subordinate legislation to the executive. Although the most sweeping of these, the National Recovery Act, was struck down in the courts as 'delegation run riot', this by no means meant the end of delegated legislation. The U.S.A., no less than other modern governments, has found such delegation essential and through successive rulings of the courts has established a code of acceptable governing principles which makes possible an extent and diversity of delegated legislation not dissimilar to Britain's.

The high point of Roosevelt's legislative leadership was not long maintained, as factional and personal disagreements overtook the initial community of purpose of the New Deal. But the mutual dependence which he established could never again be totally undone and even in the most exasperated days of Harry Truman's dealings with the 'Do-nothing 80th Congress' and in Dwight Eisenhower's diffident assertions of the presidential will, a level of executive–legislative co-operation was maintained which many earlier generations would have considered downright improper. In this connection the development in the use made of the President's State of the Union Message is of particular interest. Under Truman the practice was established of using this to do more than set out a general theme or policy; instead he incorporated in it a set of specific legislative recommendations, in effect a legislative agenda for Congress. When Eisenhower, reverting to previous custom, omitted this procedure Congress, so far from rejoicing in this return to *laissez-faire*, complained of his failure to keep them informed of his programme and in the following year the Truman procedure was revived, to become henceforward standard practice. This is not to say that Congress feels the presidential agenda to be binding, still less all-inclusive. It merely reflects the fact that even in their primary task of planning their work Congress has now accepted that the complexity of modern government requires a statement of the executive's intentions and requirements.

This still leaves open the question of how much cooperation a President will in fact be able to secure from his Congresses. Harry Truman, who knew whereof he spoke, observed: 'I sit here all day trying to persuade people to do the things they ought to have sense enough to do without my persuading them. . . . That's all the powers of the President amount to.' Vis-à-vis Congress this is substantially true, if those few specific powers such as the veto, which we have already noted, are discounted. Put another way, an institutional jealousy between legislature and executive guarantees, if all else fails, that President and Congress will not naturally pull in a common direction. If they cooperate it will be because a positive effort has been made to see that they do. And if only because the President is one and Congress are many, it is from the President's side that this effort will ordinarily have to come. What instruments are available to the President to help him in this task?

Time was when the lever of patronage might have headed the list. As in eighteenth-century Britain when a monarchical executive had to secure cooperation from a separated legislature, the distribution of loaves and fishes had its accepted place among the instruments of government. A key figure in any administration would be the Post-master-General, not because of the cruciality of the mail service, but because his department, in the days of 'small' government, was alone in having at its disposal jobs spread over the face of all the congressional districts and states of the U.S.A. So the Postmaster-General has nearly always been a person holding a high-level post in the party – most frequently, Chairman of the National Committee – and his advice on all matters of politics and patronage, within and without his department, would carry weight with the President. However, even in the Post Office, the steady encroachment of 'merit' on 'spoils', added to the general clumsiness of patronage as an instrument of political control, has caused a marked decline in reliance on this weapon throughout the century. The New Deal, conservative in this respect while innovatory in so many others, gave way to one last glorious flare-up of the old addiction. It has been estimated that it created, through the medium of its vast expenditures on public works etc., 89,000 new jobs available for 'political' appointment, and there is no doubt that under the master-minding of James Farley, 'FDR''s campaign manager and Postmaster-General, these were used to assist the President in his control of Congress. Astutely, they were not all expended at one go, but were spread over the maximum period to produce the maximum results, on the principle that in politics the only gratitude is the expectation of favours to come. But even while the New Deal was thus with one hand reviving the political squalors of an earlier age, it was with its other cutting away at their roots. By hastening America's evolution towards a welfare state with low unemployment and diffused affluence it was robbing political jobs of the appeal which made them attractive, while by bringing its own creations into the merit system it prevented their being used again for the purpose it created them.

Thus it has come about that the modern President, despite the vast scale of the federal government, has at his disposal comparatively few jobs with which to tempt congressmen or appeal to their constituents. What he does have, of course, is something different, less flexible but still on occasion very valuable. The vast level of government expenditure, which makes even the New Deal look small, provides a range of potential political favours to which even the most affluent of societies will not be indifferent. However, these are by no means exclusively at the President's disposal. They are the result of appropriations voted by Congress and Congress is at least as eager and in general just as capable as the President of indicating on whom it wishes the fountain of public beneficence to play. Indeed the Lockeian principle (which in any case was never wholly applicable in the U.S.A.), by which the taxpayers' legislature seeks to curb the extravagances of the executive, has now gone into reverse. It is now generally the President whose budget proposals are aimed at economies, while it is Congress which seeks to spend where spending will most please. The closing of a redundant Brooklyn Navy Yard or the cutting back of excessive farm price supports – these are distasteful tasks that Congress prefers to leave to the executive branch. And although the President may remind a forgetful congressman of the benefits which some federal programme has brought to his own district, he can seldom reinforce the reminder with a threat to withdraw such aid if the congressman's vote goes the wrong way; the man who is President of 'all the people' operates under the inhibitions which derive from his quasi-monarchical role.

There is however another instrument at the President's disposal – his prestige as party leader. The fact that he is in the White House at all is evidence of his political potency. (Even if he has arrived there direct from the Vice-Presidency some potency remains evident; even the vice-presidential nomination does not go to a total nonentity.) His party has identified itself with him in the contest for power; some-times, as with 'FDR' or Eisenhower, the party has clearly owed its success at the elections to its identification with his name and image, and congressmen and senators have ridden into office, as the phrase has it, on the President's coat-tails and will be hoping to do so again. Sometimes, of course, like Kennedy, or Nixon in 1968, the President has run, not ahead of, but behind most of his party; even so, if he has the skill he can use the presidential office, once he has won it, to enhance his own prestige as party leader and to convert the narrowest of electoral margins into a good base for political persuasion. This is especially true during his first term, when Congress knows he will be re-nominated and will personify his party once more at the polls. It has some validity in respect of the congressional elections half-way through his second term. It is a sharply diminishing asset after that. Time was when the separation between legislature and executive was carried down to electoral levels, each branch fighting its own battles; indeed until comparatively recently it was thought improper for the President to intervene in the mid-term elections for Congress. However not only is presidential endorsement generally sought in leap years at every level; increasingly the President is under pressure to campaign for governors, senators, and congressmen of his party who are facing the electors at mid-term on issues which, by an earlier constitutional theory, were exclusively local and non-presidential.[1]

So the President vis-à-vis his own party in Congress can invoke these common experiences and expectations of battles fought and to come. How does he translate these loyalties into day to day cooperation with his party in Congress? His main instruments are of course the Speaker, the Vice-President, the majority leaders and the party caucus. He must

[1] Can the President throw his weight *against* a member of his own party whom he regards as a rebel? Roosevelt's attempt to 'purge' dissident Democrats in 1938 was a resounding failure, largely because his intervention was treated as in-trinsically improper. The impropriety is no longer so axiomatic, but it remains hazardous for the President to pit his prestige against a popular renegade.

not, of course, ever give the *impression* of treating them as instruments; institutional jealousy would flare up at any such suggestion. But he will be a poor President who has not been consulted on the selection of the principal congressional leaders of his party and his influence may be decisive in their selection. He will, like 'FDR', consult them and take them into his confidence on all important issues, but equally he must be careful not to expose them to the damaging charge of being merely his 'errand boys'. If his party is in a minority in either or both Houses the President is, of course, at a serious disadvantage, as Truman and Eisenhower both discovered. Here, however, the diffused and loose-jointed character of the American parties may come to the President's aid; Eisenhower was, in fact, able to carry much of his programme by a series of coalitions, constructed *ad hoc* for each specific measure, between Republicans and sympathetic Democrats.

In eliciting such extra-party support the President can draw on another weapon in his armoury; he can present himself as not merely a party leader, but as the national leader. Here the fusion of Chief Executive and Head of State stands him in good stead, enabling him to make smooth and imperceptible the switch from one personality to another. An emergency address to Congress may dramatize this role. Or he may utilize his press conference. Or, most effective perhaps of all, he may speak to the nation direct by radio and television. In so doing he may, if direct persuasion has failed with Congress, appeal to the people and even incite them to put pressure on Congress in support of his programme. To do this, as for example Truman did in respect of his 'Do-Nothing 80th Congress', involves a risk; it involves admitting a failure to cope with Congress directly and it implies great faith in one's own capacity to turn the sovereign people against their own elected legislators. It requires in consequence both boldness and finesse; the crudity of the operation must not appear in the explicit appeal, and yet a sufficient dint must be made on the public mind for the required popular response to emerge. And it must not be done too often. It must be a reserve power, an extraordinary device for an emergency situation.

Indeed it is a measure of the slowly intensifying solidity of the American party that such appeals by the President over the heads of Congress are increasingly confined to issues such as foreign affairs to which, in any case, party programmes have only a limited application. In Congress, as outside, party labels have only a limited significance upon which a President can normally rely. On the one hand it is rare for voting to coincide exactly with party labels – indeed this occurs virtually only on issues involving the organization of Congress. There are indeed, by British standards, a surprisingly large number of bills on which the parties do not divide, but these are those private bills or measures of merely local application which are commonly passed by unanimous consent, on a live-and-let-live basis. But this leaves a hard core of important measures on which Democrats and Republicans take clearly opposing sides – that is to say, each party has its own centre of gravity, and however much the periphery of each party may overlap with the others, these centres of gravity do not. The sort of issues which bring out these basic differences are those associated with the spending and taxing powers – deficit budgeting, social welfare programmes, the allocation of tax burdens and the like. Here the 'class' bias of the congressional parties reveals itself. It is to this that the President appeals or, put it another way, it is this that he elicits. The solidarity on such issues is in general stronger among Democrats (despite the big sectional group of Southern Democrats) than it is among Republicans – i.e. the Democrats of modern America are more of a positive party, while the Republicans are more a collective of critical, even negative, individualists.

The more one contemplates the complexities of the American party system the more one is struck by the paradox that, on the one hand, the President helps to consolidate and rationalize it, giving leadership to his own party and sharpening (in general) its contrast with its opponent, and yet, on the other, the separation of powers is simultaneously creating and maintaining lines of institutional conflict which cut across the doctrinal divisions. Not only in Congress itself but also among the electorate there is in each party a division between those who are Congress-minded, i.e. the particularists, the localists, the 'nay-sayers', and those who are President-minded, the delegators of power, the nationalists, the believers in positive government. Thus one may say, with some truth, that America has four parties – the Presidential Democrats, the Presidential Republicans, the Congressional Democrats, and the Congressional Republicans. Of these the first is in general the most powerful, both because of the predominant pressures of the age, and because in general the Democrats tend to be the more presidentially-minded party. The Presidential Republicans, a minority in the Republican Party, assert their individuality most clearly in the context of foreign affairs. The Congressional Democrats are overwhelmingly a party of the South, a region whose voting consistency has given it bastions of power in House and Senate such as it can never win in the executive branch and which are indeed out of proportion to its numerical strength in the nation. It lives or dies by its hold on Congress. Finally the Congressional Republicans are a rearguard party whose basic contradictions are harshly revealed every leap year, but whose power as a negative or braking force reflects that deep-seated element of anti-governmentalism which is one of America's oldest traditions.

There are those who, contemplating this chequerboard of opposed attitudes and constitutional severances, have despaired of the prospects for American democracy and abandoned hope of eliciting the amount of unity and consent necessary to make the system work. Any number of proposals for reform have been advanced, ranging from the substitution of a British parliamentary system to a four-year term for Congress or a presidential power of dissolution. There is no good reason to suppose that any of these proposals will get very far. The complicated structure of American party politics reflects the complexity of America itself. The demands it makes on those who lead the parties and work the system are indeed severe. With one exception – and that is in the peculiar context of last century's civil war – these demands have not proved more than the American political genius can supply. If they do, there are emergency resources in the institution of the Presidency which have been exploited before and would doubtless be exploited again. However, such limited emergencies apart, the untidy, wasteful, multiple process of check and countercheck, aggression and concession, push and pull which characterizes American politics today will probably continue to dominate it for the foreseeable future.

Further Reading

Becker, Carl L., *The Declaration of Independence: a Study in the History of Political Ideas.* New York, new edn. 1942.

Binkley, W. E., *American Political Parties: Their Natural History.* New York, 4th revised edn. 1965.

Brogan, D. W., *An Introduction to American Politics.* London, 1954.

Bryce, James, *The American Commonwealth.* Ed. Louis M. Hacker. New York, 1959.

Cummings, Milton C. and Wise, David, *Democracy under Pressure.* New York, 1971.

Galloway, George B., *The Legislative Process in Congress.* New York, 1953.

Hartz, Louis, *The Liberal Tradition in America.* New York, 1955.

Hofstadter, Richard, *The American Political Tradition and the Men Who Made It.* London, 1962.

Key, Vladimir O., Jr., *Politics, Parties and Pressure Groups*. New York, 5th edn. 1964.

Lewin, Leonard C., *A Treasury of American Political Humor*. New York, 1964.

Rossiter, Clinton L., *Conservatism in America*. New York, 2nd revised edn. 1962.

Sorauf, Frank J., *Party Politics in America*. Boston, Mass., 1968.

White, William S., *The Citadel: The Story of the U.S. Senate*. New York, 1957.

Wilson, Woodrow, *Congressional Government*. Originally published 1885; New York, 1956.

9 The Emergence of an American Literature

DOUGLAS GRANT

Literature in the Colonial Period

A discussion about when American literature can be said properly to begin is usually quite idle. American literature began as soon as pamphlets and poems, and other convenient forms of literature, began to be written by men who made their home in America. Some accounts of American literature start with George Sandys (1578–1644), the translator of Ovid's *Metamorphoses*, but Sandys is only recruited into the American ranks for the sake of the elegant and surprising impression he makes on the newcomer to American letters. He was not an American, he was only a visitor to Virginia (1621–5); and his interest in this connection is that men of culture and attainments were not stopped from crossing the Atlantic.

George Sandys is an English poet. Edward Taylor (*c.* 1644–1729) was born in Leicestershire and may have spent some time at the University of Cambridge before sailing for New England in 1668, but he is an American poet. After graduating from Harvard College in 1671, he received a call to become minister at the new frontier town of Westfield in Massachusetts, and there he stayed until his death – a great span, putting it against the background of events in Europe.

Taylor was by far the most considerable American poet of this period, but he was quite unknown until 1937, when his poems were published from manuscript for the first time. He wrote in the general style of the English devotional poets who were in fashion when he was young: Joshua Sylvester – the translator of Du Bartas's *Divine Weeks and Works*, George Herbert, Richard Crashaw, Francis Quarles. He overuses conceits and hyperbole in an effort to say the utmost, and he largely keeps to a rather monotonous stanza, but his series of 'Preparatory Meditations', in which he privately fixed his attention on God's wonders and the mysteries of the Christian faith before administering the Lord's Supper, are marked by their unvarying sincerity and occasional beauties and solemnities.

> My shattered Phancy stole away from me,
>   (Wits run a wooling over Edens Parke)
> And in Gods Garden saw a Golden Tree,
>   Whose Heart was All Divine, and gold its barke.
> Whose glorious limbs and fruitfull branches strong
> With Saints, and Angels bright are richly hung.

As he lay unpublished, Taylor had no effect at all, of course, upon American poetry, but he is of the greatest interest in illustrating the poetic temperament responding to the circumstances of American life. He shows no development as a poet: the last of his 'Meditations', of 1725, could as well have been the first, written forty-three years earlier; but this could have been expected, living as remotely as he did and far from the stimulus of any centre of literary culture – a disadvantage that was to depress American writers for many years yet to come. He was isolated in another profounder sense: as a responsible individual in relation to his God and the moral order of the universe. In spite of this transcendental interest and the exotic trappings of his imagery, mostly collected from the Bible, there is a marked strain of realism in his verse. An inhabitant of Westfield could not have escaped the stern facts of ordinary life.

Taylor may have been the best, but Anne Bradstreet (1612–72) was the best-known of the New England poets until his discovery. She, too, was born and bred in England, not arriving in Massachusetts until she was eighteen, in the company of her husband and her father, Thomas Dudley, the Governor of the Massachusetts Bay Colony. Her first collection of poems, *The Tenth Muse Lately Sprung Up in America*, was published in London in 1650, when it would have caused as much surprise for being written by a woman as by an American. A second collection, containing better and later work, appeared at Boston in 1678. On the scores of both sex and nationality it has proved possible to magnify Mrs Bradstreet's achievement, but several of her shorter, domestic, poems remain more clearly in the memory, on account of their affectionate and godly simplicity, than the more sonorous and far-searching verses of Taylor. When she addresses her 'Dear and Loving Husband' she avows her affection with the same forthrightness as she declares in her excellent verses 'Upon the Burning of our House', that what she lost by fire was God's, to be taken back when He rightly chose:

> And when I could no longer look,
> I blest his Name that gave and took,
> That layed my goods now in the dust;
> Yea so it was, and so 'twas just,
> It was his own; it was not mine;
> Far be it that I should repine.

She makes an effect as much by strength of character as by skill in metre; another early anticipation of a distinctive trait in later American verse.

Taylor and Mrs Bradstreet are poets, but their more renowned contemporary, Michael Wigglesworth (1631–1705), the author of the popular set of admonitory stanzas on *The Day of Doom* (1662), which was widely read in New England for a hundred years, seems now more of a name than a poet. And in the course of the next hundred years Wigglesworth was followed by other names, one of the brightest and latest being that of Joel Barlow. Barlow wrote *The Hasty Pudding*, a famous mock heroic poem on a favourite dish of his boyhood, and *The Vision of Columbus* (1787: revised and published as *The Columbiad*, 1807), an epic which has been shown to be not entirely impervious to intelligent criticism. But all the names that could be collected would only serve to indicate the poverty of the colonial imagination.

The imagination was poor because men were taxed to the limit by reality – of heaven as well as of earth. The English settlers transferred to North America the customs and institutions of their homeland, but the new land made new demands and offered new opportunities and the settlers were fully occupied in trying to adapt themselves to these new circumstances, or in bringing in the necessary innovations. The forest had to be cleared and settlements established, and the deeper the penetration into the wilderness, the more strenuous the labour and the greater the dangers. The colonists could have no time for so leisured a pursuit as polite letters, but as they were as much concerned with their salvation in the next world as with their survival in this, they required a learned ministry to expound the truths of Revelation and of sacred history. The writing done in the Colonies had consequently a strong practical bias, whether it was concerned with what lay at hand, or was supposed to occur on its relinquishment.

Cotton Mather (1663–1728) is the finest example of the Puritan ministry. He belonged to the third generation of an important Massachusetts family; his father, Increase Mather, was President of Harvard College, an influential politician, and a prolific writer. Cotton Mather himself attempted to maintain the virtues and beliefs of the past in the midst of a changing and increasingly secular society, though he was deeply interested in the new science and affected by its rationalism. He was elected to the Royal Society in 1714, a proof of his sympathy with the modern. He wrote more than four hundred and fifty works, and manfully kept up a voluminous diary, but his finest work, and certainly his most accessible to modern taste, is his *Magnalia Christi Americana* (1702), or ecclesiastical history of New England, in which he sought to describe 'the wonders of the Christian religion, flying from the depravations of Europe, to the American strand', with the intention of keeping the virtues of the early settlers alight. The work is a compilation of history and biography and anecdote, written with learning and force; a summary in manner as well as in matter of the Colonies' early times.

William Byrd (1674–1744) is a figure comparable to Cotton Mather, from the Southerly colonies, from Virginia. He had an even larger library than Mather at a time when extensive libraries were unusual, to say the least, and he was also – like Mather – a Fellow of the Royal Society. He spent much time in England as a young man, and again later as colonial agent (1715–26), when he moved in fashionable and literary society, an experience which lent wit and grace to his style. He did not write for publication, but his writings have since been discovered and published. He was one of the party that surveyed the boundary between Virginia and North Carolina in 1729 and kept an excellent journal, published as the *History of the Dividing Line* (1841). He also kept personal diaries which are equally remarkable and observant. They give an admirable account of the character and learning and way of life of a gentleman colonist.

Mather and Byrd stand out clearly from many lesser writers of the same sort, but the first Americans of the Colonial period to achieve a wide contemporary reputation were Jonathan Edwards (1703–58), the philosopher and evangelist, and Benjamin Franklin (1706–90). The difference between them is profoundly temperamental, but it was due in part to their background. Edwards represents the finest and most uncompromising aspects of the Puritan tradition of New England. He was born in Connecticut and educated at Yale University and spent his life in the ministry. Franklin, though born in Boston, was brought up in the more liberal and pragmatic and worldly atmosphere of Phila-delphia. Edwards's attention was ultimately fixed on man's eternal welfare, Franklin's on his present comfort; and if the one naturally took to the sermon to urge his opinions, the other as instinctively turned to the more insinuating medium of the newspaper column. But this is to separate them: taking them together, as they must be taken, they can be seen as representing the main strands in the American literary consciousness.

As an evangelist Edwards affected immediately only New England; he began the Great Awakening (1734) by his fervent preaching of the doctrine of salvation through grace; but as a metaphysician he exer-cised a much wider influence. Among his sermons his *Sinners in the Hands of an Angry God* (1741) is the most notorious, a powerful depic-tion of the supposed operation of God's justice and of human depravity; his *Enquiry into the Modern Prevailing Notions of Freedom of Will* (1754) is certainly his finest metaphysical work. 'Having produced *him*', exclaimed William Hazlitt, who was greatly influenced by the *Enquiry*, 'the Americans need not despair of their metaphysicians. We do not scruple to say, that he is one of the acutest, most powerful, and, of all reasoners, the most conscientious and sincere.' Edwards's exposition of divine necessity in the *Enquiry* may seem grimly Calvinistic, but there appears in his other writings not only the same passionate logic, but a fine sense of moral beauty and a vibrant response to this world as an expression of God's power and glory, which help him to stir the imagination more than might appear from his desolating theology. As Hazlitt's remark may suggest, he discussed problems that were to pre-occupy later generations, in England as well as in New England, and his influence, while seeming to be a matter of the past, helped his American successors to grasp the significant direction of modern secular thought.

Benjamin Franklin was, in contrast to Edwards, a man of affairs. He was largely self-educated, by travel as well as by books. He was in England as a young man, from 1723 to 1725, where he worked in a London printing office, and he returned to London in 1757 as agent for Pennsylvania, staying there until 1775 – a period of crisis between Britain and her North American colonies. He was a man of versatile genius. He was an inventor (the Franklin stove was once universally known and is still used), an experimental scientist (who has not heard of his experiment in electricity with a kite?), a statesman (he was appointed American plenipotentiary to the French Court in 1778); and more besides. He was a popular and successful journalist – his *Poor Richard's Almanack* (1733–58) was a skilful compilation of humour and sound sense – and he was an effective and frequent pamphleteer. As a writer, his reputation rests, appropriately enough in view of his various interests, on his *Autobiography* (1791: first complete edition, 1868), which covers his early life down to 1757. The *Autobiography* is a candid and enlightened review of experience, even though its complacency and worldly wisdom can be exasperating. Franklin helped in the drafting of the Declaration of Independence, and his character well illustrates the self-confidence and independence that lay behind the promulgation of that document.

The break with Great Britain and the succeeding arguments over the political shape of the new nation were accompanied by some brilliant political and polemical writing. The great Thomas Paine, and Alexander Hamilton and James Madison, the authors of *The Federalist* (1787–8) – 'the best commentary on the principles of government which ever was written', according to Thomas Jefferson – were among the most skilful contributors to the debate. But once independence had been actually achieved and the turmoil had subsided, the new Americans began to demand that their nation should become, in the words of Noah Webster, the lexicographer, as great in arts as it was in arms. The urge towards the literary expression of the new consciousness was very great from the start, though it was many years before it was realized successfully.

The Beginnings of Literary Independence

The principal difficulty confronting the American writer was not so much the New World as the Old. The Frenchman, Hector St Jean de Crèvecoeur (1735–1813), who came out to Canada as a young man and later settled on a farm in New York State, had described in his *Letters from an American Farmer* (1782) – first published in English in London and a favourite among the English Romantics – what it was like to be an American and the effect of the place upon the feelings and imagination. But once the writer turned aside from description such as de Crèvecoeur's, and attempted the novel or verse or the play, he was intimidated by the sheer weight of the English tradition. He might open his mouth with the intention of sounding independent, but the voice that faintly spoke was the voice of London, with an American accent. The books he read were English books; the thoughts he had perforce to think were those flowing in from abroad; and the words he had to use to describe his own peculiar experiences were already bent to another use by English genius. None of this mattered if what he wrote sprang from political controversy – words became malleable in the heat of the moment; but once he sat down to tell a tale or to versify it became intolerable. He was dulled by a sense of his own inadequacy.

But gradually a distinctively American style began to appear, especially in poetry. The development can be seen by comparing Philip Freneau (1752–1832) and William Cullen Bryant (1794–1878). Freneau was inspired by all the fury of liberty and wrote many patriotic poems, as well as serving in the Revolutionary army, but his verse could as well be printed in an anthology of eighteenth-century English verse as in one of American, making allowance for place names and national allusions. Freneau's satiric and declamatory verse is generally interesting as a document of the times, but his reflective lyrics are more likely to stay in the memory. 'The Wild Honeysuckle' (1786) implicitly compares the flower with the transitoriness of human life, and such moral comparisons, or emblems, were to become characteristic of American verse.

William Cullen Bryant's most famous poem, 'To a Waterfowl' – 'the most perfect brief poem in the language', according to Matthew Arnold – which he wrote in 1815, at the age of twenty-one, is a complete emblem. The bird, winging its solitary way south through the gathering dusk, is meant for the soul making its predestined flight through life into eternity. The habit of thinking in terms of such emblems, to express the operation of a morally consequential universe and its effect upon the individual, was among the legacies of the Puritan past, but the influence of William Wordsworth on Bryant and upon later American poets was also strong. Wordsworth assured them that Nature was the greatest of poetic themes, and Nature lay everywhere about them in its grandest forms. American poetry is born of the Romantic Movement, and is stamped with its origins.

The American poet, with divine Nature to prompt him, was far luckier than the American novelist or dramatist. The dramatist was obviously handicapped by the moral prejudice against the stage and the lack of theatres, but the novelist had also similar difficulties to face. The novelist had to begin working within the tradition of the English novel, but the English novel, which, in all its forms, depended upon a complex society and a rich history, was an almost impossible challenge to American imitators. They looked at those about them with the candid gaze of democrats, and their beginnings lay just over the horizon. The picaresque novel, with its endless variety of incidents, was hard to realize in a country which was not yet ready, in any sense, for peregrinations; the sentimental novel could only be tepidly copied where people were not born as into prisons and shackled with obligations; the comic novel was impossible where the only jokes possible were at the cost of a smiling sameness; and the 'gothic' novel, seemingly, must lie beyond the reach of writers without any castle to command or ruined priory for meditation. The sets of Henry Fielding, Samuel Richardson, Lawrence Sterne, and Mrs Ann Radcliffe standing on American shelves walled in the native American imagination.

The latest of the novel's forms, the 'gothic' novel, was the one that improbably offered the best opportunity. Charles Brockden Brown (1771–1810), under the influence of William Godwin as both a political theorist and a novelist, wrote four novels in two years, in which he partially succeeded in translating the psychological elements of the 'gothic' novel into American terms. The best of these four novels is probably the first, *Wieland* (1798), but *Arthur Mervyn* (1799), *Osmond* (1799), and *Edgar Huntly* (1799) are roughly comparable, in their faults as well as merits. Castles and priories, titled villains and ruthless inquisitors and legendary ghosts were obviously properties denied to Brown, but he found substitutes in caverns and forests and Red Indians, and as for the distressed imaginings and subconscious terrors and superstitious impulses, which are the essence of this kind of fiction, he had no reason to try and replace them; they were lodged in the American mind as well as in the European. The 'gothic' romance thus gave the American novelist greater freedom than other forms to examine the American consciousness independently, and in spite of their faults of style and construction and their constant straining of credibility, Brown's novels mark the uncertain beginnings of a native tradition.

Brown's novels made 'some noise' in England and such acclaim was of great importance to the American writer, who wanted a critical reassurance that he could not hope to find at home. The first American writer to be widely acclaimed abroad was Washington Irving (1783–1859). Irving, like Brown, began as a lawyer, but when he, too, turned to literature he brought far greater talents than Brown possessed. He wrote elegantly and wittily and in conformity with the standard of *belles lettres* set up by Joseph Addison and the eighteenth-century periodical essayists. He made his name by his contributions to *Salma-*

gundi; or, The Whim-Whams and Opinions of Launcelot Langstaff (1807-8), satirical essays on New York's tastes and manners, and by a burlesque *History of New York* (1809), purportedly the work of an eccentric Dutch–American scholar, Diedrich Knickerbocker. But the period of his great fame began after his removal to England in 1815, with the publication in 1820 of *The Sketch Book*, under the pseudonym of Geoffrey Crayon, Gent. Irving became one of the best known men-of-letters of the day and was included by Hazlitt in his literary character sketches, *The Spirit of the Age* – a sufficient tribute.

Several of Irving's essays in *The Sketch Book* are on American themes – the most famous are the folk tales, 'Rip Van Winkle' and 'The Legend of Sleepy Hollow' – but most of them concern the English models. Irving's success in playing the part of the man-of-letters in English terms accounted for his great reputation among his own countrymen, who were glad to see an American hold his own abroad, but once national fervour began to demand a distinctively American manner and a devotion to American themes, Irving began to be discounted as imitative and genteel. He was welcomed enthusiastically on his return home to New York in 1832, but a hundred years later he was in eclipse, the merits of not only *The Sketch Book* but his many other works, historical and miscellaneous, disregarded. The revaluation of American literature that has taken place in the past twenty-five years has re-established him as a talented and interesting writer and exonerated him as an American.

The fate of the reputation of Irving's great contemporary, James Fenimore Cooper (1789–1851), who also lived abroad for long periods and received wider international acclaim, has been entirely different. Cooper is recognized today as the great myth maker of American literature; the novelist of the frontier, whose description of those vast woods and wastes and the struggle between white men and red men for their possession are really metaphysical statements on the nature of the American soul. Cooper was not without pretentiousness, but he was not pretentious in that way. He began by challenging Walter Scott and had the sobriquet of 'the American Scott' bestowed on him for his pains. The title was obviously deserved by the vigorous style and loose construction of his early narratives, but there are better reasons for comparing him and Scott. Scott had managed to assert the literary independence of Scottish literature as against English literature by proving that Scottish themes and characters were sufficient for the creating of a great literature. Cooper attempted to do as much for

American literature, and the title conferred on him marks, at least, his partial success.

The novels in which Cooper sets out his mythology of the early United States are the five 'Leather-Stocking Tales', whose hero is the great woodsman and scout, Natty Bumppo – 'Leather-Stocking'. The five novels were written and published in a different order to the chronological narrative they describe, taken together. *The Pioneers* (1823), *The Last of the Mohicans* (1826), *The Prairie* (1827), *The Pathfinder* (1840), and *The Deerslayer* (1841) is the order of appearance, but in the sequence of events *The Deerslayer, The Last of the Mohicans, The Pathfinder, The Pioneers, The Prairie* ought to follow one another; in this way Natty Bumppo can be followed from youth to old age and death.

Each of the stories has its own separate tale of adventures, in which the course of romantic love is entangled in the vagaries of frontier conflicts, but rather than details of plot the reader remembers the descriptions of the wilderness and one or two of the more dramatic scenes, in which the characters seem to behave with a ritualistic significance, and, above all, Natty Bumppo and his Indian comrade, Chingachgook, the Mohican. Natty Bumppo dies unmarried; he is a celibate of the frontier, devoted to the wilderness which forever yields before him, retreating westwards, an unattainable ideal. And in his lonely idealism, and sense of a mystical brotherhood transcending race, and desperate search, he becomes, in an extreme interpretation, a symbol of the American psyche itself and, in a more ordinary interpretation, a pattern of pioneer life. Cooper has many faults of varying seriousness – innumerable faults, some have said – but the strange, intense vision of the 'Leather-Stocking Tales' comes through unimpaired.

The 'Leather-Stocking Tales' gave Cooper, as the 'gothic' romances had earlier given Brockden Brown, the chance of developing a narrative on his own terms. The sea offered him an equal opportunity, and his sea stories hardly fell short of the other series in popularity or achievement. *The Pilot* (1823) and *The Red Rover* (1827) are two of his early sea stories; *Afloat and Ashore* (1844) is a later one. The sea, like the forest, inspired Cooper's romantic imagination with symbols of energy and grandeur, and offered him equal scope for the confident unrolling of the narrative. But once he came ashore he complained, as bitterly as any other American writer, that American society was too limited and impoverished to support a novelist. In part, he was complaining under the guise of criticism against developments in American society which he deplored on political grounds as an aristocrat, but he was also expressing the desperation that the American novelist felt as he tried to write realistically about his optimistic, levelling, disrespectful, society. *Homeward Bound* (1838) and *Home as Found* (1838) are only two of the novels in which he expressed his disillusionment. Truth seemed, for Cooper, to lie on the frontier with Natty Bumppo, or out at sea; for other writers it was even more distant, in the past.

The Literature of New England

Walter Scott had an extraordinary vogue in the United States. 'I have read all Scott's novels . . .' one young man wrote in 1820; 'I wish I had not, that I might have the pleasure of reading them again.' The writer was Nathaniel Hawthorne (1804–64), at the time a student at Bowdoin College. Hawthorne's first apprentice novel, *Fanshawe* (1828), is sufficient evidence of Scott's influence. *Fanshawe* was a complete failure, but one good effect of Scott was to encourage Hawthorne to consider, with deep personal interest, the history of New England and the effect of Puritan traditions upon the New England character. Hawthorne's interest can be called personal as well as historical since he belonged to a family established in Salem since the seventeenth century. Among his forbears was one of the judges at the notorious Salem witchcraft trials, which polluted the last years of that century.

After *Fanshawe* Hawthorne turned to the short story – though allegory would be a far apter description of the studies in the Puritan mind and temperament which he wrote in retirement at Salem. He collected them together under the title of *Twice-Told Tales* (1837; enlarged edition, 1842). Whether he draws upon the past in New England or touches upon the present, he succeeds with telling economy in suggesting the melancholy and uneasiness that lie at the centre of the Puritan conscience – at least, of the Puritan conscience as it was in decline. He speaks of guilt and hints at sins so monstrous that the simple consciousness of their unspecified existence infects the whole world, draining it of its joy and vitality. A lack of vitality is the chief fault of these stories, leading to an insubstantiality in the characterization and a relaxed hold upon commonplace realities. They are otherwise perfectly fashioned and soberly acute.

Hawthorne published a second collection of allegorical stories in 1846, *Mosses from an Old Manse*; more mature and ambitious stories than the earlier ones. He had come out of retirement at Salem in 1836 and after an interval of hack writing, he took up a post in the Boston Custom House in 1839. He also married. This experience of the world, as well as his greater proficiency as a writer, were reflected in such admirable stories as 'Young Goodman Brown', 'Rappaccini's Daughter', and several others. The allegory is still as strong as ever, but it is now accompanied by a more intimate and feeling sense of the suffering that accompanies guilt.

Guilt and suffering are the themes of *The Scarlet Letter* (1850), his first novel since *Fanshawe*. The influence of Scott is as clearly to be seen in this novel as in the early one, but the indebtedness is that of a master to his old teacher and not that of an insolvent debtor. *The Scarlet Letter* is entirely Hawthorne's own: in its construction, which is built upon his practice of the short story; in its exceedingly disciplined form; in its allegory; and in its relentless but sensitive probing of the Puritan conscience. The novel is set in Boston in the mid-seventeenth century, but by using the action to identify the historical cause of the temperamental malaise of the nineteenth-century New Englander, and by making the heroine, Hester Prynne, a forerunner of emancipated womanhood, Hawthorne gave his tale a sharp moral and social relevance.

Hawthorne repeatedly affirmed that he wrote romances rather than novels. The novel, he argued, kept faithfully to 'the probable and ordinary course of man's experience'; the romance has 'the right to present the truth under circumstances, to a great extent, of the writer's own choosing or creation'. The quotation occurs in the Preface to Hawthorne's next novel, or romance, *The House of the Seven Gables* (1851). The *Seven Gables* may be a romance under the terms of Hawthorne's nomenclature, but in directing its attention towards the 'probable and ordinary course' of contemporary experience, Hawthorne showed that he was dissatisfied with the romance and wished to write a novel, to the extent that American society allowed him.

The House of the Seven Gables begins in the past, with a gross and cruel injustice committed in the seventeenth century. The ultimate consequences of this old crime are worked out in Salem in the nineteenth century. In spite of the real difficulty of making the effects of seventeenth-century wizardry plausible under nineteenth-century conditions, Hawthorne tells the story well and succeeds both in illustrating the moral ambiguities that lurk under ordinary appearances and in creating more substantial characters than he had ever done before, especially his delightful heroine, Phoebe Pyncheon. The difficulty of the book lies in the disconcerting way in which it wavers between realism and allegory. The two never coincide as they should and the reader is consequently left wondering whether the blurred focus is his own fault or Hawthorne's.

Hawthorne retreated even farther from the past in *The Blithedale Romance* (1852). The romance is an extremely interesting one, especially in its description of the passionate and intellectual Zenobia and in its play of ideas, but the same failure to weld together the allegorical and the ordinary is apparent, resulting in a loss of moral coherence and in an air of unreality. The romance can, no doubt, be defended critically, but the fact remains that it is the least popular of Hawthorne's works and is the last romance that he published until 1860, when *The Marble Faun* appeared – an interval that illustrates his own dissatisfaction.

The Marble Faun is not only a retreat from the Puritan past with which Hawthorne began; it is a retreat from the American present. The characters are principally Americans, but they are expatriate Americans living in Rome. The theme is again the 'unpardonable sin' and the restless conscience, but it is woven into the carnival gaieties and Catholic pomps of Rome. A complete coincidence between Hawthorne's moral vision and the action itself is again wanting, as it is in all of the novels after *The Scarlet Letter*. The moral dilemma of the Americans does not exactly square with the facts of Italian life, but the story has a strange and memorable richness. And in removing Americans from America to Europe the better to study the national character, Hawthorne showed the way to his great pupil, Henry James. If the social complexities needed to support the novel could not be found at home, then they must be sought elsewhere, in Europe.

The Blithedale Romance was based on Hawthorne's own experience at Brook Farm, a cooperative community run by the Transcendental Club. The Transcendentalists who ran the community were optimists, and while it was strange that such a dark pessimist as Hawthorne should have decided to place himself on the Farm for so long a term as six months, it was not remarkable that an ambitious writer should have been interested in the most powerful intellectual movement in the United States at that time, especially since he counted many Transcendentalists among his friends, including their leader, Ralph Waldo Emerson.

The Transcendentalists drew their principles ultimately from the transcendentalist philosophy of Immanuel Kant and his German followers, but this philosophy entered New England through the writings of S. T. Coleridge and Thomas Carlyle, both of whom enjoyed a great vogue in the United States in the 1820s and 1830s. But though they may have derived their principles from abroad, the Transcendentalists flourished because they expressed the hitherto unexpressed ambition of young American intellectuals to escape from the narrow formal teaching of the church and the commonsensical, materialistic attitudes of a provincial society into more spacious fields of speculation and idealistic action. The principles may have been fashioned abroad and imported, but they only succeeded in their task of liberation because they could be naturalized into the native intellectual tradition, without requiring those who adopted them to break with the past.

The development that occurred can be seen perfectly in the career of Ralph Waldo Emerson (1803–82). Emerson was born the son of a Unitarian minister in Boston. Unitarianism was in New England a reaction against Calvinism, in response to the more liberal and scientific intellectual currents of the late eighteenth century. Emerson followed his father into the Unitarian church, but in 1832, a year after the death of his first wife to whom he had been married for only two years, he felt compelled to resign his pastorate in Boston on grounds of conscience. He travelled in Europe for a year and through his meetings with Coleridge and Carlyle, as well as from his wide reading in philosophy and history and literature, he discovered in Transcendentalism the system he needed to satisfy his temperamental optimism and support his idealism and intellectual curiosity. He remained a preacher, but he now had a doctrine that he could expound with conviction and one which deeply appealed to all the other young men who were dissatisfied with established forms and conventional responses.

Emerson preached, no longer from the pulpit, but from the lecture platform. The lectures that he began giving in Boston after his return from his decisive year in Europe, in 1833, had an effect on many of his young audience similar to that of evangelical conversion. And he continued to lecture all his life, to wider audiences, in the United States and in England. He lectured on many subjects – on 'The Philosophy of History' and 'Spiritual Laws' and 'Love' – but his themes were always the same. He taught that an Over-Soul unified and explained even apparently contradictory phenomena, that reality was spiritual, that the individual's duty was to fulfil to the limit all the noble possibilities open to him, and that he could succeed in this self-realization if he would. He looked far ahead, in time and space, and urged his listeners to follow him, supremely confident in their success, and even when his speculations were most nebulous and his optimism most bland he disarmed their scepticism by his shrewdness and his pithy style.

Emerson began to keep journals and notebooks in 1820, when he was at Harvard, a practice that he maintained throughout his life; and these voluminous observations and collections were the foundation of all his work. He would prepare his lectures from the materials in his notebooks, and in due course, after being widely exercised, the lectures would become essays and be published. His first book was *Nature* (1836), based on his early lectures, and in it he expressed his philosophy once and for all. He never succeeded in bettering its admirable prose, or in surpassing its idealistic call to everyone to adopt a finer, more self-reliant life, or in shrouding in a blaze of feeling imagery the enormous, inconvenient gaps in his bridging system between the world of appearances and the unifying spiritual reality. Anyone mastering *Nature* has no difficulty in following anything that Emerson was to say later in his long and honoured career.

He published a first series of *Essays* in 1841 and a second in 1844. *Representative Men* – six essays on his special heroes, which were originally given as lectures in Boston and in London – appeared in 1850. While *Representative Men* was certainly inspired by Carlyle's *Heroes and Hero-Worship*, it illustrates a typically Emersonian notion, that man is a corporate being and that certain great men represent the greatest possibilities of each of the human faculties; thus, Plato is man the philosopher, Shakespeare man the poet, and so on through the six chosen.

Emerson visited England again to lecture in 1847 and on his return he lectured on England and the English themselves. These lectures were published as *English Traits* in 1856. To those who are impervious to Emerson's luminous appeals to idealistic action, this is undoubtedly his best book. The nature of the subject itself keeps him closer to reality than his usual procedure, and he expresses shrewd thoughts with wit and energy; in fact, his practicality would come as a disconcerting surprise to anyone who had judged him only by *Nature*.

Emerson's style is brilliant, but it is seldom continuous: 'poetic' would be a jaded, but accurate description, provided we meant by 'poetic' not something that was rapt and loosely eloquent, but terse and imagistic. Emerson himself said that he was a poet, however 'husky'; an unduly modest claim. He published his *Poems* in 1847 and *May-Day and other Pieces* in 1867, and though the two volumes do not add up to much in bulk, they contain some memorable verses – compact, speculative, and distinct: 'The Rhodora', 'The Snow-Storm' and 'The Sphinx' are among them – and, of course, the 'Concord Hymn', Emerson's famous celebration of national independence.

Emerson greatly helped to make the United States' literary independence recognized abroad. He spoke in his own highly individual voice, but the virtues he preached were native ones, and in their emphasis upon independence they made a deep appeal to the youth of Britain as well as of America. Matthew Arnold has described how he and many of his contemporaries responded to Emerson's message and, in fact, no account of nineteenth-century social thought in England could disregard Emerson. But his message was addressed primarily, of course, to his own countrymen.

The most famous of Emerson's disciples was Henry David Thoreau (1817–62), another New Englander. After graduating from Harvard in 1837 he came under Emerson's influence and was included in the Transcendental Club, the group of intellectuals who met occasionally after 1836 under Emerson's tutelage to discuss a variety of topics, literary and philosophical. Thoreau so identified himself with Emerson's principles that he lived in Emerson's household as a handyman for two years, from 1841 to 1843. But the most famous period of his short life was the two years he spent from July 1845 to September 1847 living alone in a cabin in the woods at Walden Pond, near Concord. He published an account of this experience in *Walden* (1856), his second book – his first had been an account of a trip made in company with his brother in 1839, *A Week on the Concord and Merrimack Rivers* (1849).

Thoreau attempted at Walden to put Emerson's teaching of individualism and self-reliance into practice. He lived as simply as possible and worked hard in his clearing in the woods, but he was not engaged in an exercise in self-survival; he was trying to show how little a man needed in order to be himself and be happy. He was challenging in the manner of a secular, or, at least, a transcendental, hermit the materialistic assumptions of the age, and in his account of his residence, which, for the sake of art, he has compressed into a calendar year, he sets out his own principles and ironically and wittily condemns the self-stultifying condition to which his neighbours have voluntarily reduced themselves. And the truth of his enquiry is illustrated in the harmony he discovers between himself and nature, in association with the great minds of the past.

Thoreau stood out against the state. He was imprisoned for a day for refusing to pay a poll tax in support of the Mexican War and he explained the philosophy behind this refusal in his essay on 'Civil Disobedience' (1849), which has had a great influence on the theory of non-violence as a means of political action. He supported the Negroes in their struggle for emancipation; and every other good liberal cause.

He was also Emerson's disciple in his practice of keeping a journal, and drew on his journals in writing *Walden*. The journals, which were not published completely until 1906 when they appeared in fourteen volumes, show Thoreau at his best as both a man and a writer. He writes an exceedingly clear and musical prose, which catches exactly the appearances of nature and his own deep response to them. Hardly one of his innumerable sketches and descriptions is not more poetic than the formal verses that he also wrote. And without a touch of ostentation he constantly asserts his independence and integrity – with a touch of the moral chilliness of the natural celibate.

Thoreau was a sound scholar and an adventurous reader, and in these respects he was typical of the energetic and resourceful intellectual life of New England in the twenty or so years before the outbreak of the Civil War. The Transcendental Club itself was not so completely dominated by Emerson that it tamely echoed his opinions at different pitches. No one could have tamed Margaret Fuller (1810–50), the ardent feminist who edited *The Dial* – the magazine of the Transcendentalist movement – for two years from its beginning in 1840. And Bronson Alcott (1799–1888) carried Transcendentalist idealism to extremes in education and social living that were beyond even Emerson's conceiving, though they evoked his admiration, such was the fineness of Alcott's intellect and character.

The more ordinary intelligence of New England was as sincerely, though less radically, excited with the hope of excelling in letters and more successful in realizing its ambitions. W. H. Prescott (1796–1859) published his *History of the Conquest of Mexico* in 1839; John Lothrop Motley (1814–77), another Harvard graduate, published *The Rise of the Dutch Republic* in 1856; and though Francis Parkman (1823–93), these great historians' great successor, had published only the first of his histories of the settlement and Christianization of North America – his *History of the Conspiracy of Pontiac* (1851) – before the Civil War, he belongs in spirit entirely to this earlier period of self-reliant and idealistic endeavour.

The writings of Prescott and Motley illustrate how incorrect it would be to think of the New England writers as being narrowly concerned with their own nationality. They were critically aware of their independence, and assured in it, but they also felt themselves as belonging still to Europe and needing to accept its cultural standards. Henry Wadsworth Longfellow (1807–82) is the great example of this position in poetry. He is unmistakably an American poet, but as his nationality is essential rather than radical, and has to be appreciated in an unobtrusive tone and attitude, he also falls acceptably into the romantic tradition of nineteenth-century English verse without seeming at all out of place, as his extraordinary popularity among English readers of the time shows.

Longfellow was a professor of French and Spanish at Harvard for eighteen years and his knowledge of these and other languages is shown everywhere in his work – indirectly, but also in his many translations, of course, particularly in his late translation of Dante's *Divine Comedy* (1867). But in spite of their air of conventional accomplishment, his better poems – and each of his frequent and regular collections of verse contained a few good poems – have a distinct character, which can be briefly described as 'American'. His narrative poem on the Acadians, *Evangeline* (1847), and the later narrative poem *The Courtship of Miles Standish* (1858) are patently American; *Hiawatha* (1855) notoriously so; but the quality is declared more subtly among his lyrics by an air of upright individualism and strenuous self-reliance. In this he shows his kinship with Emerson and Thoreau; and also in a certain air of chill refinement. He feels deeply – he suffers, too – but it is ideas that teach him and not his passions. He is always competent, but his competence comes to be suspected at last as the monotonous effect of emotional neutrality.

Longfellow's successor in the chair of French and Spanish was James Russell Lowell (1819–91), and Lowell's career as a poet illustrates not unfairly the lack of vitality that seemed often to inhibit and sometimes to threaten the New England imagination. Lowell's usual verse is fluent and correct, but lacks character; only in his satires, *A Fable for Critics* (1848), a review of polite letters in the United States, and *The Biglow Papers* (1st series, 1848; 2nd series, 1867), a pungent, liberal commentary on American politics written in the Yankee vernacular, does he succeed in being original. In spite of the pleasant Quaker poet, John Greenleaf Whittier (1807–92), whose simple, customary verse is lifted into eloquence and genuine feeling by those typically Quaker qualities, charity to man and responsiveness to nature, the instance of

Lowell proves that a future for American poetry lay outside the scope of the New England temperament.

Romanticism: Poe and Melville

James Fenimore Cooper had been called the 'American Scott', and in his turn William Gilmore Simms (1806–70), one of the two distinguished writers from the South, was known as a 'Southern Cooper'. The title is a rough and ready indication of Simms's standing as a novelist. His many novels can be separated into two main groups, with the remainder making a miscellaneous third: the Border Romances, which are concerned with the society and traditions of the South, and the Revolutionary Romances, which are again about the South in the period of the Revolution. But only an enthusiast would read through Simms's novels from beginning to end, while discriminating between them categorically. The ordinary reader will be content with the two or three good novels – even, perhaps, with only *The Yemassee* (1835), an exciting and well-written account of Indian warfare in South Carolina.

Simms conscientiously upheld the values of the South, including slavery, in all his work, and as a critic and journalist he strongly argued the cause of a national literature, but as a Southern man-of-letters and as a national literary figure he has been entirely overshadowed by another writer from the South – Edgar Allan Poe.

> There comes Poe, with his raven, like Barnaby Rudge,
> Three fifths of him genius and two fifths sheer fudge

Such was Lowell's perspicuous comment on Edgar Allan Poe (1809–49) in *A Fable for Critics*, and he went on to defend Longfellow against Poe's contemptuous attacks. Poe was temperamentally the opposite to the New Englander. He may have been born at Boston, the child of itinerant actors, but he was brought up in the South, in Richmond, Virginia – by a foster father after the death of his widowed mother in 1811. Poe was educated for five years at a school in Stoke Newington in England, and after his return to the United States in 1820, at the University of Virginia. He was supposed to prepare himself for the law, but after joining the U.S. Army under an assumed name and being dismissed from West Point in 1831 for gross neglect of duty, he set out upon an erratic career as a magazine editor and hack writer.

All American poets of the nineteenth century must necessarily be classed as romantic, but Poe was a romantic in ways that would make the term quite inappropriate as a description of Emerson, or even of Jones Very (1813–80), another Harvard graduate whose mystical exaltation verged on insanity. Poe was romantic in his conflict with the world of staid realities; in his excessive craving after sensation, in his fatal love for his child bride and cousin, Virginia Clemm, in his pre-occupation with dreams and hallucinations, and in his early death, brought on by despair and excesses. But he thought systematically and coherently about his own work and literary theory, and was a calculating writer, in both verse and prose, and a shrewd critic.

He published his first volume of poems, *Tamerlane*, at his own expense, as early as 1827. A second collection, *Al Aaraaf*, appeared in 1829. A third volume, *Poems*, which came out in 1831, contained such famous pieces as 'Israfel', 'To Helen', and 'The City in the Sea', which were to be committed to memory by scores of readers on both sides of the Atlantic throughout the century as the absolute expression of romantic verse. Poe's verse is frequently meretricious and artful, and monotonous in its obvious manipulation of vowels and stresses, but at its best it seems uncannily to release certain emotions in the reader which force him to submit to its musical evocation of phantoms hovering on the verge of death, in a limbo lying between beauty and deliquescence. The raven's croak of 'Nevermore' in his most famous and often parodied poem 'The Raven', which Poe proudly claimed to have begun by writing the last stanza first in conformity with his theory of effective composition, may no longer chill us, but the concluding stanza of 'The Sleeper' – the one that begins,

> My love, she sleeps! Oh, may her sleep,
> As it is lasting, so be deep!

– would fail to stir only the most hardened realist.

Poe claimed that the most poetical of all subjects was the death of a beautiful woman, and this indication of the necrophilic cast of his imagination suggests the limited range of his verse. But he has had a stature conferred upon him far above his intrinsic deserts by being adopted into the symbolist movement in European poetry through the patronage of Baudelaire. Baudelaire responded to Poe's dark visions and admired his deliberate verbal harmonies, and by placing him in the context of a literary tradition far more catholic and sympathetic than his own, lent him a significance that it took his unwilling countrymen many years to perceive.

Poe's tales are comparable to his poems. They seek to achieve their effect with the same brevity and deal with similar themes – with love that macabrely persists beyond the body's death, and compulsive guilt, and other psychological and superstitious horrors. The same charge of being contrived and methodically horrible could also be brought against the tales, but in the better ones, as in the better poems, he starts common and ineradicable fears, or insinuates his own peculiar phobias under the pretext of exact science. 'The Fall of the House of Usher', collected in *Tales of the Grotesque and Arabesque* (1840), may be his finest story – at least, it seems to be unfolded for its own sake and not for the sake of the credit it will bring the writer for cleverness – but there are other possibilities: 'The Masque of the Red Death', 'The Pit and the Pendulum', 'The Cask of Amontillado', or 'Hop-Frog'; or, in a more scientific vein, 'The Gold-Bug', and at greater length and with weirdly prophetic millenary fervour, *The Narrative of Arthur Gordon Pym* (1838).

Poe may have been the most dissolute of American men-of-letters of the first half of the nineteenth century, considered as a person; as a writer he was the most complete. His poetry and his tales and his criticism all exactly fit together into a complementary whole. He almost seems to have bought this achievement at the cost of his private affairs. The situation for writers in the United States in Poe's day was very much better than it had been in Charles Brockden Brown's, but it was still hard for a writer to make his way unless he was able to act as the editor of one of the large newspapers, or had the advantages of some form of patronage – the university, or the church, or a political sinecure – or enjoyed a private income, which so often fell to the lot of the fortunate writers from New England. The pressure under which Poe had to live as a hack writer and editor accounts for many of his difficulties; that he should choose under the circumstances to sacrifice himself rather than his work indicates the seriousness of his literary ambitions.

Poe was not the only writer of the time to experience the perils of trying to become a professional writer. Herman Melville (1819–91) also failed as a writer, though he began with greater chances of success than Poe, and appeared for a season to have almost achieved his ambition. And then his hopes, too, collapsed and he retired into the obscurity of a post in the U.S. Customs. He was almost forgotten for many years, except by a handful of English admirers.

Melville was a sailor and a traveller. He came from a good family, but after the death of his cultured but unsuccessful father he was forced to look out for himself and among various shifts he shipped as a cabin boy in 1839 for Liverpool. He sailed next on the whaler *Acushnet*, in 1841, and after cruising in the South Seas he jumped ship in the Marquesas and, after a series of adventures, made his way home as an ordinary seaman in the U.S. frigate *United States*. He landed at Boston in 1844. He never sailed again, but these voyages gave him the experience for all his books – at least, his greatest books.

Once finally ashore he determined to become a writer. He began with apparently factual accounts of his experiences among the islands of the South Pacific. In *Typee* (1846) he described how he and his friend Toby, having jumped ship upon arriving in the Marquesas, escaped to the Typees, a tribe of natives, and lived with them in the greatest uncertainty as to whether or not they were cannibals. At first glance the book may seem to be an engaging autobiographical account of Melville's own adventures, in which truth is liberally dashed with fiction, but on closer study it becomes an acute and personal dialogue on the nature of primitivism and civilization and the relativity of good and evil. But high spirits and a fine eye for striking and amusing detail concealed the metaphysics, and, as the South Sea islands were topical, *Typee* was well received by both the critics and the public – in England as well as in the United States, which was greatly to the advantage of Melville's standing.

Sensing his opportunity, Melville immediately followed up *Typee* with a sequel, *Omoo* (1847), in which he described beachcombing among the islands in company with an odder and more intellectual friend than the simple Toby – Dr Long Ghost. *Omoo* is another excellent book, interesting both for its adventures and descriptions and for its undercurrent of critical speculation on the nature and burdens of civilization. The book was again well received and Melville was now confirmed as a young writer of the greatest promise. Anything might be expected of anyone who could so adeptly satisfy public taste.

Melville's third book, the novel *Mardi* (1849), which was again set among the islands of the South Pacific, was very much not to public taste. Its involved allegory and exacting symbolism were not sufficiently compensated for by striking scenes and fine description. Disaster lay that way, as far as Melville's popularity was concerned – and popularity was now necessary, since Melville had recently married and was determined to live by writing. He quickly recovered himself with *Redburn* (1849), an account of his first voyage to Liverpool as a cabin boy, which, though written deliberately as a potboiler, touches simply and movingly upon the theme of seemingly unmotivated evil – a theme which was to recur in Melville's last work, *Billy Budd*.

The last phase of Melville's experiences afloat was used in *White Jacket; or, The World in a Man-of-War* (1850), which is based upon his voyage home in the frigate, *United States*. The book is the best account of life afloat under harsh nineteenth-century naval discipline, but it is also a subtle allegorical enquiry into the nature of experience, as its sub-title would suggest. *White Jacket* is not Melville's greatest book, but it could be fairly described as his best; a satisfactory balance being struck between factual description and symbolic interpretation. The characters of the officers and men are exactly drawn.

Melville moved to a farm in Massachusetts in 1850, where he became a neighbour of Nathaniel Hawthorne. Hawthorne's friendship and influence had a liberating, but also a strangely disturbing effect upon Melville, turning him away yet farther from reality into allegory and encouraging him to read experience under the terms of evil – of 'the power of blackness', as Melville described it in his review of Hawthorne's *Twice-Told Tales*. The unsettling effect can be seen in the composition of the book on which he was engaged – a book that started as an account of his experiences on a whaler in the South Pacific and was completed with difficulty as an epical account of the hunting of a phantasmal white whale – a 'hell-fired' book, in Melville's own phrase.

Moby-Dick; or The Whale (1851) is now regarded, for all its faults of construction and uncertainties of tone, as one of the greatest American books of the century, but its combination of realism and symbolism, action and metaphysical speculation, pathos and 'Carlylese' humour, description and encyclopaedic information, greatly disturbed the contemporary public, who now began to desert him. They were hurried on in their desertion by his next book, a novel, *Pierre; or, The Ambiguities*, which exactly fulfilled the threat in the sub-title – a novel of genius, of course, but one too mannered and eccentric to appeal to contemporary taste. Melville and the public began from this point increasingly to diverge, and though *The Piazza Tales* (1856) included some admirable stories – especially 'Benito Cereno' and 'The Encan-tadas', a strangely beautiful series of sketches that strike the imagination like chamber music – and *The Confidence Man* (1857), a satire on the age, showed him re-establishing his confidence in the face of reality, he was gradually forced into silence and was forgotten.

He was never entirely silent, however. He wrote and published poetry, and at the time of his death he was engaged on finishing *Billy Budd*, a tale of the victimization of innocence by demoniacal malevolence, which, when it was first published from manuscript in 1924, helped to begin the extraordinary revival of Melville's fame after it had been utterly eclipsed.

Melville's early books are now comparatively disregarded in favour of *Moby-Dick* and the later writings, but though this reversal of choice would be hard to justify critically, it is explicable in terms of taste. The early books belong unmistakably to the nineteenth century, but the later anticipate the future. They seem modern, in both their range of speculation and their disregard for conventional forms. They share the quality of being modern with other American writing of the same period.

Whitman, Poet of the Modern

D. H. Lawrence asserted in his brilliant and radical *Studies in Classic American Literature* (1923) that only Walt Whitman (1819–92) could be called 'the poet of the modern', exploring to the limit of his genius the possibilities of the modern sensibility. Whitman's acclaim by Lawrence was not a rehabilitation like Melville's, for Whitman had never enjoyed anything like Melville's early popular success, but it marked the last phase in the steady growth of his original reputation, which already owed greatly to the percipience of earlier English critics. Whitman had long been a potent influence in English radical thought.

Walt Whitman's earliest writings could not have revealed by any process of divination his later fame. He was born on Long Island and after following a number of different occupations, including printing and school teaching, in the manner of so many nineteenth-century American writers, he more or less settled down to political journalism in New York in the Democratic Party's cause. He published poetry of no merit whatsoever and even worse fiction, but he read widely, went to the opera and loafed about New York. Whitman later affirmed that it was a reading of Emerson's *Essays* that brought him 'to the boil'. His discovery of himself was sudden, certainly, but there is no reason to endorse a theory tantamount to that of spontaneous combustion to account for the change. Emerson encouraged him to dare to be himself as a man and to throw off 'the courtly Muses of Europe' as a poet. The result was extraordinary.

Whitman published *Leaves of Grass* at New York in 1855, at his own expense. He did not name himself on the title page, but facing the title was a portrait of him leaning out at the reader – slouch hat on head, shirt Byronically unbuttoned, arms carried akimbo; a nonchalant, democratic poet. He printed twelve poems in this edition, the first being the longest: the poem later entitled 'Song of Myself'. He sent a copy to Emerson, who praised it enthusiastically, and he used this praise to try and puff the second and enlarged edition which he published in the following year. *Leaves of Grass* continued to grow over the years, almost in accordance with the natural law implicit in its title, and enlarged and revised editions appeared in 1860, 1867, 1871, 1876, 1881, 1889, and, ninthly and lastly, in 1891, when the poet was a 'good gray bard', a very different personage from the 'rough' who had gazed speculatively out at the world in 1855, confident that he had 'arrived' at last.

Leaves of Grass is, especially in its earlier editions, strikingly original. Many and diverse influences abound everywhere – from the Bible, Shakespeare, Macpherson's *Ossian*, Scott, Thomas Carlyle, and Plato, the Upanishads, and Goethe in translation – but they are so absorbed into the esemplastic vision and declamatory style that their identification is often uncertain. Whitman's unqualified reception of the ideas of his age, which accounts for his poetry's wide relevance, was not, however, uncritical. The ideas were always organically related and subordinate to his own highly individual vision. He wrote as a democrat, assuming on those generous principles that when he wrote about himself he was also writing about others – that the 'body politic' was a phrase to be taken sociably and affectionately, as well as politically. He wrote as a mystic, revealing the correspondences in nature and the reverberant harmonies running through space and time, and shared alike by the smallest consciousnesses and vast intelligences. And he wrote as an individual, displaying his weaknesses and passions, either in open bravado or in symbols. But these elements are all orchestrated and inseparable.

The second edition of *Leaves of Grass* contains, among other notable additions, 'Crossing Brooklyn Ferry', a poem which completely expresses Whitman's democratic pleasure in the bustling crowds and the river's activity, but also his solemn awareness of the onward rush of time into eternity, symbolized by the Hudson flowing into the Atlantic. The third edition of 1860 added two important sections, 'Children of Adam', a celebration of love between man and woman, and 'Calamus', whose complementary theme is 'comradeship', or love between man and man. 'Calamus' is, if considered in terms of elementary appetites, a series of homosexual poems, but taken in the wider political and social context of 'comradeship', it attempts to assert the emotional and spiritual cohesion which is essential to the establishment of a true democracy among a people of many different creeds and races. The poems are difficult even today, both interpretatively and morally, and they hardly appeared to qualify Whitman as the proper bard for the American people, even among the handful who were bothering to read him.

Whitman's belief in American democracy and its future, which he had not only assumed in his poems but asserted in an extremely chauvinistic prose introduction to the first edition of *Leaves of Grass*, was brutally put to the test at the outbreak of the Civil War. At first, the Northern cause seemed so just and the heroism of the young soldiers so ennobling that Whitman accepted the war as a vindication of the finest democratic principles. He took up a post in government in Washington, but his real service was unofficial, as a visitor to the wounded in the military hospitals. He found a deep emotional satisfaction in his self-imposed duties. He was with young men and, under the circumstances, could show affection without embarrassment, and he could put the healing power of his great energy and sympathy to good use. Many young men were recovered from the edge of death through his ministrations – practical poetry. But as the war continued and the casualties mounted, and idealism and self-sacrifice gave way to cynicism and profiteering, his own confidence in American democracy began to waver. It never recovered in the materialistic climate that prevailed after the war. He later published, in 1875, *Memoranda during the War*, a prose account of his experiences during this period.

He wrote several poems during the war, describing scenes in the hospitals or on the battlefield, and these were published as *Drum-Taps* in 1865, and incorporated in the fourth edition of *Leaves of Grass* in 1867. *A Sequel to Drum-Taps*, published in 1866, included 'When Lilacs last in the Door Yard Bloom'd', his elegy on the death of Abraham Lincoln, one of his finest poems – one of the great elegies in English poetry. The poem expresses all that Whitman had believed in, democracy and comradeship under the figure of Lincoln, the leader and brother; it evokes his loneliness and yearning towards death; and it employs symbols unerringly, and moves freely and musically without hesitation from opening to close. It is the crowning triumph of the first and great period of his career.

Whitman wrote some good later poems, but many are strident and verbose, and in his revisions of his earlier work he often obfuscated its immediacy. The period from 1873, when he suffered a paralytic stroke (though largely recovering from it through his remarkable courage), and 1892, when he died, was a period of discipleship. He had imagined himself in 1856 as the poet of the many; he became the poet of the few. But these few found such a deep solace in his verse, and such a clear illustration of the major tendencies of the modern mind, that they wrote about him and praised him whenever they could. He was especially lucky in his English admirers, who helped him at a time when he was disregarded at home. Through their efforts, he was able at the time of his death to prove the delayed truth of Emerson's prophecy: 'I greet you at the outset of a great career.'

Whitman was the greatest poet of the Civil War. The Southern poet, Henry Timrod (1828–67), who had published his *Poems* in 1860, wrote an 'Ode' on the Confederate Dead in 1867, and the touching simplicity of the verses, which seem to belong in style and sentiment to the earlier century, showed, by comparison with Whitman's verse, how far Whitman was in advance of his time. Sidney Lanier (1842–81), another Southerner, who had served in the Confederate Army, was a more considerable poet than Timrod. He was a good musician, as well as a scholar of English literature, and his better lyrical poems successfully attempt musical effects. 'The Marshes of Glynn' is the best example of Lanier's self-conscious style and romantic melancholy. His *Poems* were first published in 1884.

Western Humour and Mark Twain

New England and the South were established and traditional societies, but the American imagination was always supposed to turn West, if not to the frontier itself, then to the frontier in metaphor – the sea, in the case of Melville's *Moby-Dick*, or the boundary between vision and reality, the spiritual region of such a pioneer as Whitman. And it was out of the West, with its vast opportunities and spaciousness, that a native American literature was expected to emerge.

The first typically Western literary form to emerge was not the anticipated epic, but the joke. 'Tall tales' have always been told everywhere – one has only to think of the famous Baron Munchausen – but they were specially appropriate to the dangerous and laborious circumstances of the frontier, where they allowed their tellers to master, at least psychologically, the forces threatening them. They depended upon a skilful mixture of exaggeration and realism and upon the contrast between the fantasy of the action and the practicality of the moral. At first, they belonged to the oral tradition of the folk tale, but they later became the favourite of writers trying to express the spirit of life as it had once been lived in the backwoods. Augustus Baldwin Longstreet's *Georgia Scenes* (1835) was the first of many such books, and one of the best. But the 'tall tale' was especially one of the properties of the frontier journalists, who filled the newspapers with their squibs and who, if they were particularly talented, made national names for themselves, both by being reprinted in newspapers across the country and by lecturing. Lectures were the most popular form of public entertainment of the century, and good comedians were most highly in demand.

The most popular comic journalist at about the time of the Civil War was Charles Farrar Browne (1834–67) – 'Artemus Ward' – whose papers in the Cleveland *Plain Dealer* delighted President Lincoln. He was an even greater success as a lecturer. His manner was similar to the other comic journalists of the time, such improbably-named characters as Josh Billings and Petroleum V. Naseby. He relied on exaggeration of incident and description and exploited the vernacular to the full both on the platform and on the page, in the shape of atrocious and risible misspellings. But running through all this flummery was a delicious vein of hard common sense: 'A. Ward and A. Linkin' exchanged pictures after an interview, 'so we could gaze upon each others' liniments when far away from one another – he at the hellum of the ship of State and I at the hellum of the show-bizness – admittance only 15 cents.'

Artemus Ward and his fellow humorists have long since lost their brightness. They could not last, according to Artemus Ward's most famous pupil, because they lacked moral seriousness. 'I have always preached,' Mark Twain argued, 'That is the reason I have lasted thirty years.' Mark Twain was given his first chance of success by Artemus Ward, who asked him in San Francisco in 1865 to contribute to a volume of comic sketches. Mark Twain sent in 'The Celebrated Jumping Frog of Calaveras County', a 'tall tale' if ever there was one, and when it arrived too late for inclusion he printed it in the New York *Saturday Press*, from which it was copied into newspapers all over the country, making him famous.

Mark Twain – or Samuel Langhorne Clemens (1835–1910) as he was properly called – had only been a journalist for three years, under his pseudonym, when he scored a success with the 'Jumping Frog'. He had spent his childhood in Hannibal, Missouri, on the Mississippi, worked as a journeyman printer, trained as a steamboat pilot on the Mississippi, and, after seeing a week or two in the Confederate forces at the beginning of the Civil War, had prospected unsuccessfully for silver in Nevada, all before he had found himself as Mark Twain. He began as a Western humorist in the style of Artemus Ward and his colleagues, but from the 'Jumping Frog' on there was a range and coherence and sense of style that put him in a different category to the others – in literature rather than in journalism, to put it simply.

The 'Jumping Frog' was enough to make a name with, but hardly to support a reputation, and Mark Twain's first great success was *The Innocents Abroad* (1869), in which he hilariously and brashly described the confrontation between a party of American tourists and the conventions and mysteries of Europe and the Holy Land. By this time Mark Twain had married and settled in the East and had proved himself to be one of the most skilful lecturers of the age. He was never to look back, either with respect to popularity or financial success, though his extravagance often threatened to bring him to grief and his Presbyterian conscience warned him that he was living always under retributive disaster.

Mark Twain's writings fall roughly into three groups. The least interesting today are his comic tales and sketches and books in the spirit of *The Innocents Abroad. Roughing It* (1872) – though this is rather special because of its account of his experiences as a prospector in the West – *A Tramp Abroad* (1880), and *Following the Equator* (1897) are the most important of the books. The second group consists of historical fantasies, in which he attacks under cover of the past the abuses and deceptions of his own day, while praising the practicality and freedom of democracy. *The Prince and the Pauper* (1882), which describes the adventures of young Prince Edward and Tom Canty, his whipping boy, when they change places on the eve of the Prince's accession to the throne as Edward VI, is a pleasant enough fable, but its successor *A Connecticut Yankee in King Arthur's Court* (1889) has a far wider and darker meaning. The Yankee sets out to reform and modernize Arthurian England, in the face of the entrenched opposition of chivalry and superstition, but all his laudable motives and technical ingenuity end in disaster – a conclusion that Mark Twain seems to have been compelled to reach instinctively, rather than by logic. The book shows the vacillation of purpose that was to harass Mark Twain's later years as a writer. *Personal Recollections of Joan of Arc* (1896) is the last historical book – 'distressingly sentimental' is the only possible description.

The third group of books is the one on which Mark Twain's reputation as a great writer can alone be based and includes his masterpiece. Mark Twain made only one serious attempt to describe his own age in fiction and the seriousness of this attempt may be doubted, since it began as a bet and was written hastily in collaboration with a friend, Charles Dudley Warner. Except, then, for *The Gilded Age* (1873), a satire on the corruptions in government and society of the time, Mark Twain's fiction returns to the past – to the world he had known as a boy and young man on the shores and waters of the Mississippi.

The Adventures of Tom Sawyer (1876) is a boy's book – at least, Mark Twain's critical friends thought it was written for boys. Mark Twain himself thought that he had written a book for adults, and there is about the story an air of hazy sentimentality which suggests that these childhood adventures have become falsified in recollection. They lack the sternness of reality, though the conclusion, in which Tom and his sweetheart, Becky Thatcher, wander lost among the labyrinthine caves where the murderer, Injun Joe, is also a wanderer, illustrates the frightening truth that sometimes lies in dreams. The setting of the story is Hannibal and Mark Twain drew on many of his childhood friends for the characters. He returned to the river and his experiences in *Life on the Mississippi* (1883), but in autobiography and description, not in fiction. He described at the beginning how he had trained as a steamboat pilot and he only bettered once the terse characterization, the appropriate humour, and the eloquent but unaffected description of these sections. The rest of the book is interesting, but conventional by comparison.

Life on the Mississippi was the forerunner of *The Adventures of Huckleberry Finn*, the greatest American novel of the century. In following the adventures of Tom Sawyer's street-Arab companion, Huck Finn, in flight from a civilization that would enslave his Negro companion, Jim, and tame him, Mark Twain was able to bring to bear all his remarkable talents: his ability to tell a good yarn, his humour, his power of characterization, his use of the vernacular, practised for many years on the lecture platform, and his moral vision. Only the conclusion can be criticized – a protracted joke, on the earlier level of Tom Sawyer's ingenious adventures. The book is otherwise a vindication of man's best spirit, in spite of the folly and corruption of which man is capable; a humorous, but tragic allegory, that is the only real literary achievement of the literary spirit of the American West.

Mark Twain lived energetically into the twentieth century, but his great books were all set in the period before the Civil War and belonged in spirit to it, the classic age of American literature. 'Hawthorne and Melville and Whitman reached a point of imaginative or visionary adjustment to America,' D. H. Lawrence once wrote, after he had published his great *Studies in Classic American Literature*, 'which, it seems to me, is again entirely lost, abandoned.' Lawrence's judgement may have been extreme, but the destructive shock of the Civil War and its disillusioning aftermath – the 'Gilded Age' – were so great on the older American spirit that many years were to pass before American literature could fully recover its spirit and renew its great tradition.

Further Reading

GENERAL

The following works are relevant not merely to this chapter but to the following chapters as well, although they will not be listed again there. See also the Checklist of Essential Works of Reference, p. 507.

Bewley, Marius, *The Complex Fate*. London, 1952.

——, *The Eccentric Design*. New York, 1959.

Bode, Carl (ed.), *The Young Rebel in American Literature*, London, 1959.

——, *The Great Experiment in American Literature*. London, 1961.

Brown, John Russell *et al.* (eds.), *American Poetry* (Stratford-upon-Avon Studies no. 7). London, 1965.

Chase, Richard, *The American Novel and its Tradition*. New York, 1957.

Cunliffe, Marcus, *The Literature of the United States*. Harmondsworth, 1954; revised 1967.

Feidelson, Charles and Brodtkorb, Paul, Jr. (eds.), *Interpretations of American Literature*. Gloucester, Mass., 1959.

Fiedler, Leslie, *Love and Death in the American Novel*. New York, 1960; revised 1966.

——, *No! In Thunder*. Boston, Mass., 1963.

Foerster, Norman, *American Criticism, A Study in Literary Theory from Poe to the Present*. Boston, Mass., and New York, 1928.

—— (ed.), *The Reinterpretation of American Literature*. New York, 1928.

Marx, Leo, *The Machine in the Garden: Technology and the Pastoral Ideal in America*. New York, 1965.

Maxwell, D. E. S., *American Fiction: The Intellectual Background*. New York, 1963.

Parrington, Vernon L., *Main Currents in American Thought*, 3 vols. New York, 1927–30.

Pearce, Roy Harvey, *The Continuity of American Poetry*. Princeton, N.J., 1961.

Poirier, Richard, *A World Elsewhere: the Place of Style in American Literature*. New York, 1967.

Rahv, Philip, *Image and Idea*. New York, 1949; revised and enlarged 1957.

Rees, Robert A. and Harbert, Earl N. (eds.), *Fifteen American Authors before 1900*. Madison, Wis., 1971.

Rourke, Constance, *American Humor: a Study of National Character*. New York, 1939.

Smith, Henry Nash, *Virgin Land: the American West as Symbol and Myth*. New York, 1950.

Spiller, Robert E., Thorp, Willard and Johnson, Thomas H. (eds.), *Literary History of the United States*. New York, 1948.

Stovall, Floyd (ed.), *Eight American Authors: a Review of Research and Criticism* (Poe, Emerson, Hawthorne, Thoreau, Melville, Whitman, Mark Twain, Henry James). New York, 1956; revised 1963; and by James Woodress, 1971.

Trilling, Lionel, *The Liberal Imagination*. Gloucester, Mass., 1950.

Waggoner, Hyatt H., *American Poets from the Puritans to the Present*. Boston, Mass., 1968.

Wilson, Edmund (ed.), *The Shock of Recognition: the Development of Literature in the United States Recorded by the Men Who Made It*. New York, 1943, 1955.

Winters, Yvor, *In Defense of Reason* (including *Maule's Curse*, *Primitivism and Decadence*, and *The Anatomy of Nonsense*). New York, 1947.

Zabel, M. D., *Literary Opinion in America*. Gloucester, Mass., revised 1951.

Useful monographs on American authors will be found in the following series:

(*a*) Twayne's United States Authors Series
(*b*) University of Minnesota Pamphlets on American Writers
(*c*) Writers and Critics (Edinburgh, Oliver & Boyd)

Collections of critical essays on individual authors are available in the following series:

(*a*) The Critical Heritage (London, Routledge)
(*b*) Twentieth-Century Views (Englewood Cliffs, N.J., Prentice-Hall)

WORKS RELEVANT TO CHAPTER 9

Allen, Gay Wilson, *The Solitary Singer: a Critical Biography of Walt Whitman*. New York, 1955.

Arvin, Newton, *Herman Melville*. New York, 1950.

Brooks, Van Wyck, *The Flowering of New England: 1815–1865*. New York, 1936.

Canby, Henry S., *Thoreau*. Gloucester, Mass., 1939.

Chase, Richard, *Walt Whitman Reconsidered*. New York, 1955.

Cox, James M., *Mark Twain: the Fate of Humor*. Princeton, N.J., 1966.

Davidson, Edward H., *Poe: a Critical Study*. Cambridge, Mass., 1957.

Dekker, George, *James Fenimore Cooper the Novelist*. London, 1967.

Dutton, G., *Whitman*. Edinburgh, 1961.

Feidelson, Charles, *Symbolism and American Literature*. Chicago, Ill., 1953.

Granger, Bruce Ingham, *Benjamin Franklin: an American Man of Letters*. New York, 1964.

Grant, Douglas, *Twain*. Edinburgh, 1962.

Grossman, James, *James Fenimore Cooper*. New York, 1949.

Harding, Walter, *A Thoreau Handbook*. New York, 1959.

Hoffman, Daniel G., *Form and Fable in American Fiction*. New York, 1961.

Humphreys, A. R., *Melville*. Edinburgh, 1962.

Lawrence, D. H., *Studies in Classic American Literature*. London and New York, 1922.

Levin, Harry, *The Power of Blackness: Hawthorne, Poe, Melville*. New York, 1958.

Lewis, R. W. B., *The American Adam*. Chicago, Ill., 1955.

Matthiessen, F. O., *American Renaissance: Art and Expression in the Age of Emerson and Whitman*. New York, 1941.

Miller, Perry, *Jonathan Edwards*. New York, 1949.

——, *The Raven and the Whale: the War of Words and Wits in the Era of Poe and Melville*. New York, 1956.

Rans, G., *Edgar Allan Poe*. Edinburgh, 1965.

Sanford, Charles L. (ed.), *Benjamin Franklin and the American Character*. Lexington, Mass., 1955.

Smith, Henry Nash, *Mark Twain: the Development of a Writer*. Cambridge, Mass., 1962.

Spiller, Robert E., *The American Literary Revolution, 1783–1837*. New York, 1967.

Stewart, Randall, *Nathaniel Hawthorne*. New Haven, Conn., 1948.

Tyler, Moses Coit, *A History of American Literature during the Colonial Period*, 2 vols. New York, revised edn. 1897.

——, *The Literary History of the American Revolution, 1763–1783*, 2 vols. New York, 1897.

Waggoner, Hyatt H., *Hawthorne: a Critical Study*. Cambridge, Mass., 1955; revised edn. 1963.

10 The Literature of Realism

DENNIS WELLAND

The Gilded Age

It was Mark Twain in the 1870s who so felicitously christened the period 'The Gilded Age'. In the novel of that name he collaborated with Charles Dudley Warner to pillory the commercialized materialism, the political corruption, and the debasement of moral values that were making Americans suspect that their golden world was at best gilt and at worst guilty. It was scepticism of this nature, modulating not infrequently into pessimism, that set the tone of much American literature of this period. The writer's concept of his role changed significantly. An earlier generation of authors had felt that society had no place for them: Melville criticized his world obliquely in the symbolism of such tales as 'Bartleby the Scrivener' and 'The Tartarus of Maids'; Hawthorne deplored the thinness of American life which, in his view, made the romance a vehicle more appropriate than the novel; Poe turned inward on the darker recesses of his own psyche and revitalized 'gothic' horror to represent man's alienation. After the Civil War the writer came to feel that he had a more definable social role. The growth of population and the increase of civilized amenities which gave more time for leisure enlarged the reading public. The increase in newspapers and periodicals created professional posts for writers; the expansion of the American publishing industry together with the popularization of subscription publishing and magazine serials increased the demand for novels. Experimentation in fiction in the Old World challenged emulation in the New, and for the social protest to which events were prompting so many men of letters the novel was the obvious form. It was an age of prose: little that was lasting or vital found expression in poetry and less in drama.

In 1879 a political economist published a work the title of which epitomized a conjunction that may seem platitudinous today but which was then deeply disturbing to many: *Progress and Poverty*. The theme of the book is summed up in these extracts:

> This fact – the great fact that poverty and all its concomitants show themselves in communities just as they develop into the conditions toward which material progress tends – proves that the social difficulties existing wherever a certain stage of progress has been reached, do not arise from local circumstances, but are, in some way or another, engendered by progress itself. . . . It is true that wealth has been greatly increased, and that the average of comfort, leisure, and refinement has been raised; but these gains are not general. In them the lowest class do not share. . . . This association of poverty with progress is the great enigma of our times. It is the central fact from which spring industrial, social, and political difficulties that perplex the world, and with which statesmanship and philanthropy and education grapple in vain. From it come the clouds that over-hang the future of the most progressive and self-reliant nations.

Henry George's impact was international – Bernard Shaw claimed that an address by George in the 1880s 'opened my eyes to the importance of economics' – but to his own self-reliant nation, accustomed to conceiving its whole history as uninterrupted progress, his discovery was especially traumatic. Moreover, he reinforced his argument by non-economic reference:

> It is difficult to reconcile the idea of human immortality with the idea that nature wastes men by constantly bringing them into being where there is no room for them. It is impossible to reconcile the idea of an intelligent and beneficent Creator with the belief that the wretchedness and degradation which are the lot of such a large proportion of human kind result from His enactments; while the idea that man mentally and physically is the result of slow modifications perpetuated by heredity, irresistibly suggests the idea that it is the race life, not the individual life, which is the object of human existence.

Tennyson – whom George quotes – and many other Europeans were similarly distressed by what they understood as the implications of Darwinian ideas of creative evolution, and Herbert Spencer had applied those ideas to society, but American Transcendentalist optimism found such theories particularly hard to assimilate. As late as 1925 in the celebrated Scopes trial at Dayton, Tennessee, attempts were being made to repudiate a doctrine that seemed not only un-Christian but un-American.

Viewed from a different angle the situation in the 1880s looked capable of a very different interpretation. Andrew Carnegie, the steel magnate, became its spokesman in his essay *Wealth*:

> We accept and welcome, therefore, as conditions to which we must accommodate ourselves, great inequality of environment, the concentration of business, industrial and commercial, in the hands of a few, and the law of competition between these, as being not only beneficial, but essential for the future progress of the race.

This was consolatory to the fortunate few in whose hands business was concentrated, and to those theorists to whom the progress of the race was more important than the poverty of a whole social stratum. Carnegie had seen 'great scope for the exercise of special ability in the merchant and in the manufacturer who has to conduct affairs upon a great scale': clearly those who remained poor lacked either this ability or the energy to apply it, and the evolution of society, as of nature, seemed to encourage the survival of the fittest. To others this analogy suggested the jungle, in which the survivors are the predators, and writers were quick to exploit this imagery or to speak of the great tycoons as the Robber Barons. Carlyle's more flattering title for them, Captains of Industry, was to be given a mordant twist by the economist Thorstein Veblen in such books as *The Theory of the Leisure Class* (1899) with a witty, though ponderously polysyllabic, irony that still has its attractions and its influence. Carnegie, in his writings, and even more in his philanthropic library-endowing practice, had sought to give his Gospel of Wealth an element of social responsibility:

> This, then, is held to be the duty of the man of Wealth: First, to set an example of modest, unostentatious living, shunning display or extravagance; to provide moderately for the legitimate wants of those dependent upon him; and after doing so to consider all surplus revenues which come to him simply as trust funds, which he is called upon to administer . . . in the manner . . . best calculated to produce the most beneficial results for the community.

This, Veblen recognized, was expecting altogether too much of human nature which, when it has acquired wealth, prefers the fact to be as widely known as possible and is remarkably inventive in devising methods for achieving this end. The process we now know as 'keeping up with the Joneses' is very close to what Veblen called 'conspicuous consumption' – the very opposite of the 'modest, unostentatious living' for which Carnegie asked. Another outward and visible sign of wealth is, of course, leisure, but the tycoon will often be unwilling or even constitutionally unable to allow himself to indulge in this (the connection between the Puritan conscience and a zealous dedication to the massing of wealth was becoming increasingly apparent). He will therefore, Veblen saw, fall back instead on 'vicarious leisure'. The paradigm for this may be found as early as 1878 in Henry James's 'Daisy Miller', where the family of a *nouveau riche* American travel, with tragic results, in a Europe for which they are totally unprepared. Daisy's atrocious younger brother explains their situation with archetypal brashness: 'My father's name is Ezra B. Miller. . . . My father ain't in Europe; my father's in a better place than Europe. . . . My father's in Schenectady. He's got a big business. My father's rich, you bet.' With a sensibility and an imagination quite outside Veblen's range (and, perhaps, outside his needs) James was to explore, over the next thirty years with increasing depth, the dilemma, social, cultural, and moral, of the monied American, especially in relation to the Old World.

In the Gilded Age the American Dream, as it had been formulated by Jeffersonian agrarianists, had changed radically. The Civil War had intensified the need for industrial and technological expansion, and to reverse this was economically impossible. The frontier was still open and the homestead farm, supporting merely the needs of its family, survived in areas like Wisconsin and Nebraska, to be chronicled, lovingly but nostalgically, by Hamlin Garland, Willa Cather and others. It was, however, becoming anachronistic in some respects, and while the movement west continued (and continued to fascinate the American imagination, as Henry Nash Smith has shown in *Virgin Land*), a counter-movement away from the land gained impetus. Opportunity and wealth now seemed to beckon from the cities; Chicago lured alike the young Middle-Westerner such as the heroine of Theodore Dreiser's *Sister Carrie* and the impoverished European immigrants of, for example, Upton Sinclair's *The Jungle*. Fiction became increasingly urban-oriented and increasingly disillusioned with urban experience. The ambivalence of attitude towards technological capitalism which makes Mark Twain's *Connecticut Yankee* so difficult to evaluate as a novel and as a satire makes it the more central as a document of the age.

Henry Adams and Henry James

Henry James's celebrated remark 'It's a complex fate, being an American' has been made something of a cliché by over-quotation, but it is inescapable. All the works mentioned so far have been preoccupied with aspects of that fate; and the search for a national identity, which may be seen to have begun in the eighteenth century when Crèvecoeur asked 'What is an American?', continues unabated in the literature of this period. Crèvecoeur's own answer had been 'The American is a new man, who acts upon new principles; he must therefore entertain new ideas, and form new opinions.' When James entitled one of his early novels *The American* and christened its affluent business-man hero Christopher Newman he seems almost to be punning on Crèvecoeur's words, but a comment by Constance Rourke in her *American Humor* sets it in the necessary perspective:

> Who ever heard of a significant English novel called *The Englishman* or an excellent French novel called *Le Français*? The simple and aggressive stress belonged to an imagination perennially engaged by the problem of the national type.

The problem was as perennial in non-fiction as in the novel. It is part of the concern of economists like George and Veblen, of social reformers and journalists (the immigrant Jacob Riis published his autobiography in 1901 under the title *The Making of an American*), and especially of historians. One of the most influential of these was, of course, Frederick Jackson Turner whose Frontier Thesis drew on an imagination in some ways more poetical than historical. A more complex and more stimulating enquiry was to come from the agonized conscience of a very different kind of historian, Henry Adams, who was especially exercised by the new ideas which Crèvecoeur saw the American obliged to entertain, who certainly formed new opinions, and who was disqualified in Crèvecoeur's definition only by inability to satisfy himself as to the new principles on which he might effectively act. His statement of the dilemma, idiosyncratic, extreme and even perverse as it sometimes is, remains an important 'abstract and brief chronicle of the time'.

In one important particular Adams is quite untypical of the generality of Americans: his great-grandfather and his grandfather had both been President of the United States, and his father had been Minister to Great Britain during the Civil War. When, with a lineage like that, you are unable to secure any political or diplomatic office, two explanations are open to you: either the world has changed out of all recognition in its ability to appreciate true merit, or you are a failure. Adams chose both, the former with more real and less affected conviction than the latter, but his detached willingness to entertain the possibility of both gives his work its relevance. Benjamin Franklin had written his autobiography as a success story, exhibiting a course of action that he believed worthy of imitation by others. Adams wrote his in a more masochistic spirit, and more as a warning to others. His models were English rather than American, Edward Gibbon the historian and Anthony Trollope. As early as 1883, after reading the latter's *Autobiography*, he wrote to a friend 'I mean to do mine. After seeing how coolly and neatly a man like Trollope can destroy the last vestige of heroism in his own life, I object to allowing mine to be murdered by anyone except myself.' He waited twenty-two years before writing it, it was published posthumously in 1918 and has grown steadily in reputation ever since, its anti-heroic stance appealing particularly to the modern temper.

Its title, *The Education of Henry Adams*, indicates its characteristics. Throughout the author refers to himself in the third person, achieving thereby a blending of self-disparagement, detachment, and self-absorption which, by virtue of its sophisticated irony, is bewildering to some readers, to others irritating in its latent narcissism, but to many fascinating in its complexity of range and shift of viewpoint. Primarily concerned with the growth of the author's mind, it is highly selective in its use of facts, omitting entirely, for example, the twenty-year period which included his married life and his most sustained attempts to enter public office. Adams is a master of paradox who sees education as a process of continual and often painfully sudden adjustment to new situations for which nothing in his earlier experience has prepared him. Posing as a historian who distrusts history ('When the historian fully realizes his ignorance – which sometimes happens to Americans – he becomes even more tiresome to himself than to others, because his *naïveté* is irrepressible'), he nevertheless clings tenaciously to the belief that there must be some coherent pattern in the life of the race if not of the individual. Bewildered by the rapid strides made by nineteenth-century science, he is fascinated by scientific method and tries to apply it to historical study; scorning 'the sink of history – antiquarianism', though for seven years he was a medieval historian at Harvard, he persuades himself that it ought to be possible to project scientifically into the future the lines of force determining human development in the past. *The Education*, 'A Study of Twentieth Century Multiplicity', was conceived as a companion volume to the earlier *Mont-Saint-Michel and Chartres: A Study of Thirteenth Century Unity*. This unity he attributes to a deeply-held religious belief which he symbolizes by the figure of the Virgin; such belief seems to him no longer possible but to have been replaced by a faith in science and technology which he symbolizes by the Dynamo. The juxtaposition is fruitful, far-ranging and provocatively developed as a chapter of intellectual history. In a more conventional field, his strictures on the administration of President Grant (a theme that he also exploited brilliantly in an anonymous novel, *Democracy*) remain as stimulating as does his discussion of the ways in which his training and upbringing had educated him only for the past.

Henry Adams and Henry James were friends for the greater part of their lives, though each viewed the other's work more with respect than with complete sympathy. At some risk of over-simplification, they may be contrasted as representing two main streams of contemporary thought. If we sustain the distinction between the individual life and the life of the race, James may be said to have been uncompromisingly dedicated to the former, Adams more – though not exclusively – interested in the latter. For Adams education was primarily a matter of 'taking the stamp of one's time': in the terminology of David Riesman's *The Lonely Crowd* Adams was 'other-directed' where James, to whom education was the evolving of a personal morality through self-knowledge and the exposure to experience, was 'inner-directed'. Adams, in his concern with the forces at work in human history, comes very close to a determinist position; the opening and closing chapters of his monumental *History of the United States during the Administrations of Jefferson and Madison* enclose the nine volumes of narrative between descriptions of the 'sanguine and self-confident' buoyancy of the nation in 1800, its future and its opportunities limitless before it, and of its state in 1817 when the 'traits of American character were fixed; the rate of physical and economical growth was established': the suggestion is that circumstances have dictated the line of development through factors quite outside the control of individuals. The characters in *Democracy* and his other novel *Esther* do not exhibit the same degree of freedom of moral choice that is available to James's characters and live in a world in which a *Zeitgeist* governs their behaviour in a non-Jamesian manner.

Heredity and upbringing led Adams to think in terms of power, prestige, and politics; his poem 'Buddha and Brahma' allegorizes an uneasy feeling that his choice of the contemplative life was a betrayal of his heritage and his responsibility. For James the contemplative life was what he had been brought up to: for his family, wealth conferred not the patrician responsibility of office but the opportunity for the cultivation of one's sensibilities. His father, Henry James Senior, a New Yorker of independent means, had been influenced by Emerson and Swedenborg, and had transmitted to his children a belief in the sanctity and integrity of the individual. He educated them privately, inculcating in them ideas of morality unallied to any formal religious denomination. The novelist's elder brother William was to achieve eminence as a psychologist and philosopher: in *The Varieties of Religious Experience* (1902) and *Pragmatism* (1907) he took an anti-dogmatic position, arguing that morality must be empirically-based and that 'ideas (which are themselves but parts of our experiences) become true just in so far as they help us to get into satisfactory relation with other parts of our experience'. Experience is similarly of paramount importance in the thinking of Henry James, and in his novels. The initiation from innocence into experience which is the theme of so much of his fiction is sometimes destructive of the individual (*The Turn of the Screw* is an obvious, if extreme, example) and will usually involve an exposure to evil. Such evil may be deliberately induced by the machinations of the evilly-intentioned, but more characteristically James's position is close to that defined by his English friend George Meredith:

> In tragic life, God wot,
> No villain need be! Passions spin the plot:
> We are betrayed by what is false within.

Thus, in one of his best-loved novels, *The Portrait of a Lady* (1881), the theme may be said to be the betrayal of Isabel, the 'young woman affronting her destiny' in James's phrase; but neither the betrayal nor the destiny ought to be too simply stated. Gilbert Osmond and Madame Merle deceive her, but they are not therefore to be defined as villains. Of Madame Merle the worst that Isabel says, agreeing that she has 'done something very bad', is 'She made a convenience of me.' It could be argued that the worst harm is done to Isabel by her cousin Ralph who, in altruistic affection for her, persuades his father to settle on her the fortune that makes her at once attractive and vulnerable to Osmond and his partner, but this is not James's point, though Ralph's conversation with his dying father is crucial to an understanding of James. Ralph's purpose in enriching Isabel is to enable her 'to meet the requirements of her imagination' which he recognizes as considerable. To have withheld the money would have been to deny her the freedom of opportunity to realize her full potential as an individual. His father concurs, though with the important reservation 'I don't know that it's right to make everything so easy for a person'. The freedom that money confers on Isabel is the opportunity of choosing how, in spending it, she shall spend her life. That she utilizes it to purchase, unintentionally, a loss of freedom is the central irony of a novel in which, as in all James's work, irony of varying degrees of subtlety is an important solvent. The choice that Isabel is called upon to make is one for which her experience is not adequate, but she makes it freely and with all the conscious awareness of which she is capable. 'What is false within' is in Isabel's case her judgement of human nature and the motives of others. She errs through a generous and unselfish idealism. Yet the act of exercising choice is the truest form of freedom; though the outcome for Isabel is regrettable and irrevocable, it is not utterly disastrous. It leads to, even though it conditions, further choices, and though her future is not what Ralph or Isabel herself would have wanted, she retains her integrity, she acquires responsibilities that give her life some purpose, and she remains in the deepest sense a free agent, exercising that choice that is, for James, the essence of the human condition.

Throughout his literary career with increasing sophistication, subtlety, and stylistic complexity James was preoccupied with the interrelatedness of consciousness and conscience in the sensitive person with aesthetic inclinations. Frequently, since it was to Europe that such Americans were drawn, Europe is the setting of his novel and provides the 'international theme' for which his fiction is so justly celebrated. By virtue of his artistry as much as by his long residence in England and his wartime adoption of British citizenship, James belongs in a tradition of English fiction extending, as F. R. Leavis has shown, back at least as far as Jane Austen. The richness and significance of James's contributions to the development of the art and the craft of the novel and of the short story, both in creative practice and in carefully-pondered critical theory; his dedication to and unhappy experimen tation with the drama; his autobiographical writings and his literary friendships – adequate discussion of all these requires far more space and a wider context than the present chapter. To some people, indeed, his presence at all in a book of this nature would seem questionable.

Henry Adams's wife Marian dismissed him sceptically as 'that young emigrant', and thought that 'the real, live, vulgar, quick-paced world in America will fret him and that he prefers a quiet corner with a pen where he can create men and women who say neat things and have refined tastes and are not nasal or eccentric.' Certainly when, in 1904, after twenty-five years of expatriation, James returned to the United States, he was nonplussed and even repelled by much that he saw. In *The American Scene* (1907) he perceptively characterized the temper of the age as one of 'unsettled possession'. To the extent that his novels are novels of manners they deal, almost by definition, with a small spectrum of American society and one not entirely representative. Yet James cannot be ignored in the study of American literature and American thought. His belief in the necessity of moral freedom evolved by the individual empirically and with minimal reliance on institutionalized religion has distinguished American antecedents, though his formulation and application of that belief are his own. His conviction that the most valuable lessons are those learnt from experience, and his faith that human beings have, or can cultivate, enough wisdom and basic goodness to learn from experience, and that they have the autonomy to apply these lessons, would not have commanded universal assent among his contemporaries, but it was a faith to which many continued to cling in an age of sceptical disillusion.

That the well-being of society depended upon a civilized code of manners but even more upon the goodness of the individual was the theme of *The Rise of Silas Lapham* (1885) by William Dean Howells. Howells's friendship with and admiration for both James and Mark Twain symbolizes his own literary position. Silas Lapham, a self-made manufacturer and businessman, belongs to a class below that which usually engaged the attention of James but more genteel than that of Mark Twain's rumbustious heroes. Lapham, if he has Hank Morgan's energy and business acumen, has a moral sensibility and a natural dignity that would not be out of place in a James hero; his rise is a moral one, ironically coinciding with his ruin as a businessman. His superiority to the effete patricians of Boston is established by Howells with some delicacy and without the overtones of burlesque that would have been irresistible to Mark Twain. That the novel ends with a symbolic marriage between the younger generations of the two families is sufficiently indicative of Howells's ambivalence of sympathy. He was not the technical innovator that both James and Mark Twain, in their different ways, were, and he was to develop, as will be indicated shortly, in a direction very different from both of them; but his craftsmanship deserves more credit than it sometimes receives, as does his humanity and his concern with the issues of his time.

The Rise of Realism

Howells wrote thirty-five novels, thirty-one dramas, and eleven travel books as well as short stories, poetry, and memoirs, yet in his lifetime his influence was greatest as a critic and as editor of the *Atlantic Monthly*. His reputation as an arbiter of taste was declining before his death in 1920, and that decade had predictably little time for a critic who was uneasy as to 'how much or how little the American novel ought to deal with certain facts of life which are not usually talked of before young people, and especially young ladies'. That sentiment, however, had been expressed in 1891, in *Criticism and Fiction*; to join too quickly with Sinclair Lewis in laughing at him for having 'the code of a pious old maid whose greatest delight is to have tea at the vicarage' is entirely to underrate Howells's complexity and his impact on his age. Believing that his country had a contribution to make to literature, he was not chauvinistic enough to pretend that it could do this in complete indifference to literary developments in Europe, especially those that were extending the frontiers of fiction, and he tried to keep his readers informed on these topics.

In 1884 Henry James wrote to him from Paris praising 'the effort and experiment' of Daudet, the Goncourts and Zola: 'in spite of their ferocious pessimism and their handling of unclean things, they are at least serious and honest'. Similar qualities were to attract Howells (and through him other Americans) to Tolstoy, Ibsen, and Thomas Hardy, and he spoke of 'a true arrangement of literature, in which realism has obtained the supremacy over romance'. In the preface to *The House of the Seven Gables* Hawthorne's distinction between the Romance and the Novel had a real meaning for his generation and provided Richard Chase, in ours, with the basis for a constructive theory of American fiction; but Hawthorne still demanded, in that preface, fidelity to 'the truth of the human heart'. The distinction drawn by Howells between realism and romance is less valuable because less precise in its application. In *Criticism and Fiction* he attempted another definition: 'Realism is nothing more and nothing less than the truthful treatment of material, and Jane Austen was the first and last of the English novelists to treat material with entire truthfulness.' In all these passages the question-begging word is 'truth', but Howells's comment was salutary in its insistence on realism as a literary technique at a time when it was more loosely being used to imply that the material selected for treatment ought to be unfamiliar to the genteel reader, and even uncongenial. Hesitation over the subject matter of French fiction and a faith in American democracy combined to prompt the remark for which Howells is most frequently censured: 'Our novelists, therefore, concern themselves with the more smiling aspects of life, which are the more American, and seek the universal in the individual rather than the social interests. It is worthwhile, even at the risk of being called commonplace, to be true to our well-to-do actualities.' Realistic treatment of the 'well-to-do actualities' was ungrudgingly conceded to be the province of Henry James by younger writers whose own outlooks and techniques were very different from his, but who admired him as a writer and in some cases enjoyed his friendship. James's characters were privileged to enjoy the amenities of a high civilization because they had the money to buy this freedom; but, to return to Henry George's lesson, there were those for whom poverty put such resources beyond reach and even beyond imagination.

Howells was not blind to this. His own Ohio origins had been humble, and he was profoundly disturbed by the deprivations and the labour unrest precipitating such events as the Chicago Haymarket Riot of 1886. In a letter of 1888 to Henry James he expressed the uneasiness that was to lead him in some of his later writings into Socialism: 'After fifty years of optimistic content with "civilization" and its ability to come out all right in the end, I now abhor it, and feel that it is coming out all wrong in the end unless it bases itself anew on a real equality.' Convinced that the novelist had a social responsibility, Howells addressed himself in his novels to a whole range of social problems as conscientiously as he could, but his solutions are moralistic rather than political or economic, and he did not feel the need to develop new techniques of fiction to suit its new subject matter. *Annie Kilburn* (1888) explores the difficulties, practical and ideological, confronting a young woman trying to improve social conditions in Massachusetts by well-intentioned philanthropy. *A Hazard of New Fortunes* (1890), which he thought 'the most vital of my fictions', paralleled his own removal to New York by a story of a New York magazine editor whose liberal conscience leads him to a principled opposition to his capitalist employer in defence of a socialist member of his staff; the employee's son and the socialist are subsequently killed when intervening in a strike of street-car men in the hope of restoring order. Howells was at least sufficient of an economist to avoid the patrician paternalism of Henry Adams's friend John Hay who, in *The Breadwinners* (1884), had shown the workers as merely duped by malicious union leaders, much as Dickens had done in *Hard Times* thirty years earlier; realistically aware here, as in *Annie Kilburn*, that goodwill, though essential, is not enough, Howells nevertheless ends the novel on a note of reconciliation, allowing his hero to comment '*I* don't know what it all means, . . . though I believe it means good.'

In 1894, the year when U.S. troops were sent to Chicago to break the Pullman strike and when the country was going through another financial depression, Howells published a deceptively urbane Utopian romance, *A Traveller from Altruria*. The traveller's apparently naïve questions are met by the narrator's genteelly unimaginative defence of things as they are: irony verges on satire, but clearly Howells shares the visitor's hopes: ' "I imagine", he went on, "that the difference between your civilization and ours is only one of degree, after all, and that America and Altruria are really one at heart".' As a modern critic has remarked, 'Altruria is what America would be if it really took to heart the principles of the Declaration.' It is this thought, none the less poignant for its idealism, that gives such impetus to American writing of this period. Altruria is much nearer to the United States than Nowhere is to William Morris's England of 1890 in the romance to which Howell's debt is clearer in *Through the Eye of the Needle* (1907), the sequel to *A Traveller from Altruria*. Both Howells and Morris had been preceded by Edward Bellamy (1850–98) whose *Looking Backward* (1888) projected a young Bostonian into the world of 2000 A.D. to enjoy 'the blessings of a social order at once so simple and logical that it seems but the triumph of common sense'; America has 'organized as the one great business corporation in which all other corporations were absorbed: it became the one capitalist in the place of all other capitalists'. This has been brought about by 'a process of industrial evolution': 'All that society had to do was to recognize and co-operate with that evolution, when its tendency had become unmistakable.' Less convinced of evolutionary inevitability and less optimistic about human nature was Ignatius Donnelly (1831–1901), whose *Caesar's Column* (1890) looked ahead to a violent future in which the worker-slaves throw off the capitalist tyranny by revolution, only to be overwhelmed by their own greed and baser natures. Jack London (1876–1916) was to predict a similarly horrific and even more immediate future in *The Iron Heel* (1907), in which, by 1918, America has become a fascist police-state, perpetuating monopolistic business capitalism by force until the twenty-third century when collectivism eventually replaces it.

Howells's Christian Socialist principles look less for a change of system, violent or evolutionary, than for a change of heart. In *The Undiscovered Country* (1880) he had contrasted the happy, simple piety of a Shaker community with the harm done by the deceptions of spiritualist charlatans; and in his last novel, *The Leatherwood God* (1916), he returned to the Ohio of the backwoods Utopias dear to his father's dreams, in one of which Howells had spent a year of his childhood; again, simple faith is set against superstitious credulity, and Howells's confidence in man's better nature asserts itself in a context of unsophisticated rural life. A similar faith and an admiration for Howells's 'sane and wholesome fiction' led Hamlin Garland (1860–1940) to advocate a 'natural and unstrained art' based on 'local colour' in which 'the writer spontaneously reflects the life which goes on around him'. This he tried to do for his native Wisconsin in short stories such as *Main-Travelled Roads* (1891), novels, and autobiography (*A Son of the Middle Border*, 1917). His theories of literature, expressed in essays collected in *Crumbling Idols* (1894), though less iconoclastic than their title promises, were not without significance. That 'Provincialism (that is to say, localism) is no ban to a national literature' would have been readily agreed by several contemporary regionalist writers. Garland instanced, among others, George Washington Cable (1844–1925) whose *Old Creole Days* (1879) and *The Grandissimes* (1880) dealt with Louisiana, especially New Orleans; Mary Murfree (1850–1922) who was publishing stories of Tennessee pseudonymously as Charles Egbert Craddock; and Joel Chandler Harris (1848–1908) who had created 'Uncle Remus' in 1876 and who was already well-known for these Negro folk-tales as well as for other local-colour fiction set in Georgia. Constance Fenimore Woolson (1840–94), friend and disciple of Henry James, had written about the Great Lakes; Bret Harte (1836–1902) about the mining frontier; and in 1896 one of the 'local-colour' masterpieces was to appear: *The Country of the Pointed Firs* by Sarah Orne Jewett (1849–1909). Admiration for the Southern 'local-colour' fiction of Harriet Beecher Stowe (1811–96) led her to attempt something for the sea coast of Maine, winning Henry James's admiration and his brother William's praise for the book's suggestion of 'that incommunicable cleanness of the salt air when one first leaves town'. Miss Jewett was to become the acknowledged model for a more prolific writer, Willa Cather (1876–1947), whose best work is set in the Nebraska where she spent her early years. The short story is the form to which the 'local-colourist' most usually tends, but Willa Cather turns this talent into the writing of episodic novels such as *O Pioneers!* (1913) and *My Antonia* (1918) which tell of the hardships encountered by European immigrant farmers on the exposed Nebraskan prairies. A celebration of the sturdy virtues of the industriously unassuming, the novels combine honesty and nostalgia in a controlled and muted lyricism that still compels respect.

The 'local-colourist' aimed not only at the regional atmosphere but also at its speech, believing with Garland that 'Dialect is the life of a language, precisely as the common people of the nation form the sustaining power of its social life and art.' For the type of realism he was advocating Garland tried unsuccessfully to popularize the term 'veritism', in part to distinguish it from the Zola-esque realism that troubled his rather conventional mind, and to emphasize its indigenous roots. Yet he foresaw the increasing literary importance of 'the contrast of city and country, everywhere growing sharper'; and his *Rose of Dutcher's Coolly* (1895) is a novel of a Wisconsin farm-girl's aspirations towards a life of greater fulfilment and culture in the city.

Naturalistic Leanings

When other writers told him what they conceived to be the truth about the city in language more aggressive than his own and with a local colour more lurid and more sombre in its extremes, Garland, like Howells, was imaginative enough to respond with an understanding and encouragement that won for both of them the friendship and respect of these younger novelists. In 1892 a paper-bound short novel called *Maggie: a Girl of the Streets* reached Garland, who at once urged its author, Stephen Crane (1871–1900), to send a copy to Howells. This 'tale of the Bowery', as it was sub-titled, had already been rejected by at least one editor because of its uncompromising use of the dialect and the vocabulary of that area of New York. Impressed by Crane's honesty, Howells urged him to exploit this vein further and recalled later that 'It was interesting to hear him defend what he had written, in obedience to his experience of things, against any charge of convention. "No", he would contend, in behalf of the profanities of his people, "that is the way they *talk*. I have thought of that, and whether I ought to leave such things out, but if I do I am not giving the thing as I *know* it" '. This emphasis on personal experience as the basis for fiction and this 'telling it as it is' might sound highly modern in its realism; and there is no denying that Crane's theme and idiom were unconventional and, to many readers, shocking. Yet for all its perceptive rendering of the squalid realities of life in a New York slum, not even *Maggie* avoids with complete success the much-censured pitfalls of romance. Degraded by her environment and by the crude violence and passions of her companions, Maggie, having 'blossomed in a mud-puddle', is drawn into a conventional suicide in 'the deathly black hue of the river'. Crane exposes the false sentimentality of her mother's mourning but misses the sentimentality inherent in his conventionally convenient disposal of his fallen woman.

In *The Red Badge of Courage* (1895) he mingles realism and romance at first sight even more confusingly. The modern reader, expecting a war novel to be an indictment of war, will be strengthened in his expectations by the graphic brutality of the descriptions of carnage and by the unheroic conduct of the hero. The boy's leave-taking of his mother is a skilfully calculated contrast of a vernacular reality with the stereotyped sentiments of romantic fiction and reflects a truer, if more mundane, stoicism. His flight from the field of battle, and his projection of his own feelings on to the wild creatures of the wood in the belief that he is drawing a lesson from them, seem a timely refutation of more grandiose Transcendentalist notions of man's communion with nature in a benevolent and harmonious universe. Crane wrote the novel without any first-hand experience of a military campaign, yet, as Fleming comes to realize his officers' incompetence, the joys and limitations of soldiers' rough camaraderie, and the part played by chance in war, the author seems to be anticipating the soldier-novelists and poets of the First World War. It should not be assumed, however, that his aims were identical with theirs. Howells found 'a good deal of floundering' in this novel and thought 'the dialect does not so much convince' as in *Maggie*. The floundering is due less to the dialect than to the dialectic. For much of the novel Crane's stance is Hardy-esque: man is a stranger in an implacable universe, a prey to chance, deluded into believing himself autonomous when in fact his behaviour is conditioned by circumstance and his own nature. The boy's flight is dictated by the instinct of self-preservation as much as is the flight of the squirrel he meets; his capture of the flag at the end of the novel is described with so much animal-imagery that that action too seems instinctive. Yet the closing paragraphs of the book are in a quite different key:

He felt a quiet manhood, non-assertive but of sturdy and strong blood. He knew that he would no more quail before his guides wherever they should point. He had been to touch the great death, and found that, after all, it was but the great death. He was a man.

So it came to pass that as he trudged from the place of blood and wrath his soul changed. He came from hot plowshares to prospects of clover tranquilly, and it was as if hot plowshares were not. Scars faded as flowers.

. . . He had rid himself of the red sickness of battle. The sultry nightmare was in the past. He had been an animal blistered and sweating in the heat and pain of war. He turned now with a lover's thirst to images of tranquil skies, fresh meadows, cool brooks – an existence of soft and eternal peace.

Over the river a golden ray of sun came through the host of leaden rain clouds.

This technicolour prose is not merely self-conscious and over-written, not merely at odds with the racier vernacular of the dialogue: it is at odds with the book's whole theme. The mixture of biblical overtones ('So it came to pass . . .'), the expansive romanticism ('a lover's thirst . . . tranquil skies, fresh meadows, cool brooks') and the final benediction of Nature all evoke associations the validity of which the narrative seemed to have been at pains to deny. To see in this ending the irony that is at work elsewhere in the novel, exposing Fleming as a self-deceiver to the last, is to ignore the tone of the passage and to beg the question why, if irony is intended, it is achieved less competently than elsewhere. The manuscript suggests uncertainty on Crane's part as to how to end the novel but no hint of irony. More convincing is the argument that the conflicts of tone indicate an unresolved conflict of authorial views. This has wider implications for our understanding of the literature of this period, and makes Crane's work more interesting than that of Ambrose Bierce (1842–1914?), whose *Tales of Soldiers and Civilians* (1891) are brilliantly-executed Civil War stories with a Poe-like element of horror (the English edition was titled *In the Midst of Life*). Their accomplished irony is, however, in its cynical nihilism, ultimately less satisfying and more perfunctory than Crane's ambivalence. Crane reflects better the debate between free-will and determinism that was exercising so many minds in direct relation to the varying factors seen as affecting human life. Darwinian biology suggested evolution and heredity; economic determinists suggested the social environment; Henry Adams's concept of scientific history came near to seeing man conditioned by the historical past. Earlier notions of original sin still had considerable force for some people but not for the most enquiring; such notions assigned to the individual a preeminence in the scheme of things which experience just did not seem to justify. The survival and development of the species, the type, the society, the class, was what seemed to matter. Out of such social Darwinism came the literary movement known as Naturalism.

The process has been traced by Malcolm Cowley in a symposium, *Evolutionary Thought in America*, and its characteristics defined. He emphasizes its pessimism, because, convinced that the forces governing man are outside his control, the Naturalists cannot accept the possibility of the reform of society or of man, either by individual or collective action, any more than they can allow the possibility of a character consciously exercising moral choice. *Maggie*, it will be seen, fits this prescription fairly closely. In his painstaking efforts to render accurately the dialect and manners of the Bowery Crane may also be seen as fulfilling the Naturalist's expectation that a novel should have a documentary significance; he tries also to preserve towards his characters the detached objectivity, as of the zoologist towards specimens, that Naturalism expected. Cowley comments also that the Naturalists rarely show their characters as having histories, antecedents, or roots in the past, and this too is true of Maggie. (It might seem true also of Garland's remark: 'To the veritist, therefore, the present is the vital theme. The past is dead, and the future can be trusted to look after itself.' On the other hand, this trust in the future and his general optimism mark Garland decisively off from strict Naturalism.)

The Red Badge of Courage fits less consistently still into the rigid Naturalistic framework: the hero is capable of spiritual development and, to some extent, of choice affecting his situation. He is more of an individual, less of a type, and he is spoken of as having a soul which is capable of change. Yet another aspect of the book is even more fundamentally Naturalistic than *Maggie*: the imagery frequently represents the army as an organism with an independent existence, and the individual soldiers, not as cogs in a machine, but as cells in an organism. The novel does not protest against this state of affairs any more than it protests against war: it merely implies that this is the human condition, and that to wish it were otherwise is futile in the face of facts such as these. This, and Crane's tendency to refer to his hero not by name but as 'the youth', exemplify the Naturalist's objective presentation of the universal type rather than the sharply-delineated individual.

Yet discussion of this as a war novel obscures its concern with one particular conflict, the American Civil War, which had been fought thirty years earlier. An historical subject might seem a non-Naturalistic choice, but Crane objectifies and neutralizes it by his deliberate refusal to discuss the issues for which that war was fought and its impact on the American conscience as, for example, John William de Forest had done in *Miss Ravenel's Conversion from Secession to Loyalty* (1867). Nor does Crane sentimentalize the causes involved as so much subsequent Civil War fiction has done, with considerable popularity. He had, however, in 1894 written for Decoration Day a more conventional piece of journalism, celebrating the patriotic dedication of the men who fought in 'the great war for freedom and union'. This awareness of what the war meant to his contemporaries may have made him chary of adopting in the novel a Naturalistic stance that might offend by seeming to disparage that war and its historic significance. Realism of presentation (in de Forest as much as in Crane) exemplified the conditions in which the war was fought, but the philosophical implications of Naturalism might call into question the value of fighting it at all. The qualified note of optimism introduced at the end by the youth-become-man seeing the sun break through the clouds may have been intended to offset such misgivings.

For the clouds of Naturalism to be irradiated by some form of sun is so usual in American fiction as to merit attention for a moment longer. The case of Frank Norris (1870–1902) is instructive. In *Criticism and Fiction* Howells expressed his belief that 'fiction would be incomparably stronger, incomparably truer if once it could . . . frankly dedicate itself to the service of all the passions, all the interests, all the facts' but he was not convinced that the public was yet ready for such candour. Norris seemed determined to meet this prescription with novels about passions very different from those in genteel fiction and with a reliance on 'all the facts' that will be discussed later. *McTeague* (1899) is a grim study of cupidity and avarice leading to the destruction of human relations and even of human lives in murder and violent death. The eponymous hero is a San Francisco dentist, of limited intelligence but considerable strength, placidly content in his marriage to a woman for whom he no longer feels any passion. He is obliged to abandon dentistry when his lack of qualifications is discovered, and the decline in their fortunes drives him into morose alcoholism, her into excessive economies and deception in order to increase her secret savings: 'Trina's emotions had narrowed with the narrowing of her daily life. They reduced themselves at last to but two, her passion for her money and her perverted love for her husband when he was brutal.' Anger is McTeague's strongest passion and it is expressed in violence, bringing out 'The brute that in McTeague lay so close to the surface'; angered he gives vent to 'the hideous yelling of a hurt beast, the squealing of a wounded elephant . . . an echo from the jungle'. Imagery and action combine to emphasize the thinness of the veneer separating man from the animals: McTeague is the precursor of Eugene O'Neill's Yank in *The Hairy Ape*, Tennessee Williams's Stanley Kowalski, and similar manifestations of an American syndrome defined by Wyndham Lewis as 'the Dumb Ox' (though Lewis's application of the term to Hemingway's heroes is much more open to question).

This stress on man's sub-humanity does more than give credibility to McTeague's murder of his wife: it consorts well with the views of man as dominated by irresistible external forces and barely capable of independent willed action. The idea received another formulation when a character says of him: 'Might as well try to stop a locomotive. . . . The man's made of iron.' The image is revealing: the Naturalistic view of a universe governed by forces larger than man leads to a veneration for force itself, and force such as that embodied in the locomotive (or Henry Adams's Dynamo) acquires symbolic value. An engine made by man generates this force but the force, being bigger than its maker, reminds him of his relative puniness. Leo Marx, in *The Machine in the Garden*, provides a brilliant study of 'Technology and the Pastoral Ideal', in the phrase of its sub-title. He speaks of the American 'habit of defining reality as a contradiction between radically opposed forces', and Norris exemplifies this even more fully than it is relevant to Marx's purpose to demonstrate. Moreover it is precisely in this contradiction that undiluted Naturalism ceases to satisfy the American imagination. *McTeague* is a predominantly urban novel, and Norris even speaks of Nature as 'a vast, unconquered brute of the Pliocene epoch, savage, sullen, and magnificently indifferent to man'; the dentist dies in the arid desert of Death Valley in search of gold (the major part of his journey thither having been made, significantly, by train). Usually, however, it is quite another feature of the Californian landscape that engages Norris's imagination: the pastoral fertility of the wheat-lands which he planned to celebrate in a trilogy called 'The Epic of the Wheat'.

Like all his work, even this is characterized by a double vision. The concept of the epic, with its heroic overtones, is hardly consistent with Naturalism, and among the other conventions Norris takes over from the epic is the heroic fight with a monster. This monster, however, is no mythical beast like Beowulf's Grendel, but the railway and the capitalist finance behind it, and it is not a monster that can be slain as readily as Grendel. The metaphor of the monster is imposed by the title of the first of the only two novels of the trilogy that Norris completed, *The Octopus*. Thus to identify the railroad with a marine predator is to remove it further from the possibility of human control, but the reverse process is also at work in a passage such as this:

> Nature was, then, a gigantic engine, a vast Cyclopean power, huge, terrible, a leviathan with a heart of steel, knowing no compunction, no forgiveness, no tolerance; . . . [a] prodigious mechanism of wheels and cogs.

Nature and the machine become interchangeable in the equality of their mythologized monstrousness, yet man cannot withhold from either a grudging admiration. The machine-harvester cutting the wheat becomes 'some prodigious monster, insatiable, with iron teeth . . . snarling and slobbering . . . a hippopotamus . . . a dinosaur . . . incessant, ravenous, and inordinate' in a description like Steinbeck's of the tractors in *The Grapes of Wrath* nearly forty years later. (Like Norris also, Steinbeck found symbolic analogies between marine biology and human life.)

Stretching its rapacious tentacles across the Californian wheat ranches, the railway-octopus is even more irresistibly insidious in the poison it injects into men's systems: it corrupts its agents and its opponents alike into machinations so unscrupulous as to be dehumanizing and self-destroying. Norris weakens his point by the crudeness of his invention and the obviousness of his symbolism. The pursuit of the fugitive and the subsequent gun duel, obligatory in the Western, are given a variation more symbolic than credible by substitution of locomotives for horses; the alternation of scenes between an extravagant dinner-party and a woman dying of starvation on the San Francisco streets is over-obvious; while the death of the ruthless capitalist, accidentally buried in the grain cascading into the ship's hold, is in its triteness almost as suffocating to the novel as to the tycoon. More to

Norris's credit is the unexpected revelation of another tycoon, Shelgrim, as a man of humanity, taste and even sentimentality instead of a rapacious monster.

The measure of Norris's difficulty is the problem he creates for himself in utilizing his hero. Presley is a good-natured man on friendly terms with all and universally respected, a champion of the oppressed, and an idealist fired by his poetic ambition to write the epic of the American West – an obvious *persona* for his author. Yet Norris can find for him no role more positive than that of a choric observer. Desperately aware of the need for action, Presley is equally conscious of the inefficacy of action, and is reduced to a stasis parallel to that of Henry Adams in *The Education*. 'Chaos was the law of Nature; order was the dream of man', Adams was to discover. Presley precedes him; he makes two half-hearted and wholly unsuccessful attempts to bring about that order by action – he attempts an assassination and, more characteristically, he addresses a mass meeting – but he quickly abandons his flirtation with socialism in the belief that there are no enemies, only 'Forces, conditions, laws of supply and demand'. Norris's difficulty in finding a role for Presley highlights the problem of the compatibility of Naturalism and literature. If the lives of men are so determined by immutable forces, what purpose is served by art and by the creative writer? The problem is solved by these novelists only in the extent to which they move (or are moved) away from Naturalism in their fiction, but conviction may be weakened in the process. Thus Presley, at the end of *The Octopus*, surveying the toll of death and havoc taken by the twin forces of the railroad and grasping human greed, is buoyed up in the final two paragraphs by reflections such as these:

> *But the* WHEAT *remained*. Untouched, unassailable, undefiled, that mighty world-force, that nourisher of nations, wrapped in Nirvanic calm, indifferent to the human swarm, gigantic, resistless, moved onward in its appointed grooves. . . .

> Falseness dies; injustice and oppression in the end of everything fade and vanish away. Greed, cruelty, selfishness, and inhumanity are short-lived; the individual suffers, but the race goes on. . . . The larger view always and through all shams, all wickednesses, discovers the Truth that will, in the end, prevail, and all things, surely, inevitably, resistlessly work together for good.

Noble words, but less comforting than they are intended to be. The wheat is a force hardly less blind than the railroad, so can it really be any more benevolent? The humane capitalist, Shelgrim, has already warned Presley of this: ' "The Wheat is one force, the Railroad, another, and there is the law that governs them – supply and demand. Men have only little to do in the whole business. . . . Blame conditions, not men".' D. H. Lawrence's advice, 'Never trust the artist; trust the tale', applies every bit as much to the Naturalistic novel as to the romance, and the tale of *The Octopus* is too compellingly told to be set aside by the rhetoric of final-paragraph reassurances. The conditions it describes carry more conviction than the men it creates as characters. In one sense their own creed rebounds ironically on the Naturalists: they release in their stories a force larger than themselves which often undermines them and sometimes blows them up.

So much emphasis on force is inevitable. If the inconsistencies of their thought were unmatched by strength elsewhere, their work would not merit this attention. Crude as it sometimes is in its expression, there is in these novels a vigour and a dynamism that revitalize the gentility of a Howellsian plea for a new school of American realism and that divert the current of American literature into a new channel. Their inspiration is national, their material indigenous. Emerson and Whitman, asserting the challenge of the continent as itself the greatest poem, were in spirit closer to the American Dream than their successors, but the power of that dream is sufficiently attested by the inability of these novelists to reject it. The impulse behind these novels is not unlike that behind *A Traveller from Altruria* or that which led William Jennings Bryan to campaign for the Presidency in 1896 with the claim that America was being 'crucified upon a cross of gold' by financiers who would not recognize that 'the great cities rest upon our broad and fertile prairies'. Regionalism had centred on the city as Garland predicted, but it was a bitter realism, closer to the indignation which led Lincoln Steffens in 1904 to write *The Shame of the Cities*.

The Literature of Urbanism

The second novel of Norris's projected trilogy, *The Pit*, is sub-titled, as many other novels might, with equal appropriateness, have been, 'A Story of Chicago'. After a disastrous fire in October 1871 occasioned heavy losses of life and property, Chicago had been rebuilt with a rapidity dictated by its importance as a centre of transcontinental communications as well as of the meat-packing and the iron and steel industries. It was the great Chicago Exposition of 1893 that set Henry Adams speculating about the new forces of technology; and the city's bustling commercial reputation, based in part on its wheat market (the 'Pit' of Norris's title), gave it a fascination for novelists, who found this prosperity dramatically juxtaposed against the poverty that Jane Addams's Hull House settlement had been instituted to alleviate, and against the resentment that overflowed into the Haymarket Riot and the Pullman Strike. Upton Sinclair's *The Jungle* (1906) is a relentlessly Naturalistic study of the squalor and deprivation forced on immigrant workers by the economic condition of the stockyards. It ends on the up-beat note of a Socialist meeting harangued by an orator who promises to organize, drill, and marshal 'the outraged working-men of Chicago' until the tide is made to turn and Chicago will be theirs. His rhetoric is more emotive, more doctrinaire, and less idealistic than Presley's, and Sinclair is a writer less persuasive than Norris, less imaginative than Crane: nevertheless, *The Jungle* precipitated a federal inquiry and legislative action.

Sinclair and Norris had both introduced into their novels the girl driven by economic necessity to prostitution, though they treated the theme less fully than Crane in *Maggie*. That it did not need the extremes of poverty to tempt young women into illicit relations is the theme of another Chicago novel, Theodore Dreiser's *Sister Carrie*, where the lure of the city for the unsophisticated country girl involves aspects of Chicago more opulent than those of *The Jungle*. His view of life is not basically dissimilar to Sinclair's, however, and the book enjoyed an even greater *succès de scandale*. (The story of its withdrawal from publication by timorous publishers, however, seems to be apocryphal.) The title obliquely acknowledges the story's origins within the experience of Dreiser's own family and the novel has the stamp of authenticity in many other respects too. Drawn from rural Wisconsin to Chicago by dreams of the opportunities afforded in the city, the fictitious Carrie is typical of many of her generation, and the novel might be expected to fall into a familiar American genre, the novel of initiation in which a young person develops from innocence through experience into maturity. From the 1860s onwards a Unitarian minister named Horatio Alger had enjoyed a great reputation as a prolific writer of boys' books on the 'rags to riches' theme, in which a virtuous and energetic struggle against adverse circumstances reaps the inevitable reward of wealth and honour. Carrie is by no means the female equivalent of one of these paragons, for her route to wealth, though effective, is far more dubious. Though she is not without determination, hard work and industrious thrift are not for her.

She is, indeed, rescued from the necessity for them by a series of irregular liaisons, of which the main one is with Hurstwood, the middle-aged manager of a prosperous Chicago bar who robs his employer's safe and decamps with Carrie to Montreal and then New York. Unable to adapt himself to this situation, he degenerates morally and ends as a suicide, while Carrie has found a career on the stage and a succession of new admirers.

The opening chapter is entitled 'The Magnet Attracting: A Waif amid Forces', and many subsequent references make clear Dreiser's affinities with Naturalism, but the description of Carrie as a waif distracts attention from her as the victim less of outside forces than of her own good nature and her tendency to take the line of least resistance. Naïve as she is at the outset, she is so attracted by the magnet of a comfortable life that self-interest and inertia seem to motivate her more than those sensibilities and finer feelings that Dreiser assures us she possesses. She seems, for example, much more materialistically-minded and much less the innocent victim of cynical men and blind destiny than Hardy's Tess of the d'Urbervilles. She is not hounded by her author as relentlessly as the unhappy Tess, but Dreiser's grasp of female psychology is in many respects less subtle and less convincing than Hardy's. Even F. O. Matthiessen, one of the most sympathetic and constructive of Dreiser's critics, admits the novelist's limitations in presenting the inner life of his characters. Matthiessen comments shrewdly: 'The only way we could sense what Dreiser calls her "feeling mind" would be to see her deeply stirred, and this she never is. . . . She is never a woman in love.' Far from being the unconventional heroine that Dreiser thought her, she is not, Matthiessen suggests, unconventional enough. What Dreiser wants us to see as a striving towards beauty and a life of richer fulfilment will, to many readers, look uneasily like a striving towards what Veblen has taught us to call pecuniary culture and conspicuous consumption. Her highest ideals seem to be a notion that she should be reading better books and getting parts in straight plays instead of musicals.

Henry James praised Howells's work for being 'in the highest degree *documentary*'; the phrase echoes Howells's plea for fiction to 'dedicate itself to the service of . . . all the facts'. The dedication to factual documentation is especially strong in Dreiser. We learn, for example, that Chicago in 1889 had a population 'of over 500,000 . . . scattered over an area of seventy-five square miles'; that the department store was in those days a novelty and that 'The first three in the United States, established about 1884, were in Chicago'; and that the term 'drummer' was a recent slang coinage for a travelling salesman, and 'masher' (a dandy) 'had sprung into general use among Americans in 1880'. When Hurstwood makes a phone-call from a Chicago drugstore Dreiser tells us 'It was a famous drugstore, and contained one of the first private telephone booths ever erected'. That Dreiser can describe physical reality more vividly than he can dramatize the feelings of his characters suggests a limitation of artistic imagination that can be a handicap. To take a specific instance: in New York Carrie is taken by friends to a particularly opulent restaurant, and Dreiser sets the scene:

> On the walls were designs in colour, square spots of robin's-egg blue, set in ornate frames of gilt, whose corners were elaborate mouldings of fruit and flowers, with fat cupids hovering in angelic comfort. On the ceilings were coloured traceries with more gilt, leading to a centre where spread a cluster of lights – incandescent globes mingled with glittering prisms and stucco tendrils of gilt. The floor was of a reddish hue, waxed and polished, and in every direction were mirrors – tall, brilliant, bevel-edged mirrors – reflecting and re-reflecting forms, faces, and candelabra a score and a hundred times.
>
> The tables were not so remarkable in themselves, and yet the imprint of Sherry upon the napery, the name of Tiffany upon the silverware, the name of Haviland upon the china, . . . made them seem remarkable.

Little as this decor may coincide with modern taste, its heavy nineteenth-century fussiness is faithfully rendered on the factual level. The description, like the prose in which it is presented, is workmanlike rather than inspired. One might, to borrow a phrase from Coleridge, say of the various features of the room 'I see, not feel, how beautiful they are.' The reader's emotions are not greatly engaged because neither are the author's: to him it is a scene externally viewed. More significantly, the character's emotions are not conveyed in the description; it is through Dreiser's eyes rather than through Carrie's that we see it. An illuminating contrast may be made with the passage in the opening chapter of *The Great Gatsby* where Scott Fitzgerald brings his narrator for the first time into the drawing-room of the wealthy Buchanans. The furnishings are less ornate, and Fitzgerald has the advantage of a first-person narrator, but these factors do not adequately explain the difference in quality of imagination behind the two passages nor the way in which Fitzgerald can achieve the richness of felt experience in his prose, a simultaneous evocation of atmosphere and character's response to atmosphere. Dreiser's effects are painstakingly rather than brilliantly achieved, in dialogue as well as in description. The accuracy of his dialogue in vocabulary, colloquialism and phrasing reflects that zeal for verisimilitude which not infrequently led these writers into attempts to render dialect on the printed page as well. Crane tried Bowery speech in *Maggie*; Norris, Howells and others make somewhat laborious efforts at conveying the accents of German immigrant characters, just as Dreiser in this novel uses an Irish accent in the scenes of the streetcar strike. It is not that the speech lacks authenticity; what is missing is the dramatic sense that enables a novelist to give ordinary conversation significance and evocative power. Again a contrast is afforded by Fitzgerald whose use of dialogue is especially economical and imaginative. Far from leaving the dialogue to do the work, Dreiser is inclined to bolster it up with descriptive comment. For example, Hurstwood's instrumentality in launching Carrie on a theatrical career is established thus:

> Small four-line notes had appeared in all of the daily newspapers. These he had arranged for by the aid of one of his newspaper friends on the 'Times', Mr. Harry McGarren, the managing editor.
> 'Say, Harry', Hurstwood said to him one evening, as the latter stood at the bar drinking before wending his belated way homeward, 'You can help the boys out, I guess'.
> 'What is it?' said McGarren, pleased to be consulted by the opulent manager.
> 'The Custer Lodge is getting up a little entertainment for their own good, and they'd like a little newspaper notice. You know what I mean – a squib or two saying that it's going to take place'.
> 'Certainly', said McGarren, 'I can fix that for you, George'.

The conversation rings true enough, but it adds nothing to the situation or to the novel that has not already been conveyed by the two sentences preceding it.

Yet the passage is representative of Dreiser's method and, in a way, of his strength. 'The slowness with which things occur in his novels,' Matthiessen suggests, 'is one of the ways by which he gives them weight', and he rightly defines a Dreiser novel as 'more impressive in its main sweep than in all its details'. It is part of the enthusiasm for documentation. When Carrie is at rehearsal Dreiser incorporates into the text of the novel part of the play she is rehearsing with, again, little specific benefit to the novel. His later novel, *An American Tragedy* (1925), is based on an actual murder case; having narrated the events, he then goes over the whole ground again in a fully-documented account of the trial. Laboured as this may be made to sound, the ultimate effect of these novels in their density and massiveness is impressive and does convey a sense of life at a particular time and place.

The most affecting part of *Sister Carrie* is the decline and disintegration of Hurstwood which combines Naturalistic inevitability with psychological reality and at the same time provides an outlet for an aspect of Dreiser at variance with both, a basically simple religiosity. Despite his assiduous study of the different determinisms of Herbert Spencer and Sigmund Freud, Dreiser's moralistic reflections in his novels suggest a Hardy-like inability to jettison entirely the Christian notions of a morally-ordered universe. Hurstwood's downfall, fitting more accurately into a pattern of retribution for sin, is described more vividly and more movingly than Carrie's morally-undeserved social rise, with which it is counterpoised. Dreiser's reservations about the success of that rise, in any terms other than pecuniary, are justified, and had the contrast with Hurstwood's fall been managed with sharper irony it might have been better. Like Norris, however, Dreiser understands dramatic irony in its simpler manifestations but has no command of irony in style and language as a means of conditioning the reader's response. (Crane, it has been suggested already, saw the possibilities of this more clearly but could not always harness effectively the energy thus released.) Eschewing irony, Dreiser resorts to sentiment, as in the lingering apostrophe with which Carrie is dismissed. It ends: 'Know, then, that for you is neither surfeit nor content. In your rocking-chair, by your window dreaming, shall you long alone. In your rocking-chair, by your window shall you dream such happiness as you may never feel.'

Carrie's discontented restlessness, however, is the restlessness of the Gilded Age, just as the schisms in Dreiser are the schisms of the age. His latest biographer emphasizes this by speaking of *Two Dreisers: The Man and the Novelist*. The conscientious and sometimes pedestrian dedication to realism exhibited by all these writers is paralleled in work by such English novelists as George Gissing and Arnold Bennett; the strictures in Virginia Woolf's essay 'Mr. Bennett and Mrs. Brown' can often be applied to American novels with equal justice. Yet the non-American reader must not be too eager to generalize from these novels either about American fiction or about the age. The literary critic is apt to focus his sights on that part of the iceberg which represents the best and most creative achievement of an era and to take for granted the larger segment below the waterline. The icebergs surveyed in the chapters preceding and following this glitter with pinnacles brighter and higher than these, and therefore it may be appropriate to amplify this truism in this particular context. The trends identified and the works discussed here appear in retrospect the most significant, yet many readers of the time sought something quite different and found it purveyed in abundance. The restrictions of city life could be forgotten in the romanticized Wild West of dime novels in their thousands and Owen Wister's *The Virginian* (1902). Secular doubts were assuaged by Horatio Alger's profitably reiterated assurance that prosperity was still the reward for Franklinian enterprise and effort. Religious doubts were soothed for 80,000 American purchasers by the bromide of sentimental piety packaged in Elizabeth Stuart Phelps's *The Gates Ajar* (1868); Mark Twain cheerfully burlesqued the materialism of this 'mean little ten-cent heaven about the size of Rhode Island', but it reached a far larger public than did Harold Frederic's more responsibly realistic study *The Damnation of Theron Ware* (1896). Lew Wallace's *Ben-Hur* (1880) provided the most popular of all reaffirmations of Christianity for an age that needed something with which to counteract its disillusion, as well as a fictional escape from its own pressures.

Yet even at the level of the more significant and realistic fiction of Norris, Crane, and Dreiser it is all too easy for the non-American to overstress the disillusion, and to see these novels as an indictment of the American experience and the American Dream, just as non-Americans have always seen Sinclair Lewis's *Babbitt* (1922) simply as a satire. Yet Lewis stated categorically, 'I wrote Babbitt not out of hatred for him but out of love', and Dreiser said of Chicago that for him 'it seethed with a peculiarly human or realistic atmosphere. It is given to some cities, as to some lands, to suggest romance, and to me Chicago did that hourly. It sang, I thought, and . . . I was singing with it.' In the 1930s the work of the heirs of realism, John Dos Passos, James T. Farrell, and John Steinbeck, was similarly motivated. In the same way Dreiser's contemporaries in painting were (as will be suggested in Chapter 12) using a photographic realism of manner to render scenes of urban life in which they clearly found a beauty and an attraction.

This mixture of feelings is also well exemplified in the novels of Henry James's friend and disciple, Mrs Edith Wharton (1862–1937).

Though her morality is based more on manners than James's, which rests on aesthetic taste, and though her characters do not have the subtlety and exquisite sensitivity of his, she is concerned, in novels such as *The House of Mirth* (1905), *The Custom of the Country* (1913), and *The Age of Innocence* (1920), with the consequences, often verging on tragedy, of attempts to flout social conventions. Her milieu is late nineteenth-century New York, and, while recognizing its artificiality in sketches that occasionally have a satiric bite, her attitude to it is akin to that of the hero of *The Age of Innocence* who 'honoured his own past, and mourned for it. After all, there was good in the old ways'. At the end of the novel his son tells him 'I back your generation for knowing more about each other's private thoughts than we ever have time to find out about our own'. Sensible as Edith Wharton is of the dangerously accelerating pace of life which makes introspection impossible, she is also alert to the dangers of excessive introspection to which isolation can expose the individual. *Ethan Frome* (1911) conveys the inhibiting restriction of New England village life with an intensity exceeded only by some of Robert Frost's dialogue poems, or by the poet whose original, even idiosyncratic, work is the one great exception to this chapter's generalizations.

An Individual Voice

The solitary genius of Emily Dickinson (1830–86) flowered in the small Massachusetts country town of Amherst. At a time when literature was becoming increasingly urban-oriented, she set foot in Boston, Washington, or Philadelphia on only a very few occasions in her entire life. When other writers were preoccupied with the problems of society and their relationship with it, she could say firmly: 'The Soul selects her own society – /Then – shuts the Door'. This principle she made the basis both of her life ('I could not bear to live – aloud – /The Racket shamed me so') and of her work ('Publication – is the Auction/Of the Mind of Man'). If Whitman is the great public poet of the age, she is the great private poet. When others put more emphasis on experience, realism and the observation of fact, she indulges her imagination and her verbal ingenuity sometimes to the point of whimsical eccentricity, making out of her personal thoughts and imaginings a poetry as provocatively personal in form as in content. She sent a few poems to the influential critic and editor, Thomas Wentworth Higginson, who recognized their quality but was put off by 'the very wantonness of over-statement' in them and in her letters, so that when subsequently involved in their posthumous publication he insisted on regularizing language and prosody in them to the disadvantage of both. After her death, 1775 of these poems were found in curiously sewn-together bundles of manuscript, but it was not until Thomas H. Johnson's variorum edition of 1955 that a full and reliable text appeared.

Emily Dickinson's is a deeply-felt poetry, at times metaphysical, at times surrealist, in manner; it might be epitomized in her lines "Tis Coronal – and Funeral – /Saluting – in the Road – ', for in the homeliest contexts, exuberant celebration of the excitement of living and the unsophisticated enjoyment of the natural world alternate with agonized speculation on the meaning of mortality and the significance of death. Yet, despite its occasional obscurantism and the moments when simplicity lapses embarrassingly into *simplesse*, it is essentially a tough-minded poetry, non-intellectual, yet highly critical of the anodynes of sentimental religiosity and committed to a quest for truth which at times overwhelms her but at other times achieves the ringing clarity of a mysticism like Emily Brontë's. The crucial difference between them lies in Emily Dickinson's sense of humour ('The truth I do not dare to know/I muffle with a jest'). Sometimes this is impishly perverse but, at its best, it can irradiate with freshness, quizzical individuality and insight attitudes as conventional as the sense of her own unworthiness that her Calvinist background had bred in her, or her very human uncertainties about immortality and heaven, as in the poem 'I meant to have but modest needs'. What one values most in her is her ability to render the terror of 'The Subterranean Freight/The Cellars of the Soul' with the simple directness of lines such as these:

> I do not know the man so bold
> He dare in lonely Place
> That awful stranger Consciousness
> Deliberately face

Her clipped and often cryptic style can fail her at times but can produce aphorisms as memorable as 'A Bayonet's contrition/Is nothing to the Dead', or 'Parting is all we know of heaven/And all we need of hell'.

Had she lived long enough to read Stephen Crane's powerful short story 'The Open Boat' she would have fully understood the dilemma of the shipwrecked man and 'the pathos of his situation' when he realizes 'that nature does not regard him as important, and that she feels she would not maim the universe by disposing of him'. She would have sympathized with his 'desire to confront a personification and indulge in pleas, bowed to one knee and with hands supplicant', and with his doubt as to the efficacy of such an exercise. One need not leave nineteenth-century Amherst to experience that sense of disorientation in the face of a bewildering universe (as she put it in one of her poems, 'One need not be a Chamber – to be Haunted'). More convinced than Crane of a spiritual reality, of the power of love, and of the need for faith, she also knew the reality of scepticism, doubt, and despair. It is this that commends her to the modern reader – this, and her perpetual urge to question even the reality of her own identity. Yet when that questioning is expressed in such a form as 'I felt my life with both my hands/To see if it was there' the buoyancy, the resilience and the individuality of the expression will convince him that he is listening to one of the most original and imaginative artists of an age that too often took itself too seriously and placed too low a premium on the creative imagination.

Further Reading

Note: Reference should also be made to the list of General Works at pp. 339–40 and to the General Bibliography, pp. 507–8.

Anderson, Charles R., *Stairway of Surprise: Emily Dickinson's Poetry*. New York, 1960.

Brooks, Van Wyck, *Howells: His Life and World*. New York, 1959.

——, *The Confident Years, 1885–1915*. New York, 1953.

Carter, Everett, *Howells and the Age of Realism*. Philadelphia, Pa., 1954.

Dupee, F. W., *Henry James*. New York, 1951.

Geismar, Maxwell, *Rebels and Ancestors, 1890–1915*. Boston, Mass., 1953.

Gelfant, Blanche H., *The American City Novel*. Norman, Okla., 1954.

Gibson, Donald B., *The Fiction of Stephen Crane*. Carbondale, Ill., 1968.

Ginger, Ray, *Age of Excess: the United States from 1877 to 1914*. New York, 1965.

Hart, James D., *The Popular Book: a History of America's Literary Taste*. New York, 1950.

Holloway, Jean, *Hamlin Garland: a Biography*. Austin, Texas, 1960.

Jefferson, D. W., *Henry James*. Edinburgh, 1960.

Johnson, Thomas H., *Emily Dickinson, an Interpretive Biography*. Cambridge, Mass., 1955.

LaFrance, Marston, *A Reading of Stephen Crane*. Oxford, 1971.

Levenson, J. C., *The Mind and Art of Henry Adams*. Boston, Mass., 1957.

Lynn, Kenneth S., *William Dean Howells: an American life*. New York, 1971.

Matthiessen, F. O., *Henry James: the Major Phase*. New York, 1944.

——, *Theodore Dreiser*. New York, 1951.

Moers, Ellen, *Two Dreisers: the Man and the Novelist*. London, 1970.

Nevius, Blake, *Edith Wharton: a Study of Her Fiction*. Berkeley, Calif., 1953.

Persons, Stow (ed.), *Evolutionary Thought in America*. New Haven, Conn., 1950.

Pizer, Donald, *Hamlin Garland's Early Work and Career*. Berkeley, Calif., 1960.

Putt, S. Gorley, *A Reader's Guide to Henry James*. London, 1966.

Sherwood, William Robert, *Circumference and Circumstance: Stages in the Mind and Art of Emily Dickinson*. New York, 1968.

Smith, Henry Nash (ed.), *Popular Culture and Industrialism, 1865–1890*. New York, 1967.

Stallman, R. W., *Stephen Crane: a Biography*. New York, 1968.

Walcutt, Charles C., *American Literary Naturalism: a Divided Stream*. Minneapolis, Minn., 1956.

Walton, Geoffrey, *Edith Wharton: a Critical Interpretation*. Rutherford, N. J., 1970.

Ziff, Larzer, *The American 1890s*. New York, 1967.

Fiction and Poetry Since 1918

GEOFFREY MOORE

Symbolism and the Vernacular

The two most outstanding American contributions to literature in the twentieth century have both had for their object the design of pushing forward the boundaries of communication. One has been the use of the spoken language (the 'vernacular') for artistic purposes; and the other, literary experiment (especially symbolism) in a wide variety of forms.

Both of these seemingly contradictory phenomena were already implicit in the main currents of nineteenth-century American literature. By choosing to write *Huckleberry Finn* in a first-person 'conversational' style, Mark Twain became the first novelist in the English language to use the vernacular in a great way, for he wrote entirely without the kind of prosy self-consciousness which has so often marred English attempts at the same thing. In a different mode, we may see – in *The Scarlet Letter* and *Moby-Dick* – seeds of that interest in symbolism which led the American critic, Charles Feidelson Jr., to say:

> At a time when English literature was living on the capital of romanticism and increasingly given over to unambiguous narrative and orthodox meditation, American literature had turned toward a new set of problems, growing out of a new awareness of symbolic method. In the central work of Hawthorne, Whitman, Melville, and Poe, symbolism is at once technique and theme. It is a governing principle: not a stylistic device but a point of view; not a casual subject but a pervasive presence in the literary landscape.

Symbolism, Feidelson believed, was 'the coloration taken on by the American literary mind under the pressure of American literary history', and he claimed that this same pressure had forced one kind of American writer in the nineteenth century to anticipate some of the literary experiments which were not fully realized in European literature until the twentieth century. Although there are reasons for qualifying Feidelson's claim, it is certainly true that the approach of the American writer to his material has been different from that of the European, and particularly the English, writer. Americans, on the whole, have tended to use literature for their own purposes – purposes of mysticism, soul-searching and metaphysical speculation – rather than supply the reader with a heart-warming (or -rending) tale for fireside consumption. The American writer has been less interested in people than in ideas, and this we find as markedly in the twentieth century as in the nineteenth, in spite of the former's intense and much-appreciated realism.

Where in the field of contemporary English writing can one find a novelist at once as metaphysical, as self-tortured and as comic as Saul Bellow? William Golding is the obvious example which comes to mind; but Golding is a 'sport' in the English scene, and his parables – even *The Lord of the Flies* – lack the lyrical power of *Henderson the Rain King*. One senses, reading Bellow, that something is going on under the surface; with Golding the allegory is more obvious. The American explores, the Englishman points a moral. It is the same with J. D. Salinger. *The Catcher in the Rye* may be salty with adolescent slang, but this is not the whole story. As with the majority of American novelists, fiction is for Salinger an enquiry into the mystery of human existence, and not an exposé of social behaviour. *Franny, Zooey*, and *Raise High the Roofbeam, Carpenters* are not merely tales about people, however much we may be fascinated by the saga of the Glass family; they are the means by which Salinger explores his own predicament – and ours – in relation to the eternal mysteries. The 'central' character never appears, she is only mentioned – the fat lady in Dubuque, Iowa, who has cancer, eats chocolates, and watches television all day long: 'Ah, buddy. Ah, buddy. It's Christ Himself. Christ Himself, buddy.'

But what of Hemingway, the English reader might ask, the master of action and laconic dialogue – does his work not belie the assertion that the mind of the American writer is always searching below the surface? This has been, in general, the contention of English critics – for example, Wyndham Lewis, who saw Hemingway as a 'dumb ox'. But this kind of comment shows that the writer is blind to the subtle currents of Hemingway's work. The Biblical title of his first novel, *The Sun Also Rises*, was changed by his English publishers to *Fiesta*. *The Sun Also Rises* is not about a fiesta; it is about a wounded man, a hero of our time, who does the best he can in a world he never made.

Like all Hemingway's work, it is a novel about fortitude. One does not make one's life; one works with what one finds.

And Faulkner, another novelist of realism and violence, does his work not also tell a similar story? Sights, smells, and sounds leap from Faulkner's pages, but he does not write merely in order to convey the feeling of life – although that is no mean feat in itself. It is not for nothing that Joe Christmas, the half-white, half-Negro protagonist of *Light in August*, has (like Jim Casey in *Grapes of Wrath*) the same initials as Jesus Christ, or that he is crucified at the end of the novel by a brutal National Guardsman.

These are fairly obvious instances of the contemporary American writer's interest in symbolism, but there are many others subtler yet just as clear. Nor is symbolism the only form of literary experiment in which the American writer has shown interest. John Dos Passos provided a cross-section of city life in *Manhattan Transfer* and broke the story-telling surface of the novel with 'Newsreels', 'Biographies', and 'stream of consciousness' flashbacks in the *U.S.A.* trilogy. William Faulkner began telling the story of *The Sound and the Fury* in the words of the idiot Benjy; in the second section of the novel he explored another aspect of the Compson saga through the disconnected thoughts and impressions of Quentin; in the third section he told the story from the point of view of the cynical and grasping Jason; and, in the fourth, he took the point of view of Dilsey, the Negro servant who endured and who, with her brood, kept a once-important Southern family together. As Faulkner said in an interview for *The Paris Review*:

It began with a mental picture. I didn't realize at the time it was symbolical. The picture was of the muddy seat of a little girl's drawers in a pear tree where she could see through a window where her grandmother's funeral was taking place and report what was happening to her brothers on the ground below. By the time I explained who they were and what they were doing and how her pants got muddy, I realized it would be impossible to get all of it into a short story and that it would have to be a book. And I realized the symbolism of the soiled pants, and that image was replaced by the one of the fatherless and motherless girl climbing down the rain-pipe to escape from the only home she had, where she had never been offered love or affection or understanding. I had already begun to tell it through the eyes of the idiot child since I felt that it would be more effective as told by someone capable only of knowing what happened, but not why. I saw that I had not told the story that time. I tried to tell it again, the same story through the eyes of another brother. That was still not it. I told it for the third time through the eyes of the third brother. That was still not it. I tried to gather the pieces together and fill in the gaps by making myself the spokesman. It was still not complete, not until 15 years after the book was published when I wrote as an appendix to another book the final effort to get the story told and off my mind, so that I myself could have some peace from it. It's the book I feel tenderest towards. I couldn't leave it alone, and I never could tell it right, though I tried hard and would like to try again, though I'd probably fail again.

But we have been speaking of general trends. Let us now consider the variety of American literature in the twentieth century from an historical point of view.

The Novel Between the Wars

When the First World War ended only one novelist from the pre-war period could be called outstanding from the point of view of literary merit. With the publication of *Sister Carrie*, *Jennie Gerhardt*, *The Financier*, *A Traveller at Forty*, *The Titan*, *The 'Genius'*, *Plays of the Natural and Supernatural*, *A Hoosier Holiday*, *The Hand of the Potter*, and *Free, and Other Stories*, Theodore Dreiser had established himself as one of the most powerful forces in the American novel, although he was yet to publish his greatest work, *An American Tragedy*. And yet in a sense, *An American Tragedy* was already out of date by 1925. This huge, sprawling book, crammed with literary barbarisms and chapters of Court testimony, the story of a working-class American boy, of all those who hoped for room-at-the-top and could say when they read it 'There but for the grace of God, go I', was the product of a mind and a volition nurtured in the late nineteenth century. It had little in common with the mood of the Jazz Age.

In a similar way, but less obviously so, the novels of James Branch Cabell, Sherwood Anderson, and Sinclair Lewis, like those of Edith Wharton, Willa Cather, and Ellen Glasgow, must in perspective take second place to the most significant figures of fiction in the twenties – indeed, of the whole of twentieth-century American literature – F. Scott Fitzgerald, Ernest Hemingway, and William Faulkner. It is on these that we must concentrate at the expense of a roll-call of interesting but lesser names.

In these three writers the three most representative characteristics of American fiction in the twentieth century are exemplified: in Fitzgerald, the social graces, the dash, the flair, the sheer brilliance of nuance and impression; in Hemingway, the toughness and directness of the vernacular mode made into art of the highest order; and in Faulkner, the triumph of the Southern tradition at its best. Why is it, for example, that Fitzgerald is still read with delight today whereas Dreiser, Anderson, and Lewis have fallen into comparative insignificance? It is because he, like Hemingway and Faulkner, has qualities which cause his work to rise above the local and the particular, even though, like that of all good novelists, it springs directly from his environment.

Fitzgerald began badly. *This Side of Paradise* and *The Beautiful and Damned* were best-sellers at the time but they represent the side of his writing which is least appealing. They are too self-revealing and self-indulgent, the products of a fine literary talent which had not yet found itself. Only with *The Great Gatsby* and *Tender is the Night* did Fitzgerald come into his own. The story of Jay Gatsby is told by Nick Carraway, but it is Gatsby who is Fitzgerald's *alter ego*, the boy from the Middle West who is taken into the world of the Big Rich and yet is outside it, like the small boy in Fitzgerald's own image, whose nose is pressed against the windowpane. Gatsby, whose criminal activities are mysteriously kept in the background in a positively Jamesian way, is also a high romantic. He keeps a plan of would-be Good Works like Benjamin Franklin – at least so far as his own career is concerned. He loves Daisy hopelessly and romantically. He throws huge parties and yet is forever outside them. And when he is dying at the end of the novel no one comes to his aid and few to his funeral. He is the American on his own, the heir of Natty Bumppo – but a human creature, not a Deerslayer, or Nick of the Woods, or an Ahab. And that is the great merit of Fitzgerald's novel – that he has been able to continue a great American tradition, to write mythically and symbolically, and yet preserve the social surface. The eyes of Dr Eckleburg may look over the Waste Land through which Gatsby and the Buchanans drive to their respective dooms, but Fitzgerald does not, like Melville, forget a third of the way through the book that he is writing a novel and not a metaphysical tract for troubled Christians.

Tender is the Night is at once a worse and a better book – worse because it is not an intrinsic whole like *Gatsby* and better because it is more ambitious and better written. It has, for example, none of the

Gatsby passages of romanticized fine writing which one feels were left over from the days of *This Side of Paradise*. This fine novel – which should be read in its original version – begins (as one would find in real life) with Rosemary's introduction to the world of the Divers. Dick is a psychiatrist and, like Fitzgerald, an expatriate American in the South of France. Nicole, his wife, has a dark secret, which turns out to be incest. Rosemary (the young film star) and Dick are attracted to each other, but Dick, the scientific priest – and one does not have to concoct evidence of priestly imagery – is no philanderer. The study, for study it is, is one of degeneration away from one's roots. The sensibility is perhaps finer than in any other novel of the twentieth century; it shows clearly that superb ability which Fitzgerald had of capturing the nuance of a human situation. It is as if the art of Henry James had come to fruition. And yet Fitzgerald lacked what James, for all his infuriating circumlocution, had in abundance – the staying power, the ability to seize a great theme and see it through. And so *Tender is the Night* is a flawed novel, the product of a self-destructive personality; but it is a book for which one would not willingly exchange many more perfect works.

But we, like Fitzgerald, have strayed into the thirties and perhaps that is partly why *Tender is the Night* failed. It was the mid-thirties product of a member of the Lost Generation and when it appeared, American attention was concentrated on the harrowing events of the depression years. *The Last Tycoon* and *The Crack-Up*, which appeared posthumously in the forties, reveal the psychological disorder of a man who was as much out of his element as the Twain of 'The Man That Corrupted Hadleyburg' and *What is Man?*

With Hemingway, the Lost Generation's sense of alienation took a different form. The son of a doctor, born and brought up in Oak Park, Illinois – one of the most respectably conventional of Chicago's suburbs – Hemingway turned away from the life of the city to the life of the woods. But not after the pattern of a Wordsworth or a Thoreau. It was almost as if for Hemingway the landscape was something to be used – a therapeutic agent, as it is in 'Big Two-Hearted River'. Like T. F. Powys in another country, he saw the maggot in the wood and violence in the animal world. Nick is 'initiated' when he discovers that the Indian husband has quietly slit his throat while his wife is undergoing a Caesarian performed with a jacknife. Unnecessary brutality? Sensationalism? Perhaps. But one must remember that Hemingway grew up in that world of mealy-mouthed primness for which the smaller settlements of the Middle West were famous. Between Oak Park's hypocrisy and the senseless gang warfare of Cicero, there was no choice. Hemingway took another way out – the way of stoicism. You accepted your lot and worked, if you could, to get out of a bad situation, but you did not grumble. Whatever job you did, you did well – or left it for something better. But this toughness masked a sensitivity much above average. 'The three with the medals were like hunting-hawks;' he says in 'In Another Country', 'and I was not a hawk, although I might seem a hawk to those who have never hunted. . . .'

As a reporter for the *Kansas City Star* Hemingway had the advantage of a good paper and a good editor. But, judging from his High School stories, the famous style was formed, if not forged, before he became a reporter. There are few writers who show such consistency. Of Hemingway, more than most writers, it can be said that the style is the man himself. In ambulance service with the Italian Army during the First World War, he was badly wounded in the knee, and this traumatic experience was to provide, both realistically and symbolically, much of the material for his later writing. As an expatriate newspaperman in Paris he wrote in his spare time and the first result was *Three Stories and Ten Poems* and the second *in our time* – of which the first, unspoken, words are those of the Prayer Book, 'Give us peace'. It was a typical Hemingway irony, since the stories (like the one about Nick Adams and the Indian) are interspersed with gruesome and violent incidents of war, which have in them something of the pity and terror of Wilfred Owen.

There is no comment. And that is the beginning and end of the Hemingway method. Everything is suggested; nothing stated. We are at the farthest remove from the Victorian 'he expostulated vehemently' kind of style. The expression is laconic, clipped, bare to the point of over-simplicity, the product of a deliberate act of self-abnegation. As Hemingway said in *Death in the Afternoon*, the style is like an iceberg, one-fifth of which is above the water, four-fifths below. And if you do not read Hemingway's work more carefully than you would a newspaper you miss not only the mastery of the prose style but also the world of reference and meaning which is implicit in every paragraph.

Hemingway's first and perhaps his greatest novel was *The Sun Also Rises*, which on the surface is a story of disillusioned expatriates in Paris after the First World War. And yet, as has been pointed out in the general introduction, Jake Barnes is more than a newspaperman who has been sexually wounded in the war. He is the symbol of a generation – perhaps of a personal tragedy common to many. As Willy Loman is to Oedipus, so Jake Barnes is to the Fisher King – that tragic figure of myth whom, three years earlier, T. S. Eliot had made the chief character of *The Waste Land*. But, as E. M. Halliday suggests, of symbolism in the sense of *The Scarlet Letter* or *Moby-Dick* there is none. Hemingway worked through irony, and the book is a masterpiece by reason of the sheer excellence of the 'factual' recording. The words, seemingly unpoetic, are so faultlessly and brilliantly chosen that the communication they make can only be called poetic – if by poetry we understand the art of succinct and compressed expression of the human situation.

By the end of the twenties, Hemingway had produced one more novel, *A Farewell to Arms*, the star-crossed story of Frederic Henry and Catherine Barkley set against a background of war in Italy. He had also written a parody of Sherwood Anderson (*Torrents of Spring*), and a second volume of short stories, *Men Without Women* – if *in our time* be accounted the first.

The third and greatest member of the trio of important novelists in the twenties worked in a different way. Where Hemingway compressed, pared, reduced, William Faulkner enlarged and adumbrated, circling round his quarry like one of the hound dogs of whom he was so fond. And yet his method, which in description sounds so refined, comes out on the page as quite another thing. It was, to put it bluntly, because Faulkner's writing had guts as well as brilliance. Not that this was as apparent as all that in his first novel, *Soldiers' Pay*. This had a hint in it of the Georgian romanticism of *The Marble Faun*, a volume of poems and his first publication. *Mosquitoes* has something of the quality of the title about it. But in 1929 there began, with the publication of *Sartoris*, and of *The Sound and the Fury* and *As I Lay Dying* in 1930, what literary historians are pleased to call the 'Yoknapatawpha saga'.

The 'Yoknapatawpha saga' is so called because it deals in devious and sometimes mystifying ways with the history of a mythical county in a state of the deep South. This state is taken to be based on Faulkner's home state of Mississippi and Jefferson, its capital, on Oxford. That Faulkner should choose, for most of his life, to work in such detail on this theme is part of his strength, for his work is instinct with the spirit of the South – the South with its romanticism, its gothicism and, at the same time, its earthy actuality.

The Sound and the Fury is always said to be Faulkner's greatest work (the other chief contender is *Absalom, Absalom* which appeared in 1936) and, a little reluctantly, one agrees. Reluctantly, not because of any great fault in the novel but because Faulkner's achievement lies in the totality of his oeuvre – the saga as a whole.

The Sound and the Fury is the story of the Compson family – once grand, now decayed – whose mainstay is Dilsey the Negro servant, to whom the last section of the novel is devoted. The first three sections are devoted to the monologues of Benjy, the idiot son – the last-born sold into Egypt; Quentin, who loved his sister Caddy – although not carnally; and Jason, the earthy, penny-pinching curmudgeon of a brother who comments diabolically and wittily on the scandalous conduct of the other members of the family. There is no explanation. As Gide once said, it is the method of the '*roman policier dans la tragédie grècque*'. We are plunged into the intricate monologue of the idiot, who has been castrated for a supposed attack on a neighbour's wife, his story being realistic yet impregnated with symbolic references. Quentin, whose interior monologue occupies the second section, is a psycho-pathic case; his section is the richest and most ambitious of the four. In Jason's account (for we see the story from varying points of view) Faulkner's humour, which is so apparent in 'Spotted Horses', comes out clearly. Dilsey shows the statuesque dignity, the Christian resignation and the strength which is so lacking in the white family. It is Faulkner's ironic comment on the history of the South. This is what led him to make the Negro Lucas Beauchamp the hero of *Intruder in the Dust*.

As I Lay Dying is equally quixotic and, to the uninitiated, at first incomprehensible. Also told from several points of view, it tells of a poor white family whose mother and mainstay dies. The book is an account of how they take her back to the family burial ground, her body stinking in the August sun of Mississippi. It was not unreasonable of the general public to find this book, at first blush, unacceptable, or for Faulkner in a fit of exasperation to write another which would really shock them into reading him. This was *Sanctuary*, 'written for money' and published in 1931. But a great writer cannot write badly even when he writes 'for money' and the novel is as good as, for example, *No Orchids for Miss Blandish* – that British pastiche of Faulkner and James M. Cain – is bad.

At the end of the thirties, therefore, the mood was changing. In the twenties America still did not know where she stood. In *The Great Gatsby*, for example, we still see the influence of Britain. 'He's an

Oggsford man' presumably still meant something to Fitzgerald's audience in 1925. It meant nothing to the public which bought *The Grapes of Wrath* in such numbers.

But between *The Grapes of Wrath* and the period of which we have been speaking there lies almost a decade and Steinbeck was not the only writer to loom large. Perhaps the most impressive figure was John Dos Passos who, although his work began in 1920 with *One Man's Initiation* and continued with *Three Soldiers* in 1921 and *Manhattan Transfer* in 1925, did not really come into his own until 1930, with the publication of *The 42nd Parallel*.

This, the first book of the *U.S.A.* trilogy, was followed by *1919* in 1932 and *The Big Money* in 1936. Another 'saga' – this time of American life itself, rather than of a section of it – it covers the period from 1900 to about 1930. In it Dos Passos attempted the panoramic view. He communicated his sense of the multifariousness and at the same time the oneness of life in the United States by four methods. The 'story' is related in the accounts of the lives of 'Mac', 'Vag', or 'J. Ward Moore-house', that is, men and women taken from differing and representative walks of American life. 'Intercalated' with the story are the 'biographies', the 'News Reels', and the 'Camera Eye' sections. The biographies are of famous or infamous Americans, such as Ford, Debs, Veblen, or Valentino. The 'News Reels' provide a panorama of life at the time, taken from headlines or snatches of popular song. Under the rather curious heading of 'Camera Eye' Dos Passos attempts to convey a variety of things, either personal, sensitive – and sometimes over-written – impressions, or reflections on the accounts in the other sections.

The *U.S.A.* trilogy bestrides the thirties and yet it deals with a period which was over when the decade started. For all his detail, his knowledge and his grasp of the facts of the American scene, Dos Passos failed to write a book which moves the reader. The characters seldom come to life, their motives are crass or pathetic, they lack precisely what Steinbeck's characters have in too great an abundance.

Steinbeck first began to be known with the publication of *Tortilla Flat* (1935), *In Dubious Battle* (1936), and *Of Mice and Men* (1937), but it was *The Grapes of Wrath* which made him world-famous. This (yet another) 'saga' of the Okies – for sagas so many of these America-conscious novels demand to be called – tells of a dispossessed family in the 'Dust Bowl', who pile their belongings on an ancient Ford and make for California. In this modern exodus, a secular journey to the

Promised Land, the events incidental to the trip are treated with such compassion and understanding of human motive that one can forgive the occasional lapse into sentimentality and the over-simplicity of the character drawing. Like so many of the novels and poems of the thirties, *The Grapes of Wrath* has a political motive – unconscious, we may allow, since Steinbeck denied it. The people have hearts of gold and the bosses are worse than Simon Legree. It is the mood of 'We will fight them in the streets . . .' Moved by the tragedy of the Depression, America's writers were driven, through compassion, into antagonism, and the literary pendulum swung wide. There is no body of writing in the whole of American literature more consistently on one note than that of the thirties. And yet the writers of that decade are not in spirit at odds with their ancestors. Throughout almost all of its history, America's greatest writers have found themselves opposed to the society from which they sprang.

One exception to the prevailing political preoccupation was the work of Thomas Wolfe. Wolfe is one of those amphibians of American literature whose books are difficult to classify. They are no more 'novels' than *Moby-Dick* is a novel – if *Pride and Prejudice* or *Vanity Fair* be taken as yardsticks. But whereas *Moby-Dick* is a tract for the times, *Look Homeward, Angel*, *Of Time and the River*, *The Web and the Rock*, and *You Can't Go Home Again* are naked autobiography. What is more, Wolfe – like Dreiser, another novelist who, one feels, could just as easily have been an impresario – writes extremely badly. Extremely badly and extremely well. There are passages in Wolfe – like the account of Eugene Gant in the schoolroom (*Look Homeward, Angel*) or the Oxford clergyman in *You Can't Go Home Again* – so superbly descriptive that one exclaims with pleasure. Yet interspersed with this brilliance there are passages of repetitious cataloguing and sentimental claptrap. And so profound are the depths of American bad taste that his more sentimental effusions have been collected into a volume entitled *The Poetry of Thomas Wolfe*. The truth is, probably, that Wolfe did not know whether he was writing well or badly. He put it all down, pouring out his soul on hundreds of sheets of yellow paper as he wrote on the top of his refrigerator (containing only beer, of course). Some-one else could clear up the mess. And that someone was Maxwell Perkins, his editor at Scribners who, with the aid of one of that faithful team whom American publishers employ and English publishers refuse to stand the cost of, moulded and shaped the incoherent mass of Wolfean verbal effluent.

And yet one would not do without this great character, exasperating though he is – any more than one would do without Dreiser. Also, apart from the intrinsic merit and sheer exuberance of Wolfe's better writing, there is a sense in which, like Edwards and Franklin in the eighteenth century, his 'tradition' and the Jamesian one represent the two faces of the American literary coin. There are – as Fitzgerald pointed out to Wolfe in a fascinating exchange of letters – the 'putters-in' and the 'takers-out'. The United States has her share of both, but perhaps partly because of the sheer size and newness of the continent and the sense which the American writer has of communicating through a megaphone, there are more of the former than the latter. The urge is to get it all down, to number every flower, railroad-tie and turn of phrase in those United States until the pen drops from exhausted fingers. People won't know unless you shout, just as people won't know that you have crossed the Atlantic or hit the target nine times out of ten unless you can put a medal on your chest to prove it. Henry James had touched on this, as witness the following passage between Henrietta Stackpole and Lord Warburton:

> 'Do you know you're the first lord I've ever seen?' she said very promptly to her neighbour. 'I suppose you think I'm awfully benighted.'
>
> 'You've escaped seeing some very ugly men,' Lord Warburton answered, looking a trifle absently about the table.
>
> 'Are they very ugly? They try to make us believe in America that they're all handsome and magnificent and that they wear wonderful robes and crowns.'
>
> 'Ah, the robes and crowns are gone out of fashion,' said Lord Warburton, 'like your tomahawks and revolvers.'

Before we leave the thirties it must be recorded that the so-called 'novelists of the twenties' (obviously no writer fits neatly into any one decade in this way) continued to produce – although in a different vein. Fitzgerald's *Tender is the Night* has been referred to. Hemingway's contributions were *Death in the Afternoon* (1932) – an informative yet extremely personal account of bullfighting with interspersed commentary on life and the art of writing; *Green Hills of Africa* (1935), a story with similar comments (two volumes of short stories came in between); *To Have and Have Not* (1937) – a disaster and an indication of how true it was that Hemingway was his own worst imitator; a play, the collected short stories and – at the end of the decade – *For*

Whom the Bell Tolls. This novel, which is often taken by those who do not understand what Hemingway was about, to be his best, is as hollow as *The Old Man and the Sea* was to turn out to be. The reason is that both were the result of Hemingway's listening to his critics. Ostensibly, of course, the story of *For Whom the Bell Tolls* is a fine one, and it certainly made a better film than *The Old Man and the Sea*. But Hemingway could not write well unless he was writing from life. Unlike Wolfe, he changed and pared and shaped his material, but finally he had to follow what he felt in his heart. *For Whom the Bell Tolls* he felt in his head. He loved the Spanish people, he was moved by the Civil War and he listened to the voice of the period which told him that Great Novelists should write on great themes. However, the characters in *For Whom the Bell Tolls* do not really live in the sense that Jake Barnes, Brett and Robert Cohn live. Pablo, Pilar, even Anselmo, and Jordan himself, are stock characters compared with the real-life people in *The Sun Also Rises*. Also, Hemingway could not portray women (Maria) successfully because he did not, or did not want to, understand women. There is, in other words, a certain truth in Leslie Fiedler's theory in *Love and Death in the American Novel*, although one would wish Fiedler's theories to have been directed less towards the possible homosexual implications of this phenomenon than towards the solid and historical reasons for the attitude of the American male towards women.

Faulkner's contribution to the literature of the thirties had – as might be expected – little to do with politics or the state of American society. The state of the South, perhaps, but then only in a devious way, with reference to the history of its past. *Light in August* (1932), *Absalom, Absalom* (1936), and *The Hamlet* (1940) are about the South as it was and as it is – its legacy of carpet-bagging and Walter Scott romanticism, its pro-white brutalism and its Negro suffering. But in another sense they are not 'about' anything. What is important is Faulkner's superb sense of style, his rhetorical grasp of the fine mad possibilities of the English language. His Shakespearian flow of phrase, the magnificent periods of his prose, are interspersed with the earthy actuality of his groundling characters. One is caught up in the language itself. Everything is heightened, enlarged. The writing is not sur-real but super-real, so that the old question 'Is Faulkner a realistic novelist or is he a symbolic one?' begs itself. Symbolic in parts, yes – although when he wrote an overtly symbolical book, *A Fable*, in 1954 he failed completely. His South is not the real South but it is also not dream-country like the land of *The Scarlet Letter*. The stories and novels, in other words, are not written for their symbolism – that emerges out of the carefully woven mesh of events and character-studies which makes the book come alive. Caddy's 'drawers', for example (see Faulkner's comments in the introductory remarks), are not 'symbolic' in the sense that the scarlet 'A' of Hawthorne's novel is symbolic.

Since the contribution, not only of Sinclair Lewis but also of such 'neo-naturalists' as Farrell and Caldwell, has been played down in favour of that of the indisputably great novelists of the between-wars period, it might seem invidious to end with one whose name has previously been unmentioned. However, in the light of present-day satirical trends, the vogue of 'black humour', and the influence of the theatre of the absurd, the work of Nathanael West assumes an importance far beyond that which it had at the time. Although *The Dream Life of Balso Snell* (1931) explored a world as unlocated as any conceived by Poe, West, in his best novel, *Miss Lonelyhearts* (1933), projected an almost Kafka-like study of anguish through the persona of the writer of an 'agony' column. *A Cool Million* (1934) was followed by *The Day of the Locust* (1939). Using the setting of Hollywood's 'dream factory', West's last novel foreshadowed attitudes of mind which were to become all too familiar during the next seven years.

The Novel Since 1940

Two novelists who had been writing for some time came into their own in the forties. James Gould Cozzens had published *S.S. San Pedro* in 1931, *The Last Adam* in 1933, and *Men and Brethren* in 1936; but it was with the appearance of *The Just and the Unjust* (1942) and *Guard of Honour* (1948) that he became recognized as an unusually talented writer. *By Love Possessed*, a product of the fifties, was by comparison over-written. Robert Penn Warren, a younger member of the Fugitive group (see below, p. 412) and a university teacher, had also published two novels, *Night Rider* in 1939 and *At Heaven's Gate* in 1943, but it was *All The King's Men* (1946) which brought him into prominence in this field. Based on the career of Huey Long, the notorious Governor of Louisiana, this novel had the power and dramatic force which Warren's earlier work had lacked. However, the outstanding new talent of the forties was Norman Mailer. *The Naked and the Dead* appeared in 1948 and Mailer has never produced anything quite like it since. Written in his early twenties, it has all the quality of a first book, yet something more besides. The scope is large, the cross-section of American life ambitious, and the language highly realistic of the Pacific campaign in which Mailer served.

However, it was not until the fifties that the full force of Mailer's contribution became apparent. Although *Barbary Shore* (1951) was a failure, *The Deer Park* (1955) was not – although it is difficult to say precisely why. Ostensibly, it is a story of sex and sensationalism in the Californian film world, but the book lives through the character of Sergius O'Shaughnessy, who was to be the protagonist of *Advertisements for Myself* (not so much a novel as a way of life). There is, in fact, something of Hemingway in Mailer, although their styles are radically different. There is Hemingway's toughness and also the feeling that Mailer cannot write well unless he is writing about himself. *The Naked and the Dead* apart, the central characters are all unashamedly Mailer and as time goes by he emerges simply as himself. Even the occasional novel, like *An American Dream*, which is thrown into the mélange of 'philosophy' and brilliant reportage, turns out to be an account of Mailer in his favourite role – that of the man of power behind the scenes, the President's confidant ('Jack' to him), the successful murderer of unwanted wives, and the prodigious sexual athlete. Throughout all the more recent work there is an extraordinary concentration on smell, so that this becomes a device, a convention far beyond the realistic, conveying what the antennae sense.

If we compare the fiction of the years after the Second World War with that produced during the period between the First and the Second (nearly a quarter of a century in each case) we find an extraordinary difference. Whereas in the first period at least three great names emerge: those of Fitzgerald, Hemingway and Faulkner, with Dreiser, Anderson, Lewis, Steinbeck, Dos Passos and Wolfe achieving a distinction almost as great, we find that in the latter there are only two with a claim to similar stature. One is Mailer, the other Saul Bellow. For a time it seemed as if J. D. Salinger would go on to greater work after *The Catcher in the Rye* (1951), but although the history of the remarkable Glass family (*Nine Stories*, 1953, *Franny and Zooey*, 1961, and the subsequent *Raise High the Roofbeam, Carpenters* and *Seymour: an Introduction*) made something of an impact, the style – and apparently the impetus – began to degenerate.

Bellow is another matter. His first two short novels, *Dangling Man* (1944) and *The Victim* (1947) revealed the mind of the man – complicated, introspective, sensitive. It was therefore something of a shock to be presented with the huge, picaresque, many-charactered *Adventures of Augie March* in 1953. This novel revealed Bellow's gift for comedy and the richness of his language, and yet, below the surface – however much he might attempt to turn his mind from personality and the nuances of thought – the old Bellow is still there. The same is true of *Henderson the Rain King* (1959). On the surface, it is the story of a huge man who dominates his universe, goes to Africa, becomes Rainmaker for a tribe and attempts to dominate theirs. But what starts in reality ends in fantasy, and fantasy is half Bellow's world. *Herzog* (1961) revealed this clearly. Herzog, the teacher, is beset by metaphysical speculations. He has the world on his mind. Bellow, in other words, is interested not so much in character and event, the interplay of the human comedy, as in his own problems. In being this kind of novelist he is in a great American tradition, the tradition which began with *The Scarlet Letter* and *Moby-Dick*, in which the novel becomes a platform for quarrelling with God or one's own history.

It is here that we perceive an interesting, almost a fantastic link of several strands. That Bellow, the Canadian Jew, the adopted American, should use the novel in a similar way to the Anglo-Saxon Protestants of the nineteenth century arises partly from something endemic in the American environment and partly from his own nature. The Jew suffered, the gentile suffered, each in his different way. The intellectual climate of America in the nineteenth century was not conducive to the production of a *Vanity Fair* or a *Middlemarch*; the Americans of that period felt moved to harangue their fellow countrymen and debate with themselves. And at the end of the line came the Jew with his personal preoccupations and his legacy of suffering, to carry on the tradition in the twentieth century. 'The Jewish novel in America' is now a popular, if somewhat overplayed, theme for the aspiring Ph.D.s who labour in the groves of American academe. From Henry Roth and Nathanael West to Mailer, Philip Roth, Bernard Malamud, Saul Bellow, and the half-Jewish Salinger, it is the Jews who have regenerated the American novel, bringing to it not only the cry of the *schlemiel* and the prophet, but their extraordinary sensitivity for human motive, the hot-house world of the Jewish relationship, the Jewish family. Philip Roth, whose *Goodbye Columbus* and *Letting Go* brought him understandable acclaim, achieved fame and notoriety with *Portnoy's Complaint* (1969), an epic of masturbation and mother-domination.

The Jews and the Negroes. If the sixties can be called the decade of the Jew in America, the seventies may well be the decade of the Negro. The change in the type and status of Negro writing since Charles W. Chesnutt published *The House Behind the Cedars* or Zora Neale Hurston *Their Eyes Were Watching God*, reflects the change in the attitude of black Americans towards white Americans. It began to be apparent in the work of Willard Motley, William Attaway, Chester Himes, Ann Petry, and particularly of Richard Wright (*Native Son*, 1940 and *Black Boy*, 1945). But it was Ralph Ellison's *Invisible Man* (1952) which first brought the sufferings of black Americans into prominence in a great way. Since then the note has become shriller and more antagonistic. Since *Go Tell it on the Mountain* (1953), a story of religious experience in Harlem, James Baldwin has turned more and more to invective and polemic. The world of Leroi Jones and Eldridge Cleaver is the world of Black Power.

In recounting, even so briefly, the main trends of American fiction since the Second World War, the recent interest shown in Jewish and Negro writing should not blind the student of the period to the fact that other things were happening during this time. For one, the older novelists continued to produce – although hardly as successfully as before. Hemingway, who died in 1961, brought out *Across the River and Into the Trees* in 1950 and *The Old Man and the Sea* in 1952. Although the latter was a far better piece of writing – more an extended short story than a novel – it contrasted vividly with the actuality of his last book, *A Moveable Feast*, published in 1964. This is reminiscent of the style of the early stories and shows clearly that Hemingway ought never to have abandoned his true métier – that of conveying 'the way it was'. 'True' and 'truly' were his favourite words, and the ring of truth is as present in the early work as it is lacking in the epic pretentiousness of *For Whom the Bell Tolls* and *The Old Man and the Sea* – however worthy or ambitious their subjects might be.

That other stalwart of the between-wars period, William Faulkner, produced after *The Hamlet* and among other books, *Go Down, Moses* (1942), *Intruder in the Dust* (1948), *Requiem for a Nun* (1951), *A Fable* (1954), *The Town* (1957), *The Mansion* and *The Reivers* (1962). The last three were particularly interesting, carrying on as they did into comparatively recent times the story of the infamous Snopes family and other larger-than-life characters of the Yoknapatawpha township.

One should also remember that, in addition to *The Naked and the Dead*, the number of war novels produced in the late forties and fifties was much larger than after the First World War – although none of them had quite the originality of E. E. Cummings's *The Enormous Room* (1922). The best of them were John Hersey's *A Bell for Adano* (1944), John Horne Burns's *The Gallery* (1947), and Irwin Shaw's *The Young Lions* (1948).

For a period at the end of the war, it seemed as if American fiction was moving into what might be called 'The Age of Buechner'. A number of new novelists, among them Gore Vidal and Truman Capote, struck a fine fastidious note which continued well into the fifties. That Vidal should turn to the sexual fantasy of *Myra Breckenridge* and Capote to the terrifying reportage of *In Cold Blood* is as much indicative of the changed temper of the sixties as of their personal predilections. This 'changed-temper' had already been heralded by the work of Jack Kerouac and William Burroughs. But it was the success of *Catch-22* in 1961 which really made it clear which way the wind was blowing. Joseph Heller's cynical, semi-surrealistic fantasia expressed an attitude towards World War II which would not have been possible twenty, or even ten, years before. For readers who were disconcerted by Heller's cavalier transitions between fact and fantasy, however, Kurt Vonnegut's *Slaughterhouse Five* (1969) provided a far more substantial and convincing indictment of war. Vonnegut had started by flirting with the world of science fiction, but the glimpse of the world of the future which he gave his readers in *Player Piano* (1960) and *The Sirens of Titan* (1961) was replaced by the more mellow mood of *God Bless You, Mr. Rosewater* (1965). He continued in the 1970s (*Breakfast of Champions*, 1973) to expose the follies and absurdities of contemporary society.

Ken Kesey and Richard Brautigan are writers whose satire is more firmly anchored to the real world. Kesey's *One Flew over the Cuckoo's Nest* (1962) and Brautigan's *Trout Fishing in America* (1967) are two of the most forward-looking novels of the 1960s. John Barth achieved an early success with *The Sotweed Factor* (1960), an extravaganza built round the life and 'epic' poem of Ebenezer Cook. *Giles Goat-Boy* (1966), however, is spoilt by too academic a complexity. Of comparable erudition, Thomas Pynchon's *V* played a brilliant game with the notion of a symbolic letter, although the 'entropic' use of 'V' seems to owe as much to the example of Joyce as it does to that of Hawthorne. In *The Crying of Lot 69* Pynchon continued to exploit his sense of life as a series of chaotic coincidences. Another experimentalist is John Hawkes, who seems to owe a great deal to dadaism and surrealism.

However, the considerable literary pretension of *The Lime Twig* (1960) was less obtrusive in *The Second Skin* (1964), the central character of which is a contemporary example of the Ishmael-type of nineteenth-century American fiction.

In the 1950s and '70s few of the younger novelists sought even to preserve a semblance of the realism which had been the pride of the American novel since the late nineteenth century. John Updike and James Purdy did make an attempt, but the mood of the age seemed to be against them. During this period there loomed over the American scene two giants of fiction who, although neither of them was American by birth, wielded an influence far greater than that of any native-born citizen: the great contemporary interest in the 'lexical playfields' of Vladimir Nabokov and Jorge Luis Borges came, suggested Tony Tanner quoting Borges, from 'inner unrest ... inspired by the phenomenon of the outside world'.

The Short Story

What has been responsible for the unprecedented development of the short story in America? For one thing, the presence of a large number of magazines. But perhaps a deeper reason may be adduced from the number of American stories which, by reason of their tone and intention, are worthy to be called 'poetic'. They seek, through concrete detail, to suggest universal truth; they are compressed; their words and phrases are the result of the kind of attention which a poet gives to his vocabulary and effects. This is true, in the present century, of even so 'tough' a writer as Ernest Hemingway, and it is certainly true of Faulkner, Steinbeck, and Caldwell. The literary allegiances, professed and unprofessed, of Hemingway afford another insight into the patterns of the American short story. In *Green Hills of Africa* he maintained that he had been chiefly influenced by Mark Twain, Henry James, and Stephen Crane. Whether or not this is a fact, it is clear, from circumstantial evidence, that he was also affected by Sherwood Anderson and Gertrude Stein. These influences point up several interesting things: first, how natural it now is for an American writer to think in terms of his *own* literature, which has developed in response to specifically American conditions and, second, how important the idea of the 'vernacular' has been in the American short story. For both Anderson and Stein were, in their own ways, trying to realize that fundamental literary aim of a democratic people which Tocqueville had noted in *Democracy in America* – to make art out of the people's speech and the people's condition. Finally, the presence of James and Crane in Hemingway's list as well as Mark Twain illuminates the fact that nuance, subtlety and impression are not necessarily excluded by even the most rigorous realism.

If, indeed, ranging over that distinguished list of American short story writers in the twentieth century – which includes Sherwood Anderson, William Carlos Williams, Ring Lardner, Conrad Aiken, William March, Katherine Anne Porter, James Thurber, Caroline Gordon, Scott Fitzgerald, William Faulkner, Stephen Vincent Benét, Ernest Hemingway, John Steinbeck, Thomas Wolfe, Erskine Caldwell, James T. Farrell, Robert Penn Warren, John O'Hara, William Saroyan, Eudora Welty, Irwin Shaw, Carson McCullers, Wallace Stegner, Peter Taylor, Jean Stafford, Paul Bowles, J. D. Salinger, Flannery O'Connor, and John Updike – the enquiring reader attempts to pick out the main features which characterize the American short story, he would probably find that, as in the novel, the evidence of successful amalgamation of 'paleface' and 'redskin' characteristics was the most significant feature – in other words, a combination of Jamesian subtlety of reference and atmosphere with an informal 'vernacular' vocabulary and syntax. A second characteristic would be the interest in presenting, vividly yet with superb economy, the 'sensuous immediacy' of a scene or situation. A third would be a widespread tendency to objectivity of presentation. Instead of 'talking about' the situation in an omniscient way, Anderson, Hemingway, Steinbeck, Faulkner, and Caldwell keep themselves in the background and content themselves with suggesting what they wish to convey. There is also marked skill in dealing with the adolescent and the ordinary man (Lardner, Saroyan, Thurber) and, going further in this direction, an interest in presenting individuals on the periphery of human society – even violent, or semi-primitive characters (Anderson, Williams, Lardner, Faulkner, Hemingway, Steinbeck, Caldwell, Farrell, McCullers, O'Connor). Finally, a tendency towards the first person might be noted, a device adopted for the sake of conveying authenticity – that air of 'it actually happened' which assumes such a special validity in the context of American cultural development. It would not be an exaggeration to say that in the hands of contemporary American writers the short story had been given that new dimension of which Hemingway spoke. Attention has been focused, not on 'ideal Beauty' but on the realities of existence, the relation of Man to his environment, on that other kind of beauty which filled Whitman with such ineffable joy when he watched – and accepted – the foibles as well as the joys of human existence.

Poetry: the Break with Convention

The great break with convention, the *annus mirabilis* of American poetry, is often said to be 1912, when Harriet Monroe founded the magazine *Poetry* in Chicago. This not only marked the beginning of the so-called 'Middle Western Renaissance' (meaning that Miss Monroe printed and encouraged the Middle Western poets, Carl Sandburg, Edgar Lee Masters, and Vachel Lindsay); it also showed the new eclecticism of American verse. In the early pages of *Poetry* we may find the work of poets as dissimilar as Edwin Arlington Robinson, T. S. Eliot, Ezra Pound, and Wallace Stevens.

It was, in fact, Pound and Eliot who were the great 'instigators' of American – and, indeed, of all modern – poetry. They broke decisively with the insipid tradition of late-nineteenth-century romanticism, with the poetasting of Bliss Carman, Richard Hovey, and 'the sweet singer of Michigan'. There is a lot of Pound in the manifesto of Imagism, an Anglo-American movement produced under the aegis of another influential literary figure of the years before the First World War, Amy Lowell:

(1) To use the language of common speech, but to employ always the *exact* word, not the merely decorative word.

(2) To create new rhythms – as the expression of new moods. We do not insist upon 'free verse' as the only method of writing poetry. . . . We do believe that the individuality of a poet may often be better expressed in free verse than in conventional forms.

(3) To allow absolute freedom in the choice of a subject.

(4) To present an image (hence the name 'Imagist'). We are not a school of painters, but we believe that poetry should render particulars exactly and not deal in vague generalities, however magnificent and sonorous.

(5) To produce poetry that is hard and clear, never blurred or indefinite.

(6) Finally, most of us believe that concentration is the very essence of poetry.

Pound's spirit, however, could not – any more than Wordsworth's in his time – be bounded by the rigidity of a theory. Only, perhaps, in the work of H.D. do we find Imagism unclouded by personality. But personality – T. S. Eliot notwithstanding – is what makes the work of a poet distinctive. Pound's distinctions could be seen from the first. He 'struck through the mask'; he showed that poetry was life and not merely a part of life; and he insisted on the greatest models and the highest traditions. He was – like so many other American literary artists – the teacher *par excellence*. The mantle of the prophet was on him; he came, like some poetic messiah, to show the way.

And show the way he did, to generations of poets who did not wish to cling to the outworn conventions and stereotyped subjects of the past. One, in particular, who was indebted to him was T. S. Eliot, for whom he was 'il miglior fabbro', the man who helped forge *The Waste Land* into its present style. But there were others who had reason to be grateful to Pound – and not merely in a literary way. He was the great befriender, scornful of hypocrisy, but genuinely helpful to all who needed help. Whatever antagonistic things might be said about him – his un-American activities during the Second World War, his concentration on a private history of the West, his anti-Semitism – one cannot fault him in friendship or generosity. In *Personae: The Collected Poems* (1926) the best of the early lyrical Pound may be seen. And then, in successive batches, the great work of his life appeared: *A Draft of XVI Cantos* in 1925, *Cantos 17–27* in 1928, *A Draft of XXX Cantos* in 1930, up to the *Pisan Cantos* (74–84) in 1948, *Section: Rock-Drill, 85–95 de los Cantares* (1956), and *Thrones; 96–109 de los Cantares* in 1960.

Pound was not the only modern American poet to adopt the epic mode. His contemporary, William Carlos Williams, devoted a good part of his life to *Paterson*, Eliot to *The Four Quartets*, Hart Crane to *The Bridge*, and Wallace Stevens to a number of long poems, of which *Notes Toward a Supreme Fiction* was the most ambitious. It was as if there was something in the American air which demanded the great theme and the arduous task – a phenomenon which was also noted in the novel. Where Whitman had shown the way, the Americans of the first half of the twentieth century were led to follow – although with qualifications. 'I make a pact with you, Walt Whitman' said Pound. *The Cantos* – larger by far than *Song of Myself* – are also about America and the New Man, although Pound's method of approach is radically different from Whitman's. Crane's bridge was intended to span nations and psyches as well as the American continent. And what are Eliot's *Four Quartets* and Stevens's *Notes Toward a Supreme Fiction* but songs of their respective selves, each as quietly American, in its own way, as Whitman's was brashly so? Each poet is working towards those spiritual imperatives which were laid on him by the very fact of being an American in the twentieth century. Eliot's religious conclusion is as personal as Stevens's, although he chose to remain within the Anglican Church. In his very didacticism, his reaching out towards his spiritual masters rather than towards local and particular gods, Eliot showed that he was a man of the New World.

But we must not forget, in speaking of the early period in modern American poetry, to mention some other names which are also very important. If Robinson and Frost are bracketed, it is for the same basic reason that one brackets Sandburg, Lindsay, and Masters. The first two were New Englanders and the last three Middle Westerners. And, indeed, there is something in common between Robinson and Frost beyond the circumstances of their birth. Not only do both show the hardness, the grimness of their New England inheritance, but also both were steeped in the classics.

Robinson, being the older man, is more conventional in his style and subject matter. He had begun publishing as early as 1897 (*Children of the Night*), and some of his best-known poems – 'Richard Cory', 'Isaac and Archibald', 'Miniver Cheevy', 'For a Dead Lady', and 'The Man Against the Sky' – appeared in books published in the early 1900s (*Captain Craig*, 1902, *The Town Down the River*, 1910, and *The Man Against the Sky*, 1916). After this, his main books were *Merlin* (1917), two more long Arthurian poems, *Lancelot* in 1920 and *Tristram* in 1927, *Avon's Harvest* (1921), *The Man Who Died Twice* (1924), *Dionysus in Doubt* (1925), *Cavender's House* (1929), and *The Glory of the Nightingales* (1930) – although five more were published before he died, in 1935, and *Hannibal Brown* appeared the year after his death.

Robinson has always had more of a reputation in the United States than in Europe. Englishmen, in particular, have been slow to recognize the true qualities of this 'good gray poet' – mainly, perhaps, because he had none of the bravura of Stevens, the sophisticated erudition of Pound or the educated cosmopolitanism of Eliot. Perhaps another reason has been that the others to some extent 'made it new' – even Frost, who, seemingly so homespun and simple, conceals the barb beneath his image of everyman's class valedictorian. There is nothing intrinsically attractive about Robinson. He is gloomy without the tragic power of a Hardy; his pessimism is more real, and therefore less appealing, than the magnificently-turned felicities of Housman. Yet, in recent years, there are signs that this neglect has been changing to appreciation. Denis Donoghue, in particular, has written in his praise. For full-length books about Robinson, however, one has to go to the American presses, from which books and theses about this more-than-minor poet continue to pour.

It is the lyrics which have appealed most, for these, lending themselves to anthologizing, have become common property. Who does not now know about Miniver Cheevy – or Richard Cory, who was

> . . . a gentleman from sole to crown,
> Clean favoured and imperially slim

reminding us a little of the classic portrait of a Virginia gentleman which Mark Twain gives us in *Huckleberry Finn*? But there was something wrong with this quiet American. The protagonist of the poem curses him because he has everything, whereas he (the protagonist) goes 'without the meat'. And yet Richard Cory

> one calm summer night
> Went home and put a bullet through his head.

Robinson's 'portraits' are simple but powerful – better on the whole than the more 'beautiful' lyrics like 'Eros Turannos' or 'For a Dead Lady'. Yet even the latter grow on one with familiarity. One begins by asking how Robinson could have chosen such an unsuitable sing-song metre and ends by reciting the lines with a sort of endless fascination:

> She fears him and will always ask
>   What fated her to choose him;
> She meets in his engaging mask
>   All reasons to refuse him:
> But what she meets and what she fears
> Are less than are the downward years
> Drawn slowly to the foamless weirs
>   Of age were she to lose him.

One could do without the extra rhyme in the penultimate line and yet, in an almost perverse way, Robinson triumphs over the unsuitability of the metrical pattern. In some sense, he reminds one of those leviathans of American prose, Dreiser and Wolfe, who also triumphed in spite of the vehicle by which they chose to communicate. Robinson, of course, has infinitely more grace than they, but there is a similar impression of the homespun and the amateur, a quality which comes out touchingly in Robinson's slightly too long 'Ben Jonson Entertains a Man From Stratford'.

In the end, it may be the long poems – into which he put so much time and energy – that posterity may come to respect as revealing the true strength of this puzzling but basically appealing poet. Do Americans over-rate him? Probably. Too often they allow the symbolic significance of his tragic life to overshadow evaluation of his poetic contribution. Nevertheless, we may be grateful to them for their insistence on his stature, for without it we might not have taken a closer look, nor discovered the rewards.

Frost is a very different matter. A younger man – although only five years younger – he did not begin publishing until he was forty, whereas Robinson started when he was twenty-seven. There is a big cultural distance between the late nineties and the years before the outbreak of the First World War, and Frost had the advantage of the age on his side. After the first appearance of Pound and Eliot, with Stevens and Williams already on the horizon, a young poet could not look back to the 'twilight interval'. But Robinson had formed his style already, and he did not change it much in his lifetime. It is true that there is more of a conversational quality about Robinson than at first meets the eye – 'Isaac and Archibald' is a case in point – but it was Frost who much more obviously (in John Ciardi's barbarous phrase) 'captured the American box'. Or did he? Certainly he captured *one* of the voice-boxes, as Auden points out in his introduction to the *Faber Book of American Verse*. It is all in the rhythm, the cadence, the voice itself. But one might equally argue that Stevens, in his solemn or playfully colourful but always infinitely impressive, manner equally captured another kind of American voice-box. Or Eliot, with his preacher's drone, or Pound with his back-country impishness.

If we had not read *A Boy's Will* and noticed in more conventional form that quality of sentimentality and knowingness which was to pursue Frost all his life, we might imagine that he had sprung into life fully formed. *North of Boston*, first published in England, is rightly celebrated. In this book, and in *Mountain Interval* (1916) and *New*

Hampshire (1923), we may find the best of Frost: the dramatic poems like 'Home Burial', 'The Death of the Hired Man', and 'The Axe-Helve', and also the famous lyrics that he grew to hate to repeat at each public performance: 'Mending Wall' or 'Birches'. Frost is not, like Stevens or Pound or Eliot, a poet's poet. The trained sensibility balks at some of Frost's whimsicality, and yet so fine a critic as Randall Jarrell could speak of his greatness. Jarrell was, of course, writing at a time when the public were inclined to think of Frost as a simple homely poet of the countryside, whereas he pointed out the grimness of some of Frost's themes and the art of his seeming-simplicity. Jarrell, writing in the forties (the essay is collected in *Poetry and the Age*), was also at pains to point out to his German friends that Frost was indeed a *dichter* in spite of his manner, for a *dichter* does not have to write like Goethe – not today at any rate. Looking back from the vantage-point of the seventies one can see that Jarrell's criticism is dated, although he was right to redress the balance.

Frost's pessimism, the skull beneath the skin of his homely-philosophical public manner, is in the true American tradition. As Harry Levin so ably pointed out, 'the power of blackness' runs all the way through American writing. Things are going on down there, as Lawrence told us. He was speaking of the classic Americans, but since he was also writing as a forward-looking twentieth-century man, his insights may be extrapolated into the present century. The Americans are saying something other than they seem to say:

> . . . The great difference between the extreme Russians and the extreme Americans lies in the fact that the Russians are explicit and hate eloquence and symbols, whereas the Americans refuse everything explicit and always put up an art of double meaning.

Although this is more obviously true of Hawthorne, Poe, or Melville, the same currents are there in the twentieth century – in a Faulkner or a Hemingway, a Frost or a Stevens. Jarrell quotes the rather comic 'Witch of Coös' as evidence of the grimness of this reputedly pastoral poet. But he was looking for too obvious a piece of evidence, for things not of this world. The hardness of Frost's world-view is shown best in his realistic poems, like the one about the boy who lost his hand in the saw, in homely 'philosophical' meditations like 'Provide, Provide', and even in so simple a construct as 'Stopping By Woods on a Snowy Evening', with its strangely insistent:

> But I have promises to keep,
> And miles to go before I sleep,
> And miles to go before I sleep

After a time 'The Death of the Hired Man' and 'Home Burial' (neither of these, incidentally, 'pretty' subjects) begin to pall and one looks elsewhere in the fairly extensive Frost oeuvre for poems like 'The Grindstone'.

Reviewing Frost and Robinson as fellow-New England poets (not 'regional' for that is a limiting and basically pejorative term) one can see that they are nearer in their attitude to life than the surface-tension of their work reveals. However, if we are looking for 'forerunners', for poets who seem to be significant in the light of what is happening in American poetry in the seventies, it is Frost who is the more important. His manner is looser, freer; he chooses subjects from everyday life and makes poetic capital out of them, and although he wrote two 'masques', he never looked back to the Arthurian cycle.

Before passing on to Stevens, Williams, and Cummings who, like Pound and Eliot, revealed their stature in the twenties, a word must be said about the three poets of the 'Middle Western Renaissance'. They have not lasted well, but one has a certain sympathy for them. Rebecca West wrote an appreciative little book about Sandburg in the twenties and it is true that, in the light of the insipid neo-Georgianism and Sitwellian play-acting which seemed to dominate the English scene, there was a certain brash mixture of the laconic and the histrionic about Sandburg which must have been appealing. Miss West might better have turned her attention to the great Americans or to the mighty forces of Yeats or Lawrence, but there has always been an attraction to the English about the kind of poetic personality which Sandburg represented. He was a great character, but not a great poet – better on the page, certainly, than that former Western hero of the *Times Literary Supplement*, Joaquin Cincinnatus Miller; but his main feature was that he was a poet 'of the broad acres' who really knew the people and the country at first hand. But this is to confuse man and talent. In retrospect it is Masters (of *The Spoon River Anthology*) who strikes through the mask; and even Vachel Lindsay's thundering metres ('The Congo', 'Simon Legree', 'General William Booth Enters Into Heaven') seem more healthy than Sandburg's hollow invocations or folksy anecdotes. In the very flatness of some of Sandburg's more acceptable notations, there is a sort of pretension, as in:

I am riding on a limited express, one of the crack trains
of the nation.
Hurtling across the prairie into blue haze and dark air go
fifteen all-steel coaches holding a thousand people.
(All the coaches shall be scrap and rust and all the men
and women laughing in the diners and sleepers shall
pass to ashes.)
I ask a man in the smoker where he is going and he
answers 'Omaha'.

The Poetry of Stevens, Williams, and Cummings

Stevens, Williams, Cummings – no three poets could be less alike and
yet each is fundamentally and unmistakably American ('typical', if
'typical' is taken to represent one type and not '*the* type'). All continued writing until well into the post-Second World War period and
the first two, at least, have been enormously influential on younger
poets – Stevens more particularly in the late forties and fifties and
Williams in the sixties. As time goes on and 'concrete poetry', Mac-
Luhanism and the art of the visual become more important to the
young poets of the seventies, it may well be Cummings, for all the
thinness of his talent compared with that of the first two, who will
become the hero of the present age.

But first, why Stevens? The vogue for this difficult and complex
poet came at a time when American poets were writing with a
scholarly finesse which seemed to overshadow all else. In fact, some
Englishmen, like David Wright, do not seem to have noticed that a
major revolution developed in the fifties and that a completely different
kind of verse (from that of Donald Hall, Richard Wilbur, James
Merrill, Louis Simpson or W. S. Merwin) has dominated the American
poetic scene for the past ten to fifteen years. Writing in 1965 (*The
Mid-Century: English Poetry 1940–60*, Penguin Books) Wright says:

> There are no American poets in this anthology. American and
> English poetry is no longer homogeneous, although written in
> approximately the same language. Contemporary American poetry
> – which, thanks to the extensive interest taken in it by American
> universities, is now an industry rather than an art – seems to be
> wandering off in the direction of the decorative, where style and
> technique is all and thought, if anything, a peg on which to hang a
> Chinese box of semantic ingenuities.

How out of touch can one be? Readers who consult Donald M. Allen's *The New American Poetry*, which was published in 1960 and covers at least part of the period chosen by Wright, will find a vastly different state of affairs. Ginsberg can hardly be called 'academic', or James Wright, or Reed Whittemore, or Duncan or Berryman, or Gary Snyder, or Sylvia Plath – although some of them have, or have had, jobs in universities.

But we must consider Stevens's contribution *per se*, regardless of whether he has or has not been in fashion. A decade after *Harmonium* was published, Louis Untermeyer could damn it with faint praise, asserting that Stevens's poems had 'little relation to any human struggle'. Perfectly true, of course, in the sense in which MacLeish's empty platitudes had factual relation to the problems of the Depression Years (see Edmund Wilson's parody, 'The Omelette of A. MacLeish'). But Stevens's contribution goes far deeper than that. All his life, he was interested in the profoundest problems of human existence, problems which transcend national boundaries or immediate social necessities: the nature of apprehended reality and its relation to the creative imagination, and the problem of belief and order. He is a meditative poet and while he is capable of the most vivid sensual images he never uses them at random or in excess of their immediate poetic relevance. His images, like his thoughts, are complex and depend closely on the syntax of his verse – and yet his clear grammatical structure and exact use of words are a great help in understanding the more difficult poems.

A lawyer for an insurance firm in Hartford, Connecticut for nearly forty years of his life, Stevens negotiated the world of business with the same authority which invests his poems. Behind what seemed to Untermeyer a charming example of Connecticut rococco, there stands a solidity, a toughness and seriousness of mind that is equalled only by T. S. Eliot. The ambivalence of Stevens's approach to his task is revealed in some of the titles in *Harmonium*: 'Le Monocle de Mon Oncle', 'The Paltry Nude Starts on a Spring Voyage', 'The Woman Who Had More Babies Than That'. His poetic manner runs from the extravagant rhetoric of 'The Comedian as the Letter C' to the subtle seriousness of *Notes Toward a Supreme Fiction*. In some of the last poems, like 'The World as Meditation', he achieved a simple, mellow dignity of utterance which reveals his true greatness. The 'belief' poems are central. The protagonist of 'Sunday Morning' asks why she should 'give her bounty to the dead'. She feels that the things of this world are all we have and know, in contrast to the myths of after-life (Christian or pagan) which men have manufactured for themselves. After all, as Rupert Brooke put it in 'Fish':

> This life cannot be all, they swear,
> For how unpleasant if it were.

Yet the girl in the poem still feels (like all of us, presumably) the need for some 'imperishable bliss'. Death must be, Stevens answers, 'the mother of beauty'. The knowledge that death is really the end of existence should enable us to savour to the full the bitter-sweetness of the human condition. There was a man called Jesus but his tomb is only a grave. We are alone on this earth; it is wishful thinking to believe that a Supreme Being cares for the pitiful affairs of those who dwell on this tiny planet. We should enjoy what we have, for:

> Deer walk upon our mountains, and the quail
> Whistle about us their spontaneous cries;
> Sweet berries ripen in the wilderness;
> And in the isolation of the sky,
> At evening, casual flocks of pigeons make
> Ambiguous undulations, as they sink,
> Downward to darkness, on extended wings.

Notes Toward a Supreme Fiction deals with the basic philosophical and spiritual truths towards which Stevens had been moving all his life. The imagination, in its attempt to abstract truth, brings up the idea of 'major man' – not the exceptional man, like the 'MacCullough', but the best in every man. Change, as Stevens pointed out in 'Sunday Morning', is not merely a bringer of death, but a source of vital freshness. We must celebrate life by a constant and amazed delight in the unexpectedness of each moment. The 'order' ('Ideas of Order') that we seek must be flexible, organic, partaking of the freshness of transformation. Through the aesthetic experience Stevens explored the possibility of a new epistemology, pushing the boundaries of poetic communication to a new limit. The message is Lawrentian and yet he was so un-Lawrentian in his manner. Grave, imperturbable, solemn, playful, he spoke, like Henry James, of what he knew must be. Like Henry James, too, he talked of the necessity to present rather than 'talk about'. A friend of Williams, he felt instinctively that the *ding an sich*, of which he speaks in 'The Comedian as the Letter C', was the true end of poetic communication. 'No ideas but in things' – and yet, in a sense, he defeats himself because his poetry is not, like Williams's, full of things, but full of thoughts, perceptions. It is a controlled jugglery of parenthetical, qualifying, and extending impressions, to which no commentary would do justice, for as Stevens saw so clearly 'poetry is the subject of the poem' – or, in the words of Archibald MacLeish, 'a poem must not mean but be'. And yet, for all the qualifications which one feels called upon to make about Stevens's final contribution, his poetry begins where other good poetry leaves us, in a state of heightened awareness.

To come from Stevens to the world of Williams is like coming from Parnassus into the market place. Williams is *l'homme moyen sensuel*. He feels, he smells, he scratches his crotch. His poems read like notes or, as they sometimes were, jottings on the back of a prescription pad:

> *This is Just to Say*
>
> I have eaten
> the plums
> that were in
> the icebox
>
> and which
> you were probably
> saving
> for breakfast
>
> Forgive me
> they were delicious
> so sweet
> and so cold

From that poem follows so much of the writing of the sixties. Other poets whose work is relevant to the experience of the younger American writers of today are Pound and Whitman. Not Eliot, nor Stevens. Emily Dickinson, perhaps, is in the same line, but not Emerson, nor of course the 'fireside poets': Longfellow, Holmes, and Whittier. Not even Poe, who in spite of his themes is stylistically quite out of the running.

It took a long time for the message to get through. Williams had been pouring out books ever since 1909. By the twenties, with *Spring and All*, the impact was clear; but the time was not yet ripe. It was the age of Eliot. The *Collected Poems* of 1934 consolidated Williams's reputation, but he still had a coterie following. And then *Paterson*, Book I appeared in 1946 with (again) Jarrell's enthusiastic introduction, and the subsequent books of *Paterson*, ending with Book V in 1958. Meanwhile the *Collected Later Poems* in 1950 and *The Collected Earlier Poems* in 1951 had made it clear that Williams was a force to be reckoned in a far more radical way than had previously been supposed. This was at least true in the United States – less so in England, where to many in the fifties his verse still 'tasted like sawdust in the mouth'.

The difficulty lay in the rhythm and form of communication. Although it was not quite true that Williams got his speech 'from the mouths of Polish mothers', as he maintained, he certainly followed his own voice-pattern, as later American poets (e.g. Olson and Creeley) have been doing. This, of course, was a radical departure for, in spite of the ground having been broken by Whitman, in spite of Lawrence, in spite of Cummings, a certain compromise (even un-consciously) had always been made between speech in the head and speech as communication (in linear form) with others who might hear or read the verse. And with the act of 'thinking about the reader' there had gone the retention of a certain mellifluousness, a quality of memor-able utterance, a series of phrase-patterns which had some relation to what had always been regarded as the 'poetic line'. Not that modern poets (not good ones, anyway) ever attempted to write like Milton or Keats, but at least there was still an idea of a certain kind of 'beauty' at the back of their heads. One finds this compromise with what had always been accepted in the work of poets as modern as Spender, Day Lewis, and even Auden. There is a world of difference between 'Lay your sleeping head, my love' or 'Sir, no man's enemy' and Williams's 'The Locust Tree in Flower':

> Among
> of
> green
>
> stiff
> old
> bright
>
> broken
> branch
> come
>
> white
> sweet
> May
>
> again

The quality of Williams's verse is much more visual (Cummings, with his typographical experiments, and Pound with his conversational interjections, may be seen as relevant). It is also more prosy, if not prosaic. For example, in the moving poem 'Asphodel, that Greeny Flower', the second stanza could be written in prose form without much loss, except that the breaking-up of the lines concentrates the reader's attention:

> We lived long together
> a life filled,
> if you will,
> with flowers. So that
> I was cheered
> when I first came to know
> that there were flowers also
> in hell

It may perhaps be seen why it took half a century for Williams's type of verse to triumph. In the light of Allen's *New American Poetry*, his verse is central to the modern experience, to the necessity felt today of communicating without the slightest compromise with 'music'. The form is direct, designedly (one feels, sometimes) ungraceful, like some modern architecture. To write like even so recent a poet as Dylan Thomas would seem unnatural, to savour a phrase or a line would be to commit treason towards a credo in which beauty is certainly not truth, although truth may be taken to be beauty. Also, since one's apprehension of the world is many-faceted, at least some contemporary poets try to reflect this, as Pound presumably did in the *Cantos*. One single stream of rational, even connotative, communication cannot possibly do justice to the interwoven strands of our awareness.

E. E. Cummings was born a generation after Stevens and Williams, and this is reflected in his verse. In a sense, his first poem was in prose since *The Enormous Room*, written as a result of his experiences in a French prisoner-of-war camp, reflects all the attitudes later to be found in his verse. It has been said that Cummings was essentially a religious poet, in that, like Steinbeck, he celebrated life. He certainly embraced nature and naturalness, although with a good deal more acerbity than Lawrence, and one feels that although he thanked God 'for most this amazing day' he would not have been at home at the Esalen Institute. Mr Cummings did not read unsolicited manuscripts; Mr Cummings preserved his privacy. His spirit had none of the generosity of Williams's. One does not find Cummings, like Williams and Pound, befriending younger poets and writing prefaces for their ingenuous outpourings.

Something of this comes out in his verse. It has been said that his 'obscene' poems are the best ever written, but too often they are nasty, even scatological. The famous 'she being Brand/new' and 'may I feel said he' tend to pall. There is an air of shocking the bourgeois about them. His early lyrics, like 'all in green went my love riding' have a certain whimsical air, and this quality persisted until the end. Even the most successful later poems, like 'my father moved through dooms of love', are not entirely free from this strain. He is a little too ready to use those 'stock response' emotive terms on which I. A. Richards frowns so severely in *Practical Criticism*. R. P. Blackmur counted 'flower' forty-eight times in Cummings's first book, *Tulips and Chimneys* (1923), and twenty-one times in *Etcetera* (1925). His conclusion was that 'it must contain for him an almost unlimited variety of and extent of meaning. . . . The question is whether or not the reader can possibly have shared the experience which Mr. Cummings has had of this word'. Words like 'thrilling', 'delicious', or 'bright' also come very readily to his pen.

Where Cummings is at his best is in the poems which reflect, without pressure on the reader, his ear for common speech and his irony in the use of a slang which reflects the attitudes of 'mostpeople'. 'The poems to come' he says in his Introduction to the *Collected Poems*, 'are for you and me and are not mostpeople', for 'Life, for mostpeople, simply isn't.' A good example of this ironical or wry verse is the poem which begins 'ygUDuh'. Others are 'plato told', 'my sweet old etcetera', and the touching 'this little bride & groom'. Right at the end of his poetic career he could achieve the perfection of 'this little horse is newLY', so that one can forgive him some of his earlier lapses. When he achieves this note he can convey a simple, yet powerful, emotional state skilfully and poignantly, and one always comes back to the best of his verse with delight.

Where his contribution may be most important for the poetry of the seventies, however, is in the typographical experiments. Here the typography is the poem itself, so that we have an early twentieth-century example of 'concrete poetry' (an antecedent may be the emblematic poems of the seventeenth century). In many cases, the poem cannot be read aloud at all; it must be seen on the page. He will represent pigeons wheeling or, as in the following poem, the 'haeccitas' of a grasshopper:

r-p-o-p-h-e-s-s-a-g-r

who

a)s w(e loo)k
upnowgath
PPEGORHRASS

eringt(o-

aThe):l

eA

!p:

S   a

(r

rIvInG   .gRrEaPsPhOs)

to

rea(be)rran(com)gi(e)ngly
,grasshopper;

Another poet who first made her reputation in the twenties and has especial significance for the contemporary period is Marianne Moore. There is a certain irony in this, since she also recommended herself to T. S. Eliot, who, disliking as he did the poetry of William Carlos Williams, would presumably not have been at home with Olson, Creeley, or Snyder. Eliot compared Miss Moore's verse with certain eighteenth-century poetry like Gray's 'Elegy', in which 'the scene described is a point of departure for meditations on one thing or another'. The comparison, which seemed a little odd then, appears even more far-fetched today. What appealed to Eliot was clearly the dry scholarly wit of Miss Moore's writing. What appeals today is her syllabic counting, and the matter-of-fact tone of her educated speech-rhythms. 'I, too, dislike it', she says of 'Poetry':

. . . there are things that are important beyond
   all this fiddle.
Reading it, however, with a perfect contempt for it,
   one discovers in
it after all, a place for the genuine.
   Hands that can grasp, eyes
   that can dilate, hair that can rise
      if it must, these things are important not because a

high-sounding interpretation can be put upon them but because
they are
useful.

Miss Moore, it will be seen, is, like Stevens, a proponent of the
'*ding an sich*' or perhaps nearer – in her call for poets to be 'literalists
of the imagination' and to present 'imaginary gardens with real toads
in them' – to the 'no ideas but in things' theory of Williams.

One or two other names from the extraordinarily rich period of the
twenties must be mentioned before we pass on to the poetry of the
thirties. First, the 'Fugitives', a group who took their name from a little
magazine, *The Fugitive*, edited in Nashville, Tennessee from 1922–5.
The founders of the 'movement' were John Crowe Ransom, Allen
Tate, Donald Davidson, and Merill Moore. Later, there came 'agrarianism', a call for the South to defend its own values, the founding of
the *Southern Review*, edited at Baton Rouge, Louisiana by Cleanth
Brooks and Robert Penn Warren and, later, the *Kenyon Review*,
edited by Ransom from Kenyon College, Gambier, Ohio. From this
group also sprang the 'New Criticism' and the textbooks of Warren
and Brooks, which were to have such an effect on American university
education in the years immediately following the Second World War.
Of the Fugitives, with half of them dead and Ransom and Tate old
men, it is only Warren who continues to mine a rich vein of verse.
Incarnations (1968) shows that Warren – who is of course well-known
as a novelist – was writing better poetry in his sixties than he was in
his thirties.

Finally, Conrad Aiken and Robinson Jeffers were also important in
the twenties. Aiken, a friend of Eliot's, published his first book in 1914,
but it was *The Charnel Rose, Senlin and Other Poems* (1918), *Punch: The
Immortal Liar* (1921), *The Pilgrimage of Festus* (1923), and *Preludes for
Memnon* (1931) which made his reputation. Like Warren, he has also
had a career as a novelist. His verse is superbly turned, yet curiously
impenetrable. In *Senlin* Allen Tate noticed 'the external pattern of a
theme which remains throughout a point of reference and does not
become an interior motivation giving the work form'. Jeffers, by two
years the older man, did not publish his first book, *Tamar and Other
Poems*, until 1924. *The Women at Point Sur* followed in 1927, and
Cawdor in 1928. Throughout the thirties he continued to produce
poetry on the same related themes: his love of nature and dislike of
twentieth-century man, and his almost Greek feeling for the tragedy

of the human condition. In 1946 Jeffers's version of *Medea* was played on Broadway by Judith Anderson. In passionate but often loose and uncontrolled blank verse Jeffers expresses his disgust with humankind. Yvor Winters described him as an 'ecstatic-pantheist'. Like that other descendant of Scotch–Irish Calvinists, William Faulkner, his constantly recurring themes of rape and incest are symbolic of his deep Puritanism.

Poetry in the Thirties

Of all the poets of the thirties (he is always thought of as such, although *White Buildings* came out in 1926 and *The Bridge* in 1930), it is Hart Crane who dominates the scene. Born in 1899 in Garrettsville, Ohio, the son of a well-to-do manufacturer, he had an unhappy home life and little formal education. He committed suicide in 1932 by jumping overboard from a ship returning from Mexico. His first book came at a time when *The Waste Land* was making its greatest impact and Crane's reaction was that he wished to 'move toward a more positive, or (if I may put it so in a sceptical age) ecstatic goal'. Compared with Eliot, Crane is a true Romantic, using words in an incantatory way (e.g. 'laughing the wrapt inflections of our love'). 'When I speak' he wrote to Harriet Monroe, 'of "adagios of islands" the reference is to the motion of the boat through islands clustered thickly. . . . And it seems a much more direct and creative statement than any more "logical" employment of words such as "coasting slowly through the islands" '. Poor Crane – that he should feel it necessary to explain so much. The battle had already been won – by Rimbaud, by Mallarmé, by the dadaists and surrealists. If he had looked at *Harmonium*, which had appeared in 1923, he would have found a fellow spirit. But writing as he was in an American context, without benefit of that close association with other writers which helps European poets, he had to fight the good fight all over again. And the result of his isolation is, at times, too much verbiage, a wildness which arises from a subconsciously-felt necessity to counteract what James might have called the '*données*' or Lionel Trilling the 'doctrines felt as facts' of the American scene.

The Bridge was a peculiarly American compromise. It arose out of Crane's sense of the grandeur of man's achievements in the twentieth century; yet he tried also to express his sense of an accompanying flowering of the spirit. The ostensible subject is Brooklyn Bridge, but the bridge of Crane's vision is also a bridge between centuries and between men, a Whitmanesque dream of *brüderschaft*. 'I found' said

Crane, 'that I was really building a bridge between so-called classical experience and many divergent realities of our seething confused cosmos of today.' In eight parts he presents an array of panoramas and insights ranging from the time of Captain John Smith to the contemporary Depression scene. This 'epic of modern consciousness' begins with a 'proem' to Brooklyn Bridge:

> O sleepless as the river under thee,
> Vaulting the sea, the prairies' dreaming sod,
> Unto us lowliest sometimes sweep, descend
> And of the curveship lend a myth to God.

In 'Ave Maria' Columbus speaks; in 'Powhatan's Daughter' it is the poet himself. About 'Van Winkle' Crane wrote to his banker 'angel' Otto Kahn, 'The protagonist has left the room with its harbour sounds, and is walking to the subway. . . . The walk to the subway arouses reminiscences of childhood, also the childhood of the continental conquest, viz, the Conquistadores, Priscilla, Captain John Smith, etc. The parallelisms unite in the figure of Rip Van Winkle (indigenous Muse of Memory), who finally becomes identified with the protagonist and boards the subway with the reader.'

Of the subway, which also appears in 'The River', Crane said that it was 'simply a figurative, psychological vehicle for transporting the reader to the Middle West. . . . The extravagance of the first twenty-three lines of this section is an intentional burlesque on the cultural confusion of the present.' Describing 'The Dance' he said, 'Here is the one pure mythical smoky soil at last! Not only do I describe the conflict between the two races in this dance – I also become identified with the Indian and his world as a cultural factor. . . . Pocahontas (the continent) is the common basis of our meeting.' 'The Tunnel' represented the 'encroachment of machinery on humanity'; 'Cape Hatteras' was a 'kind of ode to Whitman'.

Ho-hum. At least Eliot could say 'No! I am not Prince Hamlet, nor was meant to be' – although that was before the less obtrusively pretentious but equally American high seriousness of *The Waste Land*, with its notes and its symbolism and its air of speaking *ex cathedra*. There is something in the cultural atmosphere which has made Americans try the big thing. One finds it – as has been pointed out – in the novel from *Moby-Dick* to *Of Time and the River*, and one finds it in poetry, from *The Columbiad*, through *Song of Myself*, Pound's *Cantos*,

The Bridge to Paterson – even in *The Waste Land* and *The Four Quartets*. In their different forms they have the impertinence to speak for humanity. One is awed as much by the pretension as by the effort which it cost. Crane, of course, with his half-baked symbolism and his attitudinizing ('I am Baudelaire, I am Whitman, I am Christopher Marlowe, I am Christ') has more bravado and less justification for it than his masters. Nevertheless, it is surprising how much he was able to get away with and how good he could be when he was not trying too hard, as in the lyrics of 'Voyages'.

Apart from Crane, there is nothing in American poetry of the thirties to parallel the new note of the so-called 'Pylon Poets' in England. It is true that many American writers turned to radicalism, or even joined the Communist Party, but they were for the most part not poets. There are no Audens, Spenders, Day Lewises, or MacNeices on the American scene in the thirties; only Archibald MacLeish, worthily invoking the 'social muse'. Born, like Hemingway, in a well-to-do suburb of Chicago, MacLeish had an impeccable upper-middle-class career. When he returned to the United States from the expatriate pleasures of Paris in 1928, he followed Cortez's route in Mexico in order to write *Conquistador* (in terza rima). His reward was a Pulitzer Prize in 1933. *Frescoes for Mr Rockefeller's City* (1933) and *Public Speech* (1936) deal with the Depression and the New Deal. This was followed by *America was Promises* (1939) and *Colloquy for the States* (1943). There have also been a number of verse dramas dealing with social themes, and MacLeish won another Pulitzer Prize in 1958 with *J.B.*, a treatment of the trials of Job in a modern setting. Distinguished public career, distinguished themes; MacLeish has had all the honours, including being librarian of Congress, Secretary of State, and Boylston Professor at Harvard. Why the pejorative note? Perhaps partly because of a certain hollowness which Edmund Wilson unkindly but justly parodied. He jumped on too many bandwagons; there has been too much self-conscious declamation, a tendency to Whitmanize without the ring of truth.

Kenneth Fearing, another Chicagoan, is a poet of the thirties who appeals more, despite his small output. His talent had been shown in *Angel Arms*, but it was the *Poems* of 1935 which aroused greatest public interest. This was followed by other satires of American middle-class life: *Dead Reckoning* (1938), *Afternoon of a Pawnbroker* (1943), and *Stranger at Coney Island* (1949). Fearing, in fact, did in poetry for his social group what Ring Lardner had done for his anti-heroes of the lower class in prose. Like Lardner, too, he avoids bitterness, in 'Dirge' celebrating a Depression death with:

> Wham, Mr. Roosevelt; pow, Sears Roebuck; awk, big dipper;
>   bop, summer rain;
> bong, Mr, Bong Mr, bong, Mr, bong.

Throughout the thirties, the older poets continued to publish. Among other prose works, Pound produced *ABC of Economics*, *ABC of Reading*, and *Make it New*, and more *Cantos*, from *A Draft of XXX Cantos* (1933) to *Cantos LII–LXXI* (1940); Williams published *An Early Martyr* (1935), *Adam and Eve & The City* (1936), and *Complete Collected Poems* (1938), as well as the collections of short stories, *The Knife of the Times* (1932) and *Life Along the Passaic River* (1938); Eliot brought out *Ash Wednesday* (1930), *The Rock* (1934), *Murder in the Cathedral* (1935), and *Family Reunion* (1939), in addition to prose works like *After Strange Gods* (1934); Cummings was responsible for *Viva* (1931), *No Thanks* (1935), *1/20* (1936), and *Collected Poems* (1938). These also were the years of *Eimi* (1933), a travel diary attacking the Soviet system, *CIOPW* (1931), showing (a significant point, this, in the light of the visual quality of his art) that Cummings was a painter as well as a poet, and *Tom*, a satirical ballet. Of the Fugitives, Ransom produced nothing new, but Allen Tate brought out *Poems 1929–1931* (1932), *The Mediterranean and Other Poems* (1936), and *Selected Poems* (1937). For Warren these were the years of *Thirty-Six Poems* (1936) and the novel *Night Rider* (1939), treating of the struggle between tobacco growers and manufacturers in Kentucky at the beginning of the century. Stevens reissued *Harmonium* in an enlarged edition in 1931 and produced *Ideas of Order* (1935), *Owl's Clover* (1936), and *The Man with the Blue Guitar* (1937). All in all, however, it may be said that, so far as poetry is concerned, the twenties are far more rewarding years for study than the thirties.

Poetry Since 1940

In the forties in America there is also nothing to parallel the English phenomena of *Poems from the Forces* or the *New Apocalypse*. For a time in England it seemed as if every man in uniform was writing verse, and the best of these 'war poets' – Henry Reed, Sidney Keyes, Alun Lewis, Gavin Ewart, Timothy Corsellis – hit a more-than-minor note. In the United States only Karl Shapiro and Randall Jarrell wrote good war poems. Shapiro's *V-Letter and Other Poems*, written when he was a soldier in the Pacific, won a Pulitzer Prize in 1944. Jarrell's 'The Death of the Ball Turret Gunner' is as stark a comment as any to emerge from the Second World War:

> From my mother's sleep I fell into the State,
> And I hunched in its belly till my wet fur froze.
> Six miles from earth, loosed from its dream of life,
> I woke to black flak and the nightmare fighters.
> When I died they washed me out of the turret with a hose.

On the Romantic side, with Crane dead, there was no American Dylan Thomas to dazzle the reader or New Apocalyptic pseudo-surrealists to produce manifestos. On the other hand there was much good verse, particularly towards the end of the decade. Theodore Roethke published his first book in 1941, and *The Lost Son* came out in 1948; Robert Lowell brought out *The Land of Unlikeness* (1944) and *Lord Weary's Castle* in 1946; Richard Wilbur's *The Beautiful Changes* appeared in 1947. Delmore Schwartz, whose first book, *In Dreams Begin Responsibilities*, had been published when he was twenty-five, and a translation of *Une Saison en Enfer* when he was twenty-six, produced the verse plays *Shenandoah* (1941) and *Genesis* (1943). Muriel Rukeyser's *The Soul and Body of John Brown* appeared in 1940, *Wake Island* in 1942, *Beast in View* in 1944, *The Green Wave* in 1948, and *Elegies* in 1949. John Berryman first attracted attention in *New Poems* (1941) and *Five Young American Poets* (1941). *Poems* followed in 1942 and *The Dispossessed* in 1948. These also were the years of John Frederick Nims's *The Iron Pastoral* (1947), Peter Viereck's *Terror and Decorum* (1948), John Ciardi's *Other Skies* (1947), and *Live Another Day* (1949), and Elizabeth Bishop's *North and South* (1946).

In the fifties there may be seen ample evidence of that talent for fine writing which led the English poet David Wright to make the comment already quoted above (p. 404). Robert Horan, James Merrill, and W. S. Merwin dazzled, but did not convince, their readers. Donald Hall, Louis Simpson, and Robert Pack, themselves good 'academic' poets, enshrined this line of American verse in their anthologies: *New Poets of England and America* (1957) and *New Poets of England and America: Second Selection* (1962). Among the better poets in the latter anthology were John Hollander, Anthony Hecht, Sylvia Plath, Anne Sexton, Galway Kinnell, and W. D. Snodgrass. However, no breath of revolution appears in these books. One would not know that the 'Black Mountain Poets' or the 'Beats' were, for some readers, filling

the horizon. Donald M. Allen rewrote the poetic history of the
fifties with his *The New American Poetry*, published in 1960. In the
beginning, for Allen, there was Charles Olson, and after Olson came
Duncan, and, after Duncan, Creeley. However, Duncan, as Allen
points out in his introduction, first 'emerged' as a member of the 'San
Francisco Renaissance' in the late forties, where he was associated with
Brother Antoninus, Robin Blaser, Jack Spicer, and Ferlinghetti.
Philip Lamantia was also in this group. It was also in San Francisco, in
1956, that the Beat Generation first attracted national attention. Its
leading members were Allen Ginsberg, Gregory Corso, and Jack
Kerouac, but Gary Snyder and Philip Whalen have also become better-
known since then.

In 1969 a third anthology, more discriminating than Allen's and
different from that of Hall, Simpson, and Pack, showed which way
the wind was blowing. Stephen Berg and Robert Mezey are quite
clear that in *Naked Poetry* they are defining the true nature of poetry
in the sixties, and they may well be right. The theme is 'Open Form'
verse, and in this connection Olson's rather wild and not altogether
original essay on *Projective Verse*, published by Leroi Jones in a book of
the same name in 1959, becomes the gospel according to Berg and
Mezey (the essay is reproduced in Allen's anthology). What they have
done is to bring together the work of nineteen American poets 'whose
poems don't rhyme (usually) and don't move on feet of more or less
equal duration (usually)'. The criterion for inclusion is that the work of
these poets should 'take shape from the shape of their emotions, the
shapes their minds make in thought. We began with the firm conviction
that the strongest and most alive poetry in America had abandoned or
at least broken the grip of traditional metres and had set out once again
into "the wilderness of unopened life" '. Berg and Mezey end modestly
by stating that 'most of the best poetry written in America during the
last two decades' is collected in their anthology.

Naked Poetry starts with Kenneth Rexroth, as the old god, and
proceeds, by date of birth, with Theodore Roethke, Kenneth Patchen,
William Stafford, Weldon Kees, John Berryman, Robert Lowell,
Denise Levertov, Robert Bly, Robert Creeley, Allen Ginsberg, Galway
Kinnell, W. S. Merwin, James Wright, Philip Levine, Sylvia Plath,
and Gary Snyder, and ends with Berg and Mezey themselves. It is a
fascinating collection and, as will be seen, only a few of the names
overlap with those selected by Hall, Simpson, and Pack. However, it
cuts across the distinction, made by Robert Lowell, between the 'raw'

and the 'cooked'. One would not have imagined, before Berg and Mezey, that it was possible to produce a tendentious book which could make the lamb lie down with the lion, the Merwin with the Ginsberg. And on the whole their choice cannot be faulted. Rexroth is a doubtful inclusion, but Patchen is not. They are probably right to leave out Olson who, emblem though he is, and author of that superb study of *Moby-Dick* entitled *Call Me Ishmael*, shows only a sort of Poundian pastiche in the pretentious Maximus poems.

Looking back at the years since the Second World War it is clear who – whatever camp they are said to belong to, whatever group may annex them to their own disadvantage or annoyance – are the most important younger American poets. They are: Robert Lowell, Theodore Roethke, Richard Wilbur, John Berryman, Allen Ginsberg, Sylvia Plath, and Robert Creeley. Of the rest, Duncan, Snyder, Kinnell, Wright, and Bly are better than average. Denise Levertov is much admired but (a curious case, this), apart from being about as American as W. H. Auden, her verse, although of excellent quality, does not have the edge and authority of Plath, or even Sexton.

This section cannot be allowed to end without some mention of the great contribution of American criticism in the twentieth century. In 1948 Stanley Edgar Hyman published an account of the important American critics of the twentieth century in which he put Edmund Wilson at the bottom of the class and Kenneth Burke at the top. This, however, is pure academic snobbery. Wilson, although he wrote little specifically on poetry, is a force to be reckoned with; for *Axel's Castle* alone he would be important. Burke, on the other hand, is more of a metaphysician and psychologist than a critic. *Permanence and Change* (1935) was a philosophical investigation of ideas, *The Philosophy of Literary Form* (1941), *A Grammar of Motives*, and *A Rhetoric of Motives* (1950) are linguistic analyses, interpreting human motives through literature. Not that linguistics can be left out – Noam Chomsky, it seems, must be read by all students of literature. However, we are concerned here more with criticism, and sensitive, exegetical criticism at that, than with cloudy and 'thematic' interpretations of the human condition which use literature rather than follow the delicate and intricate mutations of its form and content.

One of the most helpful and penetrating of twentieth-century American critics was the late R. P. Blackmur; another was Randall Jarrell. They were also very good writers. The titles of their chief books will be found appended to this chapter. Yvor Winters, infuriatingly,

Leavisianly cantankerous though he was, is also well worth reading. Others are: Richard Chase, Charles Feidelson, Alfred Kazin, Maxwell Geismar, Lionel Trilling, Harry Levin, R. W. B. Lewis, Cleanth Brooks, Philip Rahv, John Crowe Ransom, and Allen Tate. Finally, Marshall MacLuhan and Northrop Frye, Canadians – like Saul Bellow – though they are, cannot be left out of this list. Frye, more particularly, has been a powerful literary influence since the publication of *An Anatomy of Criticism*, encouraging Americans in their already deeply-rooted predilection for the mythical type and analogue.

Further Reading

Note: Reference should also be made to the list of General Works at pp. 339–40 and to the General Bibliography, pp. 507–8.

Aldridge, John W., *After the Lost Generation*. Farrar, Straus, 1958.

Beach, J. W., *American Fiction: 1920–1940*. New York, 1941.

Beaver, Harold (ed.), *American Critical Essays, Twentieth Century*. London, 1959.

Blackmur, R. P., *Language as Gesture*. New York, 1952.

——, *The Lion and the Honeycomb*. New York, 1955.

Bogan, Louise, *Achievement in American Poetry, 1900–1950*. Chicago, Ill., 1951.

Brooks, Cleanth, *Modern Poetry and the Tradition*. Chapel Hill, N.C., 1939.

Cambon, Glauco, *The Inclusive Flame: Studies in American Poetry*. Bloomington, Ind., 1963.

Coffman, Stanley K., *Imagism, a Chapter for the History of Modern Poetry*. Norman, Okla., 1951.

Cowie, Alexander, *The Rise of the American Novel*. New York, 1948.

Donoghue, Denis, *Connoisseurs of Chaos: Ideas of Order in Modern American Poetry*. London, 1966.

Foerster, Norman (ed.), *Humanism and America*. New York, 1930.

Frankenberg, Lloyd, *Pleasure Dome: On Reading Modern Poetry*. New York, 1949.

Gardiner, H. C. (ed.), *Fifty Years of the American Novel*. New York, 1951.

Geismar, Maxwell, *Writers in Crisis: the American Novel Between Two Wars*. Boston, Mass., 1942.

——, *The Last of the Provincials*. Boston, Mass., 1947.

Gregory, Horace and Zaturenska, Marya, *A History of American Poetry, 1900–1940*. New York, 1946.

Hoffman, F. J., *Freudianism and the Literary Mind*. Baton Rouge, La., 1945.

——, *The Modern Novel in America, 1900–1950*. Chicago, Ill., 1951, 1956.

Hughes, Glenn, *Imagism and the Imagists*. New York, 1931.

Hyman, S. E., *The Armed Vision, A Study in the Methods of Modern Literary Criticism*. New York, 1948.

Jarrell, Randall, *Poetry and the Age*. New York, 1953.

Kazin, Alfred, *On Native Grounds: An Interpretation of Modern American Prose Literature*. New York, 1942, 1956.

Lowell, Amy, *Tendencies in Modern American Poetry*. Boston, Mass., 1921.

Magny, Claude Edmonde, *L'Age du Roman Américain*. Paris, 1948.

Moore, Marianne, *Predilections*. New York, 1956.

O'Connor, W. V. (ed.), *Forms of Modern Fiction*. Minneapolis, Minn., 1948.

——, *Sense and Sensibility in Modern Poetry*. Chicago, Ill., 1948.

——, *An Age of Criticism, 1900–1950*. Chicago, Ill., 1952.

Pound, Ezra, *Make it New*. London, 1934.

——, *Polite Essays*. London, 1937.

Rajan, B. (ed.), *Modern American Poetry*. London, 1950.

Ransom, J. C., *The New Criticism*. Norfolk, Conn., 1941.

Southworth, J. G., *Some Modern American Poets*. Oxford, 1950.

——, *More Modern American Poets*. Oxford, 1954.

Straumann, Heinrich, *American Literature in the Twentieth Century*. London, 1951.

Tate, Allen (ed.), *The Language of Poetry*. Princeton, N.J., 1942.

——, *On the Limits of Poetry: Selected Essays*. New York, 1948.

——, *The Man of Letters in the Modern World*. New York, 1955.

Warren, Austin and Wellek, René, *Theory of Literature*. New York, 1945.

Weirick, B., *From Whitman to Sandburg in American Poetry*. New York, 1924.

Wells, Henry W., *The American Way of Poetry*. New York, 1943.

West, Ray B., *The Short Story in America, 1900–1950*. Chicago, Ill., 1952.

Williams, William Carlos, *In the American Grain*. New York, 1925.

Winters, Yvor, *Primitivism and Decadence, A Study of American Experimental Poetry*. New York, 1937.

——, *The Anatomy of Nonsense*. Norfolk, Conn., 1943.

12 Drama and the Arts in America

DENNIS WELLAND

The Artist and the Audience

This chapter is concerned – necessarily briefly – with a paradox that can be defined more easily than it can be resolved: despite the perennial and understandable complaint of creative artists that America is inimical, even hostile, to their work, the arts have flourished increasingly in the United States. Two explanations come immediately to mind. One is the condescending suggestion that the combination of wealth and a desire for a cultural reputation has enabled America to act as patron to the arts on a scale unparalleled elsewhere. This argument is supported by the large proportion of the world's art treasures housed either in American private collections or in museums and art galleries – more than 2300 of them – across the continent; by the acquisitions policies of the great libraries, private and public; by the existence of between thirty and forty major symphony orchestras; and by countless similarly impressive statistics. Veblenian theories of cultural emulation and 'pecuniary canons of taste' may be disparagingly adduced. The superb display techniques evolved in these galleries – the Solomon R. Guggenheim Museum in New York is an outstanding, but by no means unique example – may be attributed to similar motives. Attendance-figures may be cited to demonstrate how large a part of the national population annually avoids visiting concerts and art galleries; the role of the private philanthropist or his extension, the large Foundation, in supporting such ventures may be emphasized to show how little encouragement is given by the general public or the state; and the whole argument can be smugly manipulated to show all this effort as a costly smokescreen to conceal the deficiency of an indigenous cultural heritage. What this unworthy, though not uncommon, argument ignores is the quality and the quantity of American work displayed in these galleries, and the fact that many (notably the Whitney

Museum in New York) are devoted exclusively to such work, or (as at Colonial Williamsburg) to the re-creation, in the original environment, of a facet of the national past in which native art and artifacts are particularly important.

Another explanation of the paradox, equally facile and insidious, suggests that it is the popular arts that flourish in the democratic atmosphere of the United States rather than higher forms. Alexis de Tocqueville formulated this argument persuasively in the second part of *Democracy in America* (1840): in an aristocratic society taste combines with wealth to facilitate the commissioning of fine works of art by artists who have the training, the tradition, and the time to produce them, whereas in more egalitarian societies the useful is valued more highly than the beautiful; taste and craftsmanship are further debased by the need to make universally available the works of some prestige value which in another society would be the prerogative of the privileged few. When de Tocqueville was writing this book the American Art Union was being established. For an annual subscription of five dollars its members received an engraving of a contemporary American painting and a monthly magazine on American art; the promoters utilized part of the proceeds to buy original paintings and statues which were then raffled to subscribers. In ten years they distributed nearly 1300 original paintings and over 50,000 engravings. The same decade (the 1840s) saw the rise of the engraving firm of Currier and Ives, who produced popular coloured prints selling at fifteen to twenty-five cents; it is estimated that they lithographed some 5000 different pictures, at least one of which sold 73,000 copies. It is small wonder that when Mark Twain's Yankee found himself in King Arthur's court these engravings were prominent among the things he missed: 'I had been used to chromos for years, and I saw now that without my suspecting it a passion for art had got worked into the fabric of my being.'

The influence of popular taste on American painting of all periods and on American music will be indicated later, but popular taste alone has never dictated the pattern of American development in the arts. Had it done so in the theatre, for instance, the musical would be the dominant dramatic form. Yet, however much one admires *West Side Story*, any critical account of America's contribution to the drama of our time has to give much more prominence to names such as Eugene O'Neill (1888–1953), Arthur Miller (1915–), Tennessee Williams (1911–), and Edward Albee (1928–). It may be argued that these dramatists have acquired a higher reputation abroad than at home, where, paradoxically again, the drama has never enjoyed wide popularity. The United States, unlike the major European countries, has no long-standing tradition of theatrical vitality. Many of its large cities that support art galleries and symphony orchestras have no theatres. Broadway prices are so obviously designed for the tourist trade that few New Yorkers are likely to become habitual theatre-goers, and there is nothing comparable to the English provincial repertory system to sustain them. The development of drama schools within the universities provides a somewhat élitist audience and, like other campus cultural patterns such as the writer-in-residence, often arouses scepticism and even hostility among professionals.

There is no clearly-defined audience for American drama, and yet not only has this unpropitious soil supported dramatists of unusual talent but writers who have achieved reputations in other fields are still attracted into the theatre – Saul Bellow, Robert Lowell, and James Baldwin, for instance, in recent years. Nor would the pioneering energy and commercial bustle of America seem particularly hospitable to ballet except, perhaps, for an Agnes de Mille in the musical. Yet Isadora Duncan, Martha Graham, Merce Cunningham, and the Judson Dance Theater have all broken new ground so significantly that Cunningham's achievement has been compared to Jackson Pollock's in painting for its introduction of new concepts of spatial relations and rhythm that have exerted a stimulating influence on the other artists. Speculation on the causes of all this creative energy may be less useful here than acceptance of its existence and some assessment of it, but this last point does indicate one characteristic of the phenomenon that merits attention: the interrelatedness of the arts in America.

In some respects this is obvious enough: music, dance and drama fuse naturally in any culture; trends in pictorial art may influence stage design; theatre, cinema, and television will naturally interlock. In America literature also has established links with the other arts in interesting ways. Vachel Lindsay (1879–1931), dedicated propagandist for the American Dream, tried to popularize poetry by public performance, developing a form that he called 'the Higher Vaudeville'; his fondness for strongly-accentuated rhythms and syncopation led many people to suppose him to be drawing on the idioms of jazz, though he was not altogether pleased by this. A cartoonist whose work in some ways recalls Edward Lear, he evolved a more ambitious form of symbolic illustrations for some of his poems in what he called Hieroglyphics, the theory of which he adumbrated in *The Art of the Moving Picture*. Appearing in 1915, the year in which D. W. Griffith produced his American epic, *The Birth of a Nation*, this book is an early and enthusiastic championing of the cinema as a great art. Enthusiasm, didacticism, and eclecticism give Lindsay's work the stigma of the inspired amateur whose theory promises more than his performance achieves, but his desire for 'a few very well prepared audiences' and his efforts to create such audiences is symptomatic.

Other writers in search of an audience turned to the cinema in a spirit more mercenary and less idealistic than Lindsay's, attracted by its popularity and the fees it offered them as scriptwriters. Their disillusion with the film as art may be due to their looking at it from too literary an angle. Scott Fitzgerald, however, came to realize the relative unimportance of the writer in this predominantly visual art. Part of Fitzgerald's Hollywood experience as a scriptwriter was to furnish Budd Schulberg with material for his novel, *The Disenchanted*, and Fitzgerald himself drew on it frequently in his fiction. His last, unfinished novel, *The Last Tycoon*, is one of the best of the Hollywood novels (a genre which is otherwise much less interesting than it promises to be) because it centres on the producer as the key to this new art form. Fitzgerald's hero, transparently modelled on Irving Thalberg, is the businessman as artist, imaginatively exercising his managerial ability to create work of artistic merit. Had Fitzgerald completed the book Monro Stahr would have been an impressive counterpart to Jay Gatsby as a study of the American Dream in all its twentieth-century ambivalence. The American Dream is also the subject of the only other significant Hollywood novel, *The Day of the Locust* by Nathanael West (1906–40), in which the illusion and unreality of the cinema are used surrealistically to expose the savagery that lies so close to the surface of modern civilization, and the frustrations and sheer misery of Californian life. West's earlier splenetic satires such as *Miss Lonelyhearts* and *A Cool Million* have also gained in popularity in recent years, but *The Day of the Locust* gives the satire a different dimension by its pictorialism. Not only are the Hollywood scenes realized with a maliciously vivid visual quality, but the protagonist is a painter whose masterpiece is to be an apocalyptic 'Burning of Los Angeles'; the influence of Goya and Daumier, which West stresses, colours the writing of the novel, and is also discussed by West as a rejection of nineteenth-century American traditions in painting.

The Popular Arts

One effect of the popularization of art in a democracy foreseen by de Tocqueville was a preference among painters for 'the exact imitation of the details of private life, which they have always before their eyes; and they are forever copying trivial objects, the originals of which are only too abundant in nature'. He might be describing the fondness for *trompe l'oeil* painting of Charles Willson Peale (1741–1827) and his son Raphaelle Peale (1778–1860), the meticulous fidelity of the still lifes of W. M. Harnett (1848–92), the domestic detail lovingly lingered on by the genre painters, and the ornithological accuracy of the *Birds of America* by John James Audubon (1785–1851), delightful as those bird-pictures are in colour and design. 'The exact imitation of the details of private life' accurately defines the impetus behind much of the earliest painting in America – portraits of almost primitive simplicity, yet of real human dignity, in which unskilled artists (often sign-painters) captured a likeness of the early settlers and their immediate domestic environment. By the end of the Colonial period portrait-painters of real merit like John Singleton Copley (1738–1815) and Gilbert Stuart (1755–1828) were emerging, and the work of others, such as Ralph Earl (1751–1801), if technically less accomplished, has a native vigour and realism.

Subject and treatment of much post-Revolutionary painting were in tune with popular nationalist sentiment: the great historical canvases of John Trumbull (1756–1843), like 'The Signing of the Declaration of Independence'; the countless portraits of George Washington, the most accomplished of which are by Gilbert Stuart; the frontier genre pictures of George Caleb Bingham (1811–79), such as 'Daniel Boone Coming Through Cumberland Gap'; or the vast Rocky Mountain landscapes of Albert Bierstadt (1830–1902). There is an even more important form of popular painting in the unsophisticated 'primitives' that are the pictorial equivalents of the wood-carvings for ships' figureheads and tradesmen's signs or the weather-vanes and decorative metal-work that gives American folk-art its spontaneity and vigour. Many of these paintings are anonymous, but a Quaker sign-painter, Edward Hicks (1780–1849), was responsible for some of the most interesting. One theme fascinated him so much that he painted it at least twenty-five times. Entitled 'The Peaceable Kingdom', it is apparently an illustration of Isaiah's prophecy of the lion lying down with the lamb and a little child leading them. Every version is, however, transformed into an allegory of America by the inclusion of a small-scale imitation of 'William Penn's Treaty with the Indians', the picture in which Benjamin West (1738–1820) had celebrated the idealism behind the founding of Pennsylvania. It has been pointed out that, since Hicks's version of the picture is always laterally reversed, he must have been familiar with it not in the original but in a carelessly-printed engraving: Hank Morgan was not alone in deriving his art-education from the chromos.

That the most creative manifestations of American art have been popular art could be argued in our own time from the fact that pop art derived its name and its greatest impetus from the United States in the work of painters such as Andy Warhol (1930–), Claes Oldenburg (1929–), and Roy Lichtenstein (1923–). They have invested de Tocqueville's prediction with a new truth in their rendering of such 'trivial objects the originals of which are only too abundant' as soup-cans, advertisements, and city junk. By borrowing the techniques as well as the subject matter of the comic-paper strip cartoons Lichtenstein calls attention to the mass media as a popular American art form, a claim which might also be advanced for the cinema and, with greater reservations, for television.

Similarly in music it is often suggested that America has been particularly successful in the more popular forms. An obvious example is Stephen Foster (1826–64), the Pennsylvania-born composer of sentimental ballads celebrating an Old South that he had never set foot in until the best-known of them were already famous. 'Old Uncle Ned', 'My Old Kentucky Home', 'Old Folks at Home', and dozens of others owed more to the popular Nigger Minstrel shows than to the genuine songs of the Negro, but their plangent, nostalgic melodies found as ready and as enduring an audience as did the jaunty gaiety of his 'Camptown Races' and 'Oh! Susanna'. More nationalistic spirits were roused by the bold martial brassiness of John Philip Sousa (1854–1932), whose vigorous compositions for the concert band won him the title of 'The March King' and a popular reputation comparable to Foster's. In the changing idiom of the popular song Foster had many successors, notably Irving Berlin (1888–), Cole Porter (1892–1964), and Hoagy Carmichael (1899–), while the theatre resounded to the music of Jerome Kern (1885–1945) and the partnerships of Richard Rodgers (1902–) with successively, Lorenz Hart and Oscar Hammerstein. With the latter Rodgers wrote the especially successful *Oklahoma!* which in 1943 gave the musical new energy and new directions.

Part of the inspiration for the music of *Oklahoma!* undoubtedly came from one of the most genuinely popular musical forms, the American folksong, though Rodgers's music is much more sophisticated, not to say commercialized, than that of the folk songs so assiduously collected by John and Alan Lomax. Many of these have European origins in both words and music, but they are nonetheless genuine and often moving expressions of an indigenous folk culture centred on the cowboy, the pioneer, the labourer and the convict. More recently, of course, singers such as Woody Guthrie and Pete Seeger have revitalized the folk song to serve the needs and the social conscience of a younger generation who have in turn produced their own exponents such as Bob Dylan.

The popularity of the American folk song in Britain has been exceeded only by an even more significant American music, jazz. This originated in the Negro 'blues', with its plaintive self-pitying rhythms, and in the syncopation of the 'ragtime' in vogue at the beginning of the century. Before and during the First World War, in the red light district of New Orleans, jazz acquired a spontaneous and exciting eloquence in the hands of Negro pianists like Jelly Roll Morton, improvising with real virtuosity. Other musicians developed the trumpet, the trombone, and the saxophone as jazz instruments, and, in the 1920s, especially, jazz quickly extended to other areas, notably Chicago, and to the white community as well as the black. New techniques such as swing were constantly devised to sustain the improvisatory vitality so essential to the form and to counteract the commercialization that success inevitably brought with it. If Louis Armstrong, Bix Beiderbecke, Duke Ellington, Benny Goodman, Fats Waller, and countless others demonstrated its range and vigour, George Gershwin (1898–1937) showed that jazz was capable of adaptation, in 'Rhapsody in Blue', to the concert platform and, in *Porgy and Bess*, to folk opera.

Yet, stimulating as these popular forms have always been, if one regards originality, innovation, and energy as characteristics of American art, these qualities are by no means restricted to the music so far discussed. Charles Ives (1874–1954) has been widely recognized for his bold experimentalism, his imaginative vitality and the modernity of his idiom. Technically difficult, his first published work had to wait nearly twenty years for its first performance in America in 1939 and was still perplexing to its audience. Entitled *Concord, Massachusetts, 1840–60*, it was a sonata intended as 'one person's impression of the spirit of Transcendentalism'. Its four movements (Emerson; Hawthorne; the Alcotts; Thoreau) have often been praised for their Americanness as much as for their virtuosity; and his later work such as the *New England Scenes* suite drew on similarly native inspiration. Aaron Copland (1900–) reached a wider audience than Ives by composing for radio, cinema, ballet, and school-children as well as for the concert platform. His work shows a marked jazz influence and substitutes for Ives's New England the more discordant atmosphere of the twentieth-century city in which (in Brooklyn) Copland was born. The tradition of individualism and the strenuously exacting demands on the performers' technique have been continued by the 'new virtuosity' associated with Eliott Carter (1908–) and others.

Edgar Varèse (1885–1965), who left France for the United States in 1915, prepared the way for the *musique concrète* and electronic music which younger composers have developed even more daringly. Foremost among these is John Cage (1913–), though those familiar with the work of Harry Partch (1901–) see him as equally exciting. It is debatable whether Cage should be called a composer at all, so heavily does he rely on the random choice and equally random juxtapositioning of sounds and even, in his celebrated *4′ 33″*, on four minutes, thirty-three seconds of total silence; his intention is to make his audience aware of the ordinary noises of life as music.

In this breaking down of distinctions between art and life Cage has been in line with and even anticipated avant garde theories in more arts than music alone. At Black Mountain College, North Carolina and elsewhere he has worked closely with and influenced poets, sculptors, and painters. In 1961 he commented:

> The novelty of our work derives therefore from our having moved away from simply private human concerns towards the world of nature and society of which all of us are part.

It is, as will be shown later, an equally apposite description of contemporary developments in drama, and in *American Art Since 1900* Barbara Rose demonstrates how Cage's theories helped pop art to transcend the limitations of more popular illustration.

Aspects of American Painting and the Plastic Arts

This interrelatedness of the arts in America is not new. Although there is no exact American equivalent to the Pre-Raphaelite Brotherhood in which painters and poets grouped themselves together for the implementation of a common programme, the interconnections between painting and literature, for example, are not the less vital for being less schematic.

A celebrated oil painting by Asher Durand (1796–1886) depicts a painter and a poet confronting a wild natural scene with obviously shared enjoyment. The originals are clearly recognizable as Thomas Cole (1801–1848) and William Cullen Bryant (whose poetry is discussed on p. 315); Durand's title 'Kindred Spirits' reflects the friendship between the two. When Cole, as a successful and established painter, set out to visit Europe Bryant addressed to him a cautionary sonnet, urging him to retain

> A living image of our own bright land,
> Such as upon thy glorious canvas lies.

The European landscape, he promised him, will be 'fair, / But different': it will bear 'everywhere the trace of men' as distinct from the virgin land of America, and Cole must strive to 'keep that earlier, wilder, image bright'. Cole hardly needed the advice, for, though he had been born in England, he had established his ability to capture that wilder image with even more Romantic zest than Bryant himself. Indeed, in some respects Durand's style is closer to Bryant's than is Cole's, for although Bryant is referred to as 'the American Wordsworth' his accurate observation of detail and quietly contemplative tone, lacking Wordsworth's mysticism, suggest Thomson or Cowper and parallel Durand's painstaking literal-mindedness more than Cole's emotional response to the awe-inspiring sublimity of nature. Cole's favourite scenery was in the valley of the Hudson River and in the Catskill Mountains, where Washington Irving had set the scene of 'Rip Van Winkle' and others of the pieces that he thought of as sketches and published in *The Sketchbook of Geoffrey Crayon*. The title and many of the pictorial descriptions establish Irving as another of these 'kindred spirits', responding equally to the romantic wildness and to the lonely seclusion of the scenery.

A sufficiently powerful and original artist to inspire followers, Cole was, with Thomas Doughty (1793–1856), the guiding influence of the Hudson River School and founded a distinguished tradition of American landscape painting continued by Frederick Church (1826–1900) and George Inness (1825–94), and culminating in the well-known work of Winslow Homer (1836–1910). Homer replaced the earlier Romanticism and sentiment of painting with a detached naturalism that links him with the trend of fiction in his day in his claim to paint his subject 'exactly as it appears'. His Civil War paintings of army life inevitably suggest comparison with Stephen Crane, and his paintings of fashionable young American women of the 1860s and 1870s have been described as 'a visual counterpart of the early novels of William Dean Howells and Henry James', but it is for his vigorous and sensuous land- and sea-scapes that he is chiefly remembered. His bold use of colour seemed to some critics crude in its power and vitality, but his enjoyment of the fresh air and the unspoilt woods and coasts of America appealed to the enthusiasms that took middle-class Americans hunting and fishing. His pictures made no excessive demands on them and they responded to those pictures as to the country they depicted: Homer at least fulfils de Tocqueville's prescription. Henry James decided that although Homer is a 'genuine painter' he is 'almost barbarously simple, and to our eye, he is horribly ugly; but there is nevertheless something one likes about him. What is it?'. It was, James concluded, his unexpected success in rendering 'the least pictorial features of the least pictorial range of scenery and civilization'.

Critics have complained that American landscape painters are often overwhelmed by the inexpressible grandeur of the scenery they seek to portray and unable to sustain a definite attitude towards it or to humanize it without at the same time trivializing it. Homer is perhaps the great exception. W. H. Auden once suggested that, whereas in Europe nature is 'something with which you enter into a personal relation', in the United States 'nature is something much more savage. . . . Nature is the dragon, against which St George proves his manhood'. Homer conveys something of this savagery in, for example, two of his best-known works: 'The Gulf Stream', in which a Negro in a storm-crippled boat awaits death from exposure in the brilliant tropical heat, or 'The Fox Hunt', where a fox on a bleak stretch of snow is surrounded by predatory crows much as the Negro's boat is encircled by sharks. This is a nature as impersonal and as relentless as in Stephen Crane's 'The Open Boat'.

The literary movement towards realism is paralleled in painting initially in the work of Thomas Eakins (1844–1916) who, because he chose subjects less pleasant and less romantic than Homer's and then treated them almost clinically, encountered far more opprobrium. His insistence that his female students should work from the nude model affronted American propriety and cost him his post as a teacher. A similar zeal for an accurate understanding of muscular movement attracted him to the photographic experimentation of Eadweard Muybridge who had developed a multiple-camera technique to record motion in split-second sequence. In his pictures of boxers and wrestlers, or of oarsmen on the Schuylkill River, Eakins renders athletic physique in action with the same absorption, accuracy and interested honesty of vision that distinguish his portraits and figures, and with the same careful attention to realism of background and setting. As a young man he studied surgery and two of his most compelling pictures, 'The Gross Clinic' and 'The Agnew Clinic', depict surgical operations with an uncompromising vividness that many found distasteful. Each is a remarkably dramatic composition to which the acutely observed portraits of surgeons and medical students contribute importantly, but there is also a documentary value in such faithful recording of conditions and a salutary reminder of the unlovely and bloody actuality of surgery.

About a decade earlier, Walt Whitman as a wound-dresser had had first-hand experience of surgery even more primitive and unhygienic, and in his poems had forced his readers to look at the scene just as unrelentingly as Eakins does. Whitman's celebration of the body in action and of all forms of physical energy is also similar to Eakins's, and it is not surprising to find Whitman speaking enthusiastically of Eakins as the only artist he knew 'who could resist the temptation to see what they think ought to be rather than what is', and also saying 'Eakins is not a painter, he is a force'. That Eakins responded similarly to Whitman may be inferred from the wonderfully robust portrait he painted of the poet a few years before Whitman's death; greatly impressed with it, Whitman told his friends that 'it sets me down in correct style without feathers'.

The urban realism of the literature of this period has its pictorial counterpart in the vigorous work of a group known variously as 'The Eight', 'The New York School' or, more disparagingly, 'The Ashcan School', and whose joint exhibition in 1908 caused something of a sensation. Their leader was Robert Henri (1865–1929), whose insistence on the quality of humanity permeates all their work. Henri had studied in Paris, was interested in Impressionism, but was led by his profound admiration for Eakins into a rebellion against academic conventions. From Emerson, Thoreau, and Whitman he derived a delight in 'people in whom the dignity of life is manifest', and this found expression in portraits of Indians that recall the inspired work of George

Catlin (1796–1872), the finest and most prolific painter of the American Indian, his territories and his culture; but the Eight most characteristically sought their inspiration in the city. They might have said, with Emily Dickinson, 'I thought that nature was enough / Till Human nature came', but they would have given the lines their own particular emphasis. One of the best of this group was John Sloan (1871–1951), the Hogarthian gusto and liveliness of whose work led one newspaper to comment 'To some it is vulgar; to others it is a rescript of actual life. . . . The world is full of such people'. Sloan, too, honoured Eakins as 'the only great American painter who has yet occurred'. Another of the Eight, William Glackens (1870–1938), was clearly influenced by Renoir in such paintings as 'Chez Mouquin', but the picture could serve admirably as an illustration to *Sister Carrie*, for it has the right touch of brash opulence and slightly over-dressed pseudo-sophistication to harmonize with the restaurant interiors of that novel mentioned on p. 368 above.

Dreiser, in fact, admired the work of this group, and his novel *The Genius* draws freely on the life of one of them, Everett Shinn (1876–1953), whom he knew personally. It is not a good novel, and Sloan criticized it, justifiably, as 'so banal and sentimental and saccharine', comparing it unfavourably with Joyce Cary's *The Horse's Mouth*; yet Dreiser's hero is not only a version of Shinn, but a persona for Dreiser, an identification of interest that emphasizes the connection between the arts. Like Dreiser, Shinn found beauty, romance, and excitement in the city, as well as ugliness and squalor. Similar characteristics emerge in the different idioms of Reginald Marsh (1898–1954) and Edward Hopper (1882–1967).

Hopper had been a pupil of Henri's but he also exhibited in the famous Armory Show of 1913, which revolutionized American painting by its introduction of such attitudes and techniques as Cubism – as in Marcel Duchamp's 'Nude Descending A Staircase' – and his combination of this influence with Henri's produces an interesting result. The nineteenth-century landscape painters had been impelled to humanize the scene, to relate it to ordinary people, and the Eight had seen the city primarily in terms of its inhabitants. Hopper's pictures, like 'Early Sunday Morning', emphasize the loneliness of the city, capturing its deserted moments as though the better to concentrate on the essentials of form and line which its architectural features reveal. Hopper described his aim in painting as 'the most exact transcription possible of my most intimate impression of nature'; it is a transcription primarily in the visual terms of design, yet the pictures still convey a feeling for the city despite the absence of people.

A similar preoccupation with design and with purity of line, form, and colour characterizes the work of a group of Hopper's contemporaries known as the Immaculates. Charles Sheeler (1883–1965) was a professional photographer as well as a painter, believing that 'photography is nature seen from the eye outward, painting from the eye inward . . . they complement each other'. In both media he was fascinated with industrial architecture and farm buildings, rendered in a bright, hard light or with values of light and shade that accentuate their rectilinear form, the clarity of surface, and the spatial relationships. There is an austere coolness about this work which sees factories, machines, locomotives, boats, as beautiful in their geometry and their functionalism, manifestations of technological efficiency apparently independent of human life. His Pennsylvania barns, his domestic interiors and his still lifes are closer to abstract design than to homely documentation (his fondness for staircases is clearly linked to the ease with which they can be reduced to linear patterns and intersecting planes), and his work has been called 'Americana in a vacuum'. Yet it *is* Americana, there is a remarkable sense of accomplishment about his work, and the artist's obvious enjoyment of both the object and the problem of translating it into artistic form communicates itself readily to the viewer.

A sensitive balance between the realistically representational and the abstract is also sustained by the precisionist technique of Georgia O'Keeffe (1887–). Taking natural forms such as a white flower or a bleached cow-skull, or a simple architectural form like a white barn, she sets them sharp-edged against flat areas of colour to achieve striking and evocative effects. Her husband was Alfred Stieglitz (1864–1946), a brilliantly creative photographer and art dealer, who had exhibited Rodin and Matisse in New York for five years before the Armory Show, and who was particularly influential in encouraging American artists while at the same time keeping them in close touch with current European developments. His photographs of New York street scenes link him with the work of the Eight, while his modernist tastes and his discriminating judgement earned the unstinted admiration of connoisseurs like Gertrude Stein. Under his guidance younger painters transmuted their delight in the American scene into forms less directly representational. Joseph Stella (1880–1946), for example, depicted Brooklyn Bridge with a romanticized response to its symbolic value that closely anticipates Hart Crane's rhapsodic tribute. So did John Marin (1870–1953), whose enthusiasm for the atmosphere of Manhattan was also expressed in a phrase which Crane would have understood in its interrelating of the arts: 'There is great music being played'.

Two of the other artists stimulated by Stieglitz and by urban America, Marsden Hartley (1877–1943) and Charles Demuth (1883–1935), were, like Sheeler, to become friends of William Carlos Williams, and there are closer parallels between his poetry and their painting. Georgia O'Keeffe's description of one of her pictures as 'nothing but a simple statement about a simple thing' is not far removed from his much-quoted principle 'No ideas but in things', and in its own medium Williams's technique is also precisionist. His *Autobiography* is interesting not merely for its anecdotes about these painters and the experiences they shared with him (his poem 'The Great Figure' and Demuth's picture of it, for example) but also for its comparison between his idea of a poem and Sheeler's idea of a painting. For both of them representational accuracy is of less importance than form, and the way in which the form, the design, captures the essence of the original. Williams, who once called himself 'a writer, at one time hipped on/ painting', who entitled one of his volumes *Pictures from Brueghel*, and whose poetry is always pictorial, comes closest to the Immaculates in a poem such as 'Nantucket' which consists entirely of a painterly interest in the composition and the spatial interrelationship of objects in a particular light. In *Paterson* he speaks with enthusiasm of the work of Jackson Pollock (1912–56) in terms that also suggest affinities between the paintings and his own poems:

> Pollock's blobs of paint squeezed out
> with design!
> pure from the tube. Nothing else
> is real.

In the aggressive, raw violence and the romantic individualism of the colour and swirling rhythms of Pollock's Abstract Expressionism American painting may be seen as finally establishing its creative independence and the independence of the artist. Painters such as Thomas Hart Benton (1889–), under whom Pollock studied, Andrew Wyeth (1917–) and Grant Wood (1892–1942) continued to record the American rural scene with loving fidelity and (as in Wood's popular 'American Gothic') touches of humour and irony; Charles

Burchfield (1893-) was influenced by Sherwood Anderson's *Winesburg, Ohio* towards a more brooding, melancholy regionalism touched at times with a mysteriousness more sinister even than that which some of Wyeth's pictures convey. Enjoyment of 'the dynamics of the American scene and . . . the impact of the contemporary American environment', coupled with an enthusiasm for jazz, led Stuart Davis (1894-1964) to evolve a racy, colourful and original idiom (though with some debts to Cubism) to render this vitality. Though a pupil of Henri's, Davis moved away from the representational in the belief that 'painting is not a duplication of experience, but the extension of experience on the plane of formal invention'. Formal invention, for him, involved the manipulation of bold geometric 'colour-shapes' into what he called 'stillscapes', the introduction of words into his pictures ('because they are a part of an urban subject matter'), and an ebullience and wit which Sam Hunter interestingly sees as a pictorial equivalent to the poetry of E. E. Cummings.

The subject matter and inspiration of these painters and others are more overtly American than Jackson Pollock's, but his pioneering dynamism constitutes a contribution to modern painting more original even than Davis's, and an assertion of the independent romantic imagination previously approached in American art only by Albert Pinkham Ryder (1847-1917). Discussing Pollock's work Sam Hunter emphasizes its occasional 'intimations of terror within disorder and chaos' and draws an interesting analogy with Edgar Allan Poe. There is a similar quality in Ryder's powerful, though technically inexpert, oil paintings, one of which was inspired by Poe's 'The Haunted Palace'. Ryder's inspiration was often literary but it is for its atmosphere, not for its illustrative value, that his work is memorable. The atmosphere is achieved, especially in the seascapes, by the silhouetting of dark masses against subdued colour and by the deliberate avoidance of detail, so that the result is often very close to abstract design and in marked contrast to the seascapes of his contemporary, Winslow Homer. Six of his paintings were exhibited in the Armory Show, and in their brooding, dramatic intensity his work frequently suggests comparisons with the dark vision of Emily Dickinson. Some of Pollock's early work shows unmistakably the influence of Ryder, and one suspects that Ryder, had he lived, would have shared Pollock's interest in some aspects of surrealism, but the originality of each, not the influences on them, is what ultimately matters. To end this survey with Pollock is not to minimize what American painting has accomplished since his death but to recognize how genuinely international it has become in its influence and not in imitativeness.

American sculpture may similarly be thought of as coming of age with the work of Alexander Calder (1898–). As readers of *The Marble Faun* and *Roderick Hudson* will remember, the nineteenth-century American sculptor looked to Europe for training, idiom, and style: Horatio Greenough (1805–52), Hiram Powers (1805–73), and William Wetmore Story (1819–95) all spent much time in Italy and became proficient in a classical mode that was already becoming anachronistic, and Augustus Saint-Gaudens (1848–1907), though a greater genius, did not break wholly free. (Two of Saint-Gaudens's works have literary associations: the hooded figure on the grave of Henry Adams's wife in Washington and the memorial to Colonel Shaw in Boston which prompted Robert Lowell's poem 'For the Union Dead'.)

Calder, who was trained as an engineer, gave sculpture a direction that may not extravagantly be characterized as American in at least two respects. In America, more eagerly than in other cultures, the artist has been excited by the concept of the twentieth-century city and has tried to respond to it and to its technological implications. Both in his forms and in his materials Calder created sculptures for a machine age. His mobiles hung shaped flakes of metal on pieces of wire in such a way that, although pleasurable associations with leaves blowing on a twig may be suggested, their primary effect on the viewer is more likely to arouse admiring curiosity about the principles of tension and balance that have had to be applied in order to create them. They are metal for an age that has outgrown stone, and they are not static as sculptures have traditionally been: they change their configurations all the time:

> . . . inconstant objects of inconstant cause
> In a universe of inconstancy.

Wallace Stevens's lines were not written to describe Calder's mobiles, but the three principles he enunciated in that poem (*Notes Toward a Supreme Fiction*) serve very well to characterize the aims of Calder's work and of much American art: 'It Must be Abstract. It Must Change. It Must Give Pleasure'. Art has aimed to give, as he puts it in the title of another poem, 'Not Ideas About The Thing, But The Thing Itself' and its achievement in so doing has been that

> It was like
> A new knowledge of reality.

Calder's mobiles are free-moving in space, and space has a particular appeal to the American imagination. It is an important concept in American painting from the Hudson River School, the great canvases of Bierstadt and the seascapes of Winslow Homer to a picture like Wyeth's 'Christina's World', with its dramatic juxtaposition of a cramped life and a vast horizon. Fittingly, the most notable American contributions to architecture have grown out of this concern with space. It has been suggested that the skyscraper evolved as man's solution to the problem of utilizing to the full the restricted ground-area of Manhattan, but the skyscraper has also flourished in cities like Chicago where there is no such problem. Louis H. Sullivan, one of the greatest skyscraper architects, defined the chief characteristic of the tall building as loftiness: 'It must be every inch a proud and soaring thing, rising in sheer exultation that from bottom to top it is a unit without a single dissenting line'. A symbol at once of man's aspiration and of his mastery over matter, it is also a thing of beauty: 'The skyscraper, in the dusk, is a shimmering verticality, a gossamer veil, a festive scene-drop hanging there against the black sky to dazzle, entertain, and amaze'. Thus Frank Lloyd Wright (1869–1959), a pupil of Sullivan's, and himself the architect of such skyscraper masterpieces as the Johnson's Wax tower at Racine, Wisconsin (1950), and the Price tower at Bartlesville, Oklahoma (1956).

As early as 1904 Wright was rhapsodizing over the potentialities of urban development in the organic metaphors that we have noted in writers such as Stephen Crane: 'Thousands of acres of cellular tissue, the city's flesh outspreads, layer upon layer, enmeshed by an intricate network of veins and arteries radiating into the gloom, and in them, with muffled, persistent roar, circulating as the blood circulates in your veins, is the almost ceaseless beat of the activity to whose necessities it all conforms.' Creator of some of the most exciting urban architecture in America – one thinks again of the Guggenheim Museum in New York with its spiral ramp descending round the perimeter of a circular wall and its skilful combination of artificial light with natural light from above to enhance its spaciousness – Wright utilized space most originally and most influentially not in the vertical but in the horizontal plane. In domestic architecture from the end of the nineteenth century onwards he was developing the Prairie House, the capacious, low structure possible in rural and suburban areas where there is room for it. Abandoning the traditional idea of a house as a collection of cellular units, he broke down the interior partitions to open up the house into a series of spaces integrated with one another and yet in their variations capable of constant surprises and changing vistas. Despite the dramatic and sometimes starkly severe lines of his exteriors with their projections and intersecting planes, and despite his fondness for such materials as glass and reinforced concrete blocks, the core of Wright's domestic interiors is usually the fireplace-hearth, as though trying to preserve into the twenty-first century the familial focus of the nineteenth. A brilliant and inventive engineer whose revolutionary system of constructing the Imperial Hotel in Tokyo enabled it to survive a disastrous earthquake unscarred, Wright was also a visionary, an idealist, and above all an individualist in the best American tradition. 'The soul of the individual work of art', he insisted, was unity, and in architecture as in any other art that unity could be obtained only by one individual firmly controlling and directing the conception and execution of the entire work. 'Unity through individual creativeness' was not only Wright's watchword, but the watchword of the best in American art. It was his good fortune to combine that individual creativeness with a technical expertise, an imagination and a social idealism that enabled him to revolutionize architectural thinking and practice throughout the world. It is a role which has to some extent been inherited by another American architect, Buckminster Fuller, whose concepts of geodetic form may well be as far-reaching as Wright's sense of space.

Drama in America: O'Neill, Miller, and Tennessee Williams

The vitality of American architecture can be paralleled in American drama; its sense of open space emphatically cannot. In drama an oppressive claustrophobia is more characteristic, but as in Wright's houses, the focus is very much on the family. Drama was a late developer among the American arts. The first play by an American playwright to be given a professional production was Thomas Godfrey's *The Prince of Parthia* in 1767; Royall Tyler's *The Contrast* twenty years later was the first American comedy. The history of American drama from then until the First World War is a subject of greater interest to the theatre specialist than to the common reader, and it has to be told more in terms of the theatre than of the drama, for no major dramatist emerged in America in that period. Noting that the stage was not very popular in America, de Tocqueville attributed this to the absence of great political catastrophes in the history of the Republic and added patronizingly: 'People who spend every day in the week in making money, and Sunday in going to church, have nothing to invite the Muse of Comedy'.

That there is still no great American comic dramatist is at first sight surprising when one thinks of the quantity – and, at its best, the quality – of Hollywood comedy, but the explanation of this may be more subtle and more literary than the one just quoted. Great theatrical comedy depends primarily on language and on language used artificially. (This is much less true of comedy on the screen which will exploit situation far more.) De Tocqueville suggested that in democracies dramas are listened to, but not read, and that audiences are less concerned with literary and dramatic excellence than with entertainment, asking only that the author should write 'the language of his country correctly enough to be understood'. For whatever reason, an artificial use of language as in Congreve, Sheridan, Wilde, or even Shaw, has lain outside the interest – perhaps even outside the competence – of the best American playwrights. They have written well enough to be understood, certainly, but with a simplicity and directness that on the printed page looks banal, however eloquent an accomplished actor may make it sound. Theirs is a vernacular drama, capable of good comic touches but not of sustaining high comedy and not of rhetorical intensity.

Similarly, there is no American tradition of verse drama, though poets continue to be attracted to the theatre. William Carlos Williams and E. E. Cummings both wrote plays, though with little conspicuous success. Archibald MacLeish, rather like Louis Macneice in Britain, at first thought radio provided the natural medium for poetic drama and then in 1953 made an assault on the theatre with *This Music Crept By Me Upon The Waters*, a play which is heavily indebted to Eliot. MacLeish's *J.B.* (1958), a modernization of the story of Job cast in the form of a morality play, showed more imaginative originality in treatment, but its theme is a familiar one. J.B.'s comforters tell him 'Guilt is a sociological accident' and 'Guilt is a psychophenomenal situation / An illusion, a disease, a sickness', but his reply might have been written by Arthur Miller:

> Can we be men
> And make an irresponsible ignorance
> Responsible for everything?
> I will not listen to you.

In the three one-act verse plays collectively published as *The Old Glory*

(1964), Robert Lowell dramatized stories by Hawthorne and Melville so as to highlight the present-day relevance of their moral themes, but even there – as I shall suggest later – the strength does not lie primarily in the verse or in the language any more than in other American plays.

To recognize this is not to disparage but to praise the American dramatic achievement and to emphasize the way in which it must be approached. 'We have had', said Arthur Miller, 'more than one extra-ordinary dramatist who was a cripple as a writer, and this is lamentable but not ruinous.' The American theatre was one of the first to suggest to the twentieth century that for some purposes at least the language of the drama need not be exclusively verbal. By now the lesson has been so well learnt as almost to appear platitudinous, but one has only to look back as far as 1949, when *Death of a Salesman* opened, to see how language-conscious the reviewers were. In New York George Jean Nathan complained that the ordinariness of its diction lacked poetic grandeur, and in England the critics, surrounded by verse drama reinvigorated by Christopher Fry and others, were even more non-plussed by it.

The play is one of the landmarks in the remarkable development of American drama in the past twenty-five years. In some respects it seemed to look back to the social realism of the 1930s. Clifford Odets, in *Awake And Sing!* (1935), had made a somewhat similar criticism of the discrepancy between the aspirations of a business-oriented acquisitive society and the harsh facts of existence. 'In my day,' says the patriarchal Jacob, 'the propaganda was for God. Now it's for success. A boy don't turn around without having shoved in him he should make success'; yet Jacob knows the limitations confronting his success-hungry grandson: 'In a house like this he don't realize even the possibilities of life. Economics comes down like a ton of coal on the head.' The play is more Marxist in sympathy than Miller's, more senti-mentally optimistic in its ending, more folksy in its freshness, but its basic humanity is similar to his. Odets's shorter play, *Waiting for Lefty* (also 1935), had made bolder use of the theatre in its dramatization of a trade-union meeting at which cab drivers are determining on a strike: the audience becomes part of the meeting and is implicated in the action of the play in a way that seemed novel and exciting. Technical experiment and an assertion of faith in the ordinary man also charac-terized Thornton Wilder's *Our Town* (1938), but this had none of Odets's social indignation; a sort of *Under Milk Wood* without the poetry and the exuberant humour of Dylan Thomas, it played unashamedly for the sentimental response. 'Do any human beings ever realize life while they live it? – every, every minute?' asks the heroine, allowed to revisit earth after her death.

In *Death of a Salesman* some critics found overtones of Odets-like Marxism, others saw it as another emotive celebration of the American everyman. The Depression, during part of which he worked with the Federal Theater Project, has left on Miller's imagination an impression that persists even down to his latest play, *The Price* (1968), but *Death of a Salesman* is neither Marxist nor sentimental in its exploration of the breakdown of personality under the pressures of the success-ethic. The structure and action of the play are determined by the psychology of the hero: past and present intermingle on the stage as they do in his mind until the catastrophe is precipitated by the eventual unavoidable facing of the one episode in his past that he has hitherto managed to suppress – the episode that establishes the extent of his own responsibility for what went wrong. The play is important for its fusion of the social and the psychological interpretations of Willy Loman's death, for its skilful use for dramatic purposes of a muted vernacular idiom, and for its unerring sense of theatre. Its use of a set in which the whole interior of a house is on view at once may be traced back to Eugene O'Neill's *Desire Under The Elms* (1924), but it also echoes *Our Town* in the fluidity of action whereby other scenes – an office, a restaurant, a graveyard – are evoked by the introduction of minimal properties or merely by a nudge to the audience's imagination.

Another dramatist already prominent when *Death of a Salesman* made its impact was Tennessee Williams. *The Glass Menagerie* (1945) had links with the thirties through its choric-narrator Tom, and *A Streetcar Named Desire* (1947) was a commentary on the degradation of life in a New Orleans slum tenement, while on a larger scale both could be seen as symbolic statements of the breakdown of Southern culture and Southern values. Their central importance, however, lay unquestionably less in social significance than in their tender exploration of the springs of human loneliness and alienation, the dilemma of the emotionally-handicapped and the psychologically-disturbed. Williams's dramatic gifts are complementary to Miller's: he can achieve a lyric intensity that is outside Miller's usual range but which can sometimes become facile, pretentious, or sentimental. He does not have the moral detachment from his characters that makes Miller coldly forbidding to some audiences though challenging to others. Williams has a Poe-like preoccupation with the self-destructive urges in human nature and human psychology: one of his poems speaks of 'the passion there is for declivity in this world / the impulse to fall that follows a rising fountain' and observes 'that some things are marked by their nature to be not completed / but only longed for and sought for a while and then abandoned'. It is in this view of life that his plays take their origin. In a stage direction to *Cat on a Hot Tin Roof* (1955), he digresses revealingly:

> The bird that I hope to catch in the net of this play is not the solution of one man's psychological problem. I'm trying to catch the true quality of experience in a group of people, that cloudy, flickering, evanescent, fiercely-charged interplay of live human beings in the thundercloud of a common crisis. Some mystery should always be left in the revelation of character in a play.

The mystery in Williams's plays is frequently linked with an almost Gothic macabre gloom of corruption and decadence. Guilt, for his characters, is, to borrow MacLeish's phrase, 'a psychophenomenal situation, . . . a disease, a sickness'. Miller, though sensitive to the complexities of the human psyche, is less concerned with the creation of mystery than with the investigating of moral responsibility. One is tempted into the over-simplified contrast that if Miller is the Ibsen of the American theatre, Williams is its Chekhov.

Powerful as Williams's plays are, they have tended to fall into a pattern, and for all his accomplishment he does not seem to have the capability of surprising us by new developments. Miller has shown a wider – though not always equally effective – range of technique and subject matter as well as a strong sense of commitment. *The Crucible* (1953) is not only an oblique comment on McCarthyism but an impressive play in its own right. *Incident at Vichy* (1964), on the other hand, though equally urgent in theme, is theatrically less effective and less complex in its moral insights. Significantly, it is the play in which the family is of least importance.

In 1956, lecturing on 'The Family in Modern Drama', Miller postulated a distinction between 'the magnetic force of the family relationship within the play' that demands realistic treatment and the non-familial, social relationship 'which evokes in a genuine, unforced way the un-realistic modes'. Among other examples he instanced O'Neill:

> . . . so long as the family and family relations are at the center of his plays his form remains – indeed, it is held prisoner by – Realism.

When, however, as for instance in *The Hairy Ape* and *Emperor Jones*, he deals with men out in society, away from the family context, his forms become alien to Realism, more openly and self-consciously symbolic, poetic, and finally heroic.

The two plays Miller names (they date respectively from 1922 and 1920) show O'Neill moving in a direction similar to that of German Expressionism, as did also *The Great God Brown* (1926), which experimented with masks to dramatize psychological problems of personality within the individual. In his family dramas, however, he managed without these adventitious aids, and in *Desire Under the Elms* he had invested naturalism with the intensity of tragedy in his story of Oedipal rivalry between father and son on a remote New England farm. The play drew heavily on the Phaedra story, and in 1931, in *Mourning Becomes Electra*, he attempted a modern re-working of the *Oresteia*, the myth on which Eliot was to found *The Family Reunion*. In a post-Civil War, New England setting O'Neill works out his theme in Freudian terms: the nemesis that overtakes his Orestes and Electra is their unwilling assumption of the personalities of their dead and hated parents – a fate far more convincing and implacable than that embodied in Eliot's Eumenides. O'Neill, one is tempted to say, recognized and exploited the dramatic possibilities of the generation gap and the problem of identity long before those phrases were blurred into cliché, and before Kenneth Tynan could complain that 'in the American theatre the theme has become obsessive'.

One other play in the rich and varied O'Neill canon deserves mention in this context: the posthumous *Long Day's Journey into Night* (1956), possibly his greatest achievement. Its autobiographical origins are of less consequence than its dramatic power. Within a conventionally realistic framework and with an almost classically strict observance of the unities, this *tour de force* transmutes a protracted and bitter family quarrel, a vicious circle of resentment, jealousy and transferred guilt, into a theatrical experience of unparalleled cathartic power. His dedication of the play, seeing it as an exorcism, spoke of 'the faith in love that enabled me to face my dead at last and write this play – write it with deep pity and understanding and forgiveness': it is these qualities that come out so remarkably in performance. Like *Cat on a Hot Tin Roof*, it juxtaposes vividly the petty animosities and the deep-rooted affections on which family life is nourished, highlighting human irrationality with alternating flashes of comedy and tragedy; both plays emphasize the savagery with which we inflict misery on others and on ourselves, and the illusions and mendacity on which we depend. This theme O'Neill had explored more bitterly and pessimistically in *The Iceman Cometh* (written 1939, produced 1946), with its gallery of dropouts who have already rejected or destroyed their family ties. In *Long Day's Journey* the blackness is counter-balanced by the moments in which the characters can still approach each other with some understanding and even, briefly, with love: it is this that gives it a depth and a poignancy that *Cat on a Hot Tin Roof*, for all its verve and brilliance, cannot match. In one such moment Edmund (a persona for O'Neill himself), describing an experience to his father, comments:

> I couldn't touch what I tried to tell you just now. I just stammered. That's the best I'll ever do. . . . Well, it will be faithful realism at least. Stammering is the native eloquence of us fog people.

Inevitably and rightly the speech has come to be regarded as O'Neill's *apologia pro lingua sua*: his keen ear for idiomatic usage and the rhythms of everyday speech does give the dialogue a 'native eloquence' such as distinguishes the work of the best American playwrights.

Albee and After

At the end of the fifties American drama moved away from the friction of the family circle to larger issues, and a convenient turning point is Edward Albee's *The Zoo Story* (1959). In this play a chance encounter on a Central Park bench reveals to a happily-married New Yorker what a precarious hold on reality his supposed social and domestic stability really represent. This theme, the difficulty the two characters have in establishing any sort of communication, the incoherent and comic inconsequentiality of some of the speeches by the intruder, Jerry, have led to a bracketing of this play with the Theatre of the Absurd. The affinity is more apparent in some of his other plays like *The American Dream* (1961), but *The Zoo Story* is peculiarly complex in its effect on us and in its alternations of compassion, frustration, and moral indignation. The alienated Jerry may be seen as first cousin to Aston in Pinter's *The Caretaker* or as a sacrificial Christ-symbol or as a gentler version of the character who, in Saul Bellow's novel *The Victim* (1947), also accosts in Central Park a comparative stranger and, blaming him for the misfortunes he has suffered, moves in on the victim's life until, to preserve his individuality and sanity, the victim has to eject him. To see the complacent Peter merely as the butt of Albee's satire is to miss the crucial division of sympathy on which the play turns. The theme could be stated in terms that would be equally applicable to Williams's *The Glass Menagerie*: the stability and sufficiency of the family, restricting human development and inhibiting communication, serves to heighten the fears and delusions of the lonely and alienated in an unsympathetic society; but this disguises the essential difference. The nostalgic gentleness that gives Williams's play its lyrical quality is replaced in Albee by a puzzled, savage note; Laura Wingfield is isolated by an unkind world, but Jerry is alienated by a world of cruelty and violence. Williams's play has a localized, regional theme; Albee's constitutes a wider commentary on the American way of life.

So, too, does *Who's Afraid of Virginia Woolf?* (1962). At one level an acute observation of the tensions and stresses of American academic life (a theatrical counterpart to such college novels as Mary McCarthy's *The Groves of Academe*, Randall Jarrell's *Pictures from an Institution*, or Bernard Malamud's *A New Life*), it is capable of several different interpretations. One of them rests on the fact that its principal characters, George and Martha, have the same names as Washington and his wife, and speak jocularly of having lived in their house for a couple of hundred years or so. George, the historian and man of the past, is contrasted with Nick, the brash young biologist confident of a scientifically-determined future. Albee is still hammering at the American Dream and, like the play of that title, this one might also be described in his words as a deliberately offensive work, 'an attack on the substitution of artificial for real values in our society, a condemnation of complacency, cruelty, emasculation and vacuity'. In its skilful isolation and exposure of its characters and its observance of the unities it merits comparison with *Long Day's Journey*. In its preoccupation with the necessity of illusion and self-deception if life is to be endurable, and with the necessity of recognizing and exorcising those illusions if life is to be lived consciously, it recalls *The Iceman Cometh*, but it is an advance on that play in its use of a predominantly comic form for a profoundly disturbing and sado-masochistic exploration of human cruelty and human vulnerability. If in the history of the American theatre it occupies a position analogous to that of *Look Back in Anger* in England – and they are comparable in savagery, vigorous dialogue, virtuosity, brilliant stagecraft, grim comedy, and merciless exposure of human nature at its meanest – their final scenes suggest an important difference in quality. The muted monosyllabic exchange between George and Martha has an integrity, humanity and qualified hopefulness quite unlike the saccharine sentimentalities into which Jimmy and Alison are finally betrayed. George and Martha achieve, albeit painfully, a genuine basis for mutual respect.

Albee takes drama one step forward from the realistic mode and 'the exact imitation of the details of private life' (to apply de Tocqueville's phrase in a different context). The action and the effect of his plays constitute the invasion of the privacy of private life, the questioning of the logic on which private life is based, and the threat of its dissolution into anarchy. From this at the very last moment it is snatched back in *A Delicate Balance* (1966) and domestic equilibrium is restored, but at a price. The world has to be accepted as less rational than one supposed. From the curtain line, 'Come now; we can begin the day', it is tempting to infer a dramatic movement exactly the reverse of *Long Day's Journey into Night*, but the image of the abyss still looms in the final speech:

> They say we sleep to let the demons out – to let the mind go raving mad, our dreams and nightmares all our logic gone awry, the dark side of our reason. And when the daylight comes again . . . comes order with it.

The order that comes is not the familiar order of rationality, any more than the language of that speech is quite the language of everyday life. Where Miller uses language still as a means of communication, discussion and reconciliation, Albee uses it less hopefully – it is the best we've got, but we had better not expect too much of it. Such misgivings about the nature and efficacy of language call into question one of the fundamentals of drama as we know it, but if the American theatre has seemed especially interested in reducing the dependence on words it is not because American dramatists cannot use language effectively.

For many Americans the daylight and order that Albee posits at the end of *A Delicate Balance* are less certain than the 'demons . . . and nightmare, . . . the dark side of our reason' which he also invokes. The reasons for this may lie in social stresses. For a long while the American theatre has been a white theatre. In 1920 there was O'Neill's *The Emperor Jones*; in 1930 *The Green Pastures*, Marc Connelly's agreeably folksy dramatization of the Negro Sunday School version of the Bible, and in 1935 Gershwin's *Porgy and Bess*; but if one were watching

only the theatre one would never have guessed that America had a
colour problem. It has been remarked that even Tennessee Williams has
no leading Negro characters, and does not tackle racial issues. All this
changed in 1964 with several plays produced in that year.

James Baldwin's *Blues for Mister Charlie* is an attempt at a 'rhythm
and blues' treatment of the 1955 murder in Mississippi of the young
Negro Emmet Till. The play has a vigorously fluid movement, great
energy and great indignation. Its aggressively violent language matches
its subject matter, and the brutalized coarse range of sexual allusion
mirrors the ingrained racial antagonism that is its subject. Yet already it
seems anachronistic in its ending where black tells white 'Well, we
can walk in the same direction': it is as though Baldwin could not
bring himself wholly to accept the violence that the play's theme and
logic had generated. A much blacker play produced in the same year is
Leroi Jones's *Dutchman*. Jones may have taken a hint for this play from
the transitional scene in Ralph Ellison's powerful imaginative novel,
Invisible Man. Escaping from a series of traumatic experiences and
betrayals, Ellison's nameless Negro travels in a New York subway
train towards what he hopes – erroneously – will be a new life: 'Things
whirled too fast around me. . . . Across the aisle a young platinum
blonde nibbled a red Delicious apple as station lights rippled past
behind her.' In *Dutchman* a white apple-eating Eve on a New York
subway provokes a black Adam, crudely and brazenly taunting him
sexually and verbally. 'Embarrassed but determined to get a kick out of
the proceedings', he responds initially but eventually, revolted, rejects
her. She stabs him, the other passengers throw his body out, another
young Negro enters and the cycle promises to begin again.

1964 also saw the staging of Robert Lowell's trio of plays, *The
Old Glory*, based on stories by Hawthorne and Melville. The grimmest
of the three, *Benito Cereno*, is especially relevant here for the change
Lowell makes to Melville's ending. He follows his original closely in
extracting the maximum irony from Captain Delano's innocence, good
nature and lack of imagination which blinker him even while they are
saving both him and Cereno, but at the end, where Melville records
the due punishment of the Negro mutineers, Lowell has them massacred
by American sailors. Only their leader survives, offering surrender but
pleading 'Yankee Master understand me. The future is with us.'
Delano guns him down with the words 'This is your future!' and
empties the remaining barrels of his pistol into the dead Negro as the
curtain falls. Cereno's comment, 'My God how little these people

understand!', is almost superfluous in its condemnation of white America hell-bent on destruction.

That the American theatre should have felt impelled to handle such topics is a sign of its increasing range and maturity: since 1964 the theatre has become more and more committed, politically and socially, but this commitment has had an observable effect on the drama. From *The Zoo Story* onwards a broadly similar pattern is discernible in many plays: an initial situation, deceptively familiar and ordinary, gradually dissolves into the strangeness of nightmare while yet retaining full credibility. A crude violence of language reflects a shameless laying-bare of private emotions – alienation, hatred, lust, and sexuality. Layers of convention and affectation are remorselessly peeled away to leave the raw, naked human animal whose desperate final recourse is to a burst of gratuitous, irrational violence which ends, but does not resolve, the conflict, internal and external. Against a background of Vietnam, race riots and campus revolt such an emphasis is understandable. Convinced that the urgency of the human crisis makes spectatorial passivity an irrelevance and a luxury, dramatists are trying to break down all distinctions between actor and audience. Shock tactics have superseded rational persuasion as the dramatist's chosen method; emotions are aroused through the senses rather than through the reason. Social permissiveness and the popularization of Freudian ideas have opened up at the same time other ways of dramatizing emotional and sensory experience that seem less oblique and more vigorous in their impact than the older medium of more formal language. Drama in the theatre, as well as outside it, has become increasingly violent, abrasive, and sensational.

Though there have been references throughout this book, as in so much other contemporary comment, to violence as a characteristic of American society, less emphasis than some readers will think desirable has been laid on those causes and agencies of violence all too familiar through the daily press. Some perspective is necessary: the majority of Americans still lead orderly, civilized lives. The violence and sensationalism of modern drama, prominent and significant as they are, must nevertheless be similarly seen in perspective against a more stable background of theatrical tradition that is neither outmoded nor exhausted. Art has always found ways of fulfilling its traditional function as an agent of order without being reactionarily conservative. Writing on music in Richard Kostelanetz's symposium, *The New American Arts* (1965), Eric Salmon observed:

If, wherever we turn, we seem to be approaching extremes, that is merely in the nature of contemporary life which, for the first time, offers us the complete range of possible experience as material for artistic development. . . . The new range of potential experience has opened up new forms and new psychological validities whose potential seems limitless; the range of possible experience *is* the subject matter of the new art.

At the same time, speaking of John Cage's renunciation of 'the conscious control of sound and, finally, sound itself', he warned that such renunciations may become 'merely new forms of self-indulgence' and concluded that 'the best new music is expressive in the sense that it is again "about" something'.

The current restlessness of all the American arts, like the restlessness of the United States themselves, may be a manifestation of that impulse towards a new order that has characterized their whole history since the pilgrims first undertook their errand into the wilderness.

Further Reading

PAINTING

Baigell, Matthew, *A History of American Painting*. New York, 1971.

Barker, Virgil, *American Painting: History and Interpretation*. New York, 1950.

Bauer, John I. H., *Revolution and Tradition in Modern Art*. Cambridge, Mass., 1951.

Bode, Carl, *The Anatomy of American Popular Culture, 1840–1861*. Berkeley, Calif., 1959.

Christensen, Erwin O., *The Index of American Design*. New York, 1950.

Dickson, Harold E., *Arts of the Young Republic: the Age of William Dunlop*. Chapel Hill, N.C., 1968.

Dorra, Henri, *The American Muse: a Story of American Painting, Poetry and Prose*. New York, 1961.

Flexner, James T., *That Wilder Image: the Paintings of America's Nature School from Thomas Cole to Winslow Homer*. Boston, Mass., 1962.

Goodrich, Lloyd, *Three Centuries of American Art*. New York, 1966.

Hunter, Sam, *Modern American Painting and Sculpture*. New York, 1959.

Huth, Hans, *Nature and the American: Three Centuries of Changing Attitudes*. Berkeley, Calif., 1957.

Kouwenhoven, John A., *Made in America: the Arts in Modern Civilization*. New York, 1948.

Larkin, Oliver W., *Art and Life in America*. New York, 1949, revised 1964.

McCoubrey, John, *The American Tradition in Painting*. New York, 1963.

Rose, Barbara, *American Art Since 1900: a Critical History*. New York, 1967.

DRAMA

Bigsby, C. W. E., *Confrontation and Commitment: a Study of Contemporary American Drama, 1959–1966.* London, 1967.

——, *Albee.* Edinburgh, 1969.

Bowen, Croswell, *The Curse of the Misbegotten: a Tale of the House of O'Neill.* New York, 1959.

Brown, John Russell, and Harris, Bernard (eds.), *American Theatre* (Stratford-upon-Avon Studies, no. 10). London, 1967.

Cohn, Ruby, *Edward Albee.* Minneapolis, Minn., 1969.

Downer, Alan S., *Fifty Years of American Drama, 1900–1950.* Chicago, Ill., 1951.

—— (ed.), *American Drama and its Critics.* Chicago, Ill., 1965.

Engel, Edwin A., *The Haunted Heroes of Eugene O'Neill.* Cambridge, Mass., 1953.

Falk, Signi Lenea, *Tennessee Williams.* New Haven, Conn., 1961.

Hogan, Robert, *Arthur Miller.* Minneapolis, Minn., 1964.

Jackson, Esther M., *The Broken World of Tennessee Williams.* Madison, Wis., 1965.

Kernan, Alvin B. (ed.), *The Modern American Theater.* Englewood Cliffs, N.J., 1967.

Krutch, Joseph Wood, *The American Drama Since 1918.* New York, 1939; revised edn. 1957.

Leech, Clifford, *O'Neill.* Edinburgh, 1963.

Raleigh, John H., *The Plays of Eugene O'Neill.* Carbondale, Ill., 1965.

Tischler, Nancy M., *Tennessee Williams: Rebellious Puritan.* New York, 1961.

Weales, Gerald, *American Drama Since World War II.* New York, 1962.

——, *Tennessee Williams.* Minneapolis, Minn., 1965.

Welland, Dennis, *Arthur Miller.* Edinburgh, 1961.

MUSIC

Barzun, Jacques, *Music in American Life.* Gloucester, Mass., 1956.

Blesh, Rudi, *Shining Trumpets: a History of Jazz.* New York, revised edn. 1958.

Chase, Gilbert, *America's Music: From the Pilgrims to the Present.* New York, 1955.

Howard, John Tasker and Bellows, George Kent, *A Short History of Music in America.* New York, 1957.

Mellers, Wilfrid, *Music in a New Found Land.* London, 1964.

Sablosky, Irving L., *American Music.* Chicago, Ill., 1969.

13 American Thought

MARCUS CUNLIFFE

Problems of Definition

We cannot begin to talk about American thought without deciding what the term should mean. Intellectual history and cultural history are well-established fields. *The Journal of the History of Ideas* has been in existence for forty years, and a quite substantial number of scholars on both sides of the Atlantic could be described as intellectual historians. In the bibliography of his own *The Growth of American Thought* (3rd edn, 1964), Merle Curti lists no less than seven other general surveys, from the pioneering *Main Currents in American Thought* (1927, 1930) of Vernon L. Parrington to a crop of more recent studies; and several more have appeared in the last few years. Monographic works on ideas in American religion, philosophy, science, education, law, politics, economics, and culture now run into the hundreds; biographies and critical analyses of men who might be regarded as American thinkers, from John Cotton to Norman Mailer, are likewise numerous. In addition there are books that examine the influence of European ideas on the United States, and vice versa.

The problem of quantity, while it means that a brief account like the present chapter can be no more than an impressionistic outline, is however less perplexing than the problem of what constitutes 'thought'. Are we to concentrate upon the 'best' thought, i.e. upon rigorous and refined arguments pursued in isolation or developed in a few centres of higher learning? If so, the difficulty is that such advanced and erudite propositions – for example, in philosophy or mathematics or linguistics – may be impenetrable to all but a handful of other intellectuals in each particular field. Their impact, if any, is usually subject to a time-lag of a generation or more, and may never be on the grand scale. At the other extreme, ideas that have an immediate impact are frequently superficial and ephemeral. We could say that they belong to the province rather of social than of intellectual history.

There is a further difficulty. What is '*American* thought'? The term might carry simply a geographical limitation, and so refer to ideas that happen to have circulated in the United States – as one might discuss the fauna and flora of a region, without necessarily implying that they are peculiar to that region. Or should we be concerned with ideas that appear to have had a special force and relevance for the United States? In either case there is a risk of false emphasis; for ideas inhabit an international realm, and many of the powerful ideas of the past three and a half centuries have entered the United States from elsewhere. In the 1790s Thomas Jefferson declared that the three greatest men who had ever lived were Bacon, Locke, and Newton. A hundred years later an American intellectual might easily have confined his trio of the intellectually great to Europeans such as Charles Darwin. A twentieth-century American would probably include Sigmund Freud. And any roll-call of 'American' intellectuals embraces a quantity of men who by upbringing or subsequent career could be deemed not to be American at all. Even omitting the colonial Americans, whose nationality was British, and the refugee intellectuals of the 1930s, we would have to note the non-American aspects of, for example, Crèvecoeur; Thomas Paine the radical pamphleteer; the political theorist Francis Lieber; the scientist Louis Agassiz; the journalist E. L. Godkin; the philosopher George Santayana.

This leads to the question of whether, for long periods of their history, Americans made *any* original contributions to the loftier reaches of human intellect. In the colonial era, and for some decades afterward, American thought was inevitably somewhat derivative, and restricted by everyday preoccupations. 'Men must have bread before books', said a Western preacher. 'Men must build barns before they establish colleges. Men must learn the language of the rifle, the axe and the plough, before they learn the lessons of Grecian and Roman philosophy and history; and to those pursuits was the early American intellect obliged to devote itself, by a sort of simple and hearty and constant consecration.' Certain of his nineteenth-century contemporaries were worried by the nation's prevailing materialism, by what they took to be a cultural regression in newly settled areas, and by the apparent tendency of a democratic society to express contempt for intellectual pursuits. Clergymen like Lyman Beecher insisted on the need for a huge missionary drive to reclaim the West for Christian civilization. Timothy Flint, himself a Westerner, felt in the 1820s that 'An unwarrantable disdain' keeps back 'the better informed and more powerful minds from displaying themselves.' Examining the effects of popular religion and politics, the historian Richard Hofstadter has indeed concluded that *Anti-Intellectualism in American Life* (1963) has roots stretching back far into the past. Another historian, Daniel J. Boorstin, perceives the seeming deficiency as a strength. In *The Genius of American Politics* (1953), Boorstin argues that the United States has never produced great social and political theorists, of the order of a Karl Marx, because the nation has happily never needed to. In his view neither the War of Independence nor the Civil War was an ideological conflict; each was, socially and intellectually, a conservative movement, relying upon familiar, commonsense propositions. So instead of agonizing over their supposedly inferior cultural record, Americans should rejoice at their immunity to the brain-fevers of Europe.

Most American historians of ideas would not fully subscribe to the position either of Hofstadter or of Boorstin. In varying degrees, however, they have on the whole assumed that the United States is best understood as a culture with special features differentiating it from the civilization of Europe. By and large they have stressed those ideas which shaped (or possibly hindered) the formation of the sense of an American national identity. In this respect they have, even in discussing the same phenomena, approached their material in a fairly distinct fashion, vis-à-vis European scholars, who tend to be Europe-centred and place less emphasis on national boundaries. Thus, Merle Curti's *Growth of American Thought* is a work of wide learning, free from chauvinistic claims. It nevertheless pays close attention to American nationalistic drives, and to the American social context. This is illustrated by the titles of the seven sections into which Curti chronologically divides his material:

1. Adaptation of the European Heritage
2. The Growth of Americanism
3. Patrician Leadership
4. Democratic Upheaval
5. Triumph of Nationalism
6. Individualism in a Corporate Age
7. Diversion, Criticism, and Contraction

Another well-known text, Ralph H. Gabriel's *The Course of American Democratic Thought* (1940; 2nd edn, 1956), examines the intellectual history of the United States since 1815 – at which point, according to the author, Americans were free for the first time to devote themselves to 'North American tasks'. Gabriel believes that by then Americans had arrived at three major tenets, each a complex of ideas:

1. the dignity of human personality (with corollary beliefs in individual freedom of action, and freedom to participate in decision-making)
2. the existence of a fundamental moral law, both Platonic and Christian in origin, anterior to and higher than man-made institutions
3. the providential and universal mission of the United States to create a just society, and in so doing to offer an example for the rest of mankind.

Or, in oversimplified form, democracy, religion, universalist nationalism.

A later text, Stow Persons' *American Minds* (1958), identifies five successive (though not chronologically distinct) 'social minds' in American history. A social mind is defined as 'the cluster of ideas and attitudes that gives to a society whatever uniqueness or individuality it may have as an epoch in the history of thought'. The five epochs are:

1. The Colonial Religious Mind: 1620–1660
2. The Mind of the American Enlightenment: 1740–1812
3. The Mind of Nineteenth-Century Democracy: 1800–1860
4. The Naturalistic Mind: 1865–1929
5. The Contemporary Neodemocratic Mind.

Kindred patterns may be discerned in *American Thought Before 1900: A Sourcebook from Puritanism to Darwinism* (1966), a volume of readings edited by Paul Kurtz, a philosopher. Kurtz sees the United States as an inveterately pluralist society: 'the meeting place of divergent ideas and movements: Puritanism, deism, materialism, Unitarianism, transcendentalism, idealism, realism, and pragmatism – and most recently of naturalism, positivism, analytic philosophy, Marxism, Thomism, phenomenology, Zen Buddhism, and existentialism'. His enumeration reminds us of the international (and perhaps almost hopelessly eclectic) nature of the history of ideas, since all of these movements have their counterparts outside the United States. However, he considers that the pragmatic approach – the evaluation of ideas according to their social context and their practical consequences – *is* characteristically American. Here he is in agreement with a good many American scholars, including for instance Daniel Boorstin and (see the final chapter of *Paths of American Thought*, edited by Arthur M. Schlesinger, Jr. and Morton White, 1963) Arthur Schlesinger, Jr., who in several of his works praises the robustly empirical spirit of American pragmatism.

Despite variations, then, a broadly agreed-on interpretation is apparent. Whether or not they consider the outcome desirable, American intellectual historians tend to take for granted the 'exceptionalist' nature of their theme: they look for the features that stamp an idea as 'American', and regard certain other ideas as basically European or at any rate not-American. Among not-American ideas, for example, would be placed hierarchical and status systems, profoundly pessimistic estimates of human nature, defences of an established church and the like. Typically enough one American scholar, Clinton Rossiter, gives his book *Conservatism in America* (2nd edn, 1962) the subtitle *The Thankless Persuasion*.

Within what they identify as the mainstream of native thought, Americans usually focus upon aspects of 'Puritanism' from the early seventeenth to the mid-eighteenth century; then upon political or 'Enlightenment' ideas for the second half of the eighteenth century; and upon 'democratic', 'Transcendentalist', or 'Romantic' concerns for the first half of the nineteenth century. They reveal less unanimity in dealing with the period *c.* 1860–1920 – labelling it variously as 'Social Darwinist', the 'Gilded Age', the era of *laissez-faire*, or of the Robber Barons, and so on. Perhaps understandably, their picture of twentieth-century thought is tentative and miscellaneous, often ending on a note of sad perplexity. Many of the writings in this vast field, especially on particular topics, are ambitious and ingenious. The defect of some, at least for a non-American reader, is their preoccupation with Americanness, which leads them to neglect and on occasion distort contemporaneous movements in Europe.

However, there is no doubt that Americans in previous generations were often also absorbed in the question of what it meant to be an American. Europeans for their part concurred in the notion that to be an American was a special and complex fate. There is an interesting illustration of the point in an essay on 'The Spirit of the Age', written by the young John Stuart Mill in 1831. Mill, the redoubtable son of a redoubtable Scottish Utilitarian, felt that his epoch was above all one of transition. Everything was in flux; traditional beliefs seemed irrelevant.

At all other periods, there exists a large body of received doctrine, covering nearly the whole field of the moral relations of man, and which no one thinks of questioning, backed as it is by the authority of all, or nearly all, persons, supposed to possess knowledge enough to qualify them for giving an opinion on the subject. This state of things does not now exist in the civilized world – *except . . . to a certain limited extent in the United States.*[1]

Even with his cautious qualification, it is remarkable that to this well-informed British intellectual the United States should figure as a place in which there was a body of 'received doctrine', or what nowadays might be called ideology. A similar comment was made a few years later by a Scottish observer, Charles Mackay, in *Life and Liberty in America* (1837). The affections of the average American, Mackay felt, 'have more to do with the social and political systems with which he is connected, than with the soil which he inhabits. The man whose attachments converge upon a particular spot of earth, is miserable if removed from it; but give the American his institutions, and he cares little where you place him.' He hallowed a set of ideas ('received doctrines', 'institutions') rather than a physical habitat; and these ideas were clearly not ancient but of relatively recent extraction.

Provided, therefore, we take into account the constant transatlantic passage of ideas (commonly in a westward direction until the twentieth century), there is much to be said for following the general pattern of American surveys of the nation's intellectual biography. It seems sensible, perhaps essential, to concentrate upon those general ideas which were taken seriously by serious men at various epochs: in other words, to leave out recondite learning at one extreme and journalistic trivia at the other.

Religious ideas come first, both in chronological order and because they have continued, even in debased forms, to exercise a considerable influence. The characteristic figure within this stream of thought, which may for convenience be styled as 'The Puritan Heritage', is a *clergyman* such as Cotton Mather. Next comes the intense interest, in the last third of the eighteenth century and the first forty years of the nineteenth, in what we may call 'The Politics of Independence and Equality'. The characteristic figure here is a *statesman* such as Thomas Jefferson. Overlapping with this phase is a period of 'Romantic Individualism', symbolized by an *ex-clerical* free spirit like Ralph Waldo Emerson. The later decades of the nineteenth century defy neat

[1] Italics added.

summary; but there is little doubt that in this era of 'Business Enterprise' the most prominent figure is a successful *businessman* like Andrew Carnegie. We should however recognize that, despite wide agreement on broad issues, the nineteenth century produced sundry 'Heresies and Misgivings'. No one type embodies them all, but perhaps most are symbolized in the abstract figure of the *gentleman*. Finally comes the manifold and contradictory era of 'Twentieth-Century Confusions', whose spokesmen often think of themselves as *avant-garde rebels*. The picture is thus as follows:

1. The Puritan Heritage
2. The Politics of Independence and Equality (*c.* 1760–1840)
3. Romantic Individualism (*c.* 1800–60)
4. Business Enterprise (*c.* 1860–1900)
5. Heresies and Misgivings (*c.* 1800–1900)
6. Twentieth-century Confusions (*c.* 1900–70)

The Puritan Heritage

The word 'Puritan', which in the seventeenth century had a fairly precise meaning, widened thereafter into an almost indefinably broad range of connotations. It is even worse in this respect than a term like 'frontier', which in the American context may signify a line, a region, a number of regions, a process of settlement, or a state of mind. As with 'frontier', however, the very enlargement of the term 'Puritan' is a significant feature in the American outlook. With Puritanism, a religious doctrine initially confined to New England came by degrees to symbolize a style of thought and conduct that reached into nearly every corner of the United States. In other words, American culture was largely shaped by the 'Universal Yankee Nation' – a phrase about New England popularized in the 1820s – and New England was largely shaped by Puritanism.

The Puritans who left Old England for New England in the first decades of the seventeenth century were agreed upon the need to correct or 'purify' the Protestant faith, in particular to purge it of its persistent 'Popish' organization and ritual. The extreme wing, represented by the Pilgrim Fathers of the Plymouth settlement (1620), led by William Bradford, was 'separatist': i.e. prepared to take the drastic step of total separation from the national Church of England. The main group, represented by the more substantial Massachusetts Bay settlement of 1630 and led and ministered to by John Winthrop,

John Cotton, and Richard Mather, was 'non-separating' at the outset. Its aim, by remaining within the Church, was to bring about a 'presbyterian' reform on the lines established by Calvin in Geneva and Knox in Scotland. In this Calvinist or quasi-Presbyterian reform, the Anglican hierarchy of archbishops, bishops and so on, which seemed dangerously close to the Roman church (and therefore, in Puritan eyes, corrupt and ungodly) was to be replaced by a non-episcopal hierarchy of the elect – ministers and laymen.

Before very long the distinction between separatists and non-separatists disappeared. New England developed a pattern of 'Congregational' churches, each governed by its priest and its 'saints' (men and women who had demonstrated their religious zeal and probity), and each almost autonomous. For the first two or three generations, New England's culture was God-centred. Its townships were theocratic, not democratic. The elders of the church, in conjunction with the magistrates, dominated the community. Their religion was demanding, and they demanded allegiance to it. The child, the lukewarm worshipper and the backslider were constantly reminded of their duty to find God, to achieve conversion, to subject their lives to fierce self-scrutiny and the scrutiny of the congregation. The Puritans reacted still more sharply against those who challenged orthodoxy; the devout but over-argumentative Anne Hutchinson was expelled for 'antinomianism' and Roger Williams, who subsequently published his views in *The Bloudy Tenent of Persecution* (1644), for his 'levelling' (i.e., prematurely democratic) principles. The Quakers who began to arrive in the colonies during the 1650s were likewise persecuted by New England communities, and endured some hard times in America before their leader William Penn secured a grant of the territory that he named Pennsylvania (1681). The town he founded there, Philadelphia, was 'the city of brotherly love' – an appellation that might not have seemed appropriate for Boston, whatever its other virtues.

Still, by the latter end of the seventeenth century the severities of Pilgrim days were considerably modified. The Half-Way Covenant (1662) relaxed the requirements for acceptance into church membership. In Connecticut, though Massachusetts followed more slowly, the Saybrook Platform (1708) took an important step towards the incorporation of Congregational churches within a semi-Presbyterian organization. The advantages of such an organization became clearer to each successive generation, with the result that elsewhere in the United States Presbyterianism flourished while Congregationalism remained more or less confined to New England – and even there in an increasingly qualified 'Presbygalian' guise. It was Richard Mather, the first generation of a famous family, who felt obliged to draft the Half-Way Covenant. His son Increase Mather, a president of Harvard and the author of a prodigious quantity of histories, hagiographies and other providential testimonies, has figured as an archetypal Puritan for his part in the Salem witch trials of the 1690s. Yet Increase Mather, though a person of painful rectitude, was in many ways far more rational than his critics have realized (he was, for example, a supporter of the then-suspect practice of inoculation for smallpox). The same could be said much more strongly of Cotton Mather, the son of Increase, who has been subjected to even harsher strictures than his father for writing such works as *The Wonders of the Invisible World* (1693); he was a man of exceptional accomplishments who well deserved his invitation to become a Fellow of the Royal Society. There is no finer document of ecclesiastical New England than Cotton Mather's compendious *Magnalia Christi Americana* (1702) – obsessive, erudite, deeply pious, and moving in its conviction that the Puritans were a chosen people: 'I write the wonders of the Christian religion, flying from the depravations of Europe, to the American strand. . . .'

It is true that Cotton Mather was already something of an anachronism, unsuccessful in his bid to follow his father as president of Harvard, and forced to retreat from his previous hard position on witchcraft in face of the hostile criticism of his rationalist contemporary Robert Calef. It is also true that the Mather dynasty had almost lost its intellectual force. Samuel Mather, Cotton's son and the fourth in the line to become a minister, was by comparison a feeble preacher and a scholar whose publications declined into antiquarianism. A similar weakening is apparent in the several generations of the Winthrop family: compulsive piety modulated into worldliness. True, too, the upsurge of penitential religious feeling led by Jonathan Edwards in the 1730s, and known as the Great Awakening, failed to restore Calvinistic faith to its old glory, even if Edwards himself was perhaps the most gifted philosopher-theologian of eighteenth-century America. Recent scholars have discerned in the Great Awakening a first stirring of the libertarian principles that produced the American Revolution. There may be something in this theory. But at the time the battle-lines were not drawn in such a way. As a promoter of revivalism Edwards seemed to such intelligent opponents as Charles Chauncy to be vulgarly emotional, and a tyrannically tactless minister, who having again released the antinomian demon suffered the fitting punishment of dismissal by his congregation. Chauncy's own thought led him toward that mild, decent, minimally doctrinal faith known as Unitarianism which by the early nineteenth century had almost ousted Congregationalism among the educated citizenry of the Boston area. Yankee Puritanism was mocked outside New England, for instance in Washington Irving's burlesque *History of New York, . . . by Diedrich Knickerbocker* (1809). Its demise was also a subject for New England humour: the best-known example is Oliver Wendell Holmes's poem 'The Deacon's Masterpiece; or, The Wonderful "One-Hoss Shay"' (1858), which likened Calvinism to a carriage built to last for ever. All its parts were of equal strength, and so all collapsed together, a hundred years after they were assembled. Indeed, Perry Miller has shown that from the beginning the Puritans feared that theirs was a losing fight – against rival dogmas, against laxity and against materialism. Even Anglicanism was able to make alarming inroads during the eighteenth century, as in the terrible moment at Yale in 1722 when the president, Timothy Cutler, and several fellow-Congregationalists, apostasized to the Church of England. The 'jeremiad' or warning sermon was, as Miller shows, a standard feature of Puritan religious life, and a token of deep uneasiness.

But the roots of Puritanism remained deep. However qualified, however outdistanced by denominations like the Baptists and the Methodists and its Presbyterian near-relations, the old Calvinist spirit continued to shape American thought. From New England Puritanism developed the concern for education, in order to train ministers and church members capable of contributing to metaphysical inquiry. The foundation of Harvard College dated back to 1636; Yale, Amherst, and Williams were other Congregational establishments, and in order to compete the other denominations had to be no less active in college-founding – a concern that led to the creation of hundreds of religiously oriented colleges throughout the United States during the nineteenth century. This is not to say that American education was wholly shaped by New England influences – the old foundations of Princeton, Columbia, and Pennsylvania are a reminder to the contrary – but that New England remained in the forefront. The lyceum movement, offering popular education by means of public lectures, reached the United States via New England (1826). The most important figures in secondary education – Horace Mann, Henry Barnard, William T. Harris – were New Englanders by birth and upbringing. So were such pioneers of women's education as Emma Willard, author of *A Plan for Improving Female Education* (1819), Catherine Beecher, and Mary Lyon, who almost single-handedly established Mount Holyoke Female Seminary (1837). Oberlin College in Ohio, the first to introduce co-education and to admit Negroes, was founded (1833) by New England Congregationalists. The Yankee teacher, professor or preacher, if somewhat less celebrated in folklore, became a much more significant product of the region than the Yankee peddler.

Cultural commitment and commercial enterprise: both were facets of what Max Weber termed the 'Protestant ethic' or, in David Riesman's parlance, 'inner-directedness'. This ethnic had revealed a dual aspect even from the early days of John Cotton and Anne Hutchinson: communal and individual. The communal element was the one that particularly gave Puritanism a bad name for moralistic, self-righteous and censorious codes of conduct. The existence of his Puritan ancestors, said the novelist Nathaniel Hawthorne in one of his stories, was 'sinister to the intellect and sinister to the heart; especially when one generation had bequeathed its religious gloom, and the counterfeit of its religious ardour, to the next; for these characteristics, by being inherited from the example and precept of other human beings, and not from an original and spiritual source, assumed the form both of hypocrisy and exaggeration.' To the question, Am I my brother's keeper?, Puritanism returned an emphatic yes. The crushing weight of this communal righteousness is memorably evoked in Hawthorne's *The Scarlet Letter* (1850), whose seventeenth-century heroine is compelled to wear a large 'A' to signify to all and sundry that she has been an adulteress. Disgrace in the Puritan world carried a religious implication: it was among other things a fall from grace. The ingrained American tendency to attempt to legislate morality (for example, in the Prohibition amendment of 1919), and to find moralistic sanction for displays of national power, almost certainly owes something to this early climate of opinion: a view expounded, for instance, in David L. Larson, *The Puritan Ethic in United States Foreign Policy* (1966).

If that is so, however, it is no less important to stress the individualistic aspect of Puritanism. We have noted that this was hardly an intentional feature of primal Puritanism. There is an anecdote about a Massachusetts minister who, asked by a stranger, 'Are you, sir, the person who serves here?' replied stiffly, 'I am, sir, the person who rules here.' But ministers soon found that their parishioners and their town meetings would not tolerate autocracy. By a central paradox Puritanism, and Protestantism generally, undermined the principles of authority and orthodoxy that they set up. As *The Scarlet Letter* shows, the pressure of the community was nothing compared to the pressure of man's own conscience. Self-examination preceded and predominated over the dictates of public opinion. In the words of Anne Bradstreet's seventeenth-century *Meditations*:

> As man is called the little world, so his heart may be called the little commonwealth.... Here is also the great court of justice ..., which is always kept by conscience, who is both accuser, excuser, witness and judge.... Yea, so absolute is this court ... that there is no appeal from it – no, not to the court of heaven itself. For if our conscience condemn us, He also, who is greater than our conscience, will do it much more.

Almost every articulate Puritan – and the level of articulateness was very high – kept a journal to record his personal pilgrim's progress; and autobiography persisted as a psychological need and eventually as an art form, from the first private musings of a Thomas Shepard or a Samuel Sewall to the sophisticated late nineteenth-century self-scrutiny of a Henry Adams. Alexis de Tocqueville, visiting the United States in the 1830s, concluded that this inwardness was a crucial feature: 'in most of the operations of the mind each American appeals only to the individual effort of his own understanding'.

With it went an abiding compulsion to labour and to leave a mark. The Puritan ethic discouraged day-dreaming and dilettantism. There is something remarkably strenuous even in the writings of men like Henry David Thoreau, whose avowed purpose is to warn against a life of steady toil. Historian-contemporaries of his such as William H. Prescott and Francis Parkman, who were in comfortable circumstances and who were beset by illness and hypochondria, displayed heroic application in tackling and completing ambitious themes through long years of effort. The poet Henry Wadsworth Longfellow, far from Puritan in his life as a Harvard professor, was equally committed to scholarly industry. 'Let us then be up and doing', he enjoined his fellows in one of his most admired poems, 'The Psalm of Life'.

In achieving independence, Americans absorbed something of the old millennial, providential religious style into their new-found nationalism. God's purposes were still being worked out on the American strand. Indeed, Mormonism or the church of the Latter Day

Saints, an American variant of Christianity developed by Joseph Smith in the 1820s, maintained that Zion, God's heaven upon earth, had been prepared for the faithful 'on this continent'. *Pari passu*, religion was taken to be a basic ingredient of American nationalism (though, mainly because of its doctrine of polygamy, Mormonism was for some decades regarded as both un-Christian and un-American). Religious toleration, partly as a matter of democratic principle and partly as a recognition of necessity in a pluralist society, was also enshrined. 'Being no bigot myself . . .,' George Washington told his French friend Lafayette in 1787, 'I am disposed to indulge the professors of Christianity in the church, that road to Heaven which to them shall seem the most direct. . . .' Elsewhere he remarked that the same indulgence should be extended to Jews or Muslims. But Washington was a deist, sharing the genially non-doctrinal atmosphere of the age with men like Thomas Jefferson and Benjamin Franklin. Reacting against the French Revolution, Americans made it clear that while all religions might theoretically be equal, Catholicism was potentially subversive. The true American mode was not Catholic, not deist and certainly not agnostic, but Protestant. Above all, a proper American must profess *a* belief in religion; and the best form of belief was that expounded by one or other of the Protestant denominations.

Even more than in nineteenth-century Britain, and far more than in France, the United States equated churchgoing with civic spirit. There was virtually no anticlericalism. Despite the secularization of life, as we may see from the careers of a family like the Beechers, religion remained woven into the fabric of society. Throughout the nineteenth century, conversion, revivalism, sermonizing, private and public struggles over faith and dogma, all showed that the pulpit was as important as the classroom or the political platform in determining the direction of national thought. The Puritan heritage was still a force to be reckoned with, even if it had become so diffused that Puritanism, being a term that might be used to explain almost everything, might thereby cease to explain anything, at any rate in any precise form. In some way easier to feel than to analyse, the New England cleric still exerted a ghostly ruling influence that stretched far beyond the old geographical domain.

The Politics of Independence and Equality

As we have seen, the religious impulse pervaded American life long after Puritanism had lost its initial rigour; and, in implication if not always in intent, it led towards libertarianism and individualism. Some scholars even see the intellectual ferment of the American Revolution as a quasi-religious drama of depravity and redemption. There is no doubt some truth in this. It is clear, for example, that the political notion of Americans as a chosen people, providentially destined to uphold new standards of moral worth, was a latter-day version of the religious notion of America as an asylum for God's elect. But the quarrel with Britain necessarily was expressed in a secular vocabulary, and concerned itself with 'political' issues: issues, that is, of authority, legitimacy and representation.

This was certainly the predominant tone of American thought during the second half of the eighteenth century. Colonial grievances against the mother country generated a mass of polemical pamphlets which reached a climax in Thomas Paine's magnificently scornful *Common Sense* (1776):

> Freedom hath been hunted round the globe. Asia and Africa have long expelled her. Europe regards her like a stranger, and England hath given her warning to depart. O! receive the fugitive, and prepare in time an asylum for mankind.

Though the issues changed and grew less dire in the next decades, Americans were obliged to think long and hard about the nature of man and the nature of government. So were Europeans, in those fateful decades that witnessed the French Revolution and its complex aftermath; and of course many men of goodwill, in Britain and in continental Europe, identified themselves emotionally with the American cause.

Where did the ideas of this era come from? Or, putting the matter in another way, there was an Enlightenment in Europe: was there one in North America? The most acceptable simple answer is that educated Americans of the period were familiar with the amalgam of humane, rational, and scientific inquiry that constituted 'enlightened' thinking. In Benjamin Franklin, the colonists produced at least one figure of international renown. Most of their political lore came from the classical and British authors – Cicero, Locke and so on – with whose names they sprinkled their own writings. Similarly, they drew upon the natural-rights arguments of eighteenth-century European philosophers. But their context, in a complicated way, was British. As the dispute with the mother country sharpened, the Americans discovered that the tenets of British political orthodoxy – so much envied and admired by European observers like Montesquieu – did not suit their purposes. They turned rather to the Whiggish-radical unorthodoxy of such British intransigents as John Trenchard, Thomas Gordon, and Bishop Hoadly. In other words, the Americans selected those parts of libertarian thought that spoke to their own needs, and built upon them.

The resultant pre-Revolutionary pamphlet war did not yield any masterpieces of native political philosophy. As Bernard Bailyn notes in *The Ideological Origins of the American Revolution* (1967), the American style was less brilliant and less ferocious than that of British domestic controversy (Paine, a pamphleteer of genius, was an Englishman who did not come to the colonies until the eve of the Revolution). It was less brilliant because – then and for many years – American cultural resources were too restricted to sustain a professional class of men of letters on the model of Swift or Defoe. It was less ferocious because the Americans, then and later, did not *feel* ferocious. Their aim was not to overturn society, but to remind their transatlantic kinsmen of the common legacy of Anglo-American liberty. They spoke boldly (and by no means with one voice: there were plenty of moderates and doubters among the American pamphleteers), but on the whole with a lawyerlike shrewdness. Their tone was righteous rather than furious.

In the crucial years from 1763, when the Seven Years' War ended, to 1776, when the Declaration of Independence was drawn up, the argument however took on depth. The leaders of American opinion, nearly all trained in the law, were intelligent and articulate men. As the debate developed, the colonists found themselves examining and then repudiating the bases of British constitutional theory. The process is too intricate to recount here. The vital point is that the colonists became aware of the anomalies in their situation. The large measure of freedom they had enjoyed in practice was circumscribed in theory. They were British subjects, yet in some sense held in subjection. The British doctrine of sovereignty, comforting though it might be to men in England, tended to seem either punitive or irrelevant to men three thousand miles away. Having concluded that it could not properly apply to themselves, under present circumstances, the colonial spokesmen went on to conclude that it *should* not apply. Independence was thus not only justified, it was also, as Paine insisted, mere common sense. In drafting the Declaration, Thomas Jefferson contented himself with a brief exposition of the universal, 'unalienable' rights of man – good Enlightenment philosophy, but also tactically desirable since they were no longer claiming the protection of specifically British rights. He continued with a bill of complaints against the British crown. Eight years later, having failed to suppress the rebellion by force of arms, Britain conceded that the thirteen United States were now formally an independent nation.

Sovereignty had crossed the Atlantic. But where did it reside, and on what terms? The next stage in American political logic was to agree upon the apportionment of this sovereignty between the individual states and the entity known as 'the United States'. Simultaneously, it was imperative to devise frameworks of government for each state and at the national level. The most significant documents of this phase – most intense in the years from about 1776 to the early 1790s – are the various state constitutions; the discussions that shaped the Federal Constitution of 1787, and the arguments around this Constitution, notably the *Federalist* papers of 1787–88, pseudonymously written by James Madison, John Jay, and Alexander Hamilton; and the correspondence and political pamphlets and treatises of these men together with Jefferson, John Adams, Paine and others. On one aspect they were entirely in agreement, though they sometimes mistrusted each other: America should be a republic, with no titled or hereditary aristocracy. All, too, were generally agreed that a federal government must be a compromise. Some essential sovereignty must be entrusted to the central government (which after temporary stays in New York and Philadelphia took up office in 1800 in the new 'Federal City' named after George Washington), as representative of the whole American people. On the other hand, some degree of sovereignty must remain with the states. An American citizen owed allegiance both to the United States and to whichever state he inhabited.

The 1787 Constitution mapped out a broad division of jurisdictions, allotting primary powers to the federal government in areas like foreign policy. But the frontier between national and state power was unavoidably indistinct. The arguments for a 'broad' interpretation of the Constitution, i.e. one stressing the supremacy of the national government, were best expressed in the early state papers of Alexander Hamilton, as Secretary of the Treasury, and in some of the decisions of the Supreme Court from about 1810 to 1830, under the formidable influence of Chief Justice John Marshall. The 'strict' constructionist case, stressing the *limits* of federal authority, was developed in some of the protests of Secretary of State Thomas Jefferson, in the rather laborious *Inquiry into the Principles and Policy of the Government of the United States* (1814) by the Virginia agrarian John Taylor of Caroline, and in the subsequent extension of the 'state-rights' position at the hands of other Southerners, notably John C. Calhoun. The state-rights side of the debate was before long annexed by the South as a justification for the right of individual states to preserve the institution of slavery. As an intellectual issue it thus became distorted. A plea for the 'freedom' of state governments vis-à-vis the central government could not be brought into satisfactory harmony with the implicit egalitarian view that *all* government was a potential threat to individual liberty; and there was a bitter irony in defending a principle of liberty in order to perpetuate the enslavement of black Americans.

We shall return to this point later. For the moment, it is more germane to emphasize the generous aspects of Jeffersonianism. In the fierce political disputes of the 1790s, the 'Federalist' opponents of Jefferson and his followers tended to assume that American society would always be stratified by differences of wealth, education, and innate ability. The Federalists, as exemplified by John Adams in his *Defence of the Constitutions . . . of the United States* (1786-7) and his *Discourses on Davila* (1791), were not recommending an aristocratic order, though their assertions seemed to lend colour to this allegation. They merely took what they considered a realistic view. Certainly, all men had inalienable rights; but it was equally certain, to them, that most men were more concerned with personal interests than with abstract rights or with the general welfare. This being so, as we may see from the fascinating letters that Adams intermittently exchanged with Jefferson, the Federalists attached more importance to a stable government, administered by competent and upright men, than to the theoretical proclamations of the *Rights of Man* contained in Paine's 1791-2 treatise of that name.

American society stopped a good deal short of the thoroughgoing egalitarianism that Paine wished to see, or that was urged by some of the 'Locofoco' or radical pamphleteers of the 1830s. Revulsion against the violent phase of the French Revolution accounts in part for this refusal – as some saw it – to consummate the promise of the American Revolution. Another reason was the incompatibility of egalitarian with libertarian principles. In theory there was no discrepancy; in practice, the right of every man to enrich himself took precedence over other 'natural' rights, and left little room for the emergence of radically levelling doctrine.

However, broad assertions of democratic dogma were made and did gain acceptance in the first decades of the nineteenth century. Although

Jefferson did not work out any comprehensive defence of democracy, he and several associates did argue the logic of natural rights philosophy. In response to the Federalist picture of man as a creature who probably could not be trusted, the Jeffersonians insisted that, throughout human history, the consequences of such distrust were dismal. 'The mass of mankind', Jefferson wrote shortly before his death in 1826, 'has not been born with saddles on their backs, nor a favored few booted and spurred, ready to ride them legitimately by the grace of God.' Government of the 'wise and well-born' had invariably proved to be selfish and corrupt. True, in traditional discourse 'democracy' had signified government by the mob. But by the time Jefferson won election to the Presidency in 1800, the word 'democracy' was beginning to lose its pejorative sense. The old systems had been iniquitous and inefficient. Since America had been spared a rigid class structure, both morality and common sense suggested the establishment of a politics of equality. One essential was universal manhood suffrage; and this was provided in state after state (though with two large exceptions: women were not given the vote, and it was withheld from all Negroes who were slaves and most of those who were free). Another vital principle, reiterated in the debates of the 1787 convention that framed the Constitution and vigorously confirmed by Jefferson, was that of rotation in office. In other words, no man should remain unduly long in office, elective or appointive. 'Offices', said President Andrew Jackson in 1829, speaking as a faithful Jeffersonian, 'are created solely for the people.' Hence,

> The duties of all public officers are, or at least admit of being made, so plain and simple that men of intelligence may readily qualify themselves for their performance; and I cannot but believe that more is lost by the long continuance of men in office than is generally to be gained by their experience.

A third essential was that social and economic opportunity should accompany political opportunity. Jeffersonians and Jacksonians alike favoured free schooling and a variety of humanitarian reforms – such as the ending of imprisonment for debt. They inveighed against 'monopoly' of every kind, from banking to landholding. Radicals like Langdon Byllesby and Thomas Skidmore argued in the 1820s that America could never be a true democracy so long as inherited wealth could be passed from father to son. They drew comfort from the Jeffersonian axiom that 'the earth belongs to the living', and were fond of quoting such statements as President James Monroe's (1817) that

The earth was given to mankind, to support the greatest number of which it is capable; and no tribe or people have a right to withhold from the wants of others more than is necessary for their own support and comfort.

They applauded Jackson's 1832 veto of the Recharter Bill for the Second Bank of the United States.

Jeffersonian and Jacksonian ideas rested on a genuine belief in human potential. They were coherent enough to constitute what we may call an ideology of American egalitarianism. This ideology became dominant, most conspicuously in the political sphere, where by 1840 the two major political parties were vying with one another in the claim to embody the spirit of the common man. Jackson's Democratic party maintained that the rival Whig party still represented the old Federalist hankering after commercial aristocracy. The Whigs retorted that the Democrats were corrupt demagogues. In truth, though they took different sides on different issues, they had much the same ends in view. Thus, the Democrats tended to prefer to entrust authority to the states rather than to the federal government, in order to promote economic growth. Yet Jackson had made an extremely bold assertion of *presidential* authority, and the Whigs in the 1840s upheld the good Jeffersonian principle (one that was to be revived in the 1890s by the radical Populist or People's party) that presidents should be restricted to a single four-year term in office.

Two important features of this triumphant ideology may be noted. The first is that in becoming dominant it gradually lost its intellectual vitality – a common result when propositions cease to be challenged. Radical dissent could cite the sacred texts, either to gain respectability or to show the discrepancy between American promise and American performance; but the effect in either case was to muffle such dissent. Conservative arguments, on the other hand, became either covert or bizarre (see the later section on 'Heresies and Misgivings'). The best affirmative or pessimistic statements – in contrast to the movement of European thought – were to be found in American literature rather than in political discourse.

The second feature is that ideology became tangled up with other things: with professional politics, with nationalism, with entre-preneurial activity. Rotation was in itself a commendable principle, but was debased by its inseparable association with the patronage or 'spoils' system. Americans were apt to reassure themselves as to the soundness of their own polity by denouncing the vices of the Old World. Sometimes, as in Mark Twain's *Connecticut Yankee in King Arthur's Court* (1889), Europe served as a sort of surrogate or scapegoat; Twain's confused parable attributed to mediaeval England depravities that bothered him about the America of his own day. And broad patriotic claims to liberty and equality became adaptable to almost any purpose. They could be, and were, used to denounce 'socialism' as a confiscatory, debilitating, un-American idea. They could be used to justify exploitation. Monroe's seemingly magnanimous statement carried the implication that American farmers who intensively settled and cultivated the land had a better right to it than an Indian 'tribe or people' which, scattered across the terrain, merely pursued a hunting economy. All men were created equal; but women were not men, nor *a fortiori* were Negroes, whom pseudo-scientists solemnly defined as physiologically and mentally sub-human.

However, it has been said that ideas are not responsible for those who embrace them. Jefferson himself, to judge from his *Notes on the State of Virginia* (1784–5), did not believe that black men were truly equal to white men. Nor, for that matter, did Abraham Lincoln. Still, Jefferson deserves to be regarded as one of the finest figures of the Euro-American Enlightenment – an Enlightenment that young America seemed to be making actual. There was still the terrible anomaly of slavery; there was the impending threat posed by acquisitiveness. Even so, by the standards of the day the Americans created an exceptionally open society, and they showed that it could work – without monarchy and aristocracy, without an established church and religious disabilities, without censorship and other repressive devices. Jefferson's eclectic scholarship and sanguine temperament appeared to prove that the young United States had produced a new breed of men, remarkable alike for their intelligence and their modesty, the philosopher-statesmen of a new dispensation. If the next generation produced politicians rather than statesmen, the career of Lincoln suggested that the idea of the 'self-made' man had not lost its dignity.

Romantic Individualism

Just as intellectual historians have disagreed as to whether America experienced an Enlightenment on the European pattern, so they have been unsure about applying the term 'Romanticism' to nineteenth-century America. If we respond to Isaiah Berlin's definition of romanticism as 'the tyranny of art over life', then it could be argued that the

United States of 1800–60, as revealed in its literature and painting, demonstrated the tyranny of life over art. Romanticism embraced an enthusiasm for nature, yet also for the picturesque and the exotic, for extremes of love (leading perhaps to suicide, or at any rate to elopements and abductions), for heroism reaching to the point of monomania (as with Napoleon) or reckless extravagance (as with Byron), for feeling, intuition, sensibility, soul-searching.

If we compare the United States with Western Europe, in this light, the differences seem considerable. European romanticism, as in the poetry of 'Ossian' or the verse and novels of Sir Walter Scott, evoked the ancient, primitive, bardic folk-origins of the nations. America, as Tocqueville remarked, was born in broad daylight; and American imaginative writers, including James Fenimore Cooper and Nathaniel Hawthorne, listed with a blend of democratic pride and artistic regret the various romantic or at any rate traditional features that were missing from the American social fabric. In the absence of ruined abbeys and battlemented castles, the American metaphorical landscape could hardly be called picturesque. The political romanticism of the barricades, as expressed in the paintings of the French artist Delacroix, was foreign to the American experience of a revolution securely established. American imaginative literature, up to the Civil War of the 1860s, was strikingly apolitical. A dissenter like Henry David Thoreau recommended at most a private revolt against authority; his formula was not to overturn government, on the lines attempted in Europe in 1830 and 1848, but simply to ignore it – which was not difficult in a country whose governmental institutions were so mild and remote. The American equivalent of the wickedly flamboyant Napoleon figure was the virtuously reticent George Washington. An American counterpart to that wicked aristocrat Lord Byron was unthinkable. It seems fitting that the only well-known nineteenth-century American commentary on him should be Harriet Beecher Stowe's *Lady Byron Vindicated* (1870) – an attack on Byron's disgraceful treatment of his wife. The admiration for the criminal and the *femme fatale* evident, for example, in the poetry of Baudelaire is again a world away from the United States. The sexual candour of French or Russian literature was not to be found in American writing, except perhaps in Walt Whitman; and Americans who read him with an intent to applaud had to struggle to overcome their distaste ('it was as if the beasts spoke', said Thoreau).

Set beside the European imaginative realm of mistresses and adultery, of programmatic diabolism, the major American group of New England thinkers known as the Transcendentalists appear almost naïvely prim. Consider one of the Transcendentalist meditations of Amos Bronson Alcott: 'Greater is he, who is above temptation, than he, who, having been tempted, overcomes. . . . He who is tempted has sinned; temptation is impossible to the holy.' Or the manful yet slightly comical declaration of the greatest among the Transcendentalists, Ralph Waldo Emerson: 'If I must live by the Devil, very well I will be the Devil's child.' The American love of nature, though fundamental to men like Emerson and a central aspect of the romantic movement, likewise sounds somewhat un-European. For Europeans, 'nature' tended to connote either a charming, man-made landscape of farm and field and copse, or else a tract of moor or mountain within reach of civilization. In America, on the other hand, as Emerson beautifully observed during a visit to England, nature lay

> sleeping, overgrowing, almost conscious, too much by half for man in the picture, and so giving a certain *tristesse*, like the rank vegetation of swamps and forests seen at night . . .; and on it man seems not able to make much impression. There, in that great sloven continent, in high Alleghany pastures, in the sea-wide sky-skirted prairie, still sleeps and murmurs and hides the great mother, long since driven away from the trim hedge-rows and over-cultivated garden of England.

One feels with this passage that nature as an imaginative entity has not yet been brought into focus; the speculative categories, already formulated in Europe, have for this highly sensitive man not yet fallen into shape. The imaginative possibilities are numerous, but bewilderingly miscellaneous.

Viewed from another angle, however, we may feel that English romanticism – a 'warm intuitive muddle' in the words of one scholar – is itself very different from that of the European mainland, and that American romanticism has much in common with it. The men whom Emerson above all wished to encounter, on his first journey to Europe in 1833, were various British writers, such as Coleridge, Wordsworth, and Carlyle, whose works had stimulated him. The direct contact with British life and thought, facilitated by language, acquaintance-ships and travel, seemed appropriate because of deeper affinities of out-look. The two societies were of course far from identical; Emerson's lifelong friendship with Carlyle was in some ways an attraction of

opposites – each man impressed by the other's integrity while increasingly unimpressed by his ideas. The Transcendentalists absorbed their
doctrines from France and Germany as well as from the philosophy of
Coleridge. Nevertheless, it is useful to envisage American romanticism
as quite closely akin to that of Britain.

Throughout the nineteenth century, British authors held pride of
place on American bookshelves. For every American who read
Balzac, a hundred read Scott or Dickens. Scott seemed an object-
lesson to men like Rufus Choate of Massachusetts, who argued that the
national past was not devoid of promising material. In the year that
Emerson was paying his respects to Carlyle and Wordsworth, Choate
delivered an earnest lecture on 'The Importance of Illustrating New-
England History by a Series of Romances like the Waverley Novels'.
As Emerson emphasized in his *English Traits* (1856), the collective
mind of the mother country was vigorous, practical and unsubtle –
which might equally well have been said of his own country. In
neither nation was theoretical radicalism a subject for serious analysis.
British thinkers, like the Americans, were relatively unconcerned with
the battles against church, state, and academy that engaged European
contemporaries; there were pockets of reaction, but no entrenched
strongholds. The British too bore the marks of their Puritan heritage.
Lascivious literature upset them no less. Old Wordsworth, conversing
with Emerson, outdid him in prudishness. For Wordsworth, Goethe's
Wilhelm Meister

> was full of all manner of fornication. It was like the crossing of flies
> in the air. He had never gone farther than the first part; so disgusted
> was he that he threw the book across the room. I deprecated this
> wrath, and said what I could for the better parts of the book. . . .

In poetry, the Englishman Tennyson and the American Longfellow
seem in this regard impeccably proper when read in conjunction with,
say, Baudelaire or Alfred de Musset. Despite Byron, Don Juan and
what he stood for could not really be accommodated in the 'Victorian'
climate of Anglo-American opinion. Romantic ideas of heroism
fascinated them, and there was certainly an American cult of Napoleon.
Emerson gave a lecture on him in Boston and then in Manchester,
subsequently published in *Representative Men* (1850). But for him
Napoleon was especially significant not as a soldier but as 'the agent
or attorney of the middle class of modern society; of the throng who
fill the markets, shops, counting-houses, manufactories, ships, of the

modern world, aiming to be rich'. In short, the world of Boston and Manchester. Much closer to Emerson's own heart was the notion expounded by Carlyle in 1840 of 'The Hero as Man of Letters':

> He . . . is the soul of all. What he teaches, the whole world will do and make. The world's manner of dealing with him is the most significant feature of the world's general position.

Viewed more widely still, for all these qualifications American like British romanticism does mingle with the broad current of nineteenth-century thinking and sensibility. The mystery and morbidity of the 'Gothic' strain are represented, if awkwardly, in the novels of Charles Brockden Brown and, if with a peculiar abstract intensity, in the writings of Edgar Allan Poe which so intrigued Baudelaire. The monomaniac hero is evoked with extraordinary power in Herman Melville's *Moby-Dick* (1851). The spiritualization of femininity was nowhere more manifest than in the United States, where it sometimes appeared that moral and aesthetic standards were defined, in poetry, fiction, and the essay, by women for women. The native brand of the exotic, in the shape of the American Indian, was successfully roman-ticized in Longfellow's *Hiawatha* (1855). This also constituted part of the attempt, also fairly successful, to create an indigenous American past. The time-scale was necessarily compressed in comparison with that of Europe. James Fenimore Cooper's Leatherstocking tales deal with the quite recent past or even with the almost immediately contemporary, yet are 'historical' in mood. The same illusion of antiquity, of things being 'ancient' that are not truly so in the European sense, was created in a number of Hawthorne's stories and romances. Americans managed too to invest the deeds of their late eighteenth-century Founding Fathers with an aura of venerability. Like European nationalists, they felt their nationalism to be both modern, the emergent spirit of the age, and deeply rooted in an almost legendary past. The difference, fervently proclaimed in George Bancroft's ten-volume *History of the United States* (1834–76), was that Americans could feel that they stood in the forefront of world progress, the heir to all the ages without being trapped by them as some nations were. In this broad perspective, American attitudes to nature appear different in degree rather than in kind from those of the Old World. The word 'nature' had a score of meanings. But all conveyed one essential message for nineteenth-century mankind: seek selfhood, which will lead to Godhood, in the open air, as far away as possible from the haunts of men. Go out from the servile cities, cries Alfred de Vigny in 'La Maison du Berger' (a poem of the early 1840s), into nature:

Les grands bois et les champs sont de vastes asiles,
Libres comme la mer autour des sombres îles.
Marche à travers les champs une fleur à la main.

The loose circle of transcendentally minded men and women who lived in the neighbourhood of Boston would gladly have endorsed this injunction; they had nearly all said similar things themselves. They disapproved of big cities and formal occasions. Their own meetings were rather self-conscious and humorously deprecatory. They did not organize as a permanent club, though some of them belonged to such clubs in Boston, nor as a dogmatic movement. The most fluent talker among them, Alcott, preferred monologue to dialogue. The voluble bluestocking Margaret Fuller also seems to have exercised a somewhat paralysing influence over her companions. Emerson, Thoreau, and various less celebrated associates were happiest when alone – reading, perambulating, thinking, writing in their journals. Since they were not a unified group, there is no single account of their philosophy that covers all their philosophizings or even presents a complete statement of any one man's thought. In their eyes, this was as it should be. Each man must be his own teacher, priest, and bard. 'Life', Emerson said, 'consists in what a man is thinking of all day.' For 'Life' he might have substituted 'Literature'; for, as he observed elsewhere, 'An auto-biography should be a book of answers from one individual to the many questions of the time.' He and his fellows wrote in a vein for which there is no satisfactory label. Several were or had been Unitarian ministers. One might say that they produced sermons for a sort of pantheistic church that had not yet been organized, and whose organization they would themselves have resisted. As Emerson announced in his first oracular little book, *Nature* (published anonymously in 1836), the man who surrenders himself to true feeling becomes 'a transparent eyeball . . .; the currents of the Universal Being circulate through me; I am part or parcel of God'. Nature was the medium uniting man with his maker. Any other intermediary, such as a church or a book, was a hindrance if it did not ultimately liberate the individual to reach his own truth. Like Coleridge and other Europeans from whom they had initially drawn inspiration, they distinguished between logical reasoning and intuitive understanding – or, as Emerson called them in a lecture on 'The Transcendentalist' (1842), between materialism and idealism:

> The materialist insists on . . . the force of circumstances and the animal wants of man; the idealist on the power of Thought and of Will, on inspiration, on miracle, on individual culture. These two modes of thinking are both natural, but the idealist contends that his way of thinking is in higher nature.

In another sense the Transcendentalists produced autobiography, and even confessional autobiography. To the extent that Whitman's outlook is akin to Transcendentalism, his *Leaves of Grass* (1855), with its intent to 'put *a Person* . . . freely, fully and truly on record', is reminiscent of Rousseau's claim that his *Confessions* (1781) were meant to portray 'a man wholly true to nature; and this man will be myself'. But though the New England Transcendentalists were preoccupied with their own inner selves, their personal testimonies are extraordinarily impersonal. They sought to generalize from the individual soul to the universal Oversoul. They were keenly, sometimes amusedly aware of one another's idiosyncrasies; and there was a robustly practical side to Emerson and Thoreau. But their serious intent, arduous in the very tenuousness of the task, was to transcend everydayness, to move life to a higher plane by eliminating whatever was mediocre or extraneous. In this conviction, most of them held aloof from the politics and even the reform impulses of the day, until at length the anti-slavery cause laid hold of their consciences.

Transcendentalism was in a way always a minority position in American intellectual life. During its most active years it came in for a good deal of abuse and ridicule as a daydream indulged in by woolly-minded cranks. Yet its principal spokesman Emerson gradually became a revered figure, a grand old man of American letters. In retrospect it is easy to see why. If Whitman was the bard of American democracy, Emerson was the philosopher of American democracy. There was something at once exhilarating and reassuring in his confidence in 'the unsearched might of man'. He was severely critical of the actual 'timid, imitative' spirit of his countrymen; he did not tell them they were splendid, but that they might be. And though the quest was far more difficult than most of his listeners could realize, they did grasp that there were no external bars to advancement. They did not have to be rich or sophisticated or widely travelled or college-educated. They need no longer feel they were in cultural thrall to

Europe. They need not affect elevated diction; good writing, like the best talk of ordinary men in the street, was simple and 'blood-warm'. Here and there, an intelligent contemporary like Henry James Sr., having pondered the Emersonian creed, discerned grave inadequacies in it. Emerson, said James, was 'fundamentally treacherous to civilization, without being at all aware himself of the fact'. He was a rarified species of the noble savage, an intellectual Luddite, a saintly quack. Or so a pessimistic commentator might feel of that American brand of romantic individualism typified by Ralph Waldo Emerson. Was he not giving his sanction to a society in which democratic freedom meant *sauve-qui-peut* – every man for himself and the devil take the hindmost? In which selfhood meant selfishness?

Business Enterprise

Wordsworth had rather sententiously warned young Emerson that Americans 'are too much given to the making of money; and secondly, to politics; . . . they make political distinction the end and not the means. And I fear they lack a class of men of leisure – in short, of gentlemen, to give a tone of honour to the community.' Wordsworth also suggested, paradoxically in Emerson's opinion, that 'they needed a civil war in America, to teach the necessity of knitting the social ties stronger'. These *obiter dicta* were offered in 1833. During the next thirty years Emerson in his journal often commented on the same problems. He was himself beginning to grow old by 1861, when a civil war did break out; and in balance he did welcome it, though primarily because it would put an end to slavery, and did come to feel that the four-year war might have beneficial results in bringing the best men into positions of authority.

Intellectually speaking, however, the Gilded Age America of the last four decades of the century seemed singularly heavy, as if Wordsworth's worst fears were being borne out. In the aftermath of the Civil War there was an apparent absence of big issues. The conflict had settled one crucial point, concerning the right of a state to secede from the Union. It is true that this complex constitutional problem was re-argued after the war with great length and learning by Alexander H. Stephens, the former Vice-President of the Southern Confederacy, in his *Constitutional View of the Late War Between the States* (1867, 1870). But few outside the South considered Stephens' treatise as anything more than a rearrangement of old bones. The war had put an end to the debate, by force instead of discourse. That being so, why resort once more to discourse? The former President of the Confederacy, Jefferson Davis, recognized as much when he concluded his apologia, *The Rise and Fall of the Confederate Government* (1881), with the hope that 'on the basis of fraternity and faithful regard for the rights of the states, there may be written on the arch of the Union, *Esto perpetua*'. Davis's lawyerlike clause about the rights of the states had not much weight in the face of the inevitable: he knew well that secession could never again be seriously mooted.

Nothing remained, then, on the constitutional agenda as soon as the immediate turmoil of postwar reconstruction began to abate. The businessman and the business ethic rapidly came to the forefront of the American mind. Law was almost the only respectable career that an intellectually inclined man could turn to, and this was the route taken by Oliver Wendell Holmes, Jr., when he put aside his officer's uniform. But even law, together with politics, became subservient to business interests. Men experienced a strong psychological pressure to demonstrate their worth by plunging into commerce and industry. There was a corresponding devaluation of disinterested intellectual effort – which as we have seen had never been very securely enshrined. By the same token, creative literature occupied an equivocal position. With a certain amount of *ex post facto* exaggeration, *The Education of Henry Adams* (1907) ironically portrays the dispossession of the old patriciate. Adams' great-grandfather John Adams and his grandfather John Quincy Adams, who had both been Presidents of the United States, had both suffered for their high-mindedness while they were in public life. But at least enough of their countrymen had esteemed them enough to vote them into the White House. Henry Adams' disdainful and perplexed memoir, and still more the two volumes of his *Letters* (1930), depict him as a gentleman deprived of the chance to consort with a sufficient quantity of other gentlemen to 'give a tone of honour to the community'. Political journalism in Washington and teaching at Harvard proved to be merely temporary refuges for him. In fact, he was by no means idle – his published work included two novels and more than a dozen volumes of solid history – and his feeling of estrangement was not mere vanity: the gentleman-intellectual was truly a somewhat marginal creature in the bustle of the Gilded Age. Culture tended to be regarded as a feminine pastime. In various novels of the period, among them Adams' *Democracy* (1880), the male characters are tough but mindless, the women refined but powerless. One suspects that the desire for social acceptance no less than economic hardship impelled such writers as Mark Twain and Ambrose Bierce to act as journalists and to visualize themselves, however unconvincingly, as businessmen. Twain was awed by the new captains of industry with whom he came in contact. The radical, irreverent side of him was easily assuaged when, as in the case of the Scottish-born Andrew Carnegie, they had risen from nothing and showed some interest in social questions (Carnegie was an ardent republican, who dreamed of the abolition of the monarchy in Britain).

It cannot be said that capitalist society encountered much of a challenge in the America of the 1870s and 1880s. Social criticism was the province almost entirely of European writers; and of these the most popular were British – John Ruskin, Matthew Arnold. Famous preachers drew huge congregations, but their eloquence was more impressive than their profundity. Perhaps the most famous of all, Henry Ward Beecher of Brooklyn, merely vulgarized the crop of current ideas. In 1877, for example, at a moment of widespread economic depression, he asserted from his pulpit that 'the trade union, originated under the European system, destroys liberty', and that a poor family could subsist on a dollar a day, provided that the husband did not 'insist on smoking and drinking beer'.

Laissez-faire assumptions were dominant. Their effect is apparent even in the writings of American reformers. Henry George's *Progress and Poverty* (1879) propounded the view that 'nothing short of making land common property can permanently relieve poverty and check the tendency of wages to the starvation point' – a position appreciably in advance of that of the Reverend Beecher. But his remedy was an attractively simple panacea, the single tax, which would gradually and gently furnish society with an ample revenue for social purposes by levying a tax on the full annual rental value of all land. His proposal recalls the arguments of those Jacksonian radicals who believed that private ownership and the transmission of their wealth through inheritance would create intolerable extremes of wealth and deprivation. Yet George's plan left private titles to land intact; and subsequently, clinging to his belief that he could establish a just society by means of one basic tax, he repudiated socialism in favour of 'individualism'.

A comparable reluctance to go to real extremes is discernible, though to a lesser extent, in the movement called Nationalism which grew out of Edward Bellamy's Utopian novel, *Looking Backward* (1888). His novel painted a glowing picture of the Boston of 2000 A.D. Competitive capitalism has given way smoothly to a system of state ownership of production and distribution. Labour is supplied by an 'industrial army' of willing conscripts. Everyone is prosperous; social strife has vanished. The Nationalist scheme was certainly bold, and it had a particular appeal for worthy ex-officers who nostalgically remembered the collective spirit of the Union army of Civil War days. Bellamy thus frankly conceded that an element of compulsion would be needed to sustain his ideal order. How the order would be achieved, or precisely how it could be administered, he did not explain. Both he and Henry George combined an effective criticism of the existing order with a fantasy of an easily attainable golden era. The 'pie-in-the-sky' quality that made their schemes alluring also made them unconvincing.

Laissez-faire doctrines, by contrast, seemed to be reinforced by science as well as by common experience. The evolutionary theories of Darwin, applied to human society, postulated a process of natural selection or 'survival of the fittest'. It is possible that American businessmen of the Gilded Age were influenced by this Social Darwinism in merely indirect ways: the Protestant ethic of hard work and self-improvement was already deeply ingrained. But men who took the trouble to read Herbert Spencer, or another popular British author, Benjamin Kidd, usually felt that they had gained a new insight into the seemingly harsh yet ultimately beneficent workings of the social order. The Yale sociologist William Graham Sumner, for instance, a man of hard-headed acuteness, denounced 'the absurd attempt to make the world over'. Even if reform were desirable, it would almost certainly fail because it would bump up against the realities of objective social and economic laws. Less cheerful than Spencer, Sumner basically agreed with him that neither the state nor any other agency should tamper with the nice equilibrium of socioeconomic forces.

In the twenty years after the Civil War the great majority of American thinkers, whether optimistic or pessimistic in outlook, in effect rationalized the existing order. But it would be misleading to regard the era as intellectually inert. In *The Theory of the Leisure Class* (1899), that maverick American scholar Thorstein Veblen was to present a sardonic analysis of the 'conspicuous consumption', 'conspicuous waste', and 'pecuniary emulation' of the prosperous stratum of society. The lesson he extracted from Darwinism was that human beings behaved atavistically: primitively naïve conceptions of display and prestige flourished among polite (or would-be polite) contemporary communities. He included patronage of the arts and pretensions to higher learning in his list of characteristic features of conspicuous leisure – while noting in a subsequent book that

> For a generation past, while the American universities have been coming into line as seminaries of the higher learning, there has gone on a wide-reaching substitution of laymen in the place of clergymen on the governing boards. . . . The substitution is a substitution of businessmen and politicians; which amounts to saying that it is a substitution of businessmen.

There is an uncomfortable degree of truth in Veblen's picture, as applied to late nineteenth-century America. Yet whatever the underlying motives, wealth brought a new cosmopolitanism and professionalism into the national culture. Art museums and symphony orchestras proliferated. So did colleges and universities; and some of the brand-new foundations, such as Johns Hopkins University and the Rockefeller-endowed University of Chicago, moved with remarkable swiftness into the front rank of academic institutions. Some of the older institutions transformed themselves from conventional colleges into multifarious universities, in which the term 'higher learning' was a matter of zealous pride. As a distinguished graduate of Harvard, Emerson became interested in the upsurge of postwar discussion – a process stimulated by the increasing number of young American scholars who attended German universities and came back full of praise for the erudition and flexibility of German methods. 'At present', Emerson remarked in 1869, 'the friends of Harvard are possessed . . . by the idea of making it a University for men, instead of a College for boys.' Indeed they had already taken the first step by installing as president Charles W. Eliot, an energetic scientist. Within a few years Eliot vastly improved the level of training in law and medicine, and established new postgraduate programmes and degrees in other fields.

Eliot was one of a whole new species of outstanding college presidents. Under their aegis, academic scholarship rapidly became more rigorous and more specialized. Each academic 'discipline' (the word has an appropriate severity) organized itself into a professional body and began to produce professional periodicals. The Modern Language Association, for example, was formed in 1883, the American Historical Association in 1884, and the American Economic Association in 1885. According to Merle Curti, some 250 national learned societies came into being between 1870 and 1900, and an equivalent host of local and state societies. By 1900, no American scholar could be considered respectable until he had buried himself in years of research, and emerged with a Ph.D. A cynic might say that the pedagogues had turned into pedants. Yet they, and a still considerable number of gentleman-amateurs outside academe, were soon publishing surveys and monographs notable for their quality as well as for their total quantity. Though Henry Adams abandoned a university career after teaching history at Harvard for a few years, no less brilliant contemporaries, such as the psychologist William James, were beginning to find life intellectually congenial within the academic enclaves. Nor need they feel entirely cut off from a wider public of reasonably intelligent and well-informed citizens. They could for instance contribute reputable articles to a growing range of sober magazines: *Harper's* (1851), the *Atlantic* (1857), the *Scientific Monthly* (1871), *Century* (1881), *Forum* (1886), and so on, in addition to European publications and one or two old American standbys like the *North American Review*. In these magazines they rubbed shoulders with the occasional articulate captain of industry (notably Andrew Carnegie) or budding politicians (such as Henry Cabot Lodge and Theodore Roosevelt), and with authors (Twain, William Dean Howells, Henry James) who were likewise for almost the first time in American history able to conceive of literature as possessing the status of a profession – even if an uncertain and inadequately rewarded one. By about 1890 several American cities had disclosed the symptoms of a metropolitan culture-style – publishing houses, salons, symphony orchestras, bohemias – although only in New York, and possibly its declining rival, Boston, had the development reached a fairly advanced stage.

This expansion of the life of the mind may appear to contradict the view of the Gilded Age as intellectually complaisant and mediocre. It should indeed be emphasized that the United States continued to depend on Europe for most of its ideas on philosophy, theology, natural science, aesthetics, literary criticism, and social thought. Carnegie was ecstatic when one morning's post brought him letters from three eminent Englishmen: Herbert Spencer, John Morley the biographer, and the scholar-statesman William Ewart Gladstone. No trio of American letters could have conferred such a glow of satisfaction.

Otherwise, the apparent contradiction is resolved when we note two other factors. The first has to do with professionalism. The prodigious growth of American industry was seen in part as a triumph of technology. Emersonian individualism had placed a premium on idealism and privacy. The Gilded Age was able to derive inspiration from some portions of this idealist gospel. In general, however, it preferred materialism (in Emerson's terminology) to idealism; it worshipped fact, organization, the expert. To the extent that the academic was an expert, especially a social 'scientist', his research could gain approval from the most determinedly unintellectual of his countrymen. The same respect for 'science' is evident among the critics of American life. Reform-minded scholars and politicians began to regard the universities as vital instruments: their task was to provide the data on social, economic, and political issues. Even Veblen admired the engineer as a product of the modern age; their work was rational, disinterested, and potentially life-enhancing; their wisdom was far superior to that of the profit-oriented businessman. This trend was perfectly exemplified a few years later in the 'sociological jurisprudence' of lawyers like Louis D. Brandeis, who based pleas for humanitarian legislation not upon sentiment or the letter of the law but upon solid dossiers of research into working conditions in several countries.

The second factor is the reawakening in the 1880s of the American social conscience. It came later than in Europe because of the power of the old American ideology of self-help and minimal government, and because urbanization and industrialization, with their attendant problems, also came later than in the Old World. There were many manifestations: the effort by sociologists like Lester Frank Ward to stress the *social* instead of the *individual* aspect of evolutionism; eloquent attacks on the evils of monopoly, as in Henry D. Lloyd's *Wealth against Commonwealth* (1894); the belated emergence of the 'social gospel' among such clergymen as Washington Gladden and George D. Herron; the semi-conversion to Tolstoyan principles of William Dean Howells and other writers, who in a narrower context also championed the notion of literature as a revealer of unvarnished truth; a revival of interest in Jacksonian democracy; a new insistence, stimulated by the historian Frederick Jackson Turner, that the West was the real repository of American democracy; a new radical movement in politics, Populism, emanating mainly from the West; pleas for female emancipation, including Charlotte Perkins Gilman's brilliant *Women and Economics* (1898); and a recognition among rich industrialists, most fully defined in Carnegie's 'gospel of wealth', that they had a duty to dedicate a substantial proportion of their money to the promotion of the general welfare. In the period immediately after the Civil War, Howells reflected, America had had, 'as no other people in the world had, the chance of devoting ourselves strictly to business, of buying cheap and selling dear'. The social costs had proved to be unanticipatedly immense. When this was realized, there was a nationwide buzz of alarm, indignation, explanation, prognosis. Many believed that America was in the throes of a total transformation. Whether they were correct may be disputed. What is clear is that the intellectual atmosphere had become intellectually charged – perhaps more so than for over a century.

Heresies and Misgivings

We have already referred to an American 'ideology', whose main tenets – the equality of men, and their freedom to form their own religious, social and economic attachments – gained such swift and pervasive assent that they functioned as a quasi-religious creed or faith. Since it resembled a religious faith, those who publicly rejected the ideology were regarded with a certain horror, as if they were heretics, and probably unhinged at that. Those who publicly questioned or ridiculed some portion of the creed, unless they obviously spoke in jest, were regarded somewhat as blasphemers. The word 'publicly' is important here; there were plenty of Americans who had greater or lesser misgivings, but there was after the early years of the nineteenth century no nationwide expression of intellectual conservatism. There was no political party, or established church, to provide an institutional locus for a rationale of tradition, ritual, and deference. The cluster of associative ideas that surround the word 'gentleman' carried at best a covert, defensive, faintly disagreeable aura – when they did not (as in the case of certain Southern formulations) tumble over the edge into sheer sacrilege. It is true that conservatism is by definition instinctive and non-credal. Being concerned to defend the *status quo* as the least bad of possible worlds, it generates few analyses of any fundamental originality. Throughout the western world of the nineteenth century, the great majority of conservative theorizing sounded sour, negative, and anachronistic. It lacked the resonance of liberal and democratic doctrines – a grumbling of old men, unable to adapt themselves to the heightened tempo of existence, and unwilling to surrender their privileges. Edmund Burke's appeal to the 'unbought grace of life', though pleasing to the conservative mind, met and was apparently conquered by the rejoinder that the unbought was the unearned and therefore the undeserved.

In Europe, however, conservative thought had an entrenched institutional support. And its arguments could not be altogether dismissed, since even the celebrators of innovation could not suppress secret doubts. Was the accumulation of wealth a high enough goal for mankind? What was the ultimate point of mere activity? Was industrial plutocracy any better than land-based aristocracy? Was society shaking itself to pieces? During the latter half of the nineteenth century, in the writings of men like Ruskin, Arnold, and William Morris, such questions began to seem radical rather than conservative.

In the United States much the same doubts lay at the back of men's minds. They could be less easily expressed, however, because they ran counter to the dominant ideology of democratic progress; short of outright heresy Americans were reluctant to voice them lest they seem to undermine the very foundations of their creed. There were other, special complications. The national ideology proclaimed the idea of the United States as an asylum for the oppressed, a nation of nations. But this generous commitment was accompanied by the private conviction of most Americans that there were innate differences between nation and nation, or rather between race and race, and that some were superior to others. Moreover, there was an implicit assumption that, while religious tolerance was a *sine qua non* of the democratic faith, the United States was a Protestant country. The word 'faith' in this respect had a double sense. Democracy was itself Protestant; other religions, above all Roman Catholicism, were too hierarchical in structure to fit properly into the national ideology. Fears of engulfment and subversion by alien values thus underlay the confident assertion that American society knew no limits or prohibitions. Their avowal tended to be clandestine or oblique, and to exist – as with the anti-Catholic 'nativism' of the 1840s and 1850s – in the realm of popular prejudice rather than as serious intellectual discourse. At a more philosophical level, American conservatism in the nineteenth century was a discontinuous affair, varying in tone from the shrill to the plaintive, and circling uneasily around the problem of whether there was a place for gentlemanly leadership in the era of the common man.

The sharpest, most heretical denial of democratic ideology came from various apologists for the slaveholding South. Until the eve of the Civil War the majority of Americans regarded abolitionism as a recklessly disruptive movement; a man like William Lloyd Garrison, the New England abolitionist who publicly burned a copy of the Constitution, seemed himself to be an absolute heretic. Nevertheless, the discrepancy between the fact of slavery and the theory of democracy led more and more Northerners to disapprove of bondage even if they could see no constitutional way to bring about emancipation. Searching for counter-arguments to meet the growing pressure of Northern moral sentiment, Southern spokesmen were obliged to construct a dual thesis. On the one hand, plantation society was wholesome because it was organic, agrarian, serene, and paternal – a modern form of the 'Greek democracy' of Athens in the era of Pericles. On the other hand the America defined by the new democratic ideology was unsound because it was unstable, polyglot, commercial, ruthless, and leaderless. The notion that 'all people are equally entitled to liberty' was, according to John C. Calhoun of South Carolina, fallacious and dangerous:

> It is . . . a reward reserved for the intelligent, the patriotic, the virtuous and deserving; – and not a boon to be bestowed on a people too ignorant, degraded and vicious, to be capable either of appreciating or of enjoying it. . . . These great and dangerous errors have their origin in the prevalent opinion that all men are born free and equal; – than which nothing can be more unfounded and false.

Every Southern apologist, indeed, poured scorn upon the natural-rights vocabulary of the Declaration of Independence. Calhoun, William Harper, and George Fitzhugh were among those who went on to denounce the 'wage slavery' or 'white slavery' of industrial England, and to prophesy that the same grim fate would overtake the working men of America. Fitzhugh, in *Sociology for the South* (1854) and *Cannibals All* (1856), leaned heavily upon the strictures of Carlyle. 'Free society' was vicious and chaotic; *laissez-faire* democracy offered seductive slogans – but these were only euphemisms, masking the ethics of the jungle. In other words, democracy as extolled in the United States was fraudulent and inherently disastrous. It rested upon force, like all governments, excluding large numbers of citizens from any real share in the system; and, in the act of widening the participatory base, would only weaken the fabric. As Fitzhugh ironically observed, in *Cannibals All*:

> Even in our North, the women, children, and free negroes, constitute four-fifths of the population; and they are all governed without their consent. But they mean to correct this gross and glaring iniquity at the North. They hold that all men, women, and negroes, and smart children, are equals, and entitled to equal rights. The

widows and free negroes begin to vote in some of those States, and they will have to let all colors and sexes and ages vote soon, or give up the glorious principles of human equality and universal emancipation.

Heretical though such assertions were, and vitiated by their obvious element of special pleading, which made Southern apologists drag in every argument they could think of, at the risk of logical inconsistency, they nevertheless posed some embarrassing questions. And they were not altogether out of tune, if for different reasons, with a good deal of discussion in the North. The very idea of heresy could be regarded as Emersonian: was it not the duty of a man to be a 'nay-sayer'? The Transcendentalists too admired Carlyle, even if his message seemed too sceptically pessimistic. Certain of their criticisms of materialism ('Things are in the saddle, / And ride mankind') and of the Northern propensity to indulge in perfectionist panaceas, are almost interchangeable with remarks made by Fitzhugh. The South represented too the survival of an older brand of élitism, that expounded by such New England Federalists as John Adams and – in more extreme form – Fisher Ames. 'That all men are born to equal rights is clear', Adams insisted in a letter to that Southern Jeffersonian, John Taylor:

. . . But to teach that all men are born with equal powers and faculties, to equal influence in society, . . . is . . . as glaring an imposition on the credulity of the people, as ever was practiced by monks, by Druids, . . . or by the self-styled philosophers of the French Revolution. For honor's sake, Mr. Taylor, for truth and virtue's sake, let American philosophers and politicians despise it.

Adams did not recommend 'aristocracy', as he called it: he simply contended that societies must recognize and allow for a degree of stratification. In admitting the existence of inequalities, they would be the better equipped to avoid gross disparities between the powerful and the lowly. Ames took a bleaker view. 'Our country is too big for union,' he lamented in 1803, 'too sordid for patriotism, too democratick for liberty. . . . Its vice will govern it, by practising upon its folly. This is ordained for democracies.' The innate viciousness of a levelling ideology, for Ames, was proved by the excesses of the French Revolution. America was doomed because this ideology had enshrined itself in men's minds, driving out the unpalatable truths of conservatism. 'It is . . . a law of politics as well as of physics', said Ames in

The Dangers of American Liberty (1803), 'that a body in action must overcome an equal body at rest.'

Ames was correct in his prediction that the democratic principle would overcome all contrary propositions – at least so far as the white male American was concerned. Whether his own conception of human nature was correct continued to be an issue, flagrantly raised in the South, somewhat subterraneanly canvassed in the North, especially when educated gentlemen gathered around the dinner-table. The Federalists disappeared as a force in national political life after 1815. Elitist reservations persisted, however, among some of the Whigs of the 1830s and 1840s, and more particularly among the semi-leisured citizens in the larger Northern cities. Enthusiasts for democracy, such as the historian George Bancroft, maintained that with every year that passed the soundness of the ideology became more unmistakably clear. But other fellow-graduates of Harvard, including Charles Eliot Norton and the historian Francis Parkman, placed a different interpretation upon the American record. Political democracy had led, inevitably, to the mob spirit, to demagoguery and to corruption. Men of their class were no longer looked up to. Learning was despised, the fine arts vulgarized. Such Boston 'Brahmins' sometimes went nearly as far as their Southern contemporaries in deploring fanatical reformism. 'I would see every slave knocked on the head,' Parkman told Norton in 1850, 'before I would see the Union go to pieces and would include in the sacrifice as many abolitionists as could be conveniently brought together.' Three years later, in *Considerations on Some Recent Social Theories*, Norton attempted a refutation of democratic perfectionism:

> It is not [to the people] that we are to look for wisdom and intelligence . . . their progress must be stimulated by the few who have been blessed with the opportunities, and the rare genius fitting them to lead. Nor is their advance to depend on the discovery of any new remedies. There are now at work in the world, principles of virtue and strength enough for all the trials and exigencies of progress.

It is significant, though, that Parkman's statement occurs in a private letter, and that Norton's book – which incidentally did not arouse much stir – was published anonymously. There is a feeling of futility in these American jeremiads. Their authors are all too aware that they are swimming against the current. They appear reluctant to push their arguments to ultimates, or not quite convinced that the arguments are tenable. Calhoun and Fitzhugh are thus careful to explain that they do not advocate coercive or dynastic rule on the European model; the suffrage should be extended as widely as possible. The Brahmins for their part were never wholly committed to élitism. None favoured slavery or a strict class-basis for society; none was naïve enough to suppose that he could turn the clock backward. In the remarks quoted above, Norton speaks of the 'trials and exigencies of progress', as if progress were a burden to be borne. Yet, a little earlier, he refers to the 'progress' of the people in an orthodoxly liberal way as something both desirable and apparently feasible. The outbreak of the Civil War did not convert Parkman to abolitionism; but it did reveal him as a passionate supporter of the Northern war effort.

After the war, the tone of the critique changed. The eventual victory of the Union, in the face of the most dismal forecasts, silenced those who had insisted on the inability of American democracy to cement the nation or to prosecute a war. Circumstance reinforced theory; and this circumstance was used elsewhere to bolster the democratic cause – for example in England, in the debates preceding the Second Reform Act of 1867. The Southern brand of anti-democratic argument was likewise silenced, and did not emerge again until the late 1920s in the rather wistful and misty guise of Southern Agrarianism.

If heresy almost disappeared, misgivings of course did not. Yet in a way these were assimilated into the American creed. Modified expressions of racism became intellectually respectable. Social Darwinism supplied reassuring scientific sanction for intellectuals as well as for industrialists who wished to believe that they had attained a higher stage of evolution than other men. Only here and there did a grumbler cast doubt upon the essential optimisms of American democracy. William Graham Sumner was one. His was a determinist approach. Social facts were the product of economic facts. Societies with a high ratio of land to population are likely to be democratic; those with an extremely low 'man–land ratio' will not be:

> Democracy itself, the pet superstition of the age, is only a phase of the all-compelling movement. If you have abundance of law and few men to share it, the men will all be equal. . . . No philosophy of politics or ethics makes them prosperous. Their prosperity makes their political philosophy and all their other creeds. It also makes all their vices, and imposes on them a set of fallacies produced out of itself.

In essence this was a pessimistic thesis. So indeed was F. J. Turner's 'frontier thesis' of 1893, which in a less obviously determinist fashion attributed American democracy to the abundance of free land in the West. For if the supply of land ceased, different and presumably less libertarian attitudes would develop. We can point to other *fin-de-siècle* hypotheses: for example, those of Henry Adams and his brother Brooks Adams, who perceived man as the victim rather than the master of his fate, as the mere creature of huge evolutionary or economic processes.

But these theories were not attacks on democracy as such, even though they might offend the national *amour-propre* by minimizing the element of purposive virtue in the American ideology. Their central contention was not that democracy was a bad system, but only that all systems were mere instruments of impersonal forces. Such conjectures had no great impact on the nation's mind at the end of the nineteenth century. They were of no use to conservatives or to radicals, seeking either to resist change or to bring it about. In the twentieth century, the debate over the national creed was to ramify. The occasional heretical statements that continued to appear, such as H. L. Mencken's *Notes on Democracy* (1927), seemed as in earlier days to operate in a void, unable to gain a purchase on their theme. They could scold and warn and ridicule; but what they could offer by way of analysis seemed unreal or irrelevant.

Twentieth-Century Confusions

The word 'confusions' refers not to the quality of individual expressions of American thought, many of which have been brilliant and influential, but to the complexity of the total scene, the profusion of differing voices, and the effect of discord produced by the fact that so many of these voices announced both a dissent from other voices and a disaffection with the central assumptions of American life – however these were defined. It is not easy to summarize the main intellectual features of this era. Yet the first seven decades of the twentieth century constitute more than a third of the time-span of America as an independent nation; and at least some aspects seem to have fallen into place. A rough chronological division provides a framework, if we remember that it is schematic and approximate. This yields four subdivisions: a first period running from about 1900 to 1920; a second from 1920 to 1940; a third from 1940 to 1960; and a fourth beginning in about 1960. For simplicity's sake, though at the risk of gross oversimplification, the 1900–20 decades may be regarded as the period of 'Progressivism';

the years from 1920 to 1940 as that of 'Avant-Gardism'; from 1940 to 1960 as the era of 'Compromise' or 'Consensus'; and the years since 1960 as the era of 'Revolt'.

It should be reiterated that these divisions and labels are arbitrary. The word 'insurgency' became common at the beginning of the century. Despite alternations of radicalism and indifference, the twentieth-century American who has regarded himself as an intellectual has throughout these decades tended to think of himself as a person at odds with his society, whether his alienation took the form of retreat into personal concerns or of collective protest. Not surprisingly, the process has itself revealed a dual tendency. All societies, no matter how revolutionary in tone, are heavily conditioned by previous experience. Characteristics of American thought already sketched in this essay continued to affect the tone of twentieth-century debate inside the United States. And, as before, American argument continued to move more or less in step with that of the rest of the western world. The difference has been that in the twentieth century the United States became markedly less provincial, more cosmopolitan, more pre-eminent than in previous eras. America, in intellect as in commerce, became an exporter rather than an importer. At various stages during the century, in every field of creative and scholarly enterprise except perhaps political thought, the United States has come to set the pace instead of marching after it.

Progressivism, 1900–20

The critical and reformist spirit that began to manifest itself toward the end of the nineteenth century spread rapidly in the opening years of the twentieth. One aspect was the diffusion of socialist and ultra-radical ideas – apparent, for example, in such titles as *Our Benevolent Feudalism* (1902) and *Mass and Class* (1904) by William J. Ghent, *The War of the Classes* (1905) by Jack London, and *Anarchism and Other Essays* (1910) by Emma Goldman. These however were almost lost to view in the great outpouring of articles and books of the 'Muckraking' movement as a whole, sometimes said to have begun with *McClure's Magazine* in 1903. The American public was regaled with a flood of documented exposés of corruption in the nation's industry and politics, of which Upton Sinclair's novel *The Jungle* (1906) survives as one of the most horrifying testaments. From denunciation, intelligent journalists like Ray Stannard Baker turned by degrees to proposals for reform. Most of those who regarded themselves as 'Progressives' or 'Insurgents' were contemptuous of orthodox political parties. Unwittingly, they echoed the early fears of Jeffersonians that government would fall into the hands of the rich, and of Federalists that it would be the instrument of the unscrupulous. Their remedy was a passion for what would later be known as participatory democracy. Much energy was expended on advocating the merits of the presidential 'primary', as a means of obliging the politicos to heed the voice of the people, and on various devices – the initiative, referendum, and recall – designed to introduce popular control of legislation. A similar determination to tell the truth, and to shake off the thrall of the 'genteel tradition', began to show itself in literature, though this development was only beginning to acquire momentum. The early symptoms included the naturalistic novels of Theodore Dreiser and the Middle Western poetry of Carl Sandburg and Edgar Lee Masters. In New York, another symptom was the establishment in 1911 of *The Masses*, a magazine that tried to combine literary and social radicalism. There was a renewed emphasis on Youth, most eloquently in the essays of the New York intellectual Randolph Bourne:

> Old men cherish a fond delusion that there is something mystically valuable in mere quantity of experience. Now the fact is . . . that it is the young people who have all the really valuable experience. It is they who have constantly to face new situations, to react constantly to new aspects of life. . . . For the weakness of experience is that it so soon gets stereotyped; without new situations and crises it becomes so conventional as to be practically unconscious.

The questioning of old beliefs was a conspicuous feature of various forms of philosophical inquiry. Though they differed a good deal in their outlook, the philosophers Charles Peirce, William James, and John Dewey all expounded a 'pragmatic' or 'instrumental' position, according to which ideas were to be subjected to various empirical tests, not so much to determine their innate truth or falsity, but rather to disclose whether they were relevant to experience. This style of thinking was seemingly linked to the 'commonsense' philosophizing of the eighteenth century. Yet it also seemed to have inherited some of the open-ended and open-minded quality of Transcendentalism. This was particularly apparent in the writings of John Dewey, with his insistence (as he said in *Democracy and Education*, 1916) on the need for a 'reconsideration of the basic ideas of traditional philosophic systems, . . . because of the thoroughgoing change in social life, accompanying the advance of science, the industrial revolution, and the development of democracy'. Change was now itself a principle of life; intellectual schemes must therefore be flexible; and (in Dewey's view) 'education' was the fundamental means of organizing the ideas and ideals of mankind.

A comparable relativism evolved in another of the central institutions of social thought, that of the law. After the era of John Marshall, no great legal propositions engaged the American mind for a full half-century. But a new era of 'legal realism' came in with the work of Oliver Wendell Holmes, Jr., Louis D. Brandeis, Roscoe Pound and others. The essence of this new approach, sometimes referred to as 'sociological jurisprudence', was that law – like education – had a vital function in society, and that this function was not to uphold absolute verities, but to mediate between the 'ought' and the 'is' of human experience. The law must interpret canons of behaviour according to the changing circumstances of society. In historical scholarship too there was a new effort to explain that one's view of the past was conditioned by one's view of the present. The 'scientific' history revered by the previous generation was chimerical. In *The New History*, the title of a book by James Harvey Robinson (1912), historical truth was seen to be relative, and instrumental to the needs of the present – a position enthusiastically endorsed by Robinson's Columbia colleague Charles A. Beard, who wished to make history serve as a mouthpiece for social reform.

'New' was a key word of Progressivism. It figured characteristically in the title of a magazine, *The New Republic*, launched in 1914 with the aim 'less to inform or entertain its readers than to start little insurrections in the realm of their convictions'. The editor, Herbert Croly, and his principal early associates, Walter Weyl and Walter Lippmann, varied in age and background. What united them was the belief that American thought, liberal no less than conservative, was imprisoned in an antique brand of emotional *laissez-faire*. Croly in *The Promise of American Life* (1909), Weyl in *The New Democracy* (1913), and Lippmann in *A Preface to Politics* (1913) and *Drift and Mastery* (1914), all maintained that Jeffersonianism was an anachronism in modern America. Hoary rhetoric or talk of 'individualism' could not solve the problems of the twentieth century. Reform was needed, but it must be sophisticated. Economics could help; thus Weyl, following the theories of the economist Simon Nelson Patten, argued that the extremes of wealth and poverty were not only reprehensible but unnecessary: the United States had an economic surplus which ought to be allotted to social welfare. In retrospect the theories of this group of 'cool' Progressives may not look particularly radical. What was striking was the attempt to apply Hamiltonian means to Jeffersonian ends: in other words, to insist for almost the first time since Alexander Hamilton that the country needed a strong and active national government (although for benevolent purposes). The power of the state, and incidentally of the American President, were redefined in American political thought. Ancient bogeys were apparently banished. There was to be a new republic – said the editors of the *New Republic*.

Avant-Gardism, 1920–40

Much of what passed for Progressive thought was soon discredited and discarded; spokesmen such as Lippmann passed on to other arguments. By 1920 the great majority of American intellectuals were ready to declare themselves thoroughly disillusioned. The process had perhaps begun with the nation's drift into war in the years 1914–17. True, not many intellectuals strenuously opposed this drift. Once American involvement in the war was an established fact, Beard, Dewey and others rallied to the cause with remarkable readiness. In 1917–18 only a minority of dissidents went against the current. Randolph Bourne was one of the few to perceive that perhaps their very open-mindedness had made them too responsive to the moods of the moment. He wrote:

> To those of us who have taken Dewey's philosophy almost as our American religion, it never occurred that values could be subordinated to technique. We were instrumentalist, but we had our private utopias so clearly before our minds that the means fell always into place as contributory. And Dewey, of course, always meant his philosophy . . . to start with values. But there was always that unhappy ambiguity in his doctrine as to just how values were created, and it became easier and easier to assume that . . . any growth was justified and almost any activity valuable so long as it achieved its ends.

Among historians, Beard, Carl Becker and others were to wrestle with this dilemma – and in some instances to weaken their own work in consequence. For most thoughtful Americans, however, involvement in the European war and subsequent revulsion from it were merely items in a long list of reasons for alienation from the traditional American culture. The main significance of Bourne was that he died young (in the influenza epidemic of 1918) and could be taken as a symbol of lonely protest. The same message was gleaned from the work of other American writers, notably Herman Melville, whose novels and tales were rediscovered in the 1920s, and Henry Adams, whose *Education* (first published privately in 1907) reached a wide audience on its republication in 1918. Protest, that is, became private and aesthetic rather than public and political. Van Wyck Brooks, H. L. Mencken, and certain other literary critics spread the view that 'Puritan' and civic America was a cultural wasteland, redeemed in the past only by isolated prophets and nay-sayers like Melville and Adams and in the present by the flowering of avant-garde talent among young writers and artists. Alienation, irony, irreverence, bohemianism were the dominant modes. The America of Harding and Coolidge, of Prohibition and Wall Street, was too absurd to be taken seriously. Its politics, Mencken said, were 'an obscene farce'. The young, according to the elderly philosopher George Santayana (himself of an ironical temper) in a 1922 essay, 'all proclaim their disgust at the present state of things in America, they denounce the Constitution . . ., the churches, the government, the colleges, the press, . . . and above all they denounce the spirit that vivifies and unifies all these things, the spirit of Business'. Outside professional psychology, knowledge of the theories of Sigmund Freud was superficial. But he was one of the names invoked by the American intelligentsia in their insistence that life was at best a mystery and at worst a sham. There were no final answers; but at any rate the young, unlike the old, did not pretend to enlightenment.

The economic crash at the end of the 1920s drastically altered the tone of American thought by making the formulations of the decade appear flippant and even heartless. Early in the 1930s, Carl Becker, discussing with a student the difficulty of getting a job during the depression, asked him 'with ironical intent' what he thought of liberty as a concept. The student replied, with an irony more harsh than that of Becker: 'I've never been through it; I don't drive a car.' Economic necessity was uppermost; at least let answers be found to some of its urgent pressures. So, not surprisingly, there was a return to the consideration of social questions. Marxism and its variants were hotly debated, though never widely espoused except for a brief period in 1932–33. The danger of totalitarianism was pointed out in Sinclair Lewis's novel *It Can't Happen Here* (1935), and coolly, more heretically analysed in Lawrence Dennis's *The Coming American Fascism* (1937). Those who discerned a tragic dimension in the fate of modern man, and who believed that American thought had been shallowly affirmative, were much impressed by the theologian Reinhold Niebuhr. In *Moral Man and Immoral Society* (1932), *Reflections on the End of an Era* (1934) and other works, Niebuhr attempted to reconcile individual and communal needs, the claims of freedom and those of social regulation.

Some intellectuals, including poets and novelists, bore witness to a sort of patriotism of landscape, rather than of slogans and anthems. They turned almost instinctively to a celebration of the homeland – stimulated no doubt by the employment provided under Roosevelt's New Deal for writers and artists, whose task was to chronicle the fabric of America. Van Wyck Brooks, hitherto preoccupied with the blighting effects of the American atmosphere, had begun in the late 1920s to view the situation more appreciatively. With *The Flowering of New England* (1936) he produced the first of several volumes of an affectionate history of the writer in the United States. F. O. Matthiessen, who declared his indebtedness to Brooks, paid his own tribute to the nation's 'usable past' in *American Renaissance* (1941), a learned yet lyrical meditation on the era of Emerson and Whitman. It should be stressed that in the 1920s and 1930s such works, including the pioneering studies of Lewis Mumford, did not adhere to the genteel tradition. What they did rather was to begin to construct a special tradition, a genealogy of rebels, radicals, and neglected heroes. Vernon L. Parrington's *Main Currents in American Thought* (1927–30), in some respects a survival from the Progressive era, greatly influenced contemporary views; and though his ideas were Jeffersonian in flavour, his latter-day Jeffersonianism led him to identify dissent as a 'main current'. Quite apart from its other, literary virtues, John Dos Passos' trilogy *U.S.A.* (1930–6) contains a fascinatingly representative gallery of biographical portraits. Here is the hagiography of the old avant-garde: Debs, Veblen, Bourne and so on.

Compromise, 1940–60

As we may see from Dos Passos, intellectuals in the 1930s often thought of America as divided into two nations, 'we' and 'they'. The 'we' portion was united against and alienated from the 'they' majority by sundry *causes célèbres*, above all the extended drama of the Sacco-Vanzetti trial in Boston, which eventually brought two anarchists to the electric chair for murders that no radical believed they had committed. During the late 1930s, radicals were convinced that anti-Communist 'witch-hunts' were another proof of the implacable and mindless hostility of official America.

Such activities multiplied after 1940, especially after the end of the war in 1945, and indeed reached a crescendo in the McCarthyite inquisitions of the early 1950s. There was a second interlude of *causes célèbres* from 1948 to 1952. This included the trial of Alger Hiss, a man of apparently impeccable liberal sentiments, in effect for having concealed his former Communist affiliations, and of Julius and Ethel Rosenberg on charges of espionage. There was a world of difference, though, between the Sacco-Vanzetti situation and the later one. It had been assumed that in clashes between 'we' and 'they' the victim was, axiomatically, victimized – namely, innocent. But now American intellectuals seemed obliged to believe that those accused were in fact guilty. They might in a sense be victims: they could not be seen as martyrs. 'Innocence' is a key word for the postwar period. The intellectuals' reaction is vividly typified in Leslie A. Fiedler's *An End to Innocence: Essays on Culture and Politics* (1955). As with the 1920s, iconoclasm moved – retreated is perhaps the better word – from politics into culture. In the public sphere, the intelligentsia tended to attack its own record rather than that of the politicians and conservatives. The limits of tolerance and the problem of loyalty were intensively discussed. On the whole, however reluctantly, intellectuals agreed that once extreme dissent became 'political' it was potentially subversive and so a risk to the public safety.

There was of course a wider context: the subversion of democratic régimes by fascism and by Stalinist Russia, and the apparent failure of Socialist or Communist societies to provide either freedom or material wellbeing for their citizens. Intellectuals on both sides of the Atlantic renounced their former hopes. They concluded – Arthur Schlesinger Jr.'s *The Vital Center: The Politics of Freedom* (1949) is a persuasive example – that Communism was the god that had failed, and that the only sensible 'ism' was pragmatism. The sociologist Daniel Bell put the point in his book *The End of Ideology* (1960): political ideas had become exhausted.

The new mood was one of sober inquiry. The end of innocence meant that the United States was no longer a carefree young nation. It was burdened with domestic and international responsibilities. Many things were wrong with modern culture. Some of these were identified, as in David Riesman's *The Lonely Crowd* (1950) and William H. Whyte Jr.'s *The Organization Man* (1957), with mass society and bureaucracy. But the emphasis was on analysis rather than indignation. There was a sort of cautiously utopian hope that social or 'behavioral' scientists, perhaps working together in 'think tanks', could develop a mature new synthesis of human needs and goals. Academic communities, whose intellectual eminence had been augmented by numbers of outstanding intellectuals from Nazi Europe, took a solid pride in their scholarly achievements. They were entitled to do so: in the humanities as in the social and natural sciences American scholars ranked with the best in the world. In the literary and visual arts American contributions were no less conspicuous, though in them the element of avant-garde disaffection lay closer to the surface.

Revolt, 1960–70

A spirit of guarded optimism survived for two or three more years in the brief span of John F. Kennedy's New Frontier. Intellectuals were welcome at and even employed in the White House; the economist John Kenneth Galbraith was made ambassador to India. It seemed that they had perhaps been able to reach an acceptable compromise between the theoretically desirable and the practically attainable, and to do this without compromising themselves. Radical terminology itself used to speak of impracticable goals as 'impossibilist'. The New Frontier intellectuals were 'possibilists', and saw no need to apologise. The search for 'consensus', which did not preclude controversy and reform-mindedness, was both a need for modern America and an actual feature of the nation's past.

But not all of their fellow intellectuals were happy with this position – which was to be abruptly challenged. In the 1950s there had been isolated attempts to formulate a more thorough-going radicalism, for instance in the magazine *Dissent* and on the part of the sociologist C. Wright Mills. In *The Power Elite* (1956), Mills anticipated the chorus of subsequent criticism of the 'military–industrial complex'. In *The Sociological Imagination* (1959) he accused Talcott Parsons and other sociological system-builders of exalting methodology and making it a rationale for unregenerate capitalist society. Though less truculent than Mills, David Riesman in the same period also expressed his concern over the corrupt values of modern materialism. In literature the 'beat' writers of the 1950s, including Jack Kerouac and Allen Ginsberg, declared their indifference to or contempt for their official civilization.

The full chorus of antagonism, however, developed only after the assassination of President Kennedy at the end of 1963. It embraced a rediscovery of poverty in the United States (Michael Harrington, *The Other America*, 1962); an upsurge of militant anger among black Americans and a rediscovery on their part – stimulated by the writings of Malcolm X, Stokely Carmichael, Eldridge Cleaver and others – of the Afro-American heritage; an attack by younger historians, ranging from Eugene D. Genovese to Staughton Lynd, upon the comfortable assumptions of 'consensus' historiography; a growing impulse among academics to relate their research to 'relevant', i.e. social and contemporary, issues. It took the form, in domestic affairs, of a surge of interest in the problems of what was variously referred to as pollution, conservation, the environment, ecology; in American defence policy, a passionate critique of the 'warfare state', with the linguistic scholar Noam Chomsky (*American Power and the New Mandarins*, 1969) in the forefront of the argument. There were an outcrop of 'political' trials (the Chicago Seven, the Black Panthers) which polarized opinion once more, as in the days of Sacco and Vanzetti; and a further polarizing, sometimes known as the 'generation gap', between the orthodox old and the insurrectionist young. The vocabulary of this rebellion recalled some of the old, almost forgotten radicalisms of the 1790s, the 1830s, the 1900s, and the 1930s. It seemed unlikely to be as ephemeral as they had been, though it revealed the characteristic factiousness of left-wing intellectual discussion and a perhaps fantasized predilection for such 'un-American' revolutionists as Mao Tse-tung and Ché Guevara. There was no doubt that at the end of the 1960s America was seized with a profound spiritual and intellectual malaise. The liberal doctrines which had permeated both the 'conventional wisdom' and the radical fringe of American thought were under challenge as never before. There was now an almost institutionalized avant-garde or rebel sub-culture, with millions in its ranks, fascinated by visions of apocalypse, street warfare, 'power to the people', and semi-surrealist techniques of disruption. *Do It!*, the title of a book by Jerry Rubin (1970), was the cry of this new wave. 'It' appeared to be anything you felt like doing that would assert the freedom of the individual and the hatefulness of his society. In the terminology of Rubin's movement the other America, the one they repudiated and considered totalitarian, was spelled with a *k – Amerika*.

Conclusion

Viewing the whole scene from early Puritan times to the present, it is neither difficult nor surprising to recognize that American thought has shared the same successive climates of opinion as those of the Europe from which it sprang. There have, understandably, been particular American developments, divergences, and time-lags. These include a preoccupation with national 'uniqueness' or 'exceptionalism' more marked than that of the European nation-states. The patterns of American thought were for a long period 'colonial' or 'ex-colonial'. They revealed, that is, the derivative and provincial features of an offshoot-culture, plus a suspicion of the élitist association of high culture. Until the twentieth century, American culture was a little tame, or genteel, or middlebrow. One reason for this was the early triumph of the almost universally received ideology of democratic liberalism. The nineteenth-century United States produced no economic or political theorist as radical as Karl Marx, no theologian as outrageous as Feuerbach (who announced that God was a creation of man, and not the other way round), no wrestler with human fate as audacious as Nietzsche. American forms of radicalism were relatively muted, like the native brands of conservatism. Then and since, unorthodox American thinkers have tended to feel that something in the atmosphere smothers them – something more insidious in its indifference or even its approval than the outright persecution they might have suffered in other countries. Some American intellectuals *have* suffered for their opinions: Tom Paine, excommunicated for his deistic religious ideas, and perhaps still more for criticizing the nation's hero George Washington, was an early post-Revolutionary victim. The majority, as perhaps in other countries, have tended to modify or abandon their theories as they grew older. Thus, Orestes Brownson jettisoned his Jacksonian radicalism and joined the Catholic church; James R. Lowell, an abolitionist as a young man, ripened into a career as a gentleman of letters; John Jay Chapman, a courageous dissenter at the outset, degenerated into a crabbed and cranky old man.

With the twentieth century, American culture was no longer derivative. With maturity, and wealth, and sophistication, came a flow of more fundamental critiques. The old ideology was no longer automatically assented to. Yet Americans were still far from indifferent to it. Their critiques sometimes seemed to resemble an inverted version of the traditional dogmas. The United States was different from other nations, that is, not in being better than they but in being *worse* than they. Against the Puritan heritage the young of the 1960s thrust its flagrant negation, an anti-Puritan creed of relaxation and exhibitionism, of blasphemy and bad language, instead of industry and piety. Yet such tactics would have no meaning except as a response to the whole intellectual and emotional inheritance that has been sketched in these pages.

Further Reading

GENERAL

Note: This lists only works of fairly general scope, not already mentioned in the text. It excludes source material, other than that to be found in certain anthologies. In other words, it merely offers an introduction. For further reading, consult the bibliographies in the books listed.

Aaron, D., *Men of Good Hope: a Story of American Progressives.* New York, 1951.
Arieli, Y., *Individualism and Nationalism in American Ideology.* Cambridge, Mass., 1964.
Baritz, L., *City on a Hill: a History of Ideas and Myths in America.* New York, 1964.
Cohen, M., *American Thought: a Critical Sketch.* Glencoe, Ill., 1954.
Commager, H. S., *The American Mind: an Interpretation of American Character and Thought since the 1880s.* New Haven, Conn., 1950.
Dorfman, J., *The Economic Mind in American Civilization,* 5 vols. New York, 1954–9.
Goldman, E. F., *Rendezvous with Destiny: a History of Modern American Reform* (c. 1865–1950). New York, 1952.
Hofstadter, R., *The American Political Tradition.* New York, 1965.
Hudson, W. S., *Religion in America.* New York, 1965.
Miller, P., *The Life of the Mind in America: From the Revolution to the Civil War.* New York, 1965.
Nash, R., *Wilderness and the American Mind.* New Haven, Conn., 1967.
Schneider, H. W., *A History of American Philosophy.* New York, 1946.
Ward, J. W., *Red, White, and Blue: Men, Books and Ideas in American Culture.* New York, 1969.
Welter, R., *Popular Education and Democratic Thought in America.* New York, 1962.

THE PURITAN HERITAGE

Miller, P., *The New England Mind: the Seventeenth Century.* Cambridge, Mass., 1939.
Miller, P. and Johnson, T. H. (eds.), *The Puritans,* 2 vols. New York, 1938.
Morison, S. E., *The Puritan Pronaos.* New York, 1935; reprinted 1960 as *The Intellectual Life of Colonial New England.* Ithaca, N.Y., 1960.
Murdock, K. B., *Literature and Theology in Colonial New England.* Cambridge, Mass., 1949.
Perry, R. B., *Puritanism and Democracy.* New York, 1944.
Schneider, H. W., *The Puritan Mind.* New York, 1930.
Wright, L. B., *The Cultural Life of the American Colonies.* New York, 1957.

THE POLITICS OF INDEPENDENCE AND EQUALITY

Bailyn, B., *The Ideological Origins of the American Revolution*. Cambridge, Mass., 1967.

Blau, J. L. (ed.), *Social Theories of Jacksonian Democracy*. New York, 1947.

Nye, R. B., *The Cultural Life of the New Nation, 1776–1830*. New York, 1960.

Pole, J. R., *Political Representation in England and the Origins of the American Republic*. London, 1966.

Rozwenc, E. C. (ed.), *Ideology and Power in the Age of Jackson*. Garden City, N.Y., 1964.

Schlesinger, A. M., Jr., *The Age of Jackson*. Boston, Mass., 1945.

ROMANTIC INDIVIDUALISM

Bode, C. (ed.), *American Life in the 1840s*. Garden City, N.Y., 1967.

Cunliffe, M., *Soldiers and Civilians: the Martial Spirit in America, 1775–1865*. London, 1969.

Ekirch, A. A., Jr., *The Idea of Progress in America, 1815–1860*. New York, 1944.

Levin, D., *History as Romantic Art: Bancroft, Prescott, Motley, Parkman*. Stanford, Calif., 1959.

Miller, P. (ed.), *The American Transcendentalists*. Garden City, N.Y., 1957.

Tyler, A. F., *Freedom's Ferment: Phases of American Social History to 1860*. New York, 1944.

Whicher, G. F. (ed.), *The Transcendentalist Revolt against Materialism*. Lexington, Mass., 1949.

BUSINESS ENTERPRISE

Destler, C. M., *American Radicalism, 1865–1901*. New London, Conn., 1946.

Dorfman, J., *Thorstein Veblen and his America*. New York, 1934.

Fine, S., *Laissez-faire and the General Welfare State: a Study of Conflict in American Thought, 1865–1901*. Ann Arbor, Mich., 1956.

Fredrickson, G. M., *The Inner Civil War: Northern Intellectuals and the Crisis of the Union*. New York, 1965.

Hofstadter, R., *Social Darwinism in American Thought*. Philadelphia, Pa., 1944.

Kirkland, E. C., *Dream and Thought in the Business Community, 1860–1900*. Ithaca, N.Y., 1956.

McCloskey, R. G., *American Conservatism in the Age of Enterprise, 1865–1910*. Cambridge, Mass., 1951.

May, H. F., *Protestant Churches and Industrial America*. New York, 1949.

Ziff, L., *The American 1890s*. New York, 1966.

HERESIES AND MISGIVINGS

Cady, E. H., *The Gentleman in America*. Syracuse, N.Y., 1949.

Eaton, C., *The Mind of the Old South*. Baton Rouge, La., 1964.

Ekirch, A. A., Jr. (ed.), *Voices in Dissent: an Anthology of Individualist Thought in the United States*. New York, 1964.

Guttmann, A., *The Conservative Tradition in America*. New York, 1967.

Kirk, R., *The Conservative Mind*. Chicago, Ill., 1954.

Spitz, H., *Patterns of Anti-Democratic Thought*. New York, 1949.
Taylor, W. R., *Cavalier and Yankee: the Old South and American National Character*. New York, 1961.

TWENTIETH-CENTURY CONFUSIONS

Aaron, D., *Writers on the Left: Episodes in American Literary Communism*. New York, 1961.
Alexander, C. C., *Nationalism in American Thought, 1930–1945*. Chicago, Ill., 1969.
Beichman, A., *Nine Lies about America*. London, 1972.
Bell, D. (ed.), *The Radical Right*. New York, 1963.
Berman, R., *America in the Sixties: an Intellectual History*. New York, 1968.
Cowley, M. and Smith, B. (eds.), *Books that Changed Our Minds*. New York, 1938.
Cruse, H., *The Crisis of the Negro Intellectual*. New York, 1967; London, 1969.
Curti, M. (ed.), *American Scholarship in the Twentieth Century*. New York, 1953.
Gettleman, M. E. and Mermelstein, D. (eds.), *The Great Society Reader: the Failure of American Liberalism*. New York, 1967.
Hofstadter, R., *The Age of Reform: From Bryan to F.D.R.* New York, 1955.
Howe, I. (ed.), *The Radical Papers*. Garden City, N.Y., 1966.
Lasch, C., *The New Radicalism in America, 1889–1963: the Intellectual as a Social Type*. New York, 1965.
Rogin, M. P., *The Intellectuals and McCarthy: the Radical Specter*. Cambridge, Mass., 1967.
Schlesinger, A. M., Jr., *The Crisis of Confidence: Ideas, Power and Violence in America*. Boston, Mass., 1969.

A Checklist of Essential Works of Reference

HISTORY

Dictionary of American Biography. 20 vols. plus Index. London, Oxford U.P. and New York, Charles Scribner, 1928–36; Supplements 1944, 1958.

Dictionary of American History, ed. James T. Adams. 5 vols. plus Index. New York, Scribner, 1946.

Encyclopedia of American History, ed. Richard B. Morris. New York, Harper, 1953. Enlarged 1970.

A Guide to the Study of the United States of America: representative books reflecting the development of American life and thought, ed. Roy P. Basler *et al.* Washington, Library of Congress, 1960.

Harvard Guide to American History, ed. Oscar Handlin *et al.* Cambridge, Mass.. 1954.

Websters Guide to American History, ed. Chas. Van Doren *et al.* Springfield, Mass., Merriam, 1971.

A Guide to Manuscripts Relating to America in Great Britain and Ireland, ed. B. R. Crick and Miriam Alman. London, Oxford U.P., 1961.

LITERATURE

Bibliography of American Literature, ed. Jacob Blanck. New Haven, Conn., Yale U.P., 1955–.

Bibliographical Guide to the Study of the Literature of the U.S.A., ed. Clarence Gohdes. Durham, N.C., Duke U.P., 1959; rev. eds. 1963, 1970.

Guide to American Literature and its Backgrounds Since 1890, Howard Mumford Jones and Richard M. Ludwig. Cambridge, Mass., Harvard U.P., 1953; rev. eds. 1959, 1964.

Selective Bibliography for the Study of English and American Literature, ed. Richard D. Altick and Andrew Wright. New York, Macmillan, 1960.

A Bibliographical Guide to the Study of Southern Literature, ed. Louis D. Rubin, Jr. Baton Rouge, La., Louisiana State U.P., 1969.

The Oxford Companion to American Literature, ed. James D. Hart. New York, Oxford U.P., 1941; rev. eds. 1948, 1956, 1965.

The Penguin Companion to Literature: U.S.A. and Latin America, ed. Eric Mottram and Malcolm Bradbury; and Jean Franco. London, Penguin Press, 1972.

Articles on American Literature 1900–1950, ed. Lewis G. Leary. Durham, N.C., Duke U.P., 1954.

DICTIONARIES

A Dictionary of American English on Historical Principles, 4 vols., ed. William A. Craigie and James R. Hulbert. Chicago, Ill., U. of Chicago Press, 1944.

A Dictionary of American–English Usage, based on Fowler's Modern English Usage, Margaret Nicholson. New York and London, Oxford U.P., 1957.

A Dictionary of Modern American Usage, Herbert W. Horwill. New York and London, Oxford U.P., 1935.

Dictionary of American Slang, ed. Harold Wentworth and Stuart Berg Flexner. New York, Crowell Co., 1960.
American Dialect Dictionary, Harold Wentworth. New York, Crowell Co., 1944.

PERIODICALS *(primarily or largely concerned with American subjects)*

American Historical Review, Washington D.C., five issues a year.
American Literature, Durham, N.C., quarterly.
American Quarterly, Philadelphia, quarterly, with an annual bibliographical supplement.
Jahrbuch für Amerikastudien, Heidelberg, annually.
Journal of American History, Bloomington, Ind., quarterly.
Journal of American Studies, London, three issues a year.
Journal of Southern History, Richmond, Va., quarterly.
New England Quarterly, Brunswick, Maine, quarterly.
Pacific Historical Review, Berkeley, California, quarterly.
Studi Americani, Rome, annually.
William and Mary Quarterly, Williamsburg, Va., quarterly.

Index

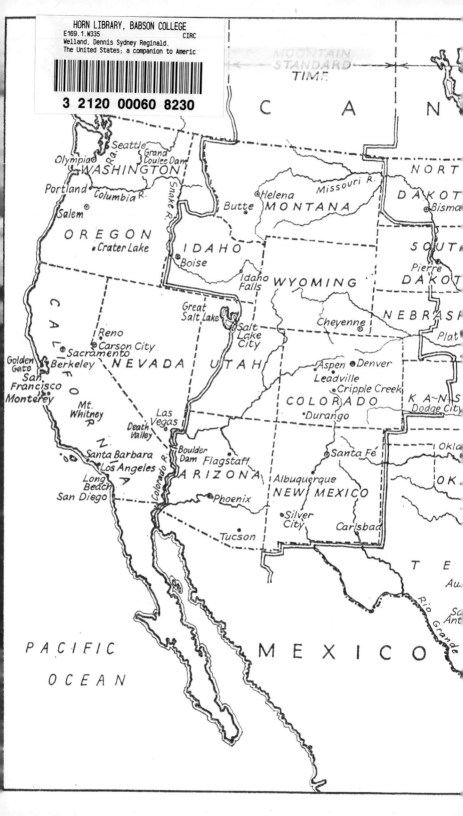

MOUNTAIN
STANDARD
TIME

C   A   N

WASHINGTON
Olympia   Seattle
          Grand
          Coulee Dam
Portland   Columbia R.
Salem
O R E G O N
   Crater Lake

I D A H O
   Boise
Snake R.

Helena   Missouri R.
Butte   M O N T A N A

N O R T

D A K O T
   Bisma

S O U T

Idaho
Falls   W Y O M I N G

Great
Salt Lake   Salt
             Lake
             City

Pierre
D A K O T

N E B R A S
   Cheyenne
             Plat

Reno
   Carson City
Sacramento
Golden
Gate   Berkeley   N E V A D A   U T A H
San
Francisco
Monterey

Aspen Denver
Leadville
   Cripple Creek
C O L O R A D O   K A N S
                         Dodge City
   Durango

Mt.
Whitney
       Death
       Valley
Las
Vegas

Santa Barbara   Boulder
Los Angeles   Dam   Flagstaff
Long   A R I Z O N A
Beach   Colorado R.
San Diego

Santa Fé   Okla

Albuquerque
N E W   M E X I C O   O K.

Phoenix

Silver
City   Carlsbad

Tucson

T E

Au.

Rio Grande

Sa
Ant

P A C I F I C

O C E A N

M E X I C O